Fengate Revisited

FURTHER FEN-EDGE EXCAVATIONS, BRONZE AGE
FIELDSYSTEMS AND SETTLEMENT AND THE
WYMAN ABBOTT/LEEDS ARCHIVES

By Christopher Evans,
with Emma Beadsmoore, Matt Brudenell & Gavin Lucas

With contributions by
Katie Anderson, Grahame Appleby, Steve Boreham, Natasha Dodwell,
Mark Edmonds, Charles French, Rowena Gale, Andrew Hall, J.D. Hill,
David Gibson, Mark Knight, Paul Middleton, Marta Moreno-García,
Quita Mould, Ricky Patten, Mark Peachey, Krish Seetah, Ellen Simmons,
Chris Stevens, Chris Swaysland, Maisie Taylor, Simon Timberlake,
Anne de Vareilles & the late Alan Vince

Principal illustrations by Andrew Hall

Interview contributions by Richard Bradley, Andrew Fleming & Francis Pryor

Cambridge Archaeological Unit Landscape Archives Series
Historiography and Fieldwork (No. 1)

Published by
the Cambridge Archaeological Unit
Department of Archaeology, University of Cambridge,
Downing Street, Cambridge, CB2 3DZ
www-cau.arch.cam.ac.uk

Distributed by
Oxbow Books, Oxford, OX1 2EW

ISBN: 978-0-9544824-8-0

This book is available direct from
Oxbow Books, Oxford, OX1 2EW, UK
(Phone: 01865-241249; Fax: 01865-794449)

and

The David Brown Book Company
PO Box 511, Oakville CT 06779, USA
(Phone: 860-945-9329; Fax: 860-945-9468)

or

via the Oxbow Books website
www.oxbowbooks.com

Page design, copy editing and typesetting by Dora Kemp.
Printed in Great Britain by Short Run Press, Exeter.

Contents

Figures

TABLES

FOREWORD

Landscape Archives Series: Historiography and Fieldwork

This book marks the first of the Cambridge Archaeological Unit's Historiography and Fieldwork Series, and is to be followed by two volumes concerned with the excavations by Margaret and Tom Jones at Mucking, Essex (1965–78). What unites these volumes (the specific linkages between Mucking and Fengate being outlined in Chapter 1 below) is their exploration of 'landscape-scale' archaeology within a specifically historiographic dimension. This is not a matter of 'landscape archives' in reference to just generic site genealogies (i.e. conceptual forerunners) or vague notions of the palimpsest of their land-use/settlement sequences. We are now so far beyond 'disciplinary origins' that all excavations within Britain must have some earlier resonance; rather it is a matter of highlighting the specific historic context of fieldwork within these particular landscapes and, in short, acknowledging that we invariably re-read landscape (and the past).

With the main excavation phases of Fengate and Mucking both ending in 1978, this is historiography catching up with the present and, accordingly, it has the advantage of participant-insights (hence the interview-section in this volume's concluding chapter). Both of these 'great' sites reflect upon the advent of Rescue archaeology in Britain and with it, to varying degrees, the impact of a 'new archaeology' in terms of sampling/recording methods and also an entirely new scale of fieldwork. Of course, in their application of techniques these projects differed greatly (with Mucking having 'pre-Winchester single-context' approaches, relying instead on notebook recording).

In the case of Fengate, there is an deeper historiographic element, that being Wyman Abbott's more 'antiquarian' efforts within its quarries during the early decades of the last century. Here, in Chapter 2, for the first time we have been able to set his notations more firmly into Fengate's landscape and, thereby, allow his findings to directly inform the results of subsequent fieldwork. Moreover, concerned with his efforts together with E.T. Leeds (and others) to formulate distinctly prehistoric pottery types, this offers a basis to explore the concept of archaeological 'type cultures' (i.e. 'people-as-types'), a vexed issue that has long plagued the subject's interpretation, but whose implications still underpin much practice. The crucial point is that an historiographic perspective — one that truly embraces the diverse histories of archaeology and is not just an exercise in ancestral disciplinary polemic (Murray & Evans 2008) — provides a broader platform to engage with excavation data than the often narrow confines of contemporary archaeological theory alone.

Finally, the underlying ethos behind these volumes is that no matter how individually renowned, sites and archaeological landscapes are/were not isolated, and our understanding of them is only enriched by a greater sense of their many contextual linkages. To this end, suggestive of time and cumulative authorship ('text-on-text'; see e.g. Figs. 1.4–1.6 below), when compared to most recent site publications these volumes are intended to have a more raw, almost scrapbook-like, quality. Our intention, on the one hand, is to convey the open-ended situation behind their production and the collective long-term endeavour of fieldwork. Equally, we think it only appropriate that a fulsome historiography embraces both the 'high' (i.e. the range intellectual implications) and 'low' of fieldwork, with the latter stretching to the impact of logistical contingency (i.e. 'chance') and a degree of personal/personnel setting; in this case, the gamut runs from Darwinian connections to the mid-'70s collapse of the pound-sterling and its effect on machine-hire costs.

Context - Preface and Acknowledgements

Fengate, thirty years on; since then the region has seen a number of significant Bronze Age 'landscape' excavations, but Fengate still retains its allure — it was *the* project of its type and it was tackled with all of Francis Pryor's larger-than-life gusto and bravado. When trying to encapsulate what is intended by this volume, from the outset a personal stake must be declared. I dug at Fengate for the last couple of seasons, variously serving as a site supervisor/draughtsman and, still then at the University of Toronto, I also then worked part-time in the winters as Pryor's assistant at the Royal Ontario Museum ('holding the fort' of its Office of European Prehistory when he stopped coming back to Canada).

Some three decades on, my initial Fengate job-interview still lingers in memory. The office wall behind Pryor was entirely covered with a floor-to-ceiling OS map, stuck together and duly dotted with the region's Bronze Age metalwork findings, and I remember thinking how these maps said everything about what it was to be an archaeologist (swords, shields and landscape). Having, from the outset, been told the job was mine, Pryor then went on to convince me of its advantages, pointing out that the Green King brewery was here, the Adnams there: this was archaeology as rock-n-roll and utterly compelling. Working with Francis was, for me, highly formative (in much the same way as doing Haddenham with Hodder was later) and entirely fun, and it is hoped that this volume conveys something of this. (William Moss' 1978 BA paper, 'Sites, circuits and benders: networks and networking on British archaeological sites' explored the 'ethnography' of Fengate and other '70s excavations in Britain: see Fig. 6.10; see also Wainwright 2000 on the era.)

Given this background, how is this book to be described? Perhaps, 'Fengate: A Critical Celebration' would be the most appropriate. Whatever, it would have to carry a hint of contradiction. Aside from praising Pryor's achievement and exploring the work's '70s context, there needs to be the perspective of subsequent excavations which results, invariably, in a measure of critical reappraisal. (As it stands, the 'revisited' title not only implies revision but, also, reflective of an era and ethos, evokes Dylan's *Highway 61*, if even then ten years too late.) Ultimately, of course, this only reflects upon the quality of the original excavation and its accrued renown. Therefore, behind its many 'in hindsight' observations, hopefully the text maintains a sense of due respect. Over the years since Fengate, Pryor and I have liaised closely on our Fenland projects, and I can only say how deeply indebted I am to him.

Subsequently, further debts must be acknowledged and these are to Mark Knight of the CAU and to Josh Pollard (sometime Unit member). Working together throughout the latter half of the '90s on the Barleycroft/Over system was a truly creative interaction for coming to terms with Neolithic/Bronze Age landscapes and how to grapple with their traces. To this should also be added Charly French. Funnily enough, our paths never overlapped at Fengate, but since his coming to the Department of Archaeology, Cambridge, collaborating with him in the Lower Ouse and Fengate landscapes has been inspiring as, indeed, has been working with both Steve Boreham (Department of Geography, Cambridge) and Mark Edmonds (sometime of Sheffield, sometime Unit, now York).

Further insights into early fieldsystem research have been generously provided by Richard Bradley and Andrew Fleming, and — together with Francis — I only hope that they feel that Chapter 6's 'dialogue' does them justice. Beyond this, we are grateful to colleagues who have supplied information concerning their projects: Richard Cutler (Sites O & Q), Tom Lane (Welland Bank), Kate Nicholson and Claire Halpin (the Broadlands Site), Leo Webley (the Parnwell Site), and David Yates provided a manuscript copy of relevant chapters of fieldsystem volume (2007) — and, obviously, other CAU staff have also 'lent' us their fieldwork, primarily, Alison Dickens, Dave Gibson, Jacqui Hutton, Mark Knight, Kerry Murrell and Ricky Patten.

Our access to Wyman Abbott's and also E.T. Leeds's archival materials has been facilitated by Megan Price, Chris Gosden, Arthur MacGregor, Alice Grayson (Searchroom Supervisor, Kendal Records Office/Clare Fell Archive), Imogen Gunn (Documentation Assistant, Museum of Archaeology & Anthropology, University of Cambridge/Abbott Archive) and Alison Roberts (Antiquities Collections Manager & Curator for Prehistoric European Collections, Ashmolean Museum, University of Oxford/Leeds Archive). Though to negative result, Graham Deacon, David Field, Dave McOmish and Robin Stewart of English Heritage aided searches to attempt to retrieve what records Abbott might have provided the Ordnance Survey, and we are grateful for Christopher Taylor's OS insights. Also, both Adrian Challands and Don Mackreth provided us with 'home-town' Abbott insights, and Kate Sharpe was forthcoming with information concerning the Clare Fell/Hawkes and Abbott archives.

In Peterborough Museum, we must thank Rebecca Casa Hatton for access to SMR/HER entries and reports, and also Glenys Wass for museum-archive searches. Jacqueline Minchinton, the Records and Resources Management Officer for Northampton Museum & Art Gallery, kindly provided with details of the career of Thomas George.

Figure 5.9 is reproduced with permission of Cumberland and Westmorland Antiquarian and Archaeological Society, and we grateful to the Society for providing illustrative materials from their Clare Fell archive. Similarly, the 'strawbear' magic lantern slide in Chapter 2 is reproduced with permission of Whittlesey Museum and the assistance of its curator, Maureen Watson, was much appreciated. Ben Robinson is also responsible for the scene-setting aerial photograph of Fengate that features in Chapter 1, and we are also grateful to Chris Going of the Geoinformation Group for allowing us to reproduce its accompanying vertical image. Aside from his much-valued advice over the years concerning matters aerial photographic, Rog Palmer is to be thanked for allowing us to reproduce his Fengate/Northey 'master-plot' that appears in Chapter 6. Wendy Brown, of the University of Cambridge Museum of Archaeology & Anthropology, kindly gave permission to reproduce

Milward's photograph of 'Jamani, a Pardhi man' (Fig. 6.8). Equally, its Rob Law's photograph of one of Edgerley's vessels that features in Chapter 4, and we benefited from his insights concerning Collared Urns generally. We are also grateful that Andrew Fleming and Dave Yates — and, of course, Pryor himself — gave their permission to variously reproduce illustrations from their many books; just as Francis, Charly French and Bill Moss also loaned us Fengate 'scrapbook' photographs.

Of the CAU excavations that feature in this volume, the Elliott and Edgerley Road Sites were jointly managed by myself and Robin Standring (Tower Works being mine alone). Throughout, Ben Robinson (Peterborough City Council Archaeological Services, PCCAS), oversaw the project's development control and, now in the long run, has only been inspiring to work with and a rich source of information. Otherwise, the funding for the excavations and their ensuing publication has been provided by the three respective developments and we are sincerely grateful to them all: the Tower Works by Marshall of Cambridge (particularly Jonathon Barker of that organization, Nick Pettit of Bidwells and Paul Mangan of R.G. Carter Building Ltd); Barnack UK Ltd for the Edgerley Drain Road Site (especially Rob Facer); and, for the Elliott Site, the Elliot Group and Bob Darwin thereof.

Unfortunately far too many to individually mention, all of us on this book's authorial by-line are grateful to the Unit's field staff for their sterling efforts. Over the years, the sites' finds have been processed with great efficiency, first by Norma Challands and, subsequently, Gwladys Monteil. With their plans variously digitized by Marcus Abbott, Iain Forbes, Bryan Crossan and Jane Matthews, the volume's graphics largely attest to the formidable skills of Andrew Hall, its finds illustrations being by Vicki Herring (augmented by Matt Brudenell and Mike Palmer) and studio photography by Dave Webb. Aside from his cited specialist contributions, the participation of Grahame Appleby throughout has been crucial to this volume, and both he, Sam Lucy and Jo Appleby greatly aided its final production.

Christopher Evans 2007–8

Herodotus, wherever he was, always tried to note the names of tribes, their location and customs. Where someone lives. Who are his neighbors. This because knowledge of the world … accrues not vertically, but horizontally, synthetically from a bird's-eye view. I know my nearest neighbors, and that is all; they know theirs; and those know others still. In this way we will arrive at the ends of the earth
(Kapuscinski 2007, *Travels with Herodotus*, 172; emphasis added)

Curiously enough, one cannot read a book: one can only reread it
(Nabokov, *Of Books and Bicycles*; see Fig. 6.8)

CHAPTER 1

Introduction — Text on Land

Christopher Evans

This is a book concerned with time and investment in land, both relating to prehistoric farming and archaeological practices. True to the announced ethos of this publication series, the context of social relations and the historiography of work (in these respective 'fields') looms large. Certainly the volume's scrapbook-like qualities are obvious, as three recent Cambridge Archaeological Unit (CAU) sites are here used as a vehicle to broach many issues. This seems perfectly justifiable, as enquiry — like landscape itself — is something that both enfolds and is open-ended; new sources illuminate old (and *vice versa*), and allow us to revisit earlier themes and places. In this case the 'destination' is, at first glance, unassuming: the Fengate industrial estate on Peterborough's eastern fen-edge. Today with its Pizza Hut, bowling alley and many car showrooms, while perhaps not quite the 'ends of world' alluded to in this volume's introductory Herodotus/Kapuscinski passage, certainly it seems an unlikely locale to lay claim to one of the most well-known prehistoric fieldsystems in Europe.

In contrast with any espousal of Geertzian 'thick description', the risk here is of being *swamped by context* and the situation rather verges on Marx's notion that 'the past lies like a nightmare upon the present'. It is a problem that will increasingly come to the fore in current developer-funded archaeology, but at Fengate has been accelerated due to the sheer cumulative quantity of fieldwork that has now been undertaken within its environs due to its early renown. This, moreover, is exasperated due to the paucity of their publications and, additionally, the frequency of evaluation- and/or watching brief-only investigations (leading, for the most part, to undistilled, 'grey matter-type' reportage).

Appropriate to archaeology's intrinsic chronological concerns and for the sake of scene-setting, the dates of this volume's coverage should be established from the outset. Lasting for eight years, the original phase of Francis Pryor's groundbreaking excavations at Fengate — those funded by the Royal Ontario Museum (ROM) and the Department of the Environment (DoE) — were completed some thirty years ago in 1978, with its final report issued in 1984. (Conducted under the auspices of the Nene Valley Research Committee, it was actually Mahany's 1969 excavation of the Site 11 enclosure that, in the wake of Peterborough's New Town status and its ensuing expansion, instigated the modern *rescue* phase of Fengate's fieldwork; see below and Pryor 1993; 2001a, 9.) This volume relates to a decade of subsequent CAU fieldwork at Fengate, spanning the period from 1997 to 2006. Although the Unit's 1992 Depot Site and 1997 Co-op Site investigations were summarily reported in Pryor's 2001 *Flag Fen*, both are referred to here, with the latter seeing more in-depth reportage.

The three main sites presented span the Fengate landscape: the Elliott investigations within its central core, Edgerley Drain Road at its northern end and Tower Works to the southwest (Fig. 1.1). Their situation relative to the fen-edge also varies, with Elliott crossing 'the edge' proper, Edgerley falling just back from that 'divide' and with Tower Works lying in the immediate hinterland, some 300–400 m 'inland' from later prehistoric marshlands. Collectively extending over some 3.5 ha, the area-coverage of these sites only amounts to approximately a third of that excavated by Pryor during the '70s:

TABLE 1.1. *Areas of Fengate investigated.*

	Total area investigated	Main site stripped area
Tower Works	7.6 ha	0.14 ha
Elliott	2.3 ha	1.7 ha
Edgerley	4.6 ha	1.7 ha
Pryor's sites	23.3 ha	*c.* 11.3 ha

Since the advent of developer-funding in the early 1990s, there has been a spate of investigations within Fengate's landscape. Most of these have been on a fairly minor scale and have often resulted in either only watching brief monitoring coverage and/or various modes of preservation *in situ*. Aside from Pryor's 1989 Power Station Site and his return to Cat's Water in 1990 (2001a, 38–47, 52–73), and also Hertfordshire

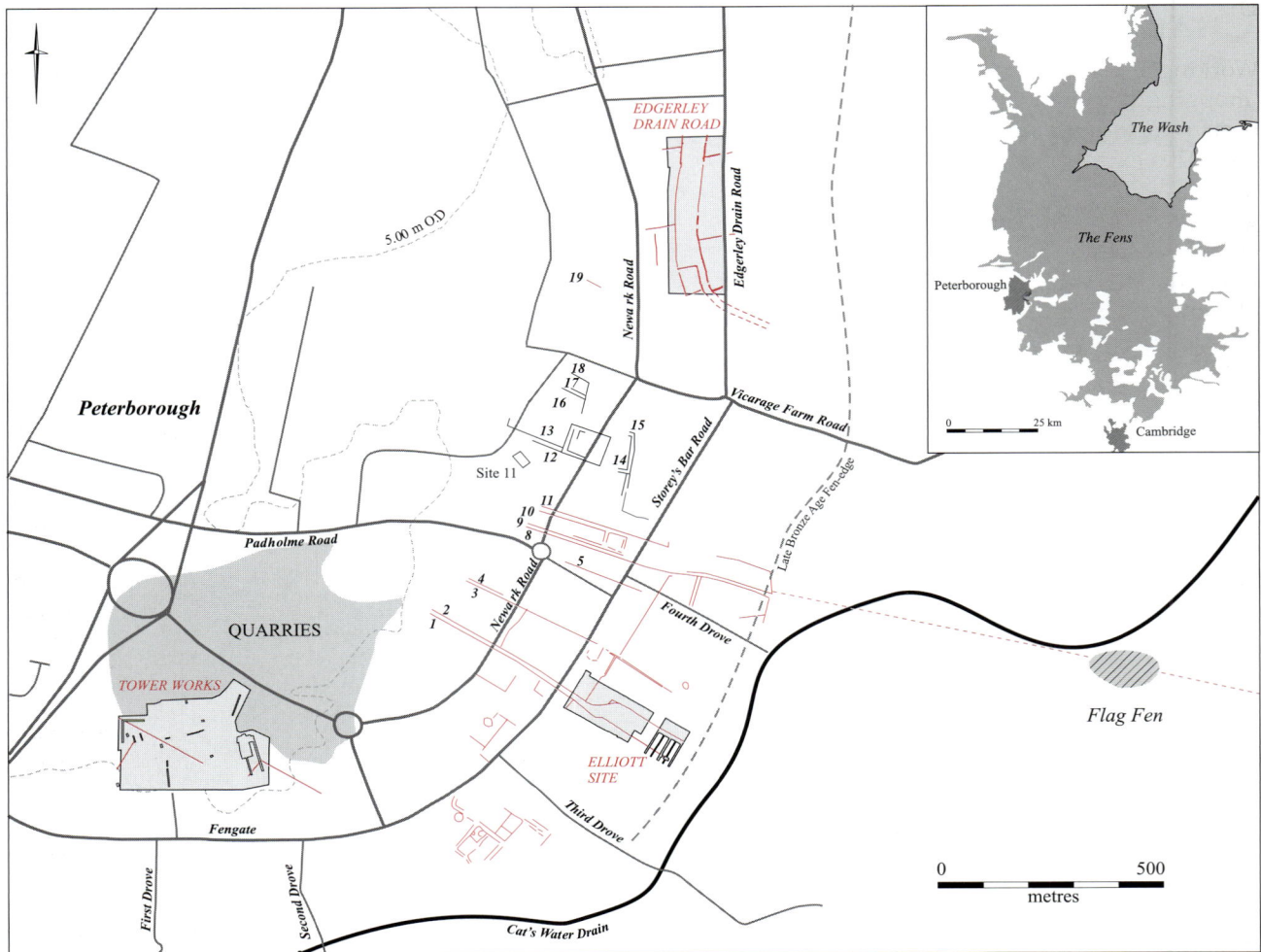

FIGURE 1.1. *The Fengate Landscape (as of c. 1999), with main CAU sites presented in this volume indicated in grey-tone (after Pryor 2001a, fig. 1.4). Note that numbers relate to Pryor's ditch system enumeration and the blackening of his Ditch 12/13 and 16–18 enclosures (and Site 11) reflects their erroneous plotting in the Flag Fen volume (and e.g. Pryor 1992, fig. 3 and Yates 2007, fig. 10.3); these are corrected, and the implications of their new layout discussed at length in Chapter 6 (see Figs. 6.1 & 6.2). (Reproduced by permission of Ordnance Survey on behalf of HMSO. © Crown copyright 2009. All rights reserved. Ordnance Survey Licence number 100048686.)*

Archaeological Trust/Archaeological Solution's work at Broadlands (HAT/AS; see Chapter 4, below), the CAU's Edgerley Road and Elliott Sites have been the only substantial excavations in the area, at least up until 2005. Typical of the vexed fortunes of commercial-sector archaeology, with at least seven different archaeological organizations having undertaken fieldwork in the area since, it is fair to say the landscape risks being chaotic (and over-crowded) in contrast to Pryor's unified fieldwork programme of the '70s. An attempt was made to make sense of recent work in the 2001 Flag Fen volume, but even that makes for a somewhat diffuse story, and since then the picture has only fragmented further.

'Post-Pryor', the CAU has undertaken much of the fieldwork within Fengate (listed at the end of this chapter). It is in an effort to bring some order into its landscape that this volume has been assembled; however, without any central-source funding, it is beyond our remit to definitively overview all of its diverse results. Therefore, it will primarily be concerned with the main CAU excavations, and will only draw upon the myriad of more minor investigations by other units as appropriate and when necessary. Otherwise this text could itself easily risk dissonance, and the mapping of the many possible projections of fleetingly exposed short ditch-lengths almost take on a convoluted 'snakes-and-ladders' quality.

Digging suburbia

Working in Fengate now carries with it an air of 'mopping-up'. Certainly, it is a landscape that has been transformed almost beyond recognition since the 1970s excavations. Then, the fieldwork occurred in a relatively pastoral setting, replete with the grazing horses of local Travellers. Today, all that is changed and the area has been subsumed beneath industrial estates (Figs. 1.2 & 1.3). Due to the vast scale of Fengate's stripping, the excavations themselves have actually contributed to this change, and certainly they have 'marked' the landscape. Led by what was then the imminent threat of Quaker Oats intending to relocate their main European headquarters to the area, the archaeology was tackled in a fairly hard-hitting manner. (Though by today's standards the plotting of individual artefacts within the fieldsystem's ditches makes it appear an almost nuanced excavation, and Fengate's exposures now seem dwarfed by the size of some current landscape excavations.) Going so far as to celebrate the rapid pace and sheer expanse of its earthmoving operations — the compelling drama of box-scrapers followed up by 360° 'grooming' — Fengate's prehistory is something that could really only come into being through the mechanization of the excavation process (Fig. 1.4; Pryor 1974b). It was the first really major site to commission its own stripping on such an industrial scale (Mucking being exposed through on-going quarrying; see e.g. Jones & Bond 1980 and Inset, this chapter). It was almost as if the *Rescue* trademark of the day — the bulldozer famously lifting Stonehenge in its bucket — was inverted with the machines instead brought to the service of archaeology. Certainly, at Fengate it was a case of size being a virtue; without such vast stripping there is no other means by which its fieldsystem-axes could have been retrieved in any kind of meaningful manner. In other words, *scale was required to appreciate pattern*.

Seeming to occur apart from any obvious theoretical 'ism' (see, though, below), the later 1970s were heady days for prehistoric landscape studies, with a real sense of pushing the research frontier. Their many conferences (and their resultant British Archaeological Report Series' volumes) not only concerned early agriculture and fieldsystems (e.g. Bowen & Fowler 1978), but the Bronze Age generally was also a focus (e.g. Burgess & Miket 1976; Barrett & Bradley 1980). Despite this, there was always an 'outsider' quality to Fengate's archaeology (i.e. non-polite/learned society). Although relatively well-funded for its day, it was never an agenda-led flagship. Nevertheless, it was *a great excavation* and what, in effect, Pryor did, was to invent a new kind of singularly modern landscape

archaeology in Britain. It was, for example, antithetical to the other main Bronze Age fieldsystem project of that decade (Mucking aside), the Dartmoor Reaves (e.g. Fleming 1988). There, due to the earthwork survival of its boundaries, Fleming's surveys (accompanied by small-scale excavations) could still be conducted in a topographic tradition: 'walking' revealed the subtleties of its landscape and, of course, they were research-led and not dictated by rescue needs (see, though, Chapter 6's Interview below). In some respects, what Pryor did at Fengate is comparable to Bersu's achievement at Little Woodbury in the immediate pre-WWII years. It was only through the scale of Bersu's exposures (though still then hand-dug; Evans 1989) that its hallmark, post-built roundhouses could be appreciated. The ubiquitous 'pit-dwelling' that previously held sway as the main house-type of British prehistory was, in part, a direct interpretative/logistical outcome of previous small-scale excavation.

The circumstances of Fengate's funding were equally as extraordinary as the excavations themselves, and that the ROM could be coerced into sponsoring such an enormous British project is, in itself, a singular achievement. The manner in which this came about and other background matters will be discussed in Chapter 6. The point to stress here is that it truly was a case of *landscape archaeology*. Typically, Fengate generated fairly meagre finds assemblages, and certainly did not yield the kind of bounty that most museums usually expect of their overseas expeditions.

The actual foundations of Fengate's archaeology *per se* are, of course, attributable to the other individual whose work looms large in this volume: Wyman Abbott (though see Chapter 2, Note 3 concerning John Evans's earlier inspection visit to the area). In the early decades of the last century, Abbott, a Peterborough lawyer, collected a wealth of prehistoric (as well as Roman) material from the then on-going Fengate quarries. He first published his findings in *Archaeologia* in 1910, with an accompanying overview contribution by R. Smith of the British Museum. Thereafter, in 1922, a further summary of his results, this time authored by E.T. Leeds, appeared in the *Antiquaries Journal*; Hawkes and Fell's appraisal of Abbott's Early Iron Age pottery was published in the *Archaeological Journal* in 1945 (see also Sharpe 2007, 8–9).

As promoted by Leeds, the impact of Abbott's researches upon Britain's prehistoric artefact studies is certainly considerable and the fact that Fengate can lay claim to three pottery types is essentially down to him. Firstly, there is the later Neolithic 'Peterborough Ware/phase' generally and then, more specifically, the 'Fengate-style sub-type' itself (Smith 1956; see also e.g. Gibson & Kinnes 1997). Beyond this, Abbott's

FIGURE 1.2. *Fengate Now — Top, looking northwestward across the line of the River Nene's embankment to Fengate's fen-edge (photograph, Ben Robinson); bottom, vertical image showing the area's suburban industrial sprawl (note that the Elliott Site area, in the lower right-centre, has still to be developed (see Fig. 3.1), whereas the Edgerley Site plot is now completely covered; reproduced by permission of Geoinformation Group).*

FIGURE 1.3. *Fengate Then — 1976 aerial photograph showing Pryor's main sites amid fields and farms (Storey's Bar Road, left; Newark Road, right; and, lower centre, Cat's Water), with the area's first industrial units making their appearance (note the dark circles of two barrows lower left; see Fig. 4.28; CUCAP RC8-BO24; north is to the right of the image). In the detail below of the same, the intensity of Pryor's excavation technique (i.e. ditch sample-interval) can be readily appreciated.*

FIGURE 1.4. *Scrapbook Sources (I) — Fengate's archaeology has provided a legacy of national coverage ranging from* The Times' *1920 report of Wyman Abbott's 'A Skeleton of 2,000 B.C.' to Norman Hammond's 1974 and '76 notices of Pryor's fieldwork (the latter phase also featuring in, for example,* Country Life). *Note the archaeological-inspired local chauvinism of the 'Prominent Citizens of Peterborough' clipping right, including 'It is worthy to mention to state [sic] that Mr. George Wyman Abbott … has made Peterborough famous for the unique Neolithic and Bronze Age pottery found, in the district …'* (The Peterborough Citizen 24/04/1928). *Central photograph, Pryor in action at the Cat's Water, 1977 (photograph, C. Evans).*

PREHISTORIC PITS AT PETERBOROUGH 339

as early as any found elsewhere in Britain. Other specimens of the same early type have been discovered on islands in the Fens, for instance, being in the Peterborough Museum. One of the of the Peterborough pits is the proo was not exclusively but was even wh ully fin of tter w the re t inst

pit n b

Antiquary Journal (vol II) 1922

THE EARLY IRON AGE SETTLEMENT AT FENGATE PETERBOROUGH
By C. F. C. HAWKES
Edited and adapted from an original study (1935-9) by

Further Discoveries of the Neolithic and Bronze Ages at Peterborough
By E. T. LEEDS, M.A., F.S.A.
[Read 12th January 1922]

FIGURE 1.5. *Scrapbook Sources (II) — Against a background of Fengate's early academic papers stands Pryor, upper right (at Over, 2004; photograph, D. Webb); middle row, left, Fengate staff c. 1975 (see Fig. 6.10 for 'cast-list'; photograph, F. Pryor); right, the Newark Road excavations (note the intensity of the ditch segment digging-interval; photograph, F. Pryor); bottom row, left, the CAU's Elliott Site staff, 2005 (photograph, E. Beadsmoore); right, Cat's Water 1976, with a Greater Peterborough Council signboard announcing in the background 'Sites to Let' (i.e. the shape of things to come; photograph, C. French).*

Early Iron Age pottery — originally assigned as of Hallstatt-type by Leeds — was recognized in Cunliffe's 'Fengate-Cromer style-zone' (1968; 1974; see also Champion 1975, 136, fig. 3). Furthermore, Abbott's findings of Beaker pottery featured in Clarke's typology and corpus of 1970 (see also Gibson's study of his Beaker material in the third Fengate volume; Pryor 1980a, 234–45). Given this strong finds-based emphasis, Abbott was little concerned with any detailed plotting of his Fengate findings and his was not really a site-oriented archaeology as such.

Though some attempt has since been made to tie down Abbott's findings, generally their provenance has been considered too imprecise to warrant area-specific appraisal. However, in the course of our current researches we have, for the first time, had access to Abbott's notebooks (apparently deposited in the University Museum of Archaeology and Anthropology in 1973 as part of the Abbott bequest, but only accessioned in 1998) and, coupled with detailed study of named-quarry locations on the historical map series, we have found that much of his material can, in fact, be allocated to distinct areas of Fengate. Perhaps most significant is the recognition that Abbott worked in two main quarry zones. Aside from the well-known swathe on the west side of Fengate, there was, in addition, another in the north, from where most of his Beaker material derived (and where he both identified a settlement and investigated a barrow of that period). Accordingly, Abbott's findings must also feature in Chapter 2 of this volume. This is not only because the latter northern quarry area directly relates to our adjacent Edgerley Road Site, but now having greater area-specific reference, his local findings reflect upon aspects of Fengate's sequences to which Pyror's work had little connection.

Themes and approaches

The three sites presented each reflect upon different facets of Fengate's sequence. Having quite distinct paddock arrangements, the Elliott and Edgerley Road Sites both provide new insights into the character of its Middle Bronze Age stock management. The latter site, furthermore, included a series of artefact-rich Neolithic and earlier Bronze Age pit groups (and, also, a Collared Urn-related structure), whose assemblages greatly contribute to the understanding of the terrace's early usage and the practices of 'type' prehistory generally. Equally, exposing a small fen-edge embayment immediately south of Pryor's Cat's Water sub-Site, the Elliott Site details 'marginal' Iron Age activities associated with Pryor's settlement of that period, as well as furthering the understanding

of occupation accompanying the earlier fieldsystem and its inter-familial operations. In fact, with its mass non-diagnostic pit activity, the Elliott Site represents the antithesis of a 'type' sequence.

Lying much further removed from the 'core' of the Fengate system (or at least the focus of its excavations to date) and seeing the only substantive exposure within that area, it is the Tower Works Site that perhaps provides the most original data. This is enhanced, moreover, by the fact that it straddled the earlier gravel workings and thereby offers further insights into the Wyman Abbott collections. The 2004 excavations there included a later Roman settlement, but more importantly, the earlier evaluation-phase identified a substantial Early Iron Age settlement. Producing very substantial finds assemblages, the latter clearly resonates with Hawkes and Fell's above-mentioned study of the material of that date from the earlier quarries (1945). In addition, we were able to scientifically test and sample-interrogate the site's 'rich' buried soils in some detail, and which offer significant insights into the generation of (quasi-) midden/'dark earth-type' deposits.

In an effort to further a 'comparative fieldwork' agenda (Evans forthcoming) and to readily appreciate the character of these sites, their respective broad finds-category statistics are outlined in Table 1.2 (with detailed breakdowns appearing in their relevant chapters). Although having respectable assemblages by the standards of British prehistory, it is immediately apparent that none were particularly finds-rich. These site-density figures can, of course, only provide a rough, 'rule-of-thumb' relative measure, as they are invariably dependent upon the specific excavation strategies employed. Nevertheless, as each of these excavations were undertaken by the same organization, their methodologies were, at least broadly, consistent. From these figures, the artefact density of the Tower Works Early Iron Age settlement is immediately striking (yet this is somewhat misleading as it represents small, area-specific, rather than site-wide, densities). What is also noteworthy is that, whilst the ratio of pottery-to-bone at the Tower Works and Edgerley is comparable and generally typical of that on most prehistoric sites, at 1:17 the Elliott Site is markedly different. It produced more than three times the quantity of bone as Edgerley, despite the fact that they are sites of roughly equivalent size. In fact, the Elliott Site generated the largest Bronze Age-attributed animal bone assemblage of any of Fengate's excavations and, accordingly, this data must feature within its interpretation.

The encounter with, and potential of, ubiquitous buried soil strata was not really recognized in the

TABLE 1.2. *Comparative site assemblages and artefact densities (per square metre).*

	Flint		Pot		Bone		Pot/Bone ratio
	No.	Density	No.	Density	No.	Density	
Tower Works							
1997 EIA (104 sqm)	23	-	455	4.4	452	4.4	1:1
2004 Roman (1400 sqm)	17	0.09	738	0.5	1115	0.8	1:1.5
Edgerley (16,700 sqm)	706	0.04	1767	0.1	1211	0.08	1.5:1
Elliott (17,300 sqm)	405	0.02	230	0.01	3948	0.2	1:17.2

course of Fengate's early excavations. Indeed, it was only really 'discovered' during the last stages of stripping the Cat's Water sub-Site in the final year, 1978 (Pryor 1984). It was up to subsequent projects, particularly Etton (Pryor 1998a) and Haddenham (Evans & Hodder 2006a) to problematize and explore various means of sampling these generic buried horizons. Accordingly, first starting with the Depot Site in 1992 (Evans 1992 and in Pryor 2001a, 17–27; see Chapter 3, below), this strata has been a focus of all the ensuing CAU investigations within the Fengate area. Not only has this involved soil micromorphology, but also metre-square sampling for the finds densities locked within them (Table 1.3). Attesting to the Unit's application of standard artefact-sampling procedures generally (e.g. Evans 2000; Gdaniec *et al.* 2008 and Lucy *et al.* forthcoming), as discussed in Chapter 6 below, this allows for a degree of broad statistical comparison between the 'background' intensity of Fengate's land-use and other prehistoric landscapes within the region.

Beyond the presentation of the sites alone, several major themes will also be addressed in this volume, primarily the nature of Bronze Age settlement and land-use, and its 'collectivity' generally. Of the first, any potential settlement component within the axes of Fengate's fieldsystem was downplayed in the '70s excavations in the expectation of 'more', the ethos being that it must have lain elsewhere. As a result of landscape-scale exposures since that time, understanding of the (low intensity) character of the period's occupation has developed significantly, and Fengate's data will be reviewed in the light of this new evidence.

The other main themes — *land-use and collectivity* — are clearly interrelated factors within the organization and operation of the fieldsystem (and its community/ies). Yet, in this case, they also find further expression, albeit negative. Namely, in contrast to other sites/systems (and given the scale of Fengate's exposures), what accounts for the apparent absence of accompanying cremation cemeteries: why aren't they there? Review will accordingly have to be made both of the ring-ditches and other monuments within the immediate area, and also, of the report of

TABLE 1.3. *Buried soil sampling, worked flint densities.*

	Depot site (11 sqm)	Tower Works (2004; 57 sqm)	Elliott (28 sqm)	Edgerley (27 sqm)
Worked flint				
Range	0–6	0–2	0–2	0–3
Mean density	2.3	0.09	0.2	0.7

Wyman Abbott's finding of an extraordinarily large and complicated mortuary complex during the early gravel workings. It will be argued that the greater degree of collectivity expressed therein might also have ramifications for the dynamics behind the Flag Fen platform.

In order to adequately consider such issues, a firm sense of framing context will need to be established. As will be outlined in Chapter 2, in the first instance this will involve other recent excavations in the wider Fengate/Whittlesey environs, specifically the quarry-related projects at Kings Dyke/Bradley Fen and, somewhat more removed, at Eye. Further afield, the results of the CAU's major excavations along the lower River Great Ouse (the Barleycroft/Over investigations) and at its immediate fen-junction at Earith will also be drawn upon. In particular, the latter project's findings have a strong resonance with Fengate. That derives not only from the striking parallels between portions of its ring-ditch-dotted fieldsystems and Fengate's, but also from the fact that it was the first major exposure of the Bronze Age fieldsystem in the region since Pryor's Peterborough work. Reference will also need to be made to a series of South Lincolnshire sites, these being, in the main, at Welland Bank and Langtoft. Finally, the findings of Yates' 2007 synthetic overview, *Land, Power and Prestige: Bronze Age Field Systems in Southern England*, will be drawn upon.

Now having a far greater degree of regional context, this study affords an opportunity to reappraise the status of Fengate's archaeology. It is fair to say that since the excavation of Flag Fen in the mid '80s, there has, in effect, been a propensity to view the later prehistory of its immediate fen-edge 'backwards' from the perspective of the latter's timber platform. In other words, informed by its apparent 'special-ness', there has been a tendency to search for and, arguably over-emphasize, the antecedents of its uniqueness amid the boundaries of the Fengate fieldsystem. Yet this risks injustice to both Flag Fen's and Fengate's archaeology, and it is essential that we try to determine just what is truly distinct within Fengate's sequence.

This being said, the circular imprint of what is evidently a pair of barrows that appear in the bottom left-hand corner of Figure 1.3's photograph effectively announces two further 'extraordinaries': to the south of these rings, a major barrow cemetery and, further southeast, the Must Farm timber platform (Figs. 2.15, 4.28 & 6.9). Outlined in Chapter 2 below, while both occur south of the Nene Washes, which otherwise effectively amounts to the southern limit of this volume's core-area study zone (Fig. 6.1; the bulk of the barrow cemetery actually falling within the Washes' embankment), they are discoveries of such magnitude that they further recast the understanding of the prehistory of the broader Flag Fen Basin/Fengate area.

From the first, the approach taken to Fengate's archaeology by Pryor was most certainly *informed* and not just data-led, and he went so far as to critique generic 'Landscape Archaeology' approaches of the day (1980a, 485). While the emphasis given to *transhumance* in the operation of Fengate's fieldsystem (e.g. Pryor 1978, 162; 1984, 202, 210) potentially had a regional precedent in patterns of long-distance medieval stock intercommoning (Darby 1940), it was equally sympathetic to the Cambridge 'Higgsian' School of Palaeo-Economic Archaeology of the 1970s. Undoubtedly offering an attractive dynamic, such 'life-on-the-hoof' interpretations provided a means of interconnecting far-flung distribution dots and, thereby, immediate context. Certainly, during that decade and into the next, modes of wetland transhumant modelling came to explain most of the major 'highlights' of the region's prehistory, variously providing the impetus for its fieldsystems, causewayed enclosures and hillforts (see Evans 1987 for review).

Amid occasional interpretative allusions verging on historicism (e.g. cattle rustling; Pryor 1976, 42), Fengate's interpretation was essentially driven by environmental determinism, although never completely ignoring socio-cultural factors (see Pryor 1980a, 176 on '*cultural* ecology'). The common south/southeast orientation of its Iron Age roundhouse doorways was, for example, explained in reference to cold fenland winds, and the ultimate abandonment of the Cat's Water settlement in Roman times was attributed to third-century AD flooding. Similarly, it was the onset of Fen Clay flooding in the later third millennium BC — and the accompanying loss of summertime

peatland pasture — that was held to first give rise to Fengate's fieldsystem (Pryor 1984, 206, 213, 230). While, of course, working in a landscape so prone to change as the Fens only the foolhardy would disavow the crucial impact of environment on its sequences, the impetus behind such explanations must invariably be local-/regional-specific. Such immediate modes of interpretation reflect a paucity of excavated parallels at that time. In other words, too little *pattern* was then available to appreciate just how widespread were such phenomena as the common orientation of Iron Age doorways, or even Bronze Age fieldsystems as a whole; accumulated knowledge invariably undermines the degree to which explanations can lie in immediate landscape factors, as opposed to deeper cultural trends and broader social factors.

Far less appreciated is the fact that much of Fengate, and most explicitly the Storey's Bar Road complex (Pryor 1978), was also interpreted within the paradigm of the *New Archaeology*; its operational logic being understood in terms of the efficiency of labour. (Hence why its ring-ditch had, *de facto*, to relate to the Grooved Ware settlement, as it represented too great an investment for the single Collared Urn cremation found within its interior and, accordingly, it could not have been a monument outright; see Evans & Pollard in Pryor 2001a, 25–6.) Variously citing Binford, Clarke and others, and endorsing the principles of Schiffer's 'Behavioural Archaeology' (albeit qualified), Pryor was much more explicit in this vein in his 1980 paper, 'Will it all come out in the Wash?'. There, he re-visited his interpretation of Storey's Bar Road and explained its deposition in reference to Schiffer's 'C'- and 'N'-transformations. In fact, Storey's Bar Road, together with Hodder's *Wendens Ambo* (1982b), is among the very few overtly '*New*' excavations to have occurred in Britain (see Evans *et al.* 2006 concerning David Clarke's Great Wilbraham excavation), and the same influences are also clearly apparent in the methodological rigour Pryor brought to Maxey's fieldwork (Pryor & French 1985).

Over the intervening years, Fengate has become a unique archaeological palimpsest through the extent of its accumulative 'over-writing' — *text upon text upon land* — and, like the incessant sprawl and infill of the area's industrial units today, much conspires to stop us today seeing Fengate as 'land' (Fig. 1.2). In the case of its archaeology, this is also a matter of *site genealogies*; to borrow Foucault's phrase, we are now 'beyond origins' and cannot appreciate Fengate's fieldsystems without the filter of earlier fieldwork. As further explored in Chapter 2, it is because we must invariably dig in relationship to what has been dug before, that an active appreciation of the deeper

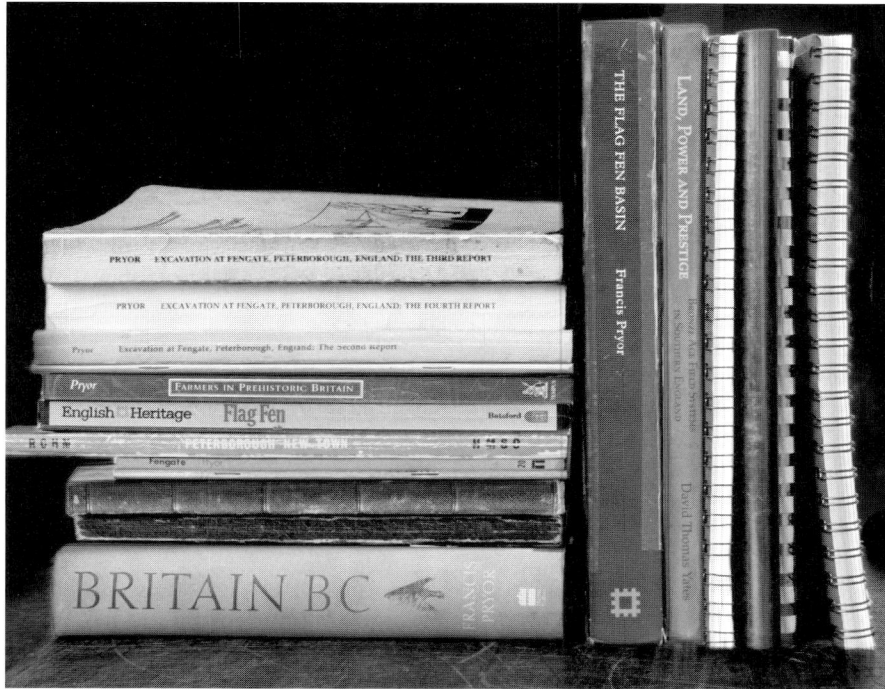

FIGURE 1.6. *The Fengate Stacks ('text-on-text') — A formidable legacy of various notebooks, papers, books and reports (photograph, D. Webb).*

historiographic framework of our researches and also the persuasion of other, non-immediate fieldwork influences, becomes imperative.

The publication of Pryor's final Fengate volume in 1984 (Cat's Water) marked a watershed within its landscape study, seeing a high level of over-arching interpretation. Certainly, its final discussion chapter can only be considered masterful and, arguably, that was last time Fengate ever saw such a unified perspective (and probably the only time it ever will). While the 2001 Flag Fen volume included a degree of Fengate overview, that was of quite a different order and considerably more fragmentary as it had to account for the myriad of small-scale investigations undertaken by other organisations during the 1990s. To this must be added Pryor's own continuing involvement in both the immediate landscape and the wider Peterborough/Welland environs. This had naturally led to a degree of revisionism and what can seem a series of somewhat contradictory 'simultaneous' (re-) interpretative trends. With his excavations at Etton, Pryor shifted toward post-processualism and, becoming increasingly 'ritualistic' in his approach, duly reinterpreted Fengate's Neolithic from this perspective (1988; 1993). Then, there was the discovery of the Flag Fen timber platform, just 'offshore' from Fengate. Certainly an extraordinary site

if ever there was one, as alluded to above, it resulted in a commensurate search for the *special* in Fengate's sequence; in effect, what 'announced' Flag Fen in both time and space. Finally, on himself becoming a sheep farmer, Pryor reappraised the operations of Fengate's fieldsystems and introduced grand-scale flock dynamics into its interpretation in his 1996 paper, 'Sheep, stockyards and field systems: Bronze Age livestock populations in the Fenlands of eastern England' (and also his volume, *Farmers in Prehistoric Britain*; 1998c). Harking back to the project's New Archaeological roots, this paper was still underscored by concepts of economic maximisation. Moreover, attempting to navigate the waters of Fengate's changing interpretation, not only Pryor's many academic papers, but also his popular syntheses have to be taken into account (e.g. 1991; 2003).

While this volume will provide, again, some degree of overview to its study, it certainly does not aspire to 'totality' (see Evans & Hodder 2006b further to this theme) and ultimately, of course, it can only amount to still another 'over-writing'. If nothing else, though, Fengate's now densely nuanced, accumulative legacy seems appropriate to landscape investigation as an open-ended interpretive project — *never seeing completion or closure* — and this is an ethos that Pryor himself has certainly embraced.

Fengate/Mucking — Project connections

It was not without some degree of irony that, during the production of this volume, the CAU also embarked upon a final, 'third-try' Mucking publication programme. Amid that project's mammoth archives, housed in the British Museum (see Clark 1993 for project history), was a file with site-related correspondence between its director, Margaret Jones, and Pryor. This gives insights into the unexpected connections between the two projects, although, in hindsight these linkages make perfect sense (and, yes, in retrospect, I can remember Margaret attending a Fengate day-seminar and asking singularly awkward questions of Francis). During the '60s Pryor had dug at Mucking, and together, it and Fengate were the only really 'big' landscape projects of their day in eastern England. Both projects, moreover, shared a major Bronze Age component, with Mucking having seven round barrows set within a series of fieldsystem 'blocks' (admittedly much simpler and more patchily traced than Fengate's) and, of course, its great 'Rings' (see below; Jones & Bond 1980). Nevertheless, the degree to which the archives' letter-exchanges convey a sense of shared research directives between the two projects was unanticipated.

Consisting of 18 letters, their correspondence started in January 1978, with Pryor asking Jones if he could see a plan of Mucking's Bronze Age fieldsystem, and continued until 1980 (with Dave Crowther and Maisie Taylor fielding queries from Jones during the following year). Whilst providing insights into how a shared research framework and context is established, much of the correspondence is fairly banal and deals with such matters as clay fabrics, pottery and loomweight types, and salt-making equipment. Indicative, however, of developing cross-North Sea research connections, in one letter (15/02/80) Pryor announces that he is about to travel to Holland and, in another (02/08/79), Jones relates that she has been in touch with Dutch archaeologists working with diatoms in pottery to establish whether clays were saline and if, on this basis, pottery can shown to have been imported. Of more immediate interest, arising as a result of Pryor's Welland Bank/Maxey Project 'manifesto' in the Rescue Newsletter (Pryor 1980b), is Margaret's reaction to his 'redundant information' stance (see Chapter 6, Inset, below):

```
Best of luck to the new project, especially
your use of computers, etc. I cannot,
however, agree with your view that much
information is redundant. In the first
place, it is only when some sites have been
completely rescued that we can realise
what can be done without - if you follow
this! (Jones 11/02/80; emphasis added).
```

At Mucking the Joneses did, indeed, attempt to dig everything and locally achieved a 75–100 per cent excavation sample. What seems extraordinary concerning that project was that the Joneses wholeheartedly embraced cutting-edge computing while still practising an outmoded notebook recording system involving a co-ordinate-based system instead of 'contexts' (this is in contrast to Fengate, which did employ single-context recording; its use of computers was, though, rudimentary and it was only in his subsequent Maxey investigations that Pryor fully adopted their usage; Fig. 1.7, see Pryor 1984, app. 1). Not until today, with readily available GIS-based programmes, have Mucking's intensive excavation/plotting techniques — with their tremendous possibilities for artefact distributional analysis — come into their own.

Also of immediate significance are Jones and Pryor's five letters, from May to August 1980, concerning the nature of their project's early fieldsystems (they sent each other colour-pencilled photocopies of their respective Bronze Age landscapes; Fig. 1.8). Their exchanges progressed, with Margaret taking Pryor to task for describing his system by its ditches and not so much as fields (01/05/80). Sending his figure in his reply, Pryor hinted of just how large he then considered Fengate to be:

```
It's almost impossible to estimate the
original extent of the field system, but
recent work by the Nene Valley Research
Committee at Orton Longueville, some
5 miles west of Fengate, has revealed
traces of straight ditch[es] associated
with Beaker barrows - presumably part of
the Fengate system. The Fengate system is
known to extend over about 1km by about
600m of land, and that is perhaps rather
a conservative estimate (Pryor 20/05/80).
```

Relating to a question still of relevance for this volume, Margaret took issue with Pryor concerning his parallel-ditch track-/droveways: fine when they bordered one side of fields, but what of when they went right the way around compounds? These she referred to as 'duplicating' circuits and went on to discuss them in relationship to Mucking's Romano-British enclosures, which did, indeed, also have such 'doubled' boundaries. Her term 'duplication', though, resulted in some confusion, with Pryor thinking that she implied that Mucking saw Roman reuse of Bronze Age ditches, an impression that Margaret later emphatically dismissed. Nevertheless, the frank exchanges this fostered, in terms of what is implied by in-/out-field for their respective systems, is illuminating for both projects (and their remarks will also feature in the forthcoming Mucking publication):

```
I find your suggestion for the use of an
infield/outfield system interesting and
convincing, but wonder, nonetheless, how
one can prove it. What sort of surface
evidence, for example, would one expect
to find in the outfield - surely we could
expect to find the occasional summer camp
or enclosure in the manner of the highland
zone sheilings? (Pryor 22/07/80).
```

That it was Dermot Bond, a legendary Fengate supervisor, who thereafter went onto to direct the North Ring excavations at Mucking for the Central Excavation Unit, provides another inter-project link (see Fig. 6.10; Jones & Bond 1980 and Bond 1988). In recent years Mucking's two Ring enclosures — the southern originally interpreted by the Joneses as an Early Iron Age 'mini-hillfort' and subsequently as, in effect, a Late Bronze Age 'stronghold' controlling both a local ridgeway route and possibly along-Thames movement (Jones & Bond 1980) — has attracted considerable reappraisal, largely focusing upon the formality of their spatial layout and the situation of their 'special' deposits (i.e. human remains and metalwork; Parker Pearson & Richards 1994 and Brück 2006). Mucking saw the end of its fieldwork in 1978 and, in effect, that marked the last excavation within its immediate environs. Alternatively, probably due to Pryor's maintained presence in the local landscape at Flag Fen and the sense of the Fengate landscape as an on-going project (i.e. an active 'directorial territory'), it has not seen the same degree of 'outside' re-interpretation.

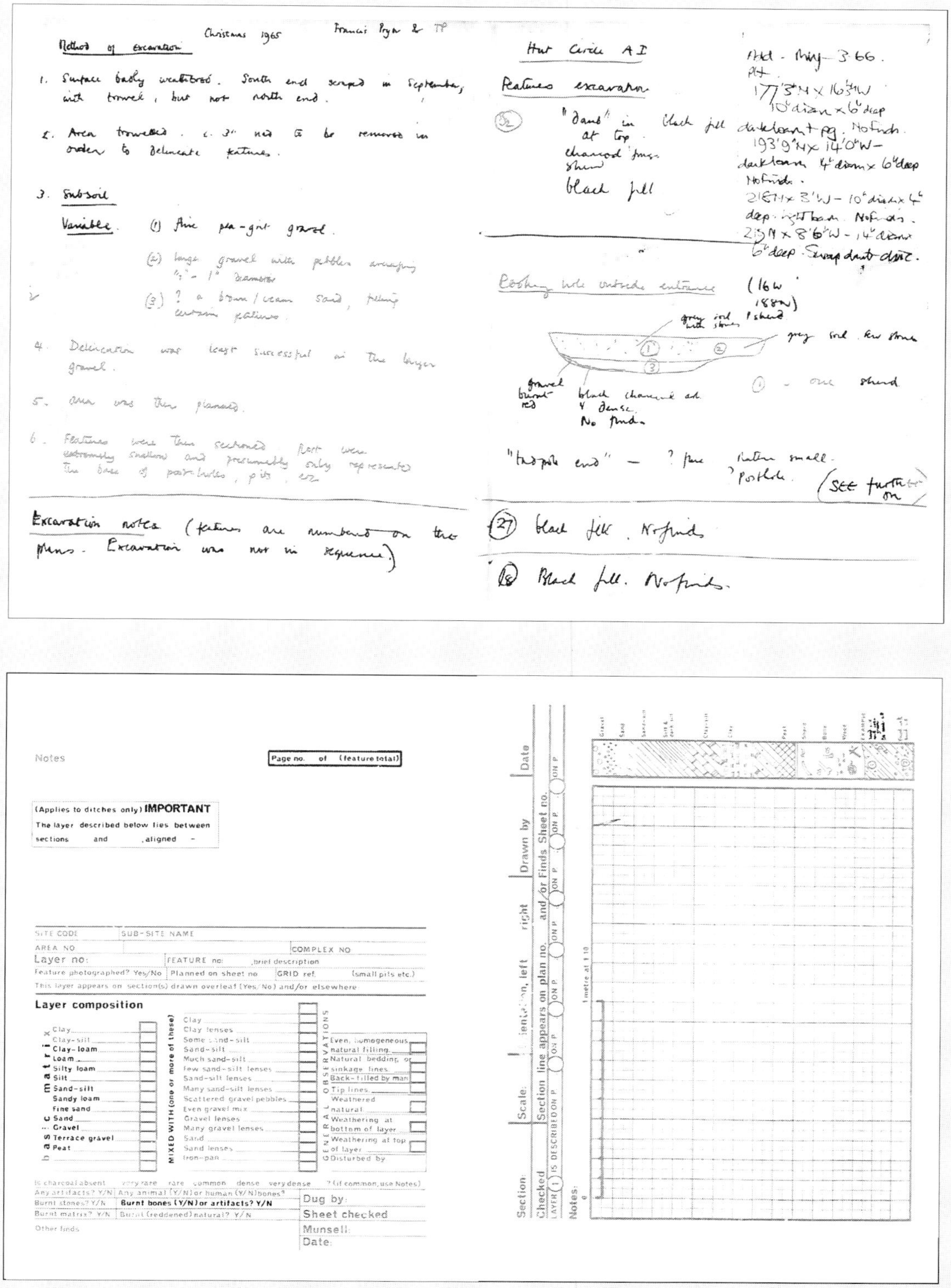
Christmas 1965 Francis Pryor & TP

Method of excavation

1. Surface badly weathered. South end scraped in September, with trowel, but not north end.

2. Area trowelled. c. 3" now to be removed in order to delineate features.

3. Subsoil

Variable. (1) fine pea-grit gravel.
(2) large gravel with pebbles averaging ½"–1" diameter
(3) ? a brown/clean sand, filling certain features.

4. Delineation was least successful in the larger gravel.

5. Area was then planned.

6. Features were then sectioned. Most were extremely shallow and presumably only represented the base of post-holes, pits, etc.

Excavation notes (features are numbered on the plans. Excavation was not in sequence)

Hut Circle A I

Features excavation

(52) "daub" in black fill at top. charcoal frags. Shu... black fill

Hut circle A I ... 3.66.

Cooking hole outside entrance (16w 188w)

gravel burnt red; black charcoal ash & dense. No finds.

grey soil with stones; 1 sherd; grey soil, few stones

(1) – one sherd

"tadpole end" – ? fine rather small. ? posthole. (SEE further on)

(27) black fill. No finds.

(28) Black fill. No finds.

Notes

Page no. of (feature total)

(Applies to ditches only) IMPORTANT
The layer described below lies between sections and , aligned

SITE CODE | SUB-SITE NAME
AREA NO | COMPLEX NO
Layer no: | FEATURE no: brief description
Feature photographed? Yes/No | Planned on sheet no | GRID ref (small pits etc.)
This layer appears on section(s) drawn overleaf (Yes/No) and/or elsewhere

Layer composition

Matrix: Clay; Clay-silt; Clay-loam; Loam; Silty loam; Silt; Sand-silt; Sandy loam; Fine sand; Sand; Gravel; Terrace gravel; Peat

MIXED WITH (one or more of these): Clay; Clay lenses; Some sand-silt; Sand-silt; Much sand-silt; Few sand-silt lenses; Sand-silt lenses; Many sand-silt lenses; Scattered gravel pebbles; Even gravel mix; Gravel lenses; Many gravel lenses; Sand; Sand lenses; Iron-pan

GENERAL OBSERVATIONS: Even, homogeneous, natural filling; Natural bedding, or sinkage lines; Back-filled by man; Tip lines; Weathered natural; Weathering at bottom of layer; Weathering at top of layer; Disturbed by

Is charcoal absent very rare rare common dense very dense ? (if common, use Notes)
Any artifacts? Y/N Any animal (Y/N) or human (Y/N) bones?
Burnt stones? Y/N Burnt bones (Y/N) or artifacts? Y/N
Burnt matrix? Y/N Burnt (reddened) natural? Y/N
Other finds

Dug by:
Sheet checked
Munsell:
Date:

Section | Scale: | Date | Drawn by | Checked | Section line appears on plan no. and/or Finds Sheet no. | LAYER (1) IS DESCRIBED ON P | ON P | Notes: | 1 metre at 1:10

Gravel; Sand; Sand-silt; Silt & dark silt; Clay-silt; Clay; Peat; Sherd; Bone; Wood; EXAMPLE

FIGURE 1.7. *Recording Systems — Top, facing pages of Tim Potter and Pryor's notebooks entries at Mucking, Essex (Notebook no. 1); bottom, early Fengate computer punchcard-based 'layer' card (see Lucas's Chapter 5 Inset concerning notebook vs context sheet recording).*

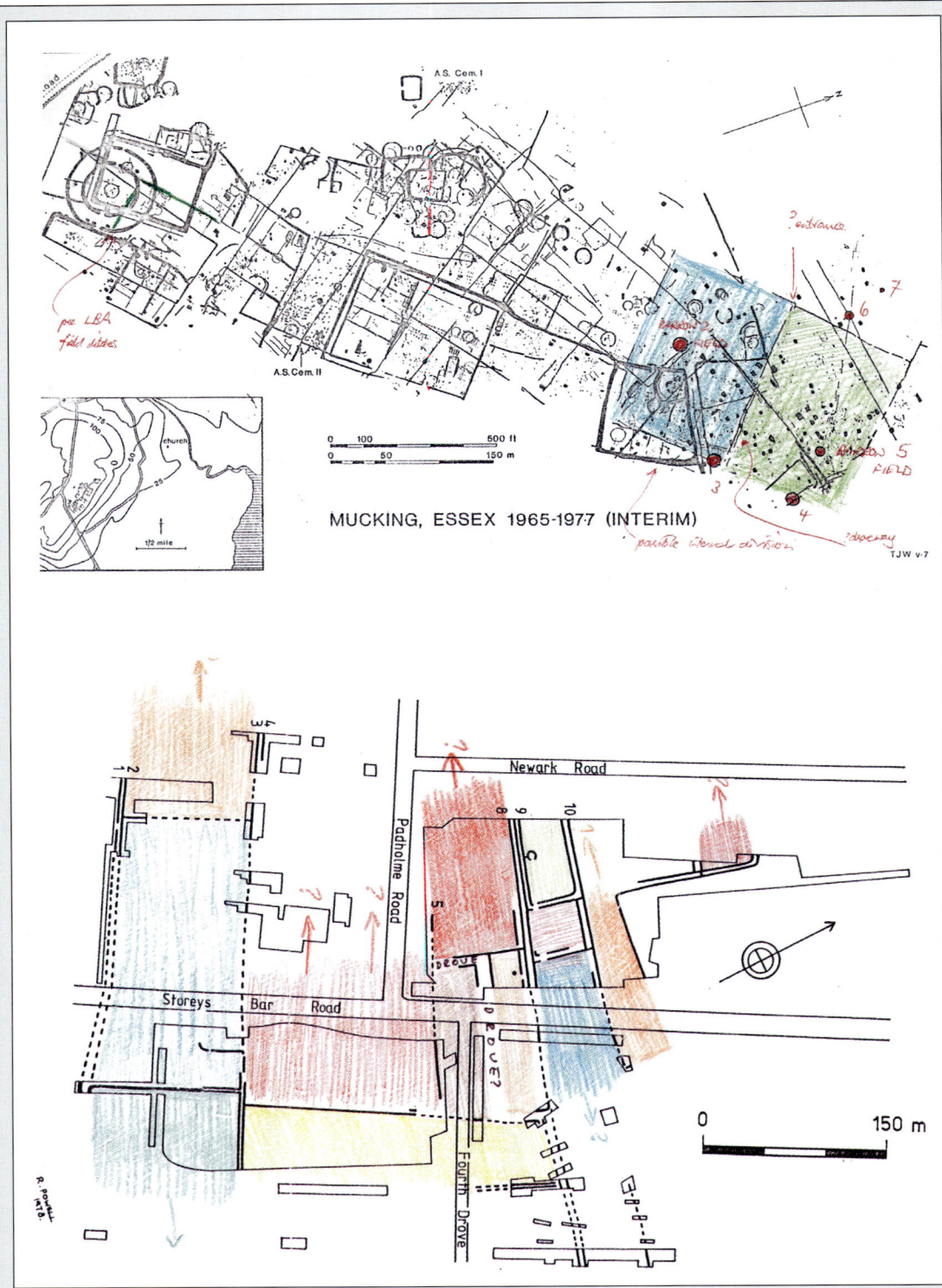

FIGURE 1.8. *A Landscape Exchange — Top, a copy of M. Jones's 1980 colour-annotated plan of Mucking's Bronze Age (note that this omits the South Rings as it was then thought to be an Early Iron Age 'mini-hillfort'); bottom, the colourful Fengate 'field-block' plan sent by Pryor (Pryor/Fengate Correspondence File, Mucking Archives, British Museum).*

Fengate's sub-sites and components

As opposed to the clean aesthetics of this volume's first map, Figure 1.9, showing all the 'interventions' to date within Fengate's core, is fairly horrific. Yet, attesting to the long-term palimpsest of fieldwork (i.e. time in landscape), it is important that it is appreciated 'un-groomed'. Indeed, with so many excavations now having been undertaken locally, it can be difficult to appreciate its many parts. This has been compounded by that fact that it is only at this juncture that its area-plans have been digitized, and the experience of having done this for Fengate (concurrently also for Mucking) demonstrates just how important the advent of computerized graphics has been for the analysis and data-manipulation of major landscape projects. Accordingly, to facilitate further discussion and establish a sense of 'base-line', here we will review the many phases/areas of excavation at Fengate, with their Bronze Age fieldsystem-related components being prioritised (Fig. 1.9). Again, for comprehension in the face of sheer numbers, this will be divided, with Mahany's Site 11 and Pryor's original 1970s sub-sites presented first (see also Pryor's cross-volume chronological gazetteer in '*Fengate Four*' (1984, 256–7), with his ditch-enumeration system used as a basis of reference (originally, 1–15 in Pryor 1974a, fig. 1; modified to 1–19 in Pryor 2001a, fig. 1.4).

Site 11 (1969)
This trench-area rescue excavation, directed by Christine Mahany on behalf of the Nene Valley Research Committee, occurred hard on the heels of the publication of the *Peterborough New Town* volume (RCHM 1969); however, aside from a note in *Current Archaeology* (Mahany 1969), it was only fully published by Pryor in 1993 (in Simpson *et al*. 1993, 127–40; see also Pryor 2001a, 9). As suggested by aerial photographs, its main component was a rectangular enclosure (30 × 50 m) defined by a 3 m-wide and 0.70 m-deep ditch. In addition, a number of settlement-related features were found within its interior (including what was probably a roundhouse eavesgully) and also cutting the main ditch's fills. The excavator, though, understood these to be generally contemporary. There is, however, considerable ambiguity concerning its dating and sequence, and this will be further discussed below (see Chapter 5, Inset). Crucially, the enclosure lay well off the orientation of the adjacent Newark Road fieldsystem and yielded little dating evidence (and much of that inconclusive: a single sherd of Beaker within its upper fills, and both a leaf-shaped arrowhead and a thumbnail scraper). Based essentially on the paucity of material recovered from it (only 17 flints from seven 'segment-cuttings') and its shared alignment with the Padholme Road Neolithic 'house', it was subsequently interpreted by Pryor as a Neolithic mortuary enclosure (see also Kinnes, in Pryor 1993, 138), with the other features being assigned to a Beaker-associated settlement.

Padholme Road (1971–72)
This included the Neolithic 'house' (see Chapter 3, Inset), two Beaker pits and Iron Age pits/wells (Pryor 1974a; 1980, 3–22; 1984, 11–12). Along the southern side of the field, ditches flanking a 4 m-wide, 'fenward' droveway were dug (1 & 2; the former having a burial

within it). A parallel ditch (3) was traced for some 145 m across the middle of the field. At its western end, a second boundary (4) ran parallel with it, *c*. 4–5 m north, suggestive of still another droveway. This may have been localized as the 'doubling' only continued over some 10 m, at which point Ditch 4 stopped. Only one cross-axial boundary running between Ditches 2 and 3 was recovered; Ditches 1–3 were exposed again within the Cat's Water sub-Site.

Vicarage Farm (1972)
This saw the excavation of a narrow double-ditch system and a series of earlier and Middle Iron Age pits (scraps of Beaker and a flake from a Group VI polished axe were recovered). No dating evidence was retrieved from the ditches, despite their near-complete, very intensive excavation. Based on their alignment, Pryor thought them unlikely to be of second-millennium BC attribution; he admitted, though, that a Neolithic date was possible (1974a, 15–22; 1984, 7–10).

Storey's Bar Road (1973)
The subject of the second Fengate report (Pryor 1978; though see also 1984, 13–18), this involved two main areas: a main eastward area of excavation (I) and, anticipating road construction, a large northeast–southwest arcing swathe (Area II). The route of a major Romano-British droveway obliquely crossed the latter and continued into the northern end of Area I; two sub-square paddocks conjoining it were obviously in part contemporary. Within Area I, this 'way' cut through a minor Iron Age settlement cluster, consisting of a length of enclosure-ditch, pits and two roundhouses. Within the extreme northeastern quarter of that area was the corner of a Bronze Age 'field' (N1). Another such setting continued northwest from this area into Area II (P18/R1); both field-paddocks ran northward into the Padholme Road field.

The focus of the excavation lay within the south-central portion of Area I. A relatively minor ditched fieldsystem extended across this area (sharing the same alignment as the main Bronze Age system; B2, B38, B43, B/R21, R2, R4/W23, W24, & Y21). This cut across the circuit of a major ring-ditch (containing two inhumations and a cremation). Also excavated were a series of pits and postholes and two later Bronze Age wells. Otherwise, due essentially to the quantity of Grooved Ware, the remainder of these features — the fieldsystem, pits/postholes and the ring-ditch — were all considered to be of later Neolithic date (the Grooved Ware settlement-related ring-ditch thought later to be reworked as an earlier Bronze Age barrow). This interpretation was, though, reappraised within the Flag Fen volume (Evans & Pollard, in Pryor 2001a); the Grooved Ware-phase was relegated to open-settlement activity (pit-/posthole-associated), with the other features all considered to be of Bronze Age attribution (see Inset, Chapter 3).

Newark Road (1975–77)
This was the main area-excavation dedicated to the core of the Bronze Age fieldsystem (certainly it produced its most coherent plan-exposure), and it was with this that *The Third Report* was largely concerned (Pryor 1980a). In the main, its paddocks/plots were organised on either side of a major fenward drove (Ditches 8/9). South thereof were identified three ditched plots (1–3), one having a well within its interior. Bounded by the next main/continuous ditch axis northward (Ditch 10, later numbered '11'), three quite regular sub-square/-rectangular compounds were arranged along the other side of the drove (A–C). The most westerly had both a roundhouse and a 'D-'shaped 'barn' within its interior.

Having, in part, double-ditch circuits (originally referred to as 'internal droves'), the layout of this portion of the system seems very formal and Pryor has since identified these as a series of 'communal stockyards' (1996, 315–17; 2001a, 409-10). Their functional operation will be discussed at length below and need not overly detain us now. It must, though, be mentioned that the excavations also

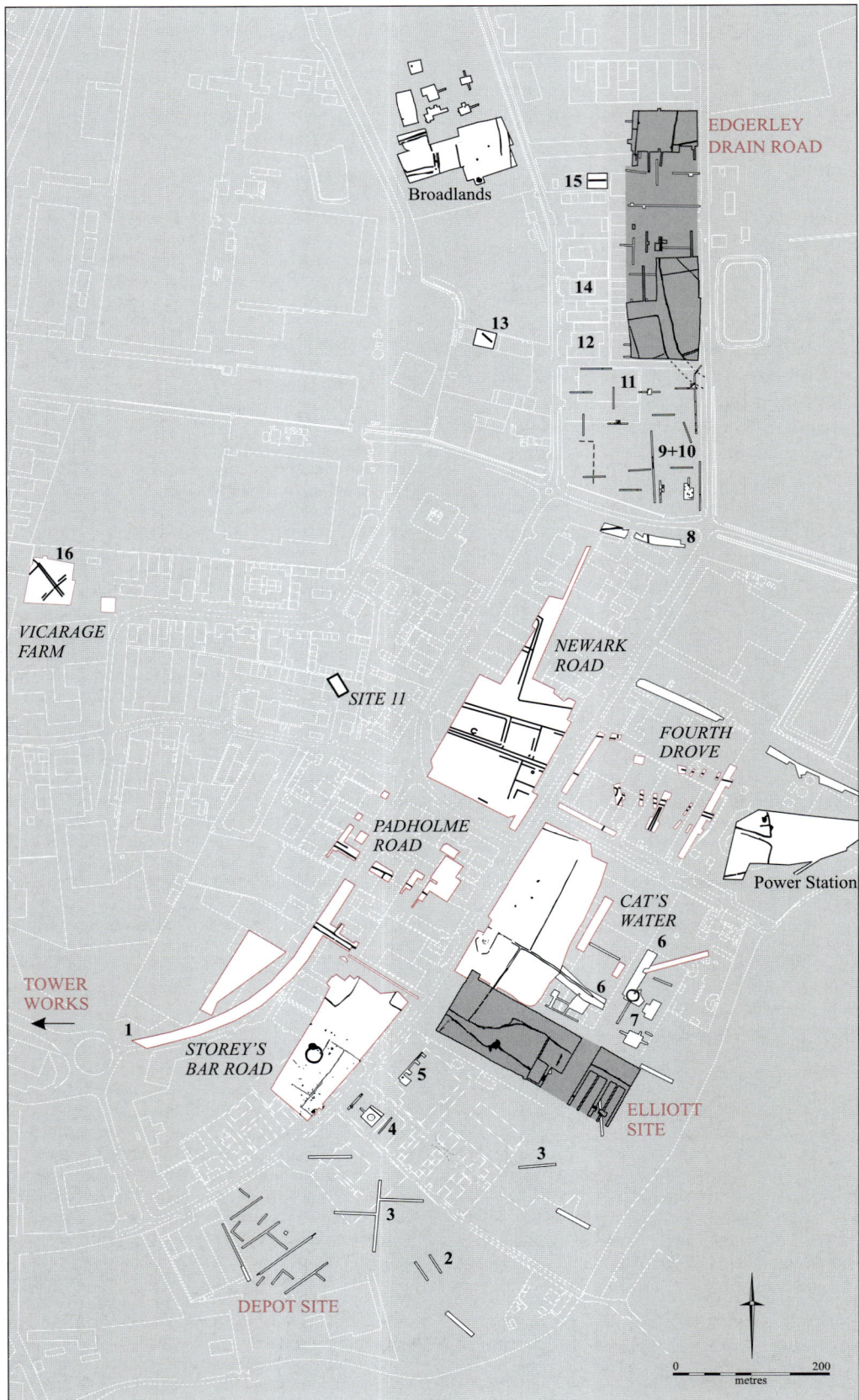

EDGERLEY
DRAIN ROAD

Broadlands

15

14

13

12

11

9+10

8

16

*VICARAGE
FARM*

SITE 11

*NEWARK
ROAD*

*FOURTH
DROVE*

*PADHOLME
ROAD*

*CAT'S
WATER*

6

Power Station

TOWER
WORKS

1

6

7

*STOREY'S
BAR ROAD*

5

ELLIOTT
SITE

4

3

3

2

DEPOT SITE

0   200
metres

Figure 1.9. *(Left) Fengate Central and North — Map showing the area's now many 'interventions', with Pryor's 1970s sub-sites indicate in red outline and main CAU excavations in grey-tone; numbered entries variously refer to small-scale trench evaluations and watching briefs: 1) Boongate Roundabout (BUFU; Cutler 1995; Pryor 2001a, 32–3); 2) Materials Recycling Centre (Gdaniec 1996b; Pryor 2001a, 32); 3) Sites O and Q (BUFU; Cutler 1998; Pryor 2001a, 30–32, 50); 4) Third Drove (Cooper 1998); 5) TP Packaging Site (Pryor & Trimble 2000); 6) Cat's Water 1990 (Pryor 2001a, 38–47); 7) The Co-op Site (Gibson 1998; Pryor 2001a, 47–50); 8) Boroughby Garage (Pryor 2001b); 9) Off-Vicarage Road (HAT/AS; Vaughan & Trevarthen 1998); 10) 'Megacars'/Barnack UK Ltd Watching Brief (CAU; Beadsmoore 2007b); 11) Barnack UK Ltd. (Northants Arch. 2001); 12) Designation Ltd, Newark Road (Pryor & Trimble 1999); 13) Global Doors (Pryor 2001a, 37); 14) Site 'T', Newark Road (Casa Hatton 1999); 15) Paving Factory (Pryor 2001a, 37–8); 16) Vicarage Farm Road (Northants Arch. 1999). (Reproduced by permission of Ordnance Survey on behalf of HMSO. © Crown copyright 2009. All rights reserved. Ordnance Survey Licence number 100048686.)*

included other components to the north. There, another fenward ditch (F.254) returning northwards conjoined with the eastern frontage of an additional large double-ditch compound (Fig. 1.1; after Pryor 2001a, fig. 1.4, Ditches 14/15). Note, however, that this has a very awkward relationship to the (unexcavated) rectangular double-ditch compound shown on the aerial photography plots just to the west (Pryor 2001a, fig. 1.4, Ditches 12/13; Pryor 1974a, fig. 1, Ditches 11/12). Long suspecting that a rectification-error may be responsible for this arrangement, this has, indeed, now been demonstrated and is corrected and discussed at length in Chapter 6 below (cf. Figs 6.1 & .2) .

Apparently of first-millennium BC/Romano-British attribution, a few scattered pits, postholes and portions of another later ditch system also occurred.

Cat's Water (1975–78)

Overlain by a series of Romano-British paddocks and arranged around a major drove (the same as exposed in Storey's Bar Road Area II), this sub-site is most renowned for its dense, compound-associated Iron Age settlement which is the primary focus of the final Fengate report (Pryor 1984). In addition, and also covered in that volume, a Neolithic multiple burial and two Peterborough Ware-associated pits has since been recovered (and another, possible, Neolithic structure has since been identified there; see Chapter 3, Inset). Of greatest relevance for our immediate purposes, two fenward fieldsystem ditch-lines were exposed: Ditch 5 at the northern end of the field and, across its middle, the projection of Ditch '4' from Padholme Road. For much of its length, a parallel boundary (Ditch '3') ran along the south side of the latter ditch, but having only a 1.5–2 m-wide 'gap' this narrow interval-setting cannot have flanked a droveway, but rather an embankment (see Chapter 2, below). A cross-axial boundary ran between Ditches '4' and 5 (Ditch iii) and another narrow interval cross-axial 'pair' continued south from Ditch '3' (F.756 & F.862); after a distance of 30 m, recut, only the eastern of these, F.862, continued southward. Within the

southwestern margin of the site, a contemporary ditched compound extended off the side of one of the main boundaries (Ditch '4') and had a post-built roundhouse within its interior (Structure 46); two wells of the period also lay 40–75 m north thereof. The use of inverted commas in the description of these boundaries relates to the fact that their enumeration appears confused; Pryor's Ditch '4' here was actually the fenward continuation of Padholme Road's Ditch 3; the narrow interval-set ditch on its southern side cannot have equated with Padholme's Ditch 3, but must have been an altogether new boundary.

As part of the investigation programme, two large trenches were dug across the field east of the main site (to negative result; two other small trench-exposures were also cut in that area) and another extended for 65 m south from the excavation to trace one of the fieldsystem boundaries. At its end, the Ditch 1/2 droveway (first exposed at Padholme Road) was encountered and an inhumation was found at the junction of the northern ditch of this pair and that running south from Cat's Water proper (F.862; see Pryor 1980a, 158–68 and 1984, 27 for the sub-site's Bronze Age phases).

Fourth Drove (1977–78)

This site involved trial trenching in the field east of the Newark Road sub-Site to further trace the main fieldsystem boundaries and its 5–7 m-wide droveway (Ditches 8 & 9). Lying 45–55 m north of the drove, the projected line of Newark Road's Ditch '10' was recovered (as originally numbered; subsequently changed to 11 in Pryor 2001a, fig. 1.4). On the southern side of the droveway the area of the field was sub-divided into three plots by two double-ditched lines: Ditch iii with a parallel boundary on its northern side and, to the east, the pairing of Ditches i and ii. It is difficult to understand the nature of these boundaries' 'doublings': estimated to lie 3–5 m apart, their plan-relations preclude a droveway function and, in all probability, they related to a 'Newark Road-type' double-ditch compound.

In Area VIII a 'D-shaped' roundhouse was found beside the main drove and, elsewhere in the same area, a fieldsystem ditch-associated bank also survived. Aside from the Post-Deverel-Rimbury-attributed well and an Iron Age ditch, the Romano-British Fen Causeway was also exposed and investigated (Pryor 1980a, 131–57).

Having outlined Pryor's original excavations, later fieldwork will now be considered. Many of these sites have already been summarized within the Flag Fen volume and the following does not include minor interventions at the Boongate Roundabout and the Global Door and Paving Factory Sites (see Pryor 2001a, 32–3, 37–8).

The Power Station Excavations (1989)

Variously undertaken by Pryor and Tim Malim (with teams from Flag Fen, Lincoln City Unit and Cambridgeshire County Council), the main area of excavation straddled the fen-edge *per se*, with the buried ground surface lying at c. 1.2–1.75 m OD (Pryor 2001a, 52–73). Aside from a possible Neolithic ditch and a series of Beaker pits, the main finding was the fenward exposure of the c. 4 m-wide Ditch 8/9 droveway (from Fourth Drove), whose ditches turned respectively south and northward, to hug and delineate the fen-edge (the former also having a southwestward return axis which might have joined with Cat's Water Ditch 5). Although roughly oriented on the line of the droveway, its ditches were superseded by the multiple-set-/-phased, Late Bronze Age, timber alignment (running east to/through the Flag Fen platform), along which had been deposited a wealth of metalwork. Traces were also found of an Iron Age 'gravel platform'. Note that two long trenches dug along the northern side of the larger area of investigation did not reveal any further fieldsystem ditches.

Cat's Water (1990)

Anticipating development, the Fenland Archaeological Trust (FAT) excavated two areas east of the Cat's Water sub-Site (Pryor 2001a, 38–47). Conjoining with and running east from the latter and down to the Parish Drain, Area 1 revealed the continuation of Bronze Age Ditches '3' and '4' (see above). While the northern ditch of this pair continued down to the Drain-side end of this area, the southern terminated and joined with it; thereby, again indicating that they could not have flanked a droveway (that the one boundary did not continue for any distance east beyond the Parish Drain was demonstrated by the later Co-op Site investigations; see below). The second area lay immediately east of, and ran parallel with, the Drain. At its southeastern end a *c.* 15 m-diameter 'ring-form' monument was excavated. This was assigned as a Class I, later Neolithic henge, essentially based on the fact that there was an 'interruption' in its southern circuit, and a small, ring-setting within its interior was considered a 'mini-henge' (Pryor 2001a, 45–7, figs. 3.3, 3.8 & 3.9); however, no firm dating evidence was recovered from the monument, nor was it ever absolutely dated. Therefore, as further discussed in the *Fengate's Monuments* section below (see Chapter 4), based on accrued regional context this is here thought more likely to have been an earlier Bronze Age ring-ditch monument.

The Depot Site (1992)

During the course of the CAU evaluation fieldwork (based on Palmer's detailed cropmark plot), aside from testing a 20 m-diameter ring-ditch, extensive traces of Iron Age and Romano-British usage were revealed (Evans 1992; Pryor 2001a, 17–27). The latter both involved a late alluvium-filled fieldsystem running parallel with the fen-edge (and Pryor's Cat's Water/Storey's Bar Road Romano-British droveway), and evidence of Iron Age fen-edge occupation (including midden-like spreads and even possible turf-stack construction). Roman features were largely restricted to the western margin of the area (Pryor 2001a, fig. 2.6, 24–5). Related occupation and prehistoric features were further exposed where, in 1997, Pryor/FAT excavated a single trench along the western side of this field (Pryor 2001a, 27–30, fig. 2.9).

The most significant finding of the CAU's '92 fieldwork related to the area's Bronze Age fieldsystem. Here, in contrast to the more elongated, reave-like layout within its Padholme/Newark Road 'core', its arrangement was more 'block-like' and was laid-out in conjoining squares, approximately 70 m across (A–D; Pryor 2001a, fig. 2.4, 23–4, 26–7). These were demarcated by double-ditched boundaries on their sides, which were thought to relate to embankment rather than droveways. Block 'D' being so-surrounded on all four of its sides. In one of the blocks (D), a ditched, sub-rectangular settlement compound (34 × 26 m) was distinguished, with two small roundhouses within its interior (Pryor 2001a, fig. 2.5). While one of these (I) was probably associated with the fieldsystem itself, the other, Structure II, seemed related to the sub-rectangular compound. The latter appeared to recut the second-millennium BC system and, otherwise yielding little dating evidence, was attributed to the Late Bronze Age/Early Iron Age.

In 1998, the eastern side of the Bronze Age 'block-system' was trenched by the Birmingham University Archaeology Unit (BUFU; see Sites O & Q below). Involving, as shown on the cropmark plots, three parallel boundaries, it is possible that the outer eastern 'pairing' may represent a major fenward droveway. In 2006 the CAU undertook watching brief monitoring when a building was erected within the central swathe of this area. This did not, though, generate any significantly different/new results (Mackay 2006a & b). However, when in 1999 Soke Archaeological Services excavated a trench across the ring-ditch, a crouched inhumation was apparently found within its ditch (probably juvenile); backfilled and left *in situ*, no other details of the burial are available.

Materials Recycling Centre (1996)

The CAU first undertook a coring survey across the field, east of the Parish Drain and south of Third Drove. Subsequently, two 20 m-long trenches were excavated beside the drain at right-angles to the fen-edge, in which the terrace deposits sloped down from *c.* 1.75 m OD to *c.* 1.35 m OD at their southeastern end (Gdaniec 1996b; Pryor 2001a, 32). The gravels carried a well-developed, 0.4 m-deep buried soil that was sealed by freshwater alluvium. Seemingly all of Middle/later Bronze Age attribution (based on the few finds recovered), a scattering of postholes and pits — including a large watering-hole — were present; in two cases, a thin skin of peat was found to fill their upper depressions/profiles.

The Co-op Site (1997)

The CAU undertook further investigation within the same east-of-Cat's Water field where Pryor had recovered his putative henge (Gibson 1998; Pryor 2001a, 47–50, figs. 3.12 & 3.13). Aside from exposing possible small fence-line settings running parallel with Ditches 3/4, and the recovery of Grooved Ware sherds from a pit in the expanded Trench 5 area, only one really significant finding was made: a sub-square Neolithic post-built structure (Trench 6), the status of which is discussed at length below (see Inset, Chapter 3). Although being a trench-based exercise, the results cannot be considered conclusive, together with the results of Pryor's 'Cat's Water East' trenching this programme also provided important negative evidence: no trace of any of Fourth Drove's south-of-droveway ditches (i & ii) were recovered.

There was some difficulty establishing the exact location of the 1990 'henge' in this area and, indeed, this was never satisfactorily resolved. In consequence, in this site's Flag Fen volume summary there was a certain degree of 'fixing' of trenches in the light of 'henge-shift' (Pryor 2001a, fig. 3.12; cf. Gibson 1998, fig. 3), with 3 and 4 shown further northeast than their actual position. What is critical in this context is that Trench 4 definitely transected the projected line of the Cat's Water Ditch 3/4 boundary, which did not continue east into it.

Sites O and Q (1998)

An evaluation was undertaken by the BUFU in the fields on either side of Third Drove, south of Storey's Bar Road (Cutler 1998; Pryor 2001a, 30–32, 50). The results of their trenches to the northeast ('Site Q') will be more appropriately considered in Chapter 3 below, as they largely coincided with the area of our Elliott Site. This summary will therefore be restricted to the evidence of the four trenches located within their Area 1/'Site O' and south beside the Depot Site. Settlement-related pits and postholes were scattered throughout and so, too, was worked flint. Sherds of earlier Neolithic pottery were forthcoming from Trench 4, with 'plain', later Neolithic/earlier Bronze Age sherds found in one feature in Trench 2. Within Trenches 3/4 were recovered two decorated, same-vessel Beaker sherds; a large rim fragment from a Collared Urn derived from a feature that also yielded fired clay and a cylindrical loomweight (Pryor 2001a, fig. 2.11).

It was only at the junction of Trenches 3/4 that the second-millennium fieldsystem ditches were exposed. These represented the northeastern end of the multiple-boundary Depot Site system (see above), and directly correlated with the area's cropmark plot where, lying parallel 5 m and 7 m apart, three ditches ran southeast–northwest while curving slightly northwards. It would, however, seem that it was within Trench 1, near Storey Bar Road, that later Bronze Age/Early Iron Age settlement activity was concentrated, as this produced 11 sherds of that date from three features.

Considerable evidence of Middle Iron Age settlement was revealed in the southern half of Trench 4, from where 115 sherds of that date were recovered. At the southern end, relating to the Depot Site's main Iron Age/Roman fieldsystem, a major ditch crossed the trench (southeast–northwest). It cut through the

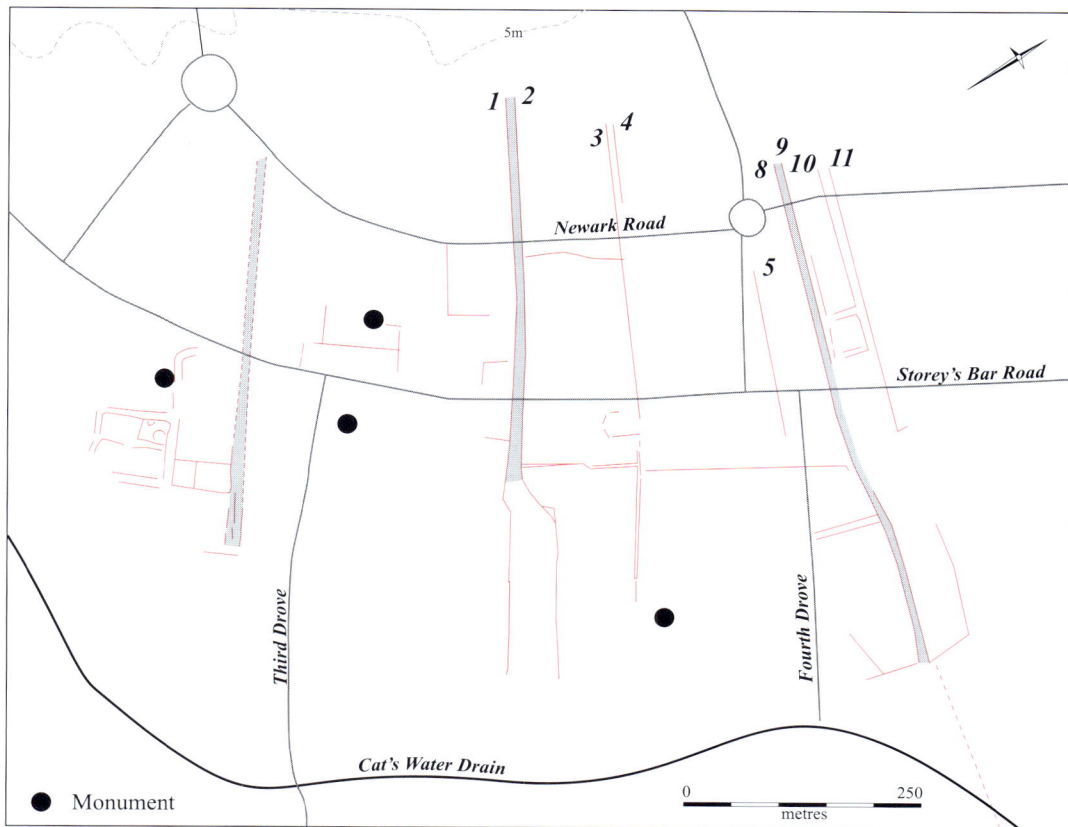

FIGURE 1.10. *Fengate Central — Droveways and Monuments, with main droveway interval indicated by grey-tone. (Reproduced by permission of Ordnance Survey on behalf of HMSO. © Crown copyright 2009. All rights reserved. Ordnance Survey Licence number 100048686.)*

buried soil, upon which an associated upcast bank survived as well as what was an obviously related axial boundary extending northeastward.

Third Drove (1998)

It was in anticipation of the construction of Walters Office World that the County Council Field Unit investigated the plot at the south-western corner of the 'field-block' beside Third Drove (and across the road from Pryor's Storey's Bar Road sub-Site; Cooper 1998). Not summarized in the Flag Fen volume overview (Pryor 2001a), this area-expanded trench-evaluation exercise eventually resulted in the excavation of a 9 m-diameter ring-ditch, which had the cremated remains of an older child/young adult set within a small pit in its centre. Despite the minor proportions of the ring's circuit (0.4–0.7 m wide and 0.2–0.4 m deep), and the absence of any dateable material from it, its construction appears to have been phased: starting as a penannular ring open on its southwestern sector, it was thereafter recut as a complete circle (this feature is also further discussed in the *Fengate's Monuments* section; see Inset, Chapter 4). Otherwise, aside from a large pit (also undated), two ditch features were exposed in the course of the work. Conceivably, both may relate to the Storey's Bar Road system; however, the paucity of dating evidence makes their attribution problematic (the modern bricks recovered from the upper fill of one may have been pressed into it).

TK Packaging Site (1999)

Operating with Soke Archaeological Services and Lincolnshire's Archaeological Project Services, Pryor undertook investigations on a plot east of his earlier Storey's Bar Road excavations, where evidence of later Neolithic activity was duly found (Pryor & Trimble 2000). With alluvium-sealed preservation throughout, at the southern end of their site was found a large Grooved Ware-associated pit, which, together with pottery, flint and animal bone, contained an aurochs skull within it. Apart from the occurrence of smaller, essentially undated, pits and two possible Iron Age ditches, they exposed a northwest–southeast oriented, second-millennium BC fieldsystem boundary.

The question of how Fengate's system was organized and, in effect, 'worked', and also just how extensive it was (the key issue being how much variance can be admitted whilst allowing it to remain a coherent 'whole'), will be returned to elsewhere in this volume. At this juncture, therefore, comments will be confined to just a few first-principle observations. To start with, it must be acknowledged that there is a natural tendency to want to 'over-regularize' its plan. Yet, upon looking closer, especially when its area-components are analysed, it is clear that even the system's 'core' displays considerable variability. Its main framework was obviously provided by its two main, northwest-southeast orientated, fenward droveways (Fig. 1.10):

A) Flanked by Ditches 1 and 2 at Padholme Road, that was again exposed at the southwestern end of the long (off-) Cat's Water trial trench tracing Ditch F.862

B) Between Ditches 8 and 9 at Newark Road and progressing through the Fourth Drove trenches, with its eastern fen-edge end exposed in the Power Station excavations; its line kinked somewhat over its eastern length.

While it is possible that Ditches 3 and 4 along the western margin of the Padholme Road Site were also drove-related, their pairing did not progress east through that field nor into the Cat's Water; the narrow-interval ditch-pair at the latter was closed at its fenward end, and they must have flanked an embankment rather than a drove (see Fig. 2.13). As noted above, it is also likely that the northernmost pair of the Depot Site's 'block-boundaries' defined a fenward drove. If so, it would have fallen at the same approximate 300 m interval to the Ditch 1/2 drove as it had to the northern Ditch 8/9 droveway (pace Pryor 2001a, 408 concerning Fengate's drove-interval).

Crucial here is the recognition that Fengate's system was organized around the spine of its droveways and that its cross-drove axes were generally weakly defined (see Pryor 2001a concerning the system's axial vs coaxial qualities). Here it is relevant that along the road-length portion of the Storey's Bar Road Site (Area II), only one ditch of probable Bronze Age attribution was found (R1), and that across the southwesternmost 225 m of its length no other fieldsystem boundary was recovered (Pryor 1984, fig. 12). Similarly, only one ditched cross-axis ran (near-) continuously between the system's Ditch 1/2 and 8/9 droves: the ditch-line (Ditch iii and F.856/862) exposed across the Cat's Water (and its ancillary southward trench). Therefore, what Fengate displays, is that its various compound/pad-docks and field-plots essentially 'hung-off' of its droves, rather than consisting of a regular, blanket area-wide fieldsystem as such. Moreover, the character of its drove-arranged enclosures clearly varied. Almost in a corridor-like manner, the Ditch 8/9 droveway series — the Newark Road compounds — were clearly distinguished by their double-ditch circuits. Although having affinities with the Depot Site's 'block-compound' layout, its organisation differed greatly from the Ditch 1/2 droveway-side paddocks.

Before progressing, two other general points warrant attention. The first is the fact that a cluster of monuments occurred in the system's southwestern sector: the Storey's Bar Road barrow/ring-ditch and the ring-ditches at both the County's Third Drove Site and the CAU's Depot Site, with Pryor's Cat's Water 'henge'/ring-ditch being the only other recently investigated monument within the area (see

though Chapter 2 and Chapter 4, Inset below, and Evans & Appleby 2008 concerning Wyman Abbott's Fengate monuments). The other point of note is that fieldsystem-contemporary settlement (albeit of a low density) has now been recovered at three locales: in the westernmost drove-side compound at Newark Road (Fig. 2.12); Structure 46 and its attendant enclosure at the Cat's Water (Fig. 2.12); and in the southern Depot Site compound (Fig. 4.3; Evans & Pryor in Pryor 2001a, 23–4, figs 2.4 & 2.5). The frequency of finds and feature-types associated with the Ditch 1/2 droveway length at Padholme Road (Area IX; Pryor 1980a, 5–9, fig. 7) could suggest another settlement locus, and this may also be true of Storey's Bar Road, Area II; the latter, again, due essentially to the occurrence of wells (during the course of their Site O investigations Birmingham found settlement evidence within a trench just to the south of that area).

Text and structure

In the final chapter of this volume an attempt will be made to more thoroughly overview Fengate's archaeology as whole, including specific facets of Pryor's sites and his broader interpretations (see also Chapter 2). Otherwise, it is the 'Fengate Central', Elliott Site that most directly interacts with his earlier excavations. In contrast, lying at a distance to Pryor's work, the Edgerley Road and Tower Works investigations rather resonate with Abbott's findings in those two areas: respectively 'Fengate North' and 'West'.

Chapter 6 also has an interview with Pryor (and Richard Bradley and Andrew Fleming). An expression of professional respect, courtesy and personal friendship, it seems only fitting that we include Francis' voice and 'take' on what has happened at Fengate (and the region's archaeology generally) over the thirty years since the main phase of its fieldwork was concluded.

In the '70s-phase of Fengate's fieldwork, the application of palaeo-environmental science generally, and also soil micromorphology, was underdeveloped. A degree of redress was made in the 2001 Flag Fen volume. This will be furthered here, as not only have all three of the main CAU sites had soil micromorphology undertaken, but also feature-specific pollen studies by Steve Boreham. Beyond this, the volume also includes wider area-sequence pollen studies: Boreham and Peachey's analyses from the Fengate Sewage Works Site (adjacent to the Tower Works; Chapter 5).

Greatly abetted by developments in computer-graphic technology over the last decade, distributional plotting of artefacts will feature in the presentation of the three CAU sites. This is appropriate as considerable emphasis was paid to artefact distributions in the original Fengate excavations and their ensuing volumes. A trait/strength also shared with Mucking (see Inset above) and prompting the intense excavation sample at both sites, this was however coupled with only a weakly defined sense of residuality and understanding of more 'open' (i.e. non-feature based) modes of land-use preceding their respective Bronze Age fieldsystem horizons. This is a crucial factor as, in the case of Fengate, it resulted in generic artefact-category plotting along its major cut features (e.g. 'pottery' and/or 'flint'). Arguably, this itself promoted the rather 'open-ended' approach taken to its dating (see Chapter 6 below), and which was most obviously expressed in the Grooved Ware-attribution of the fieldsystem at Storey's Bar Road. Moreover, it meant that there was little realization that the distribution of earlier artefact types within later cut features — whether Bronze Age field boundaries or Iron Age roundhouse gullies — could be deployed to reconstruct earlier, less feature-bound modes of utilisation (see Chapter 3 Inset below).

The 2001 Flag Fen volume reviewed Fengate's radiocarbon dating (Bayliss & Pryor, in Pryor 2001a, 390–99). Nevertheless, there is still debate as to just how early its fieldsystem was laid out. Given this, and the fact that two of the CAU sites directly reflect upon Abbott's earlier findings (which obviously were not themselves absolutely dated), each of the three sites have been radiocarbon dated (Table 1.4). These various procedures, and also, for example, the outlined buried soil artefactual and chemical trace sampling (or Vince's pottery thin-sectioning study that appears in Chapter 5), should be understood as an expression of the CAU's commitment to the idea that there need be no intrinsic difference in the nature/quality of 'research' (or state-sector) archaeology and developer-funded fieldwork. Put simply, funding sources need not necessarily determine whether excavation programmes have appropriate research directives and methodology, and all require academic prioritization.

As should be obvious, the CAU's 'grey matter' literature on Fengate now runs into many hundreds of pages. In fact, the three main sites presented here have, themselves, already generated well over 300 pages. With such an amassed background, it will not be possible to closely report these sites' many hundreds of features, but nor is it necessary here. Instead, detailed descriptions of all can be found in the relevant 'grey' reports. (Note that, as listed below, this series does not include the Unit's work within the broader 'off-terrace' Fengate/Flag Fen environs, such as the quarry work at Bradley Fen and Must Farm, Whittlesey or at Eye; their results being reviewed in Chapter 2.)

Alexander, M., 2000. *An Archaeological Evaluation of Land off Eastleigh Road, Park Lane, Peterborough.* Cambridge Archaeological Unit Report 356.

Beadsmoore, E., 2005. *Edgerley Drain Road, Fengate, Peterborough: an Archaeological Excavation.* Cambridge Archaeological Unit Report 686.

Beadsmoore, E., 2006. *Elliott Site, Fengate. Archaeological Investigations.* Cambridge Archaeological Unit Report 734.

Beadsmoore, E., 2007. *Land off Vicarage Farm Road, Fengate: A Watching Brief.* Cambridge Archaeological Unit Report 766.

Brudenell, M., 2005. *Archaeological Investigations at the Former Tower Works Site, Mallory Road, Fengate, Peterborough.* Cambridge Archaeological Unit Report 675.

Cooper, A., 2003. *Storey's Bar Road, Fengate: Archaeological Desk Based Assessment and Test Pit Survey* (Revised 2005). Cambridge Archaeological Unit Report 584.

Cooper, A., 2004a. *Mallory Road, Fengate: Archaeological Test Pit Survey.* Cambridge Archaeological Unit Report 590.

Cooper, A., 2004b. *Land at Edgerley Drain Road, Fengate, Peterborough: an Archaeological Evaluation.* Cambridge Archaeological Unit Report 635.

Evans, C., 1992. *Archaeological Investigations at Fengate, Peterborough: the Depot Site.* Cambridge Archaeological Unit Report 72.

Evans, C. & F. Pryor, 1995. *Fengate, Peterborough — The Material Recycling Site: a Statement of Potential.* Cambridge Archaeological Unit.

Gdaniec, G., 1996. *An Archaeological Investigation at Third Drove, Fengate, Peterborough, Cambridgeshire.* Cambridge Archaeological Unit Report 169.

Gibson, D., 1998. *Archaeological Excavation at the Co-op Site, Fengate, Peterborough.* Cambridge Archaeological Unit Report 264.

Knight, M. & C. Swaysland, 2003. *Fengate Sewage Treatment Works: Peterborough Auger Survey.* Cambridge Archaeological Unit Report 573.

Lucas, G., 1997a. *Tower Works, Fengate, Peterborough: a Desktop Study.* Cambridge Archaeological Unit Report 197.

Lucas, G., 1997b. *An Archaeological Evaluation at the Tower Works, Fengate, Peterborough, Cambridgeshire.* Cambridge Archaeological Unit Report 206.

Lucas, G., 1997c. *Sewage Treatment Works at Fengate, Peterborough: a Desktop Study.* Cambridge Archaeological Unit Report 234.

Mackay, D., 2006a. *Archaeological Evaluation at the Darlow Depot Site, Fengate, Peterborough.* Cambridge Archaeological Unit Report 723.

Mackay, D., 2006b. *Archaeological Evaluation and Test Pits at the Darlow Depot Site, Fengate, Peterborough.* Cambridge Archaeological Unit Report 751.

Patten, R., 2003. *Flag Fen Sewage Works, Fengate, Peterborough. a Watching Brief.* Cambridge Archaeological Unit Report 555.

Patten, R., 2004. *Fengate Sewage Treatment Works, Test Pit Survey.* Cambridge Archaeological Unit Report 643.

Williams, S., 2004. *An Archaeological Evaluation at Land Off Mallory Road (formerly Tower Works), Fengate, Peterborough.* Cambridge Archaeological Unit Report 603.

Even at the time of writing, work at Fengate is on-going and, aside from a single exception (Beadsmoore 2007b), for the sake of pragmatism post-2006 fieldwork has not been included. For much the same reason, a tight landscape focus has also had to be maintained, and evaluation/watching brief investigations down in the Flag Fen basin proper have essentially also had to be omitted (e.g. Britchfield 2001; Cooper 2003) and, at the time of writing, volumes are forthcoming on this theme (Pryor forthcoming a; Knight & Gibson in prep.).

Further, by way of introduction, should be a word concerning *naming and time*. As is apparent in the listing above and the gazetteer that preceded it, somewhere in the process of digging Fengate the historical place-names gave out (e.g. 'Cat's Water' or 'Flag Fen'). While not deeply evocative of landscape-depth, they were, nonetheless, more inspiring than the former factory or intended industrial unit titles that have since come to be applied to its sites, and certainly the *Global Doors* or *Paving Factory Sites* hold little resonance. This testifies to both the scale of present-day construction (i.e. Peterborough's sprawl) and, also, the unending quality of its underlying archaeological landscape; neither of which have 'hard' borders.

More down-to-earth matters also warrant mention. First, radiocarbon calibration, which throughout will be expressed to two sigma. Secondly, site recording; while we have come to consider the CAU investigations herein as part of a large 'Fengate Environs' project, for all logistic intents and purposes they were undertaken separately, with each having their own enumeration system (*Features*, and their constituent stratigraphic *Contexts*). This unavoidably results in a degree of cross-site numerical repetition, and one dreads to think just how many 'Feature 1s' have now been assigned to this landscape. Though no attempt has been made to amalgamate these into a unified 'master system', given the format of the sites' presentation this should not result in any undue confusion.

Finally, it is here held that *learning* should sit at the core of any post-excavation programme and, by this measure, this exercise can only be counted as successful. Put simply, if, by the end, you no longer think what you did at its outset, then it has been worthwhile. Appropriately, a sense of 'building' must inform and structure this volume; contributing to what is quite a new mapping of Fengate's prehistoric landscape and, also, its chronological framework.

TABLE 1.4. *Radiocarbon dating results.*

Laboratory no.	Context	Material	Method	Radiocarbon age (BP)	δ¹³C (‰)	Calibrated date range (cal. BC) (95% confidence)
Elliott Site						
OxA-X-2182-55	F.222	Bone	AMS	4150±37	−23.4	2880–2610
Beta-230846	F.108	Seed	AMS	4270±40	−29.4	2920–2870
Beta-230849	F.302	Wood	Radiometric	3730±60	−27.6	2300–1960
Beta-230848	F.302	Wood	Radiometric	3650±70	−26.2	2200–1880
Beta-230850	F.325	Charcoal	AMS	3340±40	−27.9	1740–1520
Beta-230845	F.2	Charcoal	AMS	3190±40	−28.8	1530–1400
Beta-230847	F.182	Plant material	AMS	2870±40	−27.8	1190–1140 and 1140–920
Edgerley Drain Road						
Beta-240340	F.323	Charred seeds	AMS	3270±40	−26.3	1630–1450
Beta-240346	F.235	Charcoal	AMS	3490±40	−25.2	1920–1730 and 1720–1690
Beta-240341	F.157	Seed	AMS	Failed	−26.6	Failed
Beta-240342	F.140	Charcoal	AMS	3730±40	−24.5	2280–2250 and 2220–2020
Beta-240343	F.193	Seed	AMS	3480±40	−24.2	1900–1690
Beta-240344	F.189	Seed	AMS	3500±40	−26.1	1930–1740
Beta-240345	F.15	Charcoal	AMS	4110±40	−27.3	2870–2570 and 2510–2500
Vicarage Farm Road						
Beta-240339	F.8	Seed	AMS	2870±40	−25.3	1190–1140 and 1140–920
Tower Works						
Beta-229355	F.13	Charcoal	AMS	2410±40	−22.8	660–640 and 590–400
Beta-229356	F.13	Charcoal	AMS	2420±40	−26.3	670–610 and 600–400
Sewage Treatment Site						
Wk-13862	-	Organic silt	Radiometric	2442±54	−30.3±0.2	770–400
Wk-13863	-	Alder wood	Radiometric	3778±42	−27.5±0.2	2340–2110

CHAPTER 2

Framing Context

Christopher Evans

This chapter is concerned with broader scene-setting, both in time and space, in order to better situate Fengate's archaeology. Largely involving Wyman Abbott's notebook accounts, but also drawing upon other related archives, its first half is primarily historiographic and its significance is two-fold. Not only do these sources detail major findings within the area during the early decades of the last century, but they also provide crucial insights into the early working practices of the discipline generally. In particular, they are of fundamental importance for the establishment of prehistoric pottery typologies in Britain. In this manner, the 'presence' of Wyman Abbott in this volume is akin to Bromwich for Haddenham (Evans & Hodder 2006b) or Tebbutt for the Colne Fen, Earith fieldwork (Evans *et al.* forthcoming).

The later portion of the chapter is, conversely, concerned with matters of much more recent relevance. It variously outlines major, post-1990 fieldwork projects, both in the wider Fengate/Flag Fen environs (including excavations at Whittlesey, Eye and in Peterborough itself) and further afield within the region (e.g. Colne Fen, Earith and Barleycroft/Over on the lower River Great Ouse). Moving outwards in the pursuit of context, these sites further our understanding of Fengate through comparison to other Bronze Age landscapes and, moreover, its neighbouring investigations potentially illuminate the role/'place' of the Flag Fen platform.

The chapter concludes by exploring themes arising from this overview and comparing the characteristics of the region's fieldsystems; rehearsing issues that will be more fully developed in Chapter 6. It may seem somewhat anomalous to begin this volume discursively, in effect, 'laying out our shop' from the outset. Yet, it is here held that such a broad context must now inform any further fieldwork in the Fengate landscape and, more generally, that interpretation is not like a 'punch-line' that only occurs at the end of study, but must underpin our investigations (and their 'books') throughout.

Building types — The Abbott/Leeds archives
(*with* GRAHAME APPLEBY)

Wyman Abbott's findings of prehistoric artefacts in Peterborough's Fengate quarries during the early decades of the twentieth century duly feature in the history of southern British archaeology. Yet, fostering such a significant contribution to prehistoric pottery studies (Abbott & Smith 1910; Leeds 1922; Hawkes & Fell 1945), Abbott himself only ever generated seven published pages in national journals concerning his thirty years of fieldwork. His 'voice' has been missing from all that his efforts inspired, due both to his specific place in the academic/disciplinary production of the day and through the fact that his primary records have been lost for more than half a century. In other words, the Abbott we have has been constructed by others, primarily *via* a museum-based nexus (variously Smith, Leeds and Hawkes & Fell). In the course of background researches for this volume, four of Abbott's notebooks were 'unearthed' in the Cambridge University Museum of Archaeology and Anthropology (Fig. 2.2). Although only accessioned in 1998 (cat. no. W11/1/1–7), these are thought to have probably been donated to the Museum as part of Abbott's 1973 bequest. These can be further augmented by Abbott's letters to E.T. Leeds from the period 1909–37, which are held in the Ashmolean Museum, Oxford. Both are a rich source of detail for Fengate's archaeology.

With its Fengate-related entries covering the period from 1906–19 (mostly 1908–13), a complete transcription of Abbott's notebooks will not be provided in this volume and, while including a period-mapping of his material, nor will we present a full gazetteer of his findings (one has, though, been prepared and is now lodged with Peterborough Museum). Instead, it will highlight a number of his discoveries, provide a sense of the flavour and scope of his records and also discuss some of the more major implications that arise from his work. In this, we will concentrate upon his in 1980 thoroughly published Abbott's Beaker material without benefit of the notebooks (in Pryor 1980a, 234–45) and a reappraisal of his Early Iron Age pottery informed by these sources is currently in preparation (by M. Brudenell), Abbott's museum artefacts have not otherwise recently been studied in detail.[2] This must await future research. Finally, it should be mentioned that, dealing with complex historiographic sources and the many rich 'byways' of their connections, this will be the one part of the volume's text that requires footnotes.

Notebook archaeology

Abbott and Leeds' life-long friendship and working partnership represents a singular amateur/professional collaboration (see Hudson 1981 and Levine 1986 on this theme generally, and Evans 2007a on lingering antiquarianism). The former (1887–1972), an eminent Peterborough lawyer, was clearly mentored and academically promoted by Leeds (1877–1955), who, appointed to the Ashmolean Museum in 1908, had been raised near Fengate at Eyebury (see *Lives* inset). Leeds was the son of a highly renowned amateur palaeontologist and, upon his graduation, served overseas with the Colonial Service. On returning home for a period of five year's convalescence due to illness, he started investigating Eyebury's gravel pits, first publishing papers on its palaeontology.[3] It was

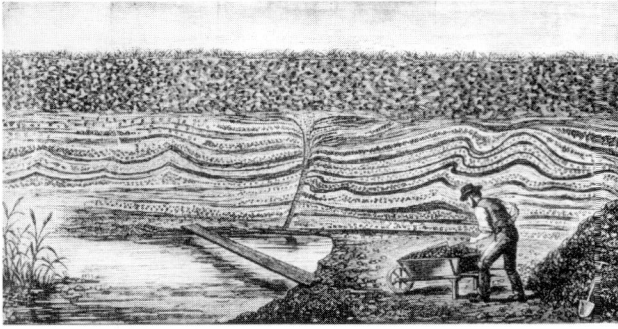

FIGURE 2.1. *Early Quarrying — Top, hand-gravel digging 'one mile West of Whittlesey' (Skertchley 1877, fig. 20); bottom, opening of a brick-pit at Peterborough (Hillier 1981, 12).*

prehistoric material and, for the sake of brevity, omit any discussion of his Roman findings.[1] While Gibson

---

1. Although not to the same extent as at Fengate, Abbott also worked in other local quarries, and one of his notebooks (W11/1/3) lists entries for Dogsthorpe, Woodston, Elton, Whittlesey and Fletton. Variously of prehistoric, Roman and Anglo-Saxon date (another notebook is entirely concerned with the Anglo-Saxon cemetery at Nassington, Northants.), these need not unduly concern us here (though see below concerning Fengate's Saxon cemetery). Of those locations then falling within the Huntingdonshire portion of Peterborough, Abbott's Woodston and Fletton findings were fully summarized within its *Victoria County History* of 1926. Northamptonshire's *Victoria*

County History (the County wherein Fengate was then situated) was published in 1904 and therefore did not include Abbott's material. Abbott, indeed, was cited as a full co-author of Burkitt and Fox's text of that volume's 'Early Human Occupation' section. However, they mention that while Abbott did not actually write any of the text, he was so accredited because his unpublished researches were so extensively drawn upon by them (Burkitt *et al.* 1926, 193, note 1). In fact, the description therein of his most important site in this area (Fig. 2.15) — the putative Early Iron Age 'pile dwellings' at the Fletton London Brick pits (associated with human remains; Burkitt *et al.* 1926, 212–13) — is so close to his original notebook entry (W11/1/3) that he must have provided them with that notebook (see Fig. 2.2 concerning the credibility of this finding).

Abbott also recovered material from Orton Longueville and Water Newton and was accredited with finding, in 1937, the inscribed sherd that first named *Durobrivae* (Wright 1940, 190).

2. At the time of his death, the former curator of Peterborough Museum, Martin Howe, was (without the benefit of the notebooks) attempting to situate Abbott's Fengate finds by working with historical maps and quarry-related documents (see also Pryor 1997), and Ben Robinson kindly provided us with copies of his researches.

3. Abbott seems to have shared these geological interests. In the notebooks there is a general entry of 'River Gravels' as well as section drawings through palaeo-channel deposits. Noting the occurrence of, for example, rhinoceros, mammoth and hippopotamus bones, he also collected Palaeolithic flints from the gravel pits (see also Burkitt *et al.* 1926, fig. 2); equally, Leeds's father is accredited with first finding the Iron Age settlement at Fletton (Burkitt *et al.* 1926, 212).

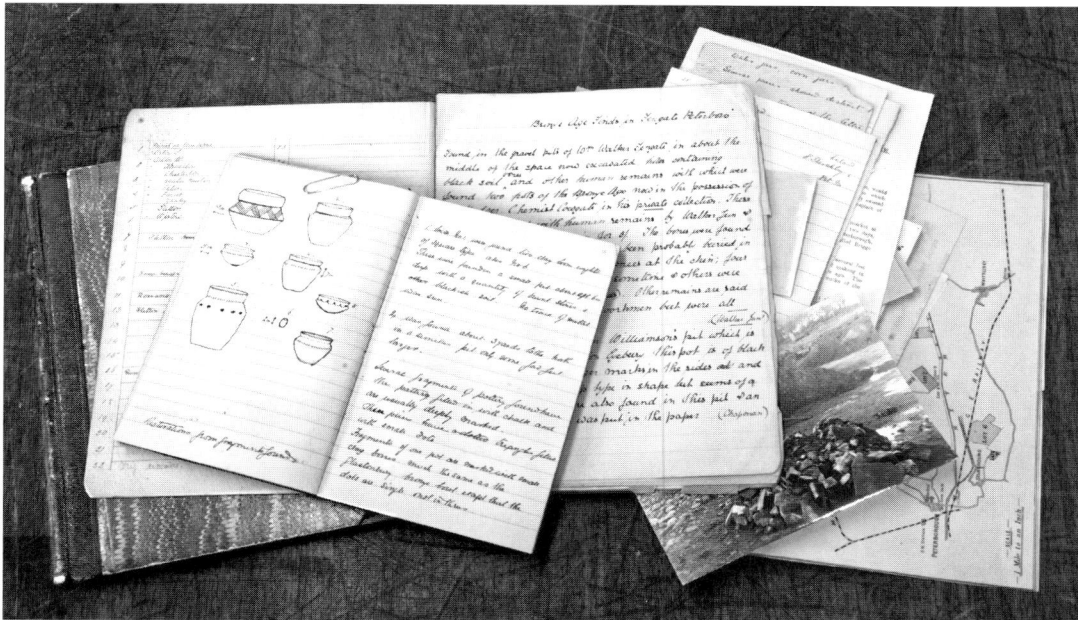

FIGURE 2.2. *Abbott's Notebooks — Top, Cambridge University Museum of Archaeology and Anthropology (photograph, D. Webb); below, extract from Abbott's notebook entry concerning the putative 'pile dwellings' at the London Brick Company's Fletton Yard (note its small sketch of timber pile: W11/1/3); in its entirety, the account reads:*

A quantity of brushwood some 2ft 6in thick was found just inside the place where the greater quantity of the bones were found. This brushwood contained no remains but a few split bones at the bottom of the layer.

In several places cut & shaped piles had been driven into pits dug below the level of the black layer. These piles were usually about 4-6in in diameter and made of oak or ash? and cut off to a V at the bottom showing notches cut at intervals to where these piles were broken off [illustration; see above]. These appeared to be at the edge of the brushwood but I was not sure of this in several cases.

A rough type of pottery was found varying from black to reddish and several pieces were ornamented with fingertip impressions round the widest part of the total of the pot. Many of these pots were handmade and not wheel turned.

In lieu of any further evidence, his description raises the possibility that the notched timber piles were actually only log ladders set within pit wells, whose waterlogged remains may then have been the source of the site's brushwood. Certainly, this would make sense given the site's 'inland' position relative to the fen. Abbott apparently investigated the site in 1908 while steam navvies were employed in its reduction; given these conditions, a degree of stratigraphic imprecision/confusion is quite understandable.

at this time that his archaeological interests took root and, aside from working on an Anglo-Saxon cemetery in Northants, between 1910 and 1914 he excavated three barrows at Eyebury (see Chapter 4 Inset; Leeds 1910; 1912; 1915; see also Hall 1987, 32).

Despite this, in examining Abbott and Leeds's partnership we should be aware that at that time any 'amateur/professional' distinction was not the rigid divide it has since become. Abbott's discoveries were carried in *The Times* (21/06/1920 & 28/04/1924) and he independently exhibited his findings at the Society of Antiquaries of London (Abbott & Smith 1910, 333). Elected a Fellow of that society in 1926 (being proposed by Peers and supported by Leeds, Clapham, Wheeler and Bushe-Fox amongst others) and a member of both the Fenland and Nene Valley Research Committees (Smith 1997), he was certainly not an 'unconnected' fieldworker.[4]

Indeed, interest in the area's prehistory could, potentially, have begun much earlier as John Evans mentions in his renowned *Archaeologia* paper of 1860, 'On the occurrence of flint implements in undisturbed beds of gravel, sand and clay', in which, having with Joseph Prestwich already established the 'deep' fossil animal-associated antiquity of Palaeolithic axes in French gravel quarries, that similar findings had come to his attention from Peterborough's quarries. Unfortunately, when the pits were inspected they failed to yield results (1860, 307). The region's Palaeolithic findings were first really highlighted by Skertchley, who provided contributions on this theme to *Nature*, *The Geological Magazine* and to the second edition of Giekie's *The Great Ice Age* (1877), as well as featuring in his and Miller & Skertchleys' *The Fenland, Past and Present* of the following year (Miller & Skertchley 1878). Evans, Prestwich and Darwin were all among the subscribers to the latter book, and Skertchley's researches were well known to Darwin, who in a letter of 16/11/1876 to Geikie wrote: 'Mr Skertchley … seems to be a first-rate observer; and this implies, as I always think, a sound theoriser' (in Darwin 1887, 227).

4.   The boundary between amateur/professional was not constant during the first half of the twentieth century, as the constitution of the discipline then changed massively. Reflective of the rise of a new university-based 'professionalism', Grahame Clark apparently wanted to oust Abbott (along with other 'locals') from the Fenland Research Committee on the grounds that they were unscientific amateurs (P. Smith pers. comm.).

   The Peterborough Citizen's 24/04/1928 outline of Abbott (Fig. 1.4) mentions that he was a 'pupil of the late Mr T.J. George, Curator of Northampton Museum, by whom his early interest in archaeology was fostered'. George (1869–1920), a fellow of the Geological Society and author of the *Victoria County History*'s account of the County's prehistory (1902), was a founding member of the local archaeological field group in 1899 ('The Northamptonshire Exploration Society') and, over the next decade, undertook a series of small-scale excavations. These, however, were apparently of a fairly poor standard, involving only limited recording and planning (Moore 1980, 16–17). Abbott was listed as being a member of the Northamptonshire Natural History and Field Club after 1904; further confirmation of a linkage between George and the Abbott family is provided in his account of the finds from Hunsbury Camp, in which it was noted that a loomweight from the hillfort had been lent to the Museum by J. Wyman Abbott, 'our' Abbott's uncle (George

Abbott's archaeology can, in many respects, be considered transitional between the nineteenth and twentieth centuries. Whilst the latter decades of the former obviously saw campaigns of a high standard, such as Pitt Rivers's work and particularly Fox and St John Hope's Silchester campaigns (e.g. 1895), most excavations then fell well short of this mark and their reportage can only be considered variously inadequate or unintelligible. Abbott's weak illustrative documentation of his researches would have been perfectly acceptable within the context of most later nineteenth-century archaeological practice (Evans 2007a; see Evans 2004 concerning archaeological 'graphic literacy' generally). In contrast, the fact that, for the most part, Abbott was concerned with settlement archaeology and not just burial monuments, could be considered a distinctly twentieth-century trait.

It was really only the 1920/30s that marked the advent of any kind of archaeological 'professionalism', with a general rise in the quality of excavation and its reportage. This was the era when various forms of fieldwork manuals were issued (see Lucas 2001b). Wheeler's work would epitomize this trend, but Leeds' Abingdon or Sutton Courtney campaigns could equally be cited. The key point is that, when compared to his earlier forays at Eyebury, the latter two sites clearly demonstrate the degree to which Leeds' fieldwork developed. The same is certainly not true for Abbott and, if anything, his recording then declined. Weighed in the balance, he perhaps is best thought of as a product of a 'long nineteenth century' and could be fitted into its tradition of the lone regional fieldworker, such as Lucas or Greenwell (although evidently lacking their intellectual vigour/ rigour). The fact that he worked on settlement remains — as opposed exclusively to barrows — essentially reflected what was locally at hand, rather than any conscious research intent (Evans 2007a).

Abbott's handwritten notebooks provide a finding-by-finding gazetteer-type chronicle. They appear to have been composed/transcribed some time after their respective fieldwork, and are not a direct or daily 'in-field' record (see Lucas' Chapter 5 Inset concerning notebook recording).[5] Though there are illustrations

---

1917, 37). Abbott's connection to George, and thereby Hunsbury, may have influenced his attribution of Fengate's Early Iron Age wares to 'Late Celtic' times, based on a familiarity with La Tène curvilinear ornament; though, obviously Glastonbury offered another parallel, albeit also mistaken (see below).

5.   It would appear that Abbott worked up these entries from rougher, immediately in-/post-fieldwork notes. A loose sheet in the archives has the 'primary' description of the semi-circular trench' in Walker's pit (Entry no. 47), the possible ring-ditch/barrow discussed below. Yet there are discrepancies between the two source-texts. While those relating to feature

of specific pottery vessels and other finds, and also sketch sections of selected pits, they do not include site plans or any mapping as such. This being said, his main 'sites' are therein enumerated by red pencil highlighting, which obviously indicates that he did, indeed, locate his material. His written descriptions do themselves provide a basis of approximate indication. Those of a cluster of Bronze Age 'pit dwellings' (see below) can be considered typical:

> These pits were about 23 yards from the hedge dividing Williamsons [&] Walkers fields pits [i.e. quarries] & about 36 yards from the hedge dividing Rippons Stone pits from Williamsons pits (W11/1/1 Entry no. 6).

In fact, his descriptions are sufficiently detailed that, through reference to the area's historical maps, his sites can now be plotted with some accuracy.

Aside from providing a site sketch-plan (discussed below), the Leeds archive includes a hand-rendered map showing the location of a number of Abbott's major findings. Moreover, in a letter to Leeds he writes concerning the loss of his maps:

> I have not been able to get any paper into shape yet as the detailed plan I had in the pre war days has been lost in the many wanderings of my belongings during the war, and the loss ties me up very badly as all my notes relate to numbers on the plan (20/05/1921).

Beyond this, some documentation of Abbott's findings must have been supplied for the 1927 OS mapping[6] and, furthermore, in his 1922 Fengate paper, Leeds further admitted to having access to an area-wide plan:

The site, as seen when set out on a rough plan is so confused that it is impossible to say that any special portion of it was occupied exclusively at one period. The recorded finds of the Neolithic and Bronze Ages, with the exception of one particular section of the Neolithic material, seem to be *distributed indiscriminately over the whole area without rhyme or reason* (Leeds 1922, 220; emphasis added).

Hawkes and Fell, similarly, remarked upon the intensity of Fengate's occupation as the reason why they did not include a map within their paper:

> *The succession of occupations which resulted from these natural advantages* [of the site's location] *has greatly confused the site-plan.* In addition to loose material including worked flint in abundance, there are Neolithic and Bronze Age pits, and burials both by inhumation and cremation, as well as the pits numerous trenches, and other disturbances belonging to the Early Iron Age occupation; and these are themselves enough to make it a wonder, as Mr. Leeds remarked, that any of the earlier features survived intact. Actually, as he was also able to record, the Early Iron Age remains are for the most part concentrated in the central portion of the site. This will be seen from the 1927 edition of the 6-in. Ordnance Survey Map (Northants sheet VIII SE.), upon which are marked the positions of the principal discoveries recorded by Mr. Wyman Abbott up to 1923.

> *It is impracticable to publish with this paper any more informative plan of the Early Iron Age remains* (1945, 189; emphasis added).

Abbott's material was thought to be 'distributed without rhyme or reason' and Fengate's overall site-plan held to be 'confused'. Certainly, given the techniques available to him Abbott's plotting was coarse, but the key point as to why Fengate's finds were not so allocated in the many papers arising from Abbott's researches is that their authors' focus was primarily upon artefact studies (i.e. building finds typologies) and that his work did not result in the kind of discrete site delineations that were then expected (and could be coped with). In other words, Abbott was generating the type of multiple-period landscape palimpsest that has really only begun to be tackled over the last 50 years, arguably starting with Mucking in the mid 1960s.[7]

---

size probably derive from subsequent quarry exposure, much more serious for this potential monument's interpretation (and, again, indicating a significant degree of basic inaccuracy), on the record sheet he notes the occurrence of human skull fragments close to the palstave within the ditch, which is omitted in the notebook entry. (On the Fig. 2.4 map he notes: 'in trench number of prob. crouched skeletons found many years ago'.) Equally, while the sheet has two 'thumbnail' section sketches, neither appeared in the notebook.

6. Preparing the 1969 *Peterborough New Town* RCHM volume, Christopher Taylor (formerly of the Royal Commission) apparently interviewed Abbott; however, he reports that Abbott (then in his early 80s) had very little memory of his Fengate fieldwork and could offer no real insights (pers. comm.). The review of Abbott's findings undertaken for that volume, therefore, had largely to draw upon the 1920s Ordnance Survey record cards. These would have been compiled by their fieldworker-researchers, who would have probably have interviewed Abbott. It is, in fact, possible that he lent or showed them his notebooks, but evidently not the 'great' ring-ditch manuscript (see below); unfortunately, searches indicate that the record cards would seem to have either been discarded or lost in the war-time bombing of the Ordnance Survey's Southampton offices (Seymour 1980, 274–85; see Pryor 1997 concerning Taylor's attempts to situate Abbott's material).

7. In his ring-ditch manuscript, Abbott (at the instigation of Leeds) cited Stephen Stone's mid nineteenth-century investigations at Standlake, Oxon (Stone 1857; Akerman & Stone 1857), it and Mortimer's *Forty Years' Researches* being the only noted sources (Evans & Appleby 2008). Held to be the first proper example of a prehistoric settlement investigation in Britain (and among the first quarry-sites not focusing on Palaeolithic findings; see below), Standlake can equally be held to be the first prehistoric landscape investigation within Britain (as

Before proceeding, just what kind of 'project' Abbott was embarked upon should be considered. Perhaps further reflective of his 'transitional' status, to what extent was he actually attempting to render a nuanced site-by-site record as opposed to generating distribution dots and, effectively, only putting Peterborough onto regional-/national-scale maps? In this he may, in fact, have been inspired by George's slim volume of 1904, *An Archaeological Survey of Northants* (see Note 4 concerning Abbott's connection with George, curator of Northampton Museum). There stating that 'The museum at Peterborough, at the other end of the county, is getting together a fair number of remains found in late years in the north-eastern end of Northamptonshire', his pull-out county map only showed two points east of the city: 'coins and miscellanea' and 'bronze weapons, etc.'. George apparently delivered this text at a meeting of the Society of Antiquaries of London (05/04/1900), and it was duly noted in their *Proceedings* (Second Series Vol. 18) that it '… will be published in continuation of the Society's series of Surveys'. The issuing of maps, intended to contribute to 'An Archaeological Survey of England by County', was a theme of the Society's 1888 conference for the Congress of Archaeological Societies, and in the early 1890s general standard surveys for Cumberland/Westmorland and Hertfordshire were published in *Archaeologia* (see e.g. J. Evans 1876 and C. Evans 2007a, 297, note 115).

In his 1910 paper, Abbott admitted that his field-work coverage was not systematic and that much had been obliterated without record. Certainly, in order to appreciate Abbott's efforts, his various recovery methods — both his own 'excavation' of features and quarry-labourer finds collection — must be appreciated. This is nowhere more apparent than when considering Gibson's study of Abbott's Beaker findings (in Pryor 1980a). Being quite fresh and unabraded, this assemblage consists of some 350 sherds, of which 47 different vessels can be distinguished based on the rims. Compare this to Abbott's notebook entries, wherein only three Beakers are mentioned. This both suggests that he was only attributing large sherds and semi-complete vessels and, also, that he obtained much more material than appears in the notebooks.[8]

It is also apparent that Abbott was himself able to dig out a number of features. This is true of both the inhumations (e.g. Entry nos. 69–71) and some of the pits, such as the Bronze Age pit-dwelling on Fengate Common, whose full text is provided below. The detail of its finds inventory and degree of recording attests to its excavation as such. In fact, on the top of the latter's manuscript it indicates that this feature was first found on 28/1/[19]06 and only finished on 25/4/[19]07; in other words, he had 15 months in which to investigate it. It would seem that the quarries mainly operated during the summer months and, as is evident in the letter to Leeds below, at other times there was scope for archaeological digging (the prime constraint being when Abbott could get away from work and, later, his many public office responsibilities):

> I have been intending to write you on some possible Neo dwellings. These are still remaining quite intact and are ready and are available for excavation and should I believe be fairly productive as such things go here. *I was wondering if you would have a care to have a dig at Xmas to see what was to be found.* They are all at Fengate near the spot which produced the curious Neo - Bronze Age pottery and flint flakes etc (20/11/11; emphasis added).

As Abbott outlined in a letter to Leeds in July, 1921 the conditions in which he retrieved his material would generally have to be considered horrific and certainly unconducive to detail:

> The pits taken out by the men [i.e. 'quarry-men'] are, as a rule, two yards by five … It is most difficult just now to be able to collect clear details, as the ground is extremely hard, and I do not get time to superintend the diggings myself, and *many of the facts have to be gathered from the workmen* (29/07/21; emphasis added).[9]

---

opposed to various barrow-/monument/related campaigns). With Pitt Rivers' Cranborne Chase researches providing the second instance of such, Abbott's Fengate — although occurring in markedly different circumstances to both — must be accredited as only the third such investigation.

8. Leeds and Abbott were apparently not the only local collectors of finds and, in his notebooks, Abbott recorded that two Bronze Age pots from Walker's pits had been sold to a Mr Bodger, a chemist on Cowgate; Messrs Hill, Shortacre and Dr Walker MD are also mentioned as collecting and buying local finds. The

latter, whose impressive collection is now housed in both the Peterborough and Wisbech Museums (see Middleton 1990), was apparently the Leeds' family doctor (Leeds 1956, 86).

Pryor spoke with Abbott shortly before his death, who then admitted that he had offered the quarrymen 'tips' of a few shillings for their artefacts. So encouraged, Pryor duly raised the possibly that some of the thus 'sold' finds could have derived from other quarry sources (i.e. non-Fengate), and Abbott said that he was always aware of this possiblity. However, the latter related that he knew his informant-suppliers well and thought any such dishonesty unlikely. Equally, having viewed the finds, given their shared condition (degree of mineral encrustation, patina, etc.), Pryor also thinks it unlikely that they derived from a variety of sources (Pryor 1997, 7).

9. During the course of the Haddenham project, the similarly mauled remains of an Iron Age enclosure that had been partially quarried-out in just such a manner was excavated, and its striped and pockmarked plan allows us to appreciate the difficulties of Abbott's work (Evans & Hodder 2006b, figs 6.16 & 6.17). Yet the degree of confusion that seems evident within Abbott's fieldwork (see below) would only have been exacerbated by

Abbott/Leeds — lives and overlap

When outlining the lives of our protagonists, for Abbott the main source must be his obituaries, whereas for Leeds it is D.B. Harden's biographic sketch in *Dark-Age Britain: Studies Presented to E.T. Leeds* of 1956 (see also its accompanying bibliography of his published works and Harden in Wilson 1988). Born in Peterborough in 1887, George Wyman Abbott was educated at Oakham School, Rutland. He thereafter entered the legal profession as an articled clerk at his great uncle's firm of solicitors in the city, himself being admitted to the profession in 1911. In 1919, he became the senior partner in the practice following the death of his uncle (the practice continued at the same premises, 35 Priestgate until recently; see Hill 1983) until his own retirement.

In October 1914, with the outbreak of the war, Abbott enlisted as a 2nd Lieutenant in the 1/1st Huntingdonshire Cyclist Battalion (A Company). Transferred to the 1/7th Battalion Royal Warwickshire Regiment, and later promoted Captain, he served in France and Italy. In 1917 he was awarded the Military Cross for 'gallant conduct' in France and, in 1918, the *Crocce de Guerra* for similar service in Italy. On demobilisation, he returned to practice and was in 1921 elected to the town council, and in the following year to the Soke of Peterborough County Council. As well as these council positions, Abbott was also Deputy Coroner for the Hundred and Liberty of Nassaburgh (essentially the Peterborough district), Secretary of Queen Anne's Bounty, No. 7 Area (Tithe, comprising the dioceses of Ely, Peterborough and Leicester), Steward of the Manors of Yaxley, Woodston and Elton, and Secretary to the Peterborough Diocesan Board of Finance Trust Committee. In 1927 Abbott married Mrs Dorothy Gladys Sampson, daughter of the rector of Barnack, and moved to Stibbington House, Wansford. It was probably this move to western Peterborough that prompted the end of Abbott's Fengate fieldwork, with the quarries there remaining in operation until the Second World War. (Abbott's collecting interests also extended beyond archaeology. Apparently Grimes used to tell a story of when, having to stay at Abbott's house while recording his collection of prehistoric pottery, he was unable to sleep at night because it was so full of clocks; mis-timed, their constant chiming kept him awake; A. Challands pers. comm.)

Created a County Alderman in 1946, Abbott died in November 1972, aged 85. It is a salutary lesson concerning the generational situation of fieldwork, to realise that he actually survived until the first years of Pryor's Fengate campaigns.

Born at Eyebury, near Peterborough, in 1877, Edward Thurlow Leeds was the second son of Alfred Nicholson Leeds, a 'gentleman farmer.' He was educated at Uppingham, Rutlandshire and thereafter read Classics at Magdalene College,

Cambridge. After graduating in 1899, Leeds embarked on a career in the Colonial Service, with a cadetship in the Federated Malay States service, preceded by two years in China. Ill health necessitated a five-year period of convalescence at Eyebury, where his father's interest and influence came to the fore. A Fellow of the Geological Society, Leeds senior had achieved a European reputation as a palaeontologist for the classification of marine reptilia and other fossils collected from Peterborough's quarries (these were later donated to the British Museum; Fig. 2.3). Leeds himself became an accomplished palaeontologist; reviewing his father's material and collecting new fossils, he published papers in 1907 and 1908 on Jurassic crocadyliforms.

It was during Leeds' field-trips that his interest in archaeology began, leading to his work on his 'home' Eyebury barrows. (Growing up at Tanholt House, there is now a certain irony that the Bronze Age fieldsystem of its namesake clearly extends onto what was the Leeds' family property; see below and Figs 2.17 & 4.26.) At the age of 31, he was introduced by Abbott to the then Keeper of the Ashmolean, Sir Arthur J. Evans, which led to his appointment in 1908 as an Assistant Keeper there. Following Evans' resignation, Leeds became Assistant Keeper in the Department of Antiquities to D.G. Hogarth. It was Leeds who introduced T.E. Lawrence (then an undergraduate) to Hogarth, with Leeds and Lawrence establishing a close friendship that continued until the latter's death in 1935 (see Wilson 1988).

With Hogarth's interests confined to the Mediterranean and Middle East, the British Isles and northern European archaeology fell to Leeds. In 1908 Sir John Evans died and his British and continental 'Dark Age' material was left to the Ashmolean. This Leeds used as the basis of his *Archaeology of the Anglo-Saxon Settlements* of 1913, the period whose studies Leeds came to dominate. While known primarily as an Anglo-Saxonist, Leeds also undertook extensive prehistoric researches. Aside from the his investigation of the Eyebury barrows, he also excavated the Neolithic enclosure at Abingdon, the Iron Age hillforts at Chun Castle and Chastleton, and the settlement site at Radley. In all, Leeds published eighteen papers on the Neolithic and Bronze Ages between 1910 and 1940, including studies on Iberian prehistory and, significantly, on Late Bronze Age cauldrons.

Despite forays into other periods, Anglo-Saxon archaeology remained the principal focus of Leeds' research and excavations. He initiated investigations at Sutton Courtney, Abingdon, Asthall Barrow, Chadlington, Frilford and North Leigh in the Thames Valley, and he essentially established the archaeological research agenda for the Oxfordshire region. Leeds' intellectual output from the period when he was appointed to the Ashmolean until his death was prolific. Producing five major publications on Anglo-Saxon archaeology,

---

Indeed, another letter to Leeds later that same year, hints of the strain Abbott evidently felt in being re-

the fact that he does not seem to have used any feature-specific enumeration/allocation system to organize his site recording. Equally, untangling his descriptions is not made any easier as he evidently employed the term 'trench' to refer to both quarry-cuttings and archaeological ditches (with 'excavations' sometimes referring to pits). An example, from his ring-ditch manuscript, reads: 'The cremated burials were scattered over practically the whole area of the trench [i.e. "ditch"] and frequently not more than 4 feet apart and sometimes as many as 6 were found in a trench [i.e. "cutting"] 6ft × 14ft' (W11/1/4).

sponsible for Fengate's archaeology (while still being otherwise employed full-time elsewhere).

> I am afraid that when I wrote last I was very much troubled over my Fengate cemetery as I found I had lost touch with the details as they are muddled and crowded.

> Your letter came as a quietening influence and since then I have not found much of interest and have been able to collect the facts and details (20/05/21).

FIGURE 2.3. *Protagonists — Top, E.T. Leeds (right, 1877–1955; reproduced with permission of the Ashmolean Museum) and G. Wyman Abbott (right, 1887–1972; from Hill 1983); below, A.N Leeds with his Eyebury fossil collection (from Leeds 1956).*

he also wrote two smaller books, ninety-two papers, various notes and reviews and was actively involved in the Oxford University Archaeological Society (which he refounded after World War I, having spent much of the war at the War Office). It is remarkable that within this relatively short period, Leeds was also able to find time to undertake an excavation at Faringdon Folly castle and contribute several articles on medieval and later archaeology, notably his *Oxford Trademen's Tokens* of 1923 and, earlier, his influential paper on the dating of wine bottles. His final posthumous publication, of 1956, was a return to his first field and concerned the Leeds family's collection of fossil reptiles.

Elected to the Society of Antiquaries in 1910 and serving as its Vice-President from 1929 to 1932, Leeds was a University of Edinburgh Rhind Lecturer (1935) and was elected a Fellow of Brasenose College (1938). He was awarded the Society of Antiquaries Gold Medal in 1946, and made an Honorary Fellow at Magdalene College, Cambridge in 1955, the year in which he died.

Having sketched something of Abbott's and Leeds's personal histories, two points need stressing, both essentially relating to Leeds's geological/palaeontological background. Firstly, aside from being a major scholar, Leeds was clearly an accomplished field archaeologist and his excavations were generally of a very high standard. Yet, in this he was apparently without any disciplinary 'mentor'. Seemingly self-taught, his understanding of fieldwork techniques and stratigraphy must essentially derive from his familial legacy. Not, in effect, serv-

ing any kind of fieldwork apprenticeship, Leeds' background connected him to the nineteenth-century 'tap-root' of the excavation process: the understanding (and depiction) of geological stratification. The second point has to do with his appreciation of his father's achievements. This he wrote of in his 1956 volume (Charles Leeds being E.T.'s uncle and also a collector of renown):

> It may appear strange that he never read deeply into the literature of his hobby ... The brothers, and more particularly Alfred Leeds, were the collectors: scientific interpretation they were content to leave to others better qualified than themselves. Doubtless Charles Leeds could with his academic training, if he had set his mind to it, have in time made himself competent to discuss scientifically the wider problems of the Jurassic fauna. As things were, Alfred Leeds could never have done so. He could observe accurately and honestly: he could mentally collate his observations; he could tenaciously argue the inferences that he had thereby been led to draw ... But with all this he could not put his knowledge on paper. It is quite impossible to conceive of him sitting down to compose a long and detailed report on a recent discovery. A two-sheet letter of widely spaced writing was the most he could perpetrate, given no more than the simplest details. That is why so much of his garnered knowledge appears under other names (Leeds 1956, 95–6).

Clearly, there is much here that echoes Leeds' own relationship with Abbott.

Accuracy and record-as-truth

Having 14 find-spot locations indicated within an area of only *c.* 30 ha (Fig. 2.4), Fengate's findings were shown in tremendous detail on the 1927 OS map, and it had far more 'points' shown than, for example, either Stonehenge or Standlake, Oxon. While generally reflective of the regard in which Abbott's material was held, this may well attest to the specific influence of O.G.S. Crawford, who was appointed the Survey's first Archaeology Officer in 1920 and was obviously familiar with the Fengate finds (e.g. Crawford 1912).[10]

In their preparation of the 1927 map, the Survey's fieldworkers would have visited Peterborough and probably interviewed Abbott in the compilation of their record cards (see Note 6); in all likelihood, Abbott would have shown them his records. Accordingly, comparing Abbott's various archival sources and the OS's indications shows the latter to be an accurate representation of his specific findings (by the time of the 1958 OS map, many of these 'spots' had simply been reduced to generic 'Neolithic to Romano-British Settlement' indications).

The Ashmolean archive map which Abbott sent to Leeds probably dates to 1921 (Fig. 2.4). Abbott's letters from that year indicate that he then sent a number of sketches and photographs of his pots as well as pit sections, presumably in anticipation of Leeds' 1922 paper (a notation on the map is dated 1920). The map, furthermore, seems to have been tailored to Leeds' immediate needs and, whilst it shows his major Neolithic and Bronze Age findings (e.g. his Entry no. 32 Beaker burial in the centre with its Beaker sketched in the bottom left-centre, and the no. 14 urn in the right margin; see Fig. 2.5:C),[11] his Iron Age material was not marked. Aside from indicating the main quarry pits in which he worked (Tebb's, Williamson's, Walker's and Rippon's), the map not only shows the location of Abbott's great ring-ditch (bottom centre-right) and the line of the Roman Car Dyke canal across the top ('C.D.'), but also annotates 'Fen'. The latter informs us of just how the quarry-site landscape was envisaged by Abbott (i.e. immediately beside the wetland, when in reality it was many hundreds of metres inland from the prehistoric marshes) and accounts for statements concerning its 'Glastonbury-like' qualities (e.g. see Note 10).[12]

---

10. It may have been Crawford's familiarity with the area's archaeology (particularly Abbott's putative Fletton timber structure; see Note 1 and Fig. 2.2) that apparently led him to initially scout out a Glastonbury-like 'lake village' as the site of the Prehistoric Society first-sponsored excavation in the later 1930s; this being the initiative that eventually led to Bersu's excavation at Little Woodbury (Crawford 1955, 252; Evans 1988, 443).

11. Abbott mistakenly marked the latter, no. 70, and otherwise did not attempt to relate the map's find-spots to his notebook enumeration.

12. In the top left-hand corner of the map are a series of dashed lines (just below there are inverted 'C's that must indicate pits)

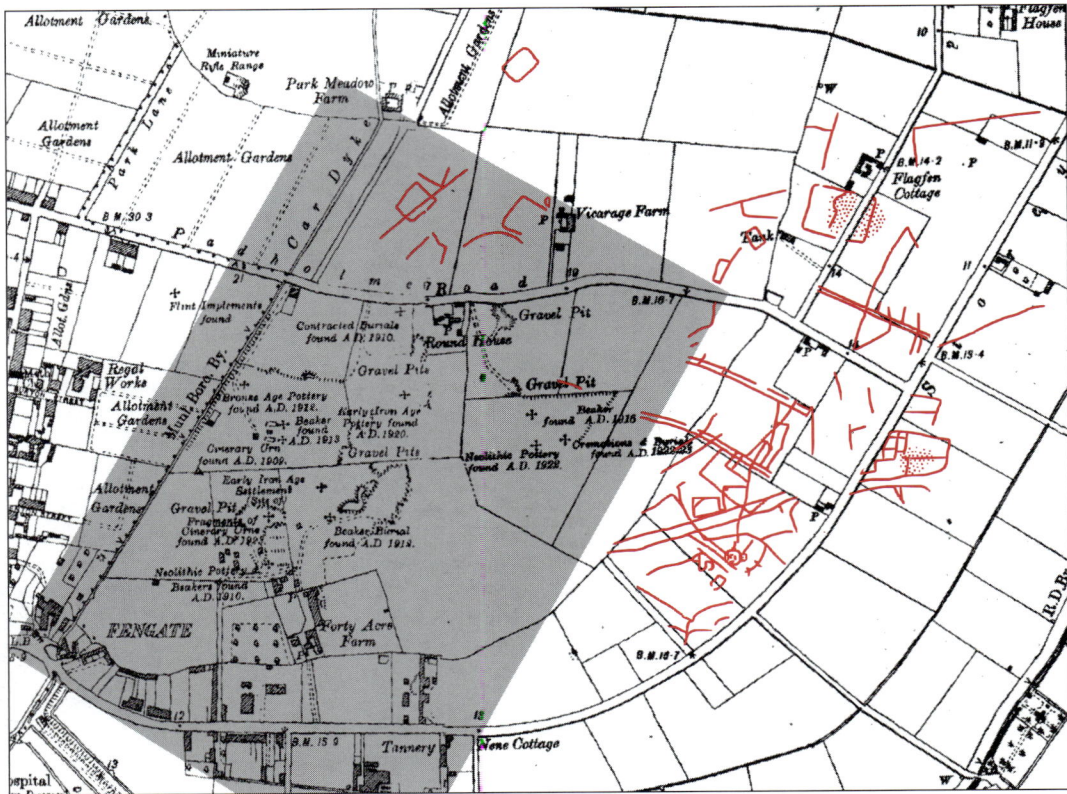

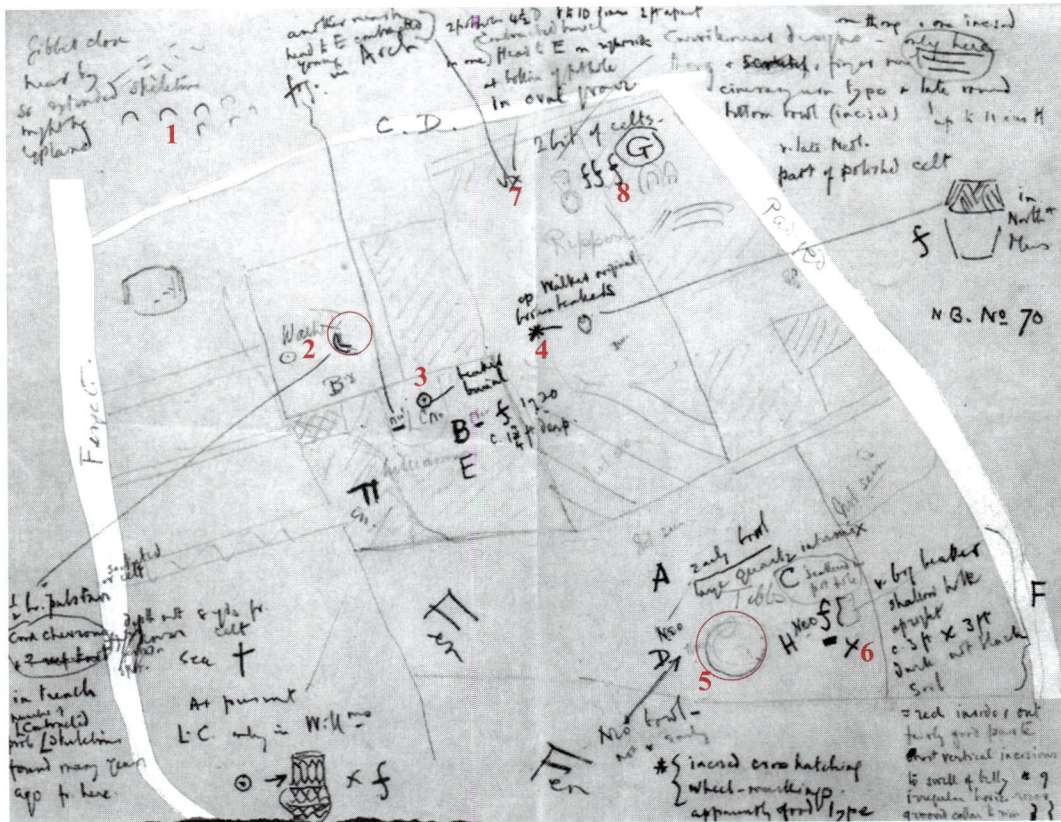

FIGURE 2.4. *(left) Abbott's Mapping — Top, shows 1927 OS map of Fengate, with the area of Abbott's map shown in grey-tone; cropmark plots in red are from the 1969 RCHM volume. The bottom figure is Abbott's Fengate sketch map of c. 1921 (Leeds Correspondence Archive, Ashmolean Museum), bounded on north by Padholme Road, Fengate in the south and, to the west, the line of the Car Dyke ('C.D.'). The location of a number of his major findings can be identified: 1) Saxon inhumation cemetery (on loose sketch plan in notebook and discussed in letter to Leeds); 2) possible ring-ditch or barrow with associated human remains and half a palstave (Entry no. 47); 3) Beaker burial (see Fig. 2.7; Entry no 32; Clarke 1970, no. 645); 4) biconical urn (Entry no 14; Leeds 1922, fig. 13); 5) the 'great' ring-ditch (notebook mss; see Fig. 2.8 and Evans & Appleby 2008); 6) beaker found in 1916 (un-numbered in notebook; Leeds 1922, fig. 5); 8) contracted Bronze Age burials (Entry no 69; note, location differs from OS map, on which these are indicated close to the 'Round House' on Padholme Road); 'cinerary urns' (Entries no. 38/40; Leeds 1922, figs. 8–11).*

FIGURE 2.5. *(right) Pottery Types and Visual Translation — Abbott's notebook vessel sketches (left; see e.g. Fig. 2.1) with various published versions (right): A) Peterborough Ware bowl, Williamson's Pit (Entry no. 15; Abbott & Smith 1910, fig. 3); B) beaker accompanying inhumation (Entry no. 32; Clarke 1970, no. 645); C) biconical urn, Rippon's Stone Pits (Entry no. 14; Leeds 1922, fig. 13); D) Early Iron Age bowl, Williamson's Pit (Abbott considering this style to be of Late Celtic date; Entry no. 23/30; Hawkes & Fell 1945, fig. 6, Q2).*

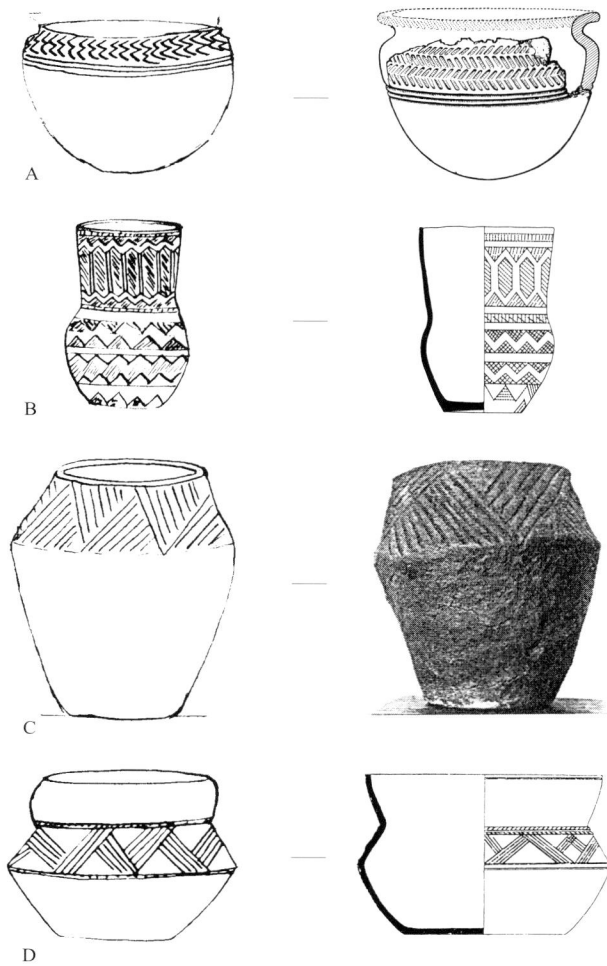

Of some 70 individual 'site' entries within his notebooks, Abbott variously assigned 21 to generic prehistoric periods: Neolithic, five; Bronze Age, seven;

with the annotation 'Gibbet close/nearby SE extended skeletons might be upland'. This must relate to a sketch plan on the back of a loose sheet in the Cambridge Abbott archive that shows an eight-grave inhumation cemetery. Two of the skeletons appear to be interred within slab-set graves (the plan also indicating that prehistoric vessels were found there). There is no reference to this site within the notebooks as such and, until viewing the Ashmolean map, we had no idea of its location, nor indeed if it actually lay within Fengate at all. Fortunately, however, the Leeds archive also includes a letter of 21/1/11 which outlines his 'Saxon' cemetery. Though not mentioning its position, its indication of a stone-lined child's grave leaves little doubt that this, in fact, is the same cemetery as that shown on the loose-sheet plan. In the letter he also records a cremation, apparently accompanied by a 'food vessel' and a jet bead necklace (the latter two being sketched; the pot is most likely a Collared Urn; M. Knight pers. comm.).

Abbott's map has, in fact, an uncanny resemblance to that produced by Frank Curtis, a local amateur, who in the 1960s excavated and recorded prehistoric sites in the area of Norfolk's Wissey Embayment (see Healy 1996, 3–4, 11–29, e.g. pl. III).

and Iron Age, nine. As shown in Table 2.1 below, this is roughly in proportion to the published attribution of his prehistoric vessels.

TABLE 2.1. *Period-/type-frequency of Abbott's Fengate pottery based on published sources (Abbott & Smith 1910; Leeds 1922; Hawkes & Fell 1945; Wainwright & Longworth 1971, 236–8, 281; Gibson, in Pryor 1980a, 234–45; Longworth 1984, 158. pl. 15b).*

Type	No. of Vessels
Peterborough Ware	13
Grooved Ware	2
Beaker	47
Biconical Urn	1
Collared Urn	1
Early Iron Age	81

Abbott's chronological attribution of his findings cannot, of course, be considered absolute, the impetus for much of his fieldwork being, after all, that prehistoric pottery types had yet to be firmly established. For example, the biconical urn from Rippon's Stone pits is said in the notebooks to be a 'Bronze Age food vessel'

(Fig. 2.5:C; Entry no. 14). Equally, the Peterborough Ware bowl recovered from Williamson's pit (Entry no. 15), illustrated and so-attributed in Abbott & Smith's 1910 paper (fig. 3), in the notebooks is described as a 'Neolithic ~~Bronze Age~~ ~~Drinking Cup~~ ~~Food~~ vessel' (Fig. 2.5:A). This entry had obviously been corrected following Smith's appraisal of Abbott's findings, which Abbott described in a letter to Leeds of 17/11/1909 (italicized emphasis added):

> I made some finds more clear when Smith was here on Sunday, I mean my Fengate lot of scraps. One pot I have is early Neolithic, he says, and only two pieces known are dredged up from the Thames last year, and one from a <u>long</u> barrow, this only scrap.
>
> I have also <u>small</u> scraps of another from the bronze age (drinking cup date) pot hole, and as this connects the two periods, which has not been done before, the find should turn out great. Also the drinking cups where restored are huge and peculiar and like some of the Scotch type I think.
>
> I have also one cinerary urn from the same locality tho' not the same hole of course.
>
> You will see of course that these pots are not new finds, but I have just been over them again, and *I am trying to restore the original shapes (drawings) to give some idea of the size of the general* [run] *of these pots in this district of this date.* Unfortunately I don't draw myself and have no useful guide for anyone else to go by so am in a somewhat difficult fix and also it is most difficult to estimate what the measurements were when one only has a base or top diameter especially when the pots are handmade. There are very many black holes turning up now, but as yet none has contained pot, but I live in hope.
>
> Two large pieces of drinking cups were lost when I was in town [?London] last year and so these are lost and gone forever with the exception of a few small scraps I saved from the heaps of crumbled pot sherds and which had been exposed for months.
>
> Also the round bottomed pot of ? black colour and well baked is of early iron age ?La Tène, and not as I thought at one time, early bronze age, another I have got all my ideas towise [?] and I must try a paper soon somewhere. I have had a promise of plates and space, which I like, in the Society of Antiquaries Journal; so come over and help me as I want ideas badly, and also knowledge as well as I am quite stale and unread now.
>
> *By the way if you see a copy of Abercrombies'* [sic] *article on Bronze Age drinking cups of about 1907 I believe, in 'Man', in a quarterly edition of the paper, I wish you could let me know the piece as I want one badly and should like if reasonable.*[13] *I of course want the plates specially as they are excellent, and most helpful in reconstruction from scrap.*
>
> I also want any reference to Neolithic pottery you may happen to see.
>
> Absolutely rushed today so please excuse scrawl.

Apart from, in effect, outlining 'the event' of the recognition of Peterborough Ware, this letter is important on two counts. Firstly, it relates that it was Smith who actually first attributed the Early Iron Age component of Abbott's assemblages (thereafter, using in his notebooks 'Early Iron Age' and 'Late Celtic' interchangeably for such material), with the latter previously thinking them of Bronze Age date. The second point is the emphasis on the reconstruction of vessel forms from 'scraps' (i.e. sherds). Reflective of how pottery typologies are constructed and accepted through convincing demonstration — by full pots and not sherds — in his notebooks generally it is full vessels and not sherds that are shown (Fig. 2.2), despite Abbott deriding his own drawing skills. Abbott, in fact, describes these as 'restorations' and clearly also restored his material himself for display purposes.[14]

Most of Abbott's material derived from pits, which he generally termed 'pot holes'. This reference was probably geologically inspired and certainly did not relate to artefact densities, as many of his so-called features lacked finds. Entirely typical of the time (see Evans 1989 for overview), in the main, he interpreted the larger of these as pit-dwellings and in the 1910 paper cited parallels to Clinch's Hayes Common 'hut-circles' (Abbott & Smith 1910, 333–4). Accompanied in the notebooks by the reconstruction drawing shown in Figure 2.6, in illustration of this is his description of one from Fengate Common (which also attests to the artefact densities from some of his features; Entry no. 1, this being the same as pit no. I in Abbott & Smith 1910, 334–7):

---

13. Abbott presumably meant Abercromby's 1902 paper in *The Journal of the Anthropological Institute*.

14. Not only is it crucial that Abbott physically reconstructed his vessels' full form, but also that he displayed them for group adjudication at the Society of Antiquaries of London: 'I shall hope to be free on the 14th January and shall do my best to get away. What do you suggest as exhibits on that day other than the lantern slides. I can bring a reasonable amount, but I don't want to carry all the fragile pieces about London if it can be avoided and the large pots are rather bulky and cumbersome' (Abbott/Leeds Correspondence 16/11/1921). Whilst, in the end, Abbott did not actually attend the Society's meeting that day (instead, this is the occasion when Leeds delivered his 'Further discoveries' and 'Beaker folk' papers; see below), the reading of his 1910 paper was evidently accompanied by exhibited finds (Abbott & Smith 1910, 333).

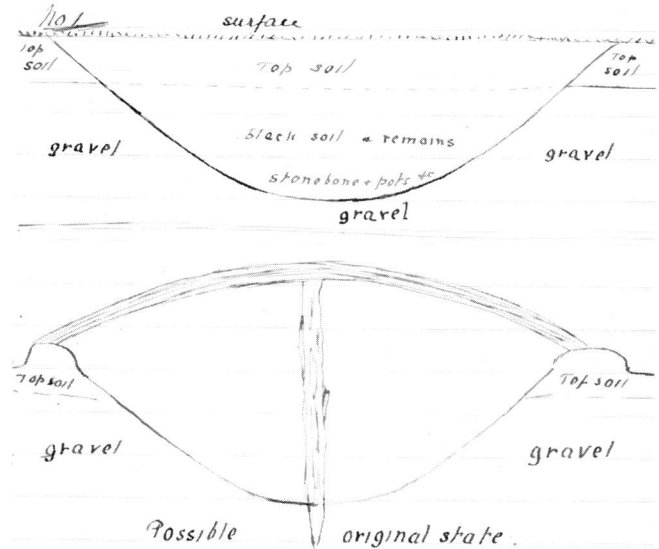

FIGURE 2.6. *Abbott's notebook account and reconstruction drawing of a Bronze Age pit-dwelling at Fengate Common (W11/1/1, Entry no. 1; Cambridge University Museum of Archaeology and Anthropology).*

This excavation which was probably a pit dwelling in Early Bronze Age times when flint was still used for ordinary purposes among the poorer people, was about 4½ ft deep in the centre & from 12–14 ft in diameter & saucer shaped with the sides at a regular slope all round to the outer edge, as far as I could see; as one side had been broken down & scattered before I saw the pit. The pit was filled with greyish black soil at the bottom which was more like the surrounding gravel & soil near the top of the pit. In this black soil which was probably composed of decayed animal & vegetable matter were found scattered all through it fragments of from 20–25 drinking cups from 5–10 food vessels & a few fragments of

[page break; disjointed text at top of page] several fragments of [**blank**] Neolithic pottery

what looked like cooking pots or rough culinary vessels of some kind; nearly all the fragments were small & had all been broken when thrown away, or else when in use as the pieces of the same pot were in quite different parts of the pit. Nearly all this pot was ornamented with the usual triangles lines & thumb marks usual to early Bronze Age pottery. There were also many worked flints including one arrow head about 35 scrapers 10 knives 3 saws about 300 rough flakes & 20 cores all made out of the usual flint nodules from the gravel; & the usual neolithic type of flints but quite dull & with none of the usual neolithic patina, All of which came form the same black soil. Also one bone pin about 4in long & sharpened at one end of the usual rough type usually found in barrows & made of the [**blank**] bone

[page break] of [**blank**]. There were also about 150 burnt stones of the usual gravel pebble type which had probably been used for pot boiling & for hearth stones most of these were broken up by the heat & so the number is only a rough guess. There were also many nut shells which had been broken. The nuts were the usual woodnut with a very thick shell. There were also a great many animal bones all the larger ones of which had been split to extract the marrow & many of them had been gnawed by animals afterwards, probably by the dogs of the makers of the pit. Many of the smaller bones had been burnt & some of the other larger bones were charred. For the list of animals as made out from the pieces of bone & teeth see p.2a. No bronze was found in this pit or other metal.

Abbott's specific assignment of pits as dwellings both related to feature morphology (see below) and, more importantly, the quantity of refuse they yielded. Interestingly, while later digging at Sutton Courtney, Berks. in the 1920s — the first 'true' excavation of a Saxon settlement in England and where sunken-building features of that period (later termed *Grubenhäuser*) were distinguished — Leeds did not consider its earlier, Bronze Age pits to be dwellings, essentially due to their paucity of finds and the lack of evidence of burning (1923, 151–4). In contrast, when in that same decade he also excavated the Neolithic causewayed enclosure at Abingdon, he interpreted its debris-strewn ditch segments as 'habitations' (1927, 443–5; see Evans 1988).[15]

With the vast majority of its illustrations relating to pottery, the main Fengate notebook only includes seven section drawings and these only pertain to its first ten entries (Fig. 2.7). Having established that this was not a raw fieldwork chronicle, but accounts worked-up after the fact, it is telling that the sketch-drawings on the 'primary' loose-sheet record for Entry no. 47 did not appear in the notebook (see Note 5); this surely suggests that other entries must also have had record-sketches that were not included within the bound volume account. Therefore, not being a body of 'face-value' observations, just what kind of record is it that Abbott provides?

Of the notebook sections, two are only very rough sketches. Of the remaining five, two are of individual features (one, Entry no. 5, being the flat-bottomed 'type' cited in Abbott & Smith 1910, 334), with the other three showing adjacent pairs of larger and small pits. Of the latter, that from Williamson's pit (Entry no. 3) is the same that was illustrated in Abbott and Smith's 1910 paper's figure 1 (Fig. 2.7), with the notebook sketch obviously providing the basis for the engraved version in *Archaeologia*. Of these pit pairings, Abbott identified the larger as the dwelling, with the smaller being a store-pit. Having set the parameters of their respective sizes (the larger measuring 12–13 ft across and 6 ft deep; the smaller, *c.* 4–6 ft in diameter and with the same depth range), after these first few notebook entries, he then stopped describing them in

any detail and generally only stated that they were of the usual smaller or larger type (or, variously, somewhat larger/smaller thereof). As is apparent in a ten-page long statement he sent to Leeds concerning a *long* Neolithic pit-dwelling that he dug out in 1911 in Rippon's Pit (and in which he himself 'types' its three classes of pottery), Abbott's sense of 'typing' even extended to the chronological development of this subterranean house-form; in it he states:

> The shape of the pit dwelling also helps to date the site & objects found. The people who made the long barrow[s] probably copied such a dwelling as this in making their funereal mound or they may even have covered the deceased['s] dwelling and this way made a long mound.
>
> Therefore I suggest that round barrow makers lived in the circular pit dwelling with the centre post and made their barrows in the same form as the house in which the dead had lived.[16]

In short, and related to allied themes further discussed below, Abbott's was evidently *a 'type-driven' record* (in this case, distinguishing pattern/type on the basis of single 'long' occurrence).[17]

Despite stating in 1910 that 'There were no surface indications of human habitation, and no barrows noticed on the [Fengate] promontory or in its neighbourhood' (Abbott & Smith 1910, 333), a number of monuments are described in Abbott's notebooks. As this facet of his work has already been published, it need not be detailed here (Evans & Appleby 2008; see also Chapter 4, Inset concerning the Herdsmen's

---

15. Hawkes and Fell, based on Bersu's Little Woodbury findings (1940) rejected Abbott's pit-dwelling interpretation of Fengate's Iron Age pits (1945, 193–4).

16. The size and shape of this feature (14 × 9 ft and 4.5 ft deep/*c.* 4.25 × 2.75 × 1.35 m), and the various 'earths', 'seats/benches' and ridges said to be within it, are reminiscent of Leeds' description of Abingdon's ditch-segment pit-dwellings (e.g. 1927). This raises the intriguing possibility of whether Abbott's 'long pit-dwelling' could actually have been the segment of a causewayed enclosure ditch; however, his description of its pottery suggests Peterborough Ware and his long pit could, instead, have been the by-product of intercutting pits and, perhaps, a tree-throw.

17. The fact that his notebooks include the section for his early Site Entry no. 3 itself indicates that his notebook accounts cannot have been worked up at a much later date than their original field recording (e.g. specifically for either Leeds' 1922 or Hawkes & Fell's 1945 papers); otherwise, he would not have bothered reproducing the section that appears in the 1910 paper (equally, as outlined above, the Bronze Age to Neolithic amendment of Abbott's Entry no. 15 pottery must have followed Smith's 1909 viewing of his material.) It is equally notable that Leeds did not, in his 1922 paper, illustrate or expound in any detail on Fengate's subsequent features, saying of its Neolithic pits: 'The discoveries were made for the most part in pits, of varying diameter and depth, of the *usual hut-dwelling type*. As examples have already been described in *Archaeologia* … it is unnecessary to dilate on their form here' (Leeds 1922, 221; emphasis added).

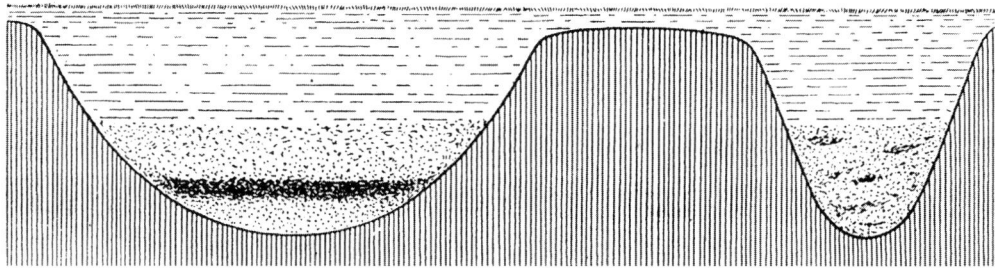

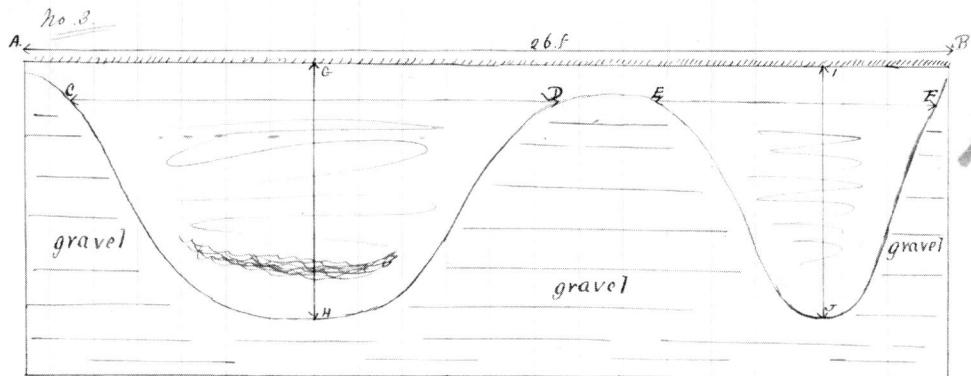

no. 3.

A ——————————— 26.f ——————————— B

C
G
D
E
F

gravel

gravel

gravel

H

A – B = 26 feet   E – F = 6 ft   = dark charcoal & band.
C – D = 13 ft   G – H = 6 ft
           I – J = 6 ft   about 1 ft. from bottom of pit.
                                              gw/a 29/1/00.

This pot hole was on the boundary between Walkers & R. Williamson's pits & about
20 yards from Rippon's corner fence boundary.

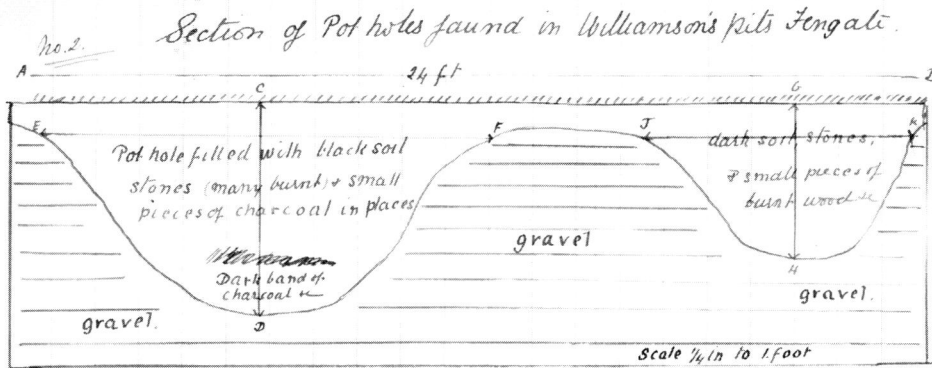

no. 2.   Section of Pot holes found in Williamson's pits Fengate.

A ——————— 24 ft ——————— D

C
G
E
F
J
K

Pot hole filled with black soil
stones (many burnt) & small
pieces of charcoal in places

dark soil stones,
& small pieces of
burnt wood &c

gravel

Dark band of
charcoal &c

gravel.

gravel.

H

D

gravel.

Scale 1/4 in to 1 foot

A – B = 24 feet   G – H = 4 ft   = layer of stones & ashes
C – D = 6 .   J – K = 6 ..   marking fire place
E – F = 12 "

These pot holes were about 40 yards from the hedge dividing williamsons
and Walkers pits & were about 15 yards north from the level of Walkers house,
& nearly at the top end of the pits

FIGURE 2.7. *Pit Types — Top, figure 1 from Abbott & Smith's 1910 paper; middle and bottom, notebook 'pot hole' sections (W11/1/1, Entry nos. 2 & 3).*

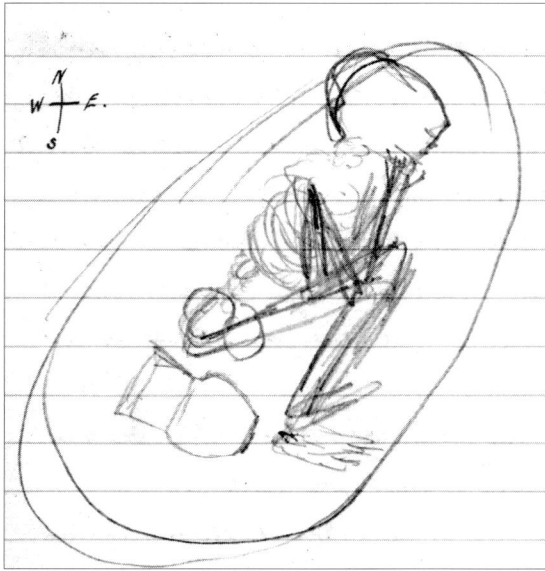

Figure 2.8. *Abbott's Beaker burial (W11/1/1, Entry no. 32; see also Fig. 2.4:B; Cambridge University Museum of Archaeology and Anthropology).*

Hill Barrow). His main finding in this category was a great oval ring-ditch, which, remarkably, apparently had upwards of 100 interments (see Chapter 6 below). Outlined in Hawkes & Fell's paper (1945, 190), the Cambridge Museum archives include an 11 page-long draft paper devoted to it[18] and, moreover, it was also the subject of five letters by Abbott to Leeds held by the Ashmolean (and shown on the map he sent to him; Fig. 2.4; see also Figs. 2.9 & 4.28:A).

In his notebooks, Abbott also related the exposure of a semi-circular ditch ('trench') over 16 yds in length (*c.* 14.6 m), 6 ft deep and 12 ft across (*c.* 1.8 × 3.65 m). Having, amongst other finds, half a palstave and human skull fragments recovered from it (see Note 5 above), this could well have related to another ring-ditch or barrow (W11/1/1, Entry no. 47; Fig. 2.4:2). The same might even also be true for some of the six 'isolated' inhumations recovered dispersed throughout the quarries. One, a crouched 'old adult' (later, added in pencil, 'probably female'), was accompanied by a complete beaker of the 'usual "a" form' (i.e. Abercromby's type A, e.g. 1902; W11/1/1, Entry no. 32; Figs. 2.8 & 2.5:B; see also Clarke 1970, no. 645). Yet Abbott was clearly aware of the potential monu-

ment-association of such interments and in this case noted that 'there was no trace of a rise in the surface soil and no trace of a ditch'.

As demonstrated in the study of Abbott's great ring-ditch (Evans & Appleby 2008), there is considerable discrepancy in the basic description between his separate manuscript account and that provided in Hawkes & Fell's 1945 paper (deriving from information supplied to the latter by Abbott). Not only does its measurement differ markedly (respectively, 84 × 90 ft/*c.* 25.6 × 27.4 m and 28 × 38 yds/*c.* 25.6 × 34.75 m), but where Abbott's version states that there were 80 cremations and 28 inhumations, in the 1945 account these figures are respectively given as 130 and 20. This cannot be explained through further quarry-exposure of this monument subsequent to the 1919–20 manuscript and additional information that Abbott might have later given Fell. Additional digging might have resulted in the increase of its length and the number of cremations in the 1945 account, yet the number of inhumations accorded in the latter is almost a third less and this must suggest a certain lack of control of data on Abbott's part. Indeed, the only 'detailed' illustration we have of this monument is a sketch of half of its ring in a letter to Leeds (Fig. 2.9), which only indicates the position of nine cremations and four inhumations.

In the case of that monument, the remarkable nature of Abbott's findings (i.e. the number of burials) must either markedly break with subsequent regional precedent or are grossly exaggerated. They do, after all, rely on the accounts of quarry labourers and, in the end, all we have is plan-documentation of a handful of cremations, where so many such interments are claimed. The unease this gulf inspires is fundamental to the entire notion of *record-as-truth*. Yet, just because something was, effectively, 'undocumented' (i.e. plotted) does not necessarily make it a falsehood.[19]

A 'typed' archaeology

On January 12th, 1922, on behalf of Abbott, Leeds apparently read two papers by him to the Society of Antiquaries of London: 'Further discoveries near Peterborough' and 'Where did the beaker folk land' (as noted in *The Antiquaries Journal* 1922/2, 175). It is the latter of these that concerns us here, as it clearly reflects the 'invasionist' prehistory of the time. Whilst we lack its manuscript, Abbott was equally explicit

---

18. Note, also, that stuck within the same notebook as this manuscript is another, loose, three-page long, pencil-written account of this same site, 'Report on a Burial Ground at Fengate, Peterborough'. Much shorter and less detailed than the main manuscript, it seems an earlier rough draft; it includes, though, a thumbnail sketch plan of the 'circle' in its upper title-page margin (see Evans & Appleby 2008).

19. In the context of archaeological documentation and issues of veracity, the laxness of Abbott's documentation as opposed to Pitt Rivers' — with both sharing legal backgrounds or, at least, experience in the case of the General — could argue against any judicial basis of *archaeological proof* (cf. Evans 2007a); there would be no court in the world that would accept Abbott's records as 'truth'.

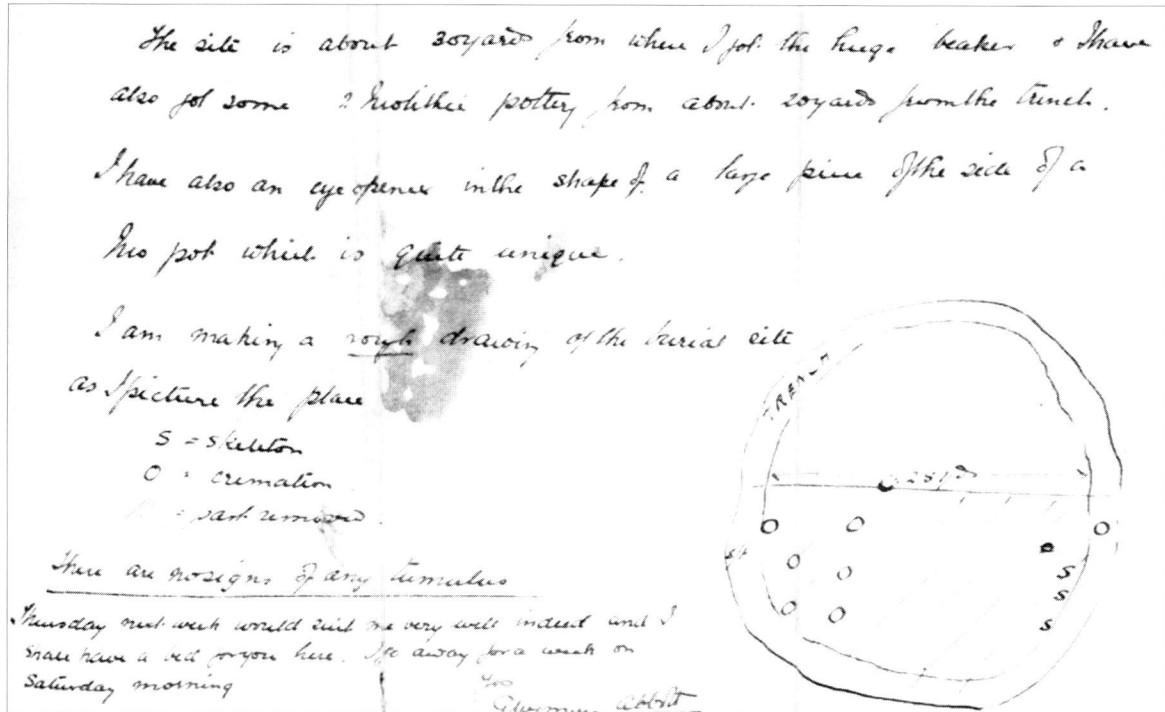

FIGURE 2.9. *Sketch plan of Abbott's 'great' ring-ditch in a letter to Leeds (13/08/1920; Leeds Correspondence Archive, Ashmolean Museum); see Figure 4.28.*

on this theme in the introductory paragraphs of his ring-ditch manuscript:

> This is probably by reason of the position of the site[,] which is just east of the first crossing place of the River Nene before this river enters the actual fens and consequently the promontory would be a natural station to protect the ford. Further[,] any tribe or people invading from the east and entering the Wash could come by boat to this point and could here establish a 'bridge head' on the promontory and[,] provided they were masters of the water[,] would only have to protect themselves on the north western side where the site is linked up by a narrow neck of land to the 'mainland'.[20]

Crucial to this is what is understood to be Fengate's 'bridge-head' location in relationship to the Continent (*via* The Wash) and, with it, early overseas 'introductions'.[21] This is an ethos which Leeds also shared, as is apparent in his first Eyebury barrows paper.

> Taken, however, in connexion with those found in Herdsman's Hill, Newark, and Mr. Abbott's discoveries at Fengate, this tumulus may with some high degree of probability be assumed to indicate a burial belonging to the earliest period of the Bronze Age, if not the actual transition from the neolithic period. Thus affording further evidence of *the use of part of the Wash route by the invaders who introduced the knowledge of metal into Britain* (1912, 92; emphasis added).

This, in turn, is comparable to Abbott's earlier remarks concerning Beakers:

> From these potsherds the date of the settlement can be fixed at the end of the neolithic period, when the first invasion of which we have any tangible evidence

---

20. In their 1945 paper Hawkes and Fell noted a remark by Abbott concerning the site's Iron Age occupation: 'It appears that the settlement was always small, and may have decreased in numbers as the community spread, as it seems to have done, upstream and round the Fen islands. I imagine that the waterways were the means of access and travel, almost entirely; and *the community could in some respects be compared with the Glastonbury type in manner of living in the fens*' (1945, 222; emphasis added).

21. An account of Abbott's ring-ditch discoveries in the *Peterbor-

ough Advertiser of 14/08/20 appeared under the by-line, 'Bronze Age Invaders at Peterborough'. With its narrative almost prefiguring Fox's *The Archaeology of the Cambridge Region* of 1923 (i.e. 'cold, forested claylands' *vs* 'light, open gravels'; see also Evans 2002), Burkitt & Fox's *Victoria County History* outline of Huntingdonshire's prehistory was equally punctuated by invasions, with both the Beaker and Early Iron Age incursions thought to originate from the area of the Rhine-land (1926, 209). Of the former, the finding of an Abercromby B-type Beaker at Stanground was held to indicate: '... that the right bank of the Nene in the neighbourhood of Peterborough (as well as the left) was occupied by the round-headed invaders' (Burkitt & Fox 1926, 210, note 2).

THE OLDEST BRONZE-AGE CERAMIC TYPE IN BRITAIN.

Map shewing localities in the County of Cambridge, whence ancient Skulls, of Romano-British and East Anglian origin, have been obtained. The specimens are now in the Anatomical Museum.

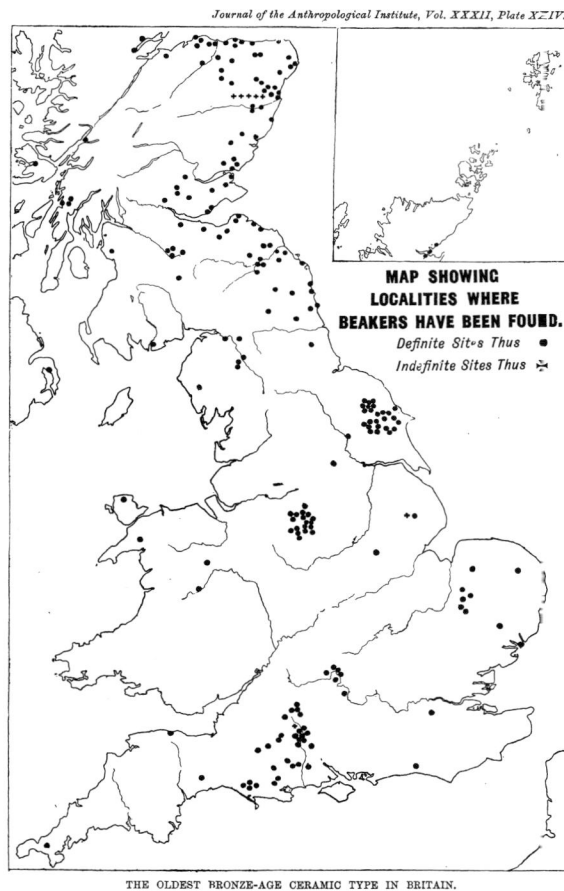

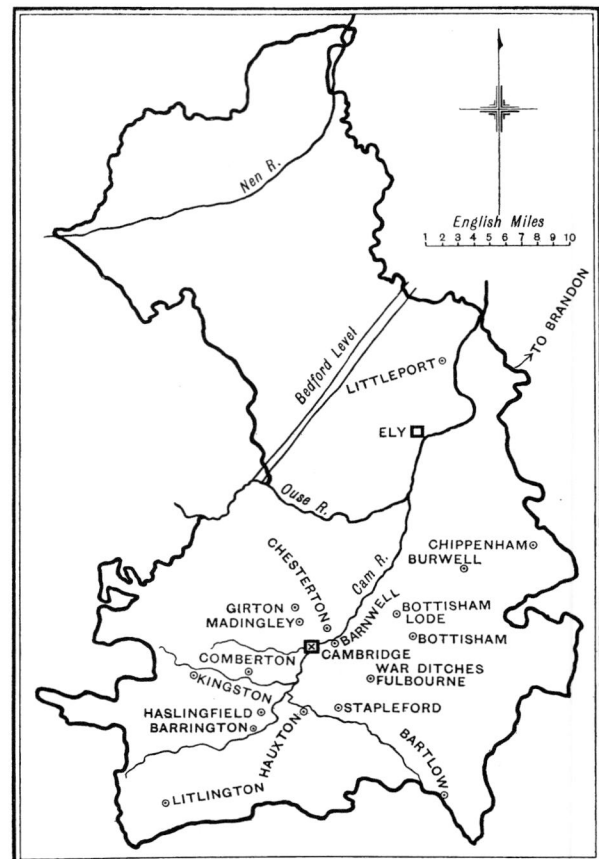

FIGURE 2.10. *'Type Maps' — Right, Abercromby's 1902 Beaker distribution maps (pl. XXIV); left, Duckworth map showing location of 'racial-type skulls' finds in Cambridgeshire (1904).*

was taking place. *The new-comers introduced the beaker or drinking cup, and landed on our eastern shores, conquered and drove inland the aboriginal dolichocephalic population* (1910, 337; emphasis added).[22]

As emphasized in these passages, it is necessary to recognize that such evidence of 'the foreign' did not just rely upon artefacts, but also drew upon skeletal evidence. Again, we have Leeds writing of his Eyebury burial:

> A report on the skull and other parts of the skeleton … shows that in the matter of height and cephalic index the skeleton has more affinities with known Bronze Age types than with those of the neolithic

inhabitants of Britain, though there is an absence of the pronounced brachycephalic characteristics met within in many of *the skulls of the immigrant race* (1912, 92; emphasis added).

This, of course, is generally reflective of the evolutionary ethnography/comparative craniology that held sway in the latter half of the nineteenth century and lingered into the early decades of the next, and is evident, for example, in the archaeology of Pitt Rivers and Canon Greenwell, with skeletal types providing a ready extra-regional/-national dynamic (see e.g. Rowley-Conwy 2007 for overview).[23] As will be discussed in this volume's concluding chapter, we ourselves should be wary of any lingering sense of

22. In the notebooks Abbott remarked of his Beaker-accompanied crouched inhumation: 'The skull which was much damaged was of a debased type and longshaped & in consequence the burial was of one of the Neolithic people contra distinguished to the Bronze Age. The nose is very wide & the jaw heavy & I quite think the teeth were in part decayed' (W11/1/1, Entry no. 32).

23. See also, for example, Duckworth 1904, 249–51 on the region's ancient skulls (Fig. 2.10); telling of the lack of popular impact of recent archaeological interpretation, skull-type succession even still underpins the story of farming presented in Whitlock's *The English Farm* of 1983 (p. 31).

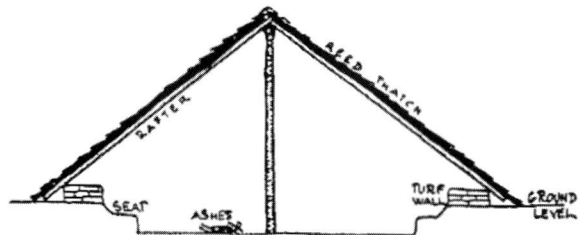

FIGURE 2.11. *Edwardian Peterborough (and archaeology) — Top, The City's Aldermen in their full regalia (with Abbott standing in the back row third from right); lower left, a magic lantern slide showing begging for Whittlesey's Strawbear procession of c. 1909 (Whittlesey Museum); lower right, reconstruction of a pit dwelling as figure 13 in* The Victoria County History of Huntingdonshire *of 1926. Entitled an 'Iron Age Hut', in the accompanying text it is, however, clear that its source was, instead, 'ethnographic' and that its sketch was made 'from memory':*

> *Some of these shallow pits were undoubtedly hut sites. The occurrence of such on the Fenland borders recalls a visit the writer made twenty-five years ago with Dr. L. Corbett of Cambridge, to a fenman's hut used to temporary shelter for tools, in the fens, near Cambridge, which closely resembled, it may be, the permanent dwellings of Iron Age and earlier folk in our district. That this hut was, at all events, a direct survival of primitive Fenland habitation need not be doubted (Burkitt et al. 1926, 210, Note 6).*

Equally, telling of the degree of assumed continuity that often pervades studies of farming practice, Whitlock's history of The English Farm *(1983) has a picture of a Victorian farm worker 'using a sickle as did his Bronze Age ancestors' (p. 33) and a photograph of what is probably a family of nineteenth-century labourers/tinkers posed in front of their crude 'bender-type' shelter has a caption comparing it to Neolithic housing (p. 25).*

'folk' association when discussing 'Grooved Ware' or 'Beaker pit groups/settlement', etc. and, even if implicitly, directly associating ethnicities/'peoples' with material cultural types (i.e. do we really mean 'Grooved Ware people' when we discuss Grooved Ware as a cultural complex?). Indeed, any such direct linkages were first discredited during the later nineteenth century (see Stocking 1987, 59; see Chapter 6). It could, nevertheless, be argued that, in contrast to today's vague reference to artefactual types alone, the essentially racialist formulation of much later nineteenth/early twentieth-century archaeology was, at least in theory, on somewhat surer ground by its broader association of both skeletal- *and* artefact-types and peoples (this being underpinned by the interpretative confidence that only minimal data can inspire).

Fengate's prominence in these early explanatory 'stories' does, itself, reflect upon the importance of Abbott's findings. Take, for example, Crawford's 1912 paper, 'The Distribution of Early Bronze Age Settlements in Britain'. Also underpinned by an invasionist and racialist-/skeletal-type dynamic, at that time Fengate featured as one of only three Beaker settlement sites known in England (1912, fig. 2). In it he postulates, based on artefact distributions and geographic factors, that a major trade route must have run between Ireland and Denmark, writing: 'The eastern terminus of the road may well have been at Peterborough, where an undoubted beaker settlement has been found' (Crawford 1912, 196); obviously The Wash, again, was considered the gateway from the Continent.

All this highlights that local landscape researches never existed in any kind of empirical vacuum, and have always been subject to wider 'outside' interpretative influence: there is always something *beyond the immediate*. It equally reflects upon how deeply engrained 'type' reasoning has been to the formulation of the archaeological process. We are familiar with the idea that the need for chronologies drove the construction of pottery (and metalwork) typologies. Yet, in the case of Fengate, this pottery emphasis existed within a spectrum of other *types* — skeletons and pits — and a desire to create order that owes as much to nineteenth-century classificatory systems generally as 'modern' approaches to an any more systematic archaeology. Indeed, the early decades of the twentieth century saw the last gasp of what can be considered a 'totalizing archaeology', variously involving excavation/earthwork survey, folklore and craniology/physiology studies (see e.g. Urry 1984). This eclecticism saw the shared involvement of both amateur and university/museum academics, and was a 'mix' that, at least regionally, survived until the advent of the more scientifically-based archaeological professionalism of the 1930s (Smith 1997; Evans 1989).

Regional Bronze Age fieldsystems and landscapes

In recent years, much fieldwork has occurred within the wider Peterborough/Fengate environs. With little of it seeing any publication to date, summaries of relevant projects are required if the context of Fengate/Flag Fen is now to be appreciated. Equally, further afield within the Fenlands, there have been a number of major landscape projects, which have resulted in vast exposures of Bronze Age fieldsystems. Though not to the same degree, for much the same reasons these also require overview. It goes without saying that the restrictions of volume length preclude comprehensive review and, inevitably (given access to source-materials), this will be somewhat biased towards recent CAU investigations. Fortunately, however, Yates's recent book (2007) provides greater 'umbrella' coverage (and lists many more ambiguous fieldsystem 'sightings' arising from minor-scale investigations; see also Malim 2001), with Garrow's *Pits, Settlement and Deposition during the Neolithic and Early Bronze Age in East Anglia* (2006), summarizing the pre-Middle Bronze Age usage of a number of these sites.

As shown on Figure 2.12's version of Yates's 2007 distribution map, our focus here essentially coincides with those fieldsystems that 'pocket' the terraces of where the region's great rivers debouched into the western Fens: the River Great Ouse, the Nene and the Welland (with the Block Fen system lying adjacent to what was the main southern-mid Fenland palaeochannel course of the Ouse). Otherwise, the only other substantive exposure of a fieldsystem within the region proper has been at Brandon, along the eastern fen-edge (Gibson *et al.* 2004). Yates's map also shows fieldsystems extending upstream from the Fens, along the River Cam, to Cambridge. This, however, is largely based on limited, single ditch-boundary exposures and it has really only been through recent work in the Addenbrooke's Environs, on the south side of Cambridge, that truly convincing fieldystems of the period have been delineated at any scale (Hinman 2001b; Evans *et al.* 2008).

Before progressing, two points need to be made. The first, as will be apparent below, relates to the sheer scope available today of Fengate's comparative context. This simply did not exist when it was dug in the '90s and in Pryor's 'Fengate Four' Discussion of 1984 the only sites that could be drawn upon in Eastern England were Ardleigh and Mucking. The second point pertains to fieldsystem *nomenclature* (see

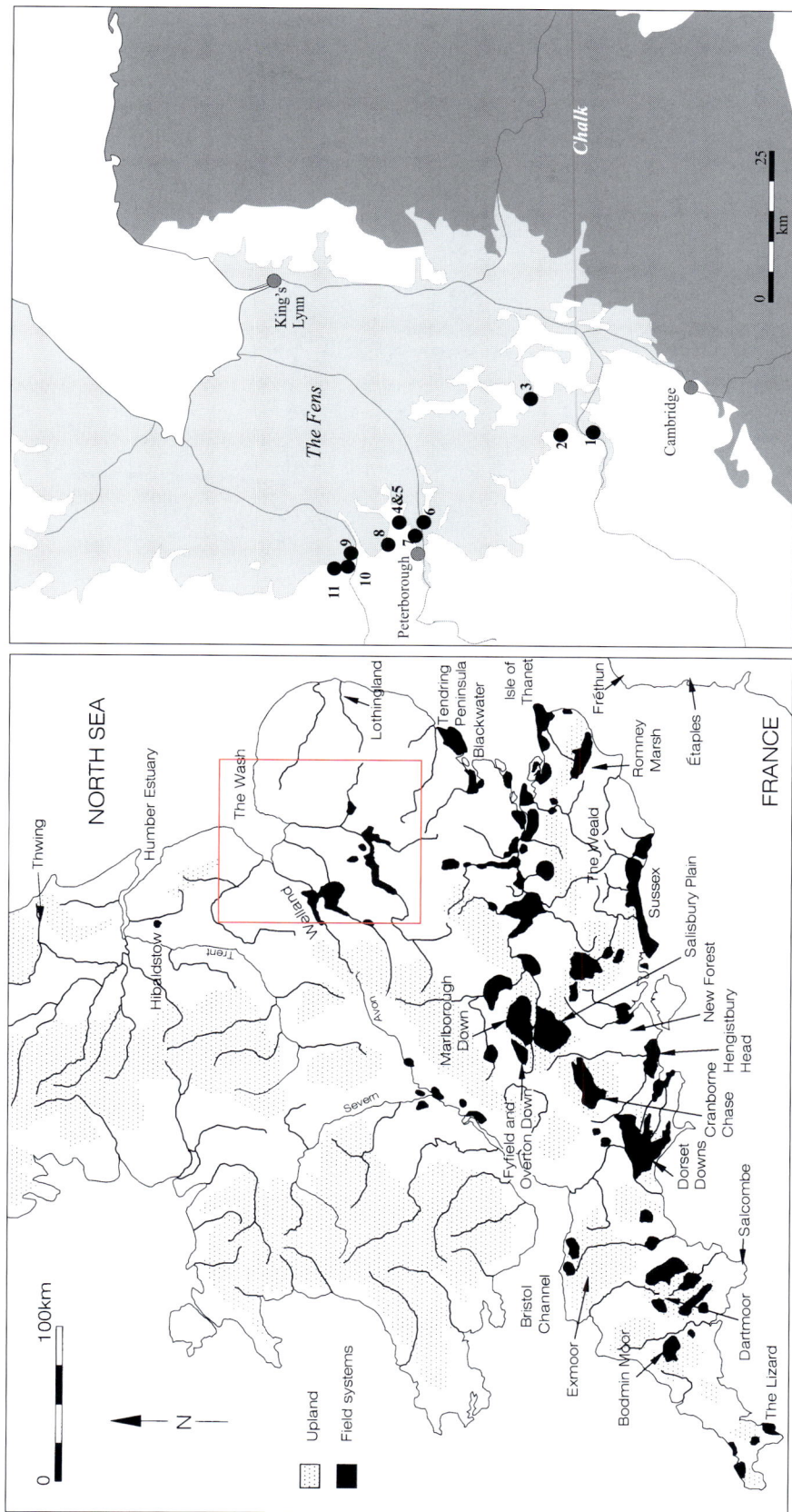

FIGURE 2.12. *Bronze Age fieldsystem distributions and site locations — Left, Yates' 'pocketed' distribution map (2007, fig. 12.2); right, location of main Fenland fieldsystems discussed in text: 1) Barleycroft/Over; 2) Colne Fen, Earith; 3) Block Fen, Mepal; 4) Pode Hole, Thorney; 5) Tanholt Farm, Eye; 6) Bradley Fen and Must Farm, Whittlesey; 7) Fengate; 8) Newborough; 9) Welland Bank; 10) Market Deeping; 11) Langtoft. (Reproduced by permission of Ordnance Survey on behalf of HMSO. © Crown copyright 2009. All rights reserved. Ordnance Survey Licence number 100048686.)*

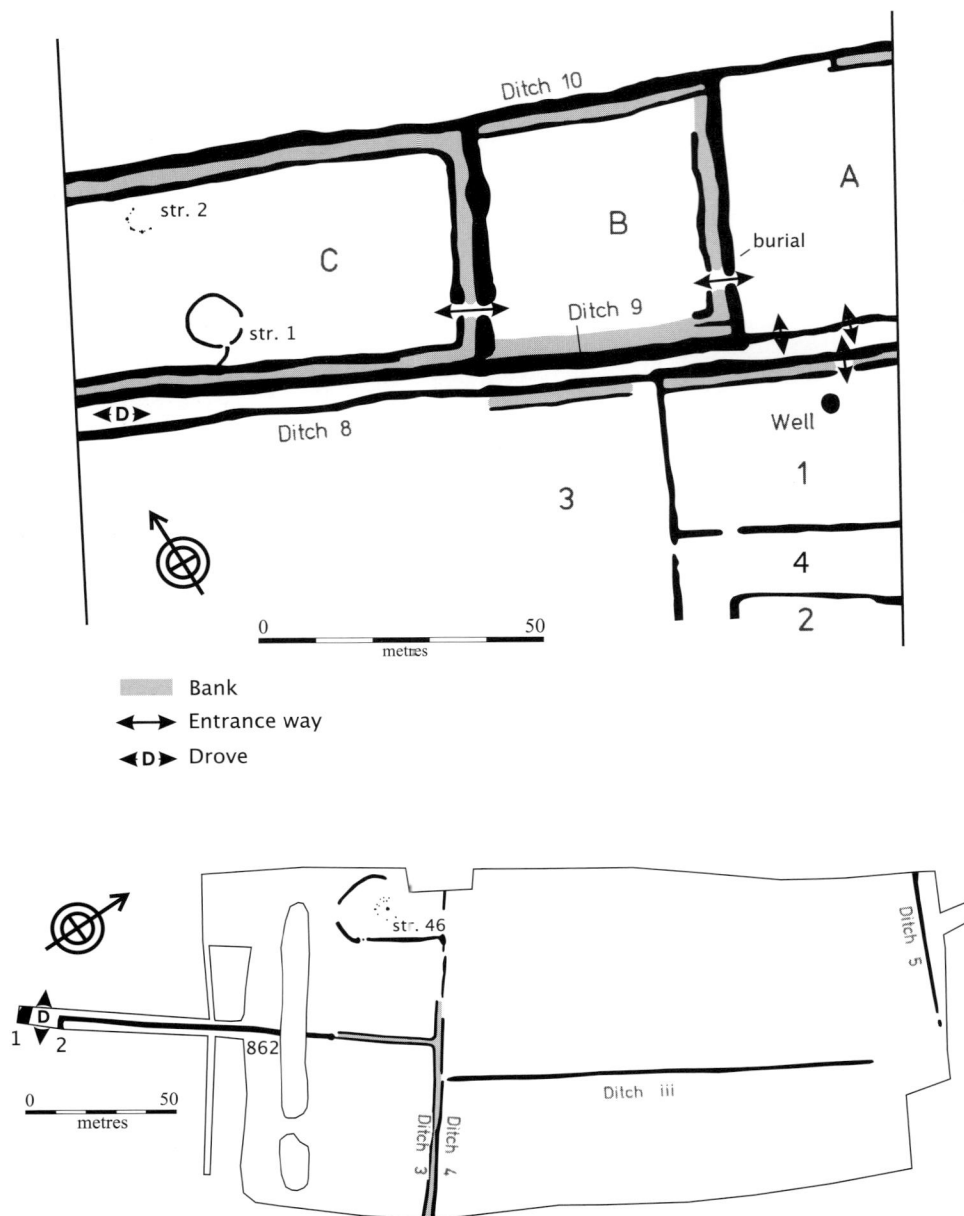

FIGURE 2.13. *Fengate's Droves and Embankments — Top, the Newark Road compounds and plots arranged alongside the Ditch 8/9 droveway. Although originally thought to indicate 'internal droves' (Pryor 1980a, 23), the double-ditch perimeter of Compounds B and C surely rather attests to their embankment; the 'single' more minor parallel boundaries in 'plots' 1 and 3 must similarly have been in relationship to drove-side banks. The 'doubling' of the compound-interior ditches in the southeastern corner of Compound B could, in fact, suggest that the main boundary-parallel banks in relationship to Ditches 9 and 10 occurred prior to the embankment of the entire circuit of B (though its western interior side may not have been so marked as this would have been provided by the eastern 'front' of Compound C, the establishment of which appears to have pre-dated it); below, Cat's Water's Bronze Age, in which the narrow-interval double-line of Ditches 3/4 and F.862 cannot have demarcated droves, but rather flanked embankments and which may have been hedge-capped. Further demonstrating their non-droveway function, in Pryor's 1990 Area 1 extension, Ditches 3/4 effectively converged and actually conjoined c. 60 m east of the site.*

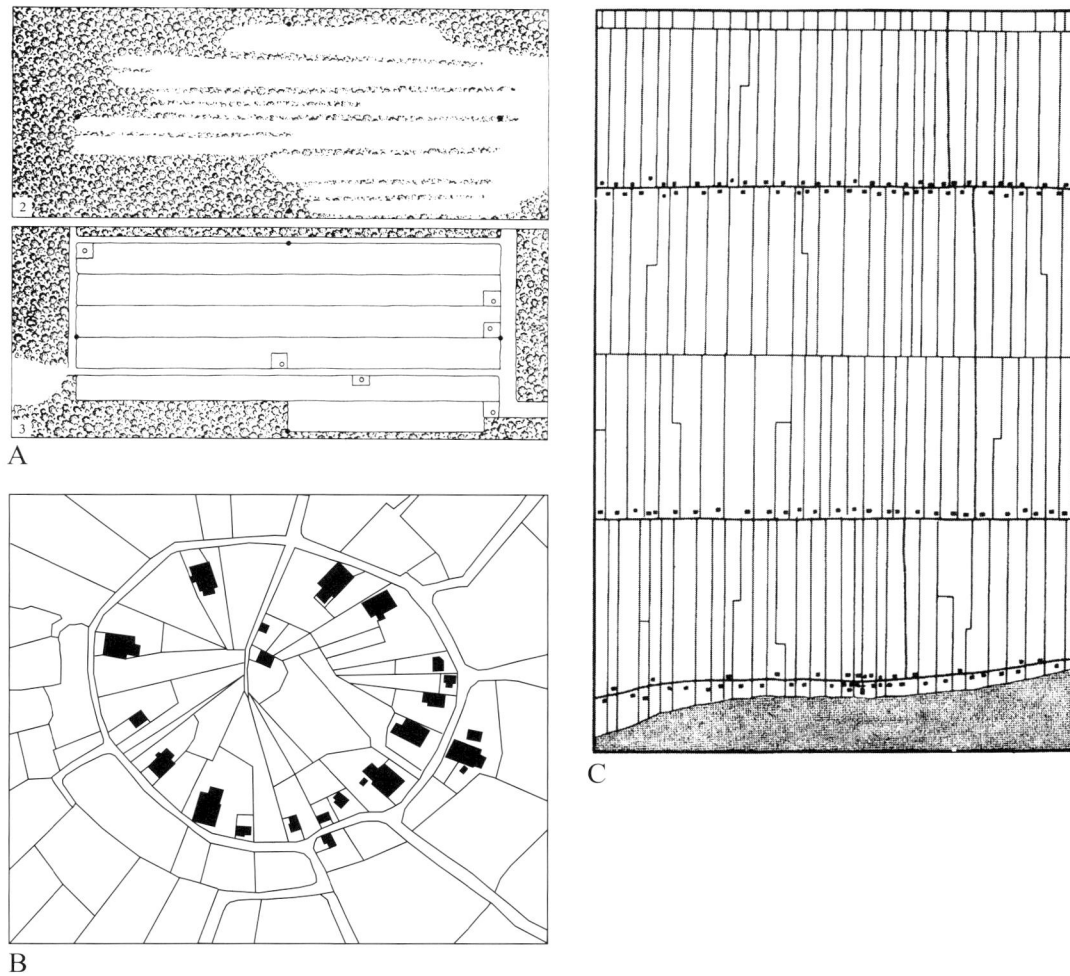

FIGURE 2.14. *Model Fieldsystems — A) Fowler 'strip model' of landscape clearance and allotment (1983, fig. 42); B) radial-type plot-divisions on Dutch terpen (Biessum; after Boersma 2005, fig. N4): C) French Canadian long-lot system stretching down to the St Lawrence River (after Harris & Warkentin 1974).*

also Fowler 1983, 107–11; Yates 2007, 15–17). In other words, what are the main 'type-components' that occur at Fengate and that we need to be aware of in the other landscapes outlined below? This is best tackled in reference to plans of Fengate's main sub-sites (Fig. 2.13). Though at risk of stressing the obvious, the first are *droveways*. Variously facilitating the through-field passage of animals and people and flanked by ditches, these were *c.* 4–10 m across (although elsewhere they also occur up to nearly 20 m wide; see Earith below). In contrast, are *narrow parallel-ditch boundaries*. With only a *c.* 1–2 m gap between them, as discussed below, based on the experience of excavating the Barleycroft Farm/Over system (Evans & Knight 2000; 2001), we would hold — in contrast to Pryor's sheep-crush/-run arguments (1996; see Chapter 6 below) — that these would have flanked hedge-capped embankments.

Finally, there are *double-ditch compounds*, such as those present at the Newark Road sub-Site (Fig. 2.13). With all of their sides marked by parallel ditches (2–3.5 m apart), their perimeters, by extension, were presumably embanked (see Welland Bank below). The crucial question of interpretation, and a theme that will be returned to on more than one occasion in this volume, is whether these were stock compounds or settlement-related. Whilst not a major feature of the original Fengate investigations (though see Pryor's 1990 Cat's Water investigations; 2001a, 45–7, fig. 3.8), another component to recognize are fence-lines. These are now, elsewhere, being recovered with some frequency, including within the immediate Flag Fen environs and potentially reflect upon the role of the Flag Fen post alignment (the cumulative evidence also attests to the importance of coppicing and the management of woodland resources to supply their timber; see Evans & Knight 2001 concerning the Barleycroft Farm alignments).

Finally, what do we imply by the term 'fieldsystem', especially as regards to which other sites/projects warrant inclusion within this category? Here, to distinguish what are just more open (or less 'formal') ditch boundary layouts, we will restrict its application to rectilinear, plot-arranged systems. While Fowler established a complicated fieldsystem typology (Fig. 2.14; 1983, 128–44), for our purposes here, the more simplified two-fold division of Yates will be adequate (2007, 15; see also Bradley 1978 and Fleming 1987). This encompasses *aggregate systems* of piecemeal or patchwork-like character without a dominant axial arrangement and, also, *coaxial systems*; the latter involving parallel, long strip-type arrangements with a single dominant alignment (although this may variously twist and/or radiate).

Peterborough and Fengate/Flag Fen environs

Pryor's limited trial trenching of the cropmarks on Northey Island, immediately opposite Flag Fen and effectively connected to Fengate by its timber alignment/causeway, were duly outlined in the Flag Fen volume (Pryor 2001a, 74–86; see also Gurney 1980). Otherwise, the most relevant investigations of recent years have been those by the CAU in Hanson's Whittlesey quarries — King's Dyke, Bradley Fen and, currently, at Must Farm — whose extraordinary results recast our understanding of the greater Fengate/Flag Fen complex and its setting. To these must now be added the on-going excavations at Stanground South. Equally, however (and, in effect, returning us to Leeds' 'home-farm' initiation of fieldwork within the area) has been the huge-scale exposure of the Bronze Age fieldsystem at Tanholt Farm, Eye. Coupled with the work at Pode Hole, Thorney, these sites certainly tell just how much of this area lay under fieldsystems during the second millennium BC.

Three smaller projects, with varying results, are also outlined (Fig. 2.15): Oxney Road, just northwest of Fengate where fieldsystem ditches were present; Parnwell on the clays alongside Eye Island, where such fieldsystem ditches were not present; and the Peterborough New Prison Site, located well 'inland' on the high ground to the west and where, surprisingly, they were (see also Mudd & Upson-Smith 2006 for the 'mid-town' Iron Age site at Alma Road).

Oxney Road
Undertaken by Soke Archaeological Services, in 2001–2, evaluation trenching and small-scale excavation occurred at Oxney Road near its junction with Eyebury Road and on the north side of the Flag Fen

embayment (TF 223006, see Fig. 4.26:4; Britchfield 2002). Not only did a series of stake-/postholes and pits (one producing a Tranchet axe) demonstrate evidence of Mesolithic to earlier Bronze Age activity (including a 'filled' Beaker pit), but two parallel ditches also seemed characteristic of a second-millennium BC fieldsystem.

Parnwell, Fengate
The Oxford Unit's 2004–5 investigations over this 12.2 ha site (TF 219012, see Fig. 2.15; Webley 2007) has been among the more intriguing projects within the broader Fengate area in recent years. Located approximately 0.8 km north of our Edgerley Drain Road Site (see Chapter 4 below), it was situated upon a low 'clayland' rise (4–6.6 m OD) on the north side of the Flag Fen basin. Seeing localized later Iron Age occupation followed by more substantial Early Roman settlement (and Anglo-Saxon charcoal-production pits), for our purposes most relevant is its evidence of Neolithic and Bronze Age activity, as this demonstrates that such 'pit-type usage' was not confined to the gravel terraces. With one feature firmly dated to c. 3600–3400 cal. BC, the former was marked by a discrete cluster of 11 pits associated with worked flint and 'decorated bowl' pottery. The earlier Bronze Age was evinced by much more dispersed irregular pits/hollows, which yielded limited quantities of flint and both Collared and Biconical Urn tradition pottery. Yet perhaps the site's most significant result from a 'Fengate perspective' is that no evidence whatsoever of any Bronze Age fieldsystem was recovered.

Peterborough New Prison (with MARK KNIGHT)
When, in 2000, the CAU excavated the 1.5 ha site of Peterborough's New Prison, located up on the cornbrash limestone (16 m OD) and some 4 km inland from the fen (TF 180003, see Fig. 2.15; Knight 2002), quite surprisingly a second-millennium BC fieldsystem was found. Essentially aligned north–south/east–west, as opposed to the site's 'open' network of quite minor fieldsystem ditches *per se*, its somewhat more robust, 'detached' boundaries appeared to demarcate settlement swathes, as defined by pits of various size and posthole clusters (a four-poster being the only recognizable structure as such). It included two major pit-well/watering-holes, 1.95 m and 2.15 m deep. Scaife's pollen analysis from one of these indicated limited background woodland and arable cultivation against a more general waste- and disturbed ground-species setting. A quantity of later Bronze Age occupation material occurred within the upper profiles of these wells, but was absent from their primary deposits. This suggests that it is possible that they were actually sunk in the earlier/Middle Bronze Age and were not directly contemporary with the settlement evidence.

Interestingly, and in reference to Table 1.2's figures, whilst the site yielded relatively little worked flint (169 pieces; density c. 0.01 per sqm), prehistoric pottery occurred in high numbers, with 906 sherds recovered (0.06 per sqm). Of the latter, more than 840 were of later Bronze Age attribution (Post-Deverel-Rimbury). Otherwise, later Neolithic Peterborough Ware was present in low numbers (18 sherds) and, apart from sherds from two Collared Urns and a Beaker, there were sherds from grog-tempered urns. The site's pre-mid second-millennium activity was restricted to two later Neolithic and two/three earlier Bronze Age attributed pits (with some later Neolithic material incidentally present within tree-throws).

The Whittlesey Quarries (with DAVID GIBSON & MARK KNIGHT)
The CAU has undertaken fieldwork in the Hanson quarries on Whittlesey since 1995, which has subsequently led to investigations extending over some 170 ha, with 25.65 ha of open-area exposure to date (Figs 2.15 & 2.16). Work originally focused on cropmarks upon the island's crown (at c. 2.8–4.4 m OD) at *King's Dyke*. Partially overlain by a network of Romano-British paddocks and the ditched line of the Fen Causeway road of that date, between 1998 and March 2000 excavations there led to the exposure of an extraordinary later

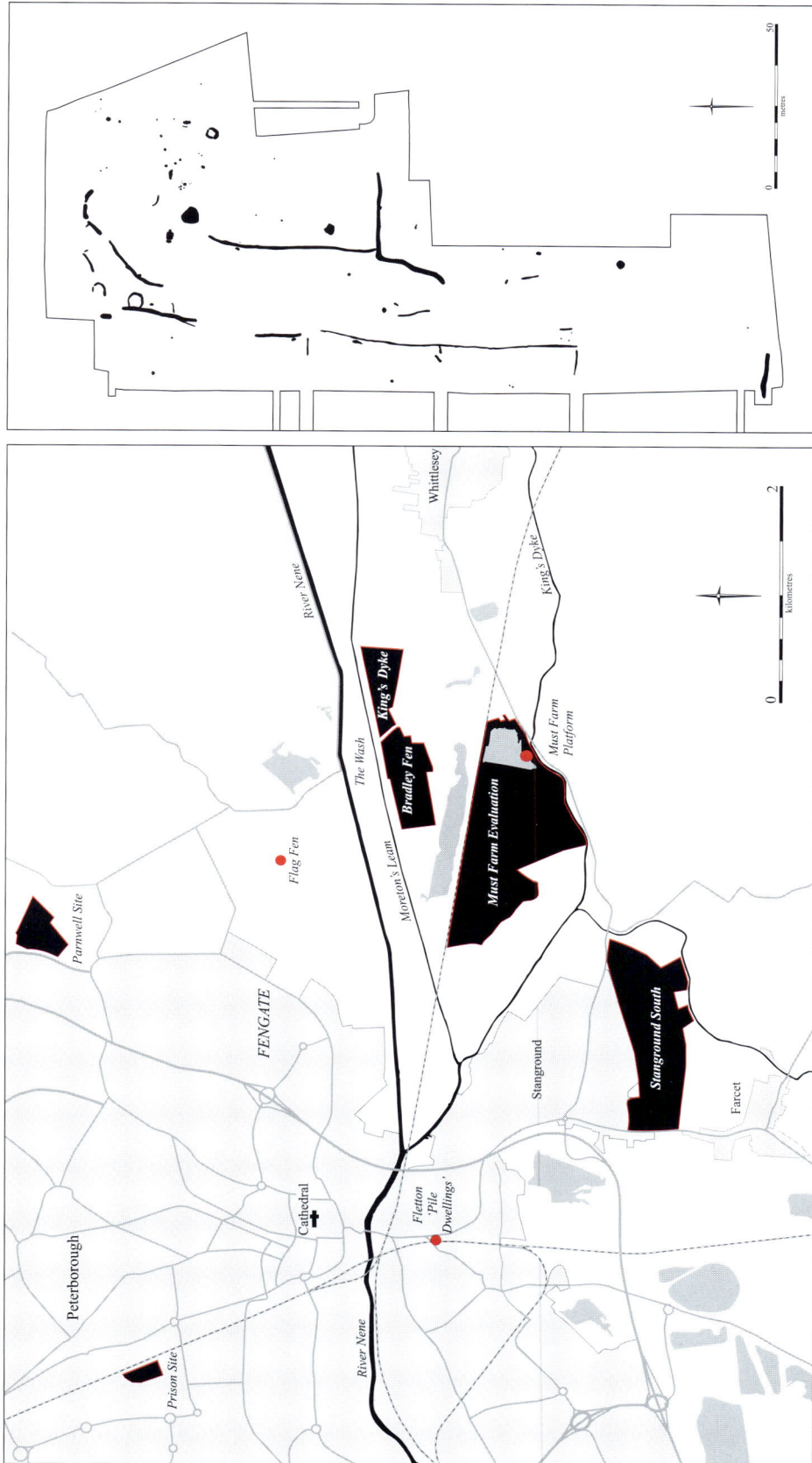

FIGURE 2.15. *Flag Fen environs investigations (left) and, right, the Prison Site plan. (Reproduced by permission of Ordnance Survey on behalf of HMSO. © Crown copyright 2009. All rights reserved. Ordnance Survey Licence number 100048686.)*

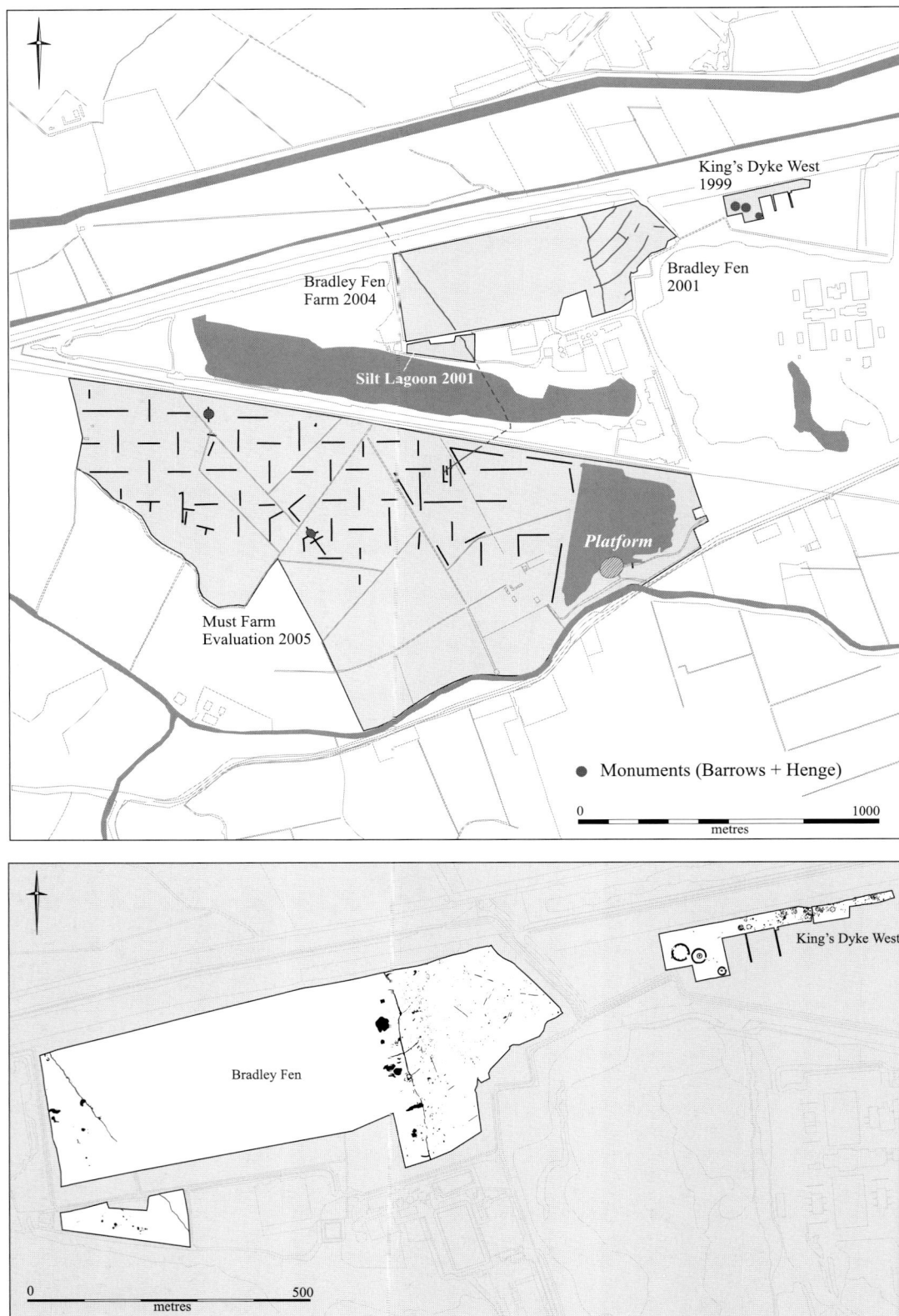

FIGURE 2.16. *Whittlesey Quarry Investigations (note: excludes The Nene Washes barrows; see Figs. 4.28 & 6.9), with detail of King's Dyke West and Bradley Fen excavations below. (Reproduced by permission of Ordnance Survey on behalf of HMSO. © Crown copyright 2009. All rights reserved. Ordnance Survey Licence number 100048686.)*

Neolithic/Early Bronze Age monument group and Bronze Age settlement complex (Knight 2000; Gibson & Knight 2002).

The earlier facet included an alignment of three monuments. At its northwestern end was a Class II henge (*c*. 30 m dia.) with an interior pit circle; quantities of Collared Urn and Food Vessel occurred in the upper fill of its ditch circuit (see Knight in Chapter 4 below concerning the Whittlesey sites' Beaker and Collared Urn assemblages). Immediately south thereof was a 'barrow' with a central inhumation surrounded by a *c*. 8.25 m-diameter trench-set post-circle. These lay just off-centre within a *c*. 25.5 m-diameter penannular ring-ditch. Three cremations were directly associated with this monument and, in addition, a small cremation cemetery lay exterior to the ring-ditch's southeastern entrance. The latter involved two cremations proper (one set within two 'conjoining' Collared Urns) and three dispersed Collared Urn findings alone; inverted, the latter were without human bone. At the southeastern end of this monument 'axis' was a smaller penannular ring-ditch (15.40m diameter). Oriented eastwards, this also had a central inhumation.

Having a stand-off of 60–70 m from the monuments, later Bronze Age settlement features extended eastwards for 260 m(+). These included pit clusters, post settings (including four-posters) and at least ten roundhouses. They also included a distinct Early Bronze Age Collared Urn-associated component, again consisting of a swathe of pits and postholes, and, in addition, a *c*. 3.5 m-diameter pit/posthole 'circle' with a southeastern porch.

Given this volume's main concerns, the site's negative evidence is equally noteworthy. Over a *c*. 400 m-long exposure across Whittlesey's 'high' ground, whilst there was extensive evidence of second-millennium BC settlement, no contemporary fieldsystem was recovered. This, however, was not the case when, in 2001 and 2004, work subsequently shifted westward and downslope to *Bradley Fen* (and the conjoining Bradley Fen Farm and Silt Lagoon sites; Gibson & Knight 2006). Extending over 24 ha, this provided an extraordinarily full (and dramatic) picture of the island's fen-edge landscape. Beaker and Collared Urn pits (and a 7.5 m dia. post/pit structure of the latter attribution) were recovered, and the 'edge' *per se* was dotted with a series of large watering-hole-associated burnt flint mounds of earlier Bronze Age date. Located somewhat further upslope, another deep pit had a cut-down length of a dug-out canoe set within its base, apparently reutilized as some variety of processing trough. Just 'above' the burnt flint features, a rather sinuous peat-filled ditch boundary snaked along what must have been the wet-/dryland divide — at *c*. 1 m OD — during the later Bronze Age. Short 'stub-length' ditches extended on either side of this boundary and, by the projection of these and similar ditch segments exposed upslope, a network of strip-type fields can be reconstructed (Bradley 2007, fig. 4.14; Yates 2007, 91–2, fig. 10.4). The main axis of this system twisted northwestward from the orientation of the southern fen-edge boundary, and would appear to have pre-dated it (i.e. the pit-wells probably date the system as a whole). Although having only fragmentary survival (and exposure), this system would seem relatively 'simple', with no evidence of any double-ditching recovered, including droveways. On its lower, fenward-side, the 'edge'-boundary was marked by a remarkable series of votive metalwork deposits: six individual spearheads (some stuck vertically into the peat with their shafts still 'in' and thereby indicating the setting of spears *per se*) and, on a low tree-mound, a 20-piece hoard containing 'killed' sword fragments and spearheads.

Four-posters (seven), roundhouses (four), and various pit/posthole settings dotted the area of the middle/lower slope (*c*. 1.2–2.59 m OD), above the 'edge'-boundary. While some were of later Bronze Age attribution, much of this settlement evidence was actually later and of Post-Deverel-Rimbury and Early-Middle Iron Age affiliation (both Romano-British and Saxon features also occurred on the site). One last deposit occurring within this area also demands mention:

the complete and articulated skeleton of an aurochs set within a rectangular pit. With evidence of skinning cuts, this obviously ritual offering was probably of earlier Bronze Age origin (thus far, attempts to date its bone have failed).

Across the western two-thirds of the site (the Bradley Fen Farm and Silt Lagoon areas), the buried ground surface fell away, over most of its length to below –0.3 m OD (where no archaeology was observed), only to rise up again to just around sea level along the western margin, where features again occurred. These included a Beaker-associated roundhouse, burnt flint mounds and watering holes, with the latter being ringed with cattle hoof-prints. This western swathe was delineated by a northwest- to southeast-oriented ditch. While essentially running straight, it wove and twisted somewhat, evidently around standing trees; a stump of one survived at one point and soil micromorphology indicates forest soils. The ditch had an accompanying upcast bank on its eastern downslope side. Sealed beneath this were the *in situ* posts of an earlier fence-line together with masses of brushwood; a post of the former has been dated to *c*. 1500 cal. BC.

In late 2004, and during the winter months of 2005, evaluation fieldwork extended southward, across the 132 ha of *Must Farm* (Evans *et al*. 2005). Bordered along its southern edge by the main palaeochannel of the River Nene, the buried ground surface across the northern half of the area — where, in effect, all of its 'dryland' archaeological findings were restricted to — lies between –0.5 m and +0.9 m OD. From there, it falls away to –3.4 m OD by the ancient course of the Nene. The present-day land surface beds at 0.5–2.5 m OD and, like the western half of the larger Bradley Fen investigations, this suggests that Whittlesey Island was not that — an *island* — but, although dissected by various palaeochannels, was originally linked by a low buried terrace to the mainland. It was thus, in effect, a peninsula (see French 2003a, fig. 10.2).

Generally, the fieldwork demonstrated a low level of early activity. What seemed to be a return-line of the Bradley Fen Farm ditch/bank and fence-line system ran along the eastern side of the terrace's 'high' ground and, west thereof (across its crown), was evidence of very dispersed/sparse later Neolithic/Bronze Age settlement activity (including, again, hoof-prints and metalled surfaces). Otherwise, the only settlement presence occurred on a sandy ridge within the area's southwestern quarter, where Neolithic and Early Bronze Age usage was evinced. This probably represents no more than temporary camps.

As will be further discussed below, it is surely relevant that no traces of any Bronze Age fieldsystem ditches were found across this upper terrace swathe, as this may well tell of the status of the land. Monuments were, however, found to be present: near the site's northwestern edge, a round barrow and, in the south-centre, a large Neolithic oval barrow were discovered, both of these being hitherto completely unknown. Arising from the recognition of these barrows (and also those two visible on aerial photographs north of the Nene; Figs. 4.28 & 6.1), the intervening area bounded by the banks of the river's washes was subsequently inspected and all available aerial imagery was scrutinized; this demonstrated the occurrence of five further definite barrows (and the same number of additional 'candidates'; see Figs. 4.28 & 6.9).

Whilst undertaking the Must Farm evaluation fieldwork, the opportunity was taken to excavate trenches along the southern edge of the neighbouring former pit immediately to the east. Largely quarried away some thirty years ago, this work was undertaken to investigate casual reports that 'early' worked timbers had been noticed there. The trenching did, indeed, confirm the validity of this information and that a major later Bronze Age timber structure still survived at that point. Subsequently, in the winter months of 2006, this was more formally test-excavated and the results surpassed all expectations, showing it to have a magnificently preserved, two-phase sequence: a later Bronze Age timber-pile platform structure overlain by a terminal Bronze Age/earliest Iron Age 'crannog' (Fig.

FIGURE 2.17. *The Tanholt Farm, Eye, fieldsystem (1), with its possible longhouse (2) and that from Barleycroft Farm (3) shown below. (Reproduced by permission of Ordnance Survey on behalf of HMSO. © Crown copyright 2009. All rights reserved. Ordnance Survey Licence number 100048686.)*

2.16; Malim & Panter 2008). Obviously, this is a finding that has major ramifications for the understanding of the Flag Fen (*et al.*) environs' archaeology, and will be the subject of a separate publication (Knight & Gibson in prep.).

Stanground South
In 2005, Northamptonshire Archaeology undertook large-scale evaluation fieldwork over 70 ha across the southern side of the

Stanground 'peninsula,' lying south of the Must Farm fields (Fig. 2.15; Taylor & Aaronson 2006). Two main foci were distinguished: in the west of the area was a Late Iron Age and Romano-British enclosure system, whereas in the south-central swathe was found earlier, late prehistoric activity. The latter included a dense, 19-interment, 'flat' cremation cemetery, with some burials within Middle Bronze Age urns. Extending over only a distance of *c.* 4 m within one trench (*c.* 2.2 m wide), it is estimated that its total burial population would be in the range of 25–30. Within the same area was also found a series of ditches and gullies (including what may have been a driveway), accompanied by scattered postholes. While essentially undated, these must be of Middle/later Bronze to Early Iron Age date. In fact, within one trench in that area was exposed an alignment of oak posts whose radiocarbon assay would fall within the latter end of this spectrum (790–420 cal. BC; Beta-213495).

In the light of arguments relating to the status of Fengate *per se*, and especially Abbott's findings, it seems extraordinary that, given the scale of Northamptonshire Archaeology's fieldwork, only one worked flint and no pre-Middle Bronze Age pottery whatsoever was recovered. At the time of writing, the excavation-phase of this project has just commenced.

Eye/Thorney (with DAVID GIBSON & RICKY PATTEN)
First starting in 1996 the still ongoing excavations by the CAU in the *Tanholt Farm, Eye Quarry* now extend over 50 ha (Figs. 2.12, 2.16 & 2.24), with traces of a rather 'piecemeal' Bronze Age fieldsystem continuing throughout (the site-exposure divides across a field in the centre-north of the area, this being preserved due to the location of a putative Roman 'villa'; e.g. Patten 2004; Yates 2007, 89–90). Lying between 3.5–4.25 m OD, it falls well 'inland' at a distance of 1 km from the fen-edge (and immediately east of Tanholt House, owned by E.T. Leeds' family). Its mid-terrace location may relate to the fact that no monuments as such have been recovered, although barrows are known to the northeast and south (see Chapter 4 Inset and Fig. 6.9; Hall 1987, 31–2, fig. 15). This being said, a 12-interment, linear-arranged, 'flat' cremation cemetery has been excavated (see Cooper & Edmonds 2007, fig. 4.38), with four other isolated cremations being found adjacent to the system's field boundaries.

Amid the twisting axes of the fieldsystem's paddocks, a *c.* 10 m-wide droveway has been traced running northeastward for 600 m, with a westward branch/return at its southern end (Fig. 2.24:3). Dotted throughout the area are a series of deep watering-holes/wells; some have been waterlogged and amongst their finds are log ladders and a fine wooden, angular-profile bowl (seemingly rendered in imitation of Late Bronze Age pottery). Although a swathe of concentrated settlement activity has now been distinguished in the mid-west of the area, what is perhaps the most relevant of the findings to date is the number of small, one/two-roundhouse Bronze Age settlement 'clusters' found scattered throughout the fieldsystem's axes. There are also a number of four-poster settings and a longhouse has been excavated (Fig. 2.17:2). In addition, one paddock has been found with an associated deeply-set fence/post-alignment.

Lying east of the course of the Catswater at Thorney (in an area of dense round barrow cemeteries; Hall 1987, 49–50, fig. 30), work was first undertaken at *Pode Hole* (*c.* 3 ha site) during the '90s by the Birmingham University Field Unit (Cutler & Ellis 2001), initially on the understanding that most of the plotted fieldsystems in the area were of Romano-British attribution (Hall 1987, 51–2, fig. 33). Indeed, at that time the fieldsystem itself was only trench-investigated, with no definite dating evidence recovered and the fieldwork, rather, focused on a *c.* 30 m-diameter round barrow. Seemingly of Early Bronze Age origin, the latter was without any encircling ditch; at least one later Bronze Age cremation was recovered from its mound.

Since that time, three neighbouring plots have been open area-stripped and excavated by Phoenix Consulting Archaeology (*c.* 43 ha in total) and, not unsurprisingly, a Bronze Age fieldsystem has been continuous throughout, the earlier Romano-British attribution being mistaken (Phoenix Consulting 2003). Running along the side of a marsh embayment and swinging on its axis northward towards Towers Fen, some of its boundaries can now be traced over a distance of almost a kilometre. Essentially, it would seem to be of a 'strip-type' layout and, though double-ditch lengths are present, it seems not to incorporate a regular series/interval of droveways.

Aside from extensive evidence of later Bronze Age settlement (including waterlogged pit-wells), an associated barrow has been dug, from which a child's inhumation was recovered set in a birch bark-lined grave.

The evidence from these sites would suggest that many of the fieldsystems plotted across the Thorney terraces are also probably of Bronze Age date; however, there are swathes that display both more 'sub-square/aggregate-type', patchwork-like patterns (see Welland Bank below) as well as portions that attest to multiple phases of allotment, which could reflect the successive overlap of both second millennium and Iron Age/Romano-British boundary systems.

South-central fens and Lower Ouse investigations

In the course of the University of Cambridge's Haddenham Project of the 1980s, primarily focused upon the fen-edge Upper Delphs terrace in the south of that parish, a mid/later second-millennium BC enclosure and a possible lynchet system were investigated (Evans & Hodder 2006b, chap. 3). However, no Bronze Age fieldsystems as such were identified there (in contrast, the understanding of that landscape's subsequent Iron Age usage was nuanced and detailed). Indeed, surely reflective of the limited scale of the project's open-area stripping, the 'absence' — or at least non-recovery — of fieldsystems at Haddenham was considered a shortcoming of that project. (In hindsight, and as a consequence of this volume's researches, one must question whether the quasi-radial fieldsystem that extents towards the fen-edge north of Willingham and immediately south of the Upper Delphs, does not, in fact, include Bronze Age components; its identified settlement 'clusters' are certainly Roman, but not necessarily all of its fieldsystem 'parts'; Evans & Hodder 2006b, fig. 8.20.)

The non-recovery of fieldsystems was quickly rectified when in the early 1990s the CAU began work in Hanson's Barleycroft/Over quarries spanning opposite banks of the River Great Ouse, just upstream from Haddenham (Fig. 2.18). Exploring the status of a major river in prehistory — as a landscape corridor and/or a 'divide' — has been that project's primary research directive. Not only has this project led to the exposure of a vast-scale fieldsystem, but it is the one whose 'formal' attributes come, in many ways, closest to Fengate's and is, moreover, associated with a range of major monument types.

This section will also include the long-term investigations at Colne Fen, Earith. Another Hanson quarry (this time straddling the fen-edge just north of where the Ouse enters the fen basin), an extensive Bronze Age fieldsystem has been also exposed there — one with substantial 'higher ground' settlement evidence — but whose layout/components differs markedly from either Fengate's or Barleycroft/Over's.

Finally, there is the Block Fen, Mepal system. It lies much further out in the fen proper (and is, again, of still

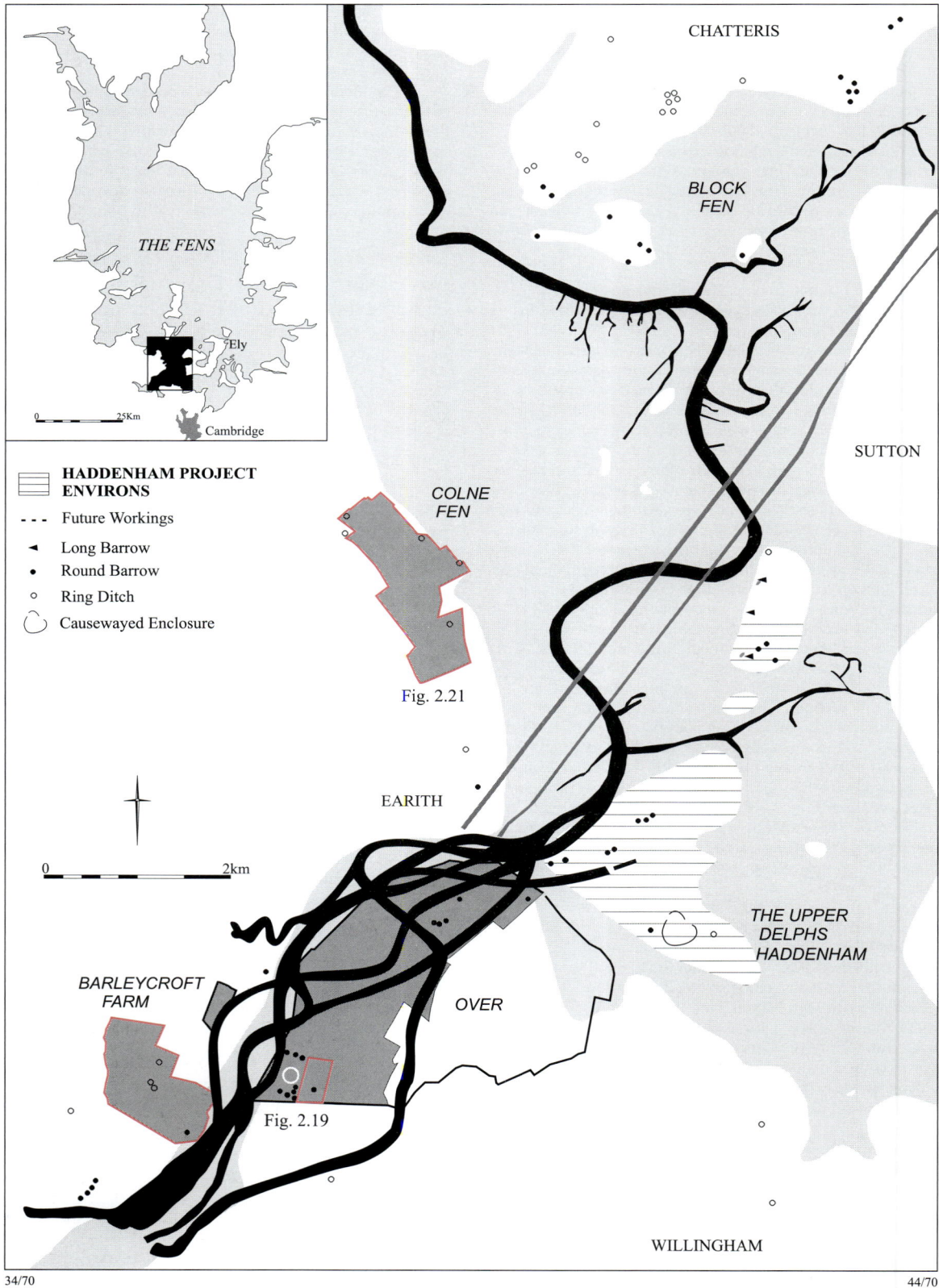

FIGURE 2.18. *The Archaeology of the Lower Ouse Environs, with Colne Fen and Barleycroft Farm/Over Investigation areas and the river's main palaeochannels indicated. (Reproduced by permission of Ordnance Survey on behalf of HMSO. © Crown copyright 2009. All rights reserved. Ordnance Survey Licence number 100048686.)*

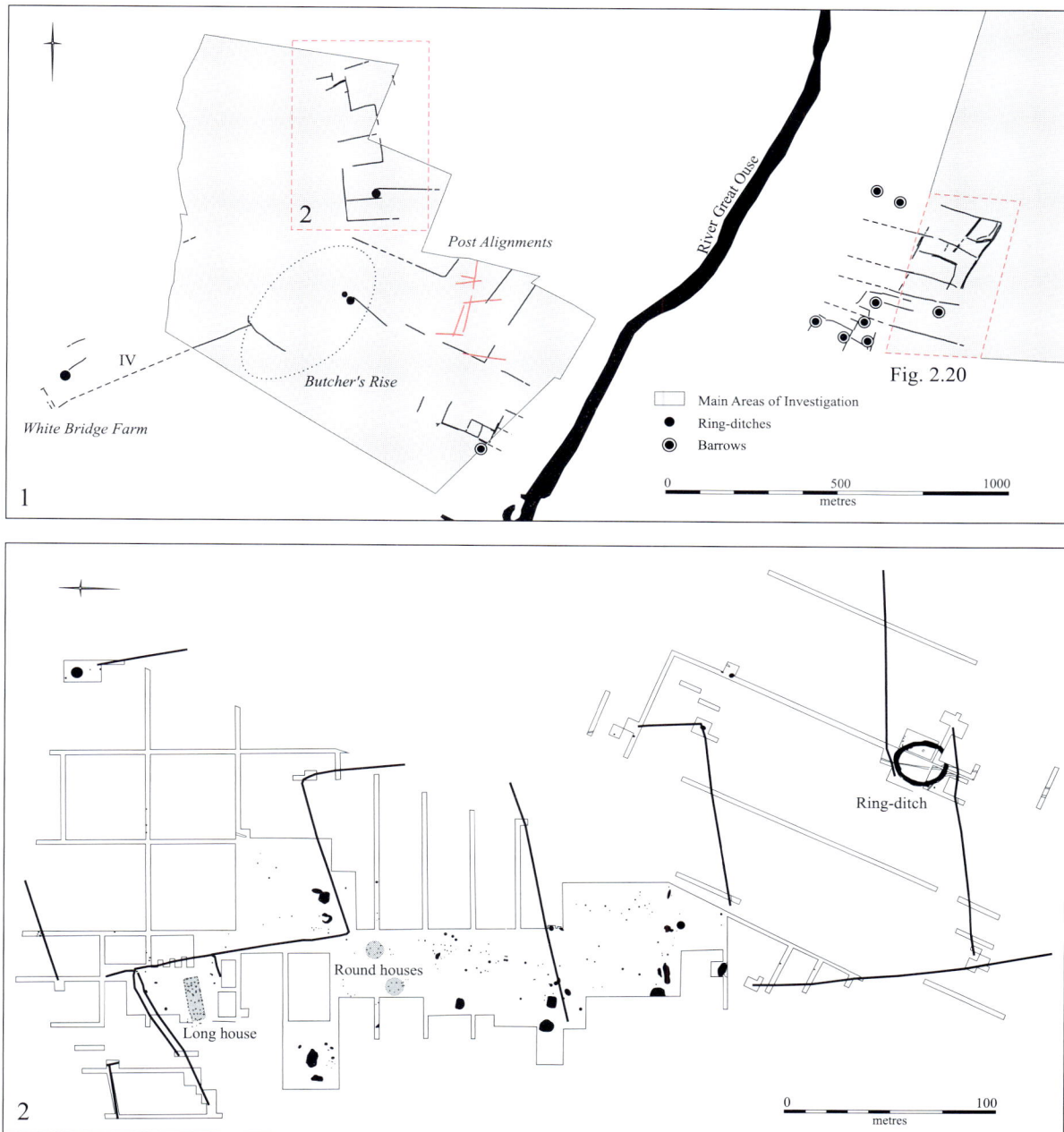

Figure 2.19. *The Barleycroft/Over fieldsystem (1), with detail of the Barleycroft Paddocks system on the west bank of the River Great Ouse, below (2).*

different character) and is here considered in relationship to the great later Bronze Age/Early Iron Age settlement complex of Langwood Ridge, Chatteris (note that prehistoric ditches which may relate to a Bronze Age fieldsystem have also been recorded on the Northern Office Site, March; Casa Hatton & Macaulay 2001).

Barleycroft Farm/Over
Spanning both banks of the floodplain of the River Great Ouse, just upstream from where it enters the fen basin, the CAU's fieldwork

in Hanson's Needingworth quarries began in 1992 (Fig. 2.18). This has since led to the recovery of a Bronze Age fieldsystem(s) extending over more than 350 ha (Figs. 2.19 & 2.20). The immediate area first came to archaeological notice through the discovery of the Over round barrow cemeteries (with 13 sited on the east bank of the river) during the course of the Fenland Survey (Hall 1996). The current programme also involves a major programme of palaeo-environmental reconstruction/research. The second-millennium BC fieldsystem is only one component of this deeply buried landscape's multi-faceted usage and, for example, a number of Neolithic and earlier Bronze Age occupation sites have now been excavated. Accordingly, it is impossible to do justice to the project

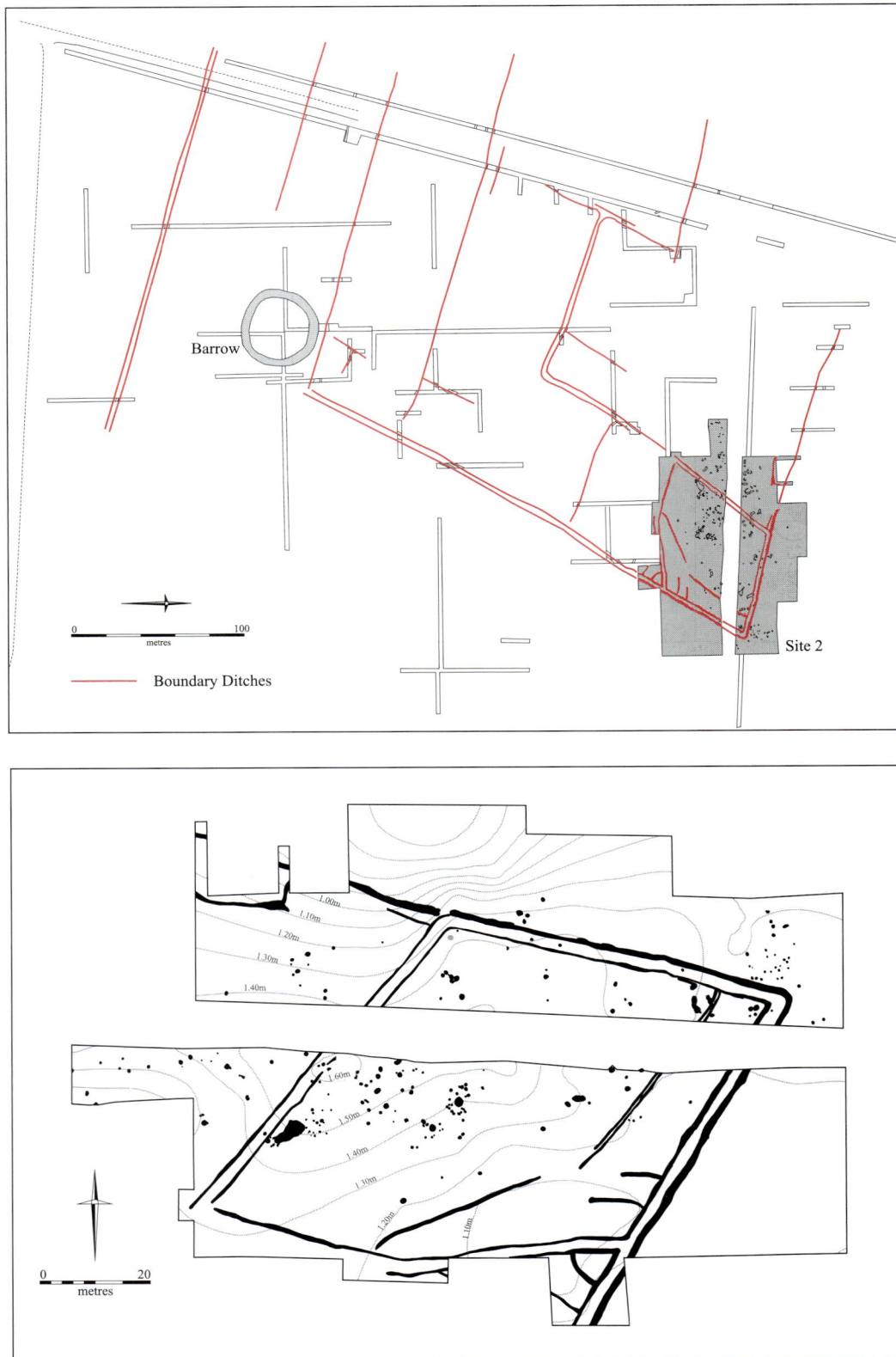

FIGURE 2.20. *Barleycroft Farm/Over — The East Bank Investigations and Over Site 2 (detail below).*

within the confines of this summary-format, but nor is this necessary as two major studies of its archaeology are already published (Evans & Knight 2000; 2001) and, its findings, furthermore, feature in a number of other recent volumes (e.g. Evans & Hodder 2006a, fig. 4.16; Garrow 2006, 27, 71–2, 93–117, figs. 4.5, 5.2, 5.10, 6.3, 6.2, 6.13–6.27; Bradley 2007, fig. 4.7; Yates 2007, 95–6, fig. 10.6).

Although it includes a longhouse set within its own compound (Fig. 2.17:3), only a relatively low density of settlement has been found in association with the fieldsystem on the river's western side (Fig. 2.19; see Evans & Knight 2000). Much denser occupation evidently occurred on the eastern riverside bank, and this included a large quasi-polygonal double-ditch settlement enclosure immediately beside the southern barrow group. (Sited upon a pond barrow, this is of both Middle and later Bronze Age attribution; an additional longhouse has been recovered therein.)

The coaxial fieldsystem has been radiocarbon dated to the second half of the second millennium BC, and probably originated 1600–1400 cal. BC. For the most part, it was arranged in a reave-like manner, with *c.* 50–80 m-wide strip-holdings oriented northwest–southeast. Whilst this pattern is common to the eastern, Over-side and across the southern portion of the western riverside at Barleycroft Farm, in relationship to the northern higher ground on the latter, its orientation shifted to a more east–west orientation (Fig. 2.19).

Thus far, three ring-ditches have been excavated, including a pair on the crown of the Butcher's Rise 'knoll' on the Barleycroft side (having two concentric rings, the monument saw an elaborate phased sequence and eventually attracted a 31-interment cremation cemetery across its southeastern sector; Evans & Knight 2001). While the ring-ditches evidently pre-dated the fieldsystem as such, they clearly influenced its layout and, occupying nodal points in the system, ditch boundaries 'spun' upon them. In contrast, the eastern bank barrows' relationship seems less sympathetic and more a matter of 'accommodation' — the field axes 'boxing' them in (Figs. 2.19 & 2.20)

Probably reflective of its riverside location, droveways were not a component of this system, suggesting that it was in effect self-contained, with little/no hinterland stock-population movement through it. This being said, a number of narrow parallel ditch-lines have been recovered that must indicate embanked boundaries. This pertains not only to the eastern and northern sides of the main fieldsystem 'block' on the eastern side of the river, but also to the smaller, individual and/or linked paddock settings; that in the southern end of the Barleycroft side is, in fact, reminiscent of Fengate's Newark Road compounds.

Among the most extraordinary findings of the work to date has been a network of long fence-/post-lines on the Barleycroft side of the river. These seemed to transgress and post-date its ditch boundaries. They were 'open' settings and did not form complete enclosures. Some, nevertheless, ended in very distinct 'T'-shaped post-set terminals and also had quite formal accessway 'interruptions'. Therefore, fulfilling no obvious functional purpose, they have been interpreted as a 'structuring device', variously framing viewer/participant lines of vision and movement between the monument groups sited on the opposite sides of the river: the main eastern barrow cemetery and, in the west, the Butcher's Rise ring-ditches (see Evans & Knight 2001 for further discussion and detail).

Colne Fen, Earith

The CAU have also investigated a major Bronze Age paddock- and fieldsystem along the fen-edge at Colne Fen, just north of where the Ouse enters the fen basin at Earith (Figs. 2.18 & 2.21; Evans *et al.* forthcoming). Although some possible Bronze Age boundaries have been found across the northern half of the area investigated, the system *per se* is restricted to its southern portion, south of the Rhee Lake embayment and across the rise of *The Holme*. Lying at

c. 4–5 m OD, the latter was a distinct marsh-surrounded island in medieval times. Although its crown, as such, had previously been quarried away, two large areas have been investigated on its flanks: *The Holme* in the south and, in the north, Rhee Lakeside South.

The Colne Fen fieldsystem, firmly radiocarbon dated to the second half of the second millennium BC, differs considerably from that at Barleycroft/Over. Many of the ditches were very substantial and robust. Up to 3 m wide and 1 m deep, some were of 'paddock-', rather than 'fieldsystem'-scale (see Fig. 2.24:4). Equally impressive is the sheer size of its droveways, being 8.5–19 m wide. That within the southern sub-site continued across the area of excavation (with a series of compounds regularly arranged along its northern side); the northern, at the Rhee Lakeside sub-site, continued eastward from the arcing perimeter of a large paddock-enclosure and is one of the very few instances where the origin or starting point of a major droveway has been exposed. Although including an element of settlement activity, the paddock at its end was presumably stock-related.

Whilst much of it has to be assigned to the Late (as opposed to the Middle) Bronze Age, there has been extensive evidence of fieldsystem-contemporary settlement at Colne Fen, with 12 post-built roundhouses and six four-posters excavated (as well as a six-post setting; Fig. 2.24:4). Although some short, localized lengths of parallel ditch-lines occur, for the most part these derive from recutting; embanked double-ditch boundaries were evidently not a component of this system.

Perhaps the main trait that distinguishes the Colne Fen system is its dual alignments (Fig. 2.21). Both of its droveways, as well as the ditch network across most of *The Holme* sub-site, were largely oriented east–west (as were the boundaries south of the drove in the Rhee Lakeside Site); however, across the centre and western half of the northern sub-site their orientation was northwest–southeast. It was within the main central area of its excavation that the seam between these two alignments occurred, with the arcing aspect of the droveway-opening paddock, in effect, bridging the two. It is difficult to satisfactorily account for these diverse alignments. They may, however, reflect the fact that the east–west orientation — that of the droveways — essentially respected the topography of the fen-edge at this point; the northwest–southeast orientation being the more 'generic' of the period (see below).

In addition to two cremations 'incidentally' recovered within the axes of the southern site and a four-interment 'flat' cemetery recovered from the paddocks of the northern Rhee Lakeside sub-site, a major cremation cemetery was associated with a *c.* 17.5 m diameter ring-ditch that lay north of the drove in the latter area. With a crouched inhumation marking the centre of the ring, 35 cremations clustered around its exterior southern aspect. Thirteen of these interments were set within Deverel-Rimbury urns. The two dates achieved from the cremations ranged from 1500 to 1200 cal. BC. Intriguingly, one of the cremations was set within the interior of a small, *c.* 4 m-diameter ring-circle that had been added to the monument's perimeter. This is reminiscent of both individual/single cremation ring-ditches that occur within the Essex region (e.g. Brown 1999) and, also, a similar ring that was found within *The Holme* sub-site. Unaccompanied by any interment, the latter might only represent some manner of landscape marker and could, therefore, potentially have even pre-dated the fieldsystem (these small ring settings are, equally, evocative of Pryor's putative 'mini-henge' at the Cat's Water, Fengate and, too, the small single cremation-associated ring-ditch dug at Third Drove; see Chapters 4, Inset below).

The Rhee Lakeside ring-ditch is one of three such monuments investigated at Colne Fen (one also being cemetery-associated). With two further ring-ditches also known within the immediate environs, these seem to have dotted the fen-edge with some regularity and originally date to one to three centuries before the fieldsystem landscape. Resonating with the evidence of the Elliott

FIGURE 2.21. *Colne Fen, Earith Investigations, with detail of southern Bronze Age fieldsystem exposures (left). (Reproduced by permission of Ordnance Survey on behalf of HMSO. © Crown copyright 2009. All rights reserved. Ordnance Survey Licence number 100048686.)*

Site at Fengate discussed in Chapter 3 below, it is here relevant that a dated pollen core from the Cranbrook Drain channel deposits in the north of the Colne Fen area indicates extensive clearance and consequent arable land-use from 1880–1620 cal. BC (Wk-21083); in other words, clearance was broadly contemporary with the initiation of the ring-ditches and, based on current understanding, pre-dated the area's fieldsystem.

Block Fen
First investigated by Tempus Reparatum in the early 1990s, and subsequently by HAT/AS, the Block Fen, Mepal fieldsystem lies on the low (and subsequently inundated) gravel terraces south of Chatteris (at *c.* 1–2 m OD). Given the available sources (the only published summary being Hunn & Palmer 1993), it is difficult to establish much sense of overview for it. Extending in total over some 180 ha, the system appears generally quite irregular and 'disjointed'. However hard it may be to see much overall pattern or structure, in the main its alignment would seem to be north/northwest to south/southeast (the somewhat more simplified, earlier Fenland Survey version of the cropmark plan shows a greater degree of 'structural coherence', at least for its southern portions; Hall 1992, 90, fig. 53.) While no substantive settlement component has been identified (and its finds densities seem extraordinarily low), the system does include droveway lengths and minor ring-ditches.

Relevant, to this volume, is the extent of later Bronze Age/Early Iron Age settlement documented on the Langwood Ridge (at *c.* 2–4 m OD), immediately 'above' and north of this system. Sample-tested during the course of the Fenland Management Project (Evans 2003), its situation and feature-density raises the question of whether it represents fieldsystem-contemporary settlement and/or reflects an upslope retreat of occupation in the face of rising marsh levels during the centuries bracketing the second/first millennium BC.

South Lincolnshire systems

In addition to those projects detailed below, other investigations in the area include Northamptonshire at Baston (A. Mudd pers. comm.) and the CAU at Langtoft. Beginning in 1998, it is only now in recent excavation seasons across the latter that a Bronze Age fieldsystem is being exposed (e.g. Hutton 2008). As it has only a weak/erratic cropmark register, at this time it is impossible to say much concerning its overall layout; however, it does seem to have marked similarities to the fieldsystem at Deeping (see below; Fig. 2.24:1 & 2). This being said, two points should be stressed concerning this project's findings. First, that later Bronze Age pits and wells (and fence-settings) were recovered dispersed across those portions to the southwest that were earlier investigated (lying beyond/without the field boundaries) and, significantly, quantities of briquetage were there recovered. Being outside fieldsystems, this potentially raises questions concerning 'allotment' and salt-making: was the latter considered a common resource, with its production possibly confined to 'open' lands? Second, settlement features associated with the eastern fieldsystem are producing substantive assemblages of Deverel-Rimbury pottery, the importance of which is further discussed in the section which follows.

Rectory Farm, West/Market Deeping
This 112 ha site was subject to intense evaluation test-excavation by Tempus Reparatum during 1993–94 (Hunn nd.). The focus of this programme was largely its Iron Age and Roman phases, and not the Bronze Age fieldsystem that extends throughout the area (Figs. 2.12 & 2.22). The cropmark plots indicate that a number of barrows/ring-ditches are associated with the fieldsystem, two of which were investigated in Tempus' fieldwork: a 25–30 m-diameter barrow (exposed only through dyke-section sampling) and an oval ring-ditch (*c.* 8 × 10 m).

The fieldsystem is clearly structured according to a series of dominant-axis/parallel, 'reave-like' droveway boundaries, some of which continue for at least 1.25 km across the area. The fieldsystem is set, in the main part of the area, with an interval of 260–370 m, which appears to narrow and lessen towards the south (see below). A few major co-axial boundary elements are apparent and, across the eastern third of the area, the cropmarks show a more patchwork-like system of paddocks and smaller enclosures. The excavator dated the layout of the system to the Middle–later Bronze Age, and two radiocarbon dates were obtained from the basal fill of one of its main boundaries: 1150–800 cal. BC and 940–780 cal. BC. One roundhouse was located, suggesting some degree of contemporary settlement.

The Deeping landscape featured in Pryor's 'mass-sheep' regional Bronze Age livestock model (Pryor 1996, 319–22, fig. 4; 2002; see also 1998c, 109–13). Essentially extrapolating from its cropmark plan (and by comparison with Fengate's Newark Road compounds), he identified a series of possible stockyard compounds attached to the western side of its main droves where, at certain times of the year, livestock would be kept off of selected pasture lands (Fig. 2.22). Yet, as none of these enclosures were actually excavated during Tempus' fieldwork, this *de facto* association remains undemonstrated (though see Welland Bank below).

When evaluating arguments as to the nature of this fieldsystem, it is crucial to recognize that, though its main droveway-dominated layout was broadly similar to Fengate's, its arrangement was actually *quasi-radial*: its interval narrows southwards down towards the Welland floodplain and would converge just west of the village of West Deeping. There would be three main ways of interpreting this layout. Firstly (and in the opinion of its excavator), these droveways were to allow the movement of stock between riverside pastures and 'upland' farms. Secondly, if following Pryor's model of in-fieldsystem stock compounds, the main swathe of contemporary settlement might have lain at the riverside. Thirdly and finally, they may have converged due to a river-crossing point. Given the layout, the latter two explanations would seem the most probable, as the first would not require axial/droveway convergence; however, the third option is considered the most likely.

Pre-Construct Archaeology is currently undertaking excavations within this quarry and, in 2007, the CAU began fieldwork within the fields bordering its southwestern side (Figs. 2.22 & 2.24:1).

Welland Bank
Extending over 18 ha, the main phase of excavation within this quarry, directed by Pryor and Tom Lane for Archaeological Project Services, occurred during 1997. Drawing upon those summaries available for it (see Pryor 1998b; 2002; 1998c, 113–23, pls. 11–16; Dymond *et al.* n.d.), it must be counted as a sample of quite a different type of fieldsystem (Figs. 2.12 & 2.23). With its cropmark plot continuing over some 1.3 km (*c.* 65 ha), the Welland Bank system as a whole seems an 'organic' or disjointed patchwork; and neither droveways or monuments are apparent amid its irregular axes. This picture of its layout did not significantly alter upon excavation; its exposed boundaries were seemingly 'incomplete' and discontinuous.

Dispersed across the area, but with a marked concentration towards its northwestern arm, the excavations revealed 15 vari-

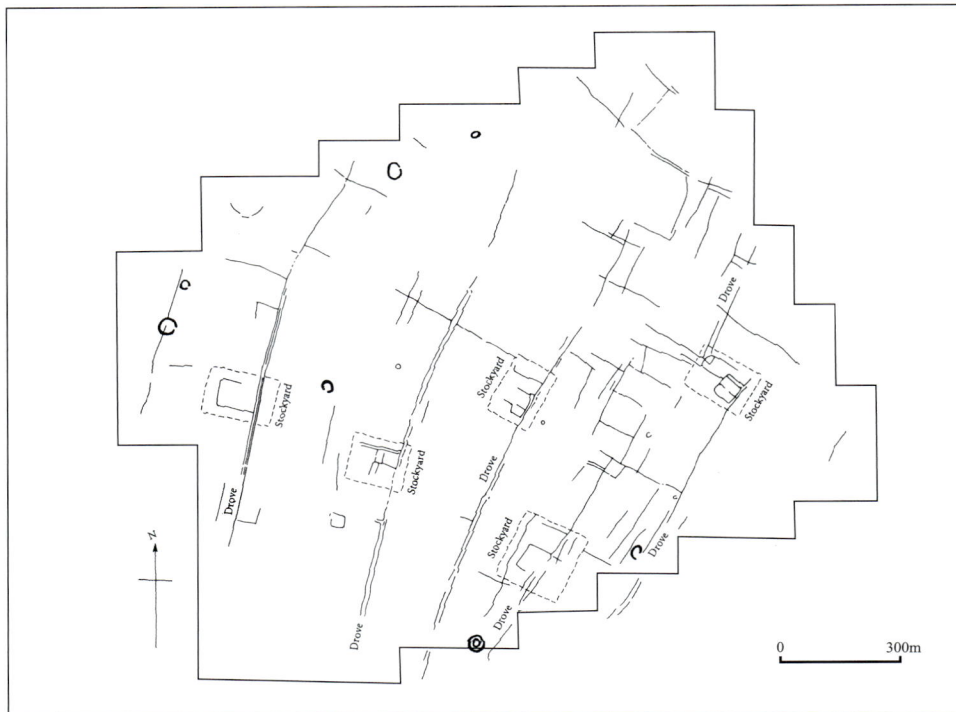

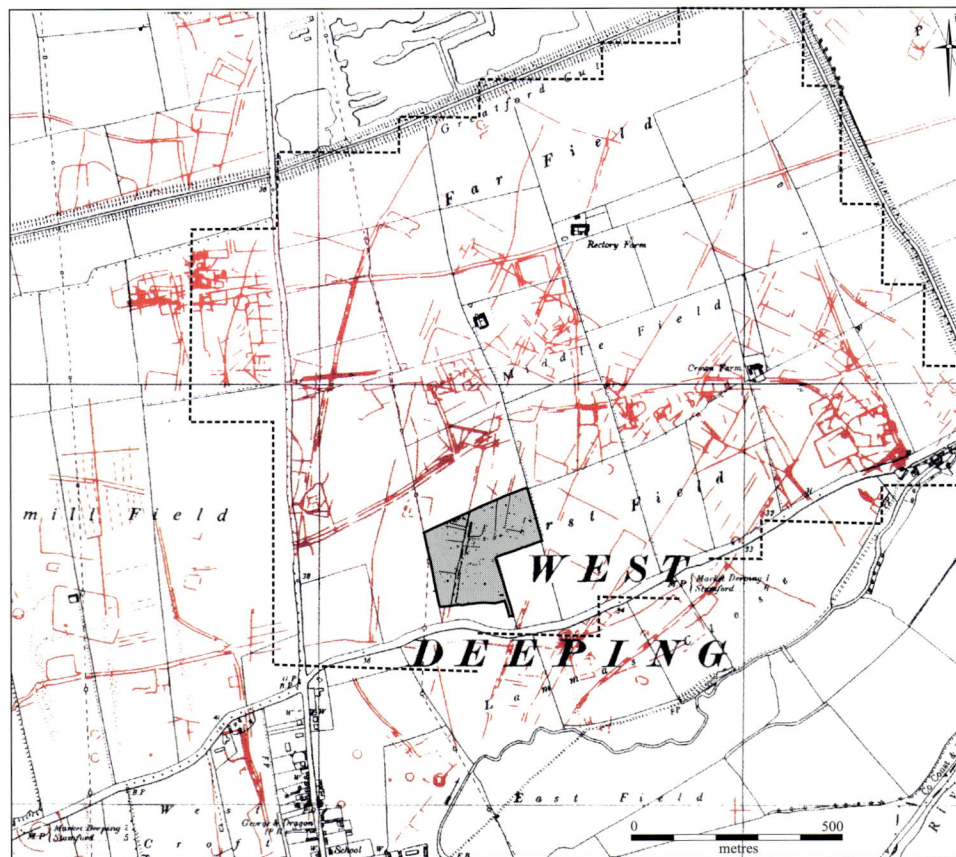

FIGURE 2.22. *The West Deeping fieldsystem (below, with CAU investigations grey-tone indicated; see Fig. 2.24:1) and, top, Pryor's interpretative plan (1996, fig. 4; 2002, fig. 3). (Reproduced by permission of Ordnance Survey on behalf of HMSO. © Crown copyright 2009. All rights reserved. Ordnance Survey Licence number 100048686.)*

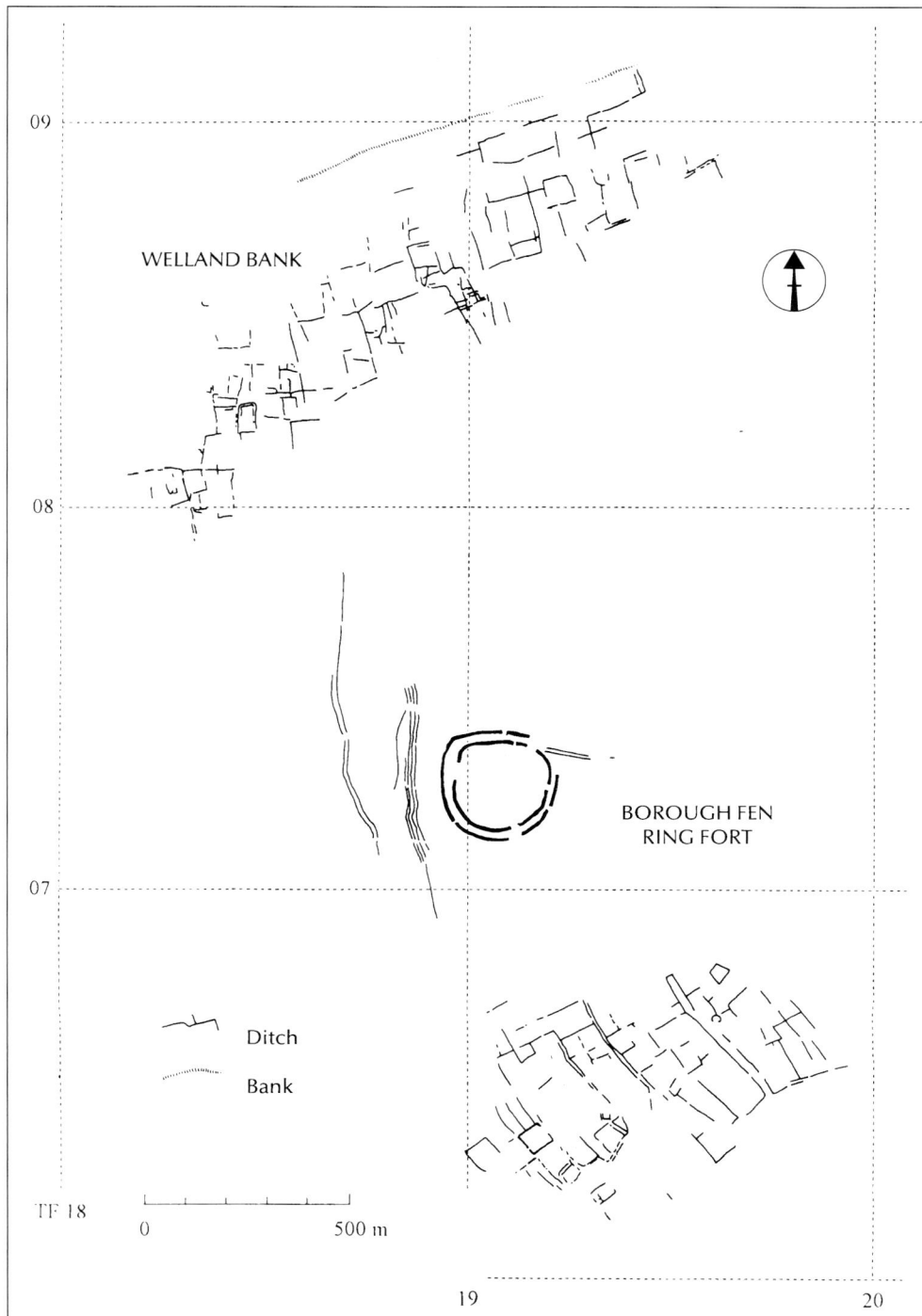

FIGURE 2.23. *The Welland Bank and Newborough fieldsystems (Pryor 2002, fig. 4). (Reproduced by permission of Ordnance Survey on behalf of HMSO. © Crown copyright 2009. All rights reserved. Ordnance Survey Licence number 100048686.)*

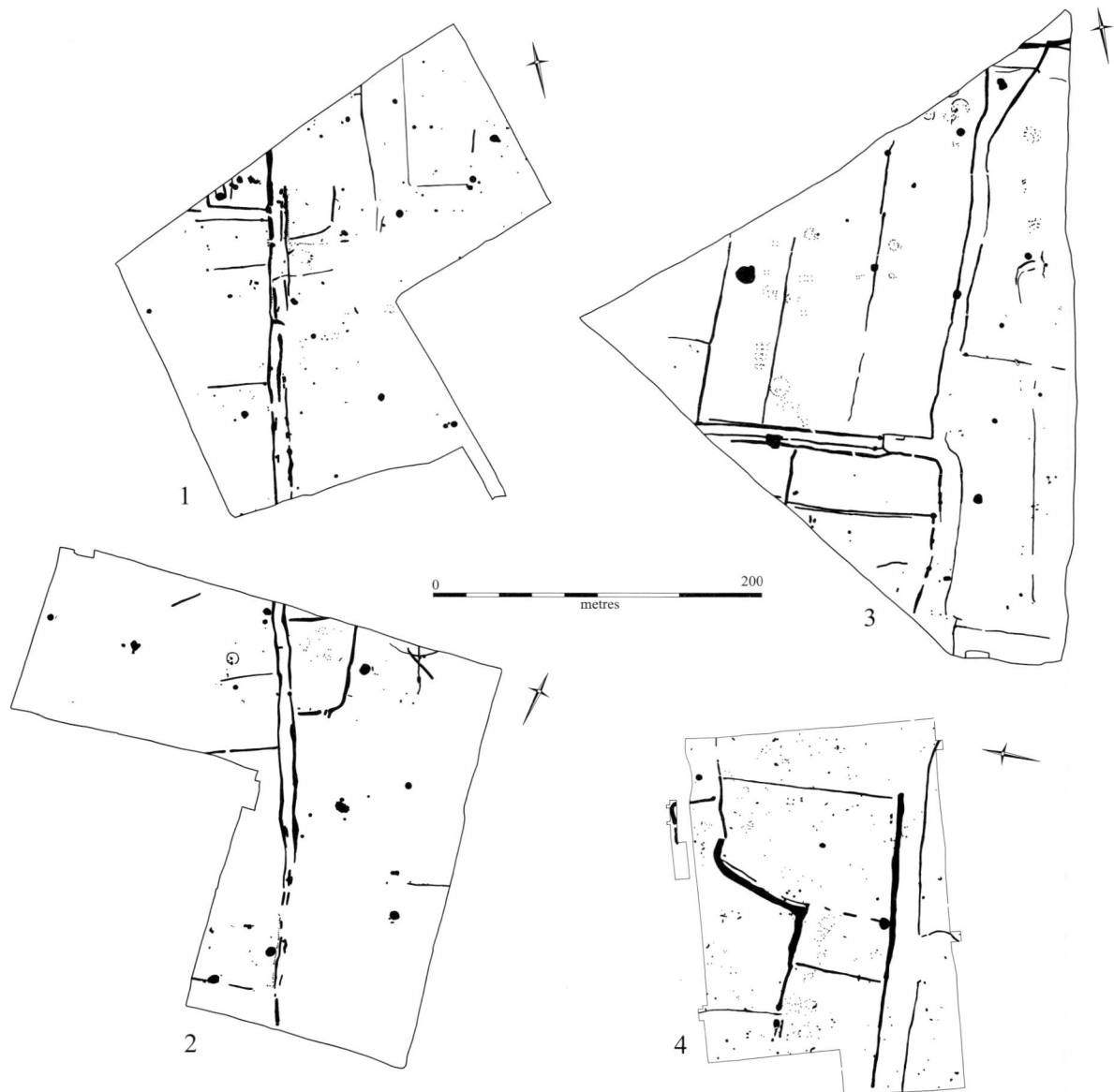

FIGURE 2.24. *Comparative Fieldsystem and Droves (not oriented to north): 1) CAU's 2007 Deeping investigations (see Fig. 2.22); 2) The Glebe Lands sub-Site, Langtoft; 3) Tanholt Farm, Eye (see Fig. 2.17); 4) The Holme sub-Site, Colne Fen, Earith (see Fig. 2.21).*

ously round and 'U'-shaped structures. Moreover, in addition to some six four-posters, three sub-square/rectangular buildings were found, including one definite longhouse. A black-stained buried soil survived over substantial portions of the site (French 2003a, 152–7), yielding quantities of domestic refuse. Although Middle Bronze Age material was recovered, most of its pottery was of later Bronze and earlier Iron Age date. Indeed, the radiocarbon determinations thus far achieved all date to the earlier first millennium BC.

Measuring 55 × 80 m, the main (discrete) enclosure that was excavated proved to be double-ditched on two of its sides and had traces of accompanying embankments on three (Fig. 6.5:4). As the only structure found within its interior was considered to be a 'U'-shaped stock pen — and otherwise the enclosure lacked obvious settlement evidence — it was interpreted as a stock compound.

Discussion — rehearsing questions

At this point it is worth outlining some of the crucial themes that arise from the preceding project overview; this, though, is a matter of rehearsal, as they will also need to be returned to in this volume's concluding chapter. Among the most pressing questions — and one also reflecting on the reappraisal of Abbott's findings — is *the nature of settlement* at Fengate. Was it a case, as has been seen across most of the Tanholt Farm, Eye landscape (Figs. 2.17 & 2.24:3), of dispersed single-household residence amid fieldsystem axes?

Alternatively, was later second-millennium BC settlement more centralized and did it occur higher up in relationship to fen-edge locales and, effectively, 'behind' fieldsystems? Any such distinction must invariably be biased by the scale on which any given prehistoric landscape is exposed (and which topographic zones/swathes are excavated). No matter how vast some recent excavations have been, they will inevitably be framed and only provide a partial 'landscape-window' — *we do not excavate totalities*. Nevertheless, the 'settlement-behind-fieldsystems' proposal could be supported by the evidence from Chatteris, where the great Lingwood Farm settlement complex sits on the ridge-top, above the Block Fen system (see Evans 2003). The same might also be true of the Colne Fen Earith system, where fieldsystem-contemporary settlement seemed to cluster on *The Holme's* island-rise, *c.* 500 m back from the fen-edge proper (Fig. 2.21).

Here it is relevant to note, in reference to the broad pattern of their layout, the observation that, in contrast to fen-edge Iron Age settlements and boundaries which appear to have been laid out in relationship to the 'wet/dry' divide' (with arable fields 'above' and water meadows 'below'), Bronze Age systems seem to have originated on their immediate high ground. In other words, whereas the Bronze Age systems extended downslope to fen marshes, in many instances Iron Age demarcation actually started at the 'wet-edge' and progressed 'back' or upwards. Conceptually, this would have had major ramifications for how land was envisaged and may well hint at the main *nexus* or locale of second-millennium BC fen-edge/-hinterland settlement.

Engendered by the scale of quarry-investigations within the region, the vast majority of the above-listed sites/fieldsystems occur on gravel and this begs the question of how real is this distribution. On the one hand, locally we have the evidence of the Parnwell Site, where no Bronze Age fieldsystems were found on the clay geology in an area where, based on precedent, they surely would have been expected. Yet, on the other hand, such systems did not occur exclusively on gravels: at the Peterborough New Prison Site they occurred on limestone cornbrash (Fig. 2.15). This does not imply that second-millennium BC activity/settlement did not take place on clays and heavier sub-soils. Evidence of such settlement includes what seem to be lengths of contemporary boundary ditches. This would be true of both the Isle of Ely (see Evans 2002 for overview) and, more recently, at Striplands Farm, Longstanton north of Cambridge (Patten & Evans 2005; Mackay & Knight 2007). The latter is particularly interesting as, falling on the interface of a Third/Fourth Terrace gravel ridge and the clay plain north of Cambridge, the site lies well inland from any riverine water sources. Though accompanied by minor ditch lengths, and having post-built roundhouses, the main features at Striplands Farm are deep pit-wells, these after all being among the great inventions of the second millennium BC, which facilitated permanent occupation in 'off-river' locales in the first place (without daily tasking for/fetching of water from springs). What was surprising at Striplands Farm was just how dense was the settlement: two of its wells alone yielded almost 4000 sherds of pottery (both were waterlogged and produced an abundance of worked timber implements, primarily axe-hafts and log ladders). Similarly, a Middle Bronze Age cremation cemetery, and what appears to be a contemporary boundary, was recently excavated on the County's claylands at Papworth Everard (Hounsell 2007).

Evidence of Middle–later Bronze Age settlement has now also been found on the clays of the East Midlands and Essex (Liddle 1982; Brooks 1993; Cooper 1994; Yates 2007, 73–7). Whilst thus far no convincing fieldsystems have been found on the region's 'heavy' lands (in contrast to its river valley/fen-edge gravel terraces), there is clearly considerable evidence of contemporary usage. In fact, it would be surprising if some such systems were not eventually encountered within these environments (although one suspects that it will be a case of a few exceptions proving the rule).

As is apparent above, the western fen margin sees a marked 'weighting' of Bronze Age fieldsystems. That investigated at Downham Way, Brandon (Gibson *et al.* 2004) and the boundaries at Fordham (Connor & Mortimer forthcoming) are the only real candidates for such fieldsystems along the southeastern and eastern fen-edge. With that area characterized by very light soils that have long been recognized as attracting dense, early 'open-scatter' settlement, but (in contrast with the west) seeing surprisingly few major monuments (e.g. causewayed enclosures and long barrows), how real is the distinction? Unfortunately, at this time the 'jury must still be out', as there have simply been too few large landscape-scale exposures in the eastern fens (as opposed to the plethora of gravel quarry-projects in the west) to resolve whether there is an actual difference in the distribution of fieldsystems (see, though, Yates 2007, 80–81, fig. 9.6 and Ashwin 2001 concerning Norfolk generally).

A further issue that this section's overview highlights is the problem of where one fieldsystem ends and another begins. This issue only comes to the fore now that it is known that such systems were so widespread in the region, and is also an inherent problem in landscape archaeology generally. Just how do we recognize the actual borders between one characteristic 'landscape-type' and another (e.g. the Fens from a river valley system debouching into its margins)? While we can distinguish *seams* within fieldsystems, primarily based upon 'off'-boundary alignment, the point where one system started and another stopped is not absolute (especially as their alignments snake around the fen-edge). Of particular relevance when trying to 'frame' Fengate's system (at least when trying to avoid being blinkered by the confines of narrow historical place-naming), the problems of multiple ditch-alignment systems are evident both at Colne Fen, Earith and Tanholt Farm, Eye (Figs. 2.17 & 2.21). Equally, what of the shared axial alignments on both sides of the River Great Ouse at Barleycroft Farm and Over (Fig. 2.19): was it a matter of one system common to both banks or do we consider the river as a sufficient divide to separate them? Ultimately, this comes down to questions of fieldsystem 'blocking' and, potentially, of socio-cultural territories and how landholding during the period is envisaged. These are, of course, major interpretative issues and, therefore, not unsurprisingly, are without ready resolve.

Common — land beyond allotment

The preceding review section's 'Cook's Tour' of Fenland projects originally concluded by relating how a landscape such as Maxey, where Pryor's investigations did not yield Bronze Age fieldsystems (Pryor & French 1985), now becomes, rather an exception; however, almost immediately upon its writing we received a copy of a report by Northampton Archaeology summarizing their recent findings across the new southern extension to that quarry. Yes, what should they have but an 'early' fieldsystem (amid a myriad of pit-features). Thus, put simply, during the Bronze Age swathes of the region were clearly parcelled up and allotted on a scale that simply would have been unimaginable for researchers to conceive of a generation ago. Not only does this have obvious implications for estimates of the period's population densities, but the apparent scale of these systems also makes it much more difficult to distinguish their 'insides' and 'outsides'. Certainly, for example, given what appears to be the spread of fieldsystems across Eye/Thorney, to reach 'the outside' (i.e. un-ditched/-allotted low ground) would not just have been a matter of a few hundred metres' traverse, but, from its 'centre', kilometres.

To be frank, having assembled the entries for the section above (at least for those along the western Fen margin) it almost comes as a relief to be able to recognize that some swathes of land were without fieldsystems. But what lay outside their limits and what was the status of land beyond — were these margins held in common? In this context it may well be relevant that at Langtoft the area of salt production, at least as indicated by the distribution of briquetage in pit-features, seemed to lay exterior to the fieldsystem. Equally, the potential role played by the Must Farm terrace within the Flag Fen basin is intriguing, as it was apparently without fieldsystem-allotment. Lying low, with its crown only at 0.9 m OD, it probably would have been inundated by the end of the second millennium BC (Fig. 2.16). Yet what of before, as it was clearly utilized and at least its eastern side was demarcated by the fence- and ditch/bank-line running south from the Bradley Fen Farm/Silt Lagoon sub-sites? While perhaps involving a minor settlement component (excavation is just commencing there at the time of writing), this low terrace might itself, aside from providing woodland resources/coppicing, have been an area of common pasture (hoof-print impressions were recovered upon its crown). Accordingly, the employment of fence-lines to delineate its side may have been a matter of keeping stock in and 'the wild' out.

The recognition that post-/fence-lines were part of the grammar of Bronze Age landscape division is itself important (see also e.g. Yates 2007, 74–6, fig. 9.2), with the Barleycroft Farm 'screens' being the most extreme example within what was clearly a spectrum (Evans & Knight 2001). Nearer at hand, the only such setting found at Fengate *per se* was discovered during the 1990 excavations at Cat's Water, where a post-alignment ran parallel to the fen-edge below the reach of its Bronze Age fieldsystem boundaries (Pryor 2001a, 45–7, fig. 3.8); to this must now be added the Early Iron Age timber-line distinguished at Stanground. These, of course, in turn resonate with the Flag Fen's own metalwork-marked post alignment (Pryor 2001a) and together, the evidence begins to suggest that much of the greater Flag Fen basin's low ground may, in fact, have been demarcated by various modes of fencing.

The status of extra-fieldsystem common 'land' (and water meadows/marsh) in a location such as the Flag Fen embayment raises specific issues of resource access, surrounded as its low ground evidently was by a series of 'fieldsystem communities'. Aside from highlighting the question of the level at which communities would have been 'resolved' — lineage, fieldsystem/herding groups or larger social networks (or all simultaneously?) — it could be anticipated that such shared common land was the location where various groups interacted and thus would have been an *arena of social/ritual negotiation*. The performance of such rights and roles in these areas may also have contributed to low/wet ground, votive metalwork deposition, such as that at the Bradley Fen 'edge' or the Power Station alignment (see also Evans 2002 for what might be comparable multi-community/-group 'shared embayment' circumstances at Coveney, Ely).

Finally, in terms of the changing framework of fieldwork and its interpretation, a degree of self-critique is here warranted. While duly questioning Pryor's direct linkage of Fengate and Flag Fen's long-term 'specialness', we, in effect, did the same as the Whittlesey quarry investigations progressed south-westwards through King's Dyke to Bradley Fen and then Must Farm, and continued to cast our sense of comparative context back to Fengate/Flag Fen. Yet, with the recognition of the Stanground peninsula's Bronze Age and its timber alignment (albeit of somewhat later, Early Iron Age date), this original 'axial linkage' demands reappraisal. Does, for example, Must Farm's timber platform in any way link to Flag Fen/Fengate (Fig. 2.15) or, much closer at hand, was Stanground its mainland 'parent' community?

Fieldsystems — origins, transmission and economic basis

Having in the preparation of this volume read so many Bronze Age landscape project reports, one cannot help but be struck by what a truism it has become that the fieldsystems of the period were predominantly livestock-related. In reference to the issue of excavation-sample percentages (see Chapters 1 & 6, Insets), one suspects that, in part, most current fieldsystem excavations generally occur at too low a density to say much that is new concerning their actual operation. This itself is understandable, as they are fairly unforgiving things to dig. Nevertheless, the net result is that most recent sites yield too few artefacts to significantly advance the study of such systems, this being especially true of their faunal remains.

Despite this, there are clear grounds to question this pastoral-based model. Primarily, there is the layout of the fieldsystems themselves. Growing up in Canada, one still remembers the High School geography lessons that drummed home the inherent differences in the layout of the historical land-division patterns between its French and British Provinces. With its strict, chain-determined grid-iron, the 'squared landscape' of the latter was largely the product of army surveyors, with little specific place/contour reference. In contrast, French-Canada — the St Lawrence River historical core of Quebec — saw Seigneurial-type, 'long-lot' allotment (Fig. 2.14:C). Stretching in strips down from higher ground arable fields to include both lower meadow pasture and riverside frontage, it was a mixed farming system that maximized the sharing of complementary landscape zone-resources

(e.g. Harris & Warkentin 1974; Butzer 2002); to me, this still seems to provide the abiding *raison d'etre* of cross-contour strip-/reave-type fieldsystems, with quasi-radial systems simply being a more extreme expression of the same (see e.g. Besteman & Guiran, in Brandt *el al.* 1987, fig. 1.4.1; see also Grove 1981 and Evans & Hodder 2006b, 3, fig. 1.2 concerning Cressey Dymock's ideal Fenland farm designs).

When reviewing the plans of the Bronze Age's fieldsystems what strikes one is, actually, the paucity of their droveway provision if they were primarily livestock-related. Of course, stock could always be driven across/through 'open' fields, but if specially organized for large-scale pastoralism then surely more inner-/cross-main 'strip' droveways would have been provided to allow animals to access individual fields. Look again, for example, at the plan of Tanholt Farm, Eye (Fig. 2.17): there simply does not seem to be sufficient droveways to allow great herds to be distributed among its fields and, equally, those portions of the Bradley Fen system excavated to date have no droveway facility whatsoever (Fig. 2.16). (The Colne Fen, Earith sites are particularly informative as regards the operation of droves (Figs. 2.21 & 2.24:4). That in the south — at *The Holme* — passed right through the excavation area and could have been accessed from the paddocks on either side; the north, at *Rhee Lakeside South*, actually started at, and directly opened onto, a settlement enclosure from where it ran eastward to the fen-edge.)

Other sources have also questioned the abiding 'stock-interpretation', the most basic being Scaife's suggestion, arising from his analysis of the Flag Fen/Fengate pollen cores, that: '*a mixed arable and pastoral economy was practiced during the Middle–later Bronze Age on the drier and better drained soils surrounding Flag Fen basin*' (2001, 381). Obviously complementing the evidence of querns and other markers of crop production (e.g. four-post granaries), cereal pollen is also documented on a number of other sites/systems of the period in the region (e.g. Colne Fen, Earith, see above). Among the most interesting of these is Striplands Farm, Longstanton. Located on heavy soils, and generally having very good environmental and waterlogged preservation, the pit-wells/watering-holes associated with its later Bronze Age settlement yielded cereal pollen levels of between 1 per cent and 3 per cent (see Boreham, in Patten & Evans 2005; Mackay & Knight 2007). It is relevant to compare these to the same site's early medieval well features, as its location lay on the north side of the historic village's core and in what would have been its in-fields. Although falling within the type of village-setting that we can readily envisage, cereals only occurred at between 9–16 per cent in these features (Mackay & Knight 2007), and the Bronze Age pollen must have undergone significant deterioration over the intervening *c.* 1500 years between the two occupation horizons. Equally, at the HAD V fen-edge Iron Age compound which, based on a wide array of data-sources (ard-marks, etc.), unquestionably practised a mixed farming economy, cereal pollen occurred at an average 4.8 per cent (Simms, in Evans & Hodder 2006b, table 5.82). This is directly comparable to Fengate's Middle–later Bronze Age cereal pollen levels of *c.* 5 per cent (Scaife 2001, 373, 375; see also e.g. Brandt & van der Leeuw 1987, 350 concerning prehistoric husbandry *vs* cultivation farming for the Assendelver Polder, Holland, where a paucity of ditch recutting was considered a trait of the latter). Equally pertinent in this context is Lewis and French's declaration, based on their study of the Fengate Depot Site's palaeosols, that there was evidence of pre-Iron Age tillage (in Pryor 2001a, 20–22).

Two more abstract arguments can also be brought to bear upon the relationship between Bronze Age fieldsystems and large-scale stock rearing. The first concerns why recourse was made to pastoralism in the first place. Linked to the advocation of pastoral transhumance models as a means by which archaeology's dispersed distribution dots can be inter-related, such as Crawford's trans-national Beaker-period 'road' (see above; 1912, 196), pastoral modes of interpretation have generally been commonplace when little (prehistoric) archaeology of any one period has been known and when far-flung phenomena demand connection. The lack of context for 1970s-excavated Bronze Age fieldsystems or Neolithic causewayed enclosures are obvious instances (see Evans 1987; 1988 for further discussion). Now, with our prehistoric landscapes becoming infilled through the intensity of excavations, we simply no longer need such overly convenient, long-distance explanatory mechanisms.

The second point to be made relates to the oft-cited rise in population that is argued to have occurred over the course of the second millennium BC (e.g. Burgess 1974, 166; Fowler 1983, 34–6). This, of course, is biased by the much greater 'obvious-ness' of later Bronze Age occupation sites when compared to, for example, the slighter traces of Beaker or Collared Urn settlement. Nonetheless, furthered by the great subsistence 'inventions' of the age — *the pit-well* (allowing for immediate/permanent 'on-site' watering sources) and *salt production* (enabling the storage of meat and meaning that the slaughter of every animal need not have involved group-feasting) — such an increase does seem apparent in the record. Accordingly, the question must be what would best account for this: a pastoral economy or an intensification of mixed farming produc-

tion fostered by the advent of fieldsystems? Based on all known historical precedent, the latter is surely far more likely (cf. Kitchen 2001, 118).

This latter issue begs the question of the origins of such systems. Based on the evidence then available, and drawing upon fieldwork results in Wessex and on Dartmoor, Fowler's model of the hypothetical stages of landscape clearance and allotment (Fig. 2.14; 1983, fig. 42), in effect naturalized the development of 'strip-type' fieldsystems. Indeed, his Stage 2 — 'clearance in swathes' — echoed the long-strip patterns of Dartmoor's Bronze Age reaves or Fengate's system (Fig. 6.4). Yet forest clearances have sub-circular configurations as often as linear (Evans & Hodder 2006a, 230–31), and the variety of prehistoric fieldsystems shows that there was no unilinear development trajectory. Moreover, in the case of prehistoric lowland Britain, the interval between landscape clearance and fieldsystem layout was such that it is difficult to see their connection (see Evans & Hodder 2006a concerning the 'archaeology of clearances'). Indeed, in the case of Fengate, its main Neolithic clearance axis/pathway arguably lay well off the alignment of its later fieldsystem (Pryor 2001a, 406–7, fig. 18.1; see Chapter 3 Inset).

There is a temptation to envisage the period's fieldsystems as some manner of 'horizon', with all being laid-out in the mid second millennium BC. Yet the system at South Hornchurch, Essex prompts caution (Guttmann & Last 2000). There, three phases of fieldsystem-development occurred between the tenth to eighth centuries BC and, with the first two associated with Post-Deverel-Rimbury pottery assemblages, it is definitely of *Late* Bronze Age attribution. (Interestingly, in its main second-phase layout, the fieldsystem's northwest–southeast droveway was clearly constructed in relationship to a roundhouse ringwork and must, thereby, essentially have post-dated it. In contrast, at Mucking the comparable South Rings settlement overlay its *Middle* Bronze Age fieldsystem; Jones & Bond 1980.)

With this dating variability, might not chronological factors account for some of the differences present in the region's fieldsystems? The most likely candidate for this is the fieldsystem at Welland Bank, which apparently had very few droveways (and those not regularly laid-out) and is of a fairly fragmentary, patchwork-like character; in other words, it is an *aggregate system*. This contrasts with the Newborough coaxial system with its regular-interval droves, which lies only *c.* 1.5 km to the south (Fig. 2.23). Analysed as a case study by Pryor (2002), his key point was that the two systems were separated by the Welland River and that its valley may have been a long-term culture boundary zone, explaining the differences in their character. Yet chronology may also have been a contributing factor. It may well be the case that the Newborough's (uninvestigated) 'classic' strip-/reave-type coaxial system is of Middle Bronze Age or even earlier attribution, whereas Welland Bank could prove to be somewhat later, at least in part (Field 2001, 59, in a Wessex context, argues that aggregate systems post-date coaxial layouts). With the latter site unpublished (though see Field 2001, 27–9, figs. 5–7), this cannot be demonstrated; however, the two radiocarbon dates from it are of Early Iron Age attribution, and the vast majority of its pottery of also of Early Iron Age and Late Bronze Age date (Dymond *et al.* n.d.). Set against this, Colne Fen's rather irregular multiple-alignment system (Fig. 2.21) is firmly radiocarbon dated to *c.* 1500/1400–1200 cal. BC, and this indicates that a fieldsystem's organizational 'style' does not offer a sound basis of chronological distinction in the absence of other evidence.

Rather than pigeonhole coaxial and aggregate fieldsystems as either/or categories, or indeed try now to develop a complicated typology for the region's fieldsystems, what seems imperative is to recognize that Fengate's fieldsystem was allied to those continuing northward into South Lincolnshire. In terms of sharing a drove-dominant 'coaxial-strip' layout, it clearly had strong affinities with the Market Deeping system (Figs. 2.22 & 6.4); this also seems true for Newborough's fieldsystem and probably Langtoft's. Whilst, pending further exposure, we must remain unsure of the overall structure of Bradley Fen's fieldsystem, the Tanholt Farm, Eye system does not seem to share the same regular coaxial layout (Fig. 2.17). Indeed, it is uncertain whether the latter should be seen as adhering to aggregate or coaxial principles, although this perhaps reflects its immediate inland/off-fen-edge situation. The crucial point is that, in comparison to the more 'corridor-like' droveside-compound/plot layout of the above-listed systems (with weak co-axes), Eye/Thorney presents a picture of a truly 'blanket' or area-wide fieldsystem *per se*. In contrast to this, the more southerly systems — Block Fen, Colne Fen and Barleycroft/Over (Figs. 2.18–2.21) — seem variously irregular. Although Colne's fieldsystem had major droves, it was without a regular coaxial structure; the latter trait the Barleycroft/Over system has (at least locally), but — and probably reflective of its river valley (*vs* fen-edge) location — it was without droveways. Given the state of current knowledge (and with published sources generally unavailable), the key issue should probably not be so much one of trying to explain the variability of these systems, but of accounting for the degree to which the Fengate/South Lincolnshire systems seem to hold together as a 'group'. Were these droves just a structural/organizational 'device', or do they reflect

a greater emphasis upon movement/transportation and, perhaps, the pastoral component of fieldsystems? Equally, was the latter also reflected in the paucity of cross-drove-axes (*vs* droveside plots/components) that seem characteristic of these systems?

The question of there being a general fieldsystem 'horizon' also extends to the layout of individual systems themselves. Here, the example must be the Dartmoor Bronze Age reaves which have been so thoroughly studied by Fleming. Basically consisting of quasi-radial, drystone coaxial systems laid out across valleys (Figs. 6.4 & 6.9), Fleming has argued for their development *en masse* in response to a 'Commons Dilemma' arising from grazing and land pressure during the Neolithic, the scale of these individual 'system-blocks' reflecting earlier intercommoning territories; this certainly implies a degree of planning (Fleming 1985; 1987; 1994). This interpretation has recently been criticized by Johnston, who rather emphasizes the 'accretive character' of the boundaries and suggests that 'the coaxial pattern emerged in a reflexive tradition', seeing the development of field systems very much as a local process relating to earlier pathways and monuments (2005, 1, 8). Whilst it must be the case that not all the components of prehistoric fieldsystems were laid out at once, at the same time they do generally seem to constitute a mass second-millennium BC 'event'. Many of the main coaxial systems of the period shared basic characteristics — such as, for example, the droveway intervals at Fengate and Market Deeping (Fig. 6.4) — indicating that they cannot just be considered as the result of immediately local community needs and traditions. This does not mean that their advent need represent any kind of migration into the region, but rather attests to the existence of *fieldsystems as an idea* — a conceptual/physical framework structuring socio-economic productive relations with the land. Fieldsystems certainly involved ancestral ties (i.e. monument incorporation/resonance), but they must also reflect *a 'phenomenon' beyond the strictly local*.

Pertaining to the very nature of transmission/invention within the archaeological record, these are clearly major issues. When, however, investigating something so deeply engrained within the fabric of the land as fieldsystems, it is little wonder that the means of their spread/distribution and dating is ambiguous.

In this capacity, it should finally be stressed that nor are ditched fieldsystems necessary for the successful practice of agriculture. Aside from 'late' Celtic fields in the north of the region, they appear to have been genuinely absent or, at least, rare in most of the Bronze Age sites/landscape of the Netherlands (though this need not exclude above-ground field-allotment (hedges and/or slight fence-lines), just any obvious below-ground component; e.g. Fokkens 2005; Harsema 2005; Arnoldussen & Fokkens 2008). Similarly, in Britain, the Trent would also seem to have delineated a northward extent of fieldsystems of the period; despite intensive and widespread investigations, within central-northern Lincolnshire and the adjacent Midlands, no such systems have there yet been recovered (Knight & Howard 2004).

Middle Bronze Age settlement — the problem

As has been outlined, definite house structures of Neolithic, Beaker, Collared Urn, later Bronze Age and Iron Age date have now all been variously recovered at Fengate and in the adjacent Whittlesey Quarry investigations. Attesting to nearly the full spectrum of later prehistory, for those prior to the mid second millennium BC the evidence is such that it could undermine arguments concerning the settlement mobility practised during those periods, otherwise based on the non-recovery of a robust 'architecture' (e.g. Pollard 1999; Whittle 1997). Yet, what of the Middle Bronze Age? No definite houses of that time have been found (as opposed to the many of later Bronze Age/post-*c.* 1200 BC attribution).

It is here held that the lack of Middle Bronze Age houses must be a problem of recognition and that we cannot seriously entertain the idea that, having established such 'rooted' fieldsystems, those communities practised some manner of non-recoverable 'light' settlement mobility that left no obvious occupation traces. Spanning the period *c.* 1500/1400–1200 BC, in other landscapes within the region their 'presence' is essentially attested to by Deverel-Rimbury urn-held cremations, which by their spatial/stratigraphic relations must have been contemporary with the usage of the fieldsystems. This non-settlement recovery pattern is a widespread phenomenon and is certainly not specific to the Fengate environs. In fact, very few settlements of the Middle Bronze Age are known within eastern England at all. There were the dump deposits of Middle Bronze Age pottery in the upper profiles of the Grimes Graves flint-mine shafts (Longworth *et al.* 1988), but only very slight settlement evidence of that date has been recovered in recent excavations; with, aside from Langtoft (see above), Ash Covert, Broom, Beds. (Cooper & Edmonds 2007) and the Blackwater sites (Wallis & Waughman 1998) proving exceptional.

The non-detection of this horizon seems essentially to relate to two factors. Firstly, the below-ground traces of buildings of the later second millennium BC are usually only postholes. Generally they were not gully-surrounded and thereby provided little 'open-catchment' for finds. This is equally true for later Bronze Age structures, which are as often dated by their associated pit assemblages as by material caught in building-features *per se*. This implies that it is conceivable that a number of the undated (and 'non-gullied') roundhouses on apparently Late Bronze Age sites could still be of Middle Bronze Age attribution, indicating that we must start to regularly radiocarbon date fieldsystem-associated buildings that do not otherwise yield dating evidence.

As to the second factor, there is still no escaping the fact that remarkably little Deverel-Rimbury pottery is being recovered from these sites (only seven such sherds were identified among the more than 3 kg of pottery recovered from Newark Road's second-millennium BC features; Pryor 1980a, 86–9, 102–3). Clearly there could not then have been much pottery in circulation (at least relative to later Bronze Age frequencies) and a proportion of what there was became 'lost' through funerary usage. Equally, communities of the time (Middle Bronze Age) could not have practised pit-deposition to any great extent. The character of the pottery itself may also have been a contributing factor. Little decorated and relatively 'feature-less', the fact that broken vessels were being reduced for the manufacture of grog-temper, both in their own time and for subsequent later Bronze Age production, would also affect their representation within the site record.

All this is a problem which cannot be readily resolved at this time, and it is one best 'side-stepped' for the moment. This being said, the generic non-/low-recovery of Middle Bronze Age material does have immediate ramifications for the understanding of Fengate's sequence, as it inevitably biases interpretation of, for example, certain compound-/paddock-'types' towards a non-settlement function, Pryor's double-ditched Newark Road compounds again being a prime instance of such. Two 'round' structures occurred within their interior (one being 'D'-shaped), which were thought to respectively represent a livestock barn/shed and a house proper (Pryor 1980a, 174, fig. 34). Yet Pryor duly noted that associated 'domestic rubbish was extraordinarily rare compared to the vast amounts encountered on the Iron Age settlement' (Pryor 1980a) and has subsequently reinterpreted their enclosures as communal stock compounds/yards (Pryor 1996), a mode of interpretation now widely adopted for similar enclosures dug by other excavators elsewhere. This may, indeed, prove a valid assignation, but — given the general non-recovery of Deverel-Rimbury settlement — we must guard against any *de facto* writing-off of hints of Middle Bronze Age occupation, however slight, in favour of animal-related explanations.

Chapter 3

The Elliott Site — Fengate Central

Christopher Evans & Emma Beadsmoore

Extending over 2.3 ha (with 1.7 ha open-area stripping) and excavated between May and August 2005, this site lay immediately south of Pryor's Cat's Water complex (Figs. 1.1 & 3.1). Providing a 250 m-long, 'transect-like' exposure of the fen-edge, it divided on either side of the Parish Drain (Areas A/B west thereof, with C to the east). The fieldwork arose following a trial trench evaluation programme by the Birmingham University Field Unit in 1998, but with their original programme occurring across a much wider area ('Sites O & Q'; Cutler 1998). Though summarized in the Flag Fen volume (Pryor 2001a, 30–32 & 50), as they have direct relevance for our work, the results of their investigations will be outlined below.

Directed by Emma Beadsmoore, in total 337 features were excavated at the Elliott Site in the course of the CAU fieldwork, with more than 5400 artefacts recovered (Beadsmoore 2006b). Despite this, the site yielded a remarkable paucity of feature-dating evidence and, for example, no sherds of any pre-Middle Bronze Age pottery were recovered whatsoever. Instead, as mentioned in Chapter 1 (Table 1.2), what distinguished this site were the relative quantities of animal bone, and to this needs to be added the frequency of its diverse pits (see Chapter 4). In short, this is a site that evidently saw considerable activity, of which little can be diagnostically/chronologically allocated with any certainty. In this respect it differs markedly from the Edgerley Site and its succession of firmly 'type-dated', pre-fieldsystem pit clusters. This being said, the site nestled in the 'hub' between Pryor's Cat's Water excavation (which lay immediately to the northeast, and was where the Co-op Site Neolithic 'house' and Pryor's putative 'henge' also lay; see Chapter 1 summaries) and both his Storey's Bar and Padholme Road investigations to the west. Indeed, elements of the site's second-millennia fieldsystem have been, at various times, previously identified in Pryor's investigations. The seemingly segmented southwest–northeast boundary extending across the northern quarter of Area A/B had actually been exposed in the course of the original Cat's Water

excavations (as F.862; Pryor 1980a, fig. 93), during which a trench was taken southwest from the main area to expose its length. Its 'patchy' or partial plan-layout in 2005 (as F.49/52/61) was evidently due to the fact that only its deepest portions survived successive machining, though during our stripping its full length was still vaguely 'ghosted'.

Pryor's Cat's Water trench actually extended to the F.862 ditch's junction with a northwest–southeast oriented (i.e. 'fenward'), double-ditch droveway, to which he allocated Ditch Numbers 1 and 2 (Fig. 2.13). In fact, he excavated a semi-crouched inhumation (F.1594) set at the junction of Ditch 2 and the F.862 boundary (Figs. 3.6 & 3.12; Pryor 1980a, 163, 168, fig. 97). (Pryor also then cut a short length of trench in the southeastern end of the site on the projected line of that droveway (1980, fig. 5); that no features were identified there is due to its 'splaying'; see below.) Although requiring a degree of 'kinked' projection, this droveway's ditches had also been excavated over a length of c. 60 m within his Padholme Road sub-Site (Area X; Pryor 1980a, figs. 6 & 7). There, the width of the drove was 4–5 m, and there can be little doubt that this was the same double-ditch system that traversed the entire length of the Elliott Site (in addition, the boundary we excavated running south from the Ditch 1-line must represent the same ditch that was exposed in the 1999 TK Packaging Site investigations; Fig. 3.2; see Chapter 1).

The three interconnecting trenches that had been dug by the Birmingham Unit (10–12) within what was to become the area of our main site (A/B; their Area 2/'Site Q') well characterized its archaeology (Fig. 3.2). They tested a range of the exposed pits and ditch lengths, and distinguished waterlogging within its more deeply cut features. Although only a single sherd of earlier Bronze Age grog-tempered pottery was recovered (Trench 12), they were able to identify the site's early, Late Mesolithic/earlier Neolithic usage: two Early Neolithic plain ware sherds were recovered from their Trench 10, as well as a microlith and end-scraper from Trench 12; blades were also recovered

FIGURE 3.1. *The Elliott Site — The last open plot within 'Fengate Central', with the Cat's Water Site (upper right) built upon. Note that the embankments across the lower, Cat's Water-side field attests to its use as a motor-cross track; the 'gun emplacement-like' settings, right, relate to testing facilities within the fireworks factory (photograph reproduced by permission of Geoinformation Group).*

there and in Trench 11, where a core and a retouched flake also occurred. In addition, 17 unretouched flakes were retrieved from these trenches (see Woodward & Bevan, in Cutler 1998, 23–5; the evidence of Birmingham's eastern, 'deep fen' trench-findings will be discussed below).

As a result of their trenching, the Birmingham Unit identified a slight fen-edge embayment within the site-area (see also Pryor 1978, fig. 3). In the main, the surface of the first terrace gravels sloped from *c.* 3 m OD beside Storey's Bar Road down to *c.* 0.9 m OD at the southeast end of the site (Fig. 3.4); however, neither the composition nor the bedding of the gravels was uniform: a 'high ground' ridge continued along the northeastern side of the site and, half-way down along its length, there was a *c.* 0.6–0.8 m-deep 'hollow' across its southwestern swathe. Deepening eastwards, the stripped gravel surface began to just rise again — by *c.* 0.1–0.2 m — along the site's southeastern edge, and it is this *c.* 50 m-wide 'depression' that constitutes the embayment. Lying to the east, beyond our area of excavation (and the current development), in two of Birmingham's trenches a series of northeast–southwest oriented palaeochannels were identified, which probably represent earlier courses of the Cat's Water proper (Trenches 8 & 9; Figs. 3.2 & 6.9). These may correlate with the relict stream channel cut by the post-

alignment (and sealed by sand deposits) in the Power Station investigations (Pryor 2001a, fig. 1.7). Equally, there could also be correspondence with the lake/pond- or slow moving stream-type horizons Scaife distinguished within the pollen from Birmingham's Trench 5 south of Third Drove (in Cutler 1998), and a possible channel was also identified nearby in the course of the CAU's Material Recycling Centre coring programme (see also Boreham & Peachey's 'edge-adjacent' channel at the Sewage Treatment Works; Chapter 5 below).

At the Elliott Site proper, the character of the terrace gravels was mixed. Not only did they include glacial tills, but also deposits of Oxford Clay. Throughout the eastern half of the site and the embayment floor, the latter rose to the surface; across the higher western ground it occurred below the surface, in distinct pockets and seams within the gravels. As will be outlined below, the presence of this clay was important for the range of activities on site, not only as a source of raw material, but also for locally perching the watertable and its water-retentive qualities.

Whilst buried soil profiles were not actually taken from the Elliott Site itself (although two were analysed from Birmingham's work; see French, in BUFA 1998), Charly French did inspect the site and provided the following summary:

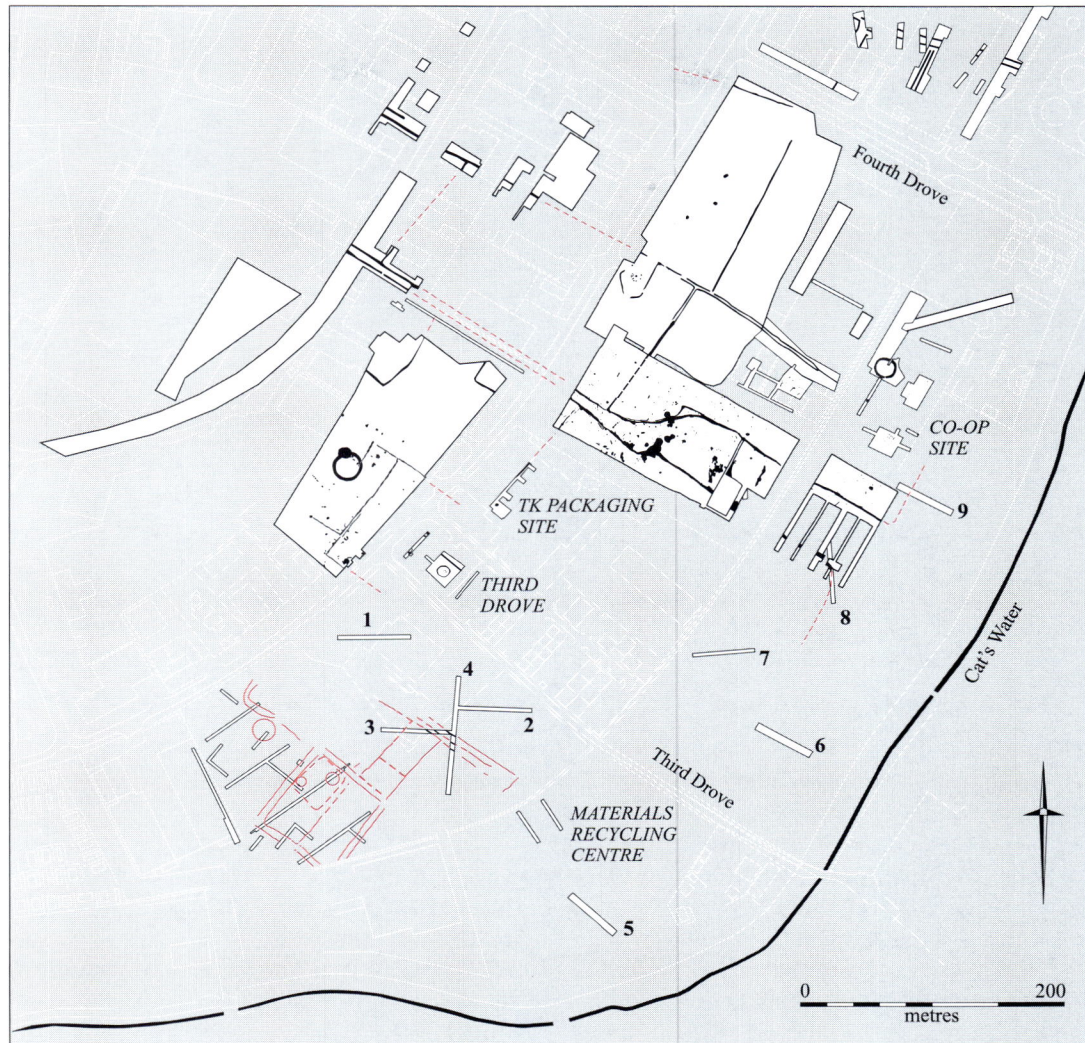

FIGURE 3.2. *Elliott Site Environs showing earlier excavations (and fieldsystem features), with 1–9 indicating Birmingham Unit trenches. (Reproduced by permission of Ordnance Survey on behalf of HMSO. © Crown copyright 2009. All rights reserved. Ordnance Survey Licence number 100048686.)*

Quite thin (<15 cm), gravel-rich buried soils were preserved on the highest parts of the site. In addition, on the margins of the small fen embayment that occupies approximately the southeastern third of the site, the palaeosol becomes almost indistinguishable from the subsequent deposition of grey freshwater sand/silts and silty clays; however, the palaeosol was much better preserved and thicker (*c.* 20–35 cm) as the site dipped eastwards towards the fen-edge and/or beneath this upstanding fieldsystem-associated banks.

The embayment sequence is essentially part of the Flag Fen basin and, from bottom to top, comprises:

1) A pale grey, sandy/silty clay indicative of alternating conditions of freshwater flooding and reed marsh.
2) Thin peat development associated with shallow standing water and reed marsh development; this unit thickens eastwards and becomes less humified and better preserved, but is now very humified.
3) Deposition of an organic silty clay alluvium, indicative of overbank flooding from the Nene and the entrained erosion of topsoils from inland and upstream.

4) A grey silty clay alluvium, derived from the entrained erosion of subsoils from inland and upstream.

With upwards of 1–1.4 m soil cover across the lower southeastern half of the site, there were some elements of feature-related stratigraphy. As shown on Figure 3.4, not only did ditch-associated upcast banks locally survive, but a patchy gravel surface lay across portions of the 'floor' of the upper embayment. For pragmatic reasons, we could not actually 'excavate' these as such; following their rapid planning, they were machine-stripped, with selected portions left for hand-dug sample-excavation. This was also true of the site's buried soils. Their main area of testing was a metre-wide transect across the Bronze Age double-ditch/droveway system at the northwest end of the site

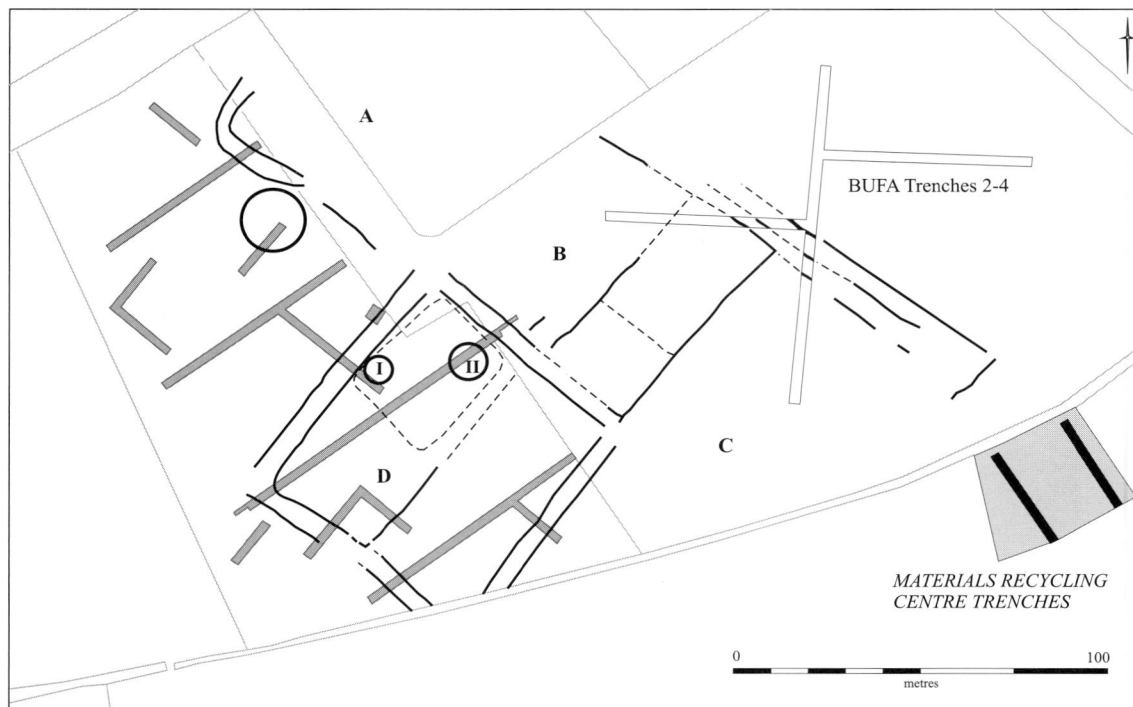

FIGURE 3.3. *The Depot Site showing 1992 and 1996 CAU trenching (and Birmingham's Trenches 2–4). (Reproduced by permission of Ordnance Survey on behalf of HMSO. © Crown copyright 2009. All rights reserved. Ordnance Survey Licence number 100048686.)*

(Fig. 3.4). There, 28 consecutive metre-squares were excavated, with five worked flints being recovered from four (0.18 m per metre mean density; see Table 1.3); among the recovered finds were a Neolithic arrowhead, an end-scraper, and what is potentially a Bronze Age core.

2005 excavations

A total of 199 pits, of various size and shape, were recorded across the Elliott Site. Of these, 133 produced no finds whatsoever. This obviously hinders their chronological attribution, as indeed does the fact that, of the remaining 66, only 10 included pottery (5 per cent of the total; 47 contained flint and the same number contained bone). As discussed below, this type of recovery pattern has not been uncommon at Fengate. More than 200 pits at Cat's Water were left unattributed due to a paucity of dating evidence (i.e. no pottery); of the 52 small pits listed in association with the Enclosure C 'settlement swathe' at Pryor's Newark Road (1980a, table 2), only 12 (23 per cent) had any finds and just seven (13.5 per cent) yielded pottery. If nothing else, what this and the Elliott evidence attest to is that these pits must have fulfilled functions other than the dumping of refuse (cf. Garrow *et al.* 2006).

The majority of the Elliot Site's assemblages derived from its pits. This included all but one of its 230 pottery sherds, 39 per cent of its worked flint and 75 per cent of its animal bone (by number; 73 per cent by weight). Given the importance of the site's faunal assemblages, it is worth noting that, of the 47 pits with bone, 25 contained 10+ fragments and only 13 contained 50 or more fragments. With 2613 fragments (22,081 g), the latter category represents 66 per cent or 63 per cent of the site's total bone assemblage (respectively by weight and number). Generally, therefore, for the purposes of 'mobilizing' the site's artefact assemblages, its pit features represent *the problem*. Accordingly, they warrant a degree of formal attribute-analysis, and whatever grounds by which they can be phased must be made explicit. It should, however, be stressed that the issue of the pits' phasing (and lack thereof) most affects the analytical potential of the site's faunal assemblage. In response to this ambiguity, in Seetah's study of the faunal assemblage (below), aside from detailing firmly phase-attributed assemblages where possible, a more general analysis is made of that animal bone which can be generically assigned to the Bronze Age as a whole.

As expressed in Figure 3.5, the site's pits varied greatly in size, from 0.05–1.14 m in depth and from

Area A

Archaeological Feature

Slot

Surface Deposit

Buried Soil Transect

0   50
metres

3.0 m

2.0 m

2.0 m

Area B

1.0 m

1.0 m   Area C

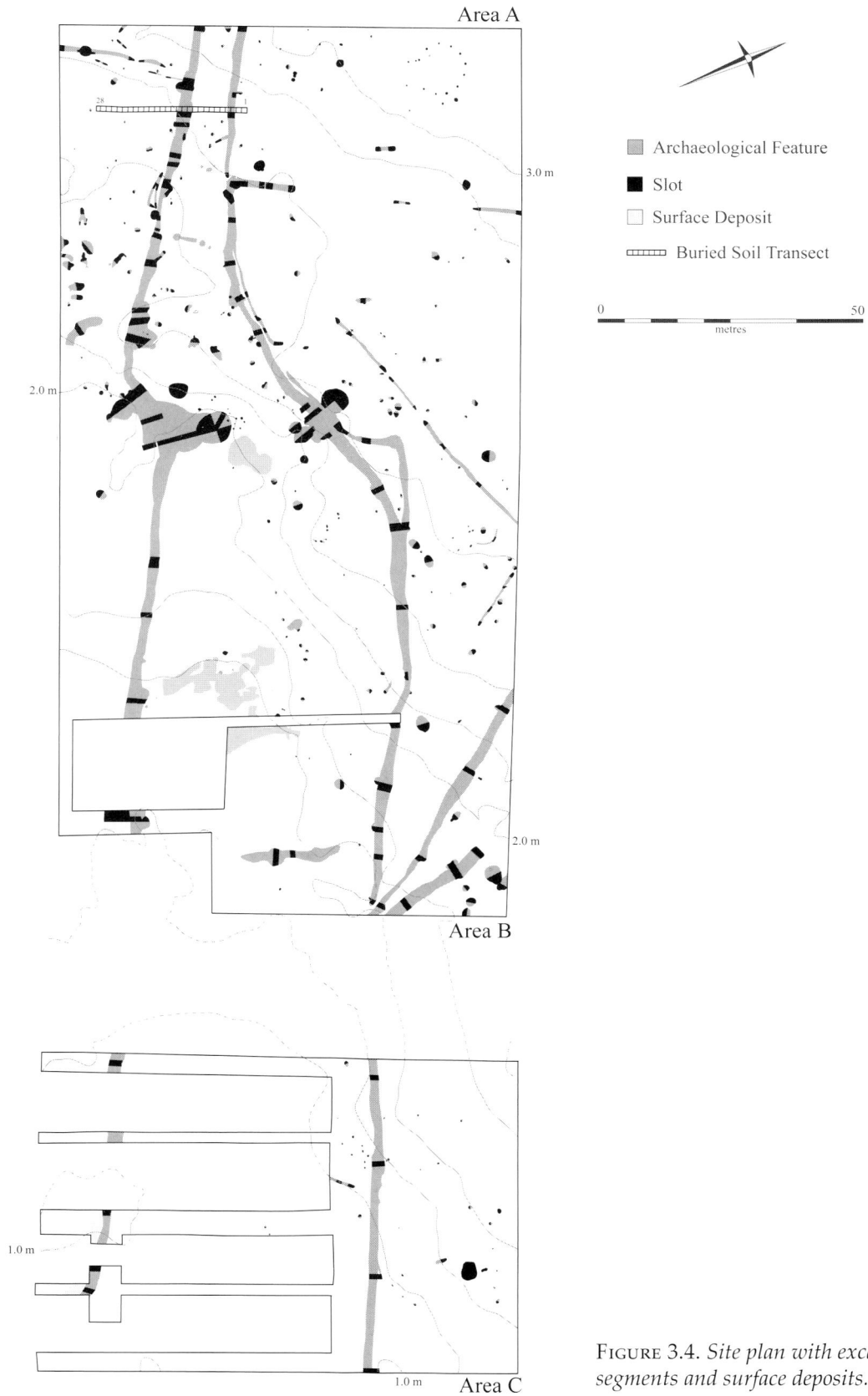

FIGURE 3.4. *Site plan with excavation segments and surface deposits.*

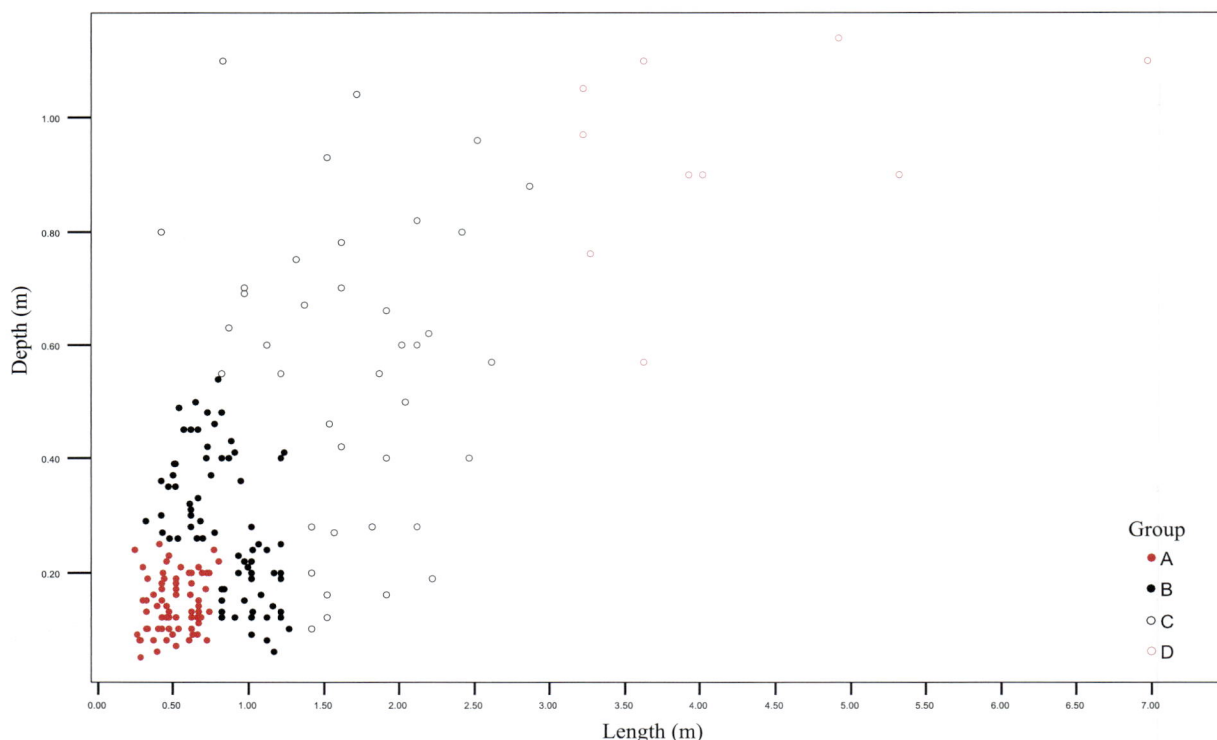

FIGURE 3.5. *Pit dimension plot.*

0.2–6.95 m across. Their plotting, however, shows a distinct concentration towards the lower end of the scale, with 148 (74 per cent) having depths less than 0.5 m and a length/diameter under *c.* 1.4 m. In fact, within this group a further 'smaller-end' clustering seems apparent, and to facilitate further analysis the pits have been sub-divided into four broad size-groupings (A–D; Table 3.1).

Twenty-two of the site's pits were described as being 'peat-filled' (as opposed to a number of others that were only peat-capped). Few of the largest category pits (C & D; seven in total) were originally dug under these evidently wet conditions; the majority — 15/68 per cent — of peat-filled pits were in group A (5) or B (10). Unsurprisingly, given the area's general environmental sequence, most of these 'peat' features were of first-millennium BC date (later Bronze

Age/Iron Age peat did not fill the second-millennium BC fieldsystem boundaries, but only locally capped them); they occurred scattered throughout all but the western quarter of the site and lay as high as 2.5 m OD (descending as low as *c.* 1.1 m OD; see Fig. 3.4).

Aside from the case of three tree-throws, wood, in varying quantities, was present in ten pits. The basal deposits of F.220 and F.302 produced the most substantial waterlogged assemblages, the latter seeing by far the best preservation on the site. The distribution of features containing wood would broadly concur with that of the peat-filled features, except that there was a marked concentration at the western end of the embayment, at the break of slope at its head. While this swathe correlates with a major junction point within the main fieldsystem (see below), the date range of these features indicates that this was a long-term focus of 'wet-edge' activity.

Radiocarbon dating

Within most site reports radiocarbon results are treated as if almost a 'punch-line' or afterthought, something that follows the presentation of the internally ordered data, and as if the phasing was not informed by any knowledge of their assays. Here, because so many of the site's features are not otherwise (or at least firmly) attributed, we need to be 'up-front' with this information.

TABLE 3.1. *Pit grouping dimensions (note that this excludes 13 severely truncated pit features for which no dimensions are known).*

	Maximum Length (cm)	Maximum Depth (cm)	Number	% of total
A	80	25	70	35.2
B	140	50	78	39.2
C	300	50+	14	20.6
D	300+	50+	10	5

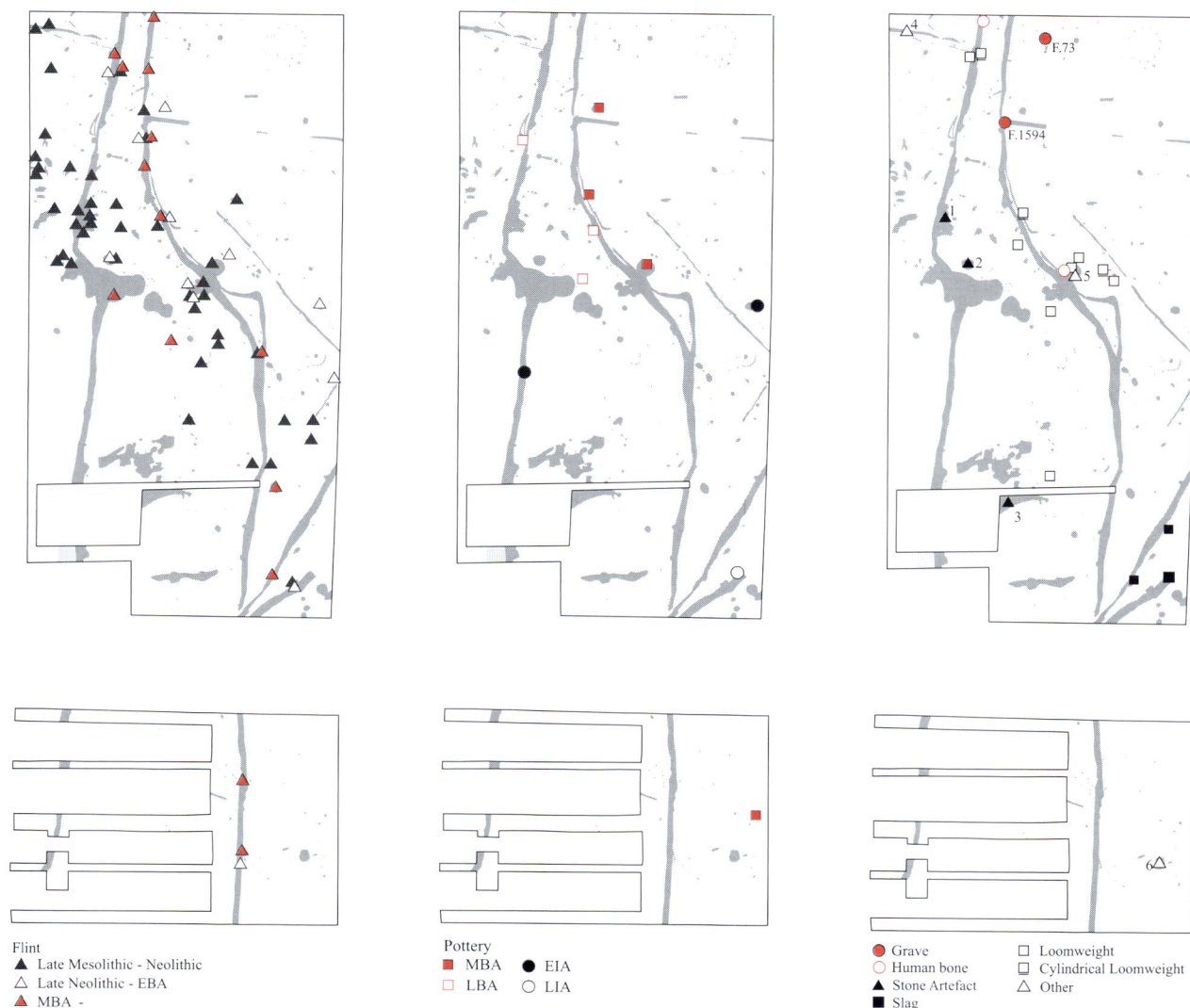

Flint
▲ Late Mesolithic - Neolithic
△ Late Neolithic - EBA
▲ MBA -

Pottery
■ MBA   ● EIA
□ LBA   ○ LIA

● Grave   □ Loomweight
○ Human bone   □ Cylindrical Loomweight
▲ Stone Artefact △ Other
■ Slag

FIGURE 3.6. *Distributions: Flint, pottery and other finds.*

Following an initial sample submitted to the Oxford Laboratory (specifically to date aurochs bone from a pit; see Lynch *et al.* 2008), six samples were processed by Beta-Analytic (all calibrated to two sigma):

1) F.222 (OxA-X-2182-55) — 4150±37 BP/2880–2610 cal. BC
2) F.108 (Beta-230846) — 4270±40 BP/2920–2870 cal. BC
3) F.302 ([1241]; Beta-230849) — 3730±60 BP/2300–1960 cal. BC
4) F.302 ([1231]; Beta-230848) — 3650±70 BP/2200–1880 cal. BC
5) F.325 (Beta-230850) — 3340±40 BP/1740–1520 cal. BC
6) F.2 (Beta-230845) — 3190±40 BP/1530–1400 cal. BC
7) F.182 (Beta-230847) — 2870±40 BP/1190–1140 and 1140–920 cal. BC.

In early 2008, a final sample, human bone from the F.73 inhumation (see below) was submitted the Oxford Laboratory; this unfortunately failed due to a lack of collagen. Otherwise, of the Beta dates, those from F.302 were both standard bulk dates from individual pieces of wood (a stake and a hedgewood piece; see Taylor below), with the remainder being AMS assays from charred materials. All are considered 'acceptable'. While it could be argued that the F.2 date (from a pit cutting the main fieldsystem droveway) seems 300–500 years too early, and that the dated charred seed might have been residual and have derived from the underlying ditch itself, a comparable assay was achieved from the Edgerley Site (see Chapter 4 below).

Later Mesolithic/Neolithic activity

As is apparent on the Figure 3.6 distribution plan (and as further discussed by Beadsmoore below), a sub-

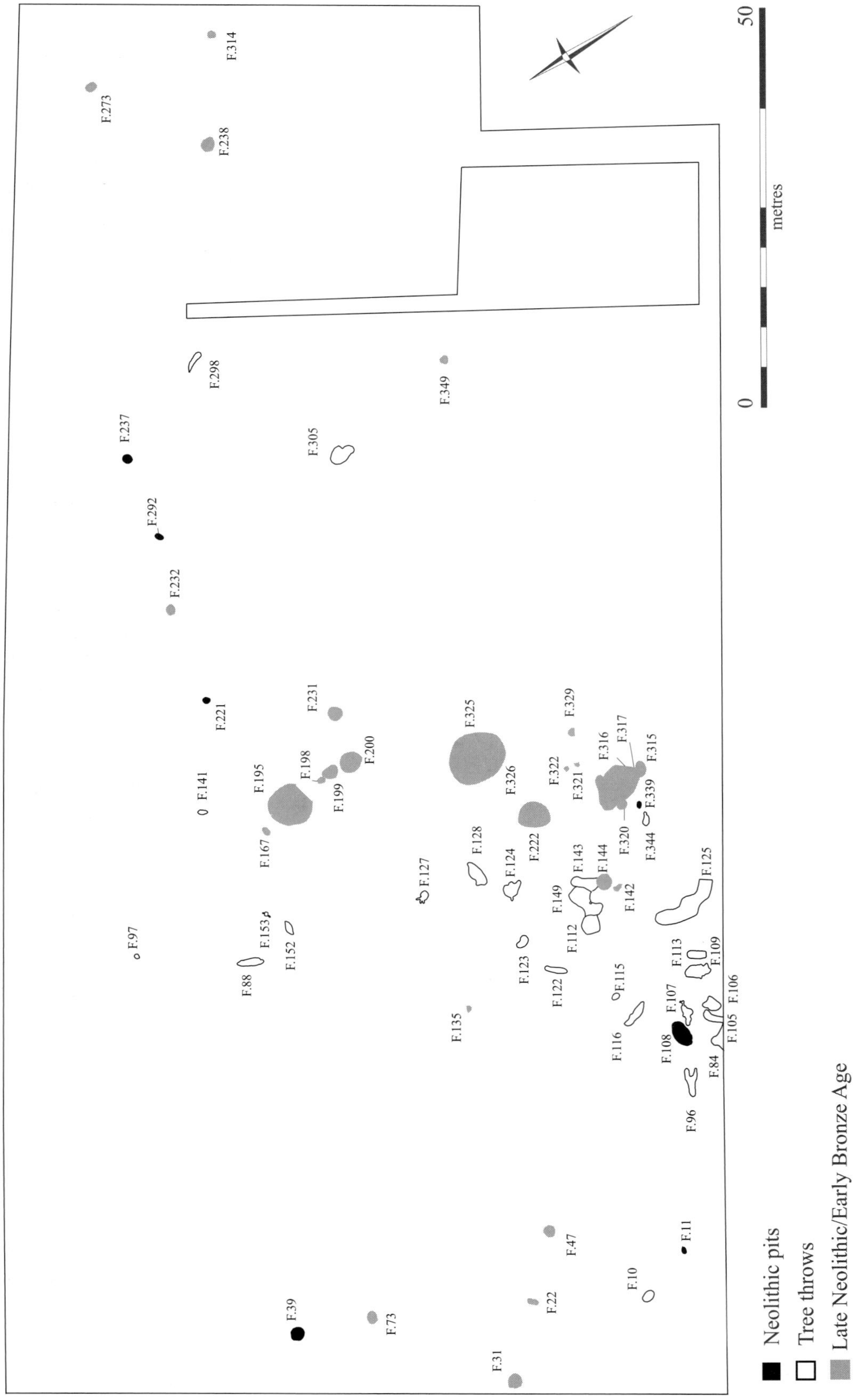

FIGURE 3.7. *Neolithic and earlier Bronze Age features phase plan.*

stantial quantity of later Mesolithic/earlier Neolithic flintwork was recovered, largely within a swathe across the northwestern third of the site and along the crest of the embayment's end. While much of this occurred residually in later contexts, some possible features of that date were identified.

Twenty of the site's 28 tree-throws yielded flint, although this mostly occurred within a cluster of ten such features along the western edge of Area A (Fig. 3.7). Despite only being 'slot-tested', three tree-throws produced more than ten pieces: F.107, F.112 and F.84. Of these, 15 and 37 pieces of the period were, forthcoming from F.112 and F.84 respectively, sufficient to suggest their potential utilization. Single microliths were recovered from both of these, with F.84 also having an end-scraper and an edge-used blade; half a polished Langdale stone axe was found in F.112.

Located amid the western tree-throw cluster was a large, sub-oval pit, F.108 (1.85 × 3.25 m; 0.75 m deep), whose complex fill sequence was half-sectioned. Although this feature produced only one flint — a flake with a worn edge, characteristic of Neolithic discoidal-core flake production — both cattle bones and hazelnuts were also recovered from it.

Six other pits at the site yielded Neolithic flint whilst containing no later material (F.11, F.39, F.221, F.237, F.292 & F.339). These varied from 0.4 m to 1.5 m across and 0.12–0.45 m deep, and all generated between one and four pieces of flint working by-products or discarded waste displaying Neolithic flake-production/core-reduction techniques. A core rejuvenation flake, a characteristic waste-product prevalent during the earlier Neolithic, was found in F.11 together with animal bone. The type of multiple-platform core recovered from F.339 was also common in that period, and the pieces from the remaining pits are broadly compatible with the period's flintworking; however, as only a few pieces were recovered from each feature, they could have been residual.

Later Neolithic/Earlier Bronze Age

It is at this point in the sequence that the paucity of dating evidence from the site's many pits — and the potential residuality of material within them — first becomes a serious interpretive issue. Apart from a few specific instances, the assignment of these features is essentially based on the fact that they were truncated by the Middle Bronze Age droveway system. As discussed below, given the frequent recutting and even extension of its boundaries, this does not though rule out the possibility that some of these pits were of somewhat later date.

Five pits were cut by the northern droveway ditch. So truncated, their original dimensions were not

FIGURE 3.8. *Pit F.222 with 'mass' of decayed wood in base.*

available and none of them yielded any finds (F.198, F.199, F.232, F.238 and F.314). Similarly, eleven pits were truncated by the line of the southern droveway (F.22, F.31, F.47, F.135, F.142, F.144, F.145, F.315–17, F.320–22 & F.329). Of those for which measurements were available, they were 0.15–0.65 m deep and 0.40–1.35 m across. No finds were recovered from two of the pits (F.22 & F.142), five just contained animal bone (F.31, F.47, F.135, F.145 & F.316), and the others flint. The flint was of generic Neolithic attribution or otherwise non-diagnostic (F.135 also produced burnt stones).

For diverse reasons, three of the larger pit features attributable to this horizon warrant specific notice. The first is F.222. Measuring 4 × 3.2 m and 0.9 m deep, its fills yielded the remains of aurochs and wild boar (see Seetah below) as well as 22 flints. The latter comprised flintworking waste and products from Neolithic flake-production/core-reduction and tool manufacturing, and included a later Neolithic oblique arrowhead as well as a flake from a Langdale stone axe. Burnt stone was a component of this feature's fills and there was a mass of very decayed and unidentifiable timber in its base (Fig. 3.8). Among plant remains recovered were brambles, elder and dogwood, evidence for nearby scrub or open woodland. This feature is assigned to the later Neolithic based on a radiocarbon date achieved from the aurochs bone: 2880–2610 cal. BC (OxA-X-2182-55; 4150±37 BP). Given this, and the occurrence of both the aurochs and wild boar, it is likely that the pit was of Grooved Ware attribution (despite the complete absence of any pottery within it). The 'wild' often features in deposits of the later Neolithic and, for example, an adult aurochs skull was found, with a complete vessel of Grooved Ware-type, at the nearby TK Packaging Plant site (Rackham 1999); the

FIGURE 3.9. *Pit F.302 with wood in base (right, detail).*

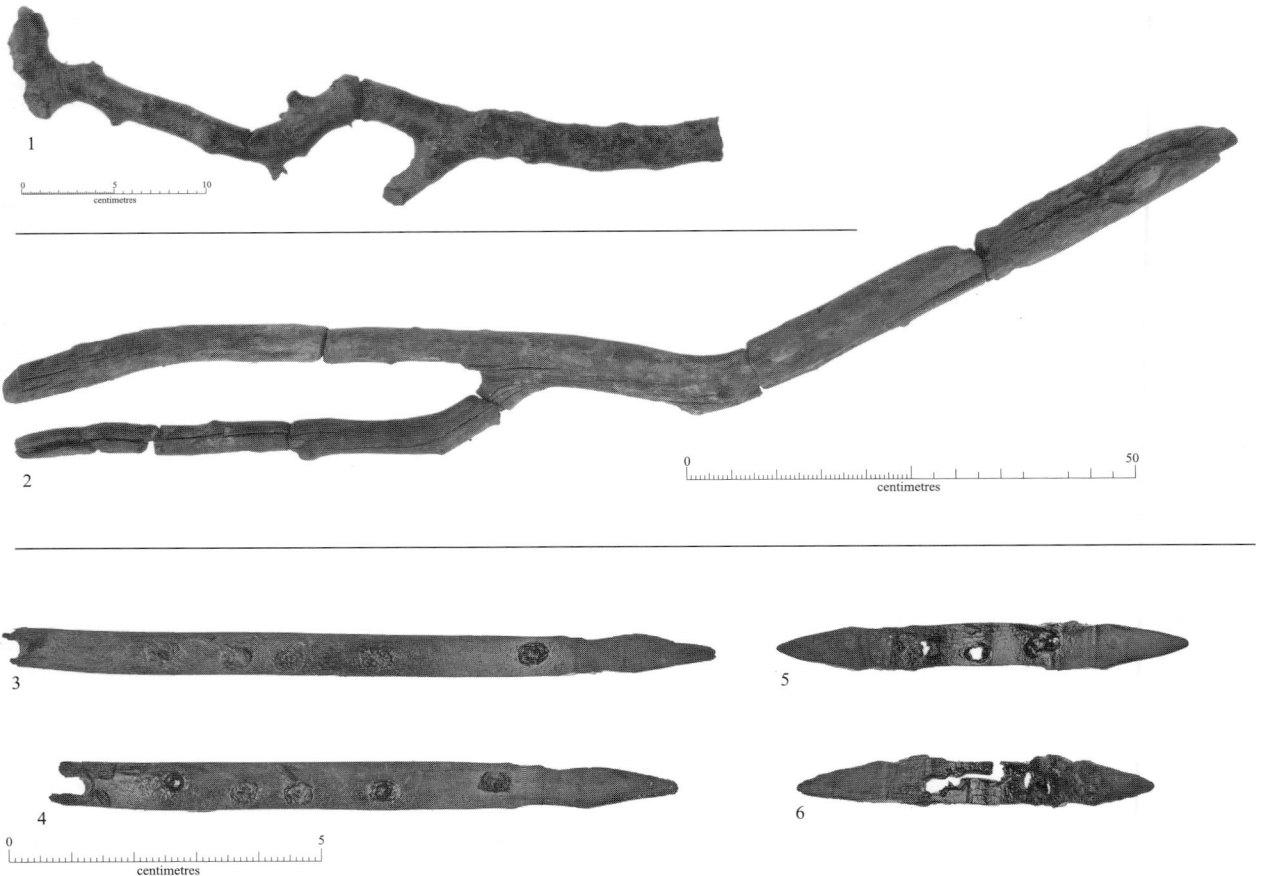

FIGURE 3.10. *The F.302 wood assemblage: 1) hedge-wood piece; 2) 'coppicers' fork; 3-6) the yew-wood straps.*

implications of this finding will be further considered in this chapter's *Concluding Discussion*.

The second feature warranting further attention, F.325, was the largest 'pit' on site and was located within the centre of the ensuing fieldsystem droveway.

Measuring 6.95 m by 6 m in extent and 1.1 m deep, with four fills (including a basal silty clay with organic material), its size and fill-sequence suggested that it may have served as a pond/watering-hole. This interpretation was supported by the recovery of the remains of water-plantain, more commonly found in ponds than wet mud deposits, from its bulk environmental samples (see de Vareilles below). Its pollen evidence, however, seems more compatible with a seasonal wet environment, and evinced pasture, meadow and arable, as well as wet and dry woodland (see Boreham below). Intriguingly, the pollen evidence included lime, whose presence would be more in keeping with a pre-Middle Bronze Age landscape and, indeed, this was confirmed by its radiocarbon date of 1740–1520 cal. BC (Beta-230850). Aside from a few pieces of wood and a probable Neolithic flake, the half-section excavation of this feature yielded more than 100 animal bones (cattle, sheep/goat and dog).

Due to its interpretative ramifications, the large pit, F.302 (2.85 × 3.6 m; 1.1 m deep), located on the northern embayment-side in Area C, is perhaps the most significant feature on the site. This is essentially due to the quality of its waterlogged preservation (Fig. 3.9), and the implications of its resultant wood assemblage in the light of its dating. Its wood, in addition to a felled tree and much coppiced roundwood, included stakes, a modified fork and also definite hedging pieces (largely of Blackthorn; Fig. 3.10; Taylor below). Otherwise yielding only two animal bones and undiagnostic flints, the feature's most extraordinary findings were four very delicate and finely carved wooden straps (Figs. 3.10 & 3.11) and these are here detailed by Grahame Appleby and Maisie Taylor:

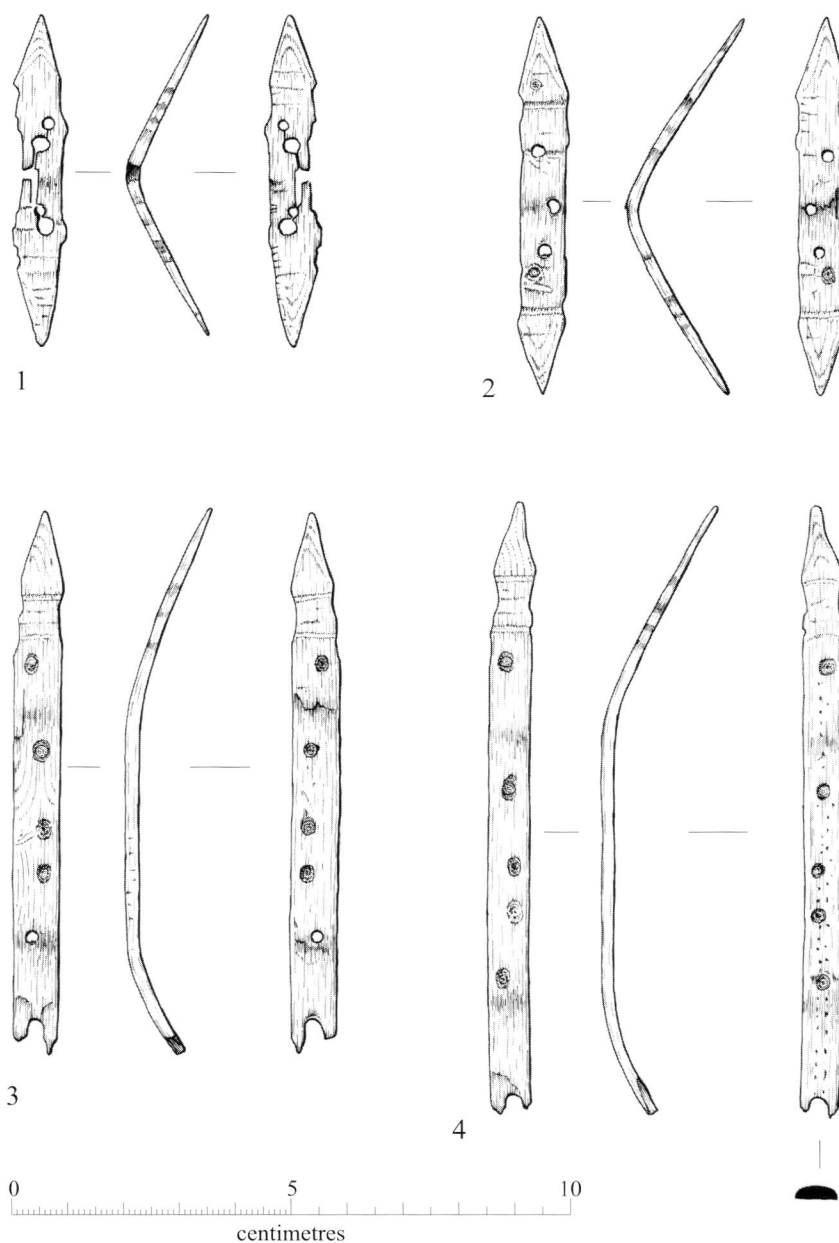

FIGURE 3.11. *Pit F.302 wood straps.*

Although the two pairs of wooden straps are different in terms of their profiles, all four constitute a distinct and coherent class of object, displaying the same manufacturing/cutting and shaping techniques and mode of fitting/attachment using small wooden pegs. All have two to three growth-rings; where it is possible to see the grain of the pegs they appear to be pared-down roundwood with pith evident, but no bark. The straps themselves are finely made and there are signs of light 'paring' on the back.

The striking, 'set-like' similarities of the straps and the recovery of all four from the same feature argue for these, as yet unique, objects having been fashioned by the same individual.

<036> i & ii (Fig. 3.11:1 & 2) – Two small, almost identical (matched pair?), narrow strips of wood, tapering symmetrically at each end to a point and angled through approximately 240° at the mid-point to form a 'winged-bracket-like' form. The larger strap (i; Fig. 3.11:2) measures 64 mm in length (between points; total length *c.* 74 mm), 7 mm wide and 2 mm thick and weighs 1 g. Three perforations, approximately 3 mm in diameter, are situated in the middle half of the strap, with the central perforation off-set from the centre-line and through the apex of the angle. The strap also possesses a further possible perforation (3 mm dia.) 22 mm from one end with an *in situ* peg. The internal

surface has two very slight transverse grooves/impressions at each end, measuring approximately 1 mm in width, just below the point where the straps begin to taper; the lateral (side) surfaces display slight indentation at these points. These impressions may be indicative of some form of fixing/binding. The smaller, very delicate strap (ii; Fig. 3.11:1) measures 58 mm in length (between points; total length *c.* 65 mm), 7 mm wide and 2 mm thick and weighs less than 1 g. There are two perforations present on the middle section of each 'wing'. They are of differing size (between 2–3 mm) and off-set either side of the centre-line. Two perforations on one wing are slightly damaged. A partially surviving fifth perforation is present on the angle of the strap. Similar lateral indentations as seen on strap i) are present and at least one impression/stain is visible on the internal surface.

<036> iii & iv (Fig. 3.11:3 & 4) – Longer than i) and ii), but of similar width and also cut along the wood-grain, these form a second matching pair of objects. Each strap has been angled through about 20° approximately 40 mm from each end, with a flat section between 45 mm (iv) and 50 mm (iii) in length, creating a 'boat'-shaped profile with up-turned prows. Both straps possess one surviving tapering end and point approximately 15 mm above the angle, the other end having broken off. The longer strap (iii; Fig. 3.11:4) is slightly narrower than the other and finished to a higher standard, possessing bevelled lateral surfaces to the external flat edge. Measuring 110 mm, its estimated total length between points is 140 mm. The strap's planar internal surface width measures 7mm, similar to i) and ii); it is 2 mm thick, and weighs 2 g. The strap possesses five surviving perforations (measuring 2–3 mm in diameter), with *in situ* pegs; four are located in the central flat section with one just above the angle. Approximately 50 per cent of a sixth perforation is present on the broken end. Two parallel lines of slight impressions are present on the external planar surface, and possibly decorative in character. A similar groove/impression to that seen on i) and ii) is present on the surviving end, although with a more pronounced flattening of the lateral surfaces. Almost identical to iii), the shorter strap (iv; Fig. 3.11:3) measures 100 mm in length (estimated complete length 120 mm), *c.* 7.5 mm in width and is 3 mm thick. Weighing 2 g, the external planar surface is flat, with sharp-angled corners and no decoration. Strap iv) also possesses five perforations in similar locations to iii), although with only four surviving rivets, as well as two bands or strips 3 mm wide, separated by 3 mm, on the external, lateral and internal surfaces, below the point where the strap tapers. There are clear indentations on the lateral surfaces.

Species identification (ROWENA GALE)

Although the waterlogged wood was fairly firm, the narrow dimensions of the straps made them very fragile and difficult to handle. The samples were prepared using standard methods (Gale & Cutler 2000), but, owing to the fine preservation of the worked surfaces, it was not possible to obtain transverse sections and thin slithers of wood were removed from the radial and longitudinal surfaces only. The anatomical structures were examined using transmitted light on a Nikon Labophot-2 compound microscope at magnifications up to ×400 and matched to prepared reference slides of modern wood.

During their construction all the straps had been cut and worked with the wood grain in the same orientation, with the sides presenting radial surfaces and the upper and lower planes presenting tangential surfaces. Although it was only possible to examine the longitudinal surfaces, the combination of diagnostic features recorded only occur in yew (*Taxus* sp.).

Originally thought to be some manner of organic box/container fittings on the grounds that, due to its non-survival, the object(s) that the straps were attached to must have been made from an even more fragile material (?leather), the critical factor informing their interpretation has proven to be this feature's date. Considered initially to probably be of later Bronze/earlier Iron Age attribution, it is now known to date to *c.* 2000 cal. BC (Beta-230848 & 230849), in other words the earliest Bronze Age. Moreover, the subsequent identification of these pieces as yew species (see Gale above) raises the possibility that they were actually manufactured from bow shavings and this, in turn, could suggest an archery connection. Being without parallel, it would be reasonable to imagine them as bindings on a bark quiver. If so, with their waisted and pointed terminals, their form may have been evocative of bows themselves (see Gdaniec 1996a concerning the miniature Early Bronze Age bone bow from Isleham).

Although the pollen from F.302 was highly oxidized (see Boreham below), what remains there were suggests that it was a small 'sedge-filled pond' and, whilst hazel scrub may have grown nearby, the landscape was essentially open and treeless. Obviously widely cleared, the evidence of open landscape complements the evidence of hedging from the wood assemblage, this being the earliest direct evidence of hedging in Britain, if not Europe.

An undated inhumation, F.73, was excavated to the north of the northern droveway ditch at the western end of the site (Figs. 3.6 & 3.12); lacking accompanying finds, unfortunately the attempt to radiocarbon date it failed. Whilst possibly of later, Bronze Age date (it lay 22 m in front of the doorway of Structure 1; see below), based on precedent, a pre-fieldsystem attribution is equally likely. The adult male was placed in a tightly flexed position within a grave pit (1.44 × 0.95 m; 0.4 m deep); his head, positioned in the west of the pit, faced southwards. He lay on his back with both of his arms flexed; his left hand was holding his right elbow and his right hand was near his right shoulder. Natasha Dodwell reports of the body in detail below:

Some post-depositional movement/disturbance of small skeletal elements of F.73 body (Skeleton [230]) had occurred in the ground: metacarpals, carpals and hand phalanges were recovered from soil inside the skull, below the left femur and in the ribcage. The skeleton is well-preserved, although all of the bones are heavily concreted with deposits of iron pan, which may mask pathological changes, and several have suffered post-mortem breaks. The skull, ribs and upper vertebrae are particularly fragmentary. Both pubic symphyses are damaged. Most of the tooth crowns, whilst present, had separated from the roots.

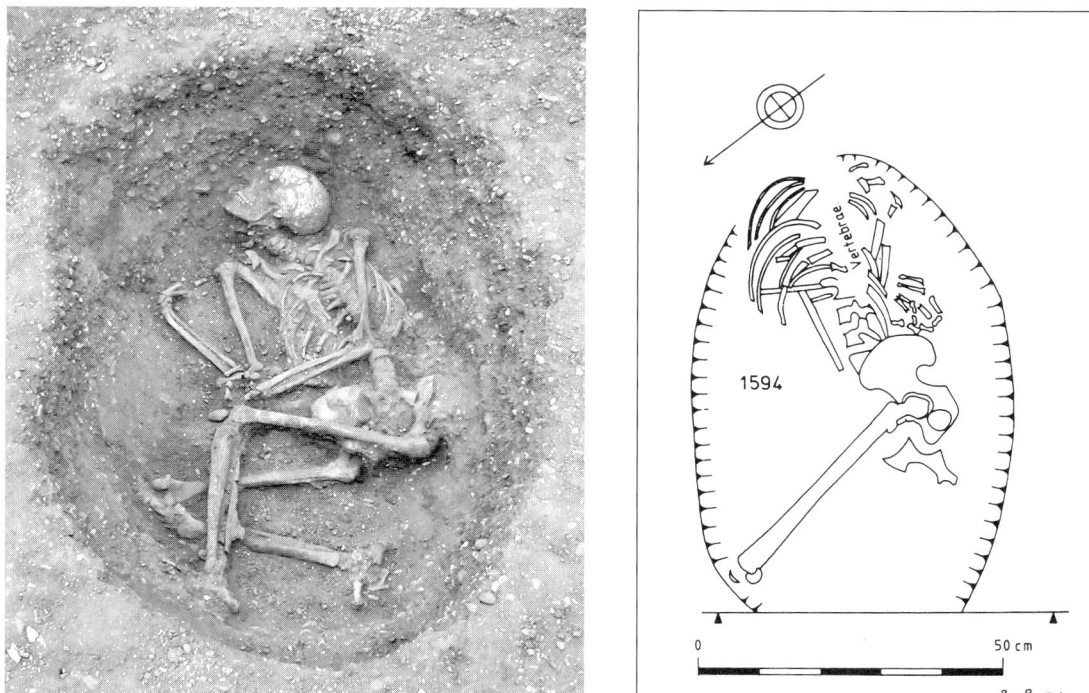

FIGURE 3.12. *Graves F.73 (left) and Pryor's F.1594 (after 1980a, fig. 97).*

An assessment of age was based on the degree of epiphyseal union, on dental eruption and attrition (Ubelaker 1989; Brothwell 1981), and on changes to the auricular surfaces (Lovejoy *et al.* 1985). The sex was ascertained from sexually dimorphic traits on the pelvis and the skull and from metrical data. An estimate of stature using the regression equations devised by Trotter & Gleser (1958) was made based on the femur length.

The body was that of an adult male, aged between 25 and 35 years and *c.* 1.66 m tall. Raised areas of new bone, characteristic of a non-specific infection, were recorded on the distal ends of both tibiae (at the fibula notch) and on the mid shaft of the left fibula. An increase of porosity at both sterno-clavicular joints was recorded, which is characteristic of incipient joint disease. The following dentition was recorded:

8	7	6	5	4	3	2	1	1	2	3	4	5	6	7	8
8	7	6	5	4	3	2	1	1	2	3	4	5	6	7	8

Slight deposits of calculus were recorded on most of the dentition, with moderate deposits on the lingual and buccal aspects of the molars.

An adult human right femur shaft was also recovered from the western end of the southern droveway ditch nearby (F.3, [046]) at the point where it had cut through and truncated pit F.22 (Fig. 3.6). Potentially, that oval feature could have been the deepest surviving trace of an inhumation comparable to F.73; the rest of the body would have been removed/dispersed when the ditch was dug.

These interments obviously resonate with the F.1594 semi-crouched inhumation of an adolescent female that Pryor recovered at the junction of his Ditches 2 and F.862 during the course of his Cat's Water trenching, which was thought to have been interred whilst Ditch F.862 was still open (Figs. 3.6 & 3.12; Pryor 1980a, 163, 168, 234, fig. 97). The implications of the many burials within this immediate area will be further discussed below.

Middle/Later Bronze Age

With only three discrete features yielding Middle Bronze Age finds, based on the paucity of dating evidence (and artefact residuality), it would be possible to outline the site's sequence as if almost no activity occurred in conjunction with the droveway/fieldsystem itself. At one end of the dating range, many of its large pit features (variously wells, quarries and hollows) could, at least in theory, be assigned to the later Neolithic/earlier Bronze Age. Equally, based on the fact that several of the 'bone-packed' pits had upper peat fills (and that the peat clearly post-dated the infilling of the system's ditches), by extrapolation the vast majority of its settlement-/activity-related features could be assigned to the later Bronze Age. Obviously a matter of much ambiguity, no hard or fast designations are possible and it is in order to convey a sense of an appropriate 'spectrum' that the Elliott Site's Middle/later Bronze Age activity is considered together. Crucial to interpretation is, of course, whether even if the fieldsystem's ditches were no longer actively maintained by the first centuries of the first millennium BC, their associated banks (probably hedge-capped) would still have structured the landscape.

Additionally, it warrants mention that, whilst relatively sparse, both the site's density and basic 'grammar' of settlement features — post-built roundhouses and four-posters (essentially without finds) — are fully in keeping with what has been found elsewhere at Fengate and what is now known to generally constitute the period's settlement evidence.

Fieldsystem ditches

When viewing the layout of the Elliott site's Bronze Age ditches, one is immediately struck by their 'ropey' character (Fig. 3.13). They had clearly been recut a number of times, both parallel to their main 'lines' and 'segmentally', or partially, along their lengths. Superficially, this seems to contrast with the established straight ditch-line 'image' of the Fengate system. Before progressing, however, it is best that this illusion is dispelled. Much of the apparent regularity of Fengate's fieldsystem relates to the illustration techniques by which its 'landscape-scale' maps were produced. Occurring prior to computerization, on these synthetic-plan versions the ditch-lines had to be hand-reduced and redrawn in straight, heavily inked lines (the legacy of the Rotring pen). Yet, looking at the detailed 'as excavated' plans of the fieldsystem dug at both the Padholme and Newark Road sub-Sites (e.g. Pryor 1980a, figs. 7 & 31), the ropily recut quality of Fengate's ditches throughout — as common to Bronze Age fieldsystems generally — can be quickly appreciated.

The overall arrangement of the Elliot Site's (enlarged) Ditch 1/2 droveway was extraordinary. Not only is it unparalleled elsewhere within the larger Fengate system, but there is no parallel with any known Bronze Age fieldsystem in southern England (Yates 2007). On entering the excavations at the western end, its ditches lay some 6.8 m apart; over the next 55 m the interval widened regularly (to *c.* 18 m), its ditches running straight in a funnel-like fashion. East of this point, the interval broadened to a maximum width of 25 m, with the ditch-lines kinking and curving northeastward. The reason for this change in alignment was the conjunction of the droveway proper with a rectangular paddock that extended across the eastern half of Area A/B and continued throughout Area C (at least for the enclosure's north ditch; just at the eastern site limits the south boundary began to turn southwards). Thereafter, extending for more than 185 m in length, its ditches were straight and *c.* 43.5–50 m apart. Clearly opening out towards

the fen, distinct corners were present in its eastern landward end (the entrance gap between the ditches there being *c.* 25 m, though on the southern side the observation of any ditch arm was confused by intense pitting). In fact, the layout of this great 'rectangle' is reminiscent of cursus monuments; however, given its layout, this must have been a major stock compound that was directly reached by the funnelling of the Ditch 1/2 drove. By the spatial arrangement of its ditches, this compound must have originally existed as a separate enclosure and may well have co-existed with the straight, western upslope portion of the drove: the ditches of the latter were only subsequently lengthened — variously by kinking and curving — to join with the landward end of the compound.

The variation incurred by the frequent recutting of the droveway/compound's boundaries is indicated in Table 3.2 and Figure 3.14. Although the ditches could locally be narrower than 1 m and broaden to *c.* 2.5–3.5 m, generally they were *c.* 1.5 m wide and 0.2–1.1 m deep (0.4–0.65 m ave. depth). Their fills variously consisted of grey and grey/brown sandy silt loam and clay silts with differing quantities of gravel inclusions. Essentially buried soil-derived, at only a single point along the eastern length of the southern compound ditch (F.102) had a skim of peat just subsided into its upper profile. Importantly, a sherd of Early Iron Age pottery was recovered from this horizon, thus dating the marsh-inundation of this area (below *c.* 2 m OD) to the first half of the first millennium BC. It should be stressed that peat did not otherwise enter the ditches' profiles, even within the lowest, eastern area of the site.

The more minor, original line of the northern ditch length, linking the droveway and the eastern compound, lay immediately parallel to and beside the main boundary (Fig. 3.13). In the west (F.168/F.159), this was only 0.55–0.65 m wide and 0.2–0.35 m deep. Continuing over some 20 m, it ended with an inturned terminal. After a *c.* 5 m access gap it then continued as F.193/F.196 (0.75 m wide; 0.2–0.55 m deep), whose curving length met with the ditch arm of the northeast corner of the compound.

Although 'pocketed' metalled spreads occurred locally across the upper landward end of the stock enclosure's interior, a formal ditch-side upcast bank (F.245) was only observed at one point: south of/exterior to the southern compound ditch at the bottom drain-side end of Area A/B (Fig. 3.4). This was approximately 4 m wide and stood 0.35 m high, with buried soil and clay silts capped by a 0.05–0.15 m layer of upcast terrace gravels.

Within the area of excavation, only one additional ditch-line directly related to the main fieldsystem. This

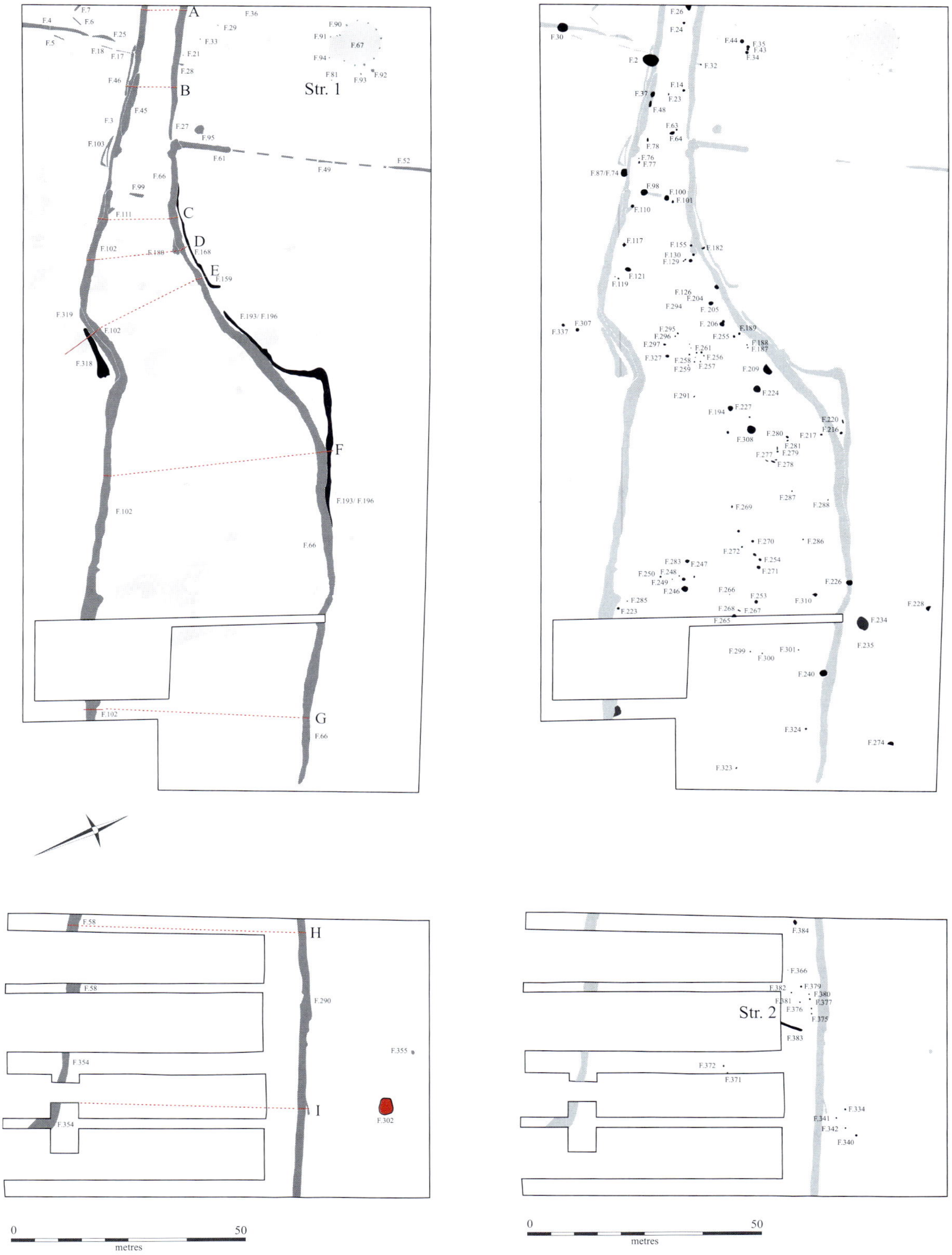

Str. 1

Str. 2

A
B
C
D
E
F
G
H
I

F.4 F.7 F.6 F.36 F.29 F.90 F.91 F.94 F.67 F.81 F.93 F.92
F.5 F.25 F.33 F.21 F.28 F.46 F.45 F.3 F.103 F.27 F.95 F.61 F.66 F.99 F.111 F.102 F.188 F.168 F.159 F.193/ F.196 F.319 F.102 F.318 F.193/ F.196 F.102 F.66 F.102 F.66
F.18 F.17 F.52 F.49

F.30 F.26 F.24 F.44 F.35 F.43 F.2 F.32 F.34 F.14 F.37 F.23 F.48 F.61 F.64 F.78 F.76 F.77 F.87/F.74 F.98 F.100 F.101 F.110 F.117 F.155 F.182 F.130 F.129 F.121 F.119 F.126 F.204 F.294 F.205 F.295 F.189 F.337 F.307 F.296 F.255 F.188 F.297 F.261 F.187 F.327 F.258 F.256 F.259 F.257 F.209 F.291 F.224 F.194 F.227 F.220 F.308 F.280 F.217 F.216 F.281 F.277 F.279 F.278 F.287 F.288 F.269 F.270 F.286 F.272 F.254 F.283 F.247 F.250 F.248 F.271 F.249 F.266 F.226 F.246 F.253 F.310 F.228 F.285 F.268 F.267 F.223 F.265 F.234 F.299 F.301 F.235 F.300 F.240 F.324 F.274 F.323

F.58 F.384
F.58 F.366
F.290 F.382 F.379
F.354 F.381 F.380 F.377
F.355 F.376 F.375
F.354 F.383
F.302 F.372 F.371
F.341 F.334
F.342 F.340

0 ————— 50
metres

0 ————— 50
metres

□ Earlier Features
▨ Middle Bronze Age Main System
■ Middle Bronze Age Primary System
...... Ditch-section Transect

▨ Middle Bronze Age Features
■ Late Bronze Age Activity

FIGURE 3.13. *Middle/Late Bronze feature base-plans (note location of Early Bronze Age pit F.302).*

TABLE 3.2. *Droveway/compound ditch characteristics (* = truncated).*

Section-transect	Southern Ditch feature	Width (m)		Depth (m)	Droveway Interval/ spacing	Northern Ditch feature	Width (m)		Depth (m)
		Feature	Total				Feature	Total	
A	F.3	1.58		0.70	6.80	F.27	2.00		0.46
B	F.46	1.00		0.43	6.90	F.27	1.62		0.6
	F.3*	1.00	2.88	0.55					
	F.47	1.72		0.76					
C	F.74*	1.25		0.47	12.7	F.66	1.56		0.34
D	F.102	1.64		0.49	18.10	F.66*	2.00		0.53
E	F.102	1.87		0.52	22.90	F.66	2.00	2.6	0.49
						F.159	0.65		0.20
F	F.102 (F.191)	1.86		0.57	43.8	F.66 (F.197)	2.30	3.4	0.88
						F.193*	1.17		0.57
G	F.102 (F.191)*	1.80		0.59	43.5	F.236	1.70		0.34
H	F.58	2.50		0.65	46.9	F.353	1.65		0.50
I	F.354	2.00*		0.55	50.7	F.290	2.50		0.67

was F.4/F.25, which ran southwest from droveway Ditch 1 of the drove across the western corner of the site (Fig. 3.13). Having an 'interruption' between its two segments (and, in fact, stopping shy of Ditch 1 itself), this was *c.* 0.55–0.8 m wide and 0.12–0.38 m deep. Just south of and roughly parallel with its line (leaving a *c.* 1.4 m gap between), was a slighter and equally interrupted ditch (F.5/F.17/F.18), only 0.25–0.3 m across and *c.* 0.1 m deep. While this may have marked a precursor of the F.4/F.25 boundary (and perhaps related to the minor, more 'trough-like' versions of Ditch 1 as discussed above), these boundaries may alternatively have together delineated a low bank, which could itself have been hedge-capped. Be this as it may, in all likelihood this ditch-line related to the paddock outlined by Pryor's second-millennium BC ditch (N1) at the Storey's Bar Road sub-Site (Area I; Pryor 1984, 15, figs. 9 & 10).

In addition to the adult human right femur recovered from the southern droveway ditch (F.3, [046]), an adult human femur shaft (left-side) was also found in the F.196 ([808]) droveway boundary (Fig. 3.6).

In order to appreciate the scale of the stock compound enclosure at the Elliott Site, we need to refer in greater detail to the Birmingham Unit's evaluation fieldwork across the eastern portion of their (larger) site area. As shown in Figure 3.2, their Trench 9 was located immediately northeast of our Area C. At its western end was excavated a 1.7 m-wide ditch (BF.204), which was probably a northward return-line of our compound ditch on that side. Generally, the ground surface there lay at *c.* 1.5 m OD. Midway along their 50 m-long trench there was a distinct slope

where, over a distance of 7 m, the terrace dropped to *c.* 1 m OD. At this edge — the fen-edge *per se* — they dug a ditch terminal (BF.203). Although this had waterlogged fills, no finds were recovered (nor were any forthcoming from this trench as a whole).

Beyond the Trench 9 'edge-slope' and to the east, the Birmingham Unit recorded a palaeochannel; unfortunately this was not excavated as such. Similar palaeochannel deposits were also observed within their Trench 8, which just overlapped into our trenched swathe at the southeastern corner of Area C. Although they recorded no features within this trench, sherds of 'plain wall' pottery, thought to be of later Neolithic/ earlier Bronze Age attribution, were recovered during machining. Water-lain horizons were also found to overlie the terrace gravels at *c.* 0.8 m OD in Trench 5, located within the extreme southeastern end of their evaluation area. No such deposits were encountered in their Trench 6, further north (again, close by the Cat's Water stream proper), with the gravels also at *c.* 0.8–0.9 m OD and overlain by a *c.* 0.3 m-deep buried soil. No features were present therein (nor any finds recovered).

Though the southward return of our compound ditch on the southeastern side did not extend into Birmingham's Trench 7 (by projection it ran further east, their trench falling some 100 m south of Area C), a major northeast- to southwest-oriented ditch, BF.205 (*c.* 2.4 m across and 0.9 m deep, with a 'V'-shaped profile), crossed their trench. Evidently associated, a *c.* 2.5 m-wide upcast bank was reported on its northeastern side. Though no dating evidence was recovered from either, in all probability this was part

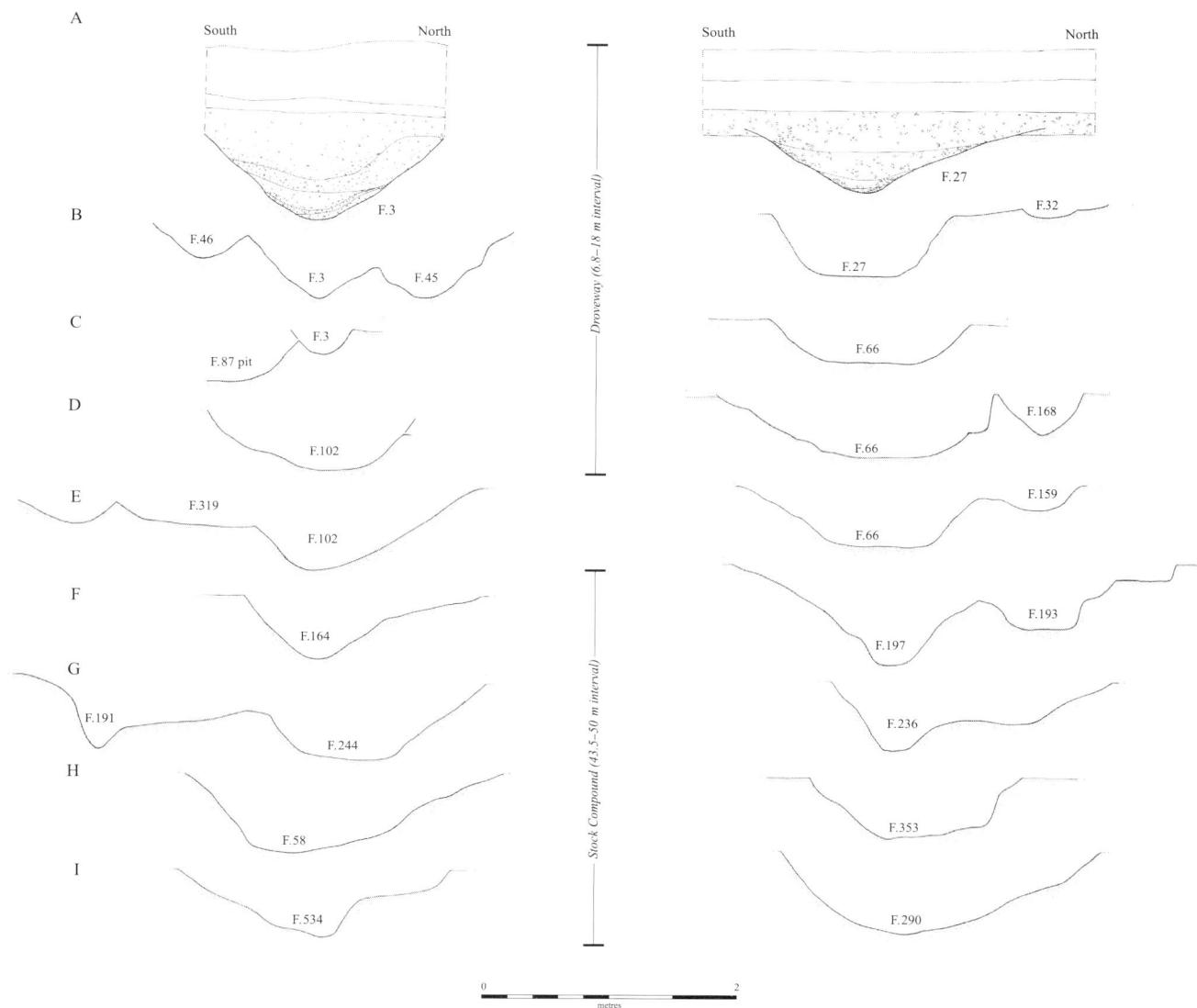

FIGURE 3.14. *Bronze Age droveway/compound ditch sections.*

of the second-millennium BC fieldsystem. In fact, if projected, BF.205 would directly correlate with the B2 boundary at Storey's Bar Road (Pryor 1978, fig. 14).

Pitting, settlement and structures

Immediately beside the Elliott Site's western, upslope, side was the post-circle of a major roundhouse (F.67; Structure 1; Figs. 3.13 & 3.15:A). The roundhouse itself was some 10 m in diameter; its 0.28–0.47 m-wide and 0.13–0.26 m-deep postholes were set at intervals of approximately 2 m. The gap between them was broader on the southwestern side and there two postholes lay some 1.6–2.5 m forward of its ring (F.90 & F.94), obviously marking the structure's entrance porch.

No interior features accompanied this building and, aside from one residual flint, no finds were recovered from its postholes. Similarly, a small pit, F.91, lying just northwest of its ring, yielded no artefacts (nor did two other postholes nearby, F.92 & F.93). In front of Structure 1's entrance lay a cluster of four small pits (F.34, F.35, F.43 & F.44) measuring 0.6–1 × 0.6–0.9 m across and 0.18–0.28 m deep. Two produced burnt stones; otherwise the only artefacts from them were undiagnostic worked flints.

Though, from its size, Structure 1 would seem to relate to a major 'residential building', the paucity of finds associated with it makes any functional interpretation purely speculative. Earlier, such 'sterile' roundhouses at Fengate were deemed 'barns' and

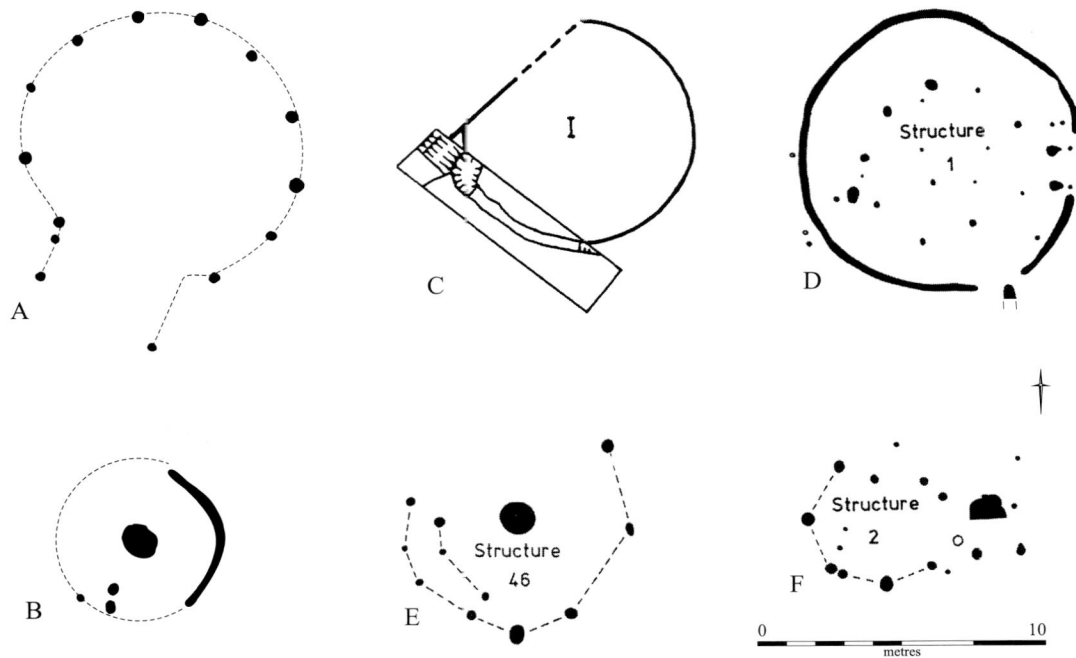

FIGURE 3.15. *Fengate roundhouses: A & B) Elliot Site Structures 1 and 2: C) Depot Site, Structure I; D) Newark Road, Structure 1; E) Cat's Water, Structure 46; F) Newark Road, Structure 2.*

not considered houses as such; however, based upon a much greater familiarity with the character of later Bronze Age settlement, this interpretation requires revision and, accordingly, will be further discussed below. In this regard, it is relevant to note that (as shown on Figure 3.19) the only two of the site's bulk environmental samples which yielded cereal remains occurred within the western quarter of the site (one, though, being from pit F.2 that cut the droveway; see below).

Although many of the site's posthole groupings are suggestive of structural patterns, only three can considered definite (or, at least, near-definite). That of which there is the greatest confidence is a four-poster configuration, Structure 2 (Fig. 3.13). With its postholes defining a 2 × 2.3–4 m 'square' (F.379–82), its situation seems somewhat incongruous. It is located 'low', between 1.3–1.4 m OD, on the side of the embayment and just inside the northern stock compound boundary in Area C. This being said, other postholes clustered within its immediate vicinity and a nearby, 'trough-like' length of ditch, F.363, might also have been building-related. Together with the other (unattributed) posthole 'lines' in this area of the site, this could suggest that this was a distinct area of settlement. Lying so low in the site's extreme northeastern quarter, it would have to have been of pre-Iron Age date.

Another possible four-post setting (Structure 3; 2–2.4 × 2.2–3 m) also lay along the site's northern side (Fig. 3.18), but this time mid-way along Area A/B at a height just above 2.6 m OD (F.169, F.171, F.174 & F.176). There is, however, greater ambiguity to its assignation as its northwesternmost posthole splays out somewhat from a 'true square'-pattern and, given its height/location, it could have been of Iron Age date.

While not sufficiently convincing to warrant formal enumeration as such, the final setting that warrants attention is a tight, quasi-circular/ovoid seven-posthole group that was located immediately north of the large pit/pond F.325 and cut into its fills. This was part of the southern stock compound terminal and lay at the end of the embayment (Fig. 3.13). Measuring 0.23–0.42 m across and 0.1–0.3 m deep, these features were peat-filled (F.215, F.257 & F.260–62). Though producing few finds, F.253 (which was more 'pit-like') yielded both animal bone and almost half of a Late Bronze pot (see Knight & Brudenell below). It is difficult to know what to make of this setting. Its 'ring' seemed too small to define any manner of roundhouse *per se*; perhaps, it related to some sort of shed or alternatively to an 'open' tripod-like arrangement.

Based essentially on the occurrence of peat within their fills, some 50 pits can be broadly assigned to the later Bronze Age (Fig. 3.13). Of these,

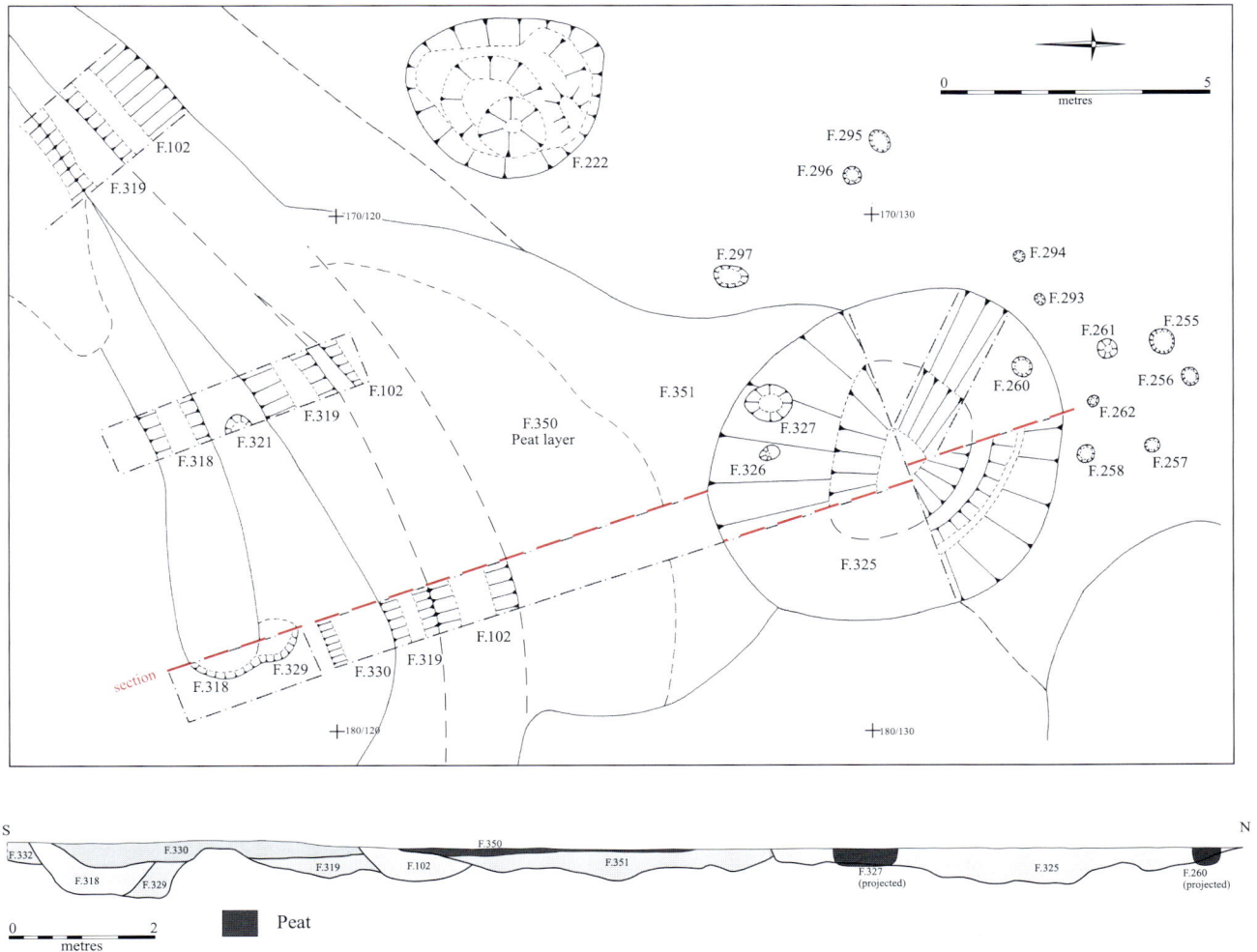

FIGURE 3.16. *Plan and section of southern droveway/compound system junction.*

nine truncated the droveway/compound system ditches and therefore there can be no doubt of their post-fieldsystem attribution. While many had animal bone within their fills (five having ten or more pieces), only two included pottery of the period (F.74/F.87 & F.157; F.182, containing Deverel-Rimbury Wares, was dated to 1190–1140 and 1140–920 cal. BC; Beta-230847). Though most of these features were *c.* 0.5–0.7 m across and 0.25–0.5 m deep, a number were larger (1–1.6 m across; 0.55–0.7 m deep).

Iron Age/Romano-British
With the Elliott Site directly bordering the southern margins of Pryor's Cat's Water complex, it would have been surprising if none of his major Iron Age or Romano-British linear features extended into it and, indeed, three did. This being said, no finds of the latter attribution, and only ten 'Early' and seven later Iron Age sherds, were recovered. The site-area's usage at

that time was clearly not intense and it can only be considered marginal to the main Cat's Water 'core'.

Oriented northwest–southeast (and running diagonally across the northeastern corner of Area A/B) was a rather sinuous/kinking ditch length (F.233–5; Fig. 3.18). Some 0.65–2 m wide and 0.35–0.6 m deep, this had evidently been recut a number of times. Though it yielded flint, animal bone and slag, no dating evidence as such was forthcoming from it. Nevertheless, it was clearly the continuation of a major Early Iron Age boundary that lay within the adjacent quarter of the Cat's Water sub-Site (Fig. 3.22; the attribution of that feature, being somewhat suspect, is further discussed below).

Later Iron Age pottery was recovered from the square-ended terminal of another ditch, immediately to the east, F.230 (2.1–2.8 m wide and 0.3–0.4 m deep; Fig. 3.18). While not exactly parallel with the line of the F.233 (*et al.*) boundary, it was sufficiently close

F.77

F.155

F.157

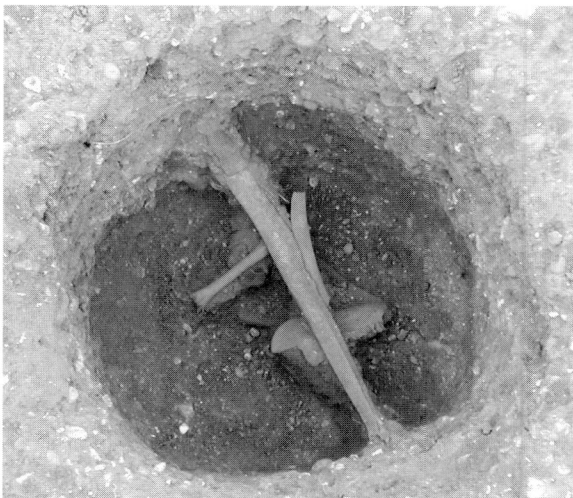

F.154

FIGURE 3.17. *'Bone-filled pits' (F.77, F.154, F.155 & F.157).*

to suggest their broad contemporaneity, with both assigned to the later Iron Age. Adjacent to the westward ditch was a small pit-hearth/-furnace, F.313, whose fills showed signs of intense firing; fragments of iron slag were recovered from it (see Timberlake below).

Aside from a sherd of Early Iron Age pottery in the upper profile of the main southern, Bronze Age, stock compound boundary, only one other feature yielded dating evidence of the period: pit F.207 (2.3 × 2.85 m; 0.9 m deep) contained a single sherd. This pit fell close to the slight remains of a roundhouse gully (F.175), that hereafter will be termed Structure 4 (Figs. 3.15:B & 3.18). Only 0.05 m deep (and 0.28

m wide), approximately a quarter of its eastern circuit survived. It is estimated to have been *c.* 5 m in diameter. Given its size and the fact that two postholes, F.186 and F.171 (though the latter might equally relate to the Structure 3 four-poster), lay in its southwestern circumference, in all likelihood this marked a small building's wall-line. No dating evidence was recovered from this structure, nor from a shallow pit in its centre, F.173, from which charcoal and burnt stones were retrieved.

As mentioned above, the register of any Romano-British activity within the Elliott Site is a matter of extrapolation and no direct dating evidence of the period has been forthcoming. Its only expression

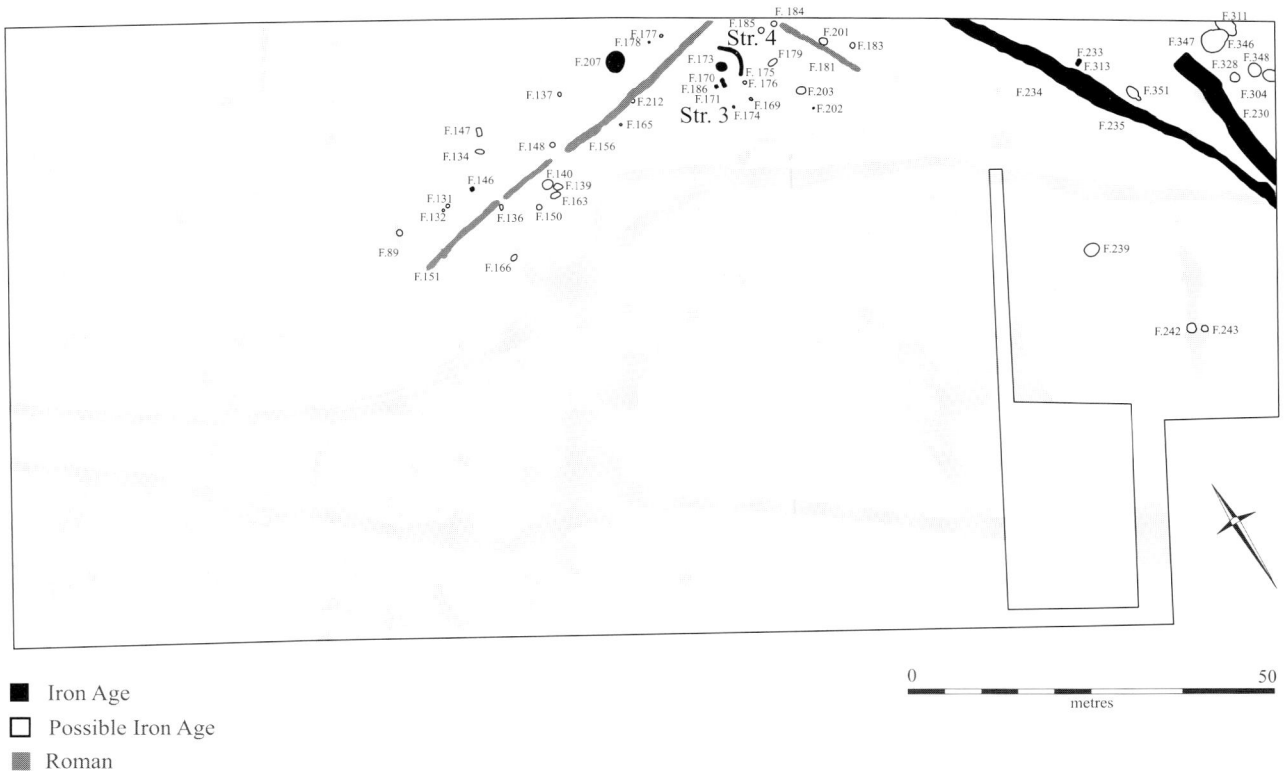

Iron Age

Possible Iron Age

Roman

FIGURE 3.18. *Iron Age and Roman feature phase-plan.*

consisted of two minor ditch-lines (0.4–0.8 m wide; 0.05–0.2 m deep), F.181 being the direct continuation of Pryor's 'off-droveway' boundary and F.151/F.156 being the interrupted southwestward return of F.18 (Figs. 3.18 & 3.22).

The above-discussed features all fell along the higher, embayment-side, ground on the north side of the site and generally lay above 1.8–2 m OD (though the southwestern end of the two Iron Age ditches descended below 1.6 m OD). Given this, it is possible that a number of the other pits within this northern swathe might well be of the same attribution and attest to Romano-British activity, but they were without any associated pottery deposition or direct dating evidence.

One intriguing possibility, given the 'reach' of the Iron Age/Romano-British linear features down into this area (and the site's low ground environmental sequence), is that the embayment might have been utilized in this period. Though then no longer ditch-delineated as such, it is conceivable that stock were driven down to this area from the Cat's Water settlement for daily watering and/or that its hollow/channel may even have served for the beaching of boats.

Distributions and depositional dynamics

Based on the quantity of the animal bone present within a substantial number of the site's pits, it has been tempting to distinguish a distinct mode of activity-specific bone/pit deposition. Indeed, in the field a series of 'bone-packed' pits were identified (Figs. 3.17 & 3.19). At least superficially, this would seem to be borne out by comparing the number of animal bones found in pit, as opposed to droveway/compound ditch, contexts: 3027 *vs.* 625; however, based on their respective excavation-ratios, this would be a false impression. Only 19 of the 49 pits producing bone were fully excavated. If the number from the remaining 28, which were only half-sectioned or otherwise sampled, are appropriately factored, then 4229 bone fragments would be expected in total from the site's pit contexts. In contrast, only some 8 per cent of the total length of the droveway/compound ditches was excavated. This would imply a total ditch population of *c.* 7800 bone fragments; in other words, and against all expectations, 46 per cent more bone fragments than were contained in the pits. Moreover, at least as indicated by average bone weight, the mean size of the bones within these two feature-categories did not vary

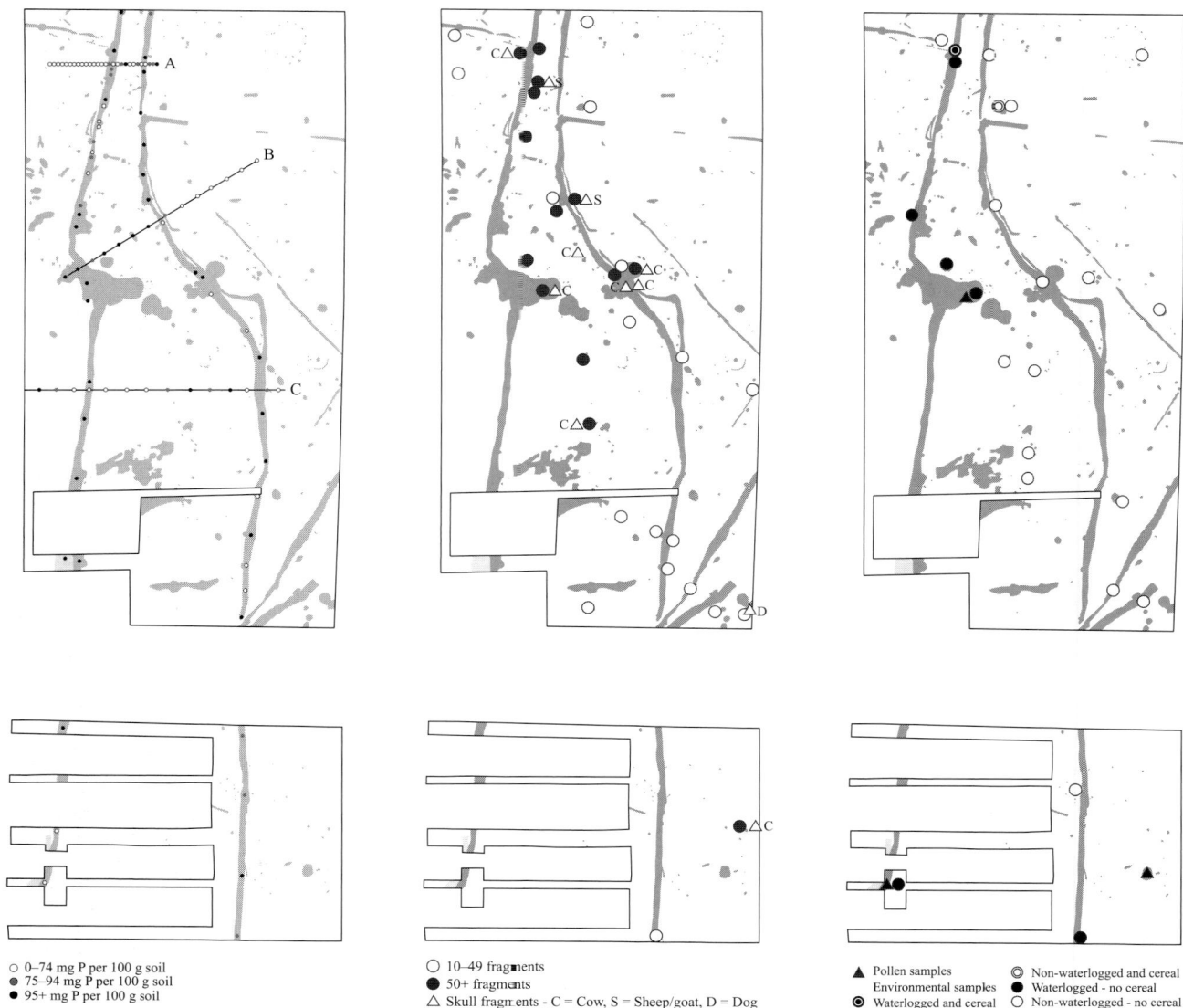

○ 0–74 mg P per 100 g soil
◐ 75–94 mg P per 100 g soil
● 95+ mg P per 100 g soil

○ 10–49 fragments
● 50+ fragments
△ Skull fragments - C = Cow, S = Sheep/goat, D = Dog

▲ Pollen samples
Environmental samples
◉ Waterlogged and cereal

◎ Non-waterlogged and cereal
● Waterlogged - no cereal
○ Non-waterlogged - no cereal

FIGURE 3.19. *Distributions: phosphate, animal bone and environmental samples.*

significantly: pits, 8.8 g and ditches, 7.45 g.

These calculations also help us gauge the scale of the bone-/animal-related activity on the site. The pits and the discussed ditch contexts would, in total, have included just over 12,000 fragments. Given this, it would seem reasonable to postulate a total site animal bone population in the range of 15,000–20,000 fragments (including other feature types and 'missing' surface deposits). Comparing this, however, to the *c.* 24,000 bones recovered from the later Iron Age household compound at Haddenham, that was occupied by a *single* extended family for a span of some 150–200 years (HAD V; Evans & Hodder 2006b), frames the scale of activity at the Elliot Site — these are certainly not terribly large numbers.

Phosphate analysis (*with* PAUL MIDDLETON)

In an attempt to further elucidate the fieldsystem's operational dynamics, and also continue a tradition of Fengate's study (Craddock 1984b), phosphate samples were obtained by two main techniques:

1) Three cross-droveway/compound transects:
A)   From the buried soil (0.5 m interval) along the main, metre-wide, artefact sampling bulk in the west of the site (on Fig. 3.19 these have been averaged and are expressed to a metre-interval);
B & C) Two further transects, located east/downslope, with samples collected every 5 m from the cleaned excavation surface.
2) Two 'chain-sets' from the primary fills of the excavated ditch segments right the way along the lengths of the northern and southern droveway/compound ditches.

In addition, a few spot samples were collected, including samples from the buried soil sealed by the bank associated with the southern compound ditch in Area C. Control samples were also taken from both the peat and the buried soil. Full details of the of the methodology employed are provided in the site's archive (see Middleton, in Beadsmoore 2006b); all phosphate levels are here expressed in terms of mg phosphorous per 100 g soil.

The control samples indicate a phosphate level of 72 mg. This is closely matched by the results from the soils sealed by the southern ditch-bank, which yielded levels averaging 76 mg. For our purposes here, we will take the average of these two figures, 74 mg, as representing the 'background'. The values from the two chain-sets of ditch samples indicate significant enhancement of phosphate above this, with the south ditch having a mean value of 108 mg; the northern, 95 mg.

Of the transect data (and using only those readings that fall between the two main ditch-lines) the samples from the easternmost (C; running across the landward head of the stock compound) had a mean value just below the background (72.5). Whilst the western, Transect A, was just above that level (77.8), Transect B — taken at the point where the droveway approached the compound proper — was very high at 142.5 mg. The latter could, potentially, have correlated with a pinch-point in the system and reflect where there might have been a 'crush' of animals funnelling into the droveway from the compound. Yet, by this reasoning, high levels should have equally been expected along Transect A and the droveway itself.

Apart from their attesting to high phosphate-related activity, as indicated on Figure 3.19, it is difficult to read the distribution of 'high swathe' values along the two ditch-lines themselves, especially their oscillation on either side of the droveway/funnel at the eastern end. The generally higher levels associated with the southern compound ditch might just reflect its more downslope location and the subsequent in-washing of phosphate/waste.

The Co-op Site and Fengate's Neolithic

Despite the fact that Fengate was, as it were, first put 'on the map' by its Neolithic pottery (see Chapter 2), relatively little archaeology of that period was forthcoming in the course of the 1970s' fieldwork. While Pryor's first sub-site at Padholme Road yielded an earlier Neolithic house, and Cat's Water later yielded a multiple burial of that date (see below), across the entire area of the Newark Road excavations only two pits of Neolithic attribution were found (with four other features producing Grooved Ware 'tradition' pottery; Pryor 1980a, 104). Otherwise, the focus of Fengate's Neolithic activity was originally held to be in the southwest: the Storey's Bar Road Grooved Ware settlement complex. Originally interpreted as being associated with that sub-site's ring-ditch/barrow and fieldsystem (Pryor 1978), its phasing dynamics were subsequently reappraised within the Flag Fen volume (Evans & Pollard 2001, 25–6). It was there postulated that, instead of being seen as contemporary components (with the later monument thought to have had a circular settlement-enclosure precursor), their interrelationship should be dismantled, with the earlier Bronze Age monument superseding the 'open' Grooved Ware settlement (and the Middle Bronze Age fieldsystem following thereafter; Fig. 3.20). Seen in this manner, with its concentration of pits and post-settings, the Grooved Ware phase becomes much more akin to other settlements of the period, such as at the Edgerley Drain Site (see Chapter 4; also Garrow 2006, Chapter 6).

What is interesting in the light of the subsequent work in the area is that, though the nearby Elliott Site obviously also saw a degree of Neolithic activity, no pottery of that period was forthcoming. Nor, as outlined above (Chapter 1), was any found in the County's Third Drove/Walters Office World investigations; only in the TK Packaging Site trenching (immediately opposite Pryor's Storey's Bar Road) was further Grooved Ware recovered (found in a pit and associated with an aurochs skull; see this chapter's *Concluding Discussion* below).

While summarily presented within the Flag Fen volume (Pryor 2001a, 47–50, figs. 3.12 & 3.13), in the light of its impor-

tance, the sub-square Neolithic post-built structure excavated by the CAU in 1997 at the Co-op Site in the east-of-Cat's Water field (Gibson 1998) deserves fuller presentation. A total of 32 postholes of varying dimensions (0.07–0.38 m deep), defined this *c.* 6.5 × 6.5 m structure (although this clearly included a degree of re-setting/-building; Fig. 3.21:A). As reported upon by Josh Pollard (1998a), the dating evidence provided by its pottery was somewhat ambiguous, as it included both earlier Neolithic plainware bowl sherds (F.1006) and Peterborough wares: a sherd in Fengate style from F.1043 and another of Mortlake type from F.1042. This admixture could be explained by recourse to residuality if it were not for the fact that the plainware sherds were in fresh condition.

The 12 pieces of worked flint from this area (six of which came from an adjacent tree-throw), included a number of blades and a blade core (Pollard 1998a); however, more typically of Late Neolithic attribution was a burnt discoidal knife on a Levallois-style flake from the buried soil (among the material from Trench 4, aside from a possible laurel leaf- and further blades/narrow flakes, was a flake from a polished axe, modified for use as a knife). The dilemma posed by this structure's assemblages is that there is simply no way that it could have stood for a sufficient length of time to span the centuries suggested by the conventional chronology of its pottery. Rather, and resonating with themes raised in relationship to Abbott's work, this raises the question of just how discrete were these pottery *types* and, particularly, whether plainware had a longer duration than it is normally accredited with.

In an effort to resolve this issue, in 1999 a sample of charred *Corylus avellana* seeds from F.1042 was submitted for radiocarbon dating. This yielded an assay of 3610–3520 and 3230–3160 cal. BC (4625±45 BP; OxA-8088) Subsequently, in anticipation of this publication, two further samples were submitted but both of these both failed.

In his *Flag Fen* summary, Pryor interpreted the Co-op Site building as a 'mortuary structure' (Pryor 2001a, 47, 406–7) and it has since entered the canon of archaeological literature under this appellation. Here, though, the record should be set straight.

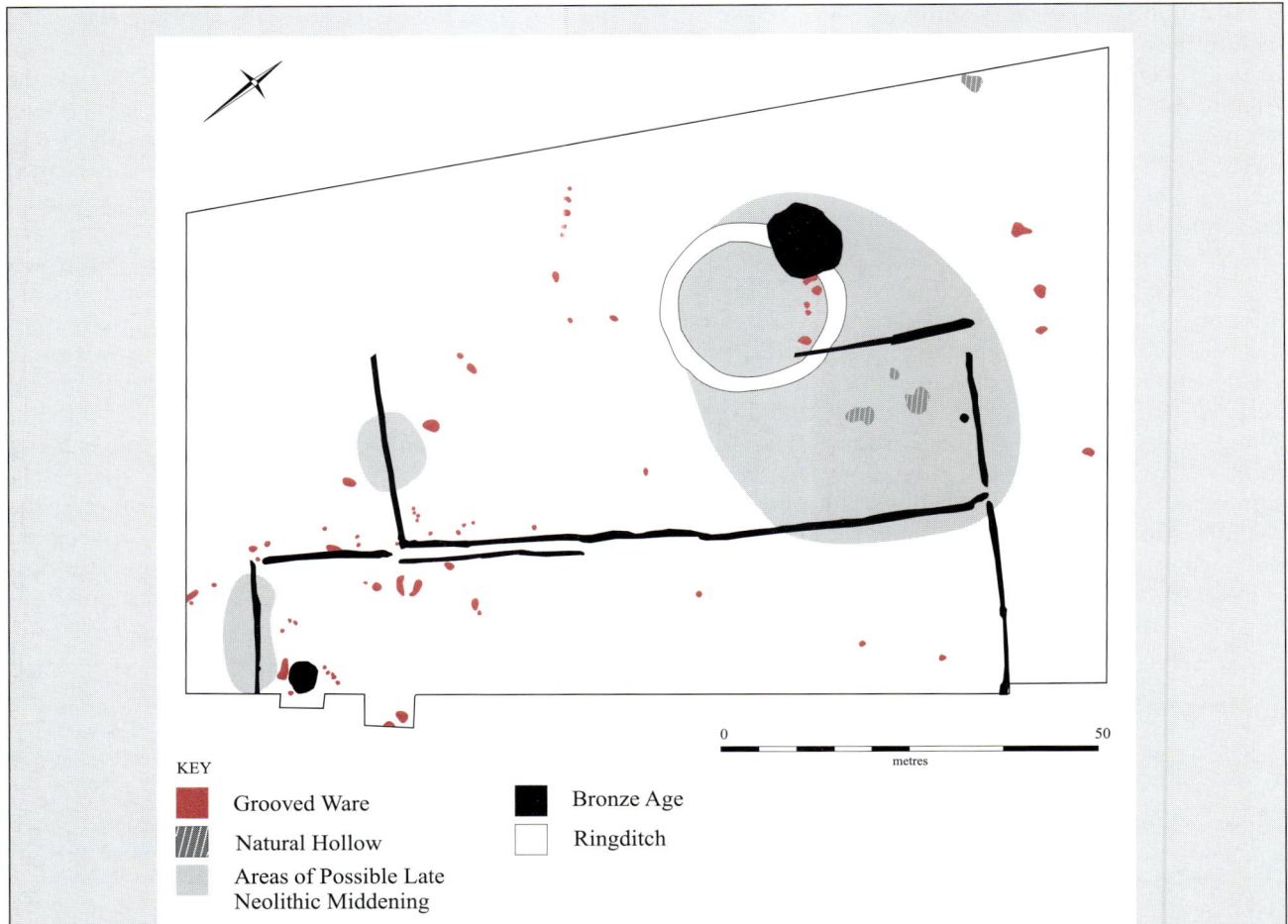

KEY

- ■ (red) Grooved Ware
- ▨ Natural Hollow
- ▨ (grey) Areas of Possible Late Neolithic Middening
- ■ (black) Bronze Age
- □ Ringditch

0 — 50 metres

FIGURE 3.20. *Storey's Bar Road Re-interpreted (after Pryor 1978, fig. 6).*

Essentially, the basis of this interpretation was the implied intentionality of the 'selection' of the structure's pottery, and a parallel with his Early Neolithic building at Padholme Road. Excavated as a 'house' in 1971/72 (Fig. 3.21:B; Pryor 1974a) and dated to 3960–3630 and 3310–2910 cal. BC (GaK-4196 & 4197; Pryor 2001a, 392), in the early 1990s Pryor re-interpreted the Padholme Road 'house' as a mortuary structure (1993, 140; see also 2003, 140). This was fostered by Pryor's analysis and publication of the 1969 Site 11 enclosure which, sealed by Beaker settlement, was assigned to the Neolithic and interpreted as a mortuary enclosure (Pryor 1988, 65; Kinnes 1993, 138); however, its period-attribution was also based on the fact that it shared the same orientation as the Padholme Road 'house' and, together, that they described a landscape axis with the Cat's Water burial (Pryor also attributed parallel cropmark ditch-lines to this alignment; their status is discussed in the Chapter 5, *Vicarage Farm* Inset, below). Thus framed by 'the dead' — respectively the Site 11 enclosure and the Cat's Water burial — the house was then duly reinterpreted as a mortuary structure. The fact that it lacked expected 'domestic accompaniments' (e.g. storage pits) and included 'special finds' (a flake from a stone axe and a jet pendant) also contributed to this attribution. More generally, this re-evaluation of the Padholme Road building's status reflects the impact of post-processualism in the mid/latter '80s and, particularly, the emphasis on ritual and ceremony that was introduced into Pryor's work with the

excavation of the Etton causewayed enclosure (1987; 1998a); it also reflected the influence of Julian Thomas' *Rethinking the Neolithic* of 1991 (Pryor 2001a, 49; 2003, 140). The key point here is that, the Cat's Water burial aside, no human remains whatsoever were recovered from either of these structures or the Site 11 enclosure. Whilst, given its 'heavy' trench-set architecture, there may be some basis for relating the Padholme Road building to the timber mortuary structures of the period (Kinnes 1992; Evans & Hodder 2006a, 194–210, fig. 3.74), there certainly no longer seems any grounds to do so for the much more lightly-built Co-op Site structure. This argument now gains greater credence through an accrued context of Neolithic domestic architecture, particularly the range of sub-rectangular/-square Grooved Ware-associated shed-like structures excavated at Over (Fig. 2.20; see Garrow 2006, figs. 6.3, 6.7, 6.15 & 6.27) and the comparably small buildings recently found at Durrington Walls (Parker Pearson pers. comm.). In short, at least for the Middle/later Neolithic, small square-ish buildings are beginning to appear to have been the norm for domestic architecture.

Straddled by these Neolithic *houses* on its western and eastern sides, the Cat's Water sub-Site obviously deserves a 'second look'. Yet, aside from its renowned, multiple/four-individual burial (the death of one presumed to be caused by the leaf-shaped arrowhead embedded within their chest; Pryor 1984, 19–22, figs. 17 & 19), remarkably little pre-second-

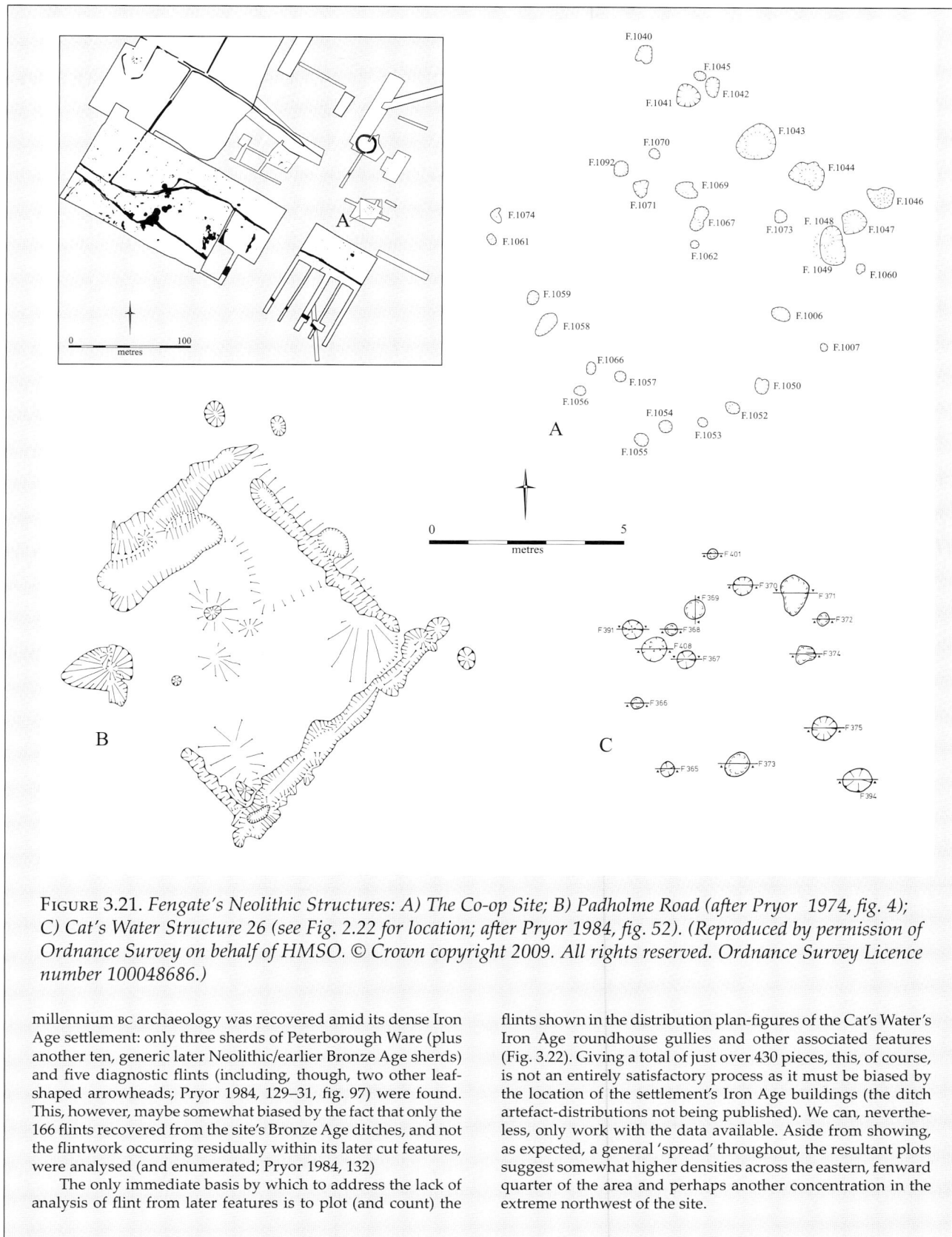

FIGURE 3.21. *Fengate's Neolithic Structures: A) The Co-op Site; B) Padholme Road (after Pryor 1974, fig. 4); C) Cat's Water Structure 26 (see Fig. 2.22 for location; after Pryor 1984, fig. 52). (Reproduced by permission of Ordnance Survey on behalf of HMSO. © Crown copyright 2009. All rights reserved. Ordnance Survey Licence number 100048686.)*

millennium BC archaeology was recovered amid its dense Iron Age settlement: only three sherds of Peterborough Ware (plus another ten, generic later Neolithic/earlier Bronze Age sherds) and five diagnostic flints (including, though, two other leaf-shaped arrowheads; Pryor 1984, 129–31, fig. 97) were found. This, however, maybe somewhat biased by the fact that only the 166 flints recovered from the site's Bronze Age ditches, and not the flintwork occurring residually within its later cut features, were analysed (and enumerated; Pryor 1984, 132)

The only immediate basis by which to address the lack of analysis of flint from later features is to plot (and count) the

flints shown in the distribution plan-figures of the Cat's Water's Iron Age roundhouse gullies and other associated features (Fig. 3.22). Giving a total of just over 430 pieces, this, of course, is not an entirely satisfactory process as it must be biased by the location of the settlement's Iron Age buildings (the ditch artefact-distributions not being published). We can, nevertheless, only work with the data available. Aside from showing, as expected, a general 'spread' throughout, the resultant plots suggest somewhat higher densities across the eastern, fenward quarter of the area and perhaps another concentration in the extreme northwest of the site.

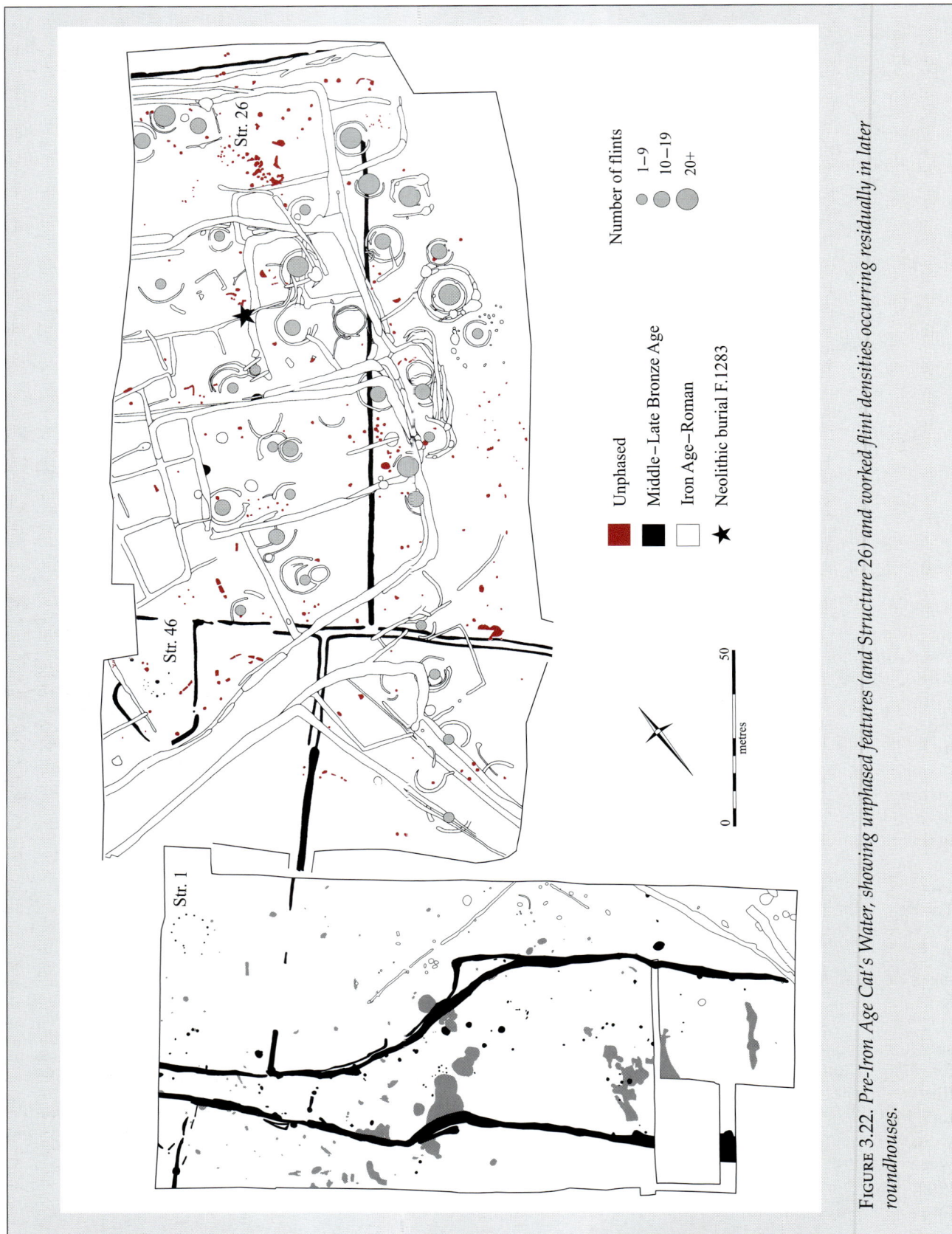

FIGURE 3.22. *Pre-Iron Age Cat's Water, showing unphased features (and Structure 26) and worked flint densities occurring residually in later roundhouses.*

Through comparison of Pryor's plan-figures 16 and 18, the number of unphased discrete features at Cat's Water can be appreciated (Fig. 3.22), their attribution (or rather the absence thereof) essentially being due to a lack of pottery (i.e. not necessarily flint; 1984, 116). Given that finds of pottery would be expected if these features had been contemporary with such a dense Iron Age settlement, it is fair to assume that a number, if not the outright majority, were of fourth- to second-millennium BC date. Again, aside from noting this possibility, further analysis cannot be advanced based on the published sources; however, one post-built setting there, Structure 26, does resemble our Co-op building (Fig. 3.21:C). Located at the northern end of the site (and some 40–45 m north of the multiple burial), its 13 postholes — plus three other possibly associated outliers — enclosed a *c.* 3 × 3 m 'square' (Pryor 1984, 69, fig. 52). Though their apparently clayish fills (with a number having charcoal) might contest such an early attribution, as discussed by Pryor, the complete absence of pottery from them seems remarkable given their situation in the core of the Iron Age settlement (Pryor 1984, 69; any flint associated with them is not detailed). This would have to suggest an earlier date and, certainly, the plan-layout of this structure markedly contrasts with the site's other settlement features.

If this attribution of this structure is correct then this is a significant 'finding', as Fengate can then lay claim to three sub-square Neolithic buildings: that at Padholme Road, the Co-op Site's and, now, Structure 26 at the Cat's Water. These need not, of course, have all been directly contemporary and there is no reason to think of them as amounting to any kind of 'hamlet-type' grouping. Equally, doubting Pryor's ritual/mortuary attribution of the first two of these buildings need not detract from his axial argument. Indeed, he first recognized their 'axis' prior to advocating a mortuary house-interpretation (1988): in other words, the two strands of his argument are not necessarily linked. Given this, how is this axis to be accounted for? Two probably interrelated factors suggest themselves. On the one hand, and to return to Pryor's original argument, their 'line' might simply relate to a progressively expanded path-side clearing amid the 'wildwood' (Pryor 2001a, 406–7; see Evans *et al.* 1998 for further discussion of clearance dynamics). On the other hand, as discussed in the Haddenham 'Neolithic' volume, northeastwards was clearly a major orientation of the earlier Neolithic monuments within the region, and would include that project's Foulmire Fen long barrow as well as that at Raunds, the Orton Meadows and Ardwincle barrows and the Grendon ring-ditch (Evans & Hodder 2006a, 197–8, fig. 3.74). By extension, it can only be presumed that the return southeast–northwest axis was also significant; however, just because landscape might have been 'organized' (or even 'ritualized') by certain spatial axes, it does not necessarily follow that all of its aligned components were 'ritual': *a house may have had a sanctified orientation, but that need not make it a shrine*.

Material culture

Producing only just over 400 flints and some 230 sherds of later prehistoric pottery, the Elliott site's assemblages were not particularly substantial. Although the flintwork attests to both Neolithic and earlier Bronze Age activity, given the scale at which the fen-edge was here exposed (and the site's proximity to the Storey's Bar Road Grooved Ware complex) — and in marked contrast to the Edgerley Drain Road investigations (Chapter 4) — it is certainly noteworthy that, in this case, no pre-Middle Bronze Age pottery was forthcoming whatsoever.

Worked flint (EMMA BEADSMOORE)

The site yielded a total of 405 (<3461 g) flints, including 326 (<2604 g) worked and unburnt flints, 44 worked and burnt (<292 g) and 35 burnt and unworked (<565 g; see Table 3.3). The majority were recovered from cut features, whilst 110 (<802 g) were from tree-throws, 14 (117 g) were a part of, or overlying compacted gravel surfaces, seven (38 g) were within surface deposits and five (51 g) were from buried soil sample squares. The flint is chronologically mixed, ranging in date from Late Mesolithic to later prehistoric. Many of the pieces were broadly contemporary with the features that they were recovered from; however, many were residual, with earlier material inadvertently incorporated into later features.

Tree-throws

The earliest evidence for flintworking was recovered from a series of tree-throws clustered around the northwestern head of the embayment (Fig. 3.7). Tree-throws F.84, F.96, F.104, F.105, F.106, F.107, F.109, F.112, F.113, F.115 and F.143 yielded a total of 87 flints, with between three and 37 flints in each. The lithic assemblages recovered from the clustered tree-throws predominantly comprised flintworking waste made up of waste flakes and blades, discarded cores and core rejuvenation flakes (Fig. 3.23:11 & 12). Material that is the product of systematic Late Mesolithic/earlier Neolithic flake production/core reduction sequences focused principally on manufacturing narrow flakes and blades. The cores were systematically worked and rejuvenation strategies were employed where possible, until the core's potential to produce the desired narrow flakes and blades was exhausted.

Although the tree-throw assemblages are dominated by the waste and products of flake production/core reduction strategies, a few flakes are the byproducts of biface manufacture or sharpening; however, both types of production/reduction sequence are incomplete. Though isolated bifacial reduction byproducts were recovered, only partial or individual components of flake production/core reduction sequences are represented, which indicates that the material was not worked directly into, or within, the features themselves. Despite this, some of the larger assemblages have a degree of coherence to them. The various stages of the reduction sequence are represented, suggesting that at least some of the flints in them were worked nearby, and this is supported by the recovery of discarded working waste, such as core rejuvenation flakes and exhausted cores.

The majority of the tree-throws in the cluster yielded at least one utilized flint, including flakes and blades, scrapers and piercers (Fig. 3.23:3 & 15). Two of the tree-throws yielded microliths, suggesting that the material is Late Mesolithic; a possible scalene triangle was recovered from F.112 (Fig. 3.23:5), whilst F.84 yielded a broken, abruptly retouched bladelet; however, such material is likely to be residual within F.112, as half a polished Langdale axe was also

TABLE 3.3. *Worked flint by feature (excluding features with less than five pieces).*

Feature	Chip/chunk	Primary flake	Secondary flake	Tertiary flake	Secondary blade	Tertiary blade	Core-rejuvenation flake	Irregular core	Single-platform core	Opposed-platform core	Two-platform core	Discoidal core	Multiple-platform core	Core fragment	Leaf-shaped arrowhead	Oblique arrowhead	Plano-convex knife	Microlith	Flake knife	Piercer	End scraper	Thumbnail scraper	Sub-circular scraper	Miscellaneous scraper	Flake from polished implement	Serrated flake	Retouched flake	Edge-used flake	Retouched blade	Edge-used blade	Unworked burnt chunk	Totals
45	1		2	3				1					1						1													9
66	1		5	1		1								1																		9
84	1		9	13		1	4	1	2	3								1									1			1		37
95			2	5																			1									8
96	1		2	1		2					1	1		1																		9
102			6	4		1		2					1																			14
105	1		1	2	1	1															1											7
107			2	4		1								1									1				1	1				11
112			2	9			1										1			1	1											15
145	2		2	3																												7
150																															5	5
159	1		6	2																												9
163																															11	11
166																															8	8
193	2	2	8	3			1	1					2																			19
197			1	2		1	1	2																								7
214	1		3					1																								5
222	2		6	5		2								1		1					2			1			1	1				22
225			2	2		1		1																								6
231	1		1	2		1		1										1		1												8
311	2												1																		2	5
Buried soil				1											1								1		1							4
Small/stray finds			3	3		2								1												1						10
Sub totals	16	2	63	68	1	8	11	11	4	4	1	1	4	6	1	1	1	2	1	2	4	0	3	1	1	1	3	2	0	1	26	245
Other features	9	3	40	38	0	9	2	5	0	3	1	0	5	3	0	0	0	0	0	0	3	1	0	0	0	0	0	3	1	0	9	135
Assemblage total	25	5	103	106	1	17	13	16	4	7	2	1	9	9	1	1	1	2	1	2	7	1	3	1	1	1	3	5	1	1	35	380

recovered from it (Fig. 3.25:5). The comparatively small, incomplete assemblages of systematically manufactured flintworking waste (focused on the production of narrow flakes and blades) recovered from the tree-throws in the cluster cannot be divided between the Late Mesolithic and earlier Neolithic. Furthermore, as both Late Mesolithic and earlier Neolithic chronologically diagnostic tools were recovered, the tree-throws and surrounding area were potentially a focus for activity during both periods. Thus, Late Mesolithic material deposited in the features was likely to be both broadly contemporary with some tree-throws and residual in others. At the time of the flints' manufacture and/or use, some of the material was deposited in contemporary tree-throws, whilst other material would have been left on the ground surface, leaving it available to become incorporated into later, earlier Neolithic features. Further evidence for background Late Mesolithic/earlier Neolithic activity at the site was provided by residual material recovered from the later, Bronze and Iron Age features, material that was concentrated in the northeastern part of the site, at the head and along the northern side of the embayment.

The remaining tree-throws were spread across Area A/B and yielded fewer flints than the clustered tree-throws. Despite its limited quantity, the flint is technologically comparable to the mate-rial recovered from the clustered tree-throws. The waste flakes and end scraper are the products of systematic Late Mesolithic/earlier Neolithic flake production/core reduction, although a flake recovered from tree-throw F.124 is more consistent with later Neolithic discoidal core reduction.

Neolithic

Evidence for Neolithic flintworking and use at the site extended beyond the material recovered from the tree-throws. Several pits yielded material of that date, which was potentially broadly contemporary with those features (Fig. 3.7). This included flake and blade blanks, core-rejuvenation flakes and discarded cores that were the product of systematic Neolithic flake production/core-reduction sequences (F.11, F.39, F.47, F.144, F.145, F.221, F.237, F.292, F.320 & F.339). Neolithic material was also found residually in later features, predominantly Bronze Age and occasionally Iron Age ditches and pits (Fig. 3.6). Neolithic flake blanks and discarded cores were also incorporated into gravel metalling and used to lay compacted surfaces. A Neolithic leaf-shaped arrowhead and scraper were recovered from the buried soil (Fig. 3.23:2); residual Neolithic material also concentrated within the northwestern part of the site.

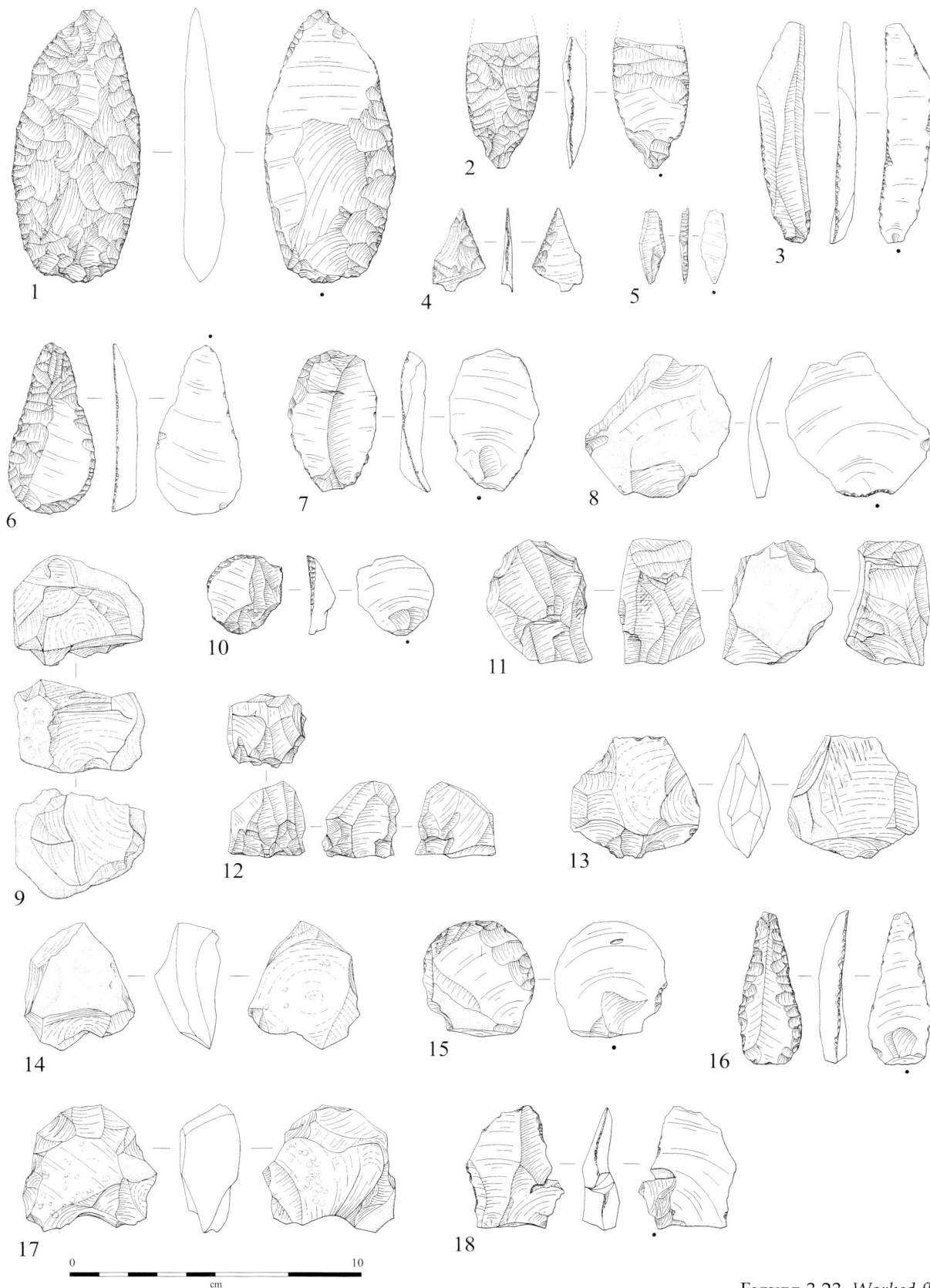

FIGURE 3.23. *Worked flint.*

Later Neolithic/Early Bronze Age

Evidence for later Neolithic activity was provided by a single flake from pit F.108, an assemblage of material from F.222 and several residual flints in later features (Figs. 3.6 & 3.7). The flake from F.108 is a classic product of discoidal core flake production/core reduction prevalent during the later Neolithic and broadly contemporary with the pit. The assemblage from pit F.222 included an oblique arrowhead (Fig. 3.23:4), scrapers (Fig. 3.23:7), utilized flakes (Fig. 3 23:18) and a flake from a polished implement (Fig. 3.23:8), material that is broadly contemporary with the feature. Residual later Neolithic flint was occasionally recovered from the Bronze Age fieldsystem, with two later Neolithic/Early Bronze Age knives recovered from ditches F.45 and F.290 (Figs. 3.23:6 & 16).

Traces of Early Bronze flint manufacture/use were recovered from seemingly contemporary features as well as from later features and layers containing residual material. A Beaker/Early Bronze Age thumbnail scraper was recovered from F.167 (Fig. 3.23:10). Pit F.273 yielded a small core comparable to types found in other Early Bronze Age contexts; three comparable cores were recovered from Collared Urn pits at a site nearby at Edgerley Drain Road, Fengate (see Chapter 4). Two further cores of this type were recovered at the Elliott Site from pit F.195 (Fig. 3.23:13) and in a later ditch, F.27. A buried soil deposit, intermixed with the gravels in the centre of the droveway, yielded a Late Neolithic/Early Bronze Age plano-convex knife (Fig. 3.23:1).

Later prehistoric

Although the fieldsystem ditches yielded earlier, residual material, flintworking waste and the products of more expedient, unsystematic Middle Bronze Age flake production/core reduction strategies and tool manufacture were also present (Fig. 3.6). Ditches F.27, F.45, F.66, F.102, F.193, F.197, F.290 and F.353 contained either roughly worked cores or expediently removed thick, broad flakes (Fig. 3.23:9, 14 & 17); a potentially Middle/Late Bronze Age core was also recovered from F.352.

A large Late Bronze Age pit that cut one of the droveway boundaries yielded an expediently reduced core that was potentially broadly contemporary with that feature. The compacted gravel surfaces within the area of the compound were locally overlain by 'buried-type' soils that contained several expediently manufactured waste flakes. These are likely to be later prehistoric and, therefore, broadly contemporary with the surfaces themselves. Tentative evidence for Iron Age flint use was supplied by expediently manufactured flakes recovered from one of the Iron Age ditches (F.230) and a pit (F.207); however, the material could also be of Middle/Late Bronze Age date, inadvertently incorporated into the later features.

The Late Mesolithic/earlier Neolithic material recovered from the tree-throws clustered at the southwestern edge of excavation and the quantities of contemporary flint residual in later features reveals an early phase of activity at the site. Additional, isolated pits and tree-throws also yielded Neolithic flint. Later Neolithic flintwork was also concentrated in the northwestern part of the excavation, in two later Neolithic features, and residually within later features. Limited evidence for Early Bronze Age flintworking and use was attested to by working waste and tools in potentially broadly contemporary features and, again, residually within later features and deposits. Flint continued to be utilized, on a reduced scale,

into the Middle/Late Bronze Age and, potentially, the Iron Age.

Worked stone (MARK EDMONDS)
Made from a large, split, fine-grained sandstone river cobble that had been dressed around its edges (perhaps to fit a frame?) and which had a small area of extra polish at one end (perhaps suggesting the direction of wear), a saddle quern was recovered as a surface-spread find (see Fig. 3.25:1). Diagnostic of pre-Middle Iron Age attribution, the stone weighed 2.4 kg and measured 22 × 13 × 6.5 cm.

Otherwise, two stone axe fragments were recovered:

<324> F.222 — Small 'tertiary flake', bearing traces of grinding/polish on one lateral edge. The colour, grain size and form of the piece strongly suggests that this is a flake detached during the reworking of a Neolithic stone axe blade, most likely one with an origin in the central Fells of Cumbria (Group VI; Edmonds 2004).

Wt	5.2 g
Length	35 mm
Width	18 mm

<154> F.112 — Fragment, including the cutting edge, of a stone axe (Fig. 3.25:5). The piece shows signs of re-sharpening prior to breakage, the latter taking the form of a classic 'end-shock' fracture. Flake scars emanating from both the cutting edge and the lateral break surface indicate that this fragment was subsequently flaked, involving the removal of c. 11 flakes. Whether or not this was undertaken to facilitate the re-hafting of a (much reduced) blade, to take the blade 'out of commission', or simply to detach flakes that could be used for other purposes, is impossible to determine from this artefact alone. Macroscopic identification indicates that the blade originates from the Group VI stone sources in the central Fells of Cumbria.

Wt	75.5 g
Length	31 mm
Width	40 mm

Later prehistoric pottery
(MATT BRUDENELL & MARK KNIGHT)
A total of 165 sherds (980 g) of Middle Bronze Age or Deverel-Rimbury pottery were recovered from four separate features (F.95, F.182, F.195 & F.355). The condition of the material was crumbly (with some pieces delaminating) and weathered, with a mean sherd weight of 5.9 g. The few feature sherds present included 16 base, five rim and two decorated fragments. The vast majority came from thick-walled vessels (up to 22 mm) with simple upright or bucket-like profiles. The temper comprised crushed shell (S1), although grog (G1) was also identified.

The 84 sherds recovered from F.182 appeared to belong to a single bucket-shaped vessel, which had a cordon or single row of diagonal fingertip/nail impressions around its body (Fig. 3.24:2). Rim sherds were only present in F.195 (along with body sherds) and these included simple out-turned as well as flattened

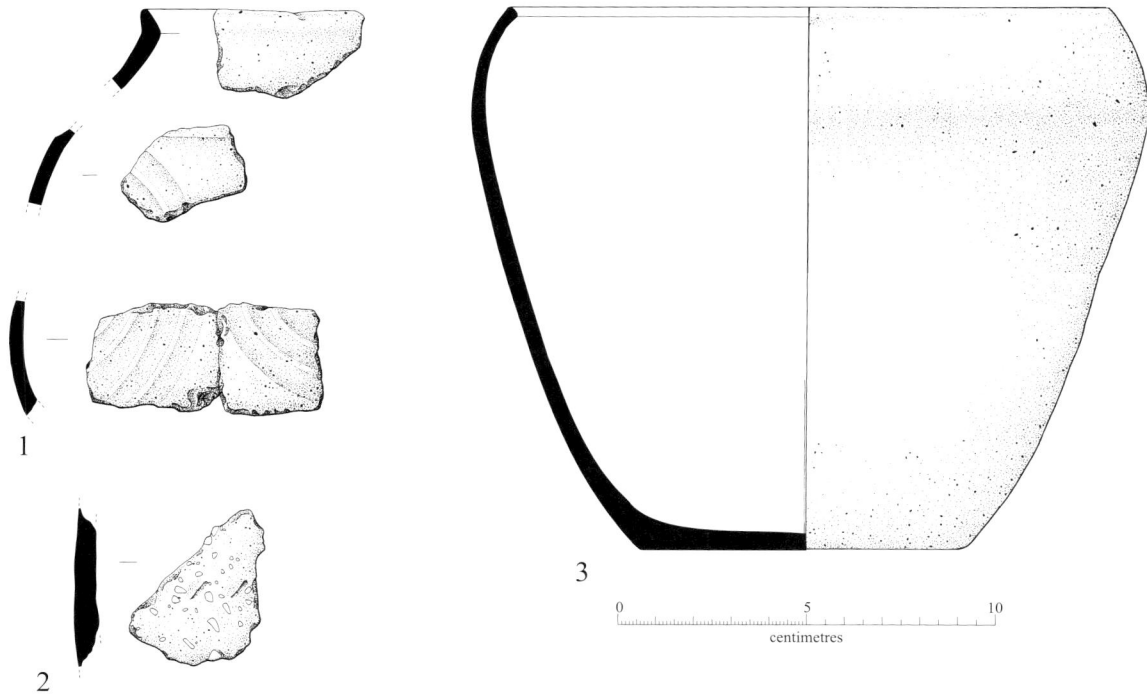

FIGURE 3.24. *Pottery: 1) Fragments of a burnt and abraded fineware tripartite bowl with smoothed dark grey surfaces; Deverel-Rimbury (Fabric F1; Ditch F.102/F.191); 2) decorated body sherd with horizontal cordon of fingertip/nail impression; 3) fineware jar with hooked rim and dark grey exterior surface; rim diameter 16 cm (50% intact) and base diameter 10 cm (40% intact; Fabric S1; Pit F.255).*

with external lip forms. One of the rim fragments belonged to a small diameter (*c.* 12 cm) thin-walled vessel that had a slightly everted profile, perhaps better described as a Post-Deverel-Rimbury form. Otherwise, the remaining pieces consisted predominantly of chunky, shell-rich slabs derived from large diameter urns.

Deverel-Rimbury pottery has an extended late second millennium currency (1400–1000 BC) which overlaps with the beginning of the Post-Deverel-Rimbury tradition (*c.* 1200–800 BC; Barrett 1976; Barrett *et al.* 1978). The identification of the small, everted form from F.195 might suggest that the assemblage, from this context at least, belongs to the Late rather than Middle Bronze Age. Similarly small assemblages of Deverel-Rimbury have been excavated at Eye, King's Dyke West and Bradley Fen (see Chapter 2 above). The nearby Newark Road excavations (Pryor 1980a) also produced fragments, some of which were recovered from parts of the fieldsystem.

Sixty-five (776 g) sherds of later, post-Middle Bronze Age prehistoric pottery were recovered from the excavation. This material was retrieved from just seven features, with a mean sherd weight of 11.9 g. Including Late Bronze Age (LBA; *c.* 1100–800 BC), Early Iron Age (EIA; *c.* 800–400/350 BC), and Late Iron Age

(*c.* 350 BC–AD 50) wares, in general the pottery was in a moderate to fair condition. Most contexts contained small- to medium-size sherds (<8 cm in size), which were moderately abraded, and quite often burnt. Only two features produced larger, 'fresher' sherds, F.255 and F.230.

Four basic fabric groups were identified based on the principal inclusions visible. Fabric S1 comprises moderate-coarse gritted fossil shell fabrics, accounting for 74 per cent of the assemblage (by weight). Frequently, the shell in this fabric was partially leached-out, leaving voids in the surface. Sherds in S1 date to the LBA/EIA, and are moderately soft to hard in texture; S2 comprised sherds with moderate fossil shell and quartz sand. These account for 21 per cent of the assemblage, and characterize later Iron Age pottery. The fabric tended to be hard to very hard. The remaining pottery contained either finely crushed burnt flint-tempered F1 (3 per cent), characterizing LBA/EIA pottery, or dense quartz sand Q1 (2 per cent), characterising later Iron Age ceramics.

Thirty-three sherds in the assemblage showed signs of burnishing (332 g). All belonged to the LBA vessel in F. 255 (Fig. 3.24:3). The leaching of shell from S1 vessels has made the identification of burnishing problematic, and several other sherds may have been so-treated. Likewise, burning had damaged or removed the surface of nine sherds, preventing identification of burnishing. In total, nine sherds in the assemblage were decorated: four EIA sherds with incised decoration, and six later Iron Age sherds with scoring. Two of the latter also displayed finger-tip impressions on the rim.

Late Bronze Age/Early Iron Age pottery

Distinguishing between LBA and EIA ceramics can often be problematic in small assemblages with few diagnostic forms. In eastern England, pottery of this time essentially forms an unbroken sequence, encompassed by the Post-Deverel-Rimbury pottery tradition (PDR). The range of forms and fabrics which typify this tradition have a long currency, transgressing the conventional LBA/EIA divide, with some formal characteristics persisting from *c.* 1100–400 BC. Closer dating within this time bracket is often difficult, and the transition from early 'plainware' PDR (LBA, *c.* 1100–800 BC) to later 'decorated' PDR (EIA, post-800 BC) is not fully understood in the region (Knight 2002). At present, distinguishing EIA pottery from that of the LBA is based on the identification of a relatively narrow range of characteristics, namely the occurrence of incised decoration, overtly angular vessels, specific rim types (including 'T'-shaped or flanged rims) and a high incidence of finger-tip/-nail decoration on the rim and shoulder. In this report, all ceramics *not* displaying these features are considered Late Bronze Age. Where possible, further justification for this dating is offered.

Three features yielded pottery datable to the LBA, totalling 48 sherds (472 g). All are in fossil shell fabrics, though most have had the shell partially leached-out. The largest assemblage came from pit F.255, comprising 33 sherds (332 g). The sherds belonged to a single, neckless, burnished PDR 'plainware' jar with a hooked rim (S1; Brudenell forthcoming a, PDR Form 13). Around 50 per cent of the jar was deposited in the pit, including at least seven large, refitting fragments. The vessel mouth is *c.* 16 cm in diameter, with a *c.* 10 cm base. Vessels of this form have been found on numerous LBA sites across eastern England, and find close parallels to vessels at Broom (Brudenell 2007), Reading Business Park (M. Hall 1992, 65–79, figs. 41-2 & 44-51) and Green Park (Morris 2004, 83–8, figs. 4.8–4.17).

Three sherds were recovered from F.74. All are likely to belong to the same vessel, including two non-refitting rim sherds displaying a direct rounded lip. Pit F.157 yielded ten body sherds, four of which were refitting. A further two LBA sherds were recovered from F.230. These were found amongst later Iron Age Scored Ware sherds and are, therefore, residual.

Two features on the site produced typologically EIA pottery, totalling ten sherds (108 g). Nine of these derived from the peat-capping of ditch F.102. All the pottery from this context was burnt, including fragments from at least two vessels. The first vessel comprises four non-refitting sherds belonged to a 'Fengate-Cromer' style bowl (Cunliffe 1978, 42). The vessel has finely crushed burnt flint inclusions (F1) and was presumably once burnished, having lost its surface when burnt. Three of the four sherds are decorated with incised grooves, forming an arching motif below the shoulder. The remaining sherd is a rim with a short everted lip, indicating that the bowl was tripartite. Bowls decorated in this style are distributed around the fen-margins, and are diagnostic of the EIA. The other sherd from the surface of ditch F.102 belongs to a jar with a concave neck and rounded rim; the voids in its fabric imply that the vessel was originally shell-tempered (S1).

A further EIA sherd was recovered from pit F.207. This comprised a single 'T'-shaped rim sherd in Fabric S1. The fabric is hard, with parallels with the LBA/EIA pottery recovered from the Tower Works Site 500 m to the northwest (see Chapter 5 below).

Later Iron Age

Seven sherds, weighing 196 g, are datable to the later Iron Age. All were recovered from a single ditch F.230. Pottery of this date is typified by a narrow range of mainly open, ovoid and globular profiled vessels, with weakly defined 'slack-shoulders'. Vessels are usually made in dense fossil shell and sand fabrics (S2), are frequently scored, and have occasional finger-tip/finger-nail impressions along the rim-top.

All bar one sherd from F.230 were scored; this includes the partial profile of an ovoid/barrel-shaped jar with everted neck and rounded rim (Hill & Horne 2003, Type D). The jar had a rim diameter of *c.* 19 cm and was embellished with rim-top finger-nail impressions. Below the neck the vessel was scored. The remaining sherd was plain in Fabric Q1. All the pottery finds parallels with the large Scored Ware assemblage from the adjacent Cat's Water site (Pryor 1984).

This is a small but informative collection of ceramics which spans the entire first millennium BC. Frequently with assemblages of this size, it is impossible to comment on anything but typological affiliation and date range; however, given the history of excavation and publication in the Fengate area, even a small collection of material can give further insight into our understanding of past settlement patterns and landscape use, particularly that of the LBA/EIA.

The nature and distribution of the LBA/EIA PDR pottery on the Elliott Site appears characteristic for Fengate fen-edge sites in general. Small quantities of pottery occurring in a small number of features typify PDR deposits in this landscape. Taken together, the quantity of PDR pottery recovered from the fen-edge is remarkably low, especially when the total area investigated is considered. At all excavated sites, only a small number of features have produced pottery of this date. For example, very few features excavated during the main Fengate excavations (1971–8) yielded EIA ceramics. Small quantities of EIA pottery were recovered at Newark Road, Fourth Drove (Pryor 1980a, 106 & 156), Vicarage Farm (Pryor 1974a, 21) and immediately adjacent at Cat's Water (Pryor 1984, 139–53). As far as can be discerned, from these sites no more than 15 features produced EIA pottery (not including residual EIA material in the later Iron Age features at Cat's Water). The largest collection derived from a cluster of substantial pits cut through the Cornbrash limestone at Vicarage Farm, (Pryor 1974a, 17; see Inset, Chapter 5 below). On the remaining sites, pottery was recovered from isolated pits and post-holes.

Only limited quantities of similarly dated LBA/EIA pottery were recovered from the large-scale excavation at Edgerley Drain Road (see Chapter 4 below) and equally minor amounts were recovered from evaluation work at the Depot Site (Evans 1992). As discussed in Chapter 5 below, it is only in the area around the former Tower Works site, Mallory Road and the pre-War gravel pits in that vicinity — *c.* 500 m west of the Elliott site and back from the fen-edge proper — that a substantial PDR assemblage, testifying to intensive LBA/EIA activity, has been recovered

Slag and ironworking debris (SIMON TIMBERLAKE)

Four samples of slag and/or ironworking debris were examined from three Iron Age features within the eastern corner of the site (Figs. 3.6 & 3.18). Two of these were later Iron Age ditches (F.230 & F.233), within which contemporary slag may have been redeposited; the third, a pit (F.313), seems to have been the base of a hearth, possibly one with an associated metalworking function.

F.313 yielded two small pieces of ferrous slag (17 g) from the upper fill of the hearth. These were found associated with burnt, redeposited natural sand and silt along with charcoal and burnt stone. The slag fragments were only poorly magnetic, the larger piece having a vitrified (slightly glazed) upper surface with its underside consisting of now fully oxidized metal, part fused to the underlying sand. This suggests the separation of a lighter and more silica-rich slag under the partially molten conditions of iron bloom formation, thus indicating that the hearth was used either for the smelting or else re-smelting of an iron bloom. The smaller fragment consists of a droplet of once molten iron-poor slag, and thus is more similar to the material recovered from the overlying layer.

The lower fills of F.313 produced a further 46 pieces of poorly magnetic ferrous slag (333 g). These have clearly been broken off (perhaps *in situ*) from a larger lump of slag-covered iron bloom, and then left discarded within the base of the hearth. The form of the slag suggests a semi-molten mass with discrete droplets forming. There are smaller 'rust' particles present as inclusions within the vesicular slag. The powdered remnants of these are significantly more magnetic, and probably represent the original metal prills, now largely oxidized to iron oxides and hydroxides (brown/yellow in colour). Again, all this material would seem to be the product of the smelting or re-smelting of an iron bloom.

F.230 contained a single lump of slightly magnetic iron slag (177 g). This seems denser and heavier than the broken slag fragments recovered from the hearth pit (F.313) and thus the iron content of this is probably higher. Nevertheless, this probably still represents discarded material. Although no appreciable degree of weathering of the lump is evident, it seems possible that this is a residual inclusion within the fill of this ditch and it could have derived from the F.313 metalworking activity.

Two pieces of slightly magnetic iron slag (38 g) were recovered from another rather similar ditch fill, F.233. A thin crust of iron hydroxide suggests the former presence of reduced metal. The iron content of this sample seems marginally higher than that of the slag pieces left within the base of the hearth (F.313).

Based on the evidence of the metallurgical debris, there is a strong likelihood that both these finds and the features with which they are associated define an Iron Age ironworking site of limited size and importance. Conceivably this may just relate to the presence of a single hearth (F.313), although the existence of others seems likely. The process seems to have involved the production of a semi-molten iron bloom with a partial accretion of slag. Whilst this would appear to be a

smelting operation, either carried out directly using an easily smelted iron ore (bog iron ore or haematite), or else by re-smelting an already part-smelted iron bloom, there is no evidence here for the production of plate slags using a tap-slagging shaft furnace (such as we find with Roman iron-smelting operations; see Jackson & Tylecote, 1988). Thus the type of slag recovered here is probably what one would expect of small-scale Iron Age production (Crew 2002).

In the absence of full metallurgical examination of the slags, or bulk sample-collection from the hearth layers, it is difficult to be absolutely certain that we are not looking at a smithing (secondary refining) process rather than the assumed smelting activity within hearth F.313. Therefore, the following is a very tentative interpretation of the excavated evidence.

Given that the hearth may already have been an abandoned, weathered and infilled feature by the later Iron Age (as is often the case with ephemeral smelting or refining furnaces), and that the remainder of this has been removed by later truncation of the archaeological layers, what survived as a 0.12 m deep and 0.8 × 0.55 m scoop in the ground surface may bear little resemblance to the original form of this structure; however, the unusual ('figure of eight') shape must reflect, at least in some way, the nature of the initial process carried out at this spot.

An area of charcoal and burning affecting the surface of underlying natural (sandy silts) at the north end of the hearth pit contrasts with a charcoal-rich layer consisting of fuel ash, fine sand and clay at the south end. This suggests that we may be looking at the raked-out contents of a roasting pit (rather than a smelting hearth) at this lower level, i.e. the roasting of an ore within an unlined open-hearth pit in order to pre-treat it and prepare it for smelting. The flames may well have been fanned by the wind rather than by a forced draught. A roasting pit is perhaps what one might expect in the first stage in the smelt reduction operation. The absence of slag or ore within this layer might simply reflect its removal after pre-treatment.

A layer of charcoal-rich silt and sand overlying the remains of this earliest operation suggests material washed into the pit from around the edges. The succeeding layer, a burnt red clay, was similarly located at the south end of the feature, suggesting this is the furnace area of the hearth pit. Based on the context description and location of the bunt clay, this would seem to be some sort of lining to a bowl hearth, or else the truncated base of a shaft furnace. Lying within the base of this, the presence of burnt 'natural', alongside charcoal, stone and slag, is perhaps not as unusual as one might think, given that the sides of earth-built furnaces crumble during their operation. However,

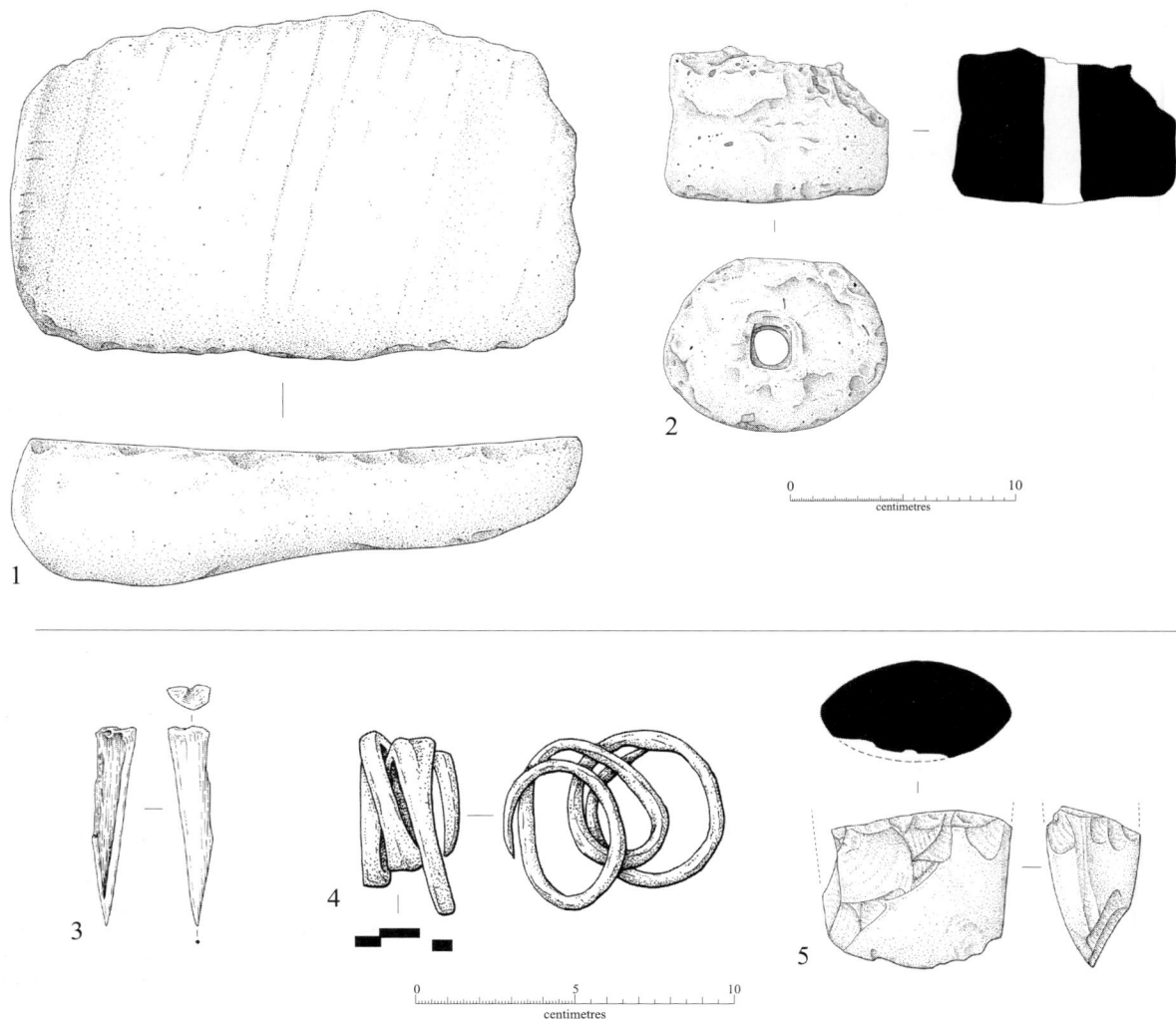

FIGURE 3.25. *Miscellaneous finds: 1) saddle quern (SmF.38); 2) loomweight (F.3); 3) bone point (F.195); 4) copper alloy coiled-ring (SmF.46); 5) stone axe (F.112).*

the complete lack of any vitrified material — either furnace lining or *tuyere* (clay bellows nozzle) ends — seems quite unusual. One of the pieces of slag recovered from this layer does show slight signs of vitrification, suggesting that it may have lain close to the clay or silt/sand lining. The layer overlying this, a dark brown-black silt with moderate amounts of charcoal packed with broken slag, seems more typical of an iron furnace. In all probability this represents the bottom of a furnace which has been abandoned, together with lumps of relatively iron-poor slag such as might have been knocked off the sides of a small iron bloom *in situ*, probably after this had cooled sufficiently. Some useful accounts of the excavation of small Iron Age furnaces as well as of experimental reconstruction smelts and the forging of iron blooms

can be found in Crew (1986; 1989; 1991; 1998; see also Serneels & Crew 1997).

Other finds

Despite the fact that during the excavation all exposed features were scanned with a metal-detector, only one metal-find was recovered (from the gravel surface, F.385):

<543> (SmF.46; Fig. 3.25:4) — Corroded and distorted copper-alloy coiled-ring, with three turns, wider at the centre with a decorative groove (16 mm long, approx. internal ring diameter 19 mm; 10 g); the patina shows some mineral loss. Coiled-rings of this form date to the Late Bronze/Early Iron Age, *c.* 1000–750 BC. A comparative example was recovered nearby at Flag Fen (Coombs 2001), although examples of coiled-rings are known from Middle Bronze Age hoards from elsewhere in Britain (e.g. Stump Bottom, Sussex; Smith 1959, 153).

Derived from ten different contexts, 40 pieces (1259 g) of burnt clay were recovered. Most were small rounded lumps with no obvious diagnostic traits, although three contexts had either semi-complete or large fragments of cylindrical loomwieghts, F.3, F.150 and F.140.

The best-preserved example of a loomweight was from F.3. This was an oval-shaped cylinder (9.5 × 9 × 7 cm) with a central axial-perforation (1.5 cm dia.; Fig. 3.25:2). It weighed 783 g and was made of hard sandy clay with frequent small-medium angular gravel and moderate small grog inclusions. The fragments from F.150 were of a similar fabric and included pieces that retained enough of a surface to suggest a similar diameter to the F.3 weight. While only one fragment came from F.140, this, too, had a curved surface; a large lump from F.224 had just the hint of a curved surface which might also suggest that it derived from a cylinder-shaped object.

Cylindrical loomweights are thought to be of Bronze Age date and a similar complete weight was recovered at the nearby Third Drove excavations (Site O) from a secure earlier Bronze Age/Collared Urn-related context (Pryor 2001a, fig. 2.11). Similar axially perforated weights have also been found in other parts of the Fengate system, including two from the Padholme Road sub-Site (Pryor 1980a) and four from Newark Road (Pryor 1980a); the other Fengate examples match almost exactly the dimensions of that from F.3.

The waterlogged wood (MAISIE TAYLOR)

The assemblage is not very large and is mostly composed of roundwood. There are, however, some other fragments, including the four strap pieces which have been described above.

All of the material comes from deeper features on the site, some on the borderline of preservation. There are 35 pieces and samples of roundwood. These range from fairly well preserved, worked pieces to some material that is either too decayed or too dry even for species identification. There are two small pieces of timber and two off-cuts/'timber debris'. There are nine pieces of bark and a woodchip.

Species

Some of the material is too decayed for species analysis. There are a few pieces of oak (*Quercus* sp.) from F.116 and F.302. There are two pieces of roundwood, one trimmed and one coppiced. The coppiced oak is very slow-grown. There is also a piece of oak timber from F.116. It is tangentially split from the outside of a tree. This piece would be generated by squaring-up a medium-sized tree. The tangential timber is 170 mm wide, so that the tree must have been at least 200 mm in diameter.

Other timber, and debris, including woodchips, is derived from alder (*Alnus glutinosa*), willow (*Salix* sp.) and poplar (*Populus* sp.). The remainder of the material divides into various sorts of

roundwood. The material derived from coppicing, including forks and a felled tree, all display the characteristics of various wet-loving species: alder (*Alnus glutinosa*), willow (*Salix* sp.) and poplar (*Populus* sp.). Other roundwood, most of which is gnarled and knobbly, is almost certainly blackthorn (*Prunus spinosa*).

The wet-loving species are used for a variety of purposes on fen sites because they would have been so ubiquitous. Willow and alder can be used for many of the same applications as hazel, having many of the same properties. Hazel can tolerate only a limited amount of waterlogging whilst in growth; in contrast, willow and alder will thrive in the wet. Many of the shrubby species used for hedging, such as blackthorn, also do not tolerate growing in very wet conditions.

Charring

There is very little burnt wood. A couple of pieces of oak debris are quite heavily charred, one from F.302 and another from F.307.

Roundwood

Of the 35 pieces of roundwood from the site, only four or five pieces appear to be 'natural'. Most of them are either worked, or show evidence of coppicing or hedging.

Felled tree
There is one possible felled tree from F.302, that is 110 mm in diameter (Fig. 3.9). The piece has the classic felled-end, with working from both sides. Yet, as 110 mm is not large, it could be 'felled' from an overgrown coppice; alternatively it may indeed have been growing as a standard tree.

Coppice
There is evidence for coppicing from almost half of the roundwood. This takes the form of long, straight stems and heels. Much of it is also trimmed. F.302 in particular contains a great deal. There are also some forks made from modified roundwood from that feature. These may have been cut from coppicing and be associated with the craft. Coppicers extensively use forks to help with bundling the rods and poles once they have been cut. The diameters of the coppiced roundwood range from 12–69 mm, but most are under 35 mm. This is relatively small material, suitable for hurdles, lightweight wattle and laying hedges.

Hedging
Other roundwood shows direct evidence for hedging, especially that from F.302. One piece could be derived from coppice, except for a sharp bend of more than 90°. Unnatural or sharp bends in wood are generally held to be evidence for laid hedges. Much of the material which has been identified as derived from hedges is Blackthorn (*Prunus spinosa*). Some has right-angled bends and much of it is knobbly and gnarled (Fig. 3.10:1). Blackthorn does not naturally grow in this fashion but, where it has been incorporated into hedges, it will grow this way when laid.

Timber and debris

The small amount of timber and debris give some indication of other woodworking activities in the area, although there is too little for any detailed analysis. There is no evidence for any working of large trees. The great timbers at Flag Fen are much larger than anything found on this site, and are derived from huge trees, the timber debris here being much smaller (Taylor 2001, tables 7.5 & 7.6).

The few woodchips suggest activity, such as sharpening of posts. The largest piece of 'timber' is quarter-split and the tree from which it derived must only have been 250–300 mm in diameter.

Bark
Although all the roundwood is quite small in diameter, most of the bark is rather thick, around 12 mm, and must be derived from a much larger tree or trees. The working of larger trees must have occurred within the area, even though there is otherwise no direct evidence of this.

Partly because of the variable, but generally poor, quality of preservation, there is only one toolmark surviving in the entire assemblage. It is partial and undiagnostic so that there is no scope for any kind of analysis.

Turning to the range of tree species, there is only a small amount of oak (7.5 per cent). The remainder consists of various wet-loving species: willow, poplar and especially alder. Alder is the dominant species in the worked wood at Flag Fen and was probably widely available all along the fen-edge (Scaife 2001, 361). The oak is very slow-grown and this may be an indicator of increasingly wet conditions close by (Brennand & Taylor 2003, 36); alternatively, it may indicate a competitive environment, such as a hedge (Taylor 1996, 106).

Material from wet-loving species is often found being used for a variety of purposes. Willow and alder can be used in much the same way as hazel. Hazel is common in damp ground, but where conditions are wetter it will gradually give way to species which can tolerate more waterlogging whilst in growth (Scaife 2001, 361). Similarly, many of the shrubby species used for hedging, such as blackthorn, do not tolerate growth in very wet conditions. This would not necessarily have been a problem, however, and is one of the reasons why hedges have always been planted on banks.

Almost half of all the roundwood from the site appears to have been coppiced. Many of the rods and poles have long, straight stems and heels. Much of it is also trimmed. Other material is knobbly and gnarled, suggesting that it is more likely to be derived from hedges. There are also some forks made from modified roundwood which were probably cut from coppice, as they have long straight handles and prongs. Simple forks may be used for a number of activities, but it should be noted that forks are used by coppicers when bundling rods and poles after cutting. It is likely that the fork from F.302 was used in this way. It is very sturdy, with a diameter on the shaft of more than 60 mm, and there is wear on the inside of one of the prongs.

The banks which have been found locally alongside Bronze Age ditches (e.g. Pryor 1980a, pl. 15, fig. 128) are indirect evidence for hedges, as is the environmental evidence where there are high levels of pollen from shrubs and thorns. Stock-proof boundaries are necessary for animal husbandry, but incontrovertible evidence is hard to find. A few shrubs planted in a row will not be impenetrable to stock. Cattle and sheep are natural browsers and will kill young trees and shrubs by stripping the leaves and bark from them in preference to eating grass. Hedges vary from area to area, but all of them are designed to contain grazing stock. One hedging practice which may leave archaeological traces is that of 'laying' the hedge. This involves partly cutting through stems, laying them down and weaving them into the hedge, normally holding them in place with light-weight stakes. The stakes only need to be strong enough to hold the stems in place until growth restarts. With the new growth, the damage caused by the partial severing of the stems will gradually heal, leaving distinctive bends and thickening of the bark.

Odd fragments of right-angled roundwood have been found on Iron Age sites, at Fisherwick, Staffordshire (Williams 1979) and Bar Hill, Central Scotland (Boyd 1984), for example. The material from this site, however, is more than just fragments, with quite substantial lengths of roundwood which has clearly been partially severed and laid. As noted above, much of the coppiced roundwood would have produced rods and poles, which would have been suitable for hedge-laying.

Although the small amount of timber and debris give some indication of other woodworking activities in the area, there is too little for any detailed analysis. The only evidence for the working of large trees is indirect, with a small quantity of thick bark amongst the debris. The timbers are all derived from small trees, unlike the 'monumental' timbers from Flag Fen (Taylor 2001, tables 7.5 & 7.6); the largest piece is quarter-split and the tree from which it was derived could only have been 250–300 mm diameter. The timber debris is from similar wood-working. The few woodchips suggest activity such as sharpening posts, or would be compatible with hedge-laying.

Economic and environmental evidence

Pollen analysis (STEVE BOREHAM)
Pollen analyses were undertaken of five samples taken from F.354, F.325 and F.302. That from the first of these (F.354; Monolith 43), a Bronze Age droveway ditch, was 50 cm long. It consisted of a dark blue-grey silty clay unit ([1566]; 0–27 cm), from which a pollen sample was taken at 5 cm, overlain by an organic grey silty clay unit ([1565]; 27–50 cm), from which a pollen sample was taken at 40 cm.

Monolith 33 from F.325, a possible pond infilling dating prior to the Middle Bronze Age, was 50 cm long

TABLE 3.4. *Pollen results.*

Pollen percentage data	F.354 ESF05 43 10 cm	F.354 ESF05 43 40 cm	F.325 ESF05 33 5 cm	F.302 ESF05 26 7 cm	F.302 ESF05 25 35 cm
Pinus	0.0	0.0	2.3		0.0
Tilia	0.0	0.0	0.8		0.0
Alnus	4.8	1.9	1.6		0.0
Corylus	0.0	3.8	0.8		4.4
Salix	1.6	0.0	0.0		0.0
Poaceae	63.5	57.7	40.6		22.2
Cereals	0.0	3.8	2.3		0.0
Cyperaceae	7.9	3.8	4.7		26.7
Asteraceae (Asteroidea/Cardueae) undif.	0.0	0.0	1.6		0.0
Asteraceae (Lactuceae) undif.	3.2	1.9	4.7		15.6
Artemisia	3.2	0.0	1.6		0.0
Caryophyllaceae	1.6	0.0	3.1		0.0
Chenopodiaceae	3.2	1.9	11.7		0.0
Brassicaceae	0.0	3.8	0.0		0.0
Filipendula	0.0	0.0	4.7		0.0
Helianthemum	0.0	0.0	0.8	*Barren*	0.0
Fabaceae	0.0	0.0	0.8		0.0
Plantago lanceolata type	0.0	0.0	7.0		0.0
Rosaceae	0.0	0.0	0.8		0.0
Saxifragaceae	0.0	0.0	0.8		0.0
Apiaceae (Umbelliferae)	0.0	0.0	0.8		0.0
Liliaceae	3.2	3.8	0.0		0.0
Veronica	0.0	1.9	2.3		0.0
Polypodium	0.0	0.0	0.0		2.2
Pteropsida (monolete) undif.	7.9	7.7	3.1		15.6
Pteropsida (trilete) undif.	0.0	7.7	3.1		13.3
Sparganium type	3.1	7.1	3.0		0.0
Total trees	*4.8*	*1.9*	*4.7*		*0.0*
Total shrubs	*1.6*	*3.8*	*0.8*		*4.4*
Total herbs	*85.7*	*78.8*	*88.3*		*64.4*
Total spores	*7.9*	*15.4*	*6.3*		*31.1*
***Main Total**	**126**	**104**	**256**		**45**
Concentration (grains per ml)	67,277	39,664	97,636	<2669	15,501

and comprised a grey silty clay ([1272]; 0–50 cm), from which a pollen sample was taken at 5 cm.

Representing infilling of a pit of Late Neolithic/ Early Bronze Age date (F.302), Monolith 26 was 50 cm long and comprised a detrital peat ([1241]; 0–50 cm), from which a pollen sample was taken at 7 cm. Overlapping the top of Monolith 26 by 7 cm, Monolith 25 (50 cm long) was also taken from that feature. It comprised detrital peat ([1241]; 0–10 cm), a grey silty clay unit ([1240]; 10–22 cm), a thin band of clayey pea grit ([1238]; 22–24 cm) and an upper grey silty clay ([1237]; 24–50 cm), from which a pollen sample was taken at 35 cm.

The five samples were prepared using the standard hydrofluoric acid technique, and counted for pollen using a high-power stereo microscope. The percentage pollen data from these samples is presented in Table 3.4.

Pollen concentrations varied widely between <2669 and 97,636 grains per ml. Preservation of the palynomorphs was rather variable. The sample from Monolith 26 (F.302) proved to be barren, and corroded pollen grains were particularly noted in the samples from Moduliths 43 (F.354) and 25 (F.302). The slides contained large amounts of finely divided organic debris, which diluted the pollen and hampered counting. Statistically desirable total counts in excess of 300 pollen grains were not achieved from assessment counts of two slides for these samples.

Monolith 43; F.354 — The basal sample from 10 cm produced a pollen signal dominated by grass (Poaceae; 63.5%), with sedges (Cyperaceae; 7.9%) and a limited range of herbs including members of the lettuce family (Asteraceae; Lactuceae), goose-foot family (Chenopodiaceae), lily family (Liliaceae) and mugwort (*Artemisia*). Arboreal taxa are represented by alder (*Alnus* 4.8%) and willow (*Salix*). Aquatic plants were represented by the bur-reed (*Sparganium*), and spores of various ferns of damp ground reached 7.9%. The sample from 40 cm was also dominated by grass (57.7%), with cereal pollen (3.8%), sedges (3.8%) and herbs including members of the cabbage family (Brassicaceae), and lily family (Liliaceae). Arboreal taxa are represented by hazel (*Corylus*; 3.8%) and alder (1.9%). A range of fern spores was present, together making 15.4% of the assemblage; bur-reed was the only representative of the aquatic plants.

Monolith 33; F.325 — The sample from 5 cm was dominated by grass (40.6%), with cereal pollen (2.3%), sedges (4.7%) and a range of herbs including members of the lettuce family, goose-foot family, meadowsweet (*Filipendula*) and strap-wort plantain (*Plantago lanceolata*). Arboreal taxa were represented by pine (*Pinus*), alder, hazel and notably lime (*Tilia*). Fern spores were present, as was pollen of the emergent aquatic bur-reed.

Monolith 25; F.302 — The sample from 35 cm was dominated by sedges (26.7%) and grass pollen (22.2%); the pollen of hazel was present at 4.4%. The abnormally high proportions of Asteraceae and fern spores in this sample indicate that this pollen assemblage has been subjected to severe post-depositional oxidation and the action of soil processes. As a consequence, interpretation of the pollen assemblage should be treated with caution. These oxidative processes have also acted on the lower part of the F.302 sequence (Monolith 26), where they have destroyed virtually all the palynomorphs.

The samples from F.354 together appear to show a post-clearance landscape dominated by pasture and meadow, with a little riparian and water-side vegetation. There is a weak signal from wet alder and willow woodland and a little hazel scrub probably grew nearby. Although the upper sample (40 cm) produced some cereal pollen, there is little evidence for ground-disturbance and arable activity nearby. It would appear that by the Middle Bronze Age, woodland clearance in this area was well-advanced, and that the droveway, possibly fringed by ditches with damp-loving vegetation, ran through an open grassland environment.

F.325 also shows an open grassland environment; however, in this sample there is evidence for arable activity and ground-disturbance as well as for the presence of woodland some distance from the site. There is also a clear riparian and diverse tall-herb vegetation signal. Taken together, this evidence suggests a patchwork of vegetation types in the landscape, including arable fields, pasture and meadow, wet woodland and distant fragments of dry forest. Although the evidence is somewhat tenuous, the presence of at least some lime pollen could suggest a date earlier than the samples from F.354. A pre-Middle Bronze Age date, therefore, fits this idea very well, although it seems most likely that this feature is of Early Bronze Age rather than Late Neolithic attribution. There is little evidence from the pollen that these are deposits from a permanent pond and it is perhaps more likely that this was a seasonally wet area in a meadow.

The sample from Monolith 25 (F.302) strongly suggests that this pit became a small sedge-filled pond, which subsequently dried out. The strongly modified pollen signal provides very little additional information. Hazel scrub may have grown nearby, but otherwise the landscape was essentially treeless. There appears to be no arable activity represented, but given the poor pollen preservation this cannot be certain. It is very hard to give an age-estimate for this sample, but the sample seems to reflect post-woodland clearance.

Bulk environmental samples (ANNE DE VAREILLES)
Twenty-two bulk soil samples were processed (Fig. 3.19). Eighteen (of which two were waterlogged) were examined using an Ankara-type flotation machine. The flots were collected in a 300 μm mesh and the remaining heavy residues washed over a 1 mm mesh. The flots were dried indoors and scanned for the presence of charred plant remains, molluscs and charcoal. The four remaining waterlogged samples were processed using a 300 μm sieve in the George Pitt-Rivers Laboratory, McDonald Institute, University of Cambridge.

Sorting and identification of macro-remains were carried out under a low power binocular microscope. Identifications were made using the reference collection of the George Pitt-Rivers Laboratory. Nomenclature of plants follows Stace (1997). All environmental remains are listed in full in Tables 3.5 and 3.6.

Of the eighteen samples with charred remains only one, pit F.95, contained cereal grains. This yielded one wheat or barley grain and a cereal fragment. The other cereal remains come from the waterlogged sample from F.2, wherein one charred hulled barley grain and a charred spelt or emmer wheat glume base were found. Only four other samples contained any charred wild plant seeds; eight species are represented by one or two seeds. Three of the charred samples have a few waterlogged seeds, indicating that their contexts were once below the watertable but had subsequently dried out. The six waterlogged samples also appear to have suffered drying or aeration events, during which many seed specimens may have been lost. The relatively low quantity of seeds can only sketch a partial image of the environment they once grew in. The water-plantain (*Alisma plantago-aquatica*) in F.325 suggests that it was probably a pond, as opposed to just wet mud (cf. Boreham above). The brambles (*Rubus* sp.), elder (*Sambucus nigra*) and dogwood (*Cornus sanguinea*) from pit F.222 attest to nearby scrub or open woodland.

Together, the plant remains from the three droveway ditches, F.17, F.32 and F.45, point towards wet mud (probably from within the ditches), with a stronger signal for waste. This indicates the presence of disturbed ground, suggesting the area around the ditches was more likely to have been used for pasture than cultivation.

The later Bronze Age pit F.2 revealed the largest array of specimens. They indicate that it lay adjacent to settlement in slightly overgrown rough ground that does not appear to have been cultivated but may have been used as pasture.

TABLE 3.5. *Plant remains.*

Sample number	<4>	<5>	<8>	<9>	<12>	<13>	<20>	<31>	<34>	<36>	<37>	<39>	<54>	<56>	<57>	<59>
Context	[332]	[312]	[748]	[848]	[902]	[891]	[1290]	[108]		[966]	[1026]	[1533]	[1136]	[1095]	[687]	[1162]
Feature	95	67	182	6	197	213	20	432	352	230	233	378	271	253	163	275
Sample volume – litres	8	8	11	6	6	35	10	10	5	11	6	5	7	12	7	9
Flot fraction examined	1/1	1/1	1/1	1/1	1/1	1/1	1/1	1/1	1/1	1/1	1/1	1/1	1/1	1/1	1/1	1/1
Cereals																
Triticum/Hordeum — Wheat/Barley	1															
Indet. cereal grain fragment	1															
Wild plant seeds																
Corylus avellana — Hazelnut shell fragments			3 WL					1 WL								
Thalictrum flavum — Common Meadow-rue									1 + 1WL							
Atriplex patula/prostrata — Common/Spear-leaved Orache									1 M							
Montia fontana ssp. *minor* — Blinks					1	1			3 WL							
Stellaria media — Common chickweed						2										
Aphanes arvensis — Parsley-piert						2										
Plantago lanceolata — Ribwort plantain									2							
Cardus/Cirsium kernels — Thistle kernels			2													
Luzula sp. — Wood-rushes			1													
Indet. wild plant seed			1													
Parenchyma tissue fragments — Undifferentiated storage plant tissue										+						
Bud			1													
Charcoal pieces																
>4 mm	-	-	++	-				-		-				-	-	+
2–4 mm	+	-	+	-				-	-	+			-	+	-	+
<2 mm	++	+	+++	-	+	++		+++	-	+	++	+	++	+++	+	++
Vitrified			-			-				-						

Key: '-' 1 or 2 items, '+' <10 items, '++' 10–50 items, '+++' >50 items; WL = waterlogged, M = modern

TABLE 3.6. *Plant remains from waterlogged samples.*

			<14>	<23>	<17>	<32>	<45>	<2>
		Sample number	<14>	<23>	<17>	<32>	<45>	<2>
		Context	[1037]	[1272]	[1222]	[1566]	[453]	[58]
		Feature	222	325	290	354	102	2
		Feature type	Pit	Pond?	Ditch	Ditch	Ditch	Pit
		Phase/Date	BA?		MBA	MBA	MBA	LBA
		Sample volume - Litres	0. 5	0. 5	0. 5	0. 5	12. 5	8
		Flot fraction examined	1/2	1/1	1/1	1/1	1/4	1/4
	Common name	**Ecology**						
Hordeum vulgare sensu lato	Hulled barley grain							1 C
Triticum spelta/dicoccum glume base	Spelt/Emmer wheat glume base							1 C
Ranunculus Subgen. BATRACHIUM	Crowfoot	On mud and in shallow water			-	++	-	-
Ranunculus sceleratus	Celery-leaved buttercup	Marshy fields, ditches, ponds			-			-
Ranunculus sp.	Buttercups		-			-		+
Urtica dioica	Common nettle	Many, including woodland, fens, cultivated ground and manured soil	-	-	++			++
Small *Chenopodium* sp.	Small goosefoots		-	++		+	-	+
Atriplex patula/prostrata	Oraches	Cultivated and waste ground		+				+
Stellaria media	Common chickweed	Cultivated and waste ground		-			-	++
Polygonum hidropiper	Water-pepper	Damp places and shallow water						-
Polygonum aviculare	Knotgrass	All sorts of open ground		-	-			+
R. conglomeratus/ sanguineus/ obtusifolius	Small seeded dock		+					++
Rubus sp.	Brambles	Disturbed ground, wood clearings	++	-	-	+		-
Potentilla anserina	Silverweed	Waste places, pastures			-	+		+
Cornus sanguinea	Dogwood	(Shrub) Woods and scrub	-					
Hydrocotyle vulgaris	Marsh Pennywort	Fens, marshes, bogs, by lakes			-			
Torilis japonica	Upright hedge-parsley	Grassy, hedge-rows, clearings						-
Daucus carota	Wild carrot	Grassy and rough ground						-
Solanum nigrum	Black nightshade	Cultivated and waste ground				+		-
Hyoscyamus niger	Henbane	Rough and waste ground, often manured by rabbits or cattle						-
Lamium sp.	Dead-nettles				-			
cf. *Galeopsis bifida*	Bifid hemp-nettle	Arable, rough ground, clearings						-
Prunella vulgaris	Selfheal	Rough ground, wood clearings			-			+
Lycopus europaeus	Gypsywort	Fens, wet fields, by water						++
Mentha sp.	Mint				-			
Sambucus nigra	Elder	Hedges, woods, rough ground, especially on manured soil	+				-	-
Carduus/Cirsium	Thistles					-	-	+
Sonchus oleraceus/asper	Sow-thistles	Cultivated and waste ground		-			-	+
Anthemis cotula	Stinking chamomile	Cultivated and waste ground			-			
Picris echioides	Bristly oxtongue	Disturbed and rough ground					- M	
Alisma plantago-aquatica	Water-plantain	In or by ponds, rivers, ditches		+				
Large *Potamogeton* sp.	Pondweeds		-					
Potamogeton sp.	Pondweeds					-		
Zannichellia palustris	Horned pondweed	Rivers, streams, ditches and ponds			-			
cf. *Cladium mariscus*	Great fen-sedge	Fens, by streams and ponds		-				
large trilete *Carex* sp.	Sedge		-				+	-
Small flat *Carex* sp.	Sedge		-	-		+		-
Indet. wild plant seed			-				-	-
Entomological remains			-	+				++
Charcoal frags. 2–4 mm			+		-		+	
<2 mm			++		++		-	

Key: '-' 1 or 2 items, '+' <10 items, '++' 10–50 items, '+++' >50 items; M = modern, C = charred

Of the eighteen samples containing charcoal, only two revealed evidence of household fires associated with cooking and eating. Although the preservation of waterlogged plant remains was not ideal, the assemblage of surviving species appears to attest to disturbed open space close to settlement, slightly overgrown with grasses, nettles and brambles. The possibility remains that small cultivated plots were present within the larger overgrown area.

Faunal remains (KRISH SEETAH)

The assemblage totalled some 3948 fragments, of which 2923 were 'assess-able'; 1587 fragments were identified to element (54 per cent) and 744 (25 per cent) further identified to species. The site represents a continuation of research in the Fengate environs that has so far appraised material from the later Neolithic (Storey's Bar Road; Harman 1978), Bronze Age (Newark Road; Biddick 1980) and Iron Age (Cat's Water; Biddick 1984). The Elliot Site was dominated by a major Bronze Age droveway funnelling into large ditched compound. Presumably designed for the management and husbandry of livestock this, combined with the size of this assemblage relative to the previous reports, indicates that the site's bone assemblage is of particular value for addressing issues of animal exploitation, local economy and management strategies. This report will briefly outline the methods used for analysing the material, before setting out the results elicited. These will initially be discussed in broad terms relative to species representation and then situated within the broader remit of the site's relative chronological phasing.

The zooarchaeological study followed the system implemented by Bournemouth University, with all identifiable elements recorded (NISP: Number of Identifiable Specimens) and diagnostic zoning (amended from Dobney & Reilly 1988) used to calculate MNE (Minimum Number of Elements) from which MNI (Minimum Number of Individuals) was derived. Ageing of the assemblage employed a combination of Grant's (1982) tooth wear stages and fusion of proximal and distal epiphyses (Silver 1969). Metrical analysis followed von den Driesch (1976; with additional measurements from Bartosiewitz *et al.* 1997 for aurochs). Elements from sheep and goats were distinguished where possible, based on criteria established for the post-cranial skeleton by Boessneck (1969) and teeth by Payne (1985) and Halstead *et al.* (2002). Identification of the assemblage was undertaken with the aid of Schmid (1972) and reference material from the CAU and the Grahame Clark Zooarchaeology Laboratory, Dept. of Archaeology, University of Cambridge. Taphonomic criteria including indications of butchery, gnawing activity and surface modifications as a result of weathering were also recorded, as were skeletal pathologies, when evident.

The assemblage was hand-collected and overall exhibited poor preservation. Of 129 separate contexts studied, 64 were 'Quite Poor' or 'Poor', indicating that extensive weathering, bone surface exfoliation and other erosive damage had occurred. In particular, and as noted on other Fengate sites (Biddick 1980; 1984), iron-rich concretions were present on the bone. The poor preservation was most detrimental for the analyses of anthropogenic modifications, such as butchery, and when attempting to decipher the taphonomic history of particular bones. Weathering and other erosive soil conditions can also adversely affect the more porous elements or parts thereof, especially the epiphyses and juvenile bone.

Species representation

The medium and large mammalian assemblage was dominated by domestic species: cow, horse, sheep/goat, pig and dog. Wild species were represented by two roe deer mandibles: a left and right pair from a juvenile individual. A possible red deer antler fragment was also recovered, although erosive damage and mineral infiltration call for caution with this identification. An aurochs metatarsal was also recovered, as was a mandible of a wild boar.

Of the domestic animals present, cattle were by far the most abundant, both within the context of NISP counts (580/78 per cent) and MNI, with at least 15 individuals recorded for the assemblage as a whole. Sheep (NISP: 126/17 per cent) and pig (NISP: 18/2 per cent) had MNI counts of five and two individual animals respectively with horse (NISP: 6/<1 per cent) having an MNI of one and dog (NISP: 11/1.6 per cent) representing a minimum of two individuals (Table 3.7 & Fig. 3.26).

Bos taurus

The cattle assemblage included all recordable carcass portions with a predominance of distal elements, particularly of the skull. This is to be expected considering that the distal bones outnumber the proximal elements (comparing metapodials to the femur and humerus); cranial bones are also more prone to post-depositional fracturing. The occurrence of skull and mandibular elements indicates either that whole animals were transported to the site 'on the hoof' and processed as needed, or that they were raised on site. One mostly complete cattle skull (Fig. 3.27) demonstrated evidence for on-site slaughter in the form of a pole-axe mark. Pole-axing can be used to serve two purposes. Firstly, it can be used to stun the animal, after which it can be slaughtered by another means such as cutting the throat. Alternatively, the blow can be driven deeper into the brain cavity to create a hole. This is then followed by 'pithing' to destroy the brain tissue. In this instance the pole-axe mark indicated that this technique was used only to stun the animal, as the puncture did not penetrate into the cranium. The blow was

TABLE 3.7. *NISP and MNI counts and percentages.*

Species	NISP	% NISP	MNI	%MNI
Cow	580	78	15	57.7
Dog	12	1.6	2	7.7
Horse	6	0.8	1	3.8
Fish	4	0.5	1	3.8
Pig	18	1.6	2	7.7
Roe	2	0.2	1	3.8
Sheep/Goat	126	17	5	19.2
Total ID Specimens	**744**			
UMM (Un.id medium mammal)	324			
ULM (Un.id large mammal)	515			
Total NISP count	**1587**			
Total fragment count	**2923**			

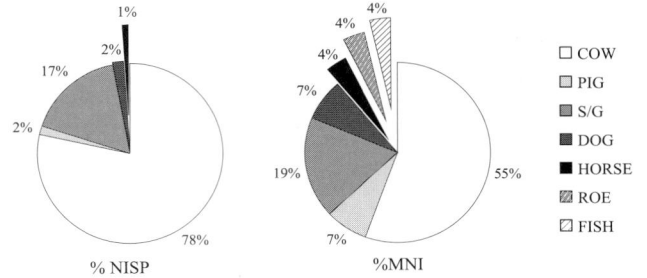

FIGURE 3.26. *Animal Bone: a) pie-chart of %NISP for main domesticates; b) pie-chart of %MNI for all species recorded.*

FIGURE 3.27. *Pole-axed cattle skull (F.2; D. Webb photograph).*

precisely delivered, slightly off-centre (Fig. 3.28 below demonstrates the ideal position for pole-axing; compare to Fig. 3.27 above). This technique for slaughter has also been reported from Iron Age contexts at Fengate (Biddick 1984).

FIGURE 3.28. *Pole-axe delivery point.*

The main meat-bearing units of the carcass, the femur for the hind quarter and the humerus/scapula for the forequarter, are both equally well-represented; however, when the distal components of the fore and hind limb are compared there is a distinct bias towards the metatarsals (hind limb: 21 records) compared to metacarpals (seven records). This is surprising as, although the metapodials as a group are extensively used for working, the metatarsal (due to its squarer shape) is usually favoured; this anomaly cannot at present be explained.

Cattle elements accounted for more identifiable bones than all the other species combined. Evidently, cattle were the most significant economic species on the site and were the main providers of meat. The ageing evidence indicated the presence of both young and old animals. A more specific age-estimation derived from the teeth (although only six mandibles were present, making the calculation of an age-profile ambiguous), indicated an average age of 30–36 months, although one of these animals had a higher Mandibular Wear Stage (MWS), which indicated an 'old adult'. This age structure would suggest that individuals were kept for traction, although the oldest range, termed 'senile', was not evident. This pays testament to the multi-purpose nature of this species and its diverse role within an economic setting.

Ovicaprids

The ovicaprid portion of the assemblage was once again composed of all the main carcass units, with a more equal distribution of hind and forelimb elements than noted for cow. Again, it would appear that animals were raised on site and killed once they were 'surplus to requirements'. Although in general it is difficult to distinguish between sheep and goats, for some elements this is far more straight-forward, the horn cores being a particularly good example. At least

three definite goat horn cores were recovered, as noted from the cross-section and overall shape of the bones. Although no definite sheep bones were identified, these two findings should not be taken to indicate that sheep were secondary to goat. It would be more appropriate to infer that goat formed part of the live assemblage simply because they are able to take advantage of resources that sheep are less adept at exploiting. The probable nature of the site, combined with structural indications of advanced husbandry, favour sheep management as opposed to goat. As with cattle, the individual animals fell within a wide age range from juvenile to adult; however, again duplicating the pattern seen in cattle, no 'senile' individuals were present. Sheep would also have been used as a multi-purpose animal, for wool, milk and meat.

Sus scrofa

While the general pattern of exploitation evidenced for cattle and ovicaprids is interesting and informative, the pig assemblage is re-markable for its paucity. Pig bones accounted for only 18 individual fragments, representing two per cent of the total assemblage. A similar paucity has been noted previously for Bronze Age contexts at Fengate (Biddick 1980). Although in general pig husbandry has traditionally been viewed as being 'woodland' based (or, in later periods with increased intensification, 'sty based'), more recent research has shed doubt on whether these are the only two modes of management used in pig husbandry. Pigs have been noted to exist in a semi-feral state (Greenfield 1985) acting as scavengers, with minimal human interference. From the evidence at this site, it would appear that pigs did not form a major part of the diet or economy and, in much the same way as goat, were present as they could take advantage of resources that other domestic animals could not.

Canids, equids and wild species

Little can be said regarding the presence of canids and equids on the site, as the element frequency was unrepresentative. All the canid bones came from cranial portions, with the exception of one fused distal tibia fragment. The evidence for one of the individuals suggested that the animal was relatively robust; the level of wear on the maxillary teeth indicated an adult animal. The presence of dogs is also evidenced from gnawing damage on cattle, horse and ovicaprid bones, although this occurred on only a small number.

Wild species were present in the form of two roe mandibles, probably from the same individual. The teeth present and level of wear indicated a juvenile animal. Unfortunately, these elements were from unphased contexts and cannot be attributed to a specific period. One aurochs metatarsal was present, along with a wild boar mandible; these will be discussed below.

Later Mesolithic/Neolithic activity
A total of 17 fragments were recorded from contexts that could be securely dated to Late Mesolithic/Neolithic activity. Of these, all identifiable fragments (four in total) were from cattle. They included the distal portion of a humerus and a complete first phalanx. Although this very small sub-set of the overall assemblage has little interpretive value, we can at least infer that the bones derive from an animal that was over 18 months old (fusion of the distal humerus occurs between 12 and 18 months; Silver 1969).

Later Neolithic/Early Bronze Age
The majority of elements from contexts that could be clearly identified to the later Neolithic–Early Bronze Age were from cattle (38 fragments), although sheep (19 fragments) were relatively well-represented proportionally to cow. For cattle, the bulk of axial elements (skull, ribs, vertebrae and pelvis) were poorly represented or absent. In particular, there was a total absence of ribs. This, combined with the proportionally well-represented 'high meat yield'

TABLE 3.8. *Measurements of aurochs metatarsal (after von den Driesch 1976; Bartosiewitz et al. 1997).*

Measurement	(mm)
DD	35.4
Bd	80.0
DFdm	36.3
Ddm	44.1
Ddl	Lateral trochlea damaged
DiSD	Diaphysis incomplete
DiDD	82.5
BFdl	35.0
Bcr	38.4
Dcm	21.3
Dcl	18.7

portions such as the femur, may indicate the preferential selection of these units, with axial elements distributed elsewhere. This pattern is repeated for sheep, although in this case it is the upper forelimb that is favoured rather than the hind limb. Once again, there is a total absence of ribs, with the dearth of axial elements reinforced by an absence of vertebrae. The above might suggest that the particular features from which the later Neolithic/EBA material comes were dumps post-*consumption*, rather than post-*butchery* processing. Dog, horse and domestic pig were also noted within these features, although the numbers in which they appear are too small to be worth further elaboration.

The aurochs and wild boar elements were recovered from features dated to this chronological period (indeed, the presence of the aurochs was an important indicator of temporality). The aurochs metatarsal was recovered from F.222 (see Lynch *et al.* 2008). The bones from this feature showed a high degree of staining indicating that they had been in waterlogged conditions for some time. The measurements (Table 3.8) from the aurochs metatarsal indicate that it was an adult male (Degerbol & Fredskild 1970). The boar was also probably an adult male (Payne & Bull 1988), but from a relatively young individual as the wear on the third molar had made little impact into the dentine. Whilst it could be speculated that the presence of these species indicates a woodland environment at that time, this would be an over-interpretation of the available data. There is certainly a possibility that woodland was present; however, these highly mobile animals are represented in numbers too small to indicate the ecological setting.

Middle Bronze Age fieldsystem ditches
North Ditch — Although the NISP count for this feature totalled some 453 fragments, only 43 bones where identifiable to species. The bulk of the material was composed of unidentifiable fragments that had undergone a high degree of fragmentation and were calcired following extensive burning. Only two species were represented: cow (32 fragments) and ovicaprid (11 fragments). Despite being a relatively small collection of cow elements, there was a reasonable distribution of skeletal parts; however, the highest meat yielding parts, particularly of the hind limb, are under-represented (only one femoral fragment was recorded). In contrast, distal limb elements are well-represented, as are distal axial portions such as the skull. Vertebrae and ribs are poorly represented compared to the frequency in which these elements occur in the body. As suggested previously, this seems to indicate that the features saw dumping of material following consumption, as opposed to what might be considered butchery waste.

The ovicaprid elements, with the exception of one racial fragment and two loose teeth, were all from the hind quarter, particularly the uppermost portion (femur and pelvis).

South Ditch — A smaller sub-set of faunal remains was recovered from this ditch feature than for the North Ditch, totalling 84 fragments. In common with the trend set by the assemblage as a whole, cattle bones predominated (15 fragments), with ovicaprids (four bones) and pig (one) also represented. Cattle fore limb elements are better represented than hind limb, although there is an under representation of the highest meat content carcass units (total absence of femur and under representation, proportionally, of uppermost forequarter elements). At least two individual animals were present; the sample size precludes further inference.

The ovicaprid elements are all potentially from the same individual. The generally porous nature of the bones and lack of fusion indicate that this was a juvenile; the bones present are predominantly from the hind limb (a left and right tibia and left femur). All elements were near 75 per cent complete, with no indications of butchery or further processing.

Later Bronze Age
The cattle assemblage from LBA features is interesting due to the predominance of distal and axial portions (particularly of the skull) over proximal (and higher meat content) units. Whilst it might be expected that distal elements would outnumber proximal ones, the proportions (132 distal fragments compared to 26 proximal) are surprising. The same trend is repeated with the ovicaprid sub-set, with only one femur and two humeral fragments recorded from an overall ovicaprid count of 59 fragments. With caveats noted regarding sample size and the use of fragment counts only (MNI counts are not viable with such small numbers of major limb elements), there would appear to be a distinct trend towards lower meat content units and, in particular, cranial portions. This represents a departure from EBA exploitation and may indicate a change in structure and function relating to animal husbandry. The assemblage would appear more directly related to carcass processing activity, rather than the waste following consumption. Both pig (10 fragments) and dog (one maxilla fragment) are present, but in numbers too small to warrant further discussion.

'Bronze Age'
The Bronze Age as a whole provides the largest grouping of bone by chronological sub-division for the overall assemblage. Some 2598 fragments were recovered. Of these, 680 were identifiable to species (27 per cent), of which 540 (20 per cent of the total assemblage/79 per cent of identifiable fragments) were from cattle. They were clearly of greatest importance during this phase as a whole, with ovicaprids present but in significantly smaller numbers (121 fragments/18 per cent of identified bones). This trend has been reported previously at Fengate, both from Neolithic levels where the assemblage was composed of 70 per cent cattle (Harman 1978) and the Bronze Age material from Newark Road, where 75.5 per cent consisted of cattle (Biddick 1980). It is not until the Iron Age that this heavy predominance of cattle over all other species is reversed: cattle account for 45 per cent of the Iron Age animal bone assemblage from Cat's Water (Biddick 1984).

The overwhelming predominance of cattle needs to be taken into account in the context of how this species functioned economically, as a beast of burden, and within the diet. Although we cannot accurately infer the numbers of animals being maintained, and a large portion of the fragment count comes from elements such as the skull (which are easily fractured and become overly represented in the NISP count), it can be suggested that cattle would have been the main meat providers and, if kept for traction purposes (as the limited ageing data hints at), would have had a major economic as well as nutritional role. Despite the presence of horse fragments during this phase, albeit in very small numbers (three fragments), it is only in the early historic period, with imported and improved stock, that the horse becomes an important traction animal. Prior to this, cattle were the primary beast of burden and providers of traction power (Albarella 2004).

Iron Age and Romano-British

Fragments from dog (eight) accounted for the majority of elements recovered from Iron Age features. These were all undoubtedly from the same individual and consisted of a fragmented cranium with maxilla. The animal was an adult and relatively robust. Cow (six fragments), ovicaprid (three) and horse (two bones) were all represented, although the numbers in which they occur preclude further inference. The potential red deer antler fragment was also from an Iron Age feature.

Only one fragment was identifiable to species from the Romano-British period: a portion of femoral head from an adult horse.

Butchery

Evidence for butchery was minimal and was present only on cattle bones (four indications of butchery were recorded in total, three of which were on cow elements). Although the evidence was minimal, and it would be a mistake to over-analyse the data, it is worth noting that in all instances the butchery was carried out with knives without any indications of a cleaver. This is particularly interesting when taken in the context of previous research, which has reported indications of butchery involving large bladed tools. Undoubtedly, the absence of butchery evidence does not indicate the absence of carcass processing: in this case the lack of cut-marks is explained by the high level of weathering and cortical exfoliation, as well as the concretions evident on the bone surface.

This assemblage has provided a useful and informative set of data, primarily for Bronze Age activity at Fengate. It is unfortunate that the state of preservation has had such a detrimental effect on the overwhelming majority of the bones; this has precluded a more in-depth appraisal of butchery and other taphonomic change, and has hampered analytical processes such as the taking of measurements and the appraisal of toothwear. Nonetheless, this assemblage has provided some useful insights into the management of animals and the patterns of exploitation used to procure faunal resources. Although the species range recovered (particularly the total lack of micro-fauna) precludes any discussion of the environmental conditions of the site, we are able to link the faunal remains with site activity. In concurrence with the observation above, we can be clear that dumping of faunal remains was *not* the main function of the pit features that typify this site: with only 47 out of 199 pits containing bone it would appear that disposal of primary processing waste (and perhaps primary processing itself) was either taking place elsewhere or on a portion of the site as yet unexcavated. This is supported by the findings of element representation in the Bronze Age as a whole: the carcass units present indicate a predominance of lower meat content portions overall. Caution needs to be exercised as the later Bronze Age evidence does indicate a shift towards evidence for butchery waste rather than consumption waste (although the later Bronze Age represents a small sub-division of the overall 'Bronze Age' assemblage). Whilst the faunal

assemblage can only indicate a negative conclusion regarding the pit features that dot the site, we can be much more convinced of the function of the parallel ditches. These would almost certainly have operated as a funnelling mechanism for the movement of livestock, as noted by Pryor (1996); however, there is no indication to support Pryor's conclusion that this was for the movement of sheep: the evidence from this site and Newark Road would indicate that cattle were the main domestic species being raised and maintained at Fengate. Unfortunately, the Iron Age sub-set is too small to observe the transition from one period to the next and although sheep numbers increase dramatically in the Iron Age, as noted at Cat's Water, they are still secondary to cattle. The function of this area as a major 'livestock thoroughfare' may also help explain why the dumping of material is sporadic and not indicative of butchery waste: the processing of animals and disposal of waste occurred elsewhere.

Concluding discussion

The pre-mid second-millennium/-fieldsystem usage of the Elliott Site is, in many respects, antithetical to that at the Edgerley Drain Road Site. The latter, with its various pit clusters (covering the full span of the earlier Neolithic to the earlier Bronze Age), essentially amounts to a 'type-series' of British prehistory. In contrast, no pre-Middle Bronze Age pottery whatsoever was recovered here. Equally, given the proximity of Pryor's Storey's Bar Road Grooved Ware site, the complete absence of any such pottery at the Elliott Site seems, at first glance, remarkable and the location can only be considered marginal to its main settlement swathe. Despite its apparent marginality, including a low ground embayment penetrating back into the fen-edge terrace, the Elliot Site certainly saw considerable activity, as is witnessed by the quantity of its pitting and its animal bone assemblage. People were clearly drawn to this locale to undertake a variety of activities, but these did not involve pottery deposition to any significant degree.

Amongst the most potentially informative of the site's many pit features is F.222, which yielded both aurochs and wild boar bone in addition to more than 20 worked flints. The latter included a later Neolithic oblique arrowhead, whose assignation would accord with the radiocarbon date achieved from the aurochs bone, 2880–2610 cal. BC (OxA-X-2182-55); though pottery did not feature in the pit's assemblages, this could suggest a Grooved Ware attribution. It, therefore, would resonate with, and could actually have been an 'edge-outlier' of, Pryor's Storey's Bar Road Grooved Ware site and which certainly continued eastwards to the area of the TK Packaging Plant Site (with its Grooved Ware and aurochs skull pit; see Inset above and, also, Chapter 1 summaries and Pryor 2001a, 407). What would then distinguish this Grooved Ware occupation would be the frequency of aurochs bone, as some 18 pieces (five MNI) were recovered from the Storey's Bar Road excavations (in addition to four possible wild pig bones/four MNI; see Harman 1978, 177–80, fig. 51 & table 60). Although it is now commonplace to associate the occurrence of 'the wild' with modes of Neolithic symbolic deposition (e.g. Pryor 1998a, 371), if this evidence is combined with the high ratio of later Neolithic arrowheads from Storey's Bar Road (26; see Pryor 1978, 138–41 and Chapter 4 below) then this larger complex might even have been some manner of hunting camp. Certainly the character of its 'occupation' from this period differs significantly from that at the Edgerley Drain Road Site and, accordingly, further discussion of this issue will be best confined to Chapter 4 below. However, by way of immediate further comparison, three of the five Grooved Ware-attributed pit clusters excavated at Over Site 2 produced what might have been comparable 'hunting-related' animal bone assemblages (Fig. 2.20). Excluding 232 unidentifiable fragments, of the 291 pieces 17 were of aurochs and four were wild pig, with there also being 23 deer elements; in other words, some 15 per cent of their assemblages were 'wild' (Higbee, in Evans & Knight 2004; see also Garrow 2006, 81, fig. 6.3). Wild species only constituted *c.* 1 per cent of the 3123 identifiable animal bones from the Etton causewayed enclosure's Neolithic phases. Of the 15 aurochs bones recovered, none were from primary ditch contexts and the majority — 12 — derived from either Phase 2 of its circuit or its interior pit features, with most seemingly associated with its later Neolithic/Grooved Ware-associated utilization (Armour-Chelu 1998a, 273–88.)

The attraction of the immediate Elliot Site area was evidently not just determined by the wet-ground topography of its embayment, but also its mixed geology, specifically, the occurrence of clay within the terrace's beds at this point. Not only would this have provided a source of raw materials for the manufacture of ceramics (daub, loomweights and potentially even pottery), but it would have also enabled water-holding. The latter — especially the raised perching of the watertable — is what allowed the waterlogging of a number of its features, which fell at absolute heights where such preservation would not normally be expected.

From these combined factors, the occurrence of tanning and retting/soaking activities can also be postulated, in addition to woodworking, food-processing,

stock-watering and butchery. In short, what this attests to is a range of *taskscape* activities: variously regular and/or daily-life subsistence needs that would, effectively, remain as a background constant despite any changes that might occur in pottery(-*type*) styles over time. This is even true during the site's main Bronze Age fieldsystem-usage, when many of these activities would have continued (augmented by gravel quarrying for the construction of its metalled surfaces).

The slow build-up of excavation (and radiocarbon) results and the 'type' predictability of accompanying material culture, of course deeply influences the interpretation of any individual (sub-)site. This invariably brings with it a reliance on *pattern*, as opposed to the *possibilities* suggested by 'rogue findings'. In the case of this site, there has, indeed, been just such an instance of the 'unexpected': the waterlogged F.302 pit. Given the hedgewood and fine-quality wooden straps recovered from it (and the lack of direct dating evidence), we anticipated that it would date to the later Bronze Age/earlier Iron Age. When its two radiocarbon results came back and it was found to date to *c.* 2000 cal. BC (Beta-230848 & 230849), suddenly any comfortable sense that the region's Bronze age fieldsystem all dated to the mid second millennium was challenged: could Pryor's consistent third-millennium BC attribution of Fengate's system be correct? Within the Elliott Site's dating sequence, taken at face-value, the F.2 assay of *c.* 1500–1400 cal. BC for the demise of its droveway ditches could support such an 'early' attribution for the system. Admittedly, as argued above, the F.2 date could always be from residual material and thus date the use of the fieldsystem ditch rather than its infilling (though comparable dating evidence from Edgerley would lend further credibility to an 'early' assertion; see Chapter 4 below). Equally, whilst F.302's assemblages attest to the fact that the landscape was already cleared and (from the evidence of its hedgewood) had seen some degree of allotment/division (agriculture would surely have been practised, as attested to by the cereal pollen within F.325; see Boreham above), this need not imply that the fieldsystem as a whole dates to the later Neolithic, or even necessarily to the earliest Bronze Age. These remain, nevertheless, crucial issues and, together with the apparent contradiction in the existence of bow-related hunting pursuits (based on the design affinities/symbolism of F.302's yew straps) at a time when the area's landscape showed evidence of extensive management, will be returned in the volume's final chapter.

The occurrence of two definite crouched burials (F.73 and Pryor's F.1594), and possibly another, disturbed third along the drove (as represented by the remains in F.3/F.22), might also reflect upon the date of the system's layout. Inhumation rites are usually associated with the earlier Bronze Age and, for example, one in a cluster of three inhumations at the Babraham Road Park-and-Ride Site just south of Cambridge has been dated to 2205–1895 cal. BC (Hinman 2001b, 36–7). Relevant here, of course, is whether the Elliott Site's inhumation grouping is considered to represent a pre-droveway cemetery, as could be suggested by the F.3/F.22 disturbed interment, or to be contemporary with it, as would seem to be the case with Pryor's F.1594 burial (lying off of the drove, F.73 does not shed any light on this issue). Crucial to this, though, is the fact that another ditch-interment was found in this drove's ditches further west in Pryor's Padholme Road exposure, this apparently occurring within the ditch itself rather than in a pit (Pryor 1980a, 5, fig. 7). As will be outlined in Chapter 4 below, a crouched burial was also forthcoming from a droveway boundary at the Broadlands Site and, therefore, there does seem to be a close correlation between Fengate's droves and inhumation burials. This being said, the frequency of inhumations along the Ditch 1/2 drove could mark its importance as a through-fieldsystem route.

Given its sheer scale and cursus-like proportions, there is certainly a temptation to stress the crucial role of the Elliot Site's 'great' stock compound in the operation of Fengate's fieldsystem. Indeed, a picture could be painted evoking the seasonal crush of animals packed into it and, also, the *en masse* culling of stock. Compelling though such a scenario may be, we should be wary of over-exaggeration. On the one hand, much higher phosphate levels should probably have been expected had many hundreds of animals been present, just as a greater degree of ground-surface churning/reduction should have been evident. Equally, whilst animal butchery clearly did occur, it did not involve vast numbers. Yes, probably on annually returning into the system from fen-edge pastures, stock would have been driven into the compound and sorted (and some culling probably occurring within the immediate area), but this would all seem to have been of a fairly modest scale. Certainly, we are not witnessing American Western 'ranch-scale' dynamics here (see e.g. Ingold 1980, 235–63).

There is also a certain 'dualism' or ambiguity to the role of the compound itself. While formally arranged and clearly linked to the Ditch 1/2 drove, at the same time (based on the evidence of the Birmingham University Field Unit's trenching), fenwards its boundaries appear to have turned to hug the terrace-side. In this manner, it would also seem to relate to a wider ditched network — like that at the Power Station sub-Site or, further afield, Bradley Fen (see Chapter 2)

— delineating the Bronze Age fen-edge. Nor should the fact that the compound effectively enclosed the terrace embayment, and that natural contours obviously participated in the general recommendation of its layout, be overlooked (this raises in turn the issue of whether the embayment's location dictated the line of the Ditch 1/2 droveway).

Accepting these caveats, the layout of the site's droveway/compound does provoke significant questions concerning the nature of the system's stock management and, particularly, the ownership of animals and access to pasture. How are we to envisage this? Was it a matter of individual families tending their stock, or were animals held communally on a mass, fieldsystem-wide basis and managed accordingly? Given the evidence of the Elliott Site's system, the latter proposition seems unlikely: there was simply no evidence of such grand-scale use. Yet, against this, the Elliott Site's layout would still suggest a larger group dynamic and something beyond the immediate, single roundhouse residential unit. In this context, lineage-based holding would offer an appropriate model, with a kinship group's animals collectively held and tended together when out in seasonal pastures. By this means, perhaps 100–200 head might be the maximum numbers involved. When returning to the 'mainland' in the autumn, driven into the compound (perhaps accompanied by culling), they could have been separated into family herds/flocks. *En route* to first being driven out in spring-time, the compound may equally have been the location where young animals were marked with their household's 'signs' (see Evans & Hodder 2006b, 247 concerning such herding arrangements; see also Fleming 1985).

By any normal standards, the paucity of occupation debris associated with the Structure 1 roundhouse and the immediate fieldsystem 'block' in which it lay can only be considered extraordinarily low. This is to the point that it might not be accredited as a house *per se*, but rather interpreted as having an ancillary function (e.g. a barn). Yet, based on the excavation of comparable second-millennium BC buildings at Fengate (e.g. the two Newark Road-compound's roundhouses; Pryor 1980a), and indeed elsewhere in the region, this is now known to be typical. The problem, essentially, derives from the remarkable paucity of settlement-associated Deverel-Rimbury pottery (the hallmark ware of the fifteenth to twelfth centuries BC) within the region: if it were not for the fact that such pottery obviously featured in the urned cremations of that time, the possibility that the period was largely aceramic could even be entertained. Given this, the very low level of Bronze Age pottery at this site could itself argue for the Middle Bronze Age-attribution of its settlement evidence; in other words, if of later Bronze Age date then far more pottery is likely to have been present. In fact, and as discussed above, the main Elliot roundhouse actually seems to have lain within a fieldsystem-associated 'settlement swathe', together with Pryor's nearby, compound-enclosed Structure 46 roundhouse at the Cat's Water Site (Fig. 3.22; Pryor 1984).

While lacking the 'obviousness' of Structure 1, it is also likely that other, broadly contemporary settlement occurred within the Elliott Site. Falling between 1.2–1.4 m OD, the cluster of postholes (including the Structure 2 four-poster) and the F.383 'trough' along the northern side of the embayment in Area C, by their absolute height/depth, certainly cannot have been of post-Bronze Age date. (Though by their proximity to the F.302 pit and their uncomfortable relationship with the main compound boundary, they may have been of earlier, pre-fieldsystem, attribution.) As to the only other readily apparent settlement cluster on the site — the Structure 4 roundhouse and possible

Structure 3 four-poster that overlapped its circle — this is tentatively assigned to the subsequent Iron Age utilization on the basis of its absolute height and 'tucked' relationship to the later fieldsystem, as well as the occurrence of other later features in the vicinity. This being said, no direct dating evidence was recovered in association with either structure, and therefore they could conceivably have also been of Bronze Age date.

Finally, little can be said of the site's Iron Age and Roman activity, as it saw so little deposition. Certainly its location on the northern side of the embayment would have to be considered marginal to the main Cat's Water settlement 'core' of that time. During the Iron Age we can, once more, envisage a number of 'off-site' water-related activities occurring, of which metalworking — as suggested by the slag from F.230 and F.233 — is but one. Whilst the notion that in Iron Age/Roman times the embayment may have served for the docking of its community's boats is appealing, in the absence of any further supportive evidence this can only remain speculative.

Chapter 4

Edgerley Drain Road — Fengate North

Emma Beadsmoore & Christopher Evans

Lying back from the fen-edge proper and along the northwestern side of the Flag Fen embayment (3.5–4 m OD; Figs. 1.1 & 1.8), this 350 m-long, 4.6 ha site is important on two counts. Firstly, it saw a full array of Neolithic and earlier Bronze Age 'pottery-typed' pits. Not only is this the first time that a recent Fengate excavation has had such a 'full' sequence — its findings thereby shedding light on Abbott's earlier investigations — but it has proved to be one of the richest multi-period prehistoric 'pit-type' sites in the region and, in fact, has produced the largest assemblages of Grooved Ware and Beaker pottery from any such site to date (see Garrow 2006 and 2007 for overview). Secondly, it lay in an area of Fengate that, thus far, has only seen limited fieldwork and generated fairly disparate results. In the light of this, the scale of the Edgerley Road Site allows a large 'block' of the second-millennium BC fieldsystem to be drawn together and discussed. In this capacity and, given its layout/location, it furthermore provides a basis from which to address the issue of *fieldsystem seams*; effectively, their beginnings and ends and, specifically, whether this was actually the same system as in Fengate's southward 'core'.

In 2004 a 5 per cent trial-trench evaluation was undertaken across the total area of the site, the location of the trenches being informed by Rog Palmer's aerial photographic survey (Figs. 4.1 & 4.2; Cooper 2004b). Archaeological remains were found in all but three of the 24 trenches, with some 75 features recorded. These proved, moreover, to be quite prolific, with 380 sherds of prehistoric pottery and more than 100 worked flints recovered.

As will become obvious, the correspondence between the aerial photographic plot and the exposed archaeology was generally inconsistent. While, in hindsight, the main axes of the fieldsystem's main 'strip-paddock' (see below) registered within the centre half of the field (and the line of an adjoining east–west boundary just west of the site can also be 'accepted'), none of its boundaries showed across the northern half. Equally, within the southern quarter of

the plot, a network of small, interlinked sub-rectangular cropmark-paddocks was visible, suggestive of Iron Age settlement. Of these, however, there was no evidence whatsoever in the ground (nor any finds of that period). Given this negative evidence, it is difficult to evaluate the status of the cropmark circle located immediately west of the field's edge at this point. This ambiguity is unfortunate for, at 16 m in diameter, though it could possibly be a large Iron Age roundhouse, this is unlikely given the paucity of any finds of that date within our nearby excavation. If 'real', a more plausible interpretation is that it marked either a small henge or ring-ditch. This being said, when this area was trial-trenched in 1999 no evidence of it was forthcoming (Pryor & Trimble 1999).

Considered within the context of the ensuing excavation, apart from the buried soil testing, there is no need to outline the evaluation results separately. Sealed beneath 0.3–0.5 m of topsoil/alluvium (locally having a 0.05–0.15 m-thick layer of peat immediately beneath), a 0.1–0.4 m-thick palaeosol survived throughout. This was duly sampled in order to appraise its finds densities, employing test pits sited at the ends of each trench (and at the mid-point of longer ones; 51 in total, 90 litres each); in addition to ten sherds of Beaker pottery from one in the north of the site, there were 14 single finds of worked flint (0.27 flints per sample ave; Fig. 4.2). Such low overall densities are typical of the Fengate landscape (see Chapter 6). What is striking, however, in this case is their 'sporadic' distribution (i.e. lacking any area-/zonal-wide clustering) given the artefact numbers associated with the site's early pits. As will be further discussed below, this surely reflects upon the nature of this occupation and could imply 'tidying-up' of its traces (i.e. pit backfilling; cf. Evans & Knight 2000 for 'scatter-site' resolution employing this same technique).

Directed by Emma Beadsmoore, the site was excavated between October 2004 and January of the following year (Beadsmoore 2005a). Perhaps the greatest bane of recent fieldwork within Fengate has been the widespread adoption of relatively light-

FIGURE 4.1. *Digging Suburbia — Looking south, in 2004, along Edgerley Drain Road evaluation trench to the Power Station; notice the industrial units that loom in the western (right-side) background and which have since progressed throughout this area (photograph: A. Cooper).*

footed, large industrial unit buildings, and the ensuing planning complications their construction entails. While laterally truncating the site's top-/buried soil strata, generally these only involve piled or sill-beam foundations. As a result, their actual destruction of archaeological features *per se* is fairly minimal and it is this that has led to so many trench-only or watching brief exercises. The problem with this, of course, lies in the future and how to ensure that their eventual demolition will not result in further destruction. Such decisions are not, however, in our hands. It does, though, have direct implications for a site such as this, as open-area excavation throughout was not thought to be justified. Instead, attempting to strike a balance, two areas were selected: in the north, Area A (0.51 ha) and, in the south, Area B (1.14 ha), with the intervening swathe being 'preserved' *in situ* beneath the new warehousing (Fig. 4.2).

Other investigations

Being removed from Fengate's original core, before proceeding other recent investigations within the immediate area need review. Mentioned in the first chapter, two minor-scale watching brief exercises occurred just west of the current site in the early '90s, both undertaken by the Fenland Archaeological Trust: the Global Doors and Paving Factory Sites (Fig. 4.3; see Pryor 2001a, 36–7). Although not dated with any assurance, single ditches were found at both and

which probably relate to the second-millennium BC fieldsystem. While that at the latter, northern site seems entirely consistent with the system's local arrangement, the northwest–southeast orientation of the ditch at the Global Doors Site does not easily tie in.

The other most significant investigation to occur within this area was by HAT/AS at Broadlands where, between 1998 and 2006, eight areas were excavated across 1.2 ha (Fig. 4.3; Nicholson *et al.* forthcoming). Lying only some 160 m west of our northern area of excavation, surprisingly little flint and no pre-Middle Bronze Age pottery whatsoever was recovered. Four parallel ditches were assigned to the fieldsystem-phase (approx. north–south) and a few Deverel-Rimbury sherds were recovered. Lying 10 m apart, the two eastern ditches probably flanked a droveway; in one a crouched inhumation lay within a pit cutting the boundary.

Interpreted directly after Pryor as a 'stockyard' (1996; see below), the square double-ditch enclosure was attributed to the Late Bronze Age/Early Iron Age. This was essentially based on a substantive dump of more than 300 sherds of pottery (1269 g, plus 2350 g daub) within one of its ditches. Surely marking its *terminus* and, essentially matching Newark Road's Compound B (see below; Fig. 6.5), this enclosure was clearly integral to the fieldsystem's axes. In addition to a scattering of pits, two large water-holes were also assigned to this phase; both were waterlogged, with one yielding log-ladder lengths. Although not dated

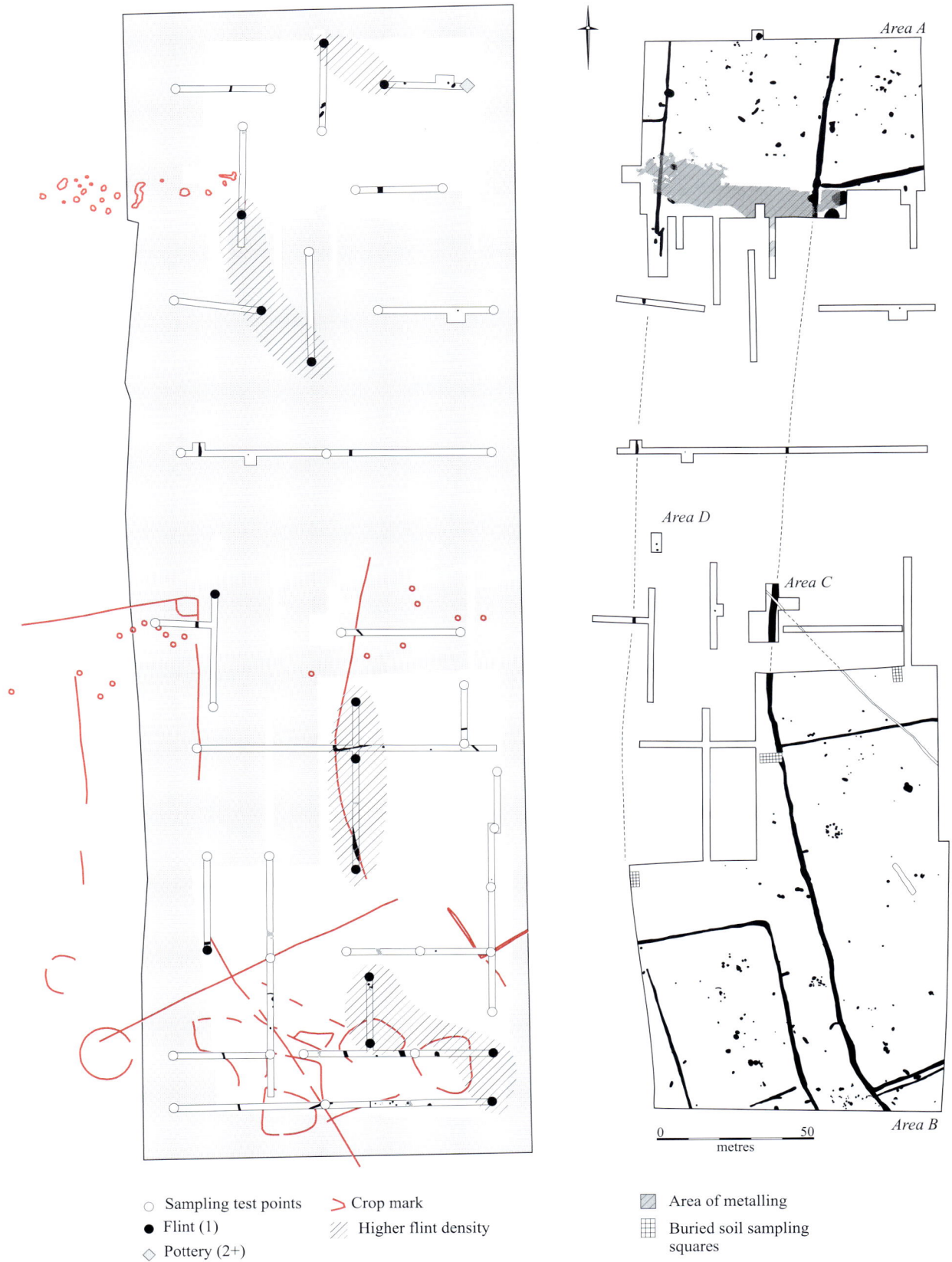

Sampling test points ○   *Crop mark* ⟩
Flint (1) ●   *Higher flint density* ⫽⫽
Pottery (2+) ◇

Area of metalling ▨
Buried soil sampling squares ▦

FIGURE 4.2. *Evaluation trenching and test point sample densities (left); right, areas of excavation and buried soil sampling units.*

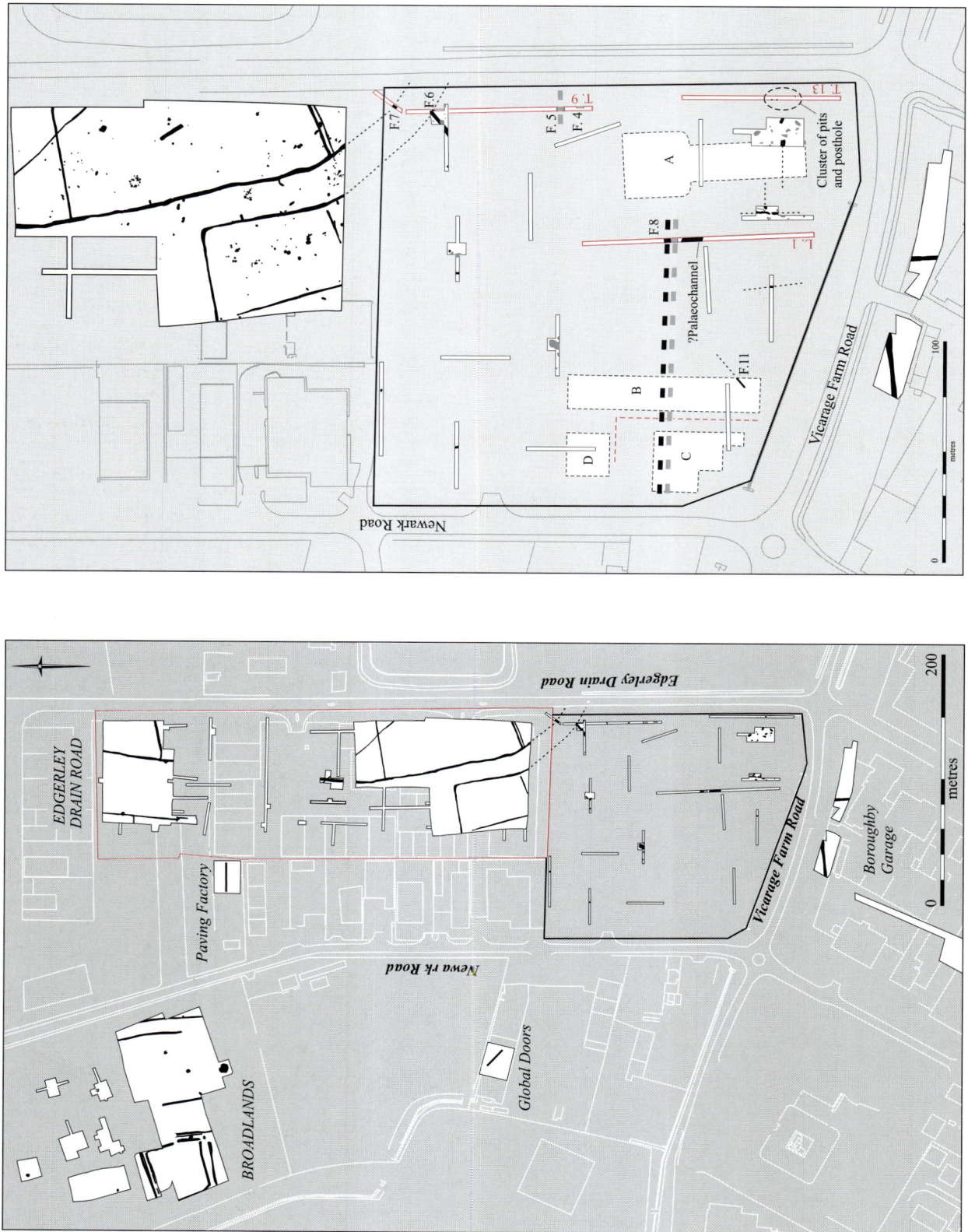

FIGURE 4.3. *Environs investigations (left), with off-Vicarage Farm Road fieldwork shown in detail left (with red outline indicating CAU trenches and monitored service-trench exposures). (Reproduced by permission of Ordnance Survey on behalf of HMSO. © Crown copyright 2009. All rights reserved. Ordnance Survey Licence number 100048686.)*

(and, thereby, left unphased), traces of three post-built roundhouses were excavated north of the double-ditch enclosure, which, in all likelihood, are of later Bronze Age date.

A localized cluster of pits was all that attested to the Late Iron Age on the site, with its Romano-British usage being far more extensive. The latter included various pits, an oven and a northwest–southeast oriented boundary ditch with a rectangular enclosure laid out on its western side.

Otherwise, most of the other fieldwork within the immediate area has been trench-based. It, unfortunately, presents something of a picture of 'mayhem' and shows the inadequacy of such minor interventions when trying to cope with such dispersed, big-scale phenomenon as fieldsystem landscapes. Undertaken by three different organizations in advance of construction, trench investigations have occurred on separate plots along the Newark Road-side of our site (Casa Hatton 1999; Pryor & Trimble 1999), with only Northamptonshire's 2001 work yielding any potential features: four possible Neolithic pits (Northants Archaeology 2001).

The only really significant findings within this area have come from HAT/AS's 1998 evaluations across the 3.4ha field immediately to the south of the current site and extending down to Vicarage Farm Road (Fig. 4.3; Vaughan & Trevarthen 1998). Discrete Beaker pits were exposed in two trenches immediately south of our area, while later Bronze Age pottery was distributed throughout, including in features associated with potential settlement. Fieldsystem ditches were identified at the extreme ends of the site, these having different alignments across its northern and southern portions. While the former generally complemented the current site's ditch-axes, those in the southern quarter lay on a more due north–south/east–west orientation (see below). Their layout appeared to divide on either side of a 'wet' inlet, up to *c.* 1.4 m deep in total, that extended across the middle of the site and in which peat and alluvium deposits were present; a possible pond or water-hole being found on the northwest side.

Anticipating car park construction for the Boroughby Garage, in 2001 a *c.* 112 m-long swathe (*c.* 12 m wide) directly south of, and parallel with, Vicarage Farm Road was excavated by Soke Archaeological Services (Fig. 4.3; Pryor 2001b). There, two fieldsystem ditches were present on the same approximate north–south alignment (and its east–west return). In addition, a number of postholes and Beaker-period pits were excavated, with 360 sherds of pottery recovered. (Soke also apparently recovered a later Bronze Age socketed axe when, in

1995, they cut trenches anticipating a new toilet block for the travellers' site 400 m northwest of the Edgerley excavations, just south of Oxney Road.)

The field immediately south of our main site area saw further fieldwork, this time by the CAU (after the main Edgerley Road excavations), during the autumn of 2005 and the first half of the following year (Beadsmoore 2007b). Consisting basically of only watching brief-cover, this involved monitoring of the groundbeam slots for a new 'Megacars' showroom building in the field's southeastern quarter (Fig. 4.3: A) and the digging of service trenches. While, due to their shallowness, the former did not penetrate to the level of archaeology, the trenches produced firm results. Although not dug under our control (and with lengths backfilled prior to recording), they effectively served as three further evaluation trenches, together spanning the north–south length of the site.

At the northern end of the northeastern trench (9) the two ditches of the main site's droveway were exposed as their line arced southeastwards (F.6 & F.7). The metre-long segment-excavation of the northernmost yielded five pieces of worked flint (including a later Neolithic-/Beaker-attributed knife); these being the only finds recovered from the investigations. In the south-centre of Trench 13 was found a 'clutch' of settlement-type features: two pits and a posthole. Though their half-sectioning generated no finds, they clearly related to the scatter of comparable features found just to the west by HAT/AS (Trench 16; Vaughan & Trevarthen 1998).

The most significant feature found was in the western drainage trench (L1; Fig. 4.3). This was a massive, *c.* 4.3 m wide and 0.7 m deep, east–west oriented, flat-/concave-based ditch (F.8), which had an associated upcast bank, sealing the buried soil, on the southern side (4.2 m wide and *c.* 0.25 m high; Fig. 4.4). No finds were recovered from its machine-excavation. While the basal deposits consisted of weathered grey clayish silt, in the main it was peat-filled and waterlogged. Yet, analysis of a bulk environmental sample from its later fills indicated that it was only intermittently 'wet', its remains attesting to a lime and alder woodland environment. The woodland may have been open and was probably damp; the molluscan evidence suggesting that the ditch feature itself had either slow-moving or stagnant water within it (see de Vareilles, in Beadsmoore 2007b).

Given its position, this major feature surely related to the inlet-deposits that occurred across the centre of the site, and delineated/bounded its southern side. Although no corresponding northern ditch was observed, in the south end of Trench 9 a comparable east–west bank-line (F.5) was present (3.2 m wide

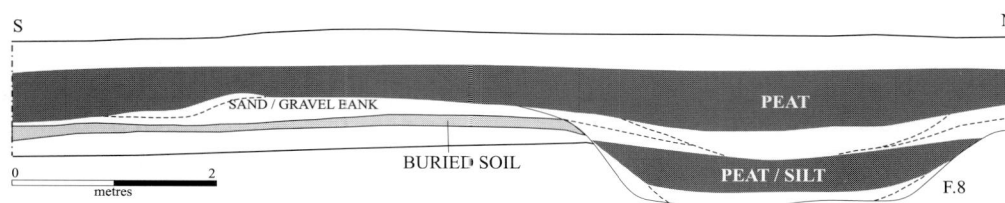

FIGURE 4.4. *Off-Vicarage Farm Road investigations 2006 showing the main F.8 ditch with its upcast bank in foreground of trench (photograph: E. Beadsmoore).*

and *c.* 0.5 m high; Fig. 4.3). In fact, another matching bank-feature (F.4) was observed in section just to the south and, together, these embankments must have bounded the inlet's northern side.

The same large ditch/channel was exposed again, some 60 m to the west, when in the following year further recording occurred. Related to the construction of three more industrial units (Fig. 4.3:B–D), whose level was to be made-up, this also essentially consisted of a watching brief exercise; aside from the controlled monitoring of contractor's drainage trenches, it only involved observations within 85 pile foundation-pad pits. Of comparable size to where it had been recorded previously, the bank and F.8 ditch was there observed to seal a 0.1–0.15 m-thick charcoal-rich buried soil. In the southern end of the drainage trench was a shallow, northeast–southwest oriented ditch (F.11; 0.6 m wide;

0.2 m deep). Filled with dark grey, alluvium-derived silty clay, this was thought to have probably been of Roman date. Between it and the main F.8 'line', a second peat-filled hollow was seen; also a gravel surface overlay the buried soil that was itself sealed by 0.5 m depth of peat. Unfortunately, the relationship between this second peat-filled hollow and the main inlet could not be determined. Equally, no finds were recovered from the main F.8/F.12/F.13 boundary that appeared to flank the inlet. Given, however, its scale, alignment and waterlogged fills, a post-Bronze Age date was always considered likely (i.e. possibly a Roman canal). Due to this ambiguity, a charred seed-sample from it was, accordingly, submitted for radiocarbon dating and produced a later Bronze Age date:

F.8 (Beta-240339) - 2870±40 BP/1190–1140 and 1140–920 cal. BC.

Clearly something extraordinary occurs within this field south of the main Edgerley Site. Seeing both an eastward twist in the northern portion of the fieldsystem, and divided by the great ditch and bank bounding the inlet, that system had quite a different alignment across the southern third of the area. Clearly, though, the many phases of trial trenching and watching brief-only investigations there have obviously been an inadequate response to the complexity of its archaeology.

2004/05 excavations

With more than 1765 sherds of pre-Iron Age pottery recovered, the chronological breakdown of the main site's pottery is shown in Chapter 6's Table 6.3. Not only does this indicate just how abundant was its period-by-period representation (it also yielded, in total, some 780 worked flints), but — and as is further discussed in that chapter — it emphasizes the problems of attributing the Bronze Age fieldsystem. These are particularly acute, for the situation, respectively, of Collared Urn and later Bronze Age features within the system's main drove appear, effectively, to bracket when it may have functioned: basically, the *c.* 300–500 years of the Middle Bronze Age. Yet, no pottery of that period was actually recovered (i.e. Deverel-Rimbury), despite every other pottery-type of the fourth to second millennia BC otherwise being present. (Strictly Middle Bronze Age flintwork, as opposed to more generally 'later' types, is essentially impossible to recognize.)

Having announced the nub of this site's 'problem', this must have implications for the phasing and the presentation of its results. Cross-cutting 'type' attributions, essentially it divides into three. First, there is its spectrum of 'open-site' pit features (and a few possibly associated structures) followed by the fieldsystem and its ubiquitous later Bronze Age aftermath, and, finally, the area's Romano-British usage (there being no significant Iron Age activity). This does not, though, rule out the possibility that the later phases of its 'open-usage' were not actually contemporary with the origins of the fieldsystem and, indeed, as discussed below, the radiocarbon dates would suggest just this.

Buried soil sampling
It is imperative that the buried soil is fully 'problematized' from the outset as it is crucial for understanding the site's depositional practices and discrete features (i.e. their full depth, etc.). In addition to the evaluation-phase test pit sampling outlined above, in Area B three limited areas (51sqm in total) were targeted for alternate metre-square hand-excavation of this

horizon (Fig. 4.2). Twenty-seven metre-squares were thus excavated, which yielded, in total, 18 flints, four sherds of pottery (Grooved Ware) and two burnt stones. With many producing no finds, the maximum number of artefacts within any single square was three. Occurring at an average density of 0.7 per metre, aside from a Late Mesolithic/earlier Neolithic blade, the recovered worked flint was essentially of later Neolithic/Early Bronze Age attribution and included a thumbnail scraper.

Consistent with studies of buried soil 'resolution' on other sites (e.g. the Haddenham Project; Evans & Hodder 2006a), it was observed that features, as such, had originally been cut from within the height/depth of its profile. They, however, could only be clearly defined at its base in the top of the terrace gravels. In this context the recovery, during the evaluation, of ten sherds of Beaker pottery from one of the test point samples is intriguing. While possibly reflecting a local midden-type deposit within the buried soil, they perhaps more likely occurred within a shallow pit that did not penetrate as deep as the terrace gravel-level.

Finally, in terms of artefact representation, it should be stressed that the sampling of this horizon was obviously inadequate to evaluate site-wide variability. Nevertheless, from what was undertaken it can be estimated that the total population of buried soil finds within the two areas would have amounted to some 11,900 flints and 2550 pottery sherds. Against this, our sampling of these assemblages — only a minuscule percentage of their 'totality' — was very limited and it is imperative that just how much surface material would have been present on a site such as this is appreciated. (These still, nonetheless, are quite low surface values; for example, within the buried soil at Over Site 3 Peterborough-Beaker sherds occurred at an average density of 1.4 per metre and flint at 10.4 pieces: almost 10–15 times the Edgerley densities; see Pollard 1998b; Garrow 2006, 111.)

Micromorphological analysis (CHARLES FRENCH)
The palaeosol that developed above a later Bronze Age metalled surface within Area A (see below) was considered appropriate for detailed study (Fig. 4.5). Accordingly, a monolith sample was taken through this context (F.334, [911]) for soil micromorphological analysis using the methodology of Murphy (1986), and the descriptive terminology of Bullock *et al.* (1985) and Stoops (2003; the detailed soil micromorphological descriptions are presented in Beadsmoore 2005a, app. 1).

The upper half of the profile (0–14 cm) was composed of a reddish/orangey-brown clay loam with a well-developed irregular blocky structure. Clay in a variety of forms is the predominant

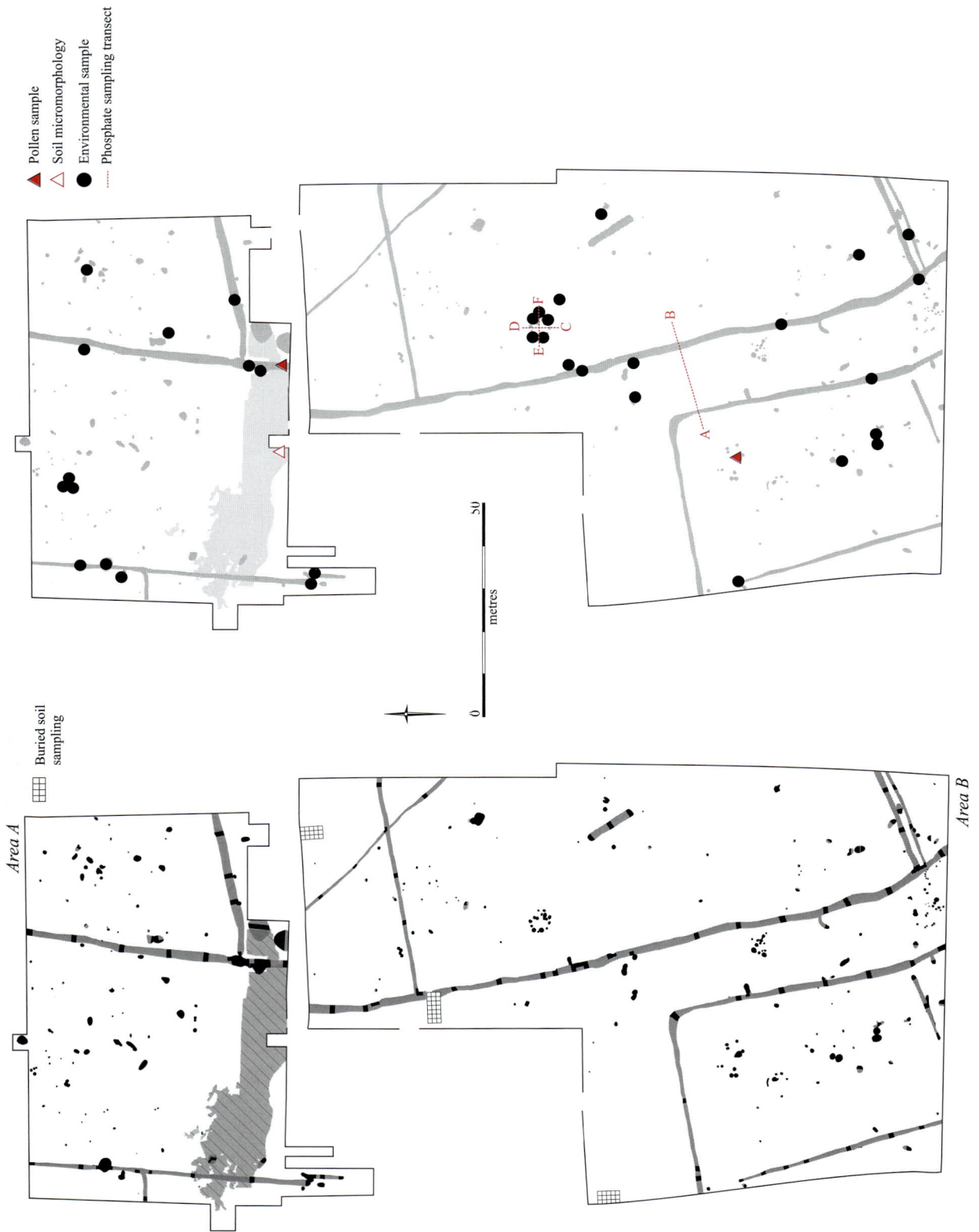

FIGURE 4.5. *Site plan showing excavation segments/'interventions' (left) and, right, location of environmental samples.*

component of this horizon. Interestingly, this clay loam contained a few fragments of fine charcoal and iron-replaced plant tissue, as well as very few occurrences of iron-phosphatic formations in the voids and a possible burnt dung fragment containing silicified grass stems. Also, there are a few irregular zones of an intrusive sandy fabric (<20% of total groundmass).

This horizon overlies an *in situ* palaeosol with two horizons evident (14–26 cm). The uppermost 8.5 cm was composed of two fabrics in an heterogeneous mixture. The predominant fabric (>60%) is a yellowish-brown sandy loam with a very minor impure (or dusty) clay component and a weakly developed small blocky ped structure. This was depleted of fine material (i.e. organic matter, silt and clay), and affected by some secondary amorphous iron impregnation. In contrast, the subsidiary fabric (<40%) was a reddish/orangey-brown clay loam which is exactly similar to the overlying horizon (0–14 cm). Other features of note were two horizontally bedded zones of amorphous iron replaced plant tissues at depths of 19.5 and 21 cm.

Defining beneath two planar voids, the lowermost horizon of the palaeosol was a 2.5–3.5 cm thickness (at *c.* 22.5–26 cm depth) of yellowish-brown sandy loam with a minor, fine flint gravel component. There was a slightly greater amount of dusty or impure clay present in the voids and groundmass at this level, and there were no intrusive or inter-mixed fabrics present.

The upper half of the profile was characteristic of alluvial fine sediments deposited through repeated seasonal, overbank floodwaters carrying and depositing silt and clay sediments from the erosion of soils upstream and inland. The minor phosphatic/dung components hint that this alluviated topsoil was frequented by animals when not seasonally flooded and, therefore, supported grassland.

This alluvium had accumulated on a thin, poorly developed brown earth-type of soil (after Avery 1980), the soil-type commonly found elsewhere in the Fengate/Flag Fen fen-edge complex (French 2001). Although there had probably been some depletion of fines from it due to subsequent rising base groundwater tables and seasonal inundation with freshwater, this poor brown earth development hints at the longer term existence of a relatively treeless landscape, at least from the Bronze Age onwards. This is certainly corroborated by the sub-regional palynological evidence from the adjacent Flag Fen basin discussed by Scaife (2001).

Unusually, this soil profile would appear to have been truncated to some extent, leaving only the poorly developed 'B'-horizon intact and *in situ*. No organic 'A'-horizon of this soil could be identified, but it is possible that the subsequent alluvial aggradation completely transformed the character of the upper half of the soil profile out of all recognition. Moreover, the distinct juxtaposition of the two fabrics in the surviving 'B'-horizon suggests that there has been some degree of physical disturbance of the contemporary soil. Although the full suite of characteristics which one would normally expect to be able to observe that would more definitively suggest that ard-ploughing

had occurred were not present (Lewis 1998), this soil would appear to have been physically disturbed, perhaps through digging over and/or livestock movement, just prior to the onset of alluvial conditions. Indeed, the two horizontally bedded zones of amorphous iron-replaced plant tissues could indicate either the base of the plough zone (much as the stubble of a modern cereal crop is found ploughed-in about 15–20 cm down profile) or trampling underfoot by people or livestock.

In conclusion, this northeastern zone of the Fengate complex, and especially the Bronze Age fieldsystems, was hitherto a relatively unknown area in terms of soil-type and land-use studies. Importantly, the post-Bronze Age soil evidence, albeit only from one surviving section, suggests that this area had probably supported pasture and livestock for a time despite being seasonally alluviated, and the soil had been physically disturbed once alluvial accumulation had begun, but there is insufficient evidence to suggest that this soil had been ploughed.

Radiocarbon dating

Seven samples were submitted for dating, their underlying logic being to provide two-assays per 'pit horizon' (Grooved Ware, Beaker and Collared Urn), with the first sample specifically directed towards dating an unusual cow-and-calf deposit within a pit cutting the fieldsystem. Of the others, the second sample (Beaker-related) failed due to modern contamination; the final, Grooved Ware-directed sample must also have included intrusive material, though in that case of earlier Bronze Age date, and its status/source is further discussed below. The submitted sample-material was all charred seeds, except that from F.323 (large charcoal fragments) and F.15 (pottery residue).

1) F.323 ([892]; Beta-240340) - 3270±40 BP/1630–1450 cal. BC;
2) F.157 ([326]; Beta-240341) - Post-0/BP assay;
3) F.140 ([287]; Beta-240342) - 3730±40 BP/2280–2250 and 2220–2020 cal. BC;
4) F.193 ([568]; Beta-240343) - 3480±40 BP/1900–1690 cal. BC;
5) F.189 ([671]; Beta-240344) - 3500±40 BP/1930–1740 cal. BC;
6) F.15 ([20]; Beta-240345) - 4110±40 BP/2870–2570 and 2510–2500 cal. BC;
7) F.235 ([549]; Beta-240346) - 3490±40 BP/ 1920–1730 and 1720–1690 cal. BC.

Aside from the failed Beaker pit sample (Beta-240341), all the dates are considered acceptable; their implications will be fully explored in the Chapter's *Concluding Discussion*.

Early pit deposits and other features

Given the site's 'type' pitting sequence and the significance of their assemblages it is crucial that the presentation of their material culture is integrated. Accordingly in the text here and that which immediately follows, the small-font sections concerned with worked flint and pottery are, respectively, contributed by Emma Beadsmoore and Mark Knight.

Before proceeding, in an attempt to avoid arbitrary distinctions of value-laden 'filled pit' depositional practices, it is crucial that we outline the inherent biases of interpreting such early pit sequences. Most relevant to the latter is the necessary loss of the buried soil strata through machine-stripping. The fact that features were clearly cut from within that horizon implies that smaller pits, with depths of 0.2 m or less, would have originally been much more substantial and upwards of twice their size/depth have been truncated.

Equally, when considering the question of whether any of the 'pitting horizons' could conceivably have been contemporary with the second-millennium BC fieldsystem, it is imperative that their attribution is not treated as if it were a stratigraphic entity (i.e. a 'layer'). Each of these 'periods' spanned hundreds of years; just because a Grooved Ware pit was cut by one of the field boundaries or the situation of a Collared Urn pit cluster within its droveway was too awkward to permit their contemporaneity, does not necessarily mean that elsewhere the period's occupation/usage may not have related to the fieldsystem. In other words, *inferential implications and stratigraphic logic should not be confused*.

Finally, there is the issue of attributing these pits to 'cultural-type' — 'Grooved Ware', 'Beaker' or 'Collared Urn' — based on pottery alone. Although this may be unavoidable if wishing a more close-grained chronology, it carries with it the presumption that there was a direct relationship between pottery and the commonly held notion that certain 'small pit'-categories were only dug to receive finds. Such interpretations usually relate to the lack of an otherwise discernable function and often leads to either 'ritual activity', 'hidden refuse' or 'marking place' explanations. But what of the comparable features without such finds? *De facto* they cannot be assigned to these pottery-/culture-type categories, but it is the very paucity of material within them that indicates that they must have had a function apart from the direct reception of finds/refuse. This issue will have to be addressed at greater length below when the site's unattributed features are considered, at least as based on pottery. There, the evidence of the flintwork will come to the fore, for generally having more generic chronological markers (e.g. 'later Neolithic'-/'earlier Bronze Age'-only), their broader categories cross-cut the strictures of 'type-reasoning' alone.

Early/Middle Neolithic

Evidence for Early Neolithic activity was supplied by one pit, F.172, in Area B (Fig. 4.6). This was bowl-shaped, 1.35 m across and 0.25 m deep, and yielded sherds of earlier Neolithic plain bowl pottery and a minor flint assemblage; the material being dispersed throughout the fill. Just to the north was another pit, F.168, of similar form and dimensions (c. 1.1 m across; 0.5 m deep). While only one artefact was recovered from it, an end-scraper, it was also cut by a Beaker-attributed feature to the west. Characteristically, no features *per se* were found associated with Peterborough Ware, the material instead deriving from tree-throw hollows in the north of the site (Fig. 4.6).

The 57 sherds of plain bowl Neolithic pottery from F.172 were small (MSW 2.1 g), abraded and had a 'corky' vacuous appearance. The majority were rounded body sherds, but also included two out-turned rim fragments, typical of Early Neolithic vessels.

Twenty-five worked flints (<123 g), five of which were also burnt, were recovered from F.172. The material included waste products and unutilized flake and blade blanks struck from the occasionally trimmed/prepared platforms of systematically reduced single-platform or methodically worked multiple-platform cores. Several of the blanks indicate a focus on the manufacture of narrow flakes and blades, a common characteristic of earlier Neolithic assemblages. The majority of the material was also small and manufactured from the local gravel. Six tools were also recovered: a fragment of a leaf-shaped arrowhead, a flake knife, an end scraper and retouched flakes (Fig. 4.9:1 & 2).

Pit F.168 yielded an end-scraper, which is only broadly datable to the Neolithic (Fig. 4.9:3).

The thirteen sherds attributed as Peterborough Ware were done so primarily on the basis of fabric (medium with frequent crushed quartz/flint) and a single 'maggot'-impressed piece from F.12 (evaluation-phase). Other Peterborough Ware-associated 'features' included the F.399 and F.402 tree-throws. Of the two flints recovered from F.402, one was a secondary flake and, the other, an edge-used flake. The latter was struck from a facetted platform and is similar to the platforms of some of the flakes recovered from Grooved Ware contexts (see below).

Grooved Ware/Later Neolithic

Thirty-four pits are assigned to this category (Fig. 4.6). Of the 11 excavated in Area A (six assigned on the basis of pottery; five from flint alone), F.7 had been fully excavated during the evaluation; F.15, F.310 and F.311 were half-sectioned, with the remaining 50 per cent removed during the excavation. The pits were in a loose/dispersed group in the northwest of the area. In Area B, 23 such pits were present (all but two assigned on the basis of their pottery); F.201, F.209 and F.211 were 50 per cent sampled during the evaluation, with the remaining half dug during the excavation. As in the northern area, the features variously lay within 'loose' clusters, pairs or isolated.

For the most part, the pits appeared as sub-circular patches of dark sandy silt; their dimensions varied from 0.28–2.2 m across and 0.09–0.46 m deep.

Area A

F.15

Plain Bowl
Peterborough
Grooved Ware

F.312   F.7   F.310   F.307
                          F.311
              F.376   F.309

F.339
F.12
F.402

F.367

F.379

F.377

F.270

0 ——— 25
metres

F.267

F.235   F.246

F.287
F.255   F.288

F.248   F.274
F.263

F.211
F.219   F.209

F.141
F.142

F.176
F.177

F.151

F.148

F. 168
F. 172

F.201
F.202   F.200
F.120

Area B

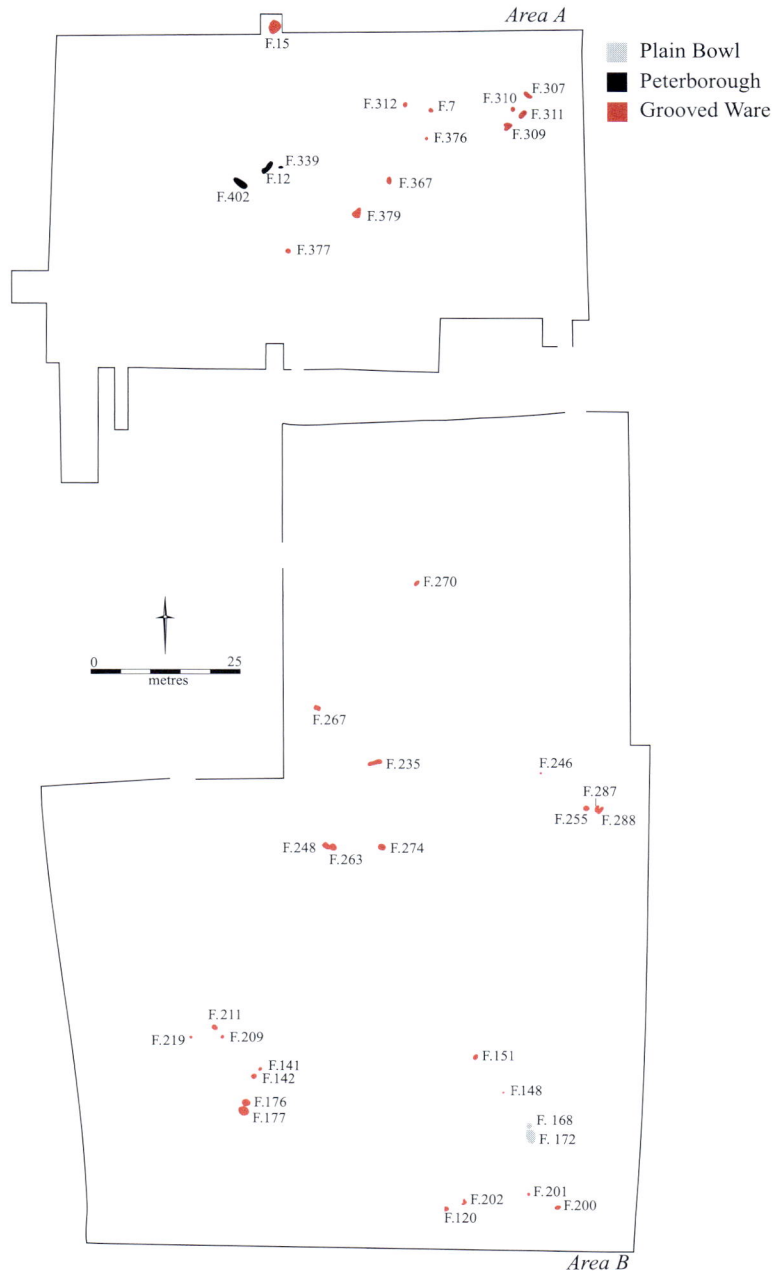

FIGURE 4.6. *Neolithic features.*

In profile they were either steep-sided with rounded bases, bowl-shaped or, shallower, with flat or irregular bases. However, two pottery-associated pits within Area B were distinctly rectangular and shallow: F.235 (cut by the later fieldsystem) and F.267, which, as well as yielding Grooved Ware pottery and flint, was also packed full of burnt stones.

The pits generally included either one or two fills. The single fills were commonly medium grey sandy silt with charcoal inclusions, whereas one of the deposits within the two-fill sequences was typically a dark grey, charcoal-rich sandy silt. The paler, single-fill pits usually contained only flint, whilst the darker deposits were more likely to also have pottery. There were, though, exceptions: F.15, a shallow pit with a pale clean fill, yielded large slabs of an almost complete Grooved Ware vessel (Figs. 4.7 & 4.8:1). In all the pits, the artefacts were commonly dispersed throughout the fills, although artefacts were often restricted to the darker deposits of the two-fill pits,

FIGURE 4.7. *Excavation of hollow F.15 with large slabs of Grooved Ware emerging (left); spiral-decorated vessel (see Fig. 4.8:1; photographs, A. Cooper).*

FIGURE 4.8. *(right) Pottery - Grooved Ware: 1) Complete profile of a barrel-shaped vessel (height: 40.8 cm, dia. 32 cm; 246 sherds from F.15), whose decoration comprises four principal zones: rim top, collar, vertical raised cordons and (intervening) body panels. The rim top was decorated with a single grooved or incised line which encircled the lip of the vessel, and the collar zone was decorated with horizontal parallel incised lines that were interrupted by concentric circle/spiral designs made by a single fingertip groove; the raised parts of the latter's circles/spirals were highlighted with small reed impressions. An incised herringbone design adorned the four vertical cordons, with the positioning of the cordons coinciding with the locations of the circles/spirals creating a 'flower on a stem' impression. The broad panels between the cordons were separated into diagonal zones infilled with a combination of parallel incised grooves or reed impressions. 2) Three decorated conjoining body sherds (F.235) with horizontal cordons defined by parallel incised lines above and below panels of incised 'zigzag' herringbone patterns; small triangular panels created by the juxtaposition of the cordons and zigzags were infilled with impressed dots. 3) Base and lower body of large tub-shaped vessel (dia. 33 cm; F.48), whose decoration comprised three incised zones: two zones of vertical herringbone divided by three horizontal and parallel grooves. 4) Rim and upper body of slightly splayed form vessel (?tub-shaped, dia. 23 cm; F.235) encircled with horizontal parallel grooves; main body has additional herringbone decoration made by filling the spaces between the horizontal grooves with opposing diagonal lines. 5) Single body sherd decorated with crudely incised spiral decoration (F.386). 6) Rim fragment with deep incised grooves over diagonal grooves (F.48; possibly the same as 8). 7) Complete profile of tub-shaped vessel (height 22 cm, dia. 26.4 cm; F.274), with decoration separated into four principal zones: collar (incised hurdle), upper body (horizontal herringbone), middle horizontal cordon (three parallel lines) and lower body (vertical herringbone); small triangular panels between the cordon and lower body were infilled with impressed dots. 8) Complete profile of a small 'stunted' tub-shaped vessel (height 16 cm, dia. 24 cm; F.48 & F.219); decorated zones included a raised collar (parallel horizontal grooves occasionally separated by rows of impressed dots), raised vertical cordons (vertical parallel lines and single thumb-print 'stop' or boss), horizontal cordons (parallel incised lines) separating central panels (horizontal herringbone) and lower body (horizontal herringbone).*

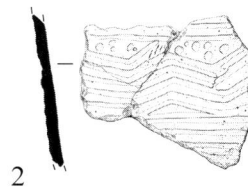

2

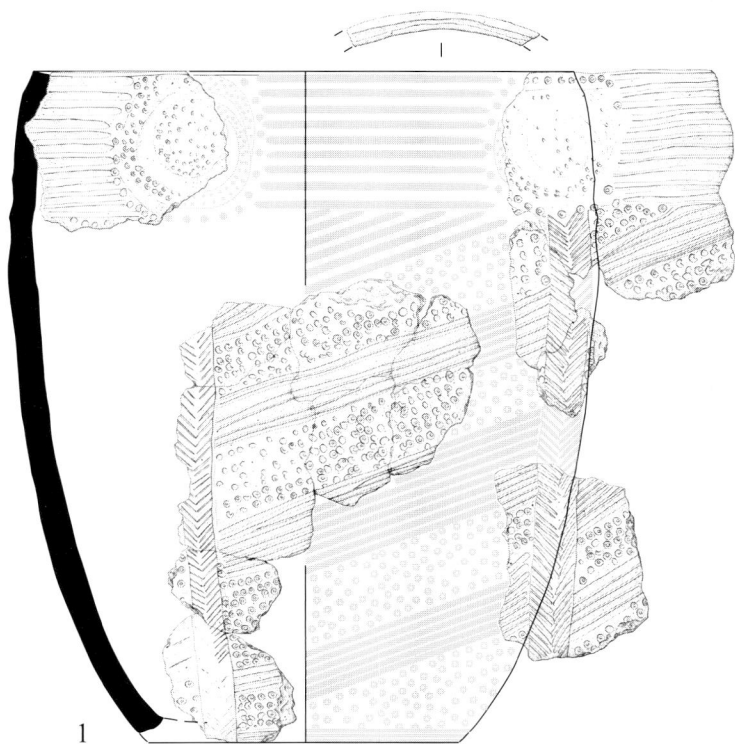

1

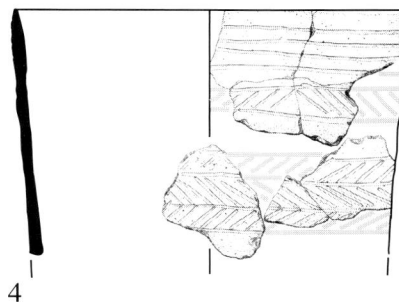

4

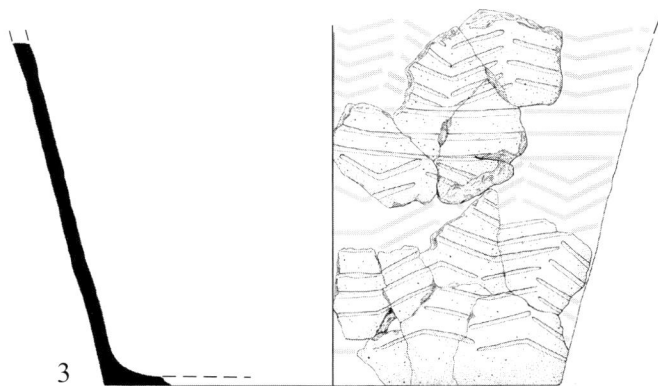

3

5

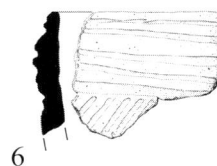

6

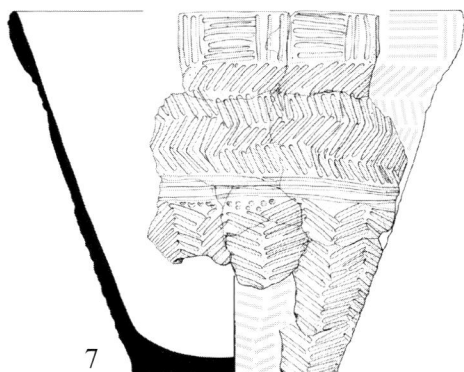

7

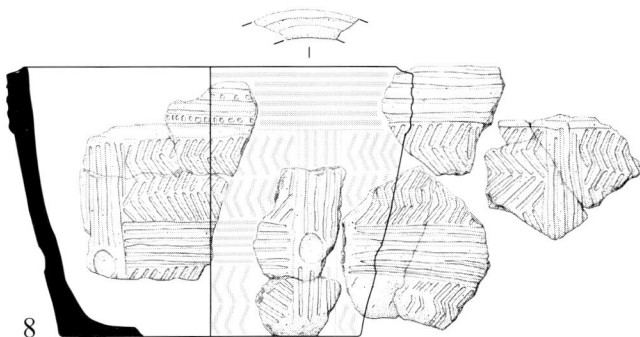

8

0   10   20

centimetres

TABLE 4.1. *Grooved Ware pit assemblages.*

Pit	Pottery	Flint	Burnt flint	Worked stone	Burnt stone	Burnt clay	Bone
Area A							
7	3 (4 g)	5 (<12 g)	3 (12 g)		2 (12 g)	3 (3 g)	5 (1 g)
15	246 (4179 g)	2 (5 g)	2 (<4 g)				
307		2 (3g)					
309	2 (2 g)	6 (27 g)					
310	16 (361 g)	13 (<112 g)	1 (<1 g)			1 (3 g)	1 (6 g)
311		2 (<16 g)					
312	20 (112 g)	4 (48 g)			1 (22 g)		
367	1 (5 g)						
376		1 (1 g)			2 (17 g)		7 (171 g)
377		1 (2 g)					
379		9 (50 g)					2 (3 g)
Area B							
120	15 (140 g)	8 (65 g)					
141	5 (20 g)				3 (115 g)		
142	5 (66 g)	3 (6 g)			9 (90 g)		
148		5 (<18 g)	1 (2 g)				
151	1 (4 g)						
176	15 (76 g)	33 (<100 g)	10 (<21 g)		6 (494 g)	3 (52 g)	
177	14 (82 g)	11 (<71 g)	1 (6 g)		6 (102 g)	4 (30 g)	
200	4 (29 g)						
201	13 (244 g)	14 (<109 g)			33 (73 g)		
202	14 (55g)	4 (18g)					
209	5 (27 g)	13 (<122 g)			2 (105g)		
211	7 (110 g)	13 (<132 g)	3 (26 g)		23 (1975 g)	2 (35 g)	
219	1 (8 g)	1 (9 g)					
235	166 (1763 g)	34 (<253 g)	6 (182 g)		60 (2000 g)		36 (65 g)
246		2 (<6 g)					
248	7 (60 g)	7 (52 g)			2 (433 g)		
255	90 (1160 g)	25 (<136 g)	2 (<35 g)		33 (1402 g)	3 (17 g)	
263	35 (264 g)	64 (<281 g)	8 (38 g)		38 (1662 g)		
267	85 (328 g)	12 (<71 g)		1 (1672 g)	80 (5146 g)		
270	83 (238 g)	27 (325 g)	2 (27 g)				
274	30 (1030 g)	3 (<21 g)	5 (46 g)		5 (138 g)		
287	13 (47 g)	25 (<228 g)					
288	8 (26 g)	4 (29 g)					

a common aspect of Grooved Ware pits generally (Garrow 2006); neither 'type' displayed any evidence of structured deposition or placed artefacts.

The pits contained a variety of materials (see Table 4.1). These were recovered in a variety of combinations, within which there seemed to be relationships between different pits; for example, within Area A pits F.7 and F.310 stood out as they were similar in form and yielded the greatest variety of materials. Overall, the pits in Area B yielded the greater quantities of artefacts. Several had considerable quantities of pottery and flint, for example F.235 and F.255; whereas some, like F.148, yielded only a few flints, or in the case of F.151, just a scrap of pottery.

The flint recovered from these contexts predominantly comprised waste from a variety of working strategies. The waste was from incomplete flake production/core reduction sequences. The Area B pits yielded cores, whilst none were recovered from Area A. Yet, full flake production/core-reduction sequences were still not present in Area B, and clearly not all of the material was getting into the pits. However, four refitting sequences were recovered from four different pits, indicating that although full or even partial

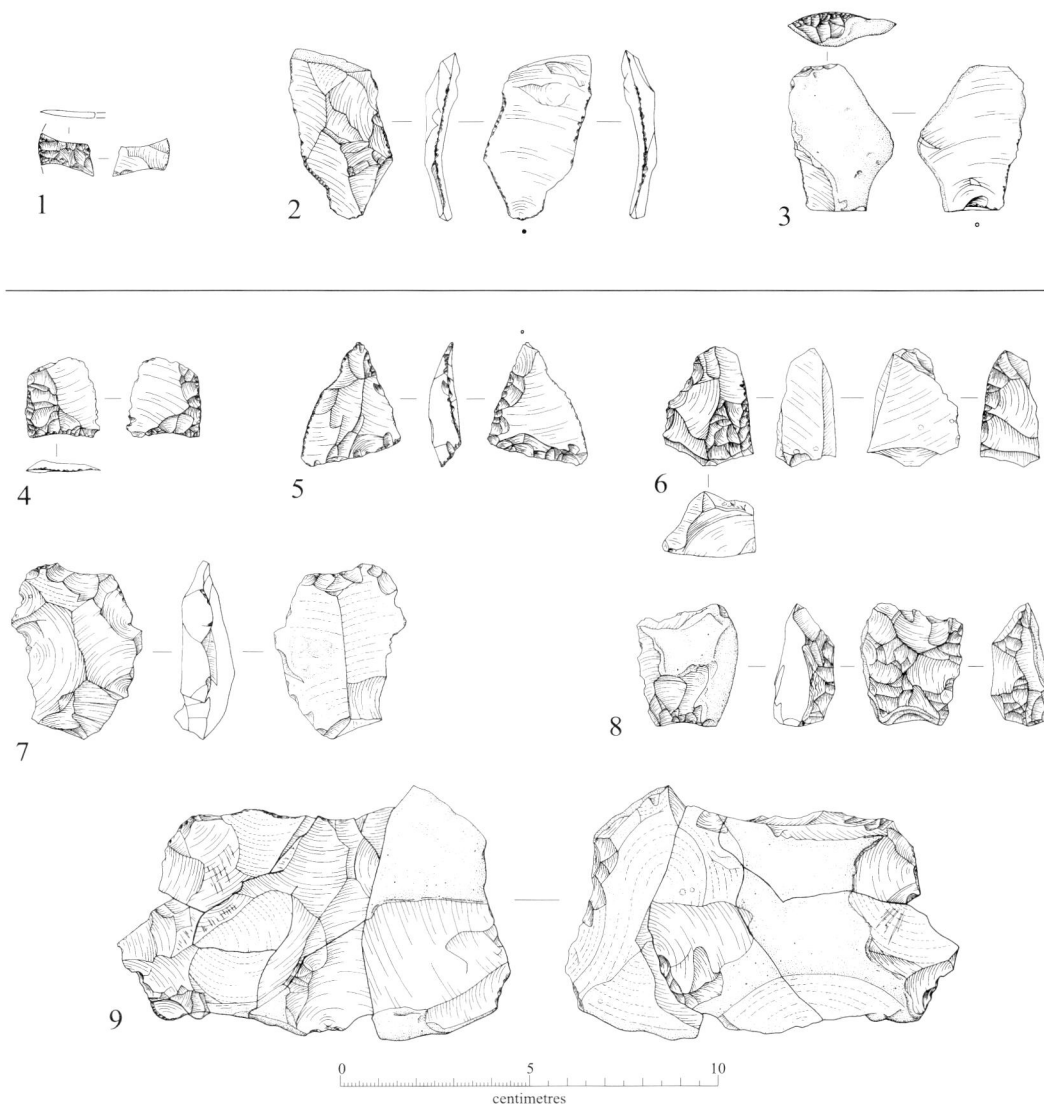

FIGURE 4.9. *Neolithic worked flint — Early Neolithic: 1) leaf-shaped arrowhead; 2) retouched flake; 3) scraper; 4–9) later Neolithic: 4) oblique arrowhead; 5) chisel arrowhead; 6–9) cores.*

reduction sequences were not recovered, elements of those sequences were sometimes deposited together. The tools comprised scrapers and utilized flakes; a broken oblique arrowhead was found in pit F.248 (Fig. 4.9:4).

The pottery consisted of rim, body and base sherds, although no complete vessels were recovered. In Area B an almost complete pot was recovered from F.274 (Fig. 4.8:7), whilst parts of at least three different vessels were recovered from F.211 and parts of four were present within F.235 (e.g. Fig. 4.8:2 & 4).

Fragments of cattle bone were recovered from these features. The bulk environmental excavation-phase samples yielded hazelnut shells, but no cereal remains; cereals had, however, been forthcoming in the evaluation samples (see below).

Over half of the 1066 sherds (11,813 g) of Grooved Ware recovered were decorated. The majority of the decoration comprised grooved or incised lines, but also included impressed dot-filled panels (F.142, F.263, F.274 & F.310) and vertical cordons (F.48 & F.211). The incised lines occurred across the vessels and incorporated horizontal (F.141, F.201, F.203, F.211, F.219 & F.263) and diagonal rows (F.15 & F.255), chevrons (F.120, F.202 & F.248), herringbone (both horizontal, F.177, F.201, F.219, F.255, F.267, F.274, F.287, F.290 & F.312, and vertical, F.209, F.263, F.274, F.288 & F.310), hurdling (F.274), 'basket-weave' (F.176) and 'mesh' designs (F.325); spirals were present on at least two vessels (F.15 & F.386).

The rim-forms were predominantly flattened or simple-rounded and many had internal horizontal grooving (F.120, F.200, F.201, F.263 & F.267). Cordon-defined collars were also present on some vessels

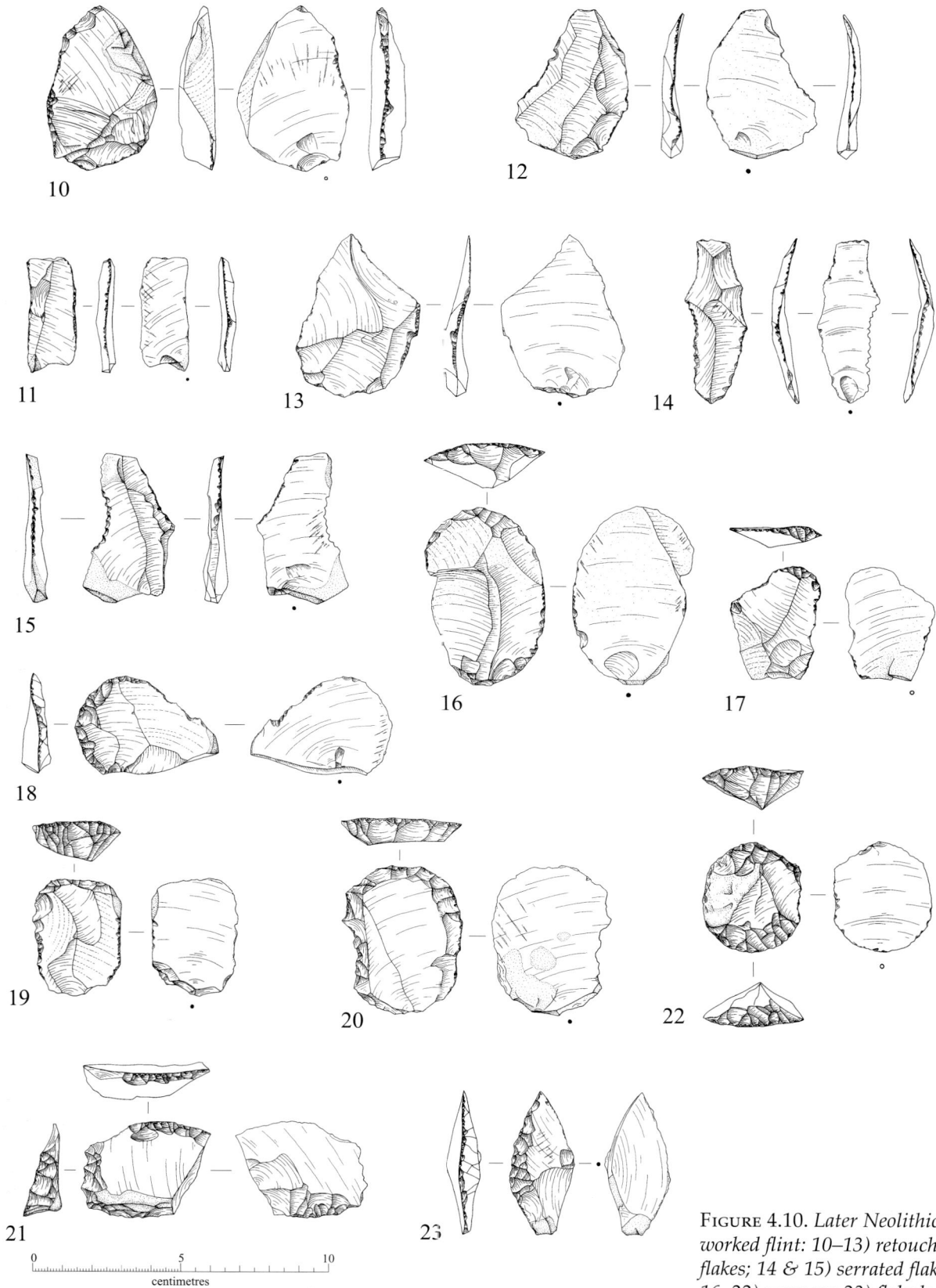

FIGURE 4.10. *Later Neolithic worked flint: 10–13) retouched flakes; 14 & 15) serrated flakes; 16–22) scrapers; 23) flake knife.*

(F.15, F.48, F.201 & F.274), and base pieces were almost as numerous as rim fragments. Reconstructed vessels varied between being straight and splayed-sided tub-like forms to taller or elongated rounded or trunco-conic forms. The principal fabric was medium-hard with common small-medium grog and common-to-abundant sand. One particular context, F.235, contained sherds that had small voids (dissolved shell?), as well as grog inclusions.

A near-complete form came from F.274 and comprised a raised collar decorated with 'hurdle design' above a zone of horizontal herringbone, which was separated from a lower zone of vertical herringbone by an incised 'cordon' made up of three horizontal grooves (Fig. 4.8:7) Small lozenge-shaped panels occurred immediately beneath the central cordon and these were infilled with small stabs. The vessel was straight-sided (24 cm high) and had a diameter of 22 cm; F.274 also produced a rim and base fragment belonging to two other vessels.

F.15 contained almost all of a single large barrel-shaped vessel that had a broad collar-zone above vertical cordons (Fig. 4.8:1). The collar was decorated with parallel horizontal grooves, that was interrupted by large spiral designs highlighted with small 'half-reed' impressions. A vertically incised herringbone design decorated the cordons, whereas the intervening panels were infilled with diagonal grooves and rows of 'whole-reed' impressions. The decoration of this vessel was sharp and fresh; its upper part was encrusted with soot as if it had been inverted over a fire, it possibly having been broken during its firing (hence its 'fresh' appearance).

In comparison, F.48 had fragments of at least three separate vessels (Fig. 4.8:3, 6 & 8). All were similar in form to that in F.15, though the sherds were less fresh and some appeared burnt. The decoration schemes were very similar and all three had horizontal grooves around their collars and decorated vertical cordons. One of the cordons had an impressed thumbprint close to the point where it met the defined collar. On two of the pots, the panels between the cordons were infilled with rows of horizontal herringbone.

F.235 produced multiple decorated sherds from at least four separate, slightly splayed or straight-sided vessels (Fig. 4.8:2 & 4). The rim-forms did not suggest defined collars as the main horizontal body decoration began almost immediately beneath the lip. The decoration on two of the vessels was executed with shallow broad grooves. Rim, body and base-angle fragments were equally represented.

The Grooved Ware pit contexts yielded the largest quantities of worked flint, 397 pieces (2679 g), of which 37 were also burnt (11 being burnt but unworked). The material is listed by type, feature and quantity in Table 4.2; the quantity recovered from each pit varied from 1–72, the material comprising flintworking waste and utilized pieces. The pits yielded a limited number of cores, seven complete and seven fragmentary (Fig. 4.9:6), which can be grouped into three broad categories: either thoroughly worked down discoidal cores (Fig. 4.9:7), that were small and must have been increasingly difficult to work, and which were potentially keeled cores at the beginning of their use-life, keeled cores proper (Fig. 4.9:8), or more expediently and less extensively reduced irregular cores. The latter frequently had incipient cones on the surfaces, indicating unsuccessful attempts to remove flakes from awkward angled edges.

The cores were either discarded because they were extensively worked and exhausted, or only partially worked, with awkward fractures/errors that remained uncorrected. Both were at the end of their use-life and consequently provide a potentially biased impression of the flake production/core-reduction strategies undertaken at the site. A core from F.270 is a good example (Fig. 4.9:9): five fragments recovered from the pit refit into a partially worked, badly fractured keeled core. The approach to flake production/core reduction focused on working the nodule in from roughly facetted keeled edges, yet the flakes and core fractured awkwardly in the poor-quality raw material; the core was consequently discarded.

Examination of the 287 flake and blade blanks recovered from the pits provides a more detailed impression of the focus of the flintworking. The material includes narrow and broad flakes, struck from unprepared or facetted platforms. In contrast to the earlier Neolithic material, the flakes either have multi-directional or single-direction dorsal scars. They could have been struck from keeled, discoidal-, irregular-, multiple- or single-platform cores, suggesting a variety of flake production/core-reduction strategies. Several chunks were also recovered, either removed in the initial stages of decortication in core-reduction sequences or tool manufacture; other chunks may have been shatter fragments, core fragments, or nodules tested as potential cores.

A group of distinctive flakes recovered from the pits comprise broad, often quite large, thin, curving flakes, typically struck from neatly facetted/prepared platforms. These were potentially the byproducts of biface manufacture, but are more likely to be the result of discoidal core preparation/reduction. The flakes are usually larger than the rest of the material, probably because they were comparatively early in the core-reduction/flake production sequences. Limited quantities of discoidal core-reduction products, from midway through the core-reduction sequence, were also identified. The flakes are broad, flat, struck from distinctive facetted platforms and potentially utilized to manufacture transverse and oblique arrowheads. Some of the flakes were broken, the distal ends being snapped off halfway across the flake, at the widest point; the distal end could have then been utilized, retouched as an arrowhead taking advantage of the original thin, sharp cutting edge, whilst the proximal end was discarded. Two of these arrowhead discard flakes were recovered from the Grooved Ware pits, F.176 and F.248, whilst others were residual in a later ditch (F.173) and pit F.323.

Utilized flakes were recovered from the Grooved Ware pit-contexts, either used as they were or after retouch (Fig. 4.10:10 & 11). A few were serrated, although the serration was heavy-toothed (Fig. 4.10:14 & 15) rather than the finer type commonly found on earlier Neolithic material (Beadsmoore 2006a). Three of the classic discoidal core products were also utilized (Fig. 4.10:12 & 13). Several of the narrower flakes, generally from early in the reduction sequence, were retouched as scrapers; the retouch was usually concentrated on the distal end, with some use-wear, but no formal retouch on one of the two sides (Fig. 4.10:16–19). Alternatively they were retouched on almost all of the available edges (Fig. 4.10:20–22). Two flake knives were also recovered (Fig. 4.10:23) as well as an oblique and a chisel arrowhead (Fig. 4.9:4 & 5).

The material was manufactured from local gravel flint, as well as primary flint, with a potential relationship between primary flint and the possible discoidal core products. To effectively manufacture a discoidal core large enough to produce suitable flakes to make transverse arrowheads, larger nodules of flint were required, sourced from more suitable raw materials, beyond the gravel flints generally available at the site.

Beaker

Four pits yielding Beaker pottery were excavated in Area A (Fig. 4.11); their assemblages are listed in Table 4.3. Unlike the Neolithic features, three of the Beaker pits intercut within a tight cluster, F.327–29. Of similar form and dimensions, these were bowl-shaped and shallow, 0.6–0.8 m across and 0.17–0.28 m deep. All three had two fills, a lower lighter and an upper darker deposit; the upper fills of all contained pottery, with no other artefacts present, although pit F.329 contained charred cereal grains. The fourth pit, F.382, had similar dimensions (0.65 m across; 0.17 m deep); it had one dark fill and contained burnt stone as well as pottery.

TABLE 4.2. *Grooved Ware flint. The table excludes the ten pit-features that yielded fewer than five flints each. Aside from a tertiary blade in F.202, an end-scraper in F.288 and a retouched flake in F.311, this variously only involved chips/chunks and secondary/tertiary flakes (F.142, F.219, F.246, F.292, F.307, F.376 & F.377); these omitted items are, however, included in the table's Grand Total.*

Area	Pit	Chip/chunk	Primary flake	Secondary flake	Tertiary flake	Secondary blade	Tertiary blade	Core-rejuvenation flake	Keeled core	Discoidal core	Irregular core	Core fragment	Retouched flake	Edge-used flake	Retouched & worn flake	Serrated flake	End scraper	Side scraper	End and side scraper	Sub-circular scraper	Miscellaneous scraper	Flake knife	Oblique arrowhead	Chisel arrowhead	Unworked burnt chunk	Total
Area A	7	1		2	4		1																			8
	15			1	1																				2	4
	309	1	1	1	1									2												6
	310	2	2	5	2		1														1				1	14
	311	1											1													2
	312			3									1													4
	379	2		3	2									1				1								9
	Total	7	3	15	12		2						2	3				1			1				3	47
Area B	120	1		2	4														1							8
	148			3	1			1											1							6
	176	3		5	33											1						1				43
	177	1		3	5	1							1	1												12
	201	4		4	4					1			1													14
	209			2	5	1		1					2												2	13
	211	4		2	5		2										1								1	15
	235	4	1	10	11		1					1	1	3		2	1								5	40
	248			3						1			1									1	1			7
	255	2	2	5	11						1	1	2	1			1			1						27
	263	4	1	10	45		2	1		1		1	4	1	1											71
	267			3	5					1			3													12
	270	1	2	8	10				1			5					1			1						29
	274			4	3												1									8
	287			7	11									4	1				1					1		25
	Total	27	6	72	163	2	6	3	1	4	1	8	13	12	2	4	4	1	3	2		2	1	1	8	334
	Overall Total	32	9	84	167	2	8	3	1	4	1	8	14	15	2	4	5	1	3	2	1	2	1	1	11	381
	Grand Total	(34)	(9)	(88)	(176)	(2)	(8)	(3)	(1)	(4)	(1)	(8)	(15)	(15)	(2)	(4)	(5)	(1)	(3)	(2)	(1)	(2)	(1)	(1)	(11)	(397)

TABLE 4.3. *Beaker pit assemblages.*

Pit	Pottery	Flint	Burnt flint	Burnt stone	Burnt clay	Bone
Area A						
327	6 (25 g)					
328	1 (24 g)					
329	12 (175 g)					
382	10 (40 g)			10 (577 g)		
Area B						
140	177 (858 g)	6 (37 g)	4 (25g)	4 (66 g)	1 (36 g)	15 (104 g)
157	34 (171 g)		1 (4g)	2 (239 g)		
169	1 (1 g)	2 (7 g)				
221	32 (66 g)	8 (64 g)				
224	5 (15 g)	1 (4 g)				
264	18 (106 g)	7 (48 g)				
265	10 (32 g)	5 (15 g)				

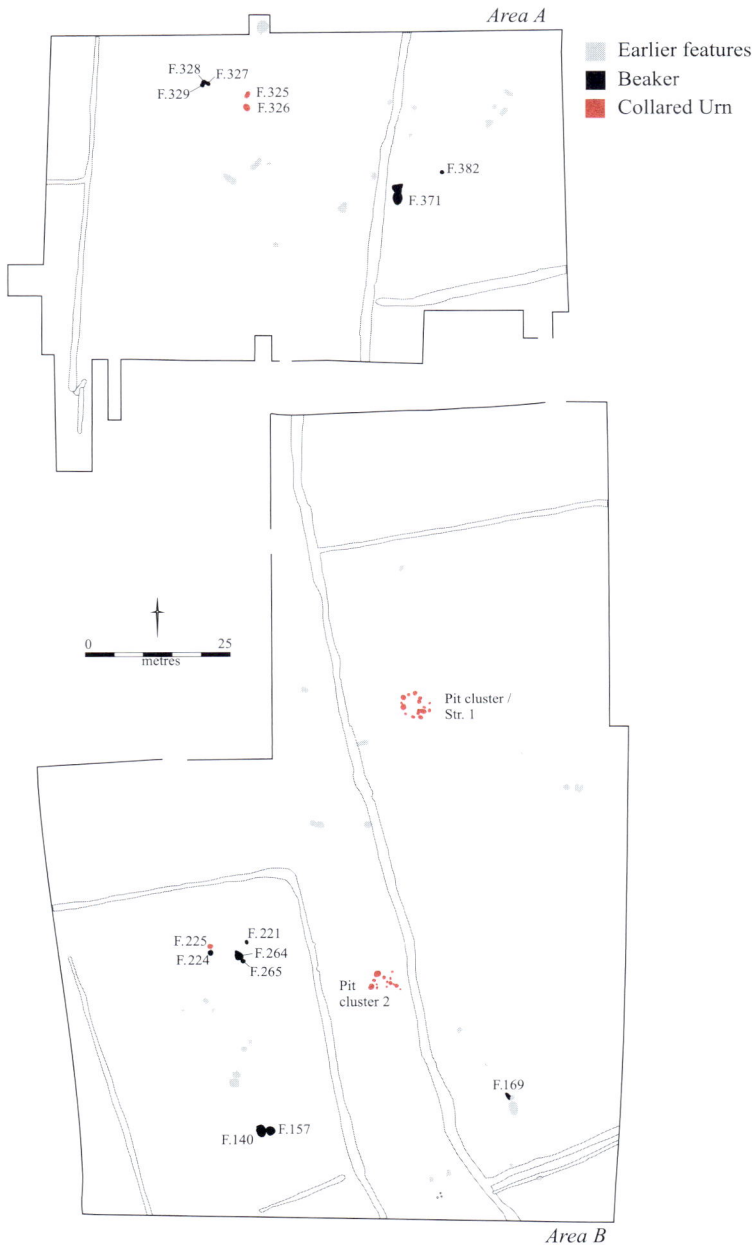

FIGURE 4.11. *Beaker- and Collared Urn-attributed features.*

FIGURE 4.12. *Beaker pits F.264 and F.265 (photograph, E. Beadsmoore).*

Beaker pottery occurred within seven pits in Area B. As was the case in the northern area, these tended to be more clustered than the Late Neolithic features (Fig. 4.11). Four seemed to be 'paired', F.157/F.140 and F.264/F.265 (Fig. 4.12). In both cases, one of the two pits was large, deep and vertical-sided with a flat base, whilst the other was shallow and bowl-shaped. The larger pits, F.140 and F.264, were 1.24–2.2 m across and 1–1.18 m deep; their fills variously attested to slumping, tipping, silting and weathering. The smaller, bowl-shaped pits, F.157 and F.265, were 0.7–1.75 m across and 0.35–0.45 m deep; their fills were dark, with no evidence of weathering. The remaining Beaker pits were also comparatively shallow and bowl-shaped, either circular or sub-circular in plan and varied between 0.6–1 m wide and 0.12–0.52 m deep.

The majority of the pits had dark grey silty sand fills; the exceptions were the two large, vertical-sided pits that saw more gravelly deposits. The shallower, bowl-shaped pits, yielding Beaker pottery and, usually, worked flint, had no clear traces of a function prior to the deposition of material within them. The pottery was generally quite weathered and, in contrast to the Grooved Ware features, the Beaker material probably had a less direct route into these pits and was not deposited within them immediately upon their breakage (F.157 contained fragments of four pots).

The bulk samples from both pits, F.140 and F.157, yielded charred wheat and barley grains, and these features may have served as storage pits.

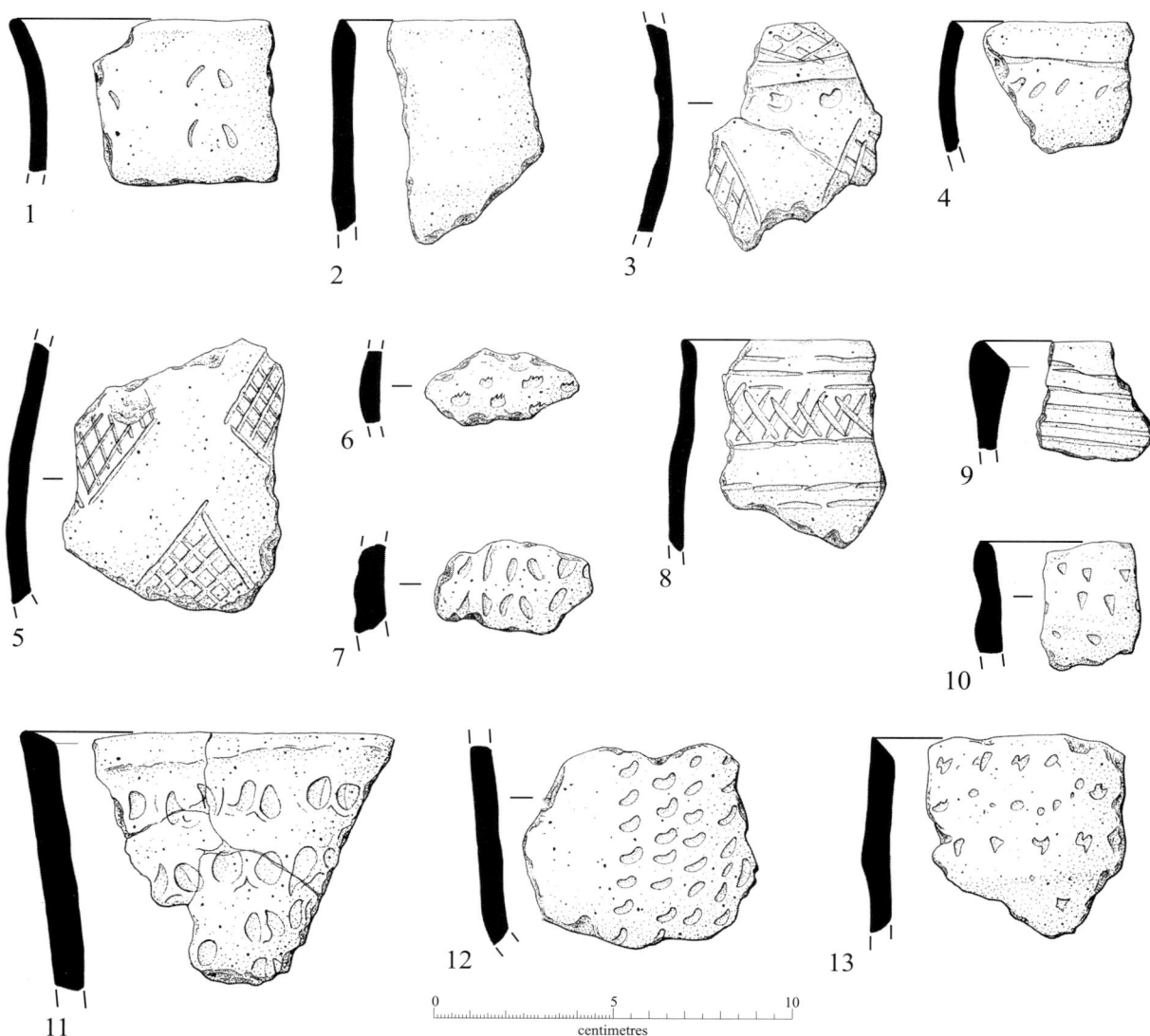

FIGURE 4.13. *Pottery - Beaker: 1–7) Mixed abraded sherds including paired fingernail impressions, plain, comb-zoned, stick and fingertip-impressed decoration (F.140); 8–10) mixed abraded sherds including comb-zoned, incised and stabbed decoration (F.157); 11–13) mixed abraded sherds including 'rusticated' paired fingertip impressions, rows of single fingernail impressions, distal-end of 'bird' bone impression (F.329).*

The majority of the 318 sherds of Beaker pottery (1534 g) derived from thin-walled vessels decorated with incised lines and/or impressed stabs and dots. As with the Grooved Ware, there was a large percentage of decorated fragments (36 per cent): an attribute of the 'all-over' decoration common to Beaker vessels. Rusticated pieces were also present and included fingernail, fingertip and finger-pinching raised plastic designs. Both decorative types occurred within the same contexts. In comparison with the majority of the Grooved Ware, the Beaker pieces appeared weathered or abraded and included sherds with a 'dissolved' appearance.

F.157 had fragments of at least four vessels, as determined by three different, internally bevelled rims and a distinctively decorated body fragment (Fig. 4.13:8–10). Each of the rim sherds was decorated differently: irregular, but broadly spaced, horizontal lines, with a band of incised lattice design; closely-spaced horizontal lines; all-over small, sharp triangular stabs. The body sherd was

'stab-covered', seemingly made with a frayed end of broken stick.

Body sherds with the same distinctive all-over design also came from F.140, along with a plain simple rim and a rounded rim decorated with diagonal incised lines (Fig. 4.13:1–7). The multiple rim and body sherds belong to a vessel decorated with spaced, roughly incised lozenges infilled with hatching, with a band of hatching near to the rim and rounded fingertip impressions. This pit also yielded rusticated fragments, including a thick-walled piece, with 'crows-feet' designs, as well as a horizontal band of fingernail impressions. The rim-forms associated with the rusticated forms were comparable with the 'finer' wares.

Further fingertip designs occurred on sherds within F.221 (a raised cordon created by heavy finger-pinching), F.327 and F.329 (multiple columns of fingernail impressions). Three thin-walled fragments from F.224 represent the assemblage's only obvious comb-impressed Beaker.

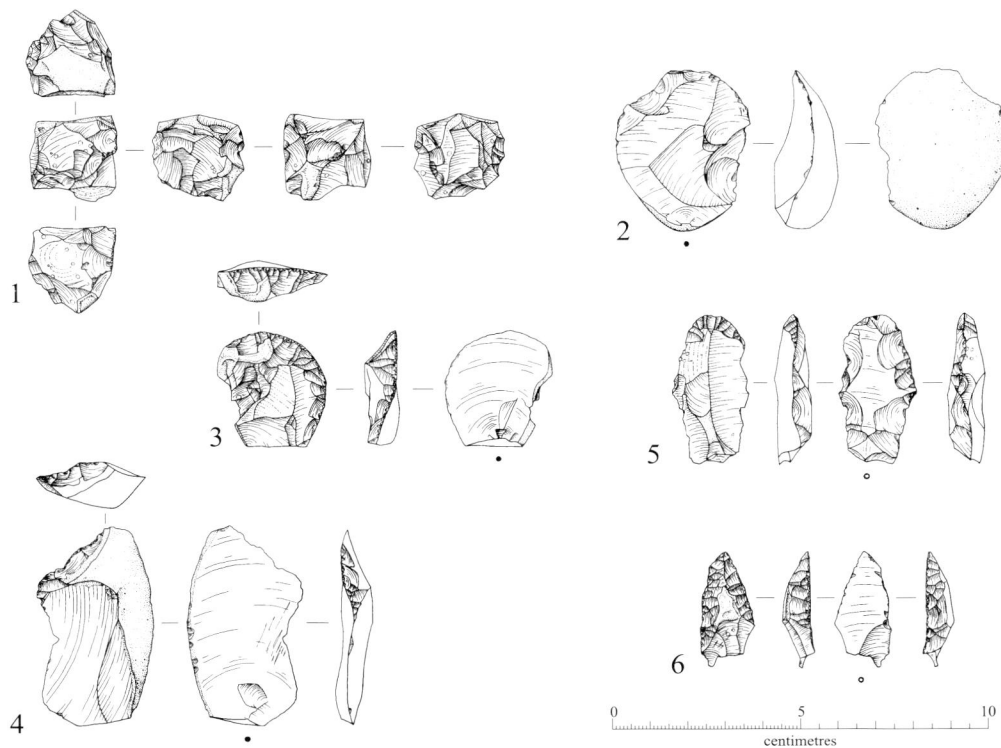

FIGURE 4.14. *Beaker-associated worked flint: 1 & 2) cores; 3–5) scrapers; 6) fabricator.*

TABLE 4.4. *Beaker pit flint.*

Type	140	157	169	221	224	264	265	Sub-total
Primary flake						1		**1**
Secondary flake	3		1	3			4	**11**
Tertiary flake	3	1	2	3	1	3		**12**
Irregular core	1			1		1		**3**
Core fragment						1	1	**2**
Retouched flake	1							**1**
Edge-used flake				1				**1**
End-scraper	1							**1**
Sub-circular scraper						1		**1**
Fabricator	1							**1**
Total	**10**	**1**	**2**	**8**	**1**	**7**	**5**	**34**

Thirty-four flints (<205 g), listed by feature, type and quantity in Table 4.4, were recovered from pits that also yielded Beaker pottery; six being burnt as well as worked. This included five cores, either irregular (Fig. 4.14:1 & 2) or just core fragments, with no traces of systematic core reduction. The majority of the flakes are compatible with the core technology; they were removed with hard-hammers from the unprepared platforms of irregular cores. The working waste generally displays no trace of systematic flake production/core reduction, nor any focus on manufacturing flakes of a particular morphology. A few of the flakes were the products of a more systematic flake production/core-reduction strategy, although with neither the earlier Neolithic's emphasis on narrow flakes and blades nor the later Neolithic's focus on broader, thinner flakes.

The pit contexts included several utilized flints: edge-used or retouched flakes and scrapers. In contrast with the later Neolithic end-scrapers, the scrapers recovered from the Beaker contexts are smaller, rounder and more extensively and invasively retouched, irregularly retouched, or re-utilized an existing core (Fig. 4.14:3–5). A fabricator was also recovered from one pit, F.140 (Fig. 4.14:6).

The combination of comparatively systematic flake production/core reduction, without a clear focus on producing flakes of a particular morphology, and more expedient flintworking, is characteristic of Beaker flint assemblages, as is the sub-circular, extensively and invasively retouched scraper. The assemblage recovered from these pits attests to partial or incomplete flake production/core-reduction sequences and included discarded flake blanks and cores, as well as utilized pieces.

Collared urn features

Lying side-by-side, two shallow pits with Collared Urn pottery were present in Area A (F.325 & F.326; Fig. 4.11), and which yielded 16/11 sherds and 3/10 flints respectively. Similar in their form and fills — pale grey sandy silt — these were 0.85–1.3 m across and 0.23–0.34 m deep.

Thirteen pits in Area B yielded Collared Urn, the majority of which were in a distinct circular cluster of 16 features (Pit Cluster 1; Figs. 4.15 & 4.16). This extended over 4 × 3.5 m in a quasi-circular layout, with several pits encroaching upon its interior. Varying between larger bowl-shaped pits and narrower steeper-sided features, they either had a single, medium-grey sandy silt fill, or two or three fills; of the latter, one usually consisted of a charcoal-rich, dark grey sandy silt overlying paler grey sandy silt. Within this grouping there were three large pits, 0.75–1.12 m across and 0.30–0.42 m deep (F.189, F.197 & F.199). Otherwise, the remainder were 0.50–0.70 m across and 0.16–0.40 m deep; the vast majority being less than 0.30 m. In addition, four distinct postholes were identified, c. 0.30–0.50 m in diameter and 0.25–0.30 m deep (F.185, F.188, F.192 & F.198); a 0.33 × 0.60 m 'silt patch' on the cluster's eastern side was 0.1 m deep (F.191).

Listed in Table 4.5, the pits contained a variety of different materials, and only F.194 had no artefacts. Two of the double-fill pits, F.189 and F.193, included unfired lumps of clay and had the largest pottery sherds (that partially reconstructed into one vessel), along with sherds recovered from one of the paler single-fill features, F.197. Collared Urn pottery occurred in 12 of the pits, while 13 produced worked and/or burnt flint; several also yielded burnt stone, burnt clay and bone. The flint recovered from them comprises both utilized pieces (including a thumbnail scraper from F.187) and working waste, attesting to partial flake production/core-reduction sequences. Some of the pottery refits involved both burnt and unburnt sherds, suggesting that the material had been involved in different post-breakage activities prior to deposition.

The bulk samples from these features yielded charred grains and flax; the latter, probably processed for fibres, is unusual but not unheard of, and flax was also found at the West Row Fen, Suffolk Bronze Age settlement (Martin & Murphy 1988). Phosphate samples were taken in two transects at right-angles across the pit cluster (Fig. 4.16) and, whilst they revealed variation in phosphate levels, no clear patterns were discernible (see below; Fig. 4.30).

While the roughly circular arrangement of this cluster is suggestive of a structure, the recovered postholes would not, unto themselves, be definitely

FIGURE 4.15. *Collared Urn-associated Pit Cluster/ Structure 1 looking east (top); below, detail of F.193 and F.194 (photographs, D. Webb).*

conclusive of a roundhouse. Other, 'non-building-related' possibilities have been explored; for example, some manner of small hengiform monument. Yet, without obvious parallels, such a 'convenient' explanation would falter on what seems to be the obviously domestic nature of its artefact assemblages. What would, however, make structural 'sense' is if two of the small pits — F.190 and F.194 — were actually dug-out postholes (the first only produced single burnt fragments of stone and clay; F.194 had no finds). In that case, F.185, F.188, F.194, F.196 and F.198 would define a c. 4 m diameter post-ring, with F.190 and F.192 relating to its eastern porch. Accepting this interpretation (and, hereafter, this setting will accordingly be referred to as Structure 1), the next question to pose, of course, is whether the other pits all lay within the floor-area of the building (whose wall-line would have presumably lain some 1 m beyond the post-ring) and were contemporary with/integral to its function, or if they reflect 'closing' deposits marking its disuse?

FIGURE 4.16. *Plan of Collared Urn-associated Pit Cluster/Structure 1, with sections below.*

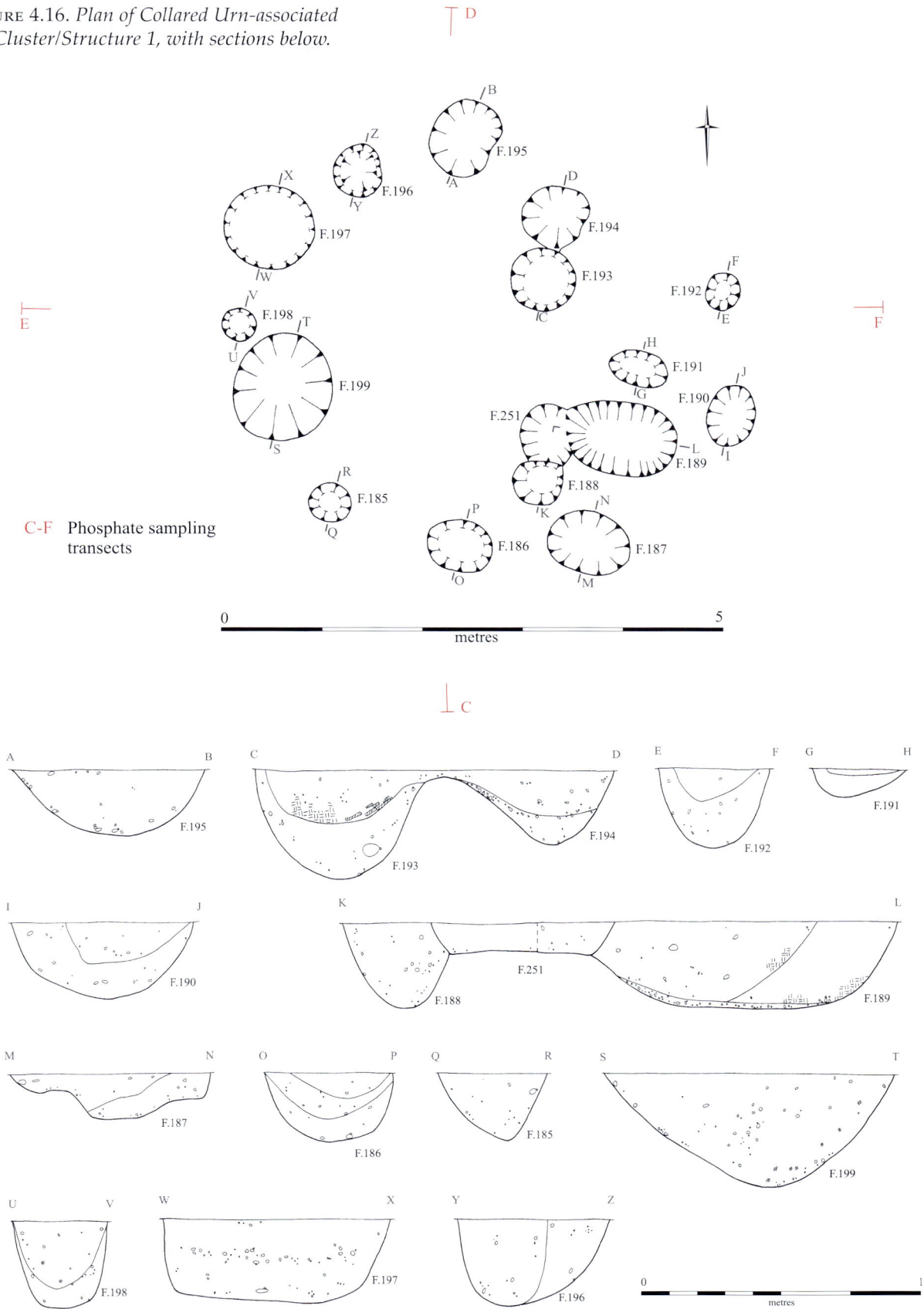

C-F Phosphate sampling transects

TABLE 4.5. *Collared Urn Pit Cluster 1 assemblages.*

Pit	Pottery	Flint	Burnt flint	Burnt stone	Burnt clay	Bone
185	4 (13 g)	3 (11 g)	1 (1 g)		5 (68 g)	
186	1 (<1 g)	1 (2 g)		1 (8 g)		
187	1 (2 g)	6 (34 g)	1 (2 g)	2 (7 g)		
188	9 (59 g)	1 (3 g)	1 (2 g)		5 (139 g)	
189	12 (237 g)	12 (<45 g)	2 (<2 g)		39 (3310 g)	12 (4 g)
190				1 (19 g)	1 (3 g)	
191			1 (1 g)			
192	1 (6 g)	1 (2 g)			7 (29 g)	
193	51 (1896 g)	2 (10 g)	2 (4 g)	2 (354 g)	23 (1113 g)	2 (<1 g)
195		7 (45 g)		1 (101 g)		
196	6 (9 g)	5 (7 g)	1 (12 g)	3 (294 g)	6 (22 g)	
197	15 (416 g)	11 (<55 g)			12 (295 g)	1 (1 g)
198	1 (12 g)	2 (13 g)	1 (8 g)		2 (7 g)	
199	1 (2 g)	1 (2 g)				
251	4 (24 g)	2 (7 g)	1 (5 g)			

TABLE 4.6. *Collared Urn Pit Cluster 2 assemblages.*

Pit	Pottery	Flint	Burnt flint	Burnt stone	Burnt clay	Bone
37				1 (79 g)		
38			1 (1 g)			
39		2 (4 g)	5 (25 g)	5 (67 g)	4 (15 g)	
40				2 (63 g)		1 (<1 g)
41						
162	2 (23 g)		1 (1 g)			
214					1 (22 g)	6 (1 g)
226	3 (45 g)	5 (56 g)		5 (236 g)		
227	1 (42 g)	1 (2 g)				

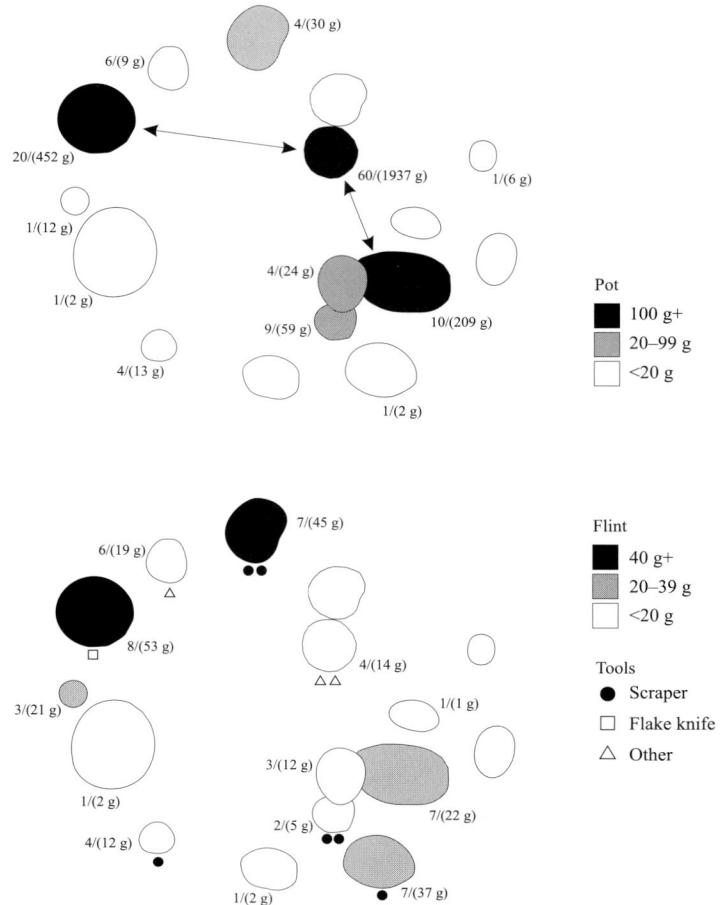

FIGURE 4.17. *Collared Urn-associated Pit Cluster/Structure 1 finds distributions: top, pottery (arrows indicate same-vessel refits); below, worked flint.*

Collared Urn pottery and flint was also recovered from an isolated pit to the southwest of Pit Cluster/ Structure 1 (F.225; 1/109 g and 2/33 g respectively); however, the remaining pits from which Collared Urn pottery was recovered (F.162, F.226 & F.227), lay within a second cluster of 14 features (Pit Cluster 2). Similar in their form and fills (medium-grey sandy silt), unlike the quasi-circular arrangement of Cluster/Structure 1, these had a more linear setting, 5.5 m long. At its western end were two larger pits, F.226 and F.227, respectively 1.15 m and 0.95–1.1 m across and 0.2 and 0.33 m deep. Also present were a series of small pits, 0.4–0.8 m across and 0.1–0.27 m deep (F.37–9, F.161, F.162 & F.220), scattered amongst which were postholes, 0.3–0.4 m in diameter and 0.1–0.18 m deep (F.41, F.161, F.214, F.215, F.228 & F.230).

Although limited in number, the flint recovered from F.38, F.39, F.226 and F.227 is broadly consistent with Early Bronze Age flake production/core-reduction strategies.

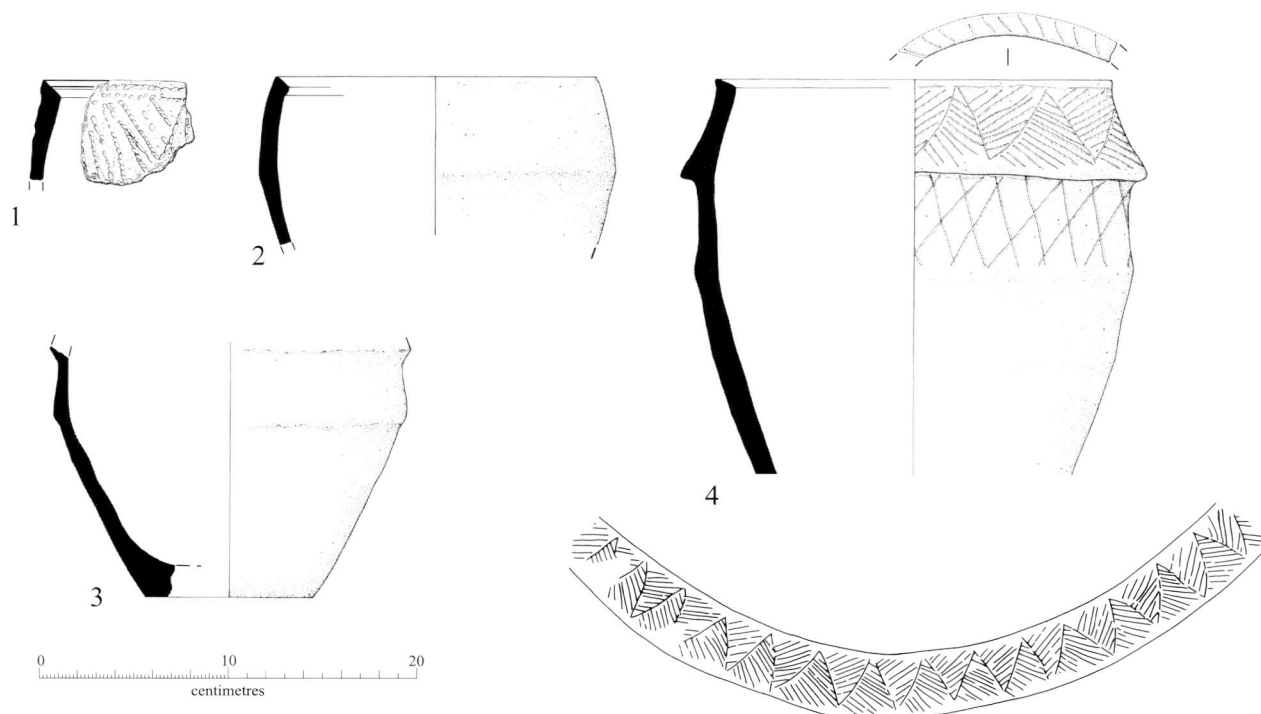

FIGURE 4.18. *Pottery — Collared Urn: 1) Single internally bevelled rim fragment, with collar surface decorated with twisted cord chevron design (F.227); 2) upper profile of plain biconical urn with 'soft' collar (dia. 13 cm; F.197), with rim inturned forming a rounded slightly hooked profile; 3) partial profile of Collared Urn made up of base and neck (F.199), with a false rim at the break between the neck and missing collar; 4) near-complete profile including rim, collar, neck, body and beginning of base-angle (height 22 cm, dia. 20 cm; F.193), and whose decoration comprised incised lines across rim top, incised filled chevrons around collar and incised cross-hatching around the neck (with detail of 'unwound' collar decoration below).*

The 119 sherds of Collared Urn (3008 g) included fragments from at least eight identifiable vessels from ten separate contexts. The largest fragments came from a single, partially reconstructible urn located within F.189, F.193 and F.197 (Fig. 4.18:4). This would have stood 22 cm high and had a diameter of approximately 20 cm. Its collar was accentuated by being slightly pinched out at its top (rim) and bottom (collar), making the top of the rim broad and flat. The rim-top was incised with short diagonal lines, whereas the collar had incised triangles filled with incised hatching. Further decoration occurred around the urn's neck as a simple incised lattice. When putting this pot back together it became obvious that some sherds had experienced different histories after the vessel had been broken. Sherds with burnt edges (as indicated by the loss of any differentiation between the internal, core and external surfaces) refitted with unburnt sherds; heat-affected sherds occurred in all three contexts.

Besides the large urn, another vessel was also present within F.193 as represented by two relatively thin-walled fragments. Similarly, F.197 also produced several sherds of a plain biconical urn (Fig. 4.18:2), as well as large fragments from a Collared Urn that had its collar section removed at the point where it joined the vessel's neck (as indicated by a broad fracture). This vessel had a gently pronounced shoulder and tapering body.

A large collar fragment, decorated with a loose incised lattice design, was retrieved from F.225; F.226 contained a single rim frag-ment impressed with diagonal lines of twisted cord, and another twisted cord-impressed collar came from an unstratified context. A pronounced shoulder/raised cordon on a sherd from F.326 shared a similar appearance and fabric to the two thin-walled pieces from F.193 and have, therefore, been included within this category.

A total of 98 flints were recovered (443 g) from the Collared Urn pits; ten were burnt as well as worked, whilst six were just burnt (see Table 4.7). The features yielded 15 cores, either single-, opposed- or multiple-platform (Fig. 4.19:1–3), discoidal, irregular or fragmentary (Fig. 4.19:4). The cores sometimes reveal a systematic approach to flake production/core reduction, yet were reduced with hard-hammers, with the scars of unsuccessful attempts to remove flakes visible on many as incipient cones. The flaking angles were not well maintained and the majority of the flake blanks produced would have been small and squat. Nevertheless, many of the cores were extensively worked.

The flakes recovered from these contexts are compatible with the core technology; commonly small and squat with a sharp *angle de chasse*, the flakes were removed with hard-hammers from unprepared platforms. Several chunks were also present, which could variously be the result of initial decortication in core reduction sequences and tool manufacture, shatter fragments, core fragments, or nodules tested as potential cores.

The pits also yielded a variety of tools and utilized flakes (Fig. 4.19:6); several of the formal tool types and utilized flints stand out

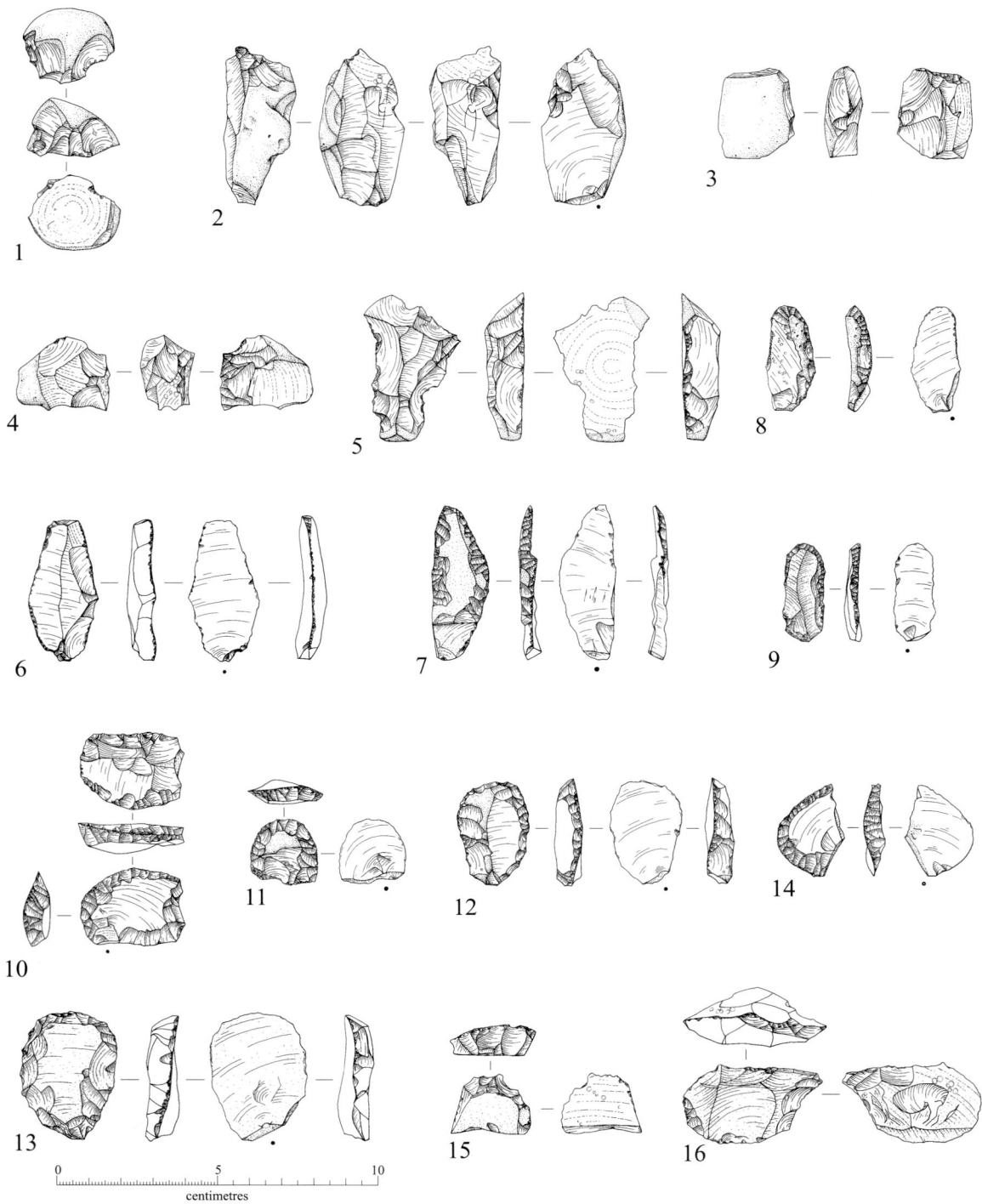

FIGURE 4.19. *Collared Urn-associated worked flint: 1–5) cores; 6) retouched flake; 7–10) flake knives; 11–15) scrapers; 16) piercer.*

TABLE 4.7. *Collared Urn pit flint.*

Pit	Chip/chunk	Primary flake	Secondary flake	Tertiary flake	Single platform core	Opposed platform core	Multiple platform core	Discoidal core	Irregular core	Core fragment	Retouched flake	Edge-used flake	Retouched & worn flake	Sub-circular scraper	Thumbnail scraper	Miscellaneous scraper	Core scraper	Flake knife	Piercer	Unworked burnt chunk	Total
38				1																	1
39			1	1																5	7
162				1																	1
225				1		1															2
226			2						2										1		5
227				1																	1
325			2	2											1			1			6
326	2		3	1	1					1				1				1			10
185	1		1	1										1							4
186	1																				1
187	2	1		1			1		1						1						7
188														1		1					2
189	3		4	4					1	1							1				14
191				1																	1
192			1																		1
193			1								1	1								1	4
195	1		1				1		1	1						2					7
196	1		2	1						1			1								6
197	1		4	2				1	1									2			11
198	1	1	1																		3
199	1																				1
251			3																		3
Total	14	2	26	18	1	1	2	1	6	4	1	1	1	3	2	3	1	4	1	6	98

against a background of comparatively expedient flake production/core reduction. The tools include four flake knives (F.197, F.325 & F.326; Fig. 4.19:7–10) and a variety of scrapers including two thumbnail scrapers (F.187 & F.325; Fig. 4.19:11) Some of the sub-circular scrapers are invasively and extensively retouched (Fig. 4.19:12 & 13), whereas the sub-circular scrapers recovered from F.188 and F.195, are abruptly retouched, smaller and almost thumbnail scrapers (Fig. 4.19:14 & 15). A piercer recovered from F.226 was worked partially as a core to remove small, squat flakes, and then retouched and utilized (Fig. 4.19:16). Two tools, a flake knife from F.197 (Fig. 4.19:7) and a piercer (F.325), were freshly retouched heavily patinated flakes; the original flakes are incompatible with the flintworking technology of the rest of the material recovered from the pits and are potentially reused Neolithic material.

The Collared Urn pit assemblages indicate that a mixture of flintworking waste, flake blanks and utilized flints were discarded in the pits. The presence of chunks, cores and flake blanks suggests that partial flake production/core reduction sequences were practised, supported by the immediacy of the core reduction strategies.

The fieldsystem

Interrelating the results of both the site's evaluation and excavation, the fieldsystem's axes can be reconstructed (Figs. 4.20 & 4.22). Of course, across the north-centre of the area, these were only trench-exposed and, there, this must be highly provisional. The system essentially consisted of a series of paddocks/fields, organized around an enormous 'strip-paddock', 40–60 m wide, which continued for more 290 m (north–south). Its eastern side was delineated by a continuous, slightly arcing ditch-line, F.173. In the main, 1.1–2.2 m wide and 0.5–0.93 m deep, this boundary showed considerable variability and clearly portions of it had been intensively recut and, at points, its line kinked (Fig. 4.21).

In Area A, the west side of this paddock was marked by Ditch F.385, whose northern length had been recut in conjunction with the establishment of a western return axis, F.322 (Fig. 4.20). Only 0.7–1.4 m wide and 0.3–0.5 m deep, the ditches on this side were much less substantial than the eastern, F.173 boundary. Ditch F.385 terminated just within the trenched zone in the southwestern corner of this area. Associated with its butt end was a posthole and pit (F.395 & F.404) and, also, a short ditch length, F.391 (*c.* 0.7 m wide; 0.2 m deep), that ran parallel with the main F.385 boundary. There can be no doubt that these related to a major westward entranceway at least 7 m+ wide (the ditch-line not being exposed again in the south until where it crossed Evaluation Trench 28).

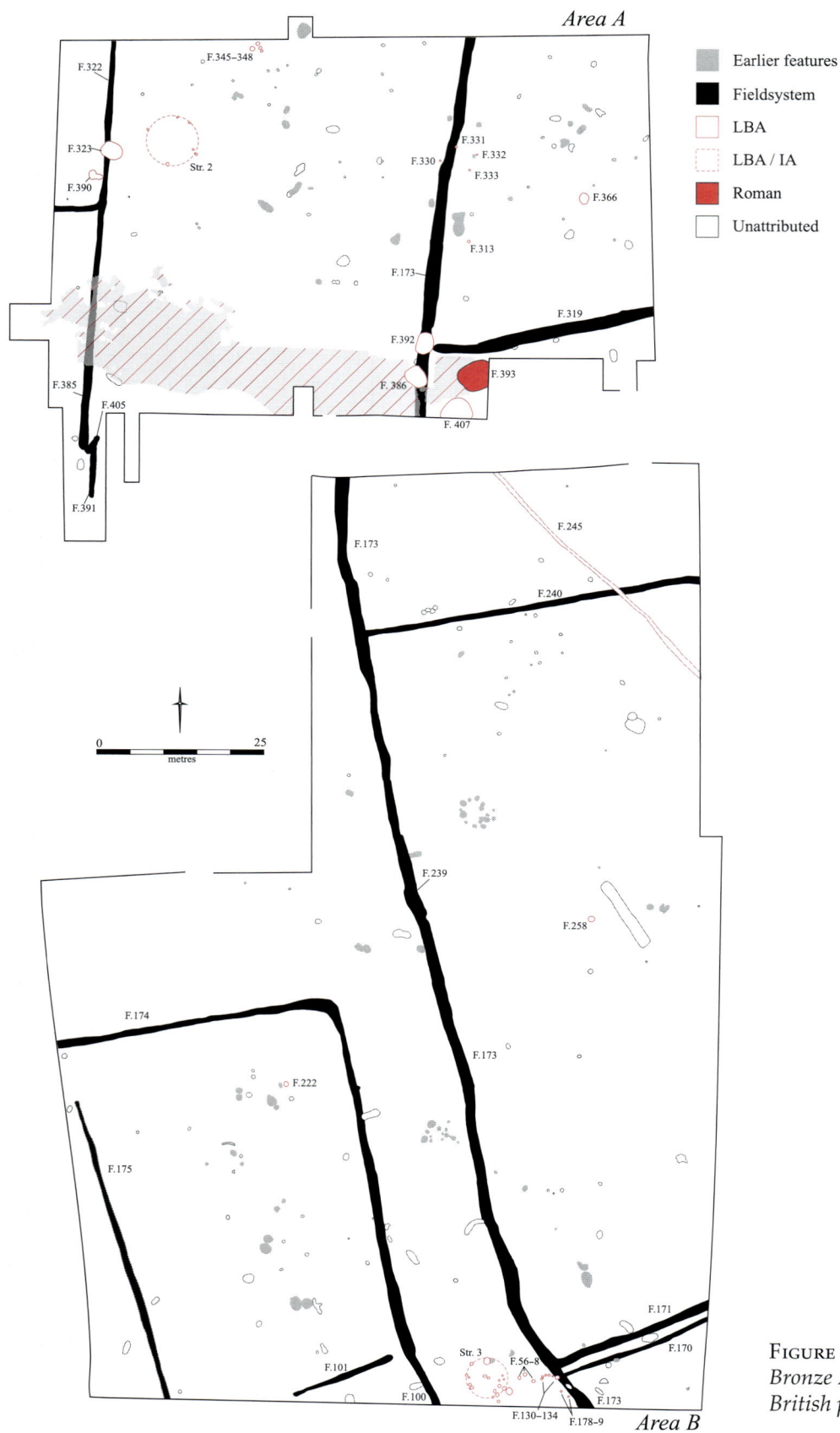

FIGURE 4.20. *The fieldsystem and Bronze Age features (and Romano-British pit, F.393).*

was defined by the side of Paddock B (35–40 × 55–60 m). There are two points of note concerning the plan of the latter. First, that the ditch length along its south side (F.101) stopped just shy of the southern edge of the site (dividing it from Paddock C) and, also, 2 m short of its eastern boundary (F.100). The latter interval was too narrow to represent any manner of entranceway and probably occurred in relationship to bank upcast along the interior western side of ditch F.100; this implies that the F.101 length was somewhat secondary. (The more bulbous terminal of F.100 apparent at this point — the ditch generally being wider north thereof — must also represent a secondary recutting in relationship to this corner.) Secondly, the gap between the northern end of this paddock's western side (F.175) and its northern boundary (F.174) was much more substantial (*c.* 8 m wide) and clearly marked an entrance as such. It is the fact that ditch F.174 continued further west than the line of F.175 which indicates that its unseen, northward return must essentially have formed the western side of the 'strip-paddock'; south of Area A, this boundary was only exposed in two evaluation trenches north of this point.

On the eastern side of the main 'strip-paddock', four paddock-fields were distinguished (D–G; Fig. 4.22). These were separated by roughly east-northeast-/west-southwest-oriented ditches (respectively from south to north):

F.171 - 1.1–1.4 m wide and 0.45–0.7 m deep
F.240 - 0.4–0.9 m wide and 0.16–0.32 m deep
F.319 - 1.4–1.9 m wide and 0.25–0.58 m deep; this ditch did not actually conjoin with the main F.173 boundary, but butt-ended just shy of it.

The southernmost boundary, dividing Paddocks D and E, was 'doubled' and had a more minor boundary running parallel, 2 m south along its side (F.170; 0.7–0.9 m wide; 0.24 m deep). As argued above, this form of ditch setting would attest to embankment, and it may well have been hedge-capped. (Note that across the north-centre of this eastern swathe — where the ditches were trench-exposed only — as defined, Paddock F would be *c.* 180 m long/wide, and it could well be the case that it was further sub-divided by another, unseen east–west boundary.)

No entranceway gaps as such were present along the length of the long eastern boundary of the 'strip-paddock'; however, based on the pattern of its recutting, as shown on Figure 4.22, the location of at least two, subsequently closed, entrance-openings can be postulated. Moreover, another can be recognized to have originally connected Paddocks F and G as, in Area A, ditch F.319 originally must have terminated *c.* 7 m short of the main F.173 boundary.

FIGURE 4.21. *The fieldsystem: top, ditch F.173 as exposed in the evaluation trenching, with buried soil-sealed metalling overlying the ditch fill; below, the main F.173 ditch-line (photographs, A. Cooper and E. Beadsmoore).*

In the south, the main 'strip-paddock' ('A') was approached by a 14–16 m-wide droveway, which turned sharply eastward adjacent to the southern limit of excavation (Fig. 4.22). While the eastern side of that 'way' was formed by the direct continuation of Paddock A's ditch on that side (F.173), its western limit

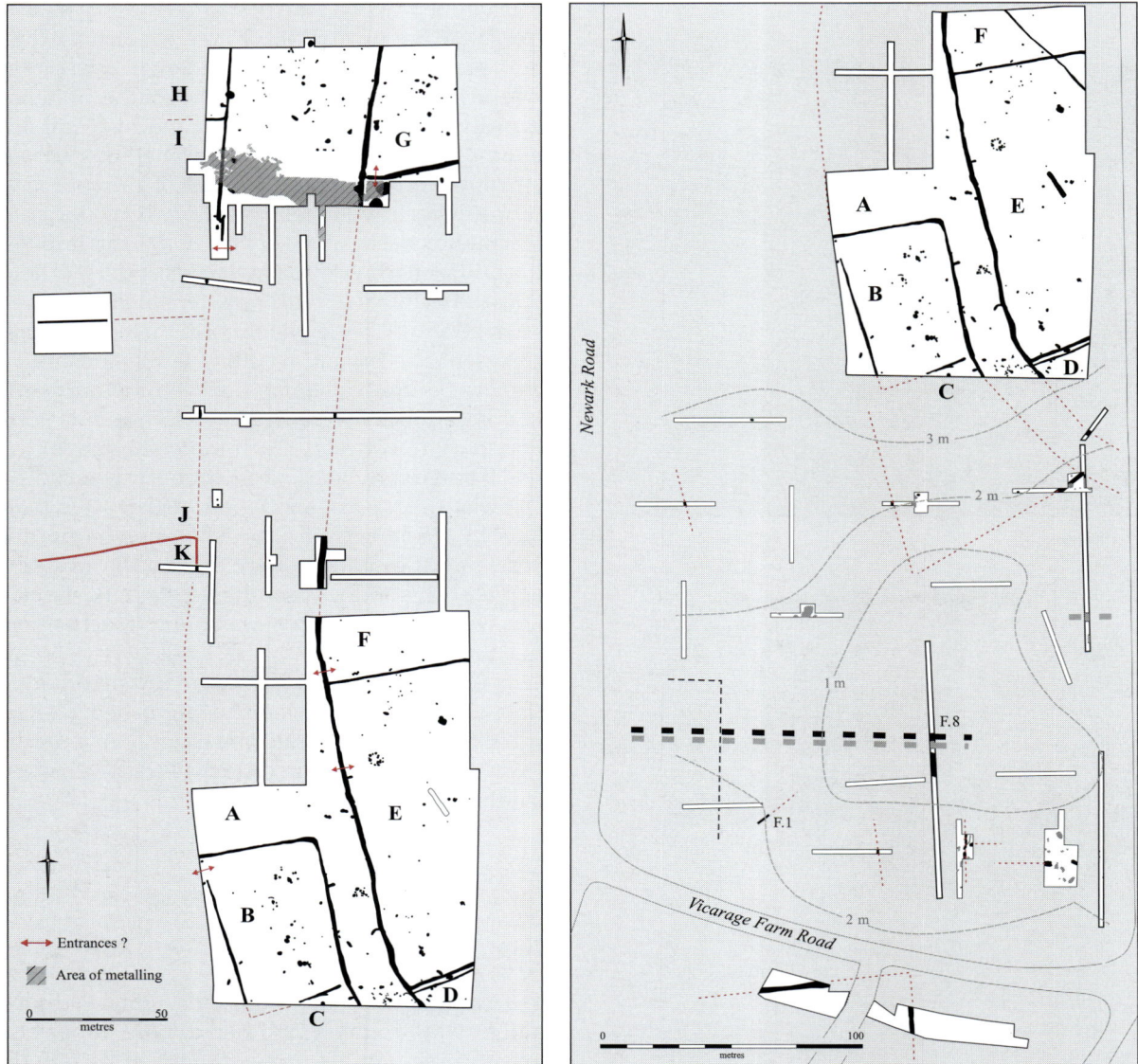

FIGURE 4.22. *Fieldsystem reconstruction. (Reproduced by permission of Ordnance Survey on behalf of HMSO.*
© *Crown copyright 2009. All rights reserved. Ordnance Survey Licence number 100048686.)*

Along the western side of the main 'strip-paddock' in Area A, Ditch F.322 was seen to separate Paddocks H and I (Fig. 4.22). While south of its line no other east–west ditches were exposed in the course of the excavation proper, drawing upon other sources two other boundaries can be proposed. The ditch that Pryor exposed within his Paving Factory investigations would mark the southern side of Paddock I (making it 88 m wide), whereas a cropmark line at this point could delineate Paddocks J and K. (The former then also being 85 m wide; Paddock K would have presumably continued south for some 110 m, and possibly ended at the projection of the northern Paddock B boundary.)

However fragmented it might seem at first, drawing upon the broader area's diverse fieldwork results now allows the wider fieldsystem to be reconstructed with some confidence. Of its northern extent, the north/south-dominated Broadlands system readily meshes with Edgerley's axes (as does also Pryor's Paving Factory Site's east–west ditch; see above). Moving south, the 'off-angle' boundaries exposed across the northern half of HAT/AS's off-Vicarage Road plot generally complement and respect the southeastward turning of the Edgerley Site's great drove and the 'swing' this would have necessitated in the paddock/fields along its western side. There

FIGURE 4.23. *The metalled surface: top, looking south (with the now ever-present Power Station in the background); below, surface detail (photographs, D. Webb).*

was then a 'return' to more due north–south (and east–west) boundaries across the southern third of that plot, beyond the line of the inlet (it being what must have caused the turning of Edgerley's drove). The only boundary that does not easily accord with this pattern is Pryor's Global Doors ditch (Fig. 4.3); oriented northwest–southeast, possibly relating to a westward fanning of the system, this is further discussed below.

Later Bronze Age and other features

A metalled surface (F.334) extended as a 13–15 m-wide east–west oriented strip along the southern margin of Area A, where it transgressed and sealed the two sides of the 'strip-paddock' (Fig. 4.20). Approximately 4 cm thick — a small/medium 'gravel nodule-worth' — this densely packed layer bedded immediately upon the truncated surface of the terrace gravels and slumped

down into the backfilled profile of the fieldsystem's ditches (Figs. 4.21 & 4.23). Although no pottery was recovered from this horizon, 47 pieces of worked flint were. While this included a number of later Neolithic pieces (e.g. two bifacially flaked knives and two flake blanks), most attested to *ad hoc* modes of Bronze Age flint production; a thumbnail scraper was among the finds.

It is difficult to be certain of the status of this gravel surface: did it just relate to a consolidation of the eroded soil horizon or a more 'intentional' construction — a 'hard' yard or even, perhaps, a trackway? Whatever the case, the apparent downcutting implied by its level may well reflect upon the 'over-representation' of later Bronze Age settlement remains (e.g. roundhouses) as opposed to the disparate traces of preceding periods.

Within Area A, a series of large pits definitely cut the fieldsystem's ditches (Fig. 4.20). On the west side of the 'strip-paddock', F.323 (2.55 × 3.30 m; 1.3 m deep; Fig. 4.25) included the articulated remains of a cow with an *in utero* calf (see Swaysland below). The eastern side boundary of the paddock was cut by F.392 (2.25m dia.; 0.9 m deep) and F.386 (2.15 × 3.15 m; 0.95 m deep). Seemingly backfilled with gravelly horizons, these pits appear to have been dug when the fieldsystem's boundaries were partially silted-up and, in the case of the latter two, shared the same upper fill as the ditches. Based on this, they have been, albeit tentatively, initially assigned to the Late Bronze Age (it being suspected that F.323 could have been considerably later, though this seems not to be the case; see below). Adjacent to the latter two features was another large pit, F.407, 4.8 m across and 1.25 m deep, whose fill sequence suggested a similar attribution.

Only one cut feature within the area yielded definite Late Bronze Age dating evidence, a small pit, F.313, with large sherds of Post-Deverel-Rimbury pottery (Fig. 4.20). Just to the north of it was a cluster of four postholes, F.330–33; though not producing dating evidence, one (F.331) cut the fills of the main fieldsystem boundary. Another tight cluster of small pits/postholes, along the northern margin of the area (F.345–8), was thought to be of the same date, but, again, this was not based on positive artefactual evidence. Also without definite assignation, located just adjacent to the F.323 cow-and-calf pit, F.390 was a small pit whose fill was distinguished by its quantity of burnt stones. It is, in fact, conceivable that this feature related to a possible 'C'-shaped setting of postholes (F.351, F.355–8), some 7 m in diameter, located just to the northeast on the other side of the 'strip-paddock' boundary at this point. Though the latter's existence is somewhat tenuous, it hereafter will be referred to as Structure 2 (Fig. 4.24).

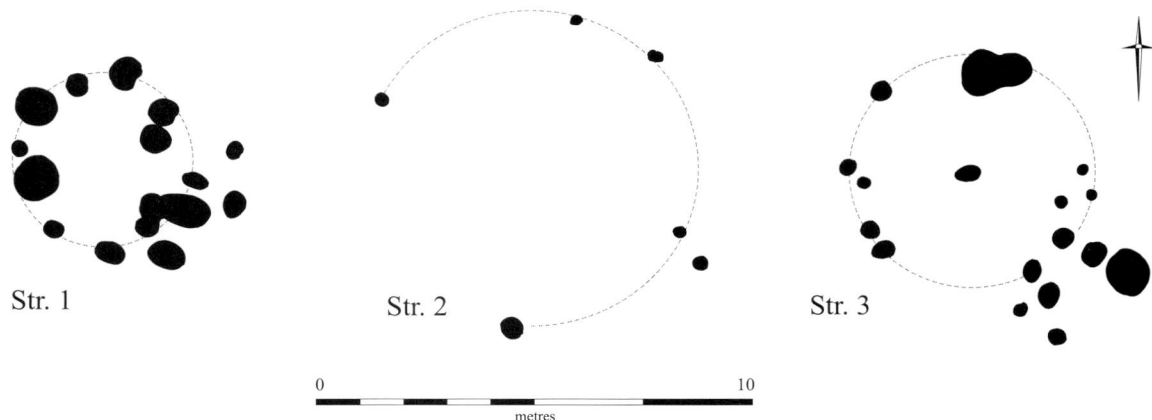

FIGURE 4.24. *Potential roundhouse structures (cf. Fig. 3.15).*

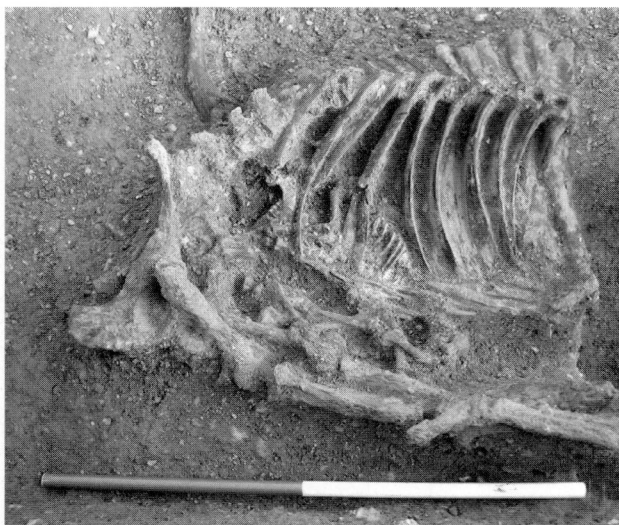

FIGURE 4.25. *Pit F.323: top, detail of the cow-and-calf deposit; below, the pit half-sectioned (photograph, E. Beadsmoore).*

No large 'late' pits were present within Area B, where, aside from a cluster of features in the extreme south, only one small, definite pit of the period was found, F.258 (Fig. 4.20). This produced large sherds of Post-Deverel-Rimbury pottery, flint and burnt flint; pit F.222 was also suspected to be of similar attribution. Only two postholes within the cluster of features on the southern side of the site, F.55 and F.56, yielded dating evidence (again, Post-Deverel-Rimbury pottery). Falling within the axes of the main droveway, these features fell into two groupings. Within the west-centre of the drove, 19 postholes (0.1–0.35 m deep) appeared to define the *c.* 4.9 m diameter of the internal post-ring of a roundhouse and its *c.* 2.2 m offset, southeast-oriented porch (Structure 3; Fig. 4.24). Just east of and beside this was the second grouping of 11 postholes (including the two with pottery), but which formed no discernable pattern.

Late Bronze Age/Post-Deverel-Rimbury pottery was recovered from six different contexts (F.10, F.55, F.56, F.173, F.258 & F.313). Features 10, 55, 56 and 173 produced only one or two small pieces, whereas F.258 and F.313 contained sizable fragments that made up the bulk of the assemblage by both number (89 per cent) and weight (99 per cent). Diagnostic pieces included small plain rims (F.173 & F.258), with shoulder fragments with diagonal slashes coming from F.313. In contrast, with the dominant grog-rich fabrics associated with the later Neolithic and earlier Bronze Age wares, this material was characterized by either lightweight vacuous fabrics or, in the case of F.313, abrasive, heavyweight quartz-rich sherds.

Only one definite Roman feature, probably a large pit-well or quarry (F.393), was present (Fig. 4.20). Truncating the eastern end of the metalled spread in Area A, this was 5.2 m across and 0.95 m deep, its upper profile being capped with alluvium. In addition to fragments of animal bone, five sherds of Romano-British pottery were recovered dating to the second to fourth centuries AD (K. Andersen pers. comm.).

Otherwise, only one other post-fieldsystem feature of any significance was present, F.245, in Area B (Fig. 4.20). The fills of this 0.3–0.8 m-wide and 0.15–0.25 m-deep, northwest–southeast oriented ditch were comparable to those of the main fieldsystem. However, lying well off of the latter's alignment and cutting across its boundaries, there was no possibility that F.245 could relate to the Bronze Age fieldsystem; lacking any alluvium/topsoil component within its fill, it is presumed to be of either Iron Age or earlier Roman attribution (a similar-sized and oriented ditch in the nearby Broadlands Site was assigned to the Iron Age; Nicholson *et al.* forthcoming).

The Herdsman's Hill barrow and Fengate's monuments

The Leeds' Archive at the Ashmolean Museum includes a statement by Abbott concerning the Herdsman's Hill barrow and which is also described by an entry in one of his notebooks (W11/1/3). These are retrospective accounts, the barrow having been quarried away by *c.* 1900. Located at the northern, Edgerley Drain-end of Fengate (Fig. 4.26), Leeds considered it as an outlier of his Eyebury barrow group (Tumulus 4; 1912, 82) and, in fact, relates that it was his father who first obtained the artefacts from it and which had since been in the Ashmolean (1912, fig. 2; see also Leeds 1956, 85). It is the notebook account that provides the most fulsome record of the monument:

Neolithic or Bronze Age Burial at Newark near Peterborough
This tumulus formerly called "Herdsman's Hill" was situate[d] on gravel land just on the edge of what was skirty fenland and was used lately as a refuge in high floods.
   The tumulus was about [**blank**] *ft long* [**blank**] *ft wide &* [**blank**] *ft high & was composed of loose top soil deep in places and the rest gravel from the surrounding gravel land. When this was removed about 1900 for gravel a large knife dagger and a spear head were found at the bottom of a "pot hole" and also a perforated axehammer was found near the same place but it is not quite certain if they were found together* [Fig. 4.27]. *Two extended skeletons were also found*[,] *one at the north & the other at the south side of the mound near the road with head to south but nothing was noticed with either of these. No bones were found to show any cremated interments & no pots of any description were noticed.*
   This mound was dug out by workmen who were very careless & who were not looked after, & so many things may have been overlooked & lost (W11/1/1, p. 10).

In the single-page archive document Abbott noted that the depth of 'the soil' (i.e. the barrow's mound) was 'from 3ft 6" to 5ft [this may account for a grave]. The workmen have an idea that the top soil had been put on top of the mound to make a safe place for cattle in time of floods, so clearly the extra depth was noticed'. Otherwise, this statement essentially reiterates the notebook's description, except for adding that the artefacts had apparently been recovered by quarry-workers; Leeds senior having presumably acquired the pieces from them.
   In that account Abbott also related that 'this hill as you remember was on a raised piece of land at Newark in a field by the side of the road leading down from the Oxney Road. The gravel was taken out by Ripon & Co in 1900'. The precise location of the monument is, unfortunately, impossible to establish with certainty and, indeed, all of the early findings within the northern end of Fengate seem somewhat ambiguous. The Commission's 1969 volume (based on the OS Record Cards) would have it sited at TL 21580030, some 165 m due north of the Edgerley Road Site (and in what was an area of 'old' gravel workings; the SMR/HER has it 75 m north of the site beside Newark Road). However, another possible location is the 'Site of Tumulus' marked on the 1924–50 OS 6" maps, almost 275

m due east of the Commission's location and beside Edgerley Drain Road (at TF 21810028). Whatever the case, there is no doubt that this barrow stood some hundreds of metres north of our site.
   The other findings reported north of the site and in the area of former gravel workings in the field northwest of the junction of Oxney and Edgerley Drain Roads, are a Collared Urn said to have been found in 1936 (Fig. 4.26:1; SMR/HER 50204) and a flint arrowhead recovered in 1912; both being reported to Peterborough Museum by Abbott (SMR/HER 2995). Much more intriguing, though, is the report in the 1969 Commission volume (p. 8), after OS Record Cards, of Abbott having found in the gravel pits there '*Bronze Age Settlement and Burials*. Beaker huts sites, Bronze Age cinerary urn and cremation ditches etc' (Fig. 4.26:2; SMR/HER 2963). One can only wonder what the 'cremation ditches' refer to, but certainly this report does appear to describe a significant Beaker/Bronze Age site: located some 850 m northeast of our excavation, it raises the question whether it was part of the same 'locale-site' or a separate settlement cluster.
   Leaving aside Abbott's 'great' ring-ditch (Fig. 4.28:A; see Chapter 2 and Evans & Appleby 2008), which was located in the fields just northwest of Pryor's later Padholme Road sub-Site area (Fig. 2.4), and also his other, possible palstave- and skull-associated ring-ditch length (see Chapter 2 above; Fig. 2.4), Fengate's fen-edge has not been particularly renowned for its monuments *per se*. Nevertheless, four have subsequently been identified. This would include both Pryor's Storey's Bar Road ring-ditch/barrow (with only a single Collared Urn-associated cremation within its interior and two inhumations in its circuit; Fig. 4.28:D; Pryor 1978 and see Evans & Pollard 2001, 25–6) and the putative later Neolithic henge dug at the Cat's Water in 1990 (Fig. 4.28:C; Pryor 2001a, 38–47). Though without any accompanying interments (and lacking direct dating evidence), the latter may well have been a Bronze Age ring-ditch. In 1992, a *c.* 20 m diameter ring-ditch was exposed at the Cambridge Archaeological Unit's Depot Site; only trench-investigated during evaluation fieldwork, no burials were recovered at that stage. During later trenching, however, a single inhumation was encountered within its ditch (Evans & Pryor 2001, 16–27; B. Robinson pers. comm.). Nearby, in 1998, a small, 9 m-diameter ring-ditch excavated (by the County Council Field Unit) off Third Drove enclosed the cremated remains of a single older child/young adult set within a pit in its centre (Fig. 4.28:B; Cooper 1998). While not dated as such, this is presumed to be of Middle/later Bronze Age attribution. (In addition, Pryor has postulated the ritual connections of a number of Fengate's Neolithic settings; all of quite ambiguous status, these were fully appraised in Chapter 3 Inset above.)
   A crucial point to be stressed here is that none of Fengate's recently investigated monuments evidently attracted substantive cremation cemeteries and nor, in contrast to other 'fieldsystem landscapes' (e.g. Tanholt Farm, Eye and Barleycroft Farm), have 'flat' Middle Bronze Age cremation cemeteries been recovered amid its boundaries. Further discussed in this

The Site

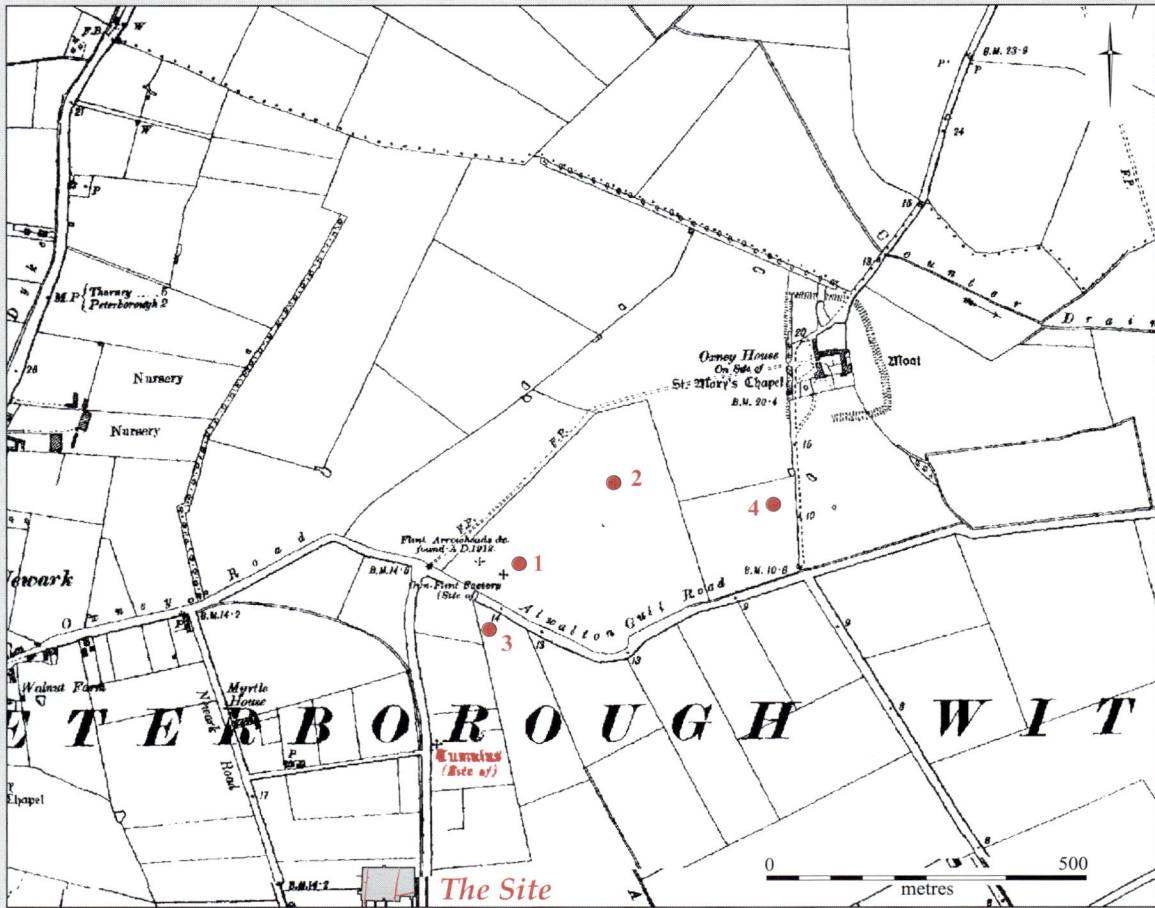

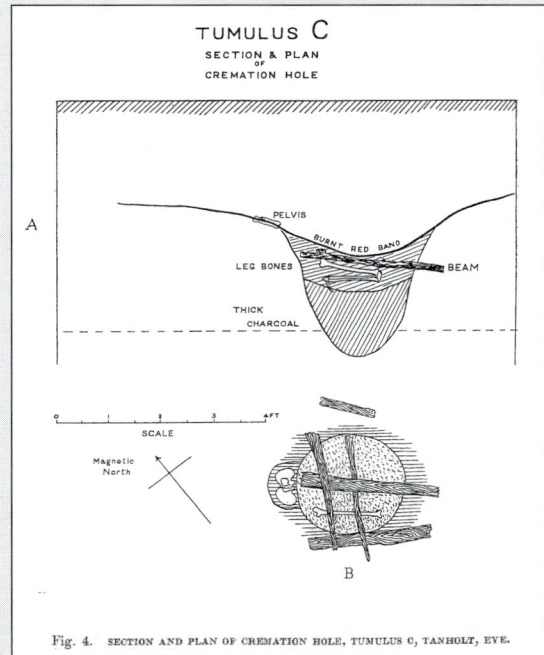

Fig. 4.   SECTION AND PLAN OF CREMATION HOLE, TUMULUS C, TANHOLT, EYE.

FIGURE 4.26. *(left) Edgerley North Environs — Top, 1927 OS map showing location of the Herdsman's Hill Barrow northwest of our site; also indicated on the map is Abbott's 1912 finds-spot of 'flint arrowheads etc.' (and the adjacent of Gun Flint Factory), with the red-dot points respectively refer to: 1) the report of a Collared Urn found in 1936; 2) Abbott's 'Bronze Age Settlement and Burials'; 3) the Travellers' Site socketed bronze axe (found 1995); 4) Soke's 2002 Oxney Road excavations; below left, Leeds's 1912 map showing Eyebury Farm area and the three barrows he excavated; right, detail of the 'cremation hole' (i.e.* in situ *pit-pyre) from his southernmost, Tumulus C (1915, fig. 4; see also Evans 1997a).*

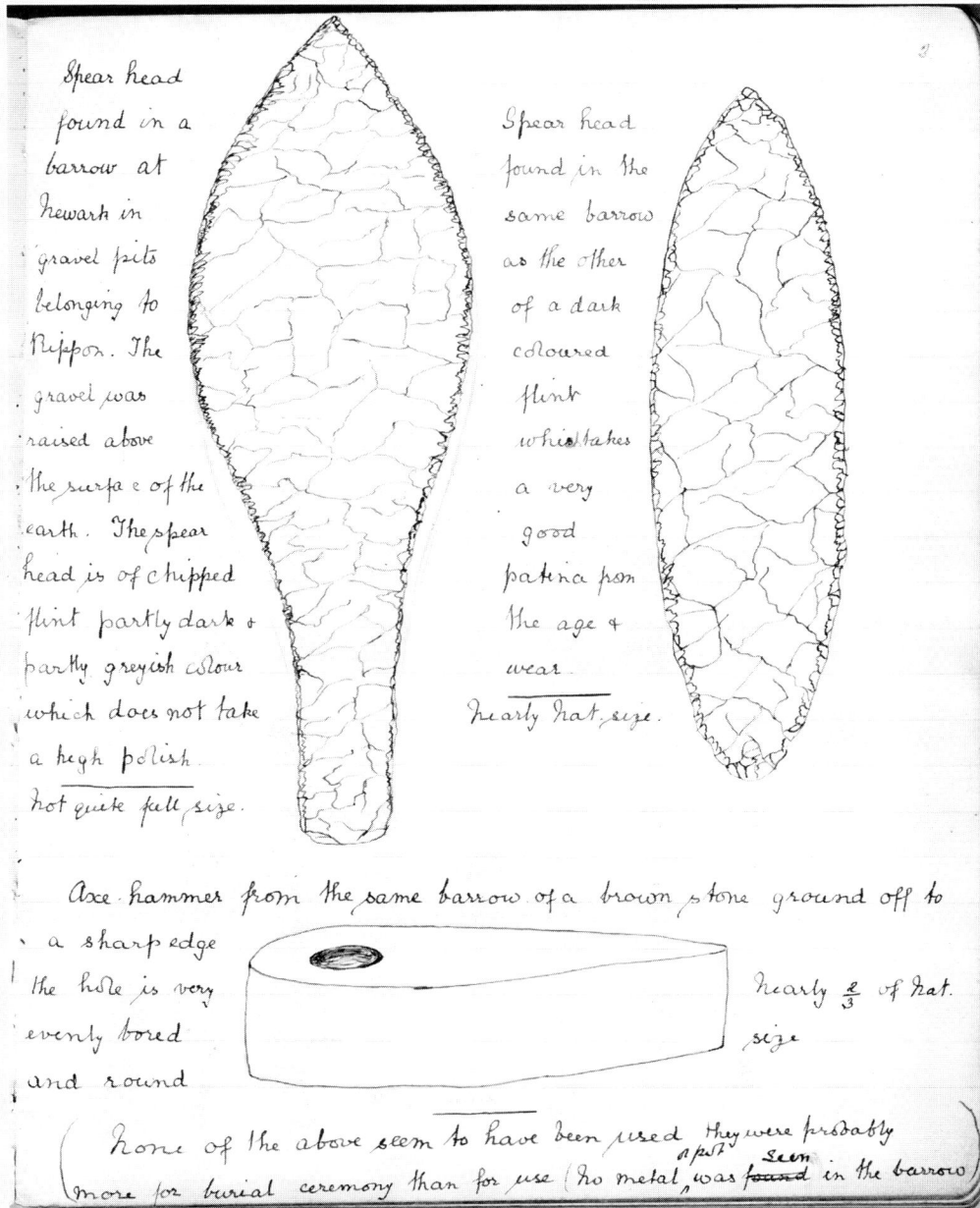

Spear head found in a barrow at Newark in gravel pits belonging to Rippon. The gravel was raised above the surface of the earth. The spear head is of chipped flint partly dark & partly greyish colour which does not take a high polish. Not quite full size.

Spear head found in the same barrow as the other of a dark coloured flint which takes a very good patina from the age & wear. nearly nat. size.

Axe hammer from the same barrow of a brown stone ground off to a sharp edge the hole is very evenly bored and round. nearly ⅔ of nat. size.

(None of the above seem to have been used they were probably more for burial ceremony than for use (no metal was seen in the barrow)

FIGURE 4.27. *The Herdsman's Hill Barrow — Abbott notebook recording of the barrow's finds (Cambridge University Museum of Archaeology and Anthropology).*

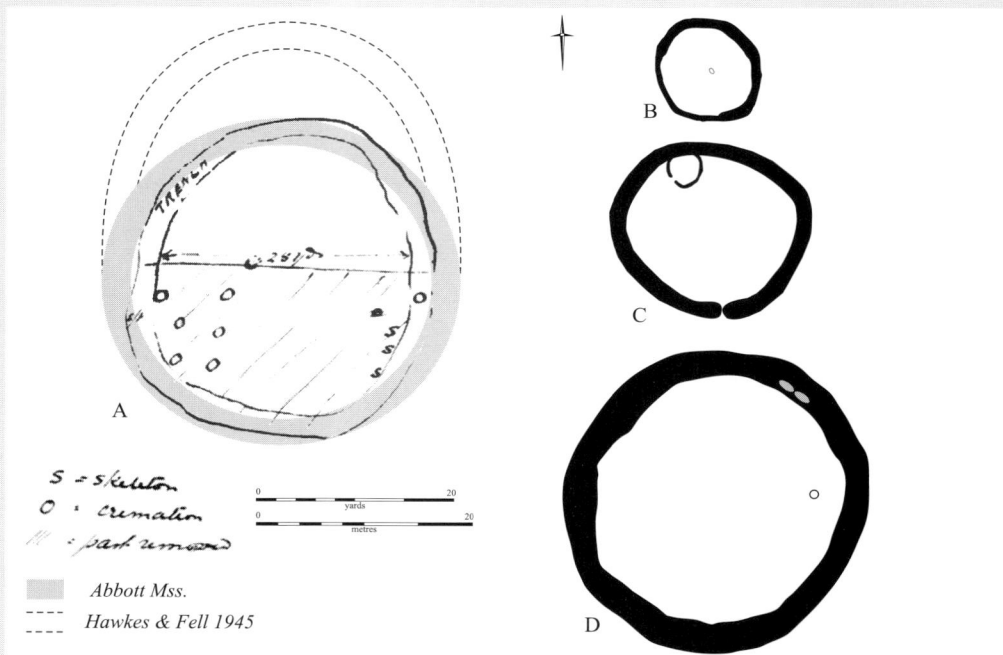

S = skeleton
O = cremation
ₘ = part removed

Abbott Mss.
Hawkes & Fell 1945

FIGURE 4.28. *(left) Fengate's Monuments — Top: A) Abbott's great ring-ditch as variously reconstructed from dimensions in his manuscript and the Hawkes and Fell paper (see Fig. 2.9); B) the Third Drove ring-ditch (after Cooper 1998); C) the Cat's Water henge/ring-ditch (after Pryor 2001a, fig. 3.9); D) the Storey's Bar Road barrow/ring-ditch (Pryor 1978); below, detail of 1976 vertical aerial photograph (from CUCAP RC8-BO243; see Fig. 1.3) showing two barrows in the field west of the later Flag Fen Sewage Works (and with larger-scale version of Number 2 inset below; see Fig. 6.1:VII & IX) that has set into present-day vertical image in which five definite round barrows are visible in the Nene Washes (3-7; see Fig. 6.9; photograph reproduced with permission of the Geoinformation Group).*

volume's final chapter, this negative evidence makes Abbott's huge ring-ditch all the more extraordinary as, together, these findings could well reflect upon the area's specific socio-political organization during the second millennium BC.

As shown on Figure 6.1, Abbott's great multiple-interment ring-ditch can be seen to lie in approximate alignment with the Storey's Bar Road ring-ditch/barrow and the small Third Drove ring-ditch (Monuments VI, I & IV respectively). Aside from Pryor's Neolithic axis, this is the only such monument alignment in the immediate Fengate landscape (though a similar claim could potentially be mounted concerning its fen-edge ring-ditches: the Depot and Third Drove Sites' and that at the Cat's Water; the latter being Pryor's putative henge). This, in itself, is interesting as this Monument I, IV and VI axis would have lain 100–150 m southwest of the line of the Ditch 1/2 droveway and been roughly parallel with it. This 'co-incidence' could lend support to the notion that that droveway may, in fact, have served as Fengate's prime axis. This argument would essentially hinge on the frequency of inhumations found along its length (perhaps echoing those in Abbott's Monument VI ring-ditch). Whilst admittedly highly speculative, this could have ramifications relating to the droveway's sympathetic relation-

ship with the Elliott Site's inlet as regards the 'recommendation' of natural topography upon cultural landscape features (i.e. the fieldsystem). This might, furthermore, find resonance in observations that a due northwest–southeast orientation seems generally to have been predominant in the region's Bronze Age fieldsystems and, presumably, this would have had ritual connotations (i.e. possibly established by sun-rise on a specific date). If this is a valid reading, then, of Fengate's main droves, the Ditch 1/2 'way' excavated at the Padholme Road and Elliott Sites most clearly followed that orientation. Equally, following this interpretative chain, it could be argued that, linked *via* the post alignment to the Flag Fen platform, the system's other significant drove — marked by Ditches 8/9 at Pryor's Newark Road and Fourth Drove Sites — only secondarily assumed the role of the system's paramount axis. This reasoning could, moreover, correlate to the fact that the latter lay considerably off the 'prime' northwest–southeast orientation, running that much closer to east–west (west-northwest/east-southeast).

To Fengate's 'core-area' monument-listing should now, however, be added the Must Farm Terrace round barrow cemetery. Not only would this include the two barrows found in the course of the 2004/05 evaluation (see Chapter 2 above; Fig. 2.16) and the pair of barrows recognized on a 1976 aerial photograph in the fields east of the Cat's Water Drain, but also the five definite (and five other 'possible') barrows distinguished on aerial photographs and in LIDAR imagery as still upstanding within the intervening Nene Washes (see Figs. 4.28 & 6.9; see Hall 1987, 60, fig. 43 concerning the 'Catswater' barrow-field; Pryor 2001a, 74–80 for Northey's monuments and Healy & Harding 2007 on wider Nene Valley distributions). Thus far entirely overlooked within the Fengate/Flag Fen 'story', the implications of this major barrow cemetery will feature in Chapter 6 below. At this juncture, though, it is worth stressing that, in relationship to arguments concerning an ancient precursor of the course of the Cat's Water Drain (see Chapters 3 & 5), the two barrows north of the Washes (Fig. 4.28:1 & .2; Fig. 6.1, Monuments VIII & IX) must have lain on the northern flank of the Must Farm terrace (Fig. 2.16). Indeed, during watching brief recording at the Flag Fen Sewage Treatment Works just to the west of these monuments, the occurrence of a gravel promontory was duly recognized (Britchfield 2001; Pryor forthcoming a).

Pit and depositional analysis

Lacking quern stone, human bone or 'small finds' generally, the site yielded few finds requiring individual distribution-point plotting and, instead, it is its pit deposits that primarily require attention. Only just over half of this site's 160 pits (excluding the one Roman feature, 393) can be assigned to a period/phase and 79 are without any real basis of attribution. Of the 82 dated pits, employing the same size-range criteria as for the Elliott Site, 65 (79 per cent) were less than 1.4 m across and/or 0.5 m deep (Tables 4.8 & 4.9). Of the remaining large pits, two categories are distinct: the four later Bronze Age-attributed quarries (F.323, F.386, F.392 & F.392) and the three Beaker pits (F.140, F.157 & F.264), with the latter not having any correlates amongst the Grooved Ware and Collared Urn features.

The unattributed pits fall into the same general size-range, with 66 (83.5 per cent) being less than 1.4 m across and 0.5 m deep (with F.269 and F.289 being the only really large undated features). As just four (4.9 per cent) of the small-medium 'attributed' pits are thought to be of later Bronze Age date, by the same measure it would have to be presumed that the vast majority of the unattributed features of this type are of pre-later Bronze Age date. Otherwise, the alternative would be to postulate substantive later Bronze Age 'pit activity' but without any real settlement-/artefact-based correlates; the site generating, after all, only very few finds of that period. This is a crucial observation. It implies that the vast majority of the site's undated pits are, in fact, probably of later Neolithic/earlier Bronze Age attribution. By extension,

TABLE 4.8. *Pits by size-range and period (see Table 4.9 for size-criteria).*

Size range	A	B	C	D	Total
Early/Middle Neolithic		2 (100%)			**2 (1.2%)**
Later Neolithic/ Grooved Ware	8 (21.6%)	22 (59.5%)	7 (18.9%)		**37 (23%)**
Beaker	4 (30.8%)	5 (38.5%)	3 (23.1%)	1 (7.7%)	**13 (8.1%)**
Collard Urn	2 (9.5%)	18 (85.7%)	1 (4.8%)		**21 (13.1%)**
Middle/later Bronze Age	3 (37.5%)	1 (12.5%)	1 (12.5%)	3 (37.5%)	**8 (5%)**
Roman				1 (100%)	**1 (0.6%)**
Unattributed	38 (48.1%)	28 (35.4%)	12 (15.2%)	1 (1.3%)	**79 (49.1%)**
Total	**55 (34.2%)**	**76 (47.2%)**	**25 (15.5%)**	**6 (3.7%)**	**161 (100%)**

TABLE 4.9. *Comparative pit-size frequency with the Elliott Site.*

	Maximum		Number		% of total	
	Length (cm)	Depth (cm)	Edgerley	Elliott	Edgerley	Elliott
A	80	25	55	70	34.2	35.2
B	140	50	76	78	47.2	39.2
C	300	-	25	14	15.5	20.6
D	300+	-	6	10	3.7	5

TABLE 4.10. *Frequency of higher artefact-value pit assemblages by period. (As listed in the phase-descriptive text-sections above, the attribution of pits to the site's 'style-period' phases is here based on a range of criteria, whereas Figure 4.38's enumeration only includes significant pit-pottery assemblages.)*

	No. of pits	Category	Range		No. with 10+ sherds/flints	No. with 80+ sherds or 20+ flints
			No.	Wt (g)		
Grooved Ware	27	Pottery	1–246	4–4179	15 (55.5%)	5 (18.5%)
		Flint	0–63	0–325	9 (33.3%)	4 (14.8%)
Beaker	11	Pottery	1–177	1–858	6 (54.5%)	1 (9.1%)
		Flint	0–8	0–64	-	-
Collared Urn	18	Pottery	0–51	1–1896	5 (27.7%)	-
		Flint	0–10	0–53	-	-

this also means that these features were dug without any express relationship to artefact deposition: neither 'ritual' or 'pragmatic' (i.e. intentional tidying-up; cf. Garrow *et al.* 2006, 75). Aside from possible instances for grain storage, well/watering holes and quarries for the larger features, we may not be able to adequately distinguish their usage — which probably included various tanning, retting and soaking purposes, and the subterranean holding of pots, leather bags and/or baskets for keeping foodstuffs and drinking water — but this does not mean that they were without function.

It can only be a coincidence that the total number of pits present at this and Elliott Site (both excavated over approximately 1.7 ha) was so close: 161 and 174. Given their relationship to the fen-edge (respectively 'behind' and 'on') and that Edgerley clearly involved much greater pottery deposition (1767 *vs* 203 prehistoric sherds), the character of their occupation/usage must surely have differed greatly: Elliott basically seeing off-/out-settlement 'taskscape' usage, whereas Edgerley was essentially a settlement locale. (While, as argued, the much greater number of animal bones at the Elliott — 2923 *vs* 324 [excluding the F.323 cow-and-calf deposit] — could reflect seasonal 'group' slaughter activities there, it surely equally attests to Edgerley's poor preservation conditions.) As demonstrated in

Table 4.9, while the trend in the frequency of the pits within the site-range criteria is broadly comparable between the two sites, a critical difference is apparent. Reflective of a need to achieve watertable depth, approximately 5 per cent more of the pits at the Elliott Site were greater than 0.5 m deep; conversely, *c.* 8 per cent more of Edgerley's pits fell within the 0.25–0.5 m depth range, presumably being related to more settlement-based activities *per se* (e.g. grain storage).

In each of the Edgerley Site's main 'pit-occupation' phases the pottery assemblages from individual features loom large and (over-) contribute to the impression of the scale of their respective occupations. Togther yielding 412 sherds (5942 g), for the Grooved Ware those from pits F.15 and F.23 produced just over half of its total. Similarly, with 177 sherds (858 g), over 50 per cent of the site's Beaker pottery came from F.140, with F.193 generating more than a third of its Collared Urn (51 sherds; 1897 g). Yet, as indicated in Table 4.10, differences in depositional practices and the *rhythm* of their change are apparent between these three main 'pit' horizons. Within its Grooved Ware contexts, higher numbers of both flint and pottery occurred within individual features. While there is a general correspondence between the two, it is by no means absolute. In demonstration, there were pits

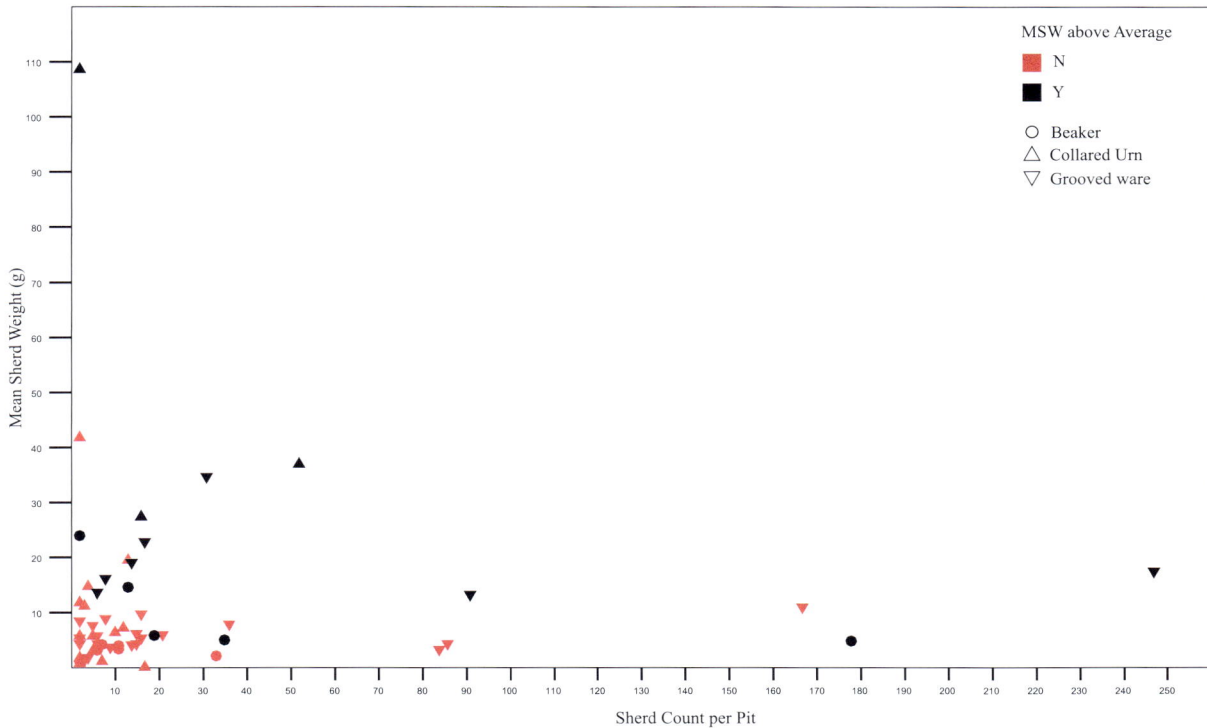

FIGURE 4.29. *Plotting of the 'typed' pits' Mean Sherd Weight (MSW) values. If excluding single sherd/pit occurrences, this shows that 13 pits (23 per cent) have values greater than the 10.4 g for the pit assemblages as a whole: Grooved Ware, eight; Beaker, one; Collared Urn, four. This measure is, however, biased against the finer lightweight Beaker fabrics and, instead, it is more representative to use the MSW of each pot-type within the pit contexts: Grooved Ware (11 g), seven pits; Beaker (4.8 g), three; Collared Urn (21.7g), two — a total of 12 pits (21 per cent). Any such gauging must, of course, be inherently biased and it could, for example, be proposed that only pits with a MSW of 20 g or more were backfilled, that corresponding to a 'reasonable' medial-size sherd which could have been readily picked up through cleaning (vs finer sweeping). In which case, only two Grooved Ware (F.274 & F.310) and two Collared Urn pits (F.193 & F.197) would meet that criteria. Yet, then again, it has to be expected that the pottery would have further broken upon impact when tossed into a pit. Nonetheless, it is crucial to note that there is a clear correlationship with the number of sherds within a pit and their size/weight, with the larger/heavier sherds generally — but not exclusively — occurring in the high pot-number features, with the result that (using the pot-type-specific MSW and excluding the two single sherd/pit instances) of the 12 higher-than-MSW pits, only two had pottery assemblages of less than 10 sherds (both Grooved Ware-associated; F.147 & F.211).*

that produced high quantities of pot, such as F.15 and F.267 (246 & 85 sherds respectively), but only very little flint (2 & 12 pieces respectively). Equally, there were instances where pits had moderately high sherd numbers (13–35; F.176, F.263 & F.287), but which had, or almost nearly so, twice the number of flints (25–63 pieces). What this implies is that, at least in some of the Grooved Ware pits, pottery and flint were being independently deposited in substantial quantities.

While through time/sequence it is clear that the absolute numbers of pottery within the pit deposits steadily decreased (possibly reflecting the relative span/intensity of their occupation), in Beaker and Collared Urn contexts some pits were clearly still backfilled with relatively high quantities of pottery.

This may, however, have entailed no more than the gathering up of large sherds for pit-deposition in the course of tidying-up (i.e. 'closure'; see Fig. 4.29 concerning mean sherd weight analysis). The key point is that, post-Grooved Ware, this depositional behaviour no longer seems to have extended to flint; the Beaker and Collared Urn pits lacked significant numbers of flint, the largest assemblage being the ten pieces from F.326 (Collared Urn-associated).

The crucial issue here, of course, is to what degree these practices/patterns were site-specific, and in this capacity it would seem that the site has relatively low numbers of worked flint generally. In total, the recovered assemblage amounted to 680 pieces. This included the 79 flints from the fieldsystem, but which was only 10 per cent sample-excavated. Factoring for this would still imply that the site's cut features would have had a total 'population' of some 1400 flints, of which only 496 (*c.* 35 per cent) would have derived from its 'typed' or attributed pits. Theoretically, to this should be added the 11,900 flints estimated to have been present within the site's buried soil horizon. Thereby reducing its 'pit occupation' flint to *c.* 3.7 per cent of the total, this certainly should promote a degree of interpretive modesty. Yet, for comparative purposes, the inclusion of the buried soil figures is not appropriate, as this horizon (and its finds) is usually just machined-off in most excavations. The most ready comparison is obviously with Pryor's Storey's Bar Road sub-Site, whose Grooved Ware occupation generated the bulk of its worked flint assemblage: *c.* 3100 pieces in total (excluding sieved contexts) — more than twice Edgerley's estimated cut-feature population (the features there essentially being 100 per cent excavated, though no buried or topsoil sampling occurred; Pryor 1978). Yet, having very few 'formal' pits as such, it generated less than 200 sherds of Grooved Ware (and one sherd each of Early/Middle Neolithic pottery and Collared Urn — in addition to its complete cremation vessel of that type — and four Beaker sherds from its ring-ditch/barrow; Pryor 1978, 91), much less than Edgerley's, and these would represent very different types of Grooved Ware usage.

Phosphates (with PAUL MIDDLETON)

A total of 110 samples were analysed in the laboratories at Peterborough Regional College. The samples fell into three groups (Fig. 4.5):

A) A single transect across the droveway;
B) Two transects taken at right angles to each other, across the area of Collared Urn Pit Cluster/Structure 1;
C) A single transect taken across buried soils overlying the metalled strip (Area A).

A control sample of the buried soil yielded a total phosphate value of 42 mg P per 100 g soil (Middleton in Beadsmoore 2005a provides details of methodology).

Droveway transect (A; Fig. 4.30)

The samples were taken at 0.5 m intervals and encompassed the defining ditches and a small swathe on either side of the droveway. Figure 4.30 illustrates the considerable variation in results obtained and, generally, the levels of phosphate are considerably above the control sample level. Phosphate levels at the western end of the sample set are markedly variable when compared to consistency of the eastern end of the transect.

Collared Urn pit cluster (B; Figs. 4.16 & 4.30)

As the two figures show, considerable variation in phosphate levels was again revealed by these samples. There do not appear to be any significant patterns, although the tight cluster of pits at the eastern side of the sampled area might be coincident with the raised levels of phosphate in Samples 75–80.

Metalling (C)

A single transect of 22 samples, taken from south to north, was analysed. With three marked exceptions, the results were uniformly low; lower indeed than the control sample, although not significantly so. Against this background, the three sample points with phosphate levels in excess of 140 mg P per 100 g soil form distinct peaks in the graph.

The results from the metalling present an intriguing picture, in which the massive peaks revealed demand explanation. Unfortunately, without further sampling to establish more conclusive patterning, any determination must remain highly speculative, since the phosphate levels will not, of themselves, give a cause. Such high levels are certainly more consistent with animal (or human) waste, rather than with being a generalized indicator of human activity. Yet, the isolated peaks against low level background readings do not seem to be consistent with animal corralling, as might be conjectured. For this, one would have expected higher background levels, resulting from the general accumulation of animal dung and urine, alongside peaks.

As noted above, the Series B samples, relating to the pit cluster/structure, need to be related to the detailed plan to see whether significant associations between phosphate levels and pits are apparent. Nothing in the results would be surprising within the context of human settlement and, at face value, it is hard to see that they are susceptible to any further interpretation.

The results from the droveway presents a tantalizing series of possibilities (Set A, Fig. 4.30). The patterning of lower levels of phosphate, particularly in Samples 33–42, and to a lesser extent, Samples 11–17, hint that these may relate to the ditches defining the droveway and that the higher levels of phosphate (>120 mg P) are focussed west of Samples 32–43 and the line of its eastern ditch. Although one transect is of limited value to rest a case on, it does seem possible that the use of the drove and enclosure to the west differed from the area east of the drove.

Excavation of a Late Bronze Age settlement and droveway system at Welland Bank, Lincs, excavated in 1997, provided a comparable opportunity to place a transect across a droveway (Middleton unpublished ms; see Chapter 2 above for summary). The results on this occasion revealed high levels of phosphate in the ditches and intermittently across the drove. This, together with bone evidence and the layout of the fieldsystem, was taken to confirm that the droveway had been used for animal management, with the ditches acting as a soakaway for the urine and dung deposited on the drove.

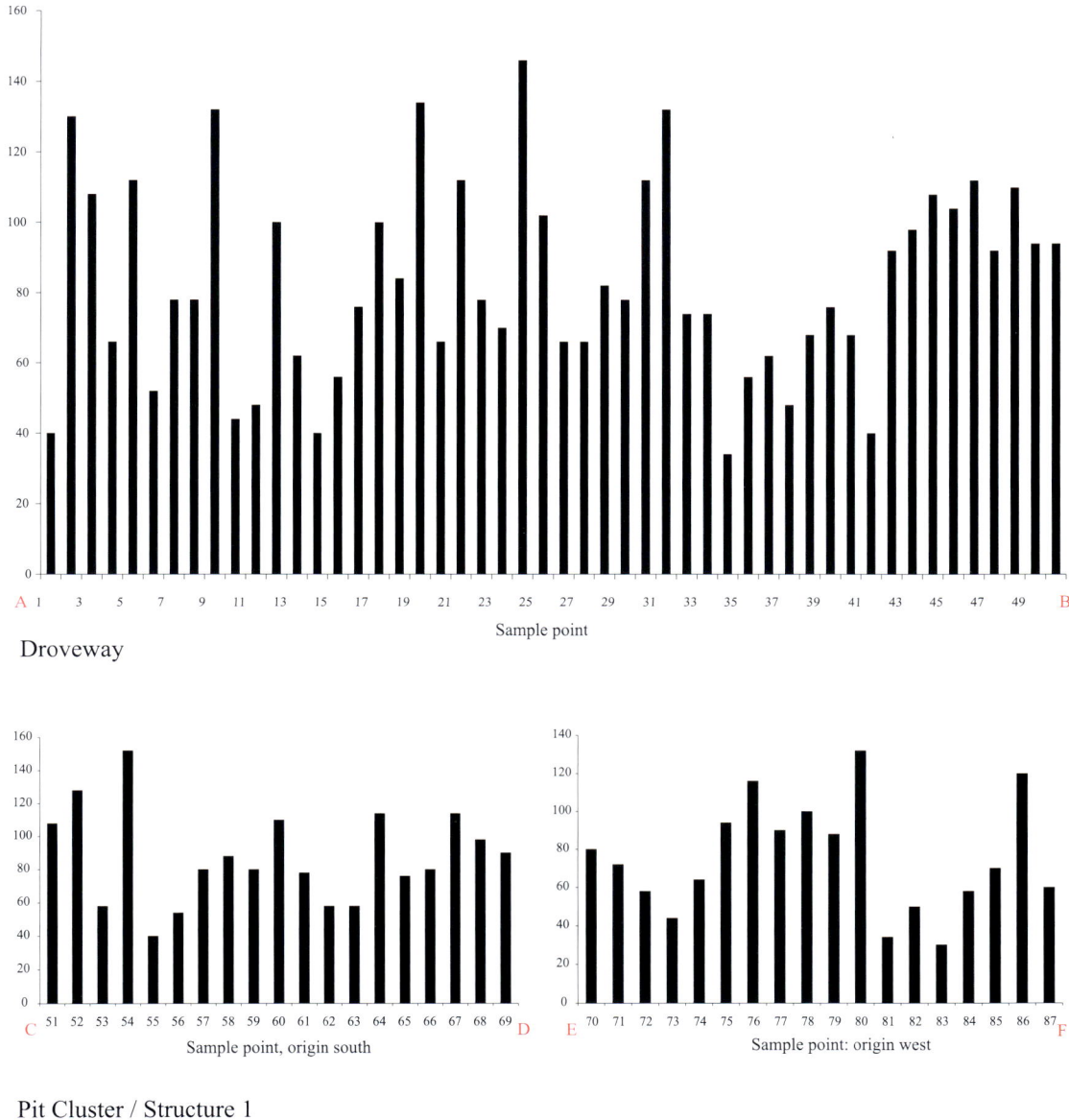

Droveway

Pit Cluster / Structure 1

Figure 4.30. *Phosphate distributions (see Figs. 4.5 and 4.16 for location).*

Material culture
Having for the sake of contextual integration already presented summaries of the site's pottery and worked flint assemblages on a phase-by-phase basis, reportage of these categories will here be confined to overview observations.

Prehistoric pottery overview (Mark Knight)
Three types of prehistoric pottery dominated the assemblage: Grooved Ware, Beaker and Collared Urn. Each represents a major assemblage in its own right that can be shown to be regionally important. Chronologically, Grooved Ware, Beaker and Collared

Urn can be seen as essentially consecutive pottery types that spanned the latter half of the Neolithic period and the first half of the Bronze Age (*c.* 3000–1600 BC; Garwood 1999; Gibson & Woods 1997). A temporal separation between these three assemblages appears to have been reflected on site spatially as there was no evidence of mixing (beyond rare residual pieces), even between neighbouring features. Markedly contrasting sherd conditions also point towards different depositional histories between types.

Similarities, as well as differences, exist between the Grooved Ware, Beaker and Collared Urn assemblages. All three comprised collections of sherds representing only the partial remains of vessels and there were no complete forms. All three types were recovered alongside other types of material culture in pit contexts. As a consequence, they could each be described as 'domestic' assemblages relating to consecutive episodes of occupation.

The term 'domestic' has frequently been used with reference to large mixed collections of Beaker sherds, especially in East Anglia (Bamford 1982; Gibson 1982; Healy 1996), but less explicitly in connection with Grooved Ware (although see Cleal 1999) or Collared Urn (Martin & Murphy 1988). The deposition of Grooved Ware potsherds has invariably been interpreted as a 'special', highly symbolic or highly structured act (Richards & Thomas 1984; Healy *et al.* 1993; Pollard 2001), whereas until recently Collared Urns have rarely been found in any quantity outside of burial contexts (Burgess 1986). Of course, the domestic and symbolic can and do co-exist, and Gibson has interpreted the incorporation of a mixed assemblage of 'domestic' Beaker sherds into pits as a 'ritually charged act' (Pendleton & Gibson forthcoming). The trouble is, however, that we end up with a catch-all interpretation that denies *difference* and ultimately suggests that all sherds buried in pits represent the end-product of a selection process driven principally by symbolic impulses. Once we have applied the 'special' or 'symbolic' tag, our interpretation comes to a shuddering halt and there is very little else to say. Surely, this is as crass as saying that all pits are rubbish pits.

Similarly, beyond stating that Grooved Ware, Beaker and Collared Urn potsherds had different profiles, decorative techniques and chronologies, do we really want to suggest that depositional practice continued unchanged throughout the latter half of the Neolithic and the first half of the Bronze Age? Alternatively, we can consider the depositional practices or post-breakage histories (Pollard 1999) of these different ceramics as ways of getting at the scale, temporality and spatial dynamics of occupation in the Late Neolithic and Early Bronze Age.

Composition

The assemblage was made up of 1767 sherds weighing 18,469 g (MSW 10.4 g). The material came from 93 separate features and comprised large well-preserved as well as small abraded fragments; overall it was in good condition. Conjoining sherds were located both within and between features. Of note was the number of rims (105), base fragments (102) and decorated pieces (534) which, when combined, made up 42 per cent of the assemblage. By way of contrast, fabric analysis (undertaken using an ×10 magnifying glass) showed little variability, with the majority of the assemblage consisting of medium-hard pieces containing grog. Fortunately, the presence of multiple diagnostic sherds distributed throughout the collection made identification of types reasonably straightforward.

The predominant diagnostic forms consisted of three main types: 1) large, thick-walled, barrel- and tub-shaped vessels, intensively decorated with grooves or incised lines occasionally interrupted by vertical and horizontal cordons and/or panels of stab impressions; 2) small, thin-walled, bell-shaped vessels decorated with incised or comb-impressed lines (parallel panels, infilled lozenges and chevrons, etc.) or 'rusticated' with rows of fingernail or fingertip impressions; 3) medium-sized, thick-walled 'urns' with heavy collars, slack shoulders and narrow diameter bases, with incised or cord-impressed decoration (predominantly triangles or lattice designs) restricted to the upper profile of the vessels.

TABLE 4.11. *Pottery assemblage breakdown.*

	Sherds	Weight (g)	MSW (g)	No. of features
Plain Bowl	57	119	2.1	1
Peterborough Ware	13	46	3.5	3
Grooved Ware	1066	11,813	11.0	42
Beaker	318	1534	4.8	14
Collared Urn	145	3147	21.7	18
PDR	59	1470	24.9	5
Unidentified prehistoric	109	340	3.5	10
Total	**1767**	**18,469**	**10.4**	**93**

Fragments of Plain Bowl Neolithic, Peterborough Ware, Grooved Ware, Beaker, Collared Urn and Post-Deverel-Rimbury were all present, although Grooved Ware (Type 1) constituted the bulk of the material by both number and weight. The second most common type in terms of sherd numbers was Beaker (Type 2), although the Collared Urn assemblage accounted for the second greatest weight (Type 3). Almost half the number of Post-Deverel-Rimbury (PDR) sherds belonged to a single vessel from an isolated pit feature. The vessel comprised 36 very hard and dense sherds weighing 1280 g; 87.1 per cent of the total PDR weight.

TABLE 4.12. *Breakdown by percentage.*

	% Sherds	% Weight	% Features
Plain Bowl	3.5	0.7	1.3
Peterborough Ware	0.8	0.2	4.0
Grooved Ware	65.3	65.6	56.0
Beaker	19.5	8.5	18.6
Collared Urn	8.2	17.0	19.3
PDR	3.6	8.2	6.7

A total of 1658 diagnostic pieces were identified, leaving 109 unidentifiable sherds. The latter small, plain fragments shared the same common grog-rich fabric generically attributable to the Grooved Ware, Beaker and Collared Urn components of the assemblage.

Fabric analysis

The bulk of the assemblage comprised relatively uniform grog-tempered medium-hard to hard sherds with contrasting light-coloured exteriors and dark interiors. Both thin- and thick-walled fragments occurred in the same fabric: the former belonging predominantly, but not exclusively, to Beaker forms and the latter principally to the heavier Grooved Ware and Collared Urn forms. The presence of thin-walled Grooved Ware and Collared Urn sherds, as well as occasional thick-walled rusticated Beaker fragments, demonstrated a complexity to the assemblage that could not easily be resolved through macroscopic fabric analysis alone. A more refined fabric definition might be achievable by microscopic analysis.

In contrast to the Grooved Ware, Beaker and Collared Urn wares, the Plain Bowl Neolithic sherds had a 'corky' appearance (through lost organic inclusions), whilst the Peterborough Ware fragments were rich with burnt flint. The heavy and extremely hard PDR sherds were also very abrasive, indicating a high sand content alongside their predominant flint filler.

Forms

Grooved Ware

The character of the Grooved Ware assemblage, with its vertical and horizontal cordons, defined 'collar' zones, horizontal and vertical herringbone and spiral motifs, locates it within the Durrington Walls sub-style (Garwood 1999). The coherency of the assemblage was reflected in the occurrence of similar decorative schemes throughout, even though there was some variation in vessel form. There were no examples of impressed cord decoration. The outstanding Durrington vessel was a large barrel-shaped form with vertical cordons and spiral designs. Others comprised squatter, and sometimes splay-sided forms which might normally be considered a Clacton-style attribute, although these also included familiar Durrington characteristics (raised collars, vertical and horizontal cordons, internal decoration, etc.), which might be indicative of a blurring of types. Equally, the adjacent Storey's Bar Road and Newark Road assemblages presented similar stylistic issues, hence the dual attribution for both sites; elsewhere in the north Cambridgeshire and southern Lincolnshire area assemblages have been similarly ambiguous to warrant being described as regional variations (e.g. Pryor *et al.* 1998).

The condition of the material (in contrast to the Beaker assemblage) was good, in that the majority of the sherds appeared 'sharp' as opposed to 'dissolved'. Many of the pit-derived assemblages had several refitting parts of the same vessel enabling the reconstruction of large parts of an individual vessel's profile. This suggests that large slabs of individual vessels, as opposed to odd fragments, were being deposited.

Substantial assemblages were recovered from 16 pits, which produced a combined total of 943 sherds weighing 11,324 g (making up 96 per cent of the total weight of Grooved Ware pottery). Thirteen of the pits were located in Area B and three within Area A. In some cases, pits contained assemblages exclusive to their confines, in others fragments from the same vessel were found in several features, indicating that the pits contained sherds derived from the same source-vessel. A minimum of 31 individual vessels were identified from the main 16 pits. Fragments of at least seven further vessels were present in some of the less substantial Grooved Ware assemblages (F.176, F.177, F.248 & F.288) and if all of the residual pieces are included (together with fragments from the fieldsystem) the best estimate is about 60 vessels in total.

The most spectacular vessel was found within pit F.15 (Figs. 4.7 & 4.8:1): 246 sherds (4179 g) were identified from a single large barrel-shaped pot (diameter 32 cm, height 40.8 cm), that had a broad collar zone above vertical cordons. The collar zone was decorated with parallel horizontal grooves interrupted by large spiral or concentric circle designs, each highlighted with small 'half' reed impressions. The spirals were made with a single finger-groove. The vessel appears to have had four 'spirals' spaced evenly around its collar and each was perched above a raised or applied vertical cordon. Each of the cordons was decorated with grooved herringbone design. The intervening panels were infilled with rows of diagonal grooves and rows of 'whole' reed impressions. The decoration of this vessel was sharp and fresh; the upper part of the pot was encrusted with soot as if it had been inverted over a fire or its contents had bubbled up and spilled over its top. One possibility is that the pot had been broken in the process of firing

(hence its 'fresh' appearance), although a base-angle fragment appeared to show signs of abrasion or wear that occurred during its lifetime. Approximately half of this vessel survived, though it is possible that more of it was lost during the initial machining of the evaluation trench (Trench 2).

F.235 produced multiple decorated sherds belonging to at least four separate slightly splayed or straight-sided vessels. All four vessels were decorated with grooved herringbone designs, either vertical (Fig. 4.8:2 & 3) or horizontal (Fig. 4.8:4), and included horizontal 'cordons' executed with parallel grooved lines. Rim, body and base-angle fragments were equally represented; both F.15 and F.235 contained 'closed' assemblages.

Refits between pits bring an extra dynamic to the assemblage. The understanding of relationships between seemingly isolated pits can be transformed by the identification of conjoining sherds from the same vessel or by fragments that do not refit but belong to the same vessel. Interestingly, vessel connections could link pits located as far as 70 m apart (F.255 and F.211; Fig. 4.31), whilst paired pits such as F.176 and F.177, that were dug side by side, are distinct by an absence of any refits between their respective assemblages (both F.176 and F.177 produced small fragmented assemblages that might be residual).

Nine features contained pottery sherds that could be 'refitted' between features. F.219 contained a few fragments from a distinctive tub-shaped vessel with panels of horizontal herring-bone and vertical cordons replete with single 'thumb' impressions, and which was also present in pit F.211 (Fig. 4.8:8). Similarly, pit F.255 had a heavily grooved rim fragment that matched exactly a rim fragment from pit F.211 (Fig. 4.8:6). A precise refit was achieved between pits F.263 and F.274 (Fig. 4.31), where a couple of body sherds with dot-filled chevrons (from F.263) could be joined with a reconstructed, semi-complete profile found within F.274 (Fig. 4.8:7). Finally, a tentative connection could be made between a sherd from F.274, with its idiosyncratic raised collar with hurdle-grooving, and a single abraded rim sherd with the same grooving pattern in F.120.

Published major Grooved Ware assemblages in East Anglia include the sub-style type site, Lion Point, Clacton, Essex (Longworth *et al.* 1971) and Grimes Graves, Norfolk (Longworth *et al.* 1988), Spong Hill, Norfolk (Healy 1988), Redgate Hill, Norfolk (Healy *et al.* 1993), Barholm, Lincolnshire (Simpson *et al.* 1993), Great Bealings, Suffolk (Martin 1993), Storey's Bar Road, Peterborough (Pryor 1978) and Etton, Peterborough (Pryor 1998a). With the exception of Etton and Grimes Graves, these are all pit sites. Unpublished major assemblages from pit sites also include Over *Sites 2, 3 & 4*, Cambridgeshire (Fig. 2.20; Evans & Knight 2004; Pollard 1998b;

TABLE 4.13. *Major Grooved Ware assemblages in East Anglia.*

Site	Sherds	Sub-style
Edgerley Drain Road	1066	Durrington Walls
Grimes Graves	590	Durrington Walls
Redgate Hill	542	Clacton
Over (Site 2)	520	Clacton
Lion Point	324	Clacton
Over (Site 4)	312	Durrington Walls
Spong Hill	210	Durrington Walls & Clacton
Storey's Bar Road	183	Durrington Walls & Clacton
Over (Site 3)	160	Clacton
Etton Causewayed Enclosure	157	Durrington Walls & Clacton
Barholm	144	Clacton
Great Bealings	131	Clacton
Barleycroft Farm (Site I)	72	Durrington Walls

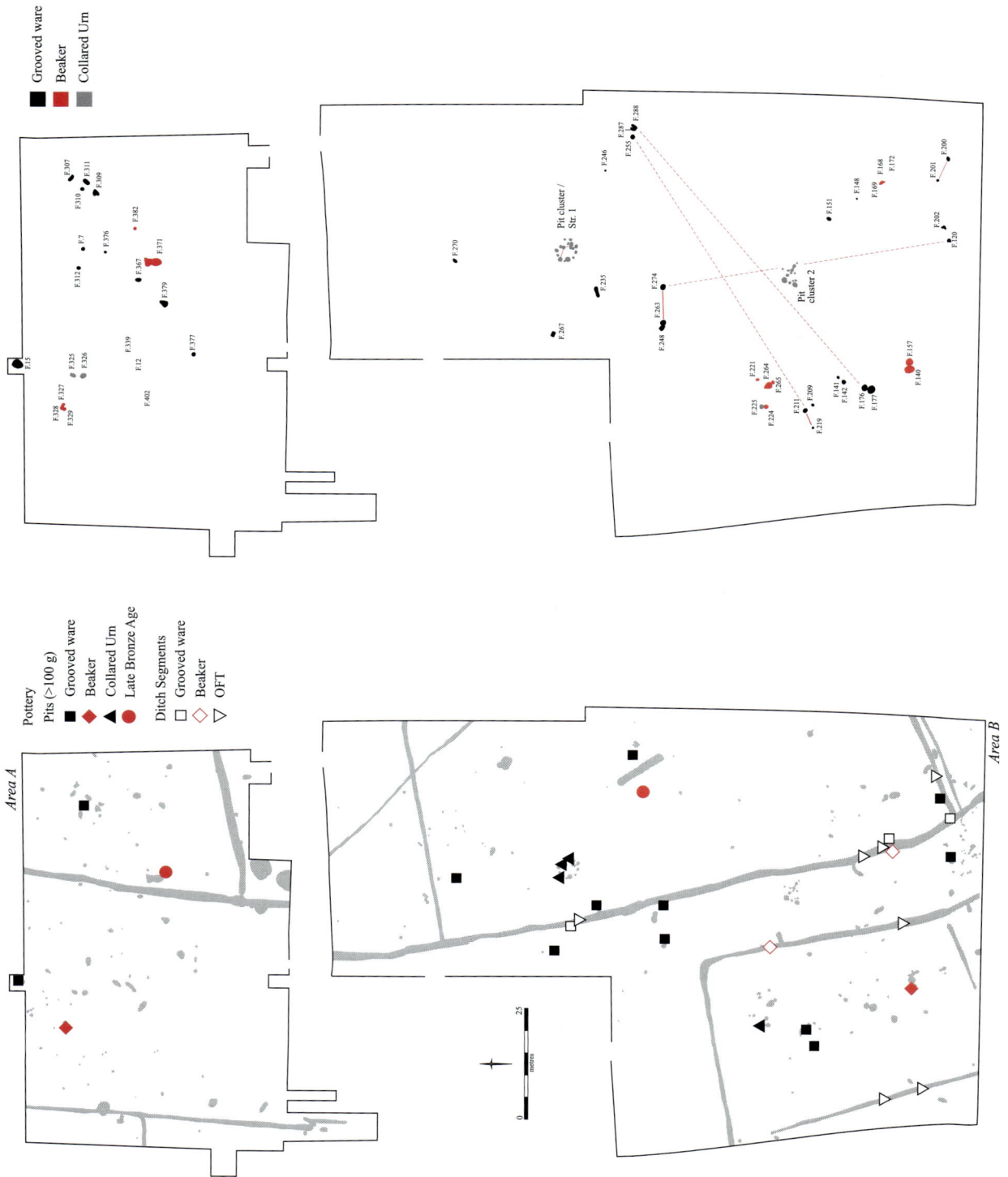

FIGURE 4.31. *'Type' pottery distributions (left); right, same-vessel connections.*

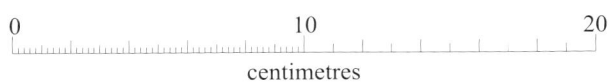

FIGURE 4.32. *'Study view' of the pottery assemblage (note size of sherds and decoration (photograph, M. Knight); below, Collared Urn (see Fig. 4.17:4; photograph, R. Law).*

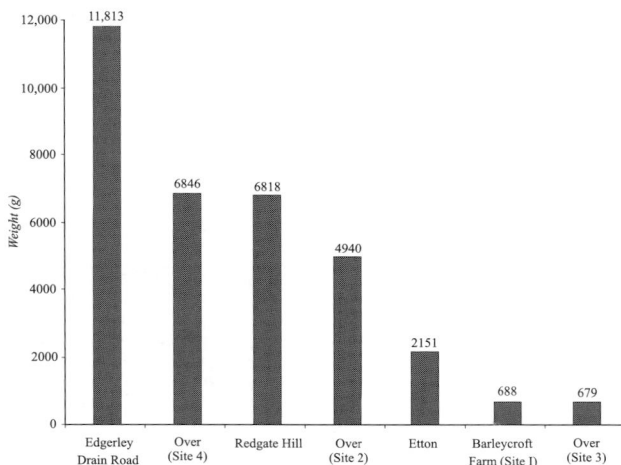

FIGURE 4.33. *Grooved Ware assemblage weights.*

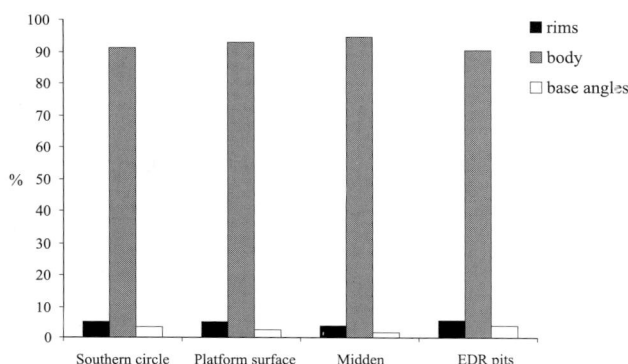

FIGURE 4.34. *Vessel representation from Durrington Walls and from Edgerley Drain Road by percentage.*

Table 4.14: *Vessel breakdown between Durrington Walls and Edgerley Drain Road.*

	Rims	Body	Base-angles
Southern Circle	109	2016	74
Platform Surface	66	1202	31
Midden	35	901	17
EDR Pits	56	899	40

Walls assemblages if the focus is placed upon which parts of vessels were represented: rim, body and base-angle. Even with the differences in assemblage size, all four contexts, *Southern Circle, Platform Surface, Midden* and *Pits* produce remarkably similar patterns (Fig. 4.34). Body sherds make up the bulk of each assemblage (*c.* 92 per cent), followed by rims (*c.* 5 per cent) and base-angles (*c.* 3 per cent). Given the basic profile of most Grooved Ware pots (mouth diameter greater than base; broad or tall body areas), it would appear that the vessel 'demographic' illustrated within Figure 4.34 reflects a normal pattern of representation with no particular bias or selection being indicated.

Given the similar representation of vessel parts at Durrington Walls and Edgerley Drain Road, does this contradict the domestic attribution given to the Edgerley assemblage or is the pattern caused by the fact that the henge-related pottery shares a similar depositional history to a pit site? Garwood has always argued that the pottery had a secondary relationship to the Southern Circle (1999), and the current campaign of work at Durrington Walls has focused on a previously undiscovered, but nonetheless substantial, settlement element, led principally by the finding of multiple house platforms (Parker Pearson *et al.* 2007). It could be suggested that the pottery reflects very similar occupation dynamics between two different kinds of site, which has, in part, been obscured by aspects of preservation, but also by levels of expectation when it comes to excavating a few circular pits on the edge of the Fens compared to the heart of a major Wessex monument.

Beaker

The pit-derived Beaker assemblage represents a characteristic fen-edge/East Anglian 'domestic' collection (Bamford 1982; Gibson 1982) as typified by the presence of fine ware comb-decorated vessels alongside fine and coarse, fingertip and fingernail-decorated Beakers. The fragmentary and dissolved nature of the material made the identification of individual vessels difficult, but a best estimate stands at 33. These were often identified on the basis of just a few small sherds. Similarly, refitting sherds were less easy to recognize in comparison with the 'fresher' looking Grooved Ware fragments, and the respective condition of the two ceramic types points towards different depositional histories.

Three principal Beaker assemblages, making up 89.6 per cent of the total number of sherds or 93.9 per cent of the total weight, came from three sets of features: the 'paired' pits, F.140 and F.157, the F.221, F.224 and F.264 'cluster', and a trio of inter-cutting pits, F.327–9.

The largest assemblage came from the first 'pair', F.140 and F.157, which together produced 211 sherds (weighing 1029 g) or 60 per cent of the Beaker pottery. Importantly, the pottery from these adjacent pits can be shown to form a comparatively 'closed' group, with fragments from certain vessels occurring across both contexts. Equally, the condition of the material from these features was similar, with the majority of the sherds showing signs of having been exposed to weathering and/or abrasion. Many of the pieces had a softened or dissolved appearance, with areas of decoration worn away or partially truncated. Occasional pieces still retained sharp decoration, which suggests that not all of the sherds had been subject to the same post-breakage histories. The fragmentary and abraded character of the assemblage indicates that there was an

Garrow 2006) and Barleycroft Farm *Site I*, Cambridgeshire (see Evans & Knight 2000). Durrington and Clacton sub-styles dominate, but possible examples of Woodlands style have been identified at Barholm and Etton, although Garwood suggests that Woodlands actually represents a continuum of the Clacton series (Garwood 1999). The division between Durrington and Clacton assemblages is roughly 50/50, with total sherd counts equalling 2314 for the former and 2095 for the latter. The sub-styles can be separated spatially, with Clacton sites occurring across East Anglia and the Durrington sites tending to cluster towards the western half of the region (with a bias of five sites to two).

The Edgerley Drain Road Grooved Ware assemblage is almost twice as large as any other found within East Anglia (by number or by weight; Fig. 4.33). In fact, its scale is much more reminiscent of some the great Grooved Ware assemblages found in Wiltshire and Dorset at the major 'henge' sites of Durrington Walls (Wainwright & Longworth 1971) and Mount Pleasant (Wainwright 1979). Its only pit-site equivalent is Yarnton *Site 7*, Oxfordshire (Hey & Muir 1997), which produced 1007 sherds from 17 pits (an average of 59.2 sherds per pit compared with 58.9 from Edgerley). Appropriately the type-site is even larger, with 5861 sherds (Longworth 1971) derived from three main contexts: *South Circle, Platform* and *Midden*, whereas the Mount Pleasant excavations produced 657.

Although very different in overall scale and context, the Edgerley Drain Road assemblage can be related to the Durrington interval between the breaking of a vessel and its eventual incorporation into the fills of a pit.

The deeper of the two pits, F.140, yielded 177 sherds (858 g) distributed throughout its four fills. The basal deposit ([288]) had 34 Beaker fragments, all of which were small and abraded, and some of which were stained 'turmeric-like' yellow, presumably by localized iron panning within the confines of the pit. The sherds appeared to represent the partial remains of at least five different Beakers. They included two small rim fragments (one decorated with incised lines bordering fingernail impressions the other with 'comma-shaped' jabs), a base-angle with pinched rustication and three body sherds decorated either with 'crow's-foot' or comb-impressed designs. The remnants of at least six other Beakers could be identified from 88 sherds (467 g) deriving from the second fill of F.140, as could further pieces of the distinctive comma-impressed vessel (Fig. 4.13:6). Of these six vessels, 36 pieces were identified from a distinctive burnt or re-fired vessel (all of the sherds were grey and lightweight) with a comb-zoned geometric motif design interspersed with areas of 'reed' impressions (Fig. 4.13:3 & 5). Parts of its rim, neck and belly survived, as did a sherd with a slightly raised cordon situated just below its rim. Other 'new' vessels located within the same deposit included parts of another comb-zoned form, as well as four largish plain sherds (including a rim; Fig. 4.13:2) from a possible undecorated Beaker.

The uppermost deposits of F.140 ([286] and [285]) added another 55 sherds (231 g) to the overall assemblage; the majority of these appeared to belong to vessels already partially represented in the lower fills. Sherds from a previously 'unseen' vessel were also present, with a widely spaced 'crow's-foot' adorned rim fragment (Fig. 4.13:1) that had been fire-blackened being particularly noteworthy. Familiar fragments included five small pieces from the burnt comb-zoned vessel, as well as more sherds of the comma-impressed Beaker. Amongst this collection was a single residual Grooved Ware rim sherd decorated with broad diagonal grooves.

The immediately adjacent F.157 continued this depositional theme, with its basal deposit yielding parts of three vessels. These included an internally bevelled rim, incised with horizontal lines of 'drag and stab', another 'crow's-foot' rusticated form and the now-familiar 'comma vessel', which was also present throughout F.140. The capping fill of F.157 incorporated minute fragments of other 'new' vessels: a rim with a raised cordon stabbed with a triangular-shaped stick (Fig. 4.13:10); a body sherd covered with half-reed or fingernail impressions; and a fire-blackened sherd with widely spaced 'crow's-foot' decoration that almost certainly came from a vessel previously identified within F.140. F.157 also included a rim fragment of collared Beaker impressed with the distal end of a ?bird bone (Fig. 4.13:13), as well as a rim with slight cordon (Fig. 4.13:8) with zoned comb-impressed decoration.

With the exception of the distinctive burnt Beaker found throughout the fills of F.140, the majority of the sherds recovered from the paired pits could only at best be used to reconstruct small parts of vessels. The 'bitty' character of the collection is typical of domestic Beaker assemblages across the East Anglia region and is indicative of material that had already been allowed to accumulate elsewhere. Previous interpretations have seen these parts of whole vessels as 'tokens' involved in a process of deliberate selection for 'special' deposition (Pollard 2006; Pendleton & Gibson forthcoming). At Edgerley Drain Road, pieces of at least 20 different broken Beakers were deposited within six different fills in two pits. Many of the sherds had a 'dissolved' appearance; some had been burnt, whilst occasionally pieces in a comparatively fresh state were also included, indicating an apparently indiscriminate 'selection'.

Analysis of the other two Beaker pit groups produced equally fragmented assemblages. The actual breakdown differed between pit groups, although the same principle applied to each, the majority of the identifiable vessels being represented by just a few scrappy sherds. Occasionally, particular vessels were represented

TABLE 4.15. *Sherd distribution through the fills of adjacent pits, F.140 and F.157.*

F.140	F.157
26 (98 g)	19 (97 g)
29 (133 g)	15 (74 g)
88 (467 g)	
34 (160 g)	

TABLE 4.16. *Minimum number of vessels from the main Beaker assemblages.*

	Weight of pottery	No. of vessels	Mean weight per vessel
'Pair'	1029 g	20	51.4 g
'Trio'	224 g	8	28.0 g
'Cluster'	187 g	5	37.4 g
Total	1440 g	33	43.6 g

by multiple sherds, as with the grey burnt comb-zoned Beaker within F.140 (43 sherds weighing 212 g), adding to the haphazard character of the collection.

By way of comparison, Bamford, Gibson and Healy have all reported on large domestic Beaker assemblages from sites in Norfolk and Suffolk (Bamford 1982; Gibson 1982; Healy 1996). The burnt mound sites of Hockwold-cum-Wilton (Bamford 1982), Northwold (Crowson 2004), Feltwell Anchor (Boast 2000) and Fordham (Connor & Mortimer forthcoming) have also established a link between Beaker pottery and 'pot-boiler' sites, and relating these to the eastern fen-edge, particularly the Wissey Embayment (see also Silvester 1991). Further north at Fairstead, Kings Lynn, a new burnt mound site continues the connection, with 45 sherds of comb-decorated or rusticated forms (Beadsmoore 2005b). Pit sites at Sutton Hoo, Suffolk (525 sherds; Hummler 2005), Worlingham, Suffolk (376 sherds; Pendleton & Gibson forthcoming), Longham, Norfolk (Ashwin 1998), Bittering, Norfolk (530 sherds; Wymer & Healy 1996), and Feltwell Quarry, Norfolk (Beadsmoore 2007a) reiterate an eastern bias, which has been furthered by Chippenham Barrow 5 (Cambs.) whose pre-mound occupation evidence produced another substantial domestic Beaker assemblage (Gibson 1980).

Garrow's recent overview of pit sites in Norfolk, Suffolk and Cambridgeshire emphasizes the same eastern 'fen-sidedness', with a lone pit containing a meagre ten sherds from Cherry Hinton, Cambridge (Garrow 2006) counting as the sole west-Fen instance. Even the addition of a pit from Haddenham, Cambridgeshire, which yielded 31 fine and rusticated sherds (Pollard 2006), does little to alter the balance. Wyman Abbott's collection of over 350 Beaker sherds recovered from across Fengate had previously been counted as a western-edge equivalent to such eastern contexts (Gibson 1980; Bamford 1982). Indeed, its scale, character and, to an extent, method of retrieval, can be directly equated to Frank Curtis's Beaker collections made from around Hockwold-cum-Wilton during the 1950s and '60s (Healy 1996). Pryor's Fengate excavations encountered occasional Beaker-related features, including a possible house structure. These have generated small domestic-type assemblages comparable in appearance, if not number, to Abbott's material (Pryor 1978). Work carried out on the opposite 'shoreline' at Northey investigated a small group of Beaker pits containing fragments from at least five vessels (Pryor et al. 2001).

As outlined in Chapter Two above, recent large-scale quarry-led excavations around the northern and southeastern edges of the Flag Fen basin at Eye and at King's Dyke West and Bradley Fen have begun to indicate the true scale of Beaker activity both in and around the embayment (Fig. 4.35). Intermittent pits, sometimes

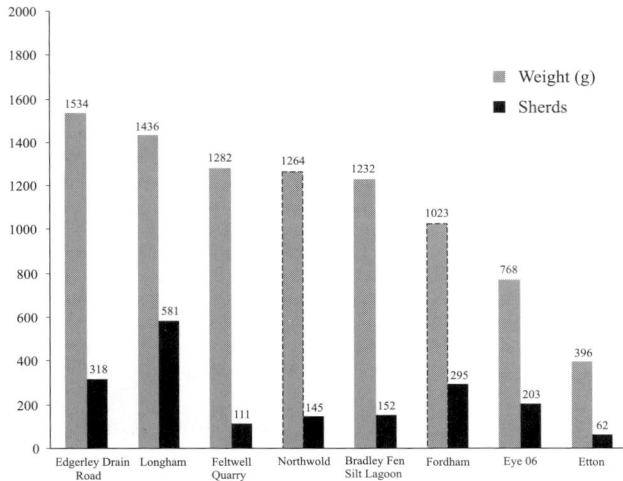

Figure 4.35. *Major Beaker assemblages from East Anglia (dashed bars indicate burnt mound sites).*

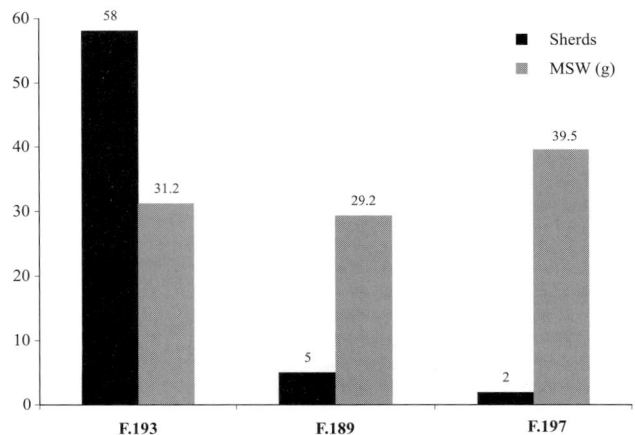

Figure 4.36. *Distribution of Pot 24 between F.193, F.189 & F.197 by sherd count and mean sherd weight.*

quite substantial and deep, have produced small, medium and large assemblages that can be traced down into the Flag Fen basin itself and beyond the fieldsystems. A very credible, and possibly regionally unique, roundhouse was located towards the bottom of the Flag Fen basin during the Silt Lagoon excavations at Bradley Fen (Gibson & Knight 2006). The building was found in relation to a collection of fine ware and coarse ware Beaker sherds and its hearth produced a radiocarbon result dating the structure to 2200–1950 cal. BC. This corresponds with dates achieved for the pit group at Worlingham, Suffolk (2410–2020 cal. BC & 2300–1880 cal. BC) that bore a bronze flat 'axe-chisel' (Class 3 type - *c.* 2150–2000 BC) as well as 408 sherds of 'domestic' Beaker (Pendleton & Gibson forthcoming). The Bradley Fen house occupied a low-lying terrace within the southeastern quarter of the basin that it shared with a burnt stone mound. The burnt mound represented one of four such features located at the site and these each delivered radiocarbon dates: the earliest being 2340–2030 cal. BC; the latest, 1930–1690 cal. BC. As well as establishing a structural domestic context for a Beaker assemblage, the Bradley Fen excavations would also appear to confirm the relationship between burnt mounds and Beaker pottery recognized along the eastern fen-edge.

Collared Urn

The bulk of the Collared Urn wares came from a single circle of features, Cluster/Structure 1. 83.4 per cent of the sherds or 87.5 per cent of the total weight were located within the 12 pits/postholes that made up the grouping. The majority of the pieces were from within a single deposit capping almost all of its features. Three features in particular, F.189, F.193 and F.197 (Fig. 4.36), yielded most of the material and these were linked by sherds from the same medium-sized urn (Fig. 4.18:4). This would have been 22 cm high and had a diameter of approximately 20 cm (Fig. 4.32). Its collar was accentuated by being slightly pinched out at its top (rim) and bottom (collar), making the top of the rim broad and flat. The rim top was incised with short diagonal lines, whereas the collar contained incised triangles filled with incised hatching. Further decoration occurred around the vessel's neck as a simple incised lattice. The base of the vessel was missing, as was part of its middle profile. Its rim and collar were complete and it appears that one side of the vessel had been re-fired when the vessel was still whole; a portion of the urn having been discoloured pale grey with a dry pumice-like appearance. The greater part of this pot derived from F.193 (58

sherds; 1812 g), with the remainder from F.189 (five sherds; 146 g) and F.197 (two sherds; 79 g). Although the vessel was unevenly spread between the three pits, the sherd-size remained consistent suggesting that they had been deposited simultaneously.

Pit F.193 also contained pieces of a thin-walled urn (body and shoulder), whereas F.197 had fragments from at least three other Collared Urns, as well as an abraded, and probably residual, rim sherd from a Beaker. The additional urns in F.197 consisted of parts of a small plain biconical form with a very slight collar (Fig. 4.18:2), about half the body, shoulder and neck of another urn that had lost its collar along a 'false-rim' break and a small collar-angle fragment from another urn (Fig. 4.18:3). A minimum of five urns, plus a single Beaker, were represented by the sherds within Cluster 1.

A second Collared Urn cluster produced a much smaller assemblage of just six sherds (110 g) dispersed between three pits, F.162, F.226 and F.227; F.227 contained a single rim fragment impressed with horizontal and diagonal lines of twisted cord (Fig. 4.18:1).

'Singular' pits, F.225 and F.326, yielded a large collar fragment decorated with a loose incised lattice design and pronounced shoulder fragment respectively; another twisted cord-impressed collar came from an unstratified context (Area A west).

Comparable 'domestic' Collared Urn assemblages are extremely rare at both a national and regional level (Longworth 1984). Nationally, excavations in advance of Manchester Airport's second runway produced a substantial collection of Collared Urn sherds from a midden-like deposit (Garner 2007), whereas regionally, West Fen Row, Suffolk is said to have generated a settlement-related assemblage (Martin & Murphy 1988). The lack of parallels beyond these two sites could be because Collared Urns are thought to be a 'specialized funerary pottery' associated 'almost exclusively with burial sites' (Burgess 1980; 1986).

It seems that, whilst equivalent Grooved Ware assemblages can be found on a national as well as regional level, and comparable Beaker sites exist in abundance across the eastern half of the region, such Collared Urn assemblages remain exceptional. Significantly, analogies do occur locally, with substantial collections coming from sites in and around the Flag Fen basin (Fig. 4.37) at Tanholt Farm, Eye (McFadyen 2000; Patten 2002; 2009) and King's Dyke West, Whittlesey in particular (Gibson & Knight 2002), but also from Bradley Fen, Whittlesey (Gibson & Knight 2006) and the Fengate sites of Newark Road, Fourth Drove and Storey's Bar Road (Pryor 1978; 1980a). Both of the Whittlesey sites also yielded complete

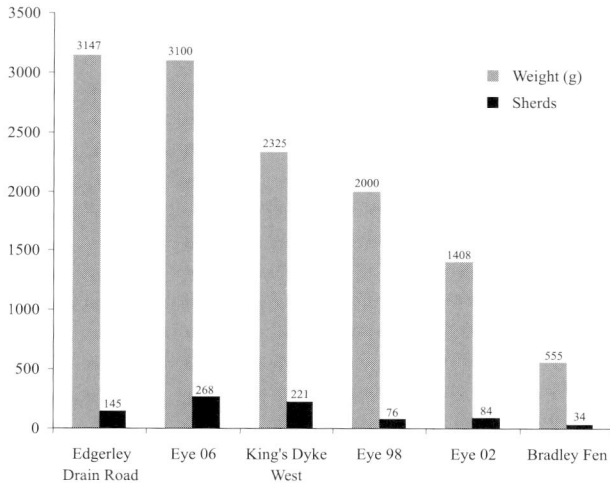

FIGURE 4.37. *Collared Urn assemblages from the Flag Fen basin.*

TABLE 4.17. *Predominant differences between pottery types.*

	Vessel representation	Sherd condition	Refits between
Grooved Ware	Large parts	Fresh	Adjacent & non-adjacent pits
Beaker	Small parts	Abraded	Immediately adjacent pits
Collared Urn	Large & small parts	Fresh & abraded	Adjacent pits

Collared Urns from funerary contexts (see Chapter 2 above), as did Storey's Bar Road.

The cinerary urns comprised both primary and secondary series forms (Longworth 1984); the primary forms being exclusive to a flat cemetery located between two barrows at King's Dyke West (Gibson & Knight 2002), with the secondary forms occurring individually within the ring-ditch at Storey's Bar Road (Pryor 1978) and in isolated burials at Bradley Fen and Bradley Fen Farm. The sherds from the various domestic assemblages appear to belong exclusively to Longworth's secondary series, although the fragmentary condition of much of the material makes identification problematic, especially when such 'types' are based on whole profiles.

One of the cremations from the King's Dyke West cemetery was contained within a pair of urns (one complete), whilst the other comprised just the body (the upper part of the vessel, from the shoulder upwards, had been removed or trimmed off leaving an even 'false-rim'). The two vessels were conjoined with the 'body-vessel' being inverted and used as a lid for the complete urn (creating a 'cocktail shaker-like' appearance). The trimming of an urn to make a lid suggests that the vessel had not been made primarily for cinerary purposes and it seems that an existing vessel had been adapted for the occasion. Elsewhere, cinerary Collared Urns have been found with repair holes, missing fragments, re-firing or signs of wear (Barclay 2002; Law 2008) indicating that the urns had not been made specifically for funerary ends and that they had had a 'use-life' prior to becoming receptacles for the dead. The domestic assemblages from the sites of Tanholt Farm, King's Dyke West and Edgerley Drain Road illustrate a different kind of depositional 'conclusion' for Collared Urns. It is possible that the difference between cinerary and domestic is chronological as well as contextual, representing a funerary-to-everyday trajectory for Collared Urns over time, similar to the trajectory proposed for Beakers (Whittle 1981). The end-use of 'old' urns for burial purposes would appear to contradict a straightforward high-to-low-status path (see Bradley 1984), as well as any obvious chronological distinction between urns found in burials and those in domestic contexts.

Temporal separation is indicated by the lack of overlap between the Grooved Ware, Beaker and Collared Urn assemblages, even though they were found in close proximity. The variation in depositional patterns and post-breakage histories also demonstrates a true distinction between types. These variations may be symptomatic of the settlement/depositional practices of the people who made, used and broke these respective wares. The different temporalities of these particular practices were, in part, reflected in the overall condition of the sherds. The Grooved Ware pieces appear to have been buried almost immediately after breakage, whereas the Beaker seems to have spent an extended period of time above ground prior to its incorporation. The mixed condition of the Collared Urn fragments could be seen as indicative of a combination of both processes, although the transformation of many of the sherds appeared to have occurred when the urns were still whole. Also it can be compellingly demonstrated that much of the Collared Urn assemblage was dumped collectively as part of a single charcoal-rich deposit into Cluster/Structure 1.

The fresh and slab-like character of much of the Grooved Ware pottery could be interpreted as suggestive of careful selection. However, the vessel demographics imply that if there was a process of selection, based upon the representation of distinctive sherds, a remarkable consistency was achieved, as all parts (rims, body & base) were presented in roughly the right proportions. If, however, adornment was the criteria then almost any sherd would have been acceptable as every vessel was profusely decorated. Perhaps at this point it would be appropriate to echo Cleal's enquiry and ask 'what features an assemblage would have to exhibit *not* to be interpreted as 'selective' or 'deliberate' deposition?' (1999, 6; original emphasis).

The freshness of much of the Grooved Ware pottery is perhaps contradicted by the occurrence of refits, especially those made between features situated as much as 70 m apart. The various conjoins would appear to rule out the possibility of things be-

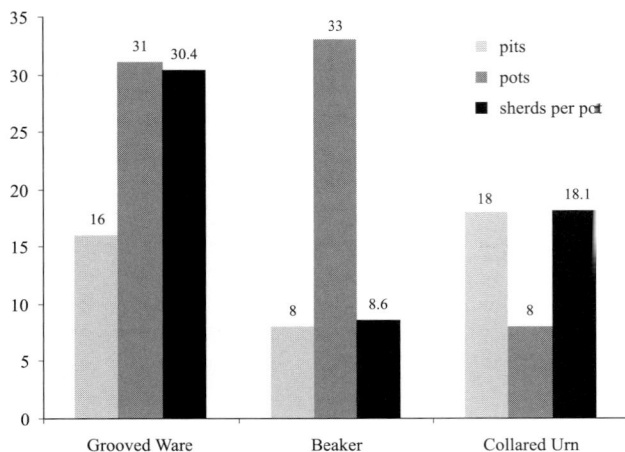

FIGURE 4.38. *Pits, pots and sherds: contrasting assemblages (note that the actual total number of Grooved Ware vessels present throughout the site as a whole was estimated to be 60; see also Table 4.10).*

ing broken at the 'pit-edge', but they do establish an important temporal connection between features so clearly detached in space. The long-distance refits suggest that the extent of the Grooved Ware assemblage occurred at the scale of the site. The short-distance Beaker and Collared Urn refits suggest that these assemblages 'resided' at the scale of the pit-cluster or even individual pit. Such a distinction might also suggest that the Grooved Ware occupation was extensive but essentially singular, whereas the Beaker and Collared Urn occupations were focused and perhaps, in terms of Beaker, episodic. The uniformity of the Grooved Ware assemblage (multiple vessels with corresponding decorative schemes) could also be seen as an attribute of a one-off 'stay'.

One final means of illustrating the different post-breakage histories between the three groups of pottery is to show the relationship between pits, number of vessels and number of sherds per vessel (Fig. 4.38). The differences are immediate, and it is hard to think of how three assemblages could have produced more divergent profiles. The fragmentary character of the Beaker assemblage, where scores of vessels are represented by just a few sherds, stands in stark contrast to slabs of pottery that represented each of the Collared Urns. Meanwhile, the Grooved Ware adds another dimension where, although it shares a similar number of pits as Collared Urn, it produced nearly four times the number of vessels (or more than seven times if the 60-vessel Grooved Ware estimate is employed).

At the scale of the Flag Fen basin and its immediate surroundings there appears to be a different dynamic between the three types, at least judging by the investigations to date. Beaker and Collared Urn fea-

tures, including structures and burials, have been found with similar regularity across most of the basin, whilst Grooved Ware appears to be unique to the northern-central reaches of Fengate. Its 'singularity', alongside the freshness of its sherds, seems to be indicating a different kind of residency to Beaker and Collared Urn that could be described as being immediate or 'momentary' (both spatially and temporally). Conversely, Beaker and Collared Urn have a widespread or extensive distribution of 'moments' or episodes — houses, pits and burials — that reside at the level of the Flag Fen basin. In a sense it could be suggested that the Edgerley Drain Road excavations succeeded in capturing the greater portion of a Grooved Ware occupation, but only small parts of Beaker or Collared Urn occupations. Considering the material this way not only demonstrates differences in scale, but helps to illustrate time/space differences between Grooved Ware, Beaker and Collared Urn assemblages.

Flintwork overview (EMMA BEADSMOORE)
The site's flint assemblages present a comparatively rare opportunity to analyse and compare material recovered from securely dated Late Neolithic–Late Bronze Age contexts in the same landscape, within a limited area and with access to the same raw materials. Although mixed material was found within the fieldsystem, a number pits from each phase were 'chronologically uncontaminated' (see Fig. 4.39 for flint densities and 'type' distributions).

The site yielded limited earlier Neolithic flint: 27 pieces, 25 of which were from one pit. In contrast, 457 later Neolithic flints were identified: 397 from pits, whilst 60 were either recovered from tree-throws, as stray finds or residually in later features. Forty-two Beaker-phase flints were recovered: 34 from pits of that attribution, seven residual in later features and one stray find. Ninety-two Early Bronze Age flints were identified: 90 from pits and two residual in later features. Only 11 identifiable later Bronze Age flints were recovered, from the large pits and also pits that yielded Post-Deverel Rimbury pottery. A total of 39 flints were identified generically as 'Bronze Age': products of expedient flake production/core reduction that could have been manufactured in the Early, but more likely in the Middle–later Bronze Age. Middle–later Bronze Age assemblages do not have characteristic formal tool types and are consequently difficult to conclusively identify. The flint numbers and tool percentages are listed by period in Table 4.18.

Earlier Neolithic

The earlier Neolithic material, although limited, is comparable to other broadly contemporary pit sites. The small assemblage

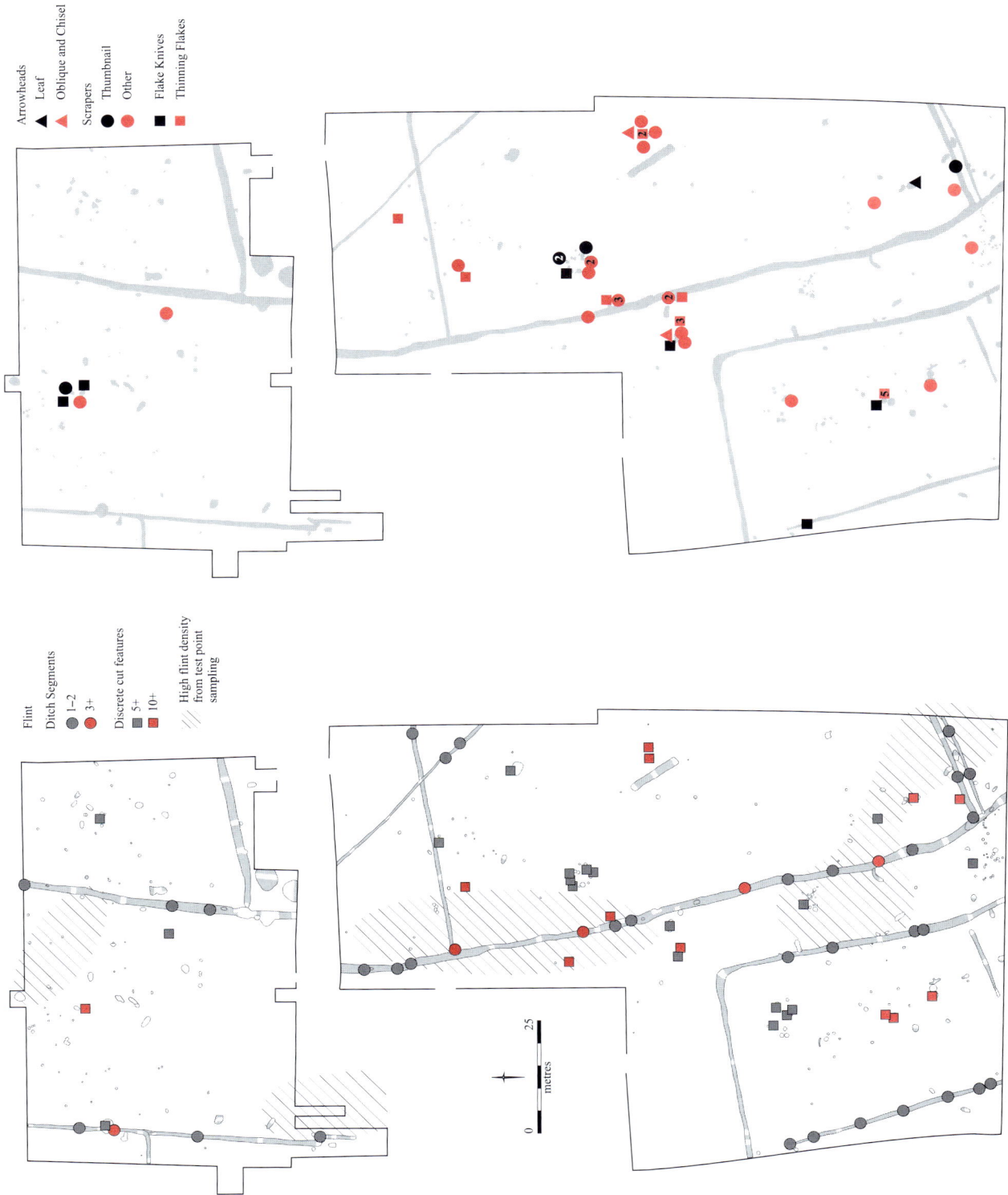

FIGURE 4.39. *Worked flint: density and type distributions.*

Table 4.18. *Pit-context flint numbers and tool percentages.*

Table 4.18. *Pit-context flint numbers and tool percentages.*

	Earlier Neolithic	Late Neolithic	Beaker	Collared Urn
Quantity	27	397	34	90
Percentage of tools	24%	13%	14%	19%

comprises an often repeated combination of flintworking waste, potentially generated by the manufacture of replacements for the few utilized and discarded tools that were also recovered from pit F.172. Fine flintworking waste recovered from that feature supports nearby flake production/core reduction.

Late Neolithic

Late Neolithic flint accounts for 55 per cent of the material, the majority of which came from Grooved Ware-associated pits. The pit assemblages include both flintworking waste, with all stages of reduction represented, and tools (13 per cent). The majority of Grooved Ware pit assemblages in East Anglia have between 1 per cent and 23.5 per cent tools, with an average of 5 per cent; near Edgerley, 18.7 per cent of the Grooved Ware pit flint assemblage at Storey's Bar Road comprises tools (Pryor 1980c, 496). Pits of the period at Over Sites 3 and 4 yielded 18.9 per cent tools (Pollard 1998b, 64–8); Over Site 2 had 4.9 per cent (Edmonds, in Evans & Knight 2004), whilst those at Barleycroft Farm had between 9.6 per cent and 36.6 per cent implements (Pollard, in Evans & Knight forthcoming). In terms of overall quantity of flint per pit, Edgerley fits in the range of other Late Neolithic pit sites on the gravels (Garrow 2006, 90).

Late Neolithic flake production/core reduction was frequently focused on the manufacture of thin, large broad flakes, rather than the finer blades prevalent during the earlier Neolithic. Large nodules of good-quality flint are required to successfully manufacture these characteristic flakes, which potentially promoted the identification and exploitation of good-quality raw material. Consequently, Grooved Ware pits on sites with comparatively small local gravel flint tend to yield less flintworking waste, with a higher percentage of tools than pits near/on good sources of raw material. Though 33 Late Neolithic pits had 397 flints at Edgerley, seven Grooved Ware pits at Linton, Cambridgeshire yielded 2703 flints, just four per cent of which are tools (Beadsmoore forthcoming). The latter site was on a sand and gravel terrace, which overlies chalk. Similarly, at Middle Harling, Norfolk, on sand and gravel with good quality raw material available, three Grooved Ware pits yielded 2005 flints, just one per cent of which were tools (Healy 1995, 33). The comparatively high percentage of tools in some Grooved Ware pit assemblages on the gravels, therefore, potentially has more to do with the limited quantities of flintworking waste in the pits, which is in turn linked to the characteristics of the raw material, rather than any kind of preferential selection of tools for deposition.

Grooved Ware pits with limited quantities of flintworking waste often correlate with limited refits. Grooved Ware flint from Barleycroft had only one small set of refits and Pollard (in Evans & Knight forthcoming) saw limited potential for further refits in the assemblage. Although five refits were identified at Edgerley, nearly all were between pairs of flints. This is potentially because either flintworking was limited at the site, only partial flake production/core reduction was carried out or, alternatively, that only limited quantities of the flint worked on site was actually being deposited in the pits. The most extensive refitting sequence comprises a core and associated chunks and flakes; the core fractured badly and was discarded along with the unused irregular working waste (Fig. 4.9:9).

Edgerley yielded a number of the characteristic large, broad flakes, struck from the facetted platforms of discoidal cores. Eight were recovered from the site: four from Late Neolithic pits, two from Collared Urn pits, whilst two were residual in the fieldsystem and a large Late Bronze Age pit. The flakes recovered from the Collared Urn pits are also likely to be Late Neolithic and residual in the later features. Six of these are broken: all in the same way, in half, at the broadest section of the flake. These distinctive flake fragments were potentially the by-products of arrowhead manufacture. Once the large broad flakes were broken in half, the proximal, thicker bulb section was discarded, whilst the original flake-edge of the distal section was turned to become the cutting edge of the transverse arrowhead. Hence, the flake blanks needed to be large and broad enough to be viable when only half of the flint was used, as well as thin enough to be effective projectiles.

Seven of these characteristic flakes were also recovered from the Elliott Site (see Chapter 3), five of which were possible transverse arrowhead byproducts. Again, all were cleanly broken halfway across the flake, at the broadest point; only the proximal sections were recovered, with the distal sections potentially retouched and utilized as arrowheads to be discarded elsewhere. Only two Late Neolithic arrowheads were recovered from Edgerley, both in Grooved Ware pits. In contrast, nearby the Storey's Bar Road Site yielded a total of 26 transverse and oblique arrowheads; whilst some were found in definite Grooved Ware contexts, others were residual in later features (Pryor 1978).

The Late Neolithic assemblage at Edgerley included some primary flint, frequently the characteristic larger, broad flakes. However, the Late Neolithic assemblage includes other tool types, not all of which required large nodules of good-quality flint and the expedient exploitation of local resources is well-represented in the material recovered from the pits: irregular cores, flake blanks, and retouched tools that utilized the local gravel flint.

The combination of flintworking waste alongside utilized and discarded tools, together with the character of the assemblage — the emphasis on scrapers and utilized flakes, the burnt flint, the limited number of arrowheads and the evidence for their manufacture — is indicative of occupation. The identification of refits suggests that the activities that generated the material were carried out near the pits, and that there was a degree of immediacy between those activities and the flint's deposition.

Beaker

The Beaker flint contrasts with the Late Neolithic material, with no trace of a close relationship between flintworking, tool-use and the deposition of the material into the pits. The Beaker pits yielded less flint than the Late Neolithic pits overall. This is not surprising, as there were considerably fewer Beaker features, but more pertinently, there was also less flint per pit; this is notable because the Beaker pits were frequently also larger than their Grooved Ware counterparts. The Beaker material has no potential for refitting and, though all of the stages of reduction are represented, the pit assemblages comprise disparate groups of flint. Of the 35 flints recovered from the Beaker pits, 14 per cent are tools.

Collared Urn

Pits of this attribution yielded 90 flints, including flintworking waste and tools: at 19 per cent, a higher percentage of the flints are tools than in the earlier pits. The tools include a variety of scraper types, knives and piercers and, when combined with the burnt flint and the flintworking waste, the assemblage is readily characterized as domestic/occupation-related. Identifiable domestic Collared Urn flint assemblages are rare, largely because all of the tool types recovered would not be out of place in Beaker, and sometimes even Late Neolithic, assemblages. In other words, if the same collection of tools were recovered without its 'type' pottery, the flint would be classed as Late Neolithic/Early Bronze Age. However, one particular type of flint — small and commonly triangular, either worked as a core to produce very small, squat flakes, or a crudely retouched scraper type tool — is identifiably Early Bronze Age (Fig. 4.19:5). Often recovered from ring-ditches, the core type was found in the Collared Urn pits at Edgerley.

Middle–later Bronze Age

Middle–later Bronze Age flint was generally spread amongst the fieldsystem ditches, the metalled surface and large pits: features that were open for some time, allowed to silt up, and that also yielded quantities of earlier material. The exceptions are the three flints recovered from F.258: all were from the same expediently worked core and two of the flakes refit, with the intervening flake absent from the pit-context. Evidence for both tool-use and flintworking at the site is provided by the expediently manufactured Middle–later Bronze Age flint. The material is both difficult to clearly define and, with the exception of the three flakes from pit F.258, gives the impression that it was manufactured, utilized and discarded, and allowed to become incorporated into the fills of large features open to the elements. The expedient character of the Middle–later Bronze Age flintworking is potentially reflected in the casual manner of its discard.

In contrast with the Middle–later Bronze Age features, all of the earlier pits display a greater immediacy between manufacture, use and discard, to varying degrees. All four 'pit-type' groups — the earlier and Late Neolithic, Beaker and Early Bronze Age — yielded evidence for flintworking and tool-use. Although all contained only partial reduction sequences, all the stages of flake production/core reduction were represented. However, the subtle variations in the assemblages provide insights into the different utilization/depositional dynamics of the respective periods. Whilst the Neolithic pits suggest immediacy between the activities that generated the flint assemblages and deposition, the Bronze Age flint followed a more complex route.

The Grooved Ware pit assemblages displayed the closest temporal/spatial relationship between flintworking, tool-use and deposition with the identification of an, albeit limited, number of refits. Although the character of the assemblages, with evidence for burning, tool-use and manufacture, is suggestive of occupation-related activities, two of the pits also yielded arrowheads; none of the later pits contained projectiles. Comparatively large quantities of arrowheads were recovered from Storey's Bar Road (Pryor 1978). Each pit at Edgerley could be seen as a unit of occupation-related activities: tasks were undertaken, including tool-use, which potentially triggered tool-manufacture, with the material generated by these tasks discarded and left to accumulate on the ground surface. At some point, potentially when a series of tasks had come to an end or when a certain amount of material had accumulated, the material was cleared into a pit.

The Beaker pit assemblages contrast markedly with the Grooved Ware material. Although flint-related activities are comparable — flintworking and tool-use — the paucity of refits and mixed character of the flint suggest that there was a temporal/spatial break between the activities and the deposition of materials in the pits. Yet the Beaker pits only yielded flint that was broadly contemporary with the features; no earlier or later material found its way in, even though the flintwork had been manufactured, utilized, discarded and later seemingly randomly incorporated into the fills of the pits. This suggests that the earlier residual material was not abundantly available on the ground surface to become incorporated into the Beaker features.

The Collared Urn pit assemblages are more comparable with the Grooved Ware than the Beaker material, although there are still subtle but significant differences. The Collared Urn-associated flint was also the product of a series of domestic activities, including flintworking and use in a variety of tasks. Yet no refits were recovered, and the pit assemblages contained a comparatively high percentage of tools. Flintworking potentially took a back-seat, sidelined in favour of other activities, and was evidently only undertaken when necessary. Alternatively, the lack of refits may reflect the character of the deposition rather than the activities that generated the material. Whereas the Grooved Ware assemblages were potentially the result of sequences of temporally and/or spatially restricted activities that were periodically cleared into pits, the Collared Urn assemblages could represent accumulated domestic debris cleared into pits in one episode within the immediate area of those activities. The gradual accumulation of material over a longer time period prior to deposition could account for the absence of refits. The clearing of accumulated material may explain the presence of the odd residual Late Neolithic flake in the Collared Urn pits, whilst the higher percentage of tools could be due to the domestic character of the activities that generated the material (i.e. carried out in a domestic space). No arrowheads were recovered from either the Beaker or the Collared Urn pits. Although there are subtle differences between the Neolithic and Early Bronze Age pit assemblages, the real break is with the Middle–later Bronze Age flint, both in terms of manufacture and deposition. The flint was generally both expediently manufactured and seemingly randomly incorporated through the gradually silting up of large features across the site.

In conclusion, the character and secure dating of the site's flint assemblages compensates for the comparatively limited quantity of material. Not only

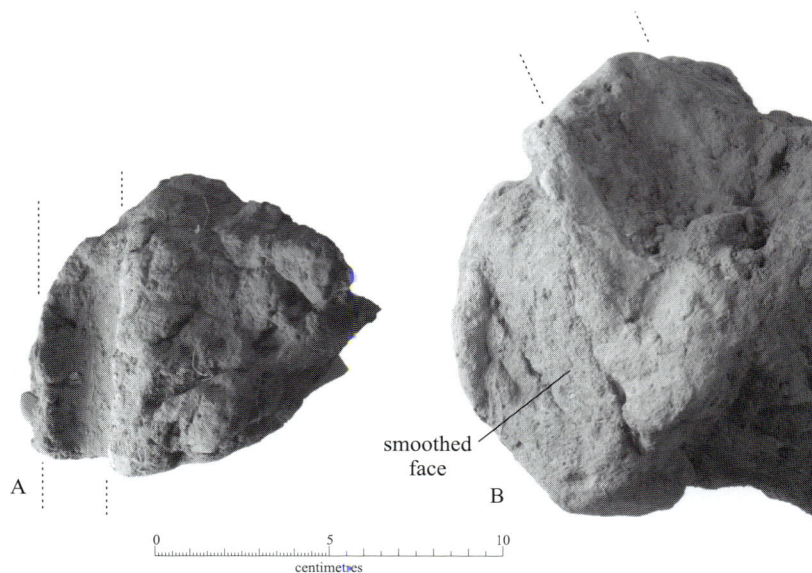

FIGURE 4.40. *Timber-impressed fired clay fragments from Collared Urn-associated Pit Cluster/Structure 1.*

do they provide details of flintworking and tool manufacture in their own right, but they contribute and contrast with the information provided by the pottery, and provide a key component in discussions of depositional practices. At a detailed level, potential byproducts from the manufacture of transverse arrowheads were specifically identified at the site and linked to raw material selection. At a more general level, the variations between the character of the Neolithic–Bronze Age pits apparent in the flint assemblages are largely mirrored in the pottery assemblages: the comparatively fresh Late Neolithic material and presence of refits contrasts keenly with the abraded and disparate character of the Beaker assemblages. Although the Late Neolithic pottery and flint refits both suggest that there was little time delay between use and deposition, the refitting flint, unlike the pottery, is the result of flint*working* rather than breakage, indicating that flint was worked, as well as utilized, adjacent to the pits. Within the Collared Urn pit assemblages only pottery refits were identified and not flint, suggesting a more complex relationship between flintworking, use and deposition in the Early Bronze Age than is seen during the Late Neolithic period.

Other finds (GRAHAME APPLEBY)

A total of 206 fragments of fired clay (9049 g) were recovered, with the majority of the smaller fragments being irregular, undiagnostic and incompletely fired. Nonetheless, some hold impressions of wattles or vegetable matter, indicative of daub. One piece from a Collared Urn-attributed pit (F.214), weighing 22 g, is a probable loomweight fragment, with a clearly defined partially surviving *lumen*, c. 15 mm in diameter, and partial exterior surface.

Nineteen fragments (216 g) were retrieved from boundary or fieldsystem ditches, 65 fragments (3634 g) from undated features, with the remainder recovered from pits and postholes.

TABLE 4.19. *Frequency of fired clay by phased contexts.*

	Grooved Ware	Beaker	Collared Urn	LBA
Pits	16 (140 g)	1 (36 g)	84 (4772 g)	-
Postholes	-	-	17 (236 g)	1 (5 g)

Fragments recovered from Collared Urn features represent the largest group of fired clay (49 per cent by number; 55 per cent by weight). Significantly, 39 fragments (3310 g) were retrieved from a single pit, F.189. The weight and size of these fragments range from 1–157 g, representing crumbs to large irregular blocks measuring up to c. 145 mm × 120 mm. Highly fired, several pieces have smooth rounded or flat surfaces, indicative of the clay having been pressed against either a post or squared-off piece of wood (Fig. 4.40). These are tentatively identified as daub, and the large irregular fragment from F.193 (316 g) possesses a partially surviving wattle *lumen*, c. 20 mm in diameter, and up to 65 mm long.

A total of 763 pieces of burnt stone (46,497 g) were recovered from 67 features across the site. Of these, 388 pieces (27,204 g; 58.5 per cent) were recovered from 23 undated features, principally pits (16). Five pieces

(591 g) were retrieved from fieldsystem ditches, with the remainder recovered from postholes.

Twenty-four Grooved Ware-associated features produced 319 pieces of burnt stone, weighing 15,604 g (33 per cent of total number; 80 per cent by weight). This contrasts with just 16 pieces from four Beaker pits (882 g), 17 pieces from nine pits of Collared Urn attribution (1082 g), two pits with Neolithic pottery (389 g) and a total of 12 pieces from five Late Bronze Age pits, postholes and ditches (1112 g).

Of the site's stone, the following items merited further description (by S. Timberlake):

<053> F.39 (Collared Urn-attributed) - Five small fragments: including two pieces of burnt flint, burnt chert (Carboniferous?), Millstone Grit sandstone, vein quartz pebble; all non-local.

<309> F.248 (Grooved Ware-attributed) - Two small cobbles: 1) The heaviest is of dolerite or diorite (basic igneous rock), a non-local glacial erratic, with the nearest outcrop being in Derbyshire; 2) Burnt sandstone/grit, a non-local erratic, possibly Carboniferous sandstone.

<678> F.392 (later Bronze Age context) - A large triangular-shaped stone with flattish top and sides that has been burnt and cracked. A quartzitic sandstone sarsen, possibly Late Eocene/Cretaceous, this non-local glacial erratic was not a quern stone, but seems as if it could have been used as a crushing anvil (both upper and lower surfaces).

<681> F.123 (undated) - Some 30 pebbles/cobbles of burnt rock and rock fragments, which include four pieces of burnt flint, two pieces of grey chert (Carboniferous?), two/three meta-quartzite pebbles (possibly Dalradian - Scottish), a pebble of Millstone Grit (Upper Carboniferous), two to three Bunter (Trias) quartzite pebbles, a fragment of fossiliferous volcanic ash (Palaeozoic?) with echinoid spines; also includes an erratic of fairly local (from east side of Fens) ferruginous carstone (Lower Greensand). Apart from this and the flint, the assemblage is non-local (glacial erratic).

Economic and environmental evidence

As the issue of the extent of arable production is central for both the study of Fengate's Bronze Age fieldsystem and the character of the earlier modes of 'open' settlement generally, the site was intensively sampled. While, as discussed by Boreham below, no positive evidence of arable activity was apparent in the pollen column from one of the fieldsystem boundaries, charred cereal remains were nonetheless present in features from all of the site's main phases (and 'type' occupations). Though the later Neolithic (Grooved Ware) economy was clearly offset by the collection of wild plant resources, hazelnut was evidently an important food source throughout the Neolithic; they, otherwise, only occurred in one later deposit (F.65, Collared Urn-attributed).

Faunal remains (Chris Swaysland)

A total of 1211 fragments (15,033 g) of animal bone were recovered from the site, including the material from the initial evaluation-phase. One pit, F.323, with the articulated remains of a cow and a calf *in utero*, yielded 887 bones (12,515 g; Fig. 4.25). This represents almost two-thirds of the entire assemblage and, otherwise, leaves only 324 bones from other contexts. Generally, the condition of the material is poor, the bone having suffered a high degree of chemical weathering; teeth are greatly over-represented and many pieces are obscured by concretions of iron-rich deposits.

No attempt has been made to distinguish between the remains of sheep and goat; however, it is assumed that the vast majority are sheep. The assemblage was quantified using a modified version of Davis (1992); in brief, all mandibular and maxillary teeth and a predetermined restricted suite of 'countable' elements were recorded. For most longbones 'countable' implies that 50 per cent of the distal articulation must be present. Any non-countable elements from less common species or elements displaying butchery marks or pathological changes were also recorded, but not used in counts. Information on gnawing, butchery and pathology was recorded where present. Butchery is recorded by 'type' (i.e. chop, knife cut, sawn), location and orientation; pathological conditions are categorized, where possible, and descriptions made as to form and location.

The age at death of the major domestic animals was analysed by mandibular tooth eruption and wear following Payne for sheep (1973) and Legge (1992) for cattle. (Note that no identifiable bone was found in association with the site's Early/Middle Neolithic features.)

Late Neolithic/Grooved Ware

Four features had identifiable bone: F.376, a distal cattle femur with light burning; F.379 and F.235 both yielded cattle tooth fragments, and a sheep/goat tibia and a dog mandible derived from F.386. In addition, small fragments of unidentified burnt bone occurred within F.7.

Beaker

Identifiable animal bone was only present in two features, F.140 and F.235: three cattle teeth and a very fragmentary section of red deer antler; a number of unidentified, small fragments of burnt bone were also recovered from F.235.

Collared Urn

Only one feature, F.197, yielded an identifiable element, a fragment of a cattle molar tooth; F.189 had 12 small, unidentified fragments of burnt bone.

Fieldsystem and Middle/later Bronze Age

Twenty-seven identifiable elements were recovered from three fieldsystem contexts, F.171, F.173 and F.174: one from horse, another from sheep/goat and 25 were from cattle; the latter were dominated by teeth (92 per cent).

While only a sheep humerus was recovered from the later Bronze Age pit F.386, F.323 contained the articulated remains of cow with an *in utero* calf (Fig. 4.25). In addition, a number of disarticulated bones were also recovered from the latter pit-feature that cut the fieldsystem in Area A. The articulated cow was skeletally mature, and the sequence of epiphyseal fusion was complete. The wear on the teeth indicated that the animal was aged three to six years at death. This age may not be reliable, however, as the animal exhibited an abnormality on both lower 3rd molars (see below). The calf was positioned in anterior presentation; that is, the normal, front feet-first birthing position, so it is probable that the cow was attempting to calf at the time of death. There is a suggestion that the calf may not have been fully developed, as its proximal metapodials were unfused and these are normally quoted as being in the process of fusing before birth (Silver 1969). The cause of death is unknown; it may have been a difficult labour, but this alone is very unlikely to result in the death of the cow. While it may seem surprising that the cow was not utilized for its meat, as its carcass would have represented a very significant amount of food, a 'birth-death' may have been bound up with concepts of 'tainted-ness'.

The articulated cow exhibited a genetic abnormality that was also present in one of the disarticulated mandibles. The 3rd cusp of the third molar (hypoconulid) was absent. This condition is reasonably common in Roman and Medieval assemblages (Dobney *et al.* 1996), but its prevalence in prehistoric material is unrecorded. It has been speculated (Dobney *et al.* 1996) that this condition is linked to breeding within a restricted gene pool, and this could imply that the articulated cow and the animal from which the disarticulated mandible came were related.

In addition to the articulated cow and calf, a number of disarticulated remains were also recovered from this pit. Cattle were represented by two mandibles (from different animals) and a humerus; sheep by a maxilla tooth and a radius.

Romano-British

Pit, F.393, yielded a sheep humerus.

When the assemblage is broken down into phase, the sample-sizes become very small. Therefore, it is beneficial to group and consider together the Late Neolithic/Bronze Age material. Analysed by this category (excluding F.323), these include both a sheep and horse bone, a fragment of red deer antler and 25 cattle bones/teeth; of the latter, 22 were teeth. The very high proportion of teeth in the cattle assemblage is a strong indication that the material has undergone severe post-depositional attrition. Teeth are the most robust of all the skeletal elements and, therefore, the most likely to survive under adverse conditions. This greatly limits the degree of information that may be gleaned from the data, particularly as many pieces are obscured by concretions of iron-derived accretions.

Plant remains (ELLEN SIMMONS & ANNE DE VAREILLES)
Forty-six bulk environmental samples were processed for charred plant remains. The methodology and nomenclature employed was essentially as that detailed in Chapter 3 above. In this case each sample was scanned under a low-power microscope in order to

assess the presence and abundance of the main classes of environmental data in all the samples (Table 4.20), with the contents of 14 then being targeted for full sorting (Table 4.22) and which included five samples analysed from the evaluation-phase (Table 4.21).

Preservation of cereals in these samples was relatively poor with many grains being heavily distorted during charring and poorly preserved due to burial conditions (e.g. abrasion, wetting and drying). As such, it should be noted that where charred plant remains were found to be absent from features this may be influenced by preservation. Some samples yielded charred wild plant seeds, and one sample, (<20>, F.172 dated to the Early Neolithic), contained chaff fragments. This indicated the potential for good preservation, as this type of material is more easily destroyed by fire than grain (Boardman & Jones 1990).

Earlier Neolithic

Sample <20>, taken from pit F.172 [359], was found to contain hazelnut shell fragments (*Corylus avellana*), as well as emmer wheat grain and chaff (*Triticum dicoccum*). The utilization of wild food plant resources from woodland or scrub is therefore indicated, alongside the cultivation of crops. Such results are consistent with charred plant remains found at other sites dated to the Neolithic (Moffet *et al.* 1989), although cereal remains are unusual in Early Neolithic contexts (Greig 1991).

Grooved Ware

The majority of samples taken from pits containing Grooved Ware pottery were found to contain hazelnut shell fragments. While no cereal remains were forthcoming from the eight excavation-phase samples, five cereal grains, along with barley chaff, were recovered from the two samples processed from the evaluation (F.9 & F.48); F.47 also yielded a whole charred sloe-berry (*Prunus* cf. *spinosa*) and an apple or pear seed (*Malus/Pyrus*).

Beaker

Five samples were processed from pits of this attribution. Those taken from adjacent pits, F.140 and F.157 in Area B (Samples <25> & <31>) yielded charred wheat and barley grains. Sample <96>, from pit F.329 in Area A, also contained charred cereal grains and was one of the few samples in this area to produce charred plant remains. Samples <93> and <94> taken from the neighbouring pits F.327 and F.328, that lay close to F.329, did not contain charred plant remains and this could possibly indicate some 'discontinuity' in deposition within these features.

Collared Urn

Pit Cluster/Structure 1 was intensively sampled (ten in total), with all but one of the samples yielding charred plant material. Charred grains of barley and wheat, which was tentatively identified as spelt (*Triticum spelta*), were present, typical crops of the Bronze Age (Greig 1991).

Charred seeds of flax (*Linum usitasisimum*) were also found in Samples <64>, <65> and <70> from pit F.193, Sample <75> (F.192) and Sample <72> (F.189), indicating some continuity of deposition between these pit contexts. Sample <84>, from the upper context of pit F.189, did not contain flax seeds, nor did samples from pits

TABLE 4.20. *Abundance estimate of main classes of environmental material in all processed samples (excludes frequency of charcoal: Key - = 1–2, + = <10, ++ = 10–25, +++> 25.*

Context	Feature	Flot (>0.3 mm)			Notes	Sample volume (litres)
		Grain + Chaff	Wild plant seeds	Other		
Early Neolithic pit						
359	172	+	-	++	Wheat and hazelnut shell fragments	10
Grooved Ware pits						
549, 578, 773	235, 263, 255			-	Hazelnut shell fragments	34.5
387	177			-	One fruit seed? Poorly preserved	9
856	312			-	Nut shell fragment?	9
718, 851	274, 310	No visible charred plant remains				26
Beaker pits						
287	140	+	-		Wheat and barley. Large Poaceae	16
326	157	+			Wheat and barley	8
900	329	+			Cereal grain, possibly barley	9
894, 897	327, 328	No visible charred plant remains				13
Collared Urn pits						
914, 697	325, 198		-, -		Wild plant seed	6, 7
568, 569, 680	193, 192	+	+	+/++	Spelt, flax, hazelnut shell fragments	35.5
570	193	+		++	Wheat grains and flax	20
671	189	+	+	+++	Barley, flax and some wild plant seeds	63
696	198	-	+		Cereal and wild plant seeds	8
694	197	+	+		Barley and other cereals; poor preservation	80
789	189	No visible charred plant remains				33
Middle Bronze Age Fieldsystem						
364	170	+	-		Barley grain; good preservation	21
429	171	-	-		Wheat grains	14
1093	391	-			Very poorly preserved cereal grain	8
640, 466, 1136, 402, 444, 877, 1145,	173–5, 385, 319	No visible charred plant remains				76
Middle Bronze Age/Late Bronze Age large pits						
392, 1072	323, 386	No visible charred plant remains				31
Late Bronze Age features						
1161	390				Large to very fine charcoal fragments	9
909	333	-	-		Barley and wild plant seed	1
911	334		-		One wild plant seed	12
847, 959	313, 322	No visible charred plant remains				15

F.198 and F.197. Flax has been identified at other Bronze Age sites in Britain, such as the fen-edge site of West Row, Mildenhall, Suffolk where it was found waterlogged (Martin & Murphy 1988), although it is still an unusual find, especially in such numbers.

The length of the flax seeds in these pits was above 3 mm, consistent with that of the cultivated variety of flax (Zohary & Hopf 1994). They, therefore, represent waste from the processing of cultivated flax for linen fibre or oil. Their intact nature suggests processing for fibre rather than oil as the seeds are crushed during oil extraction (Zohary & Hopf 1994). In addition, the presence of charred henbane seeds in Samples <64> and <72>, which are likely to have been harvested along with the 85 cm high flax, indicate a harvesting height below 80 cm, the height of the henbane plant (Stace 1997) and, thus, demonstrates the utilization of the flax stems for fibre.

Flax fibres are extracted by soaking in water in order to break down the bonds that connect the fibres to the cells and tissues of the stem; the stems are then dried and the fibres separated by pounding, before being spun into thread (Stace 1997). As suggested by Helbaek (1952), in discussing flax found at the Early Bronze Age site of Handley Down, Dorset, the evidence for the cultivation of flax for fibre at the Edgerley Site must imply a considerable time-investment by its inhabitants, in addition to that involved in cultivation.

Bronze Age fieldsystem

The majority of the ten samples taken from the fieldsystem ditches contained little or no charred plant material. The exception to this were Samples <32> and <26> from ditches F.170 and F.171 respectively, in Area B. Barley grain and emmer wheat grain were present in these, both of which are typical crops of the Bronze Age in southern England (Greig 1991); a cereal grain was also forthcoming from one of the ditch-context samples processed from the evaluation (F.16).

Later Bronze Age

Sample <90>, from posthole F.333, had barley grain, while Sample <87> from the adjacent pit F.313 contained no charred plant material.

TABLE 4.21. *Charred plant remains in fully sorted evaluation samples.*

		Trench	3	4	12	20	15
		Feature	9	16	29	57	48
		Feature type	Pit	Ditch	Pit	Posthole	Pit
		Phase/Date	LNeo	MBA	MBA	LBA	LNeo
		Sample volume - litres	8	14	14	8	12
		Flot fraction examined	1/1	1/1	1/1	1/1	1/1
Hordeum sp. grain	Barley grain					1	
Cereal grain indet.			3	1			2
Triticum dicoccum/monococcum/spelta glume base	Glume wheat chaff				0.5		
Cf. *Hordeum* sp. rachis	Barley chaff		1				
Corylus avellana (volume in ml^3 per litre of soil)	Hazelnut shell fragments		0.3		<0.01	<0.01	0.5
Corylus avellana cf. kernel fragment	Hazelnut kernel						1
Cf. *Prunus spinosa* fruit	Sloe berry						1
Malus/Pyrus seed	Primitive apple/pear seed						1
Stalk fragment							1
Rumex cf. *obtusifolius*	Broad-leaved dock				3		
Crucifereae type	Annual/perennial herb				1		
Medium Poaceae indet (*c.* 4 mm)	Medium grass family		2		2		
Small Poaceae indet (*c.* 2 mm)	Small grass family					1	1
Tuber indet.						3	

Sample <101> from pit F.390 similarly generated no charred plant material, although it was rich in charcoal. This suggests that activity in this area during the Late Bronze Age, while including burning, does not appear to be associated with the disposal of waste from the preparation and consumption of cereals; however, the poor preservation at this site should also be taken into account.

Samples <113> and <88> were also processed from Middle/later Bronze Age pits F.386 and F.323; neither contained any charred plant material. Two contexts seemingly of this attribution were also analysed from the evaluation-phase: pit F.29 and posthole F.57. Respectively, these produced wheat chaff (identified as a glume wheat and most likely emmer, *Triticum dicoccum*) and wheat chaff. The seeds of broad-leaved dock (*Rumex* cf. *obtusifolius*) and various types of grasses indicative of arable crop weeds — and probably charred as a result of crop processing — were identified in both.

A sample from buried soil over metalling (<117> F.334) did not yield any substantial charred plant material.

Extensive sampling of a variety of features at this site was carried out. Initial assessment of evaluation-phase samples indicated good potential for the recovery of unusual classes of charred plant remains, including wild apple/pear and sloe-berry seeds from Neolithic contexts. Evidence for the utilization of wild plant foods, other than hazelnut, is rare for the Neolithic in Britain and is significant for understanding the use of wild food resources during this period. The subsequent employment of sample-scanning, rather than full sorting and identification, enabled a large number of samples to be processed, thus maximizing the recovery of archaeological plant remains from all periods.

Unusual and very early evidence for the cultivation of possible emmer wheat was found in an Early Neolithic pit. The quantities of hazelnut shells and occurrence of apple/pear and sloe-berry from the Grooved Ware contexts attest to collection activities, which would have been offset by arable activity as indicated by the cereals grains and barley chaff in that period's pits.

Evidence for the consumption of emmer wheat and barley, as well as hazelnut, was present in samples taken from Bronze Age contexts. In addition, the use of 50–100 per cent sampling of a cluster of Collared Urn pits resulted in the recovery of substantial numbers of flax seeds as well as wild plant seeds providing evidence that the flax was likely to have been harvested for the extraction of fibres to make linen. This is, again, a relatively unusual find for a British Bronze Age site; the presence of charred flax seeds in samples taken from three different contexts in one pit, and from the lower context of another, out of four pits in the same cluster from which samples were processed, may also be taken as evidence of some degree of continuity in deposition between them.

Far less plant material was recovered from Late Bronze Age features, though this could be due to their lying at a distance from where waste accumulated, and from settlement *per se*.

Pollen analysis (STEVE BOREHAM)
Three monoliths from two sediment sequences were analysed: one from a Beaker-attributed pit (F.264) and two from one of the Bronze Age fieldsystem ditches (F.173). That from the F.264 pit was 50 cm long. It comprised a basal brown fine gravel unit (0–11 cm), a thin coarser gravel unit (11–20 cm), and a brown silty clay

TABLE 4.22. *Charred plant remains in fully sorted excavation samples.*

		<20>	<25>	<31>	<64>	<65>	<70>	<72>	<32>	<26>
Sample number										
Context		[359]	[287]	[326]	[568]	[570]	[569]	[671]	[364]	[429]
Feature		F.172	F.140	F.157	F.193	F.193	F.193	F.189	F.170	F.171
Feature type		Pit	Beaker pit	Beaker Pit	Collared urn pit	Collared urn pit	Collared urn pit	Collared urn pit	Ditch	Ditch
Phase/Date		ENeo	EBA	EBA	MBA	MBA	MBA	MBA	MBA	MBA
Sample volume – litres		10	16	8	20	20	2.5	63	21	14
Flot fraction examined		1/1	1/2	1/1	1/1	1/1	1/1	1/4	1/1	1/1
Triticum dicoccum sensu lato grain	Emmer wheat grain									1
Triticum cf. *dicoccum* grain			1	1						
Triticum cf. *spelta* grain	Possible spelt wheat grain				1					
Triticum sp. grain	Wheat grain		1	2					1	
Triticum sp. tail grain	Wheat tail grain	1								
Hordeum sp. grain	Barley grain			1					3	1
Hordeum sp. hulled grain	hulled barley grain								3	
cf *Hordeum* sp. grain			1.5			1		1	1	
Triticum/Hordeum sp. grain	Wheat/barley grain	3	1	2	3				3	
Triticum/Hordeum sp. tail grain	Wheat/barley tail grain				1					
Triticum cf. *dicoccum* glume base	Possible emmer wheat chaff	2								
Triticum sp. glume base	Glume wheat chaff	2								
Linum usitatissimum	Cultivated flax seeds				404	7	6	30		
Corylus avellana fragments	Hazelnut shell fragments	85	1							
Indet. fruit stone fragments					5					
Hyoscymus niger	Henbane				4			2		
Rumex cf. *pulcher*	Fiddle dock		1					1		
cf. *Rumex*	Dock/Orache							1		
Rumex sp. kernel					6					
Cf. *Spergula*	Spurrey								1	
Chenopodium sp.	Goose foot				1					
Juncus sp.	Rush									1
Astragalus sp.	Milk-vetch							1		
Small Poaceae indet.	Small grass family		1					1	1	
Medium Poaceae indet.	Medium grass family	1								
Large Poaceae indet.	Large grass family		1							
Indet. wild plant seed			1					2		1
Charcoal fragments										
>4 mm			+	+	+			-	++	+++
2–4 mm			++	++	++	-	-	++	+++	+++
<2 mm			++	+++	+++	++	+	++	+++	+++
Vitrified			+		-	-			-	

Key: '-' 1 or 2 items, '+' < 10 items, '++' 10 - 50 items, '+++' > 50 items

(20–24 cm) grading upwards into an orange/brown silt unit containing charcoal (24–50 cm), from which a pollen sample was taken at 22 cm; the infilling of this pit was generally rather oxidized.

The lower portion of Monolith 108, from F.173, was 50 cm long. It comprised a basal grey clay silt with gravel ([1064]; 0–21 cm), from which a pollen sample was taken at 5 cm. This was overlain by a sandy gravel (21–30 cm) fining upwards through silty sand (30–47 cm) to a grey/brown sandy silt-clay (47–50 cm; [063]), from which a pollen sample was taken at 48 cm. Monolith 108 'upper' was also 50 cm long; the base of this tin corresponding to c. 43 cm on the 'lower' 198 sample. Samples from this tin will be referred to relative to their height from the base of the sequence, with the height relative

TABLE 4.23. *Pollen results (* denotes very low Main Sum).*

Feature	F.264	F.173	F.173	F.173	F.173
Context	**[581]**	**[1064]**	**[1063]**	**[1062]**	**Buried soil**
Tin		**108 lower**	**108 lower**	**108 upper**	**108 upper**
Sample	**22 cm**	**5 cm**	**48 cm**	**70 cm (27 cm)**	**81 cm (38 cm)**
Trees & Shrubs					
Quercus	0.0	0.0	20.0*	0.0	0.0
Corylus	0.0	0.0	0.0	0.0	0.7
Herbs					
Poaceae	0.0	50.9	0.0	64.6	58.0
Asteraceae (Asteroidea/Cardueae) undif.	0.0	2.8	0.0	3.8	2.9
Centaurea	0.0	0.9	0.0	0.0	0.0
Asteraceae (Lactuceae) undif.	0.0	23.6	0.0	25.3	18.8
Caryophyllaceae	0.0	0.0	0.0	0.0	0.7
Chenopodiaceae	0.0	0.9	0.0	1.3	1.4
Cirsium	0.0	0.0	0.0	0.0	0.7
Brassicaceae	0.0	1.9	0.0	0.0	1.4
Plantago lanceolata type	0.0	0.0	0.0	0.0	0.7
Lower plants					
Polypodium	0.0	0.9	20.0*	0.0	1.4
Pteropsida (monolete) undif.	66.7*	4.7	60.0*	2.5	4.3
Pteropsida (trilete) undif.	33.3*	13.2	0.0	2.5	8.7
Moss spores	0.0	0.0	0.0	83.5	46.4
Summary					
Sum trees	0.0	0.0	20.0*	0.0	0.0
Sum shrubs	0.0	0.0	0.0	0.0	0.7
Sum herbs	0.0	81.1	0.0	94.9	84.8
Sum spores	100.0*	18.87	80.0*	5.1	14.5
Main Sum	3	106	5	79	138
Concentration (grains per ml)	628	17,151	821	12,782	30,076

to the base of the tin shown in square brackets. The monolith comprised an orange/brown sandy silt-clay (43–60 cm/[0–17 cm]; [1063]), a grey mottled sandy silt with pebbles (60–74 cm/[17–31 cm]; [1062]), from which a pollen sample was taken at 70 cm/[27 cm], and a brown silt-sand (74–93 cm/[31–50 cm]; buried soil), from which a pollen sample was taken at 81 cm/[38 cm]. Although it should have been present between *c.* 28–35 cm, the later Bronze Age metalled surface, F.334, was not actually identifiable within this monolith.

The five samples of sediment were prepared using the standard hydrofluoric acid technique, and counted for pollen using a high-power stereo microscope. The percentage pollen data from these samples is presented in Table 4.23.

Beaker Pit (F.264)

The sample from 22 cm ([581]) had an extremely low pollen concentration (628 grains per ml) indicating that most of its palynomorphs had been destroyed by oxidation. Only three fern spores were encountered in an entire slide, and thus this sample must be considered effectively barren. The entire sequence from this monolith was heavily oxidized.

Fieldsystem ditch (F.173)

Lower
The sample from 5 cm ([1064]) had a low pollen concentration (17,151 grains per ml). Palynomorphs were not well preserved and, in addition to the presence of corroded pollen grains, the proportion of resistant Asteraceae pollen and Pteropsida (fern spores) was unusually high. This signal is often taken to indicate oxidation from the action of soil processes. In addition, the slide contained large amounts of finely divided organic debris, which diluted the pollen and further hampered counting, resulting in a low main sum. The pollen signal was dominated by grass (50.9 per cent), with herbs including asters (26.4 per cent), members of the cabbage family (1.9 per cent) and others (1.8 per cent). Fern spores accounted for 17.9 per cent of the sample, and no arboreal or aquatic pollen was encountered. The sample from 48 cm had a very low pollen concentration (821 grains per ml). Only four fern spores and one pollen grain were encountered in a single slide, and consequently this sample is virtually barren. A tantalizing glimpse of the original pollen assemblage is given by the presence of oak, and polypody fern, both potential indicators of woodland environments; however, very little of worth can be done with such a poorly preserved assemblage.

Upper
The samples from 70 cm [27 cm] and 81 cm [38 cm] both had low pollen concentrations (12,782 & 30,076 grains per ml), and contained poorly preserved palynomorphs, and significant proportions of resistant Asteraceae pollen, hinting that oxidation had affected the

material. The slides contained abundant finely divided organic debris, which made pollen counting more difficult. The pollen signal was dominated by grass (64.6 & 58 per cent), with herbs including asters (29.1 & 21.7 per cent), members of the goosefoot family (1.3 & 1.4 per cent) and others (0.0 & 3.5 per cent). Fern spores accounted for 5 per cent and 13 per cent of the samples, and moss spores (expressed as a percentage outside the main sum) were abundant at 83.5 per cent and 46.4 per cent. The sample from 81 cm was clearly better preserved and contained polypody fern spores and pollen of hazel, thistle, campion, the cabbage family and strapwort plantain (*Plantago lanceolata*).

It is unfortunate that the sample from the F.264 Beaker pit yielded nothing of value and, from the oxidized nature of the monolith material, it seems unlikely that further pollen investigation would be fruitful.

The basal fill of the Bronze Age fieldsystem ditch (sample at 5 cm; [1064]) indicates that near-complete tree clearance had been achieved at the site, since there was not a hint of tree pollen. Indeed, there is no suggestion of aquatic pollen either, which leads to the possibility that the ditch may have remained dry for much of the time, and simply filled with 'in-wash'. Alternatively, the grass (Poaceae) signal may derive partly from reedswamp growing in the ditch, although the absence of other aquatics makes this unlikely. Also of note is the lack of cereal pollen, which could suggest that this portion of the fieldsystem was not used for arable farming. Caution must be exercised with all of these interpretations, but it is clear that meadows or grassland with tall-herb communities surrounded the ditch soon after it was dug. The fining-upwards sequence of [1063] suggests that it was waterlain. However, the upper silt unit seems to have been sub-aerially exposed and oxidized, so that the pollen sample from 48 cm was virtually barren. Little can be deduced from this sample, other than that the faint woodland signal surviving the intense oxidation could be interpreted as abandonment of the site, with the development of scrub; however, there is no firm evidence for such an interpretation.

The pollen signal from 70 cm [27 cm] is almost indistinguishable from the upper sample in the buried soil at 81 cm [38 cm], despite being apparently separated by a metalled surface. Interpretation of these samples is very similar to that for the basal sample (5 cm): meadow with tall-herb communities and no arable activity. There is a remarkably high proportion of moss spores in these samples, which suggests that the ditch soon became a mossy hollow, rather than an open water course. The absence of aquatic plants in the pollen assemblage supports this view. The uppermost sample from the buried soil (81 cm/[38 cm]) has a little evidence for the presence of scrubby woodland nearby (hazel and polypody), and for ground disturbance (strapwort plantain).

The pollen analyses from the fieldsystem ditch give 'snapshots' of the possible environments at the site during the Bronze Age. Woodland clearance seems to have been well underway in the area at that time, but no direct evidence for arable activity has been found in these samples.

Concluding discussion

Obviously resonating in relationship to Pryor's Storey's Bar Road excavations, the recovery of another Grooved Ware settlement cluster at Fengate is itself important and adds to the picture of the area's land-use during the later Neolithic. Yet, as more fully discussed in Chapter Six, the site's Beaker-phase utilization may well be more significant, as it could potentially reflect upon the origins of the area's land-allotment. It is equally crucial to recognize the frequency with which Beaker appears to occur throughout this Fengate North area as a whole. While not apparently present at the Broadlands Site, pits of the period occurred south of the Edgerley Site in HAT/AS's off-Vicarage Road plot and Pryor's Boroughby Road excavations (and, also to the north, at Soke's Oxney Road Site and Abbott's findings from that area; see '*Herdsman's Hill* Inset' above and Chapter 2). Certainly, within a western fen-edge context, this would suggest relatively dense and extensive Beaker-phase occupation. It would, for example, certainly contrast with the relative paucity of such material recovered to date from the Lower Ouse environs (Evans & Knight 2000; 2001) and, generally, Beaker sites seem far more frequent along the eastern fen margins (e.g. Bamford 1982, figs. 8–10; Hall & Coles 1994, 60–64, figs. 37 & 38); future fieldwork may however show this to be, at least in part, due to recovery bias (i.e. lighter 'east-edge' soils *vs* the west's extensive alluvial cover).

Yet, for a variety of reasons, this is not a site well-suited to advance the dating of Fengate's fieldsystem. While the Late Bronze Age-assigned metalled spread within Area A which locally sealed its ditches, and the location of the possible roundhouse (Structure 3) within the main droveway across the southern end of Area B, both seem to mark its demise, their attribution is essentially inferential and by no means absolute. Equally, at the other end of the dating spectrum, very little 'early' pottery occurred within the ditches themselves, which could, otherwise, perhaps allow for the teasing out of the system's local origins; present in just five ditch locations/segments, this only comprised 27 Grooved Ware and five Beaker sherds — just 2.5 per cent and 1.5 per cent of their respective assemblages. If to this is added the fact that no Collared Urn pottery was forthcoming from the ditches as such, and no

Deverel-Rimbury wares were recovered whatsoever, these excavations do not themselves significantly illuminate the fieldsystem's 'origins question'. In the case of the Collared Urn distributions (or better, the lack thereof) this is particularly unfortunate. Returning to the pitfall of treating 'pit occupations' as if they were stratigraphic horizons, though the situation of the period's Pit Cluster 2 within the route of the droveway would certainly suggest that it pre-dated the fieldsystem at this point, the 'comfortable' location of that period's would-be structure (Pit Cluster/Structure 1) within the system's axes could hint at their contemporaneity. It is crucial here to note that the site's Collared Urn usage was *potentially* a matter of hundreds of years and *not an event*, and 'things' — such as the layout of the fieldsystem — could have happened during its span; however, there is no distributional basis by which to progress this issue.

Having rehearsed these arguments, the site's radiocarbon assays should now be reviewed. Unfortunately, aside from for the Collared Urn, we fell short of our aim of achieving two dates from each of its main pottery-type horizons. The F.157 Beaker sample yielded a post-0/BP assay (i.e. contaminated) and the F.235 sample of 1920–1730 and 1720–1690 cal. BC (3490±40 BP; Beta-240346) is clearly upwards of a millennium too young and must have derived from the ditch that truncated the later Neolithic pit. While, therefore, giving no real sense of the date-range of the individual 'type-'/'period-occupations', the other four pit assemblage assays all fall well within the established span of their respective pottery-types:

Grooved Ware
F.15 - 2870–2570 and 2510–2500 cal. BC (4110±40 BP; Beta-240345)
Beaker
F.140 - 2280–2250 and 2220–2020 cal. BC (3730±40 BP; Beta-240342)
Collared Urn
F.193 - 1900–1690 cal. BC (3480±40 BP; Beta-240343)
F.189 - 1930–1740 cal. BC (3500±40 BP; Beta-240344).

Perhaps most singularly important are the other two dates. With its material obviously coming from the F.173 fieldsystem ditch that cut it, it is even conceivable that the charred source-material from pit F.235 came from the nearby Collared Urn occupation, as their dates essentially match each other (*c.* 1930–1600 cal. BC). Yet, the crucial point here is that both may conceivably have related to the same horizon (i.e. Collared Urn-usage contemporary with the fieldsystem), with the argument for this turning on the 1630–1450 cal. BC (3270±40 BP; Beta-240340) assay from pit F.323 that cut the fieldsystem in Area A. Taken at face-value, this could suggest that parts of the fieldsystem were no longer maintained by the mid-second millennium BC

and that the primary usage of the system could date to *c.* 1900–1600 cal. BC and the *earlier* Bronze Age. Given the ramifications of this, some might also wish to dismiss this date on the grounds that it was potentially based on residual material. However, greater assurance in this case comes from repeat-patterning; this dating would also complement that from the Elliott Site, particularly its assay of 1530–1400 cal. BC (3190±40 BP; Beta-230845) from its pit F.2 and which there also cut one of the system's droveway ditches.

As mentioned, with its succession of 'typed-pit occupations', of all Fengate's many excavations to date this site seems to approximate most closely to the kind of archaeology that Abbott investigated during the early decades of the twentieth century. As is apparent in Table 4.24, dominated by Beaker and Peterborough Ware, the 'type' frequency of his findings was, however, quite different from ours. While obviously working in an area seeing far more dense Middle Neolithic-/Peterborough Ware-associated activity, recovery-bias may well have contributed to this. For quite understandable reasons, it is clear that Abbott was generally only really distinguishing the range of larger pits — such as some of Edgerley's Beaker features — but not the smaller, 0.5 m or less deep, pits; in other words, those from which the bulk of the site's materials in these periods derived. (Recent excavations at Eye Quarry by the CAU have also had Peterborough Ware associated with larger, deep-cut features; see Chapter 2 and Patten 2009; cf. Garrow 2006, 67, tables 5.2 & 5.3.)

Edgerley's pit assemblages also offer further insights into the character of Abbott's findings, if only by way of contrast. Both in his notebooks and his 1910 paper, he only really fully detailed the inventory of one pit. At 12 ft/3.65 m in diameter and 4 ft/1.22 m deep, in addition to sherds from a number of different Peterborough Ware vessels and also Beakers, it yielded:

TABLE 4.24. *Period-/type-frequency of Abbott's Fengate pottery vessels compared to the Edgerley Site. As a relative measure of the intensity of the site's pre-Iron Age utilization, Garrow records that portions of 272, c. 200, 151 and 188 individual vessels were, respectively, recovered from Broome Heath, Hurst Fen, Kilverstone and Spong Hill's occupations from this time (2007).*

Type	No. of Vessels	
	Abbott	Edgerley Site
Plain Bowl	?	1
Peterborough Ware	13	3
Grooved Ware	2	31 (+ *c.* 29 in total)
Beaker	47	33
Collared/Biconical Urn	2	8
PDR/Early Iron Age	81	3

'1 small barbed arrow-head
3 roughly made saws
10 small knives
35 scrapers, 1/⅓ inch to 1½ inches long
20 cores, possibly slingstones'.

Moreover, aside from a worked bone implement and other animal bones, some 300 potboiler stones, baked clay fragments and a clay sling-shot were also apparently recovered from this pit; nutshells were also said to be found in its basal deposit. Only one pit at Edgerley came close to having the 69 worked flints recorded by Abbott: F.255, with 63 flints, 33 burnt stones (i.e. 'potboilers') and 90 sherds of Grooved Ware. The next largest flint assemblages only numbered in the low 30s (F.176 & F.235), but these, again, were also Grooved Ware-associated; the largest Beaker pit flint assemblage had only seven pieces. The key point here is that, at least within their pottery, *Edgerley's pit assemblages were discrete by vessel-type and showed no obvious intermixing of styles* and there was very little residuality of earlier types (the only exception being the single Beaker sherd occurring in the Cluster/Structure 1's Collared Urn assemblage). The fact that Abbott records numbers of *both* Peterborough Ware and Beaker vessels from the same feature suggests that he probably missed the intercutting of at least two pits (the nutshells probably relating to the Middle Neolithic usage).

Trying to gauge Edgerley's pre-Middle Bronze sequence, it is clear that when compared to either Hurst Fen, Barleycroft Farm or Kilverstone's 'pit-occupations' it did not see particularly intense usage (see Garrow 2007). Yet, the scale and density of these was primarily due to their Early Neolithic component, which was minimal at Edgerley. Equally, although Edgerley generated the largest pit-assemblage of Beaker pottery to date within the region, the site's widely dispersed pits of that appellation seem typical of the time (see Garrow 2006). The same, however, is not necessarily true of Edgerley's Grooved Ware. Though it also yielded the largest pottery assemblage from any 'pit site' within the region, its pit-features showed little evidence of any obvious or 'formal' settlement structure and were similarly dispersed. They occurred, for example, at a somewhat lower density than at either Storey's Bar Road, Fengate or Sites 2–4 at Over (cf. Figs. 2.20, 3.20 & 4.6; Pollard 1998b; Evans & Knight 2004; Garrow 2006, chap. 6). Moreover, it was without the evidence of small buildings present at the latter.

Although seeming to see some concentration within the southern third of Area B (across the same approximate swathe as Knight's Grooved Ware refits), Beaker features were very 'thin on the ground'; their

most obvious distributional trait being that none occurred throughout the centre-north of that area (whereas some Grooved Ware pits did). No evidence of any contemporary house architecture was recovered, comparable, for example, to that from Site 11 (Pryor 1993, 128–31, figs. 94 & 95), Bradley Fen Farm (see Chapter 2 above) and, also, Sutton Hoo (Carver 2005, 421). Yet, Beaker occupation is primarily distinguished by its paucity of pit-features, in contrast to their surface finds/middens (see Bamford 1982; Garrow 2006, chap. 7); in other words, the frequency of sub-surface features seems to attest less directly to the scale, intensity and/or duration of their usage.

To turn, finally, to the site's Collared Urn phase (see Fig. 4.11), settlements of this attribution are so rare in Eastern England that there really is no convincing basis on which to compare Edgerley. All that can be said with certainty is that the probable Structure 1 roundhouse appears to have been intentionally *closed*, with its features backfilled with 'use-related' pottery.

The Neolithic to earlier Bronze Age artefact-rich pits present at Edgerley are the kind of context now often referred to as 'filled pits' and *de facto* considered to have ritual qualities and/or to somehow evocatively mark 'place' (e.g. Pryor 1998a; Pollard 1999; see Garrow 2006, 6–8). The original basis of such arguments stems from Richards & Thomas's 1984 paper concerning Durrington Wall's Grooved Ware. It, however, hinged upon the idea that certain decorative motifs of sherds were *intentionally selected* for pit/posthole deposition, almost in a talismanic manner. As discussed by Knight above, there is no question of this occurring here; many of these pits simply seem to have been backfilled with refuse from midden spreads and must essentially reflect the 'tidying-up' of settlements. (Garrow's recent analysis of the region's prehistoric 'pit sites' demonstrates that such selection seems only potentially applicable to Grooved Ware occupations; 2006; 2007.) Such arguments have also focused upon the lack of any obvious use of these small pits and, from 'face-value' appraisal, essentially advocate that such finds-rich features were dug with the express purpose of receiving occupation refuse (Garrow 2006; 2007). Yet, it has been convincingly demonstrated above that the vast majority of the site's many unattributed pits must have related to its various later Neolithic/earlier Bronze Age 'pit occupations'. Based on the morphology of these features, in many instances there is no inherent difference between those that were 'finds-rich' and those that were devoid thereof. Only in very few cases — generally the larger pits with multiple fills — can any direct function be postulated. This surely must imply that they fulfilled a variety of functions, but which left little or no direct stratigraphic traces (see *Pit and Depositional Analysis* section above).

The moot point behind all of this, of course, is whether such pits are representative of settlement *per se* and, if so, what was their character and duration? Due mainly to their apparent lack of robust domestic architecture (i.e. convincing house structures), it is now commonplace to see them as reflecting modes of 'residential mobility' and involving various scales of 'settlement shift' (see Garrow 2006, 5–11 for overview). Based on the evidence of Fengate, it is crucial to remember the sites' buried soil strata. Now too often just machined-off without any sampling-interrogation, at Edgerley these deposits were 0.1–0.4 m deep. Where they have been found to be sealed by Bronze Age upcast horizons — beneath fieldsystem-banks both at Fourth Drove and the Depot Site — they were 0.2–0.25 m thick. Acknowledging both the truncation and compression of their profiles, then prior to *c.* 1500 cal. BC it is reasonable to presume that they would have been, perhaps, 0.25–0.35 m deep (C. French pers. comm.): more than enough to foot a timber building without it leaving any trace in the geological substrata. (Based on his experience of constructing the Flag Fen roundhouse, Pryor relates that a 0.3 m depth would be quite sufficient for a main house-post if its superstructure was supported by a ring-collar; equally, 0.35 m would be enough for the extra loadbearing capacity of a doorpost; pers. comm.) By the same token, when on these sites the traces of domestic architecture occur with some regular frequency — during the later Bronze Age — does this actually reflect the advent of more deeply footed buildings or, perhaps, the later truncation of buried soil horizons? The latter would be suggested here by the apparent down-cut situation of the metalled surface. Occupation-related soil truncation was also recorded at the 1992 Depot (see Chapter 3); the motivation behind this presumably being the establishment of consolidated horizons amid what would have been the churned character of the area's buried soil following three or more centuries of agricultural usage.

The single most critical factor that would argue against these 'pit occupations' attesting to any kind of seasonal residential mobility would be the bulky character of their pottery. Inherently large and fragile, it simply would not have been feasible to wholesale shift locale on an annual basis if having to transport either a number of Collared Urns or Grooved Ware pots. Of course, if necessary, these could always have been cached and left behind for a time. Yet, once we admit the loss of so much settlement evidence within the site's buried soil strata — potentially including even shallow-footed buildings — there seems to be

no reason to seek recourse in such 'mobility' explanations (see Chapter 6 concerning the easy persuasion of long-distance pastoral modes of interpretation). If anything, it would be the ephemeral traces of its Middle Neolithic presence — essentially evinced by only a handful of Peterborough Ware sherds in tree-throw hollows — that might rather point to 'passage' within the landscape; even that, though, need not necessarily have involved anything other than off-site 'tasking' from a nearby home-base settlement (perhaps Abbott's deep pits of the period, located to the southwest). In much the same vein, extra-settlement tasking by some members of the immediate community could well have occurred from out of the Edgerley Site locale, perhaps both on a daily basis to obtain water and more extended stays for resource procurement (variously hunting, wild foodstuff collection and pasture).

In this capacity, and as outlined above (and in Chapter 3), seeing far less pottery and apparently higher densities of worked flint, the Storey's Bar Road Grooved Ware occupation would seem to differ markedly from that at Edgerley Road. While it may have hosted various later Neolithic occupations, Storey's Bar Road's remarkable frequency of arrowheads and high representation of the 'the wild' (i.e. auroch and possibly wild pig) has even prompted speculation that, at least for part of its duration, it might have been some manner of hunting camp. If so, these activities might have extended southeastward to the area of the TP Packaging and Elliott Sites (see Chapter 3). While it would surely be too readily convenient to see that locale as a direct specialist/seasonal off-shoot from a more quasi-permanent base camp-like occupation at Edgerley, with the latter having so much more pottery (more than five times the amount) and so few arrowheads (two *vs* 26; though there is evidence of their on-site manufacture) the differences between these two Grooved Ware sites could, nevertheless, be considered complementary. Indeed, this would also appear to extend to the respective percentages of tools within their flint assemblages as a whole: Edgerley's later Neolithic having 13 per cent (compared to the site's 24 per cent Early Neolithic) as opposed to Storey's Bar Road's very high *c.* 33 per cent (Pryor 1980c, 497, note 1), and which could further suggest a more mobile component at the latter.

If the Edgerley Site saw year-round occupation prior to the Middle Bronze Age, this probably was not long based on Knight's per period minimum number of vessels, nor need it necessarily have been uninterrupted (i.e. 'episodically permanent'). Based on no more than a 'rule-of-thumb' breakage rate of two to four vessels per *annum*, then the site's Grooved Ware and Beaker occupations might have each only lasted between eight and 15 years (the range-span of the former would be doubled if the 60-vessel estimate is used); Collared Urn, perhaps just two to four years. While useful to 'think with', such logic is desperately arbitrary and presupposes a continuity of depositional behaviour, and a 10- to 20-year 'house-cluster span' might be a more reasonable basis from which to address the assemblages, especially for its potential Collared Urn structure. Whatever the estimate-measure applied, these occupations seem, at most, to have been a matter of decades and none of its 'style-type' phases may have continued for more than 50 years. Of course, relating to this is the issue of how many vessels were, at a minimum, in immediate circulation at any one time; the maximum number of vessels present within the periods' individual pits potentially provides some gauge for this. For both Grooved Ware and Beaker-associated features this would be four, with at least eight separate pots present in the Collared Urn Pit Cluster/Structure 1.

Edgerley's 'pit-occupations' broaches a series of major issues. Put simply, over time are the same people living on the site (i.e. does it show 'ancestral continuity')? At its heart sits the issue of the status of material culture (pottery) styles: what is meant by Grooved Ware, Beaker and Collared Urn occupations; is it only a matter of 'style' or do we really mean 'people'? This issue must, of course, be conditioned by the recognition of the short, episodic duration of the site's repetitive occupations; it can, though, be argued that these many short-duration settlement 'occupations' occurred within the hub of a wider area/'place' sequence generally (i.e. the 'Fengate North' area). Therefore, we should overview Edgerley's data as regards the evidence of change/continuity. Its Grooved Ware occupation sees extensive wild plant resource usage (its faunal remains being too poorly preserved for detailed determination). In contrast, apart from the demise of subsequent flint (*vs* pot) usage (see above), its Beaker occupation saw the advent of 'large pit' usage, possibly relating to grain storage. Finally, with Collared Urn and its tentatively identified house (Structure 1), we seem to witness the establishment of a more 'formal', or at least robust, domestic architecture (though Beaker-attributed roundhouses have now also been recovered in the broader Fengate/Flag Fen environs; see Chapter 2 above and Chapter 3's Inset concerning Fengate's earlier, Neolithic buildings). In short, we are witnessing significant changes in the domestic life of these 'style-periods'.

Also, as discussed above by Knight and Beadsmoore in relationship to the site's pottery and flint assemblages, major differences are apparent in the relative scales and depositional dynamics of its 'occupations'. While the Grooved Ware occupation would seem more extensive than either the Beaker or Collared Urn, it displays a greater depositional immediacy. A higher degree of its occupation debris was evidently being deposited into the pits (i.e. the site being, for whatever reason, tidied up and 'closed'), which was not true of the Beaker-associated remains; these seem to have been left to weather and accumulate — probably in midden spreads — prior to their deposition (see French & Pryor 2005, 94–8 on the Etton landscape's Grooved Ware middens). In other words, suggesting a longer duration, the site's Beaker pit assemblages appear less directly representative of the period's site-occupation as a whole and lead to a significant underestimation of its scale.

As regards to the site's fieldsystem, when compared to Fengate's southward 'core' with its fenward-aligned droves (northwest–southeast), the Fengate North area does differ in one very crucial aspect: its north–south layout (see Fig. 6.1). This shift in its axes seems more than just a matter of 'edge-related' topographic accommodation, but rather a major reorientation. Lying *c.* 220 m apart, this would be expressed in the fact that the droves of both the Broadlands and Edgerley Sites lay parallel on this alignment. While admittedly in the south of the site the latter's turned markedly eastward towards the fen, in the main, these droves ran roughly parallel with the fen-edge and fenward-access would not seem to have been the principal factor determining their arrangement.

While Edgerley's drove only continued for some 65 m into the site, there can be no doubt that the ditch which marked its eastern side (F.173) was a major axial boundary. Apparently extending for more than 350 m through the area (north–south) and generally substantially larger than the site's other fieldsystems ditches, this certainly seems to be the equivalent of Fengate's other main 'core-area' droveway boundaries and, elsewhere, could well be counted as a 'great reave' (see Chapter 6).

The continuous 'run' and evidence of subsequent closing of entranceways along this ditch's length potentially attests to changes in the fieldsystem's usage. This process has been documented elsewhere at Fengate, particularly Pryor's Newark Road compounds (1980a; 1996), but also at the Elliott Site (Chapter 3). In effect, there seems to be evidence of the widespread closure of the system's original entranceways. (This does, indeed, seem to be a matter of closure of the system, as no evidence of any secondary-dumped causeway entrances have yet to be found at Fengate.) Presumably relating to changes in the later Bronze Age usage and, particularly, animal access, what could account for this? Two explanations seem possible, but which might well prove to be interrelated. The first would be an increased emphasis on arable (as opposed to pastoral) production. While French's analysis of the buried soil sealing the metalled surface gave no positive indication of such, this horizon presumably attests to Iron Age and Early Roman usage. The second line of argument would be stock-related, as it could reflect a greater focus upon sheep-rearing. It is, of course, always possible that bridge-access was subsequently maintained at these original entrance points, but it is much more difficult to envisage cattle (as opposed to sheep) navigating their way across narrow and shaky split-plank 'ways'. Sheep are, moreover, much more adept at jumping and one could easily imagine that, in a lowland context (*vs* the stone walls of the upland zone), if seasonally taken into the 'in-fields', then their control would require more 'upstanding' elements (e.g. fence-lines and hedges). This entirely recasts the issue of the Late Bronze Age disuse/transgression of Fengate's fieldsystem, whose upstanding components may well have continued in operation after its ditches were no longer maintained.

Though, in the south, Edgerley's droveway and its immediate paddocks turned in relationship to the 'inlet' running across the off-Vicarage Road plot, it is crucial to recognize that the north–south orientation of this system continued south of that landscape feature and beyond the Boroughby Garage Site (see Fig. 6.1). In fact, the beginnings of this northward swing in the fieldsystem's orientation can be distinguished within the northern portion of Pryor's Newark Road Site. Otherwise, the trench-only exposure of features within the plot south of the site makes it difficult to reconstruct the fieldsystem there with any confidence. What can be said is that, while obviously influencing the system's layout, the inlet there does not seem to have been a focus of its axes in the way that occurred at the Elliott Site (that being apart from the watching brief-exposed F.4/5 and F.8 bank and/or ditch-lines, which seemed to frame its north and south sides). The ditch along the latter appears massive and did not yield any direct dating evidence. For a time we even seriously entertained the possibility that it might actually have been a small Roman canal and relate to the Car Dyke system; however, its radiocarbon assay of 1190–1140 and 1140–920 cal. BC (2870±40 BP; Beta-240339) would firmly place it in the later Bronze Age. Given this, how do we account for such a relatively large linear feature at this date? We are only aware of two regional parallels: the 3 m-wide and 1 m-deep ditch bounding the northern side of *The Holme* sub-Site's settlement swathe at Earith (see Chapter 2 above) and the equally impressive linear at Welland Bank (Pryor 1998c, pls. 13 & 15 and 2002, fig. 7). Associated

with Collared Urn pottery, the latter has claims to be an early, major reeve-like boundary, delineating the north side of that system's 'field block'. Although possibly comparable, the same would not seem to be true of the off-Vicarage Road system and, rather, it seems directly associated with the inlet there. Two explanations seem plausible. First, based on its non-basal fill-derived date, it may have been contemporary with the main fieldsystem and, if laid out before that area got seriously wet (the inlet's base lay at *c.* 1 m OD), then it might pertain to still another large stock compound, perhaps akin to the Elliott Site's. Secondly, if it was, indeed, of later Bronze Age date and thereby represents a modification to the fieldsystem, then this ditch and its bank (and the northward F.4/5 bank-lines) could reflect a response to flood defence — bounding the inlet's 'wet'.

As chance would have it, the closest parallel for Edgerley's great 'strip' paddock seems to be the Elliott Site's fen-edge stock compound (Fig. 4.41). Also *c.* 50 m wide, but in this case more than 100 m longer at 290 m+ length, at Edgerley this would also have to be interpreted as a stock-related facility, probably providing both pasture and somewhere livestock could be seasonally sorted. This interpretation is furthered by the scale of the droveway that accessed its southern end: 16 m wide, it was some three times wider than those within Fengate's 'core' (e.g. the Ditch 1/2 and 8/9 droves which were only *c.* 5 m across).

As is apparent in Figure 4.41, the proportion and size of the Elliott and Edgerley Road Site's stock compounds are close to that of Pryor's Newark Road compounds, which, of course, he also argued served as a communal stockyard (1996). Yet, as discussed at length in Chapter 2, these also had a number of other traits (double-ditch embankment and interior round-house structures) that would suggest a settlement component. Given this, and their overall comparable size/shape, one possibility is that Newark Road's 'long strip' arrangement was, indeed, originally stock-related, but was later modified for other purposes. Be this as it may, there would seem to be no justification for AS/HAT's ascription of their Broadlands' *square* compound as also being for stock. Apparently not directly linked to any droveway, their assignation of it as such is solely based on its double-ditched perimeter in direct reference to Pryor's Newark Road compounds (see Fig. 6.5); it, moreover, also had a substantial dump of later Bronze Age pottery within one of its ditches (Nicholson *et al.* forthcoming).

Finally, what of the site's economic evidence? Leaving aside the F.323 cow-and-calf pit deposit, only just more than 320 animal bones were recovered. As stressed by Swaysland above, due to the poor

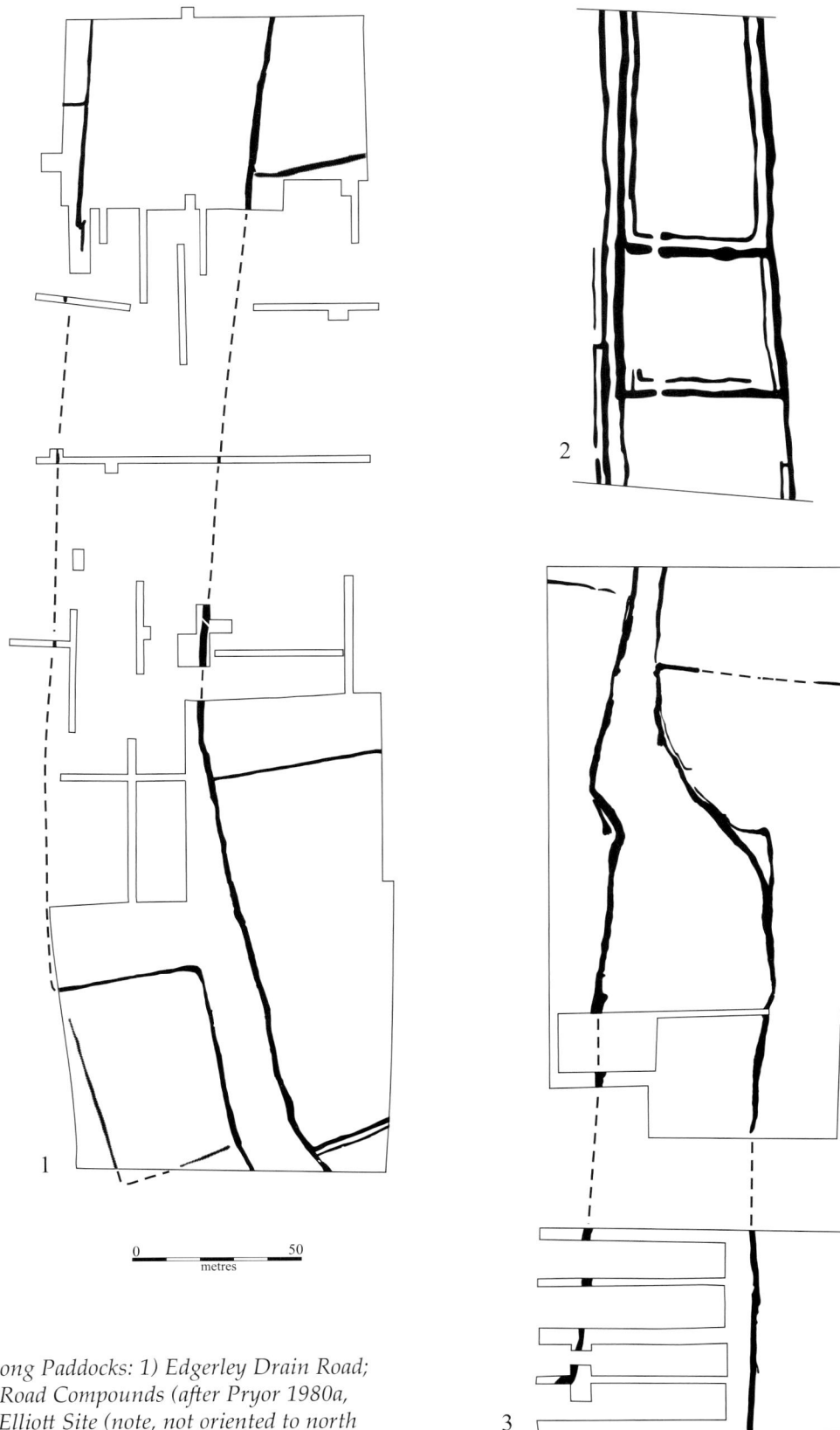

Figure 4.41. Long Paddocks: 1) Edgerley Drain Road;
2) the Newark Road Compounds (after Pryor 1980a,
fig. 19); 3) the Elliott Site (note, not oriented to north
but relative to fen-edge).

preservation of this material the assemblage does not significantly contribute to the understanding of local prehistoric stock management. Fortunately, the same is not true of the site's plant remains. Flying in the face of negative evidence of arable production based on the fieldsystem's pollen core (see Boreham above) and the non-recovery of querns, cereals featured in all of the site's major prehistoric phases (see Simmons & de Vareilles above). While these foodstuffs could, theoretically, have been brought into the locale and are not themselves necessarily markers of permanent settlement, the occurrence of chaff in the samples from both the earlier and later Neolithic, and also the later Bronze Age, would seem to indicate on-site processing and probably nearby cultivation. In this regard, the evidence of F.29 and F.57 — a Middle/later Bronze Age pit and

posthole — is particularly informative, as their samples included arable crop weeds; the extent to which the fieldsystem related to arable (*vs* pastoral) production will be a theme of this volume's concluding chapter.

Beyond this, Edgerley's samples also tell of other plant-use. This includes the degree to which wild plants featured in the Neolithic. Extending to hazelnuts during both its 'Early'- and 'Late'-phase deposits, during the latter it also involved wild sloe-berry and apple/pear. Equally important, however, is the unequivocal evidence of flax in the site's Collared Urn contexts. Presumably relating to cloth production, as will be further discussed in Chapter 6, this may well tell of the role then (or, better, lack thereof) of wool in the earlier/Middle Bronze Age and further reflect upon the cattle *vs* sheep economy issue.

CHAPTER 5

The Tower Works Investigations — Fengate West

Matt Brudenell, Christopher Evans & Gavin Lucas

Lying some 300–400 m inland from the fen-edge proper and relatively 'high' at 5–6 m OD (and well in the heart of Fengate's industrial estate; Fig. 1.1), the situation of this site differed markedly from the other two. From the outset, we were aware that it had the potential to yield significant results, as it straddled the southern margins of the quarries where Abbott had made his findings early in the last century. In short, the work offered the opportunity to set Fengate's archaeology within an earlier historical context.

Fieldwork on the site began in 1997, when Lucas directed a programme of evaluation trial trenching (Fig. 5.1; Lucas 1997). Thereafter, the development went 'cold' until 2004, when three further phases were conducted in response to revised building plans. The first, a test-pit survey, essentially confirmed the results of the early evaluation as regards the scale of the earlier twentieth-century quarrying across the northern half of the site and the widespread survival of a deep buried soil horizon elsewhere (Cooper 2004a). This was followed by still limited trial trenching across its southeastern quarter, where the brunt of the building was to occur within the area of archaeological survival (i.e. beyond the quarry limits; Williams 2004). Based on this, a seven-week long excavation then occurred throughout the latter zone under the direction of Brudenell (2005a).

Our concern in this chapter is, essentially, with the first and last of the these investigations — the 1997 evaluation and 2004 excavations *per se* — with Cooper and Williams's fieldwork only discussed as necessary within the context of the latter phase. It would not be our usual practice to so highlight and publish evaluation results as they are. Yet it is warranted in this case because the '97 evaluation delineated an area of dense Early Iron Age settlement extending throughout the site's western quarter, an area that has still yet to be developed (and, thus, excavated as such). The attention given to this sub-site is, moreover, further justified as it appears to represent an extension of the settlement of that date that was discovered by Abbott and, subsequently, brought to national notice by Hawkes and Fell's 1945 study of its material,

Aside from providing a chance to investigate in detail the area's buried soil (particularly as regards middening/'dark earth-type' formation processes), the 2004 excavations primarily focussed upon the site's Romano-British occupation and, indeed, Abbott had quarry findings of such a date nearby. Given this, the development site's archaeology — and, thereby, the format of this chapter — is effectively divided into two: the evaluation-identified westward Early Iron Age settlement and, in the east, the excavated Romano-British complex.

Finally, a summary of Boreham and Peachey's palaeo-environmental researches from the adjacent portion of the fen-edge at the Sewage treatment Site (including important pollen core results) is also presented here.

The 1997 evaluation

Prior to the twentieth century, the site-area predominantly lay under pasture. By 1910 gravel extraction had commenced, continuing until around 1940 (see Chapter 2). It was during the 1960s that the site's industrial development began, seeing the construction of the Tower Works engineering plant, whose standing buildings and 'hard' surfaces later circumscribed the location of the evaluation trenching. Nevertheless, further augmented by subsequent trenching (see below), the Unit's programme was able to firmly establish the southern limits of the quarrying area.

Through our many fieldwork phases, much attention was given to the quarries themselves. We had, as it proved optimistically, hoped that they might yield further insights into Abbott's collections, perhaps either being dug in a 'strip-style' leaving intact narrow spines of gravel natural where some archaeology would survive or, at the very least, including early finds within their backfills. Neither proved forthcoming, and clearly the quarrying was carried out with high efficiency as, despite extensive searches, no redeposited prehistoric or Roman material was found in quarry fills.

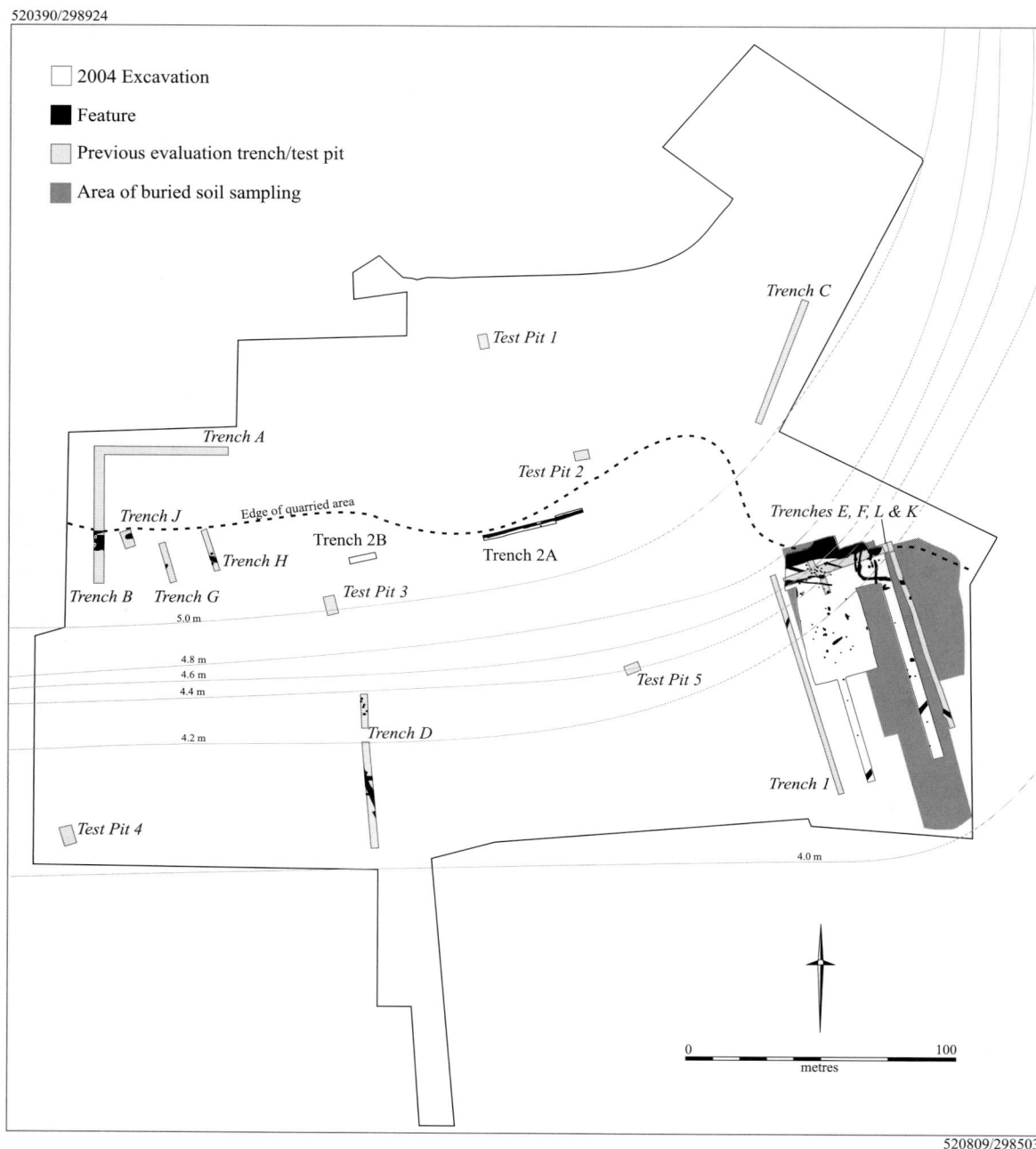

520390/298924

- ☐ 2004 Excavation
- ■ Feature
- ▨ Previous evaluation trench/test pit
- ▨ Area of buried soil sampling

Trench C

Test Pit 1

Trench A

Test Pit 2

Trench J

Edge of quarried area

Trench 2B

Trenches E, F, L & K

Trench H

Trench 2A

Trench B   Trench G

Test Pit 3

5.0 m

4.8 m
4.6 m
4.4 m

Test Pit 5

4.2 m

Trench D

Trench I

Test Pit 4

4.0 m

0   100
metres

520809/298503

FIGURE 5.1. *Site Plan.*

In response to the building plans (and immediate area 'availability'), our '97 trenches were largely confined to two areas: a series across the western half of the site and an eastern grouping (Fig. 5.1). As it was in the latter area (Trenches, E, F, L & K) that the Roman settlement was largely found (and whose results are discussed in the context of the 2004 excavations below), they need not be further outlined within this section. Rather, we will almost entirely be concerned

with those to the east (within the site's 'middle zone', aside from two possible Romano-British ditches, F.36 and F.37; Trench D only revealed features of post-Medieval/modern attribution).

Before progressing, one final caveat needs to be rehearsed. This is the recognition that we are strictly dealing with evaluation-generated results and that, due to limited trench exposure, this invariably carries a high degree of uncertainty. There is no cause,

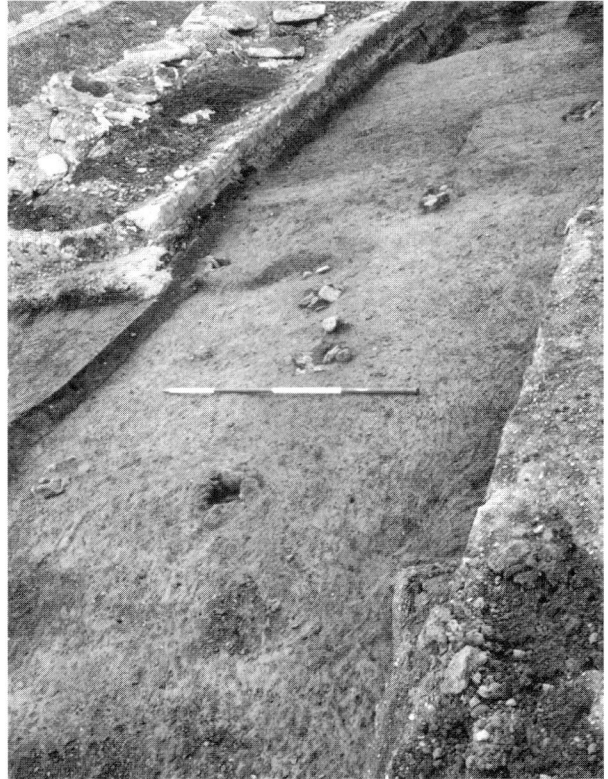

FIGURE 5.2. *Buried Soil Survival (1997): left, Trench J (with F.50, right); right, Trench E with cornbrash-packed postholes in surface (photographs: G. Lucas).*

therefore, to present the features in nuanced detail and, instead, the data can be dealt with broadly.

Within the trenches, three early 'ditch candidates' were excavated which may relate to the area-wide, second-millennium BC fieldsystem (Fig. 5.3). Of these, the attribution of F.15 (Trench F, in the east; see also Fig. 5.14 below) and F.34 in Trench G to this period are likely. Respectively 1.25 m and 1 m wide and 0.87 and 0.4 m deep, with steep-sided/'V'-shaped profiles and quite sterile, buried soil-derived fills, these seemed typical 'Fengate system' boundaries. Given its more limited exposure, there is some ambiguity about whether F.35, in Trench H (falling on the return, northeast–southwest orientation in respect to the other two ditches), was actually a ditch terminal as opposed to some manner of elongated pit. Nonetheless, with Early Iron Age pottery occurring within its upper profile, it was probably also contemporary.

Otherwise, the earliest features on the site consist of a group of pits in Trench B (there intercutting) and extending east at least as far as Trench J, but not much further (none occurred in Trench G; Fig. 5.3). They were backfilled with redeposited natural and their cuts were generally steep-sided with sharp, angular corners. Although no complete cut-plans of any were exposed, they were presumed to be of sub-rectangular or sub-square form. The paucity of weathering on the edges and the almost horizontal layering of the fills suggest fairly rapid, intentional backfilling. Some settling of an organic-rich buried soil/'dark earth' occurred in the tops of these features (see below and Figs. 5.2 & 5.4).

F.18 - A fairly steep-sided, square-cornered cut, *c.* 2 m wide with an irregular-flat base (0.45 m deep). Its basal profile was filled with an orange grey silty sand with occasional gravel and cornbrash fragments (*c.* 0.15–0.2 m thick), above which was a mid-dark brown-grey sandy silt with very rare fragments of cornbrash (*c.* 0.1–0.3 m thick). The uppermost deposit was a mid grey-brown, slightly mottled, silt with occasional pebbles (*c.* 0.1–0.15 m thick); pottery and bone were recovered from the latter two fills. As shown on Figure 5.3, this was truncated by F.16, the north-lying quarry pits.

F.17 - Separated by only a thin seam of gravel natural from F.18, was a similarly-shaped pit cut, *c.* 1.6 m wide, with a slight ridge of natural along its base (0.4 m deep). Within the hollows on either side of this ridge lay bedded a mottled orange-brown sandy silt and a mottled mid grey-brown silt. Above this, on the south side, lay a mottled mid grey-brown silt (*c.* 0.3 m thick) and, sealing all, was a mid grey silt with occasional small pebble inclusions (*c.* 0.2 m thick); bone and pot occurred throughout the feature.

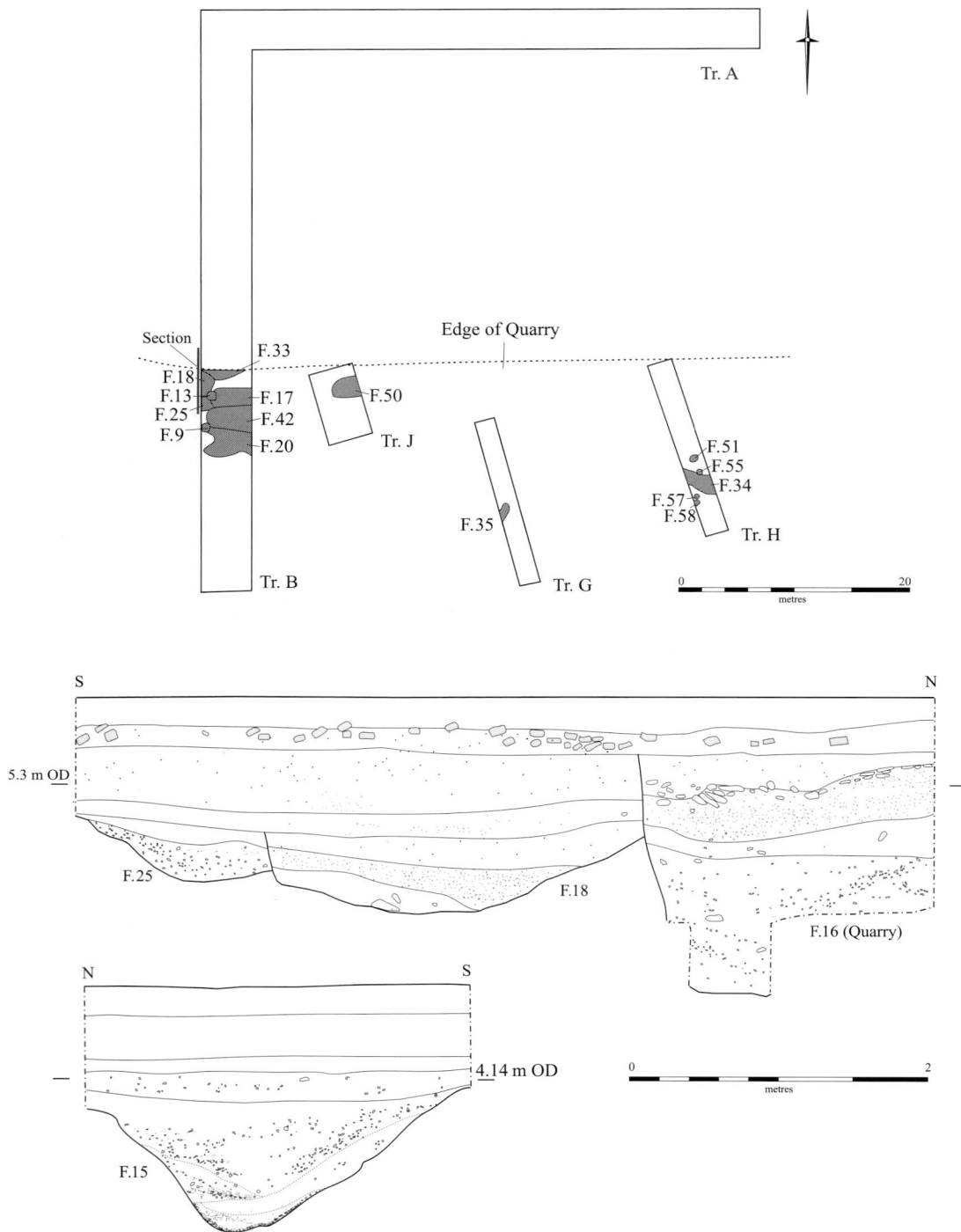

FIGURE 5.3. *West area base-plan, with F.15, F.16, F.18 & F.25 sections below.*

F.25 - A fairly gently sloping cut-edge coming down onto a flat base (*c.* 0.2 m deep), with two layered fills. The basal fill was a mixed grey silt with orange sand, *c.* 0.2–0.25 m thick. This was overlain by a mid-pale grey-brown, iron-stained sandy silt with occasional gravel and pebbles (*c.* 0.15–0.2 m thick); truncated by F.18.

F.33 - The northernmost of these pits (0.3 m deep), like the last had a gentle slope and was filled by a mixed grey-brown sandy silt with occasional pebbles and orange sandy mottling (*c.* 0.3 m thick); truncated by F.18.

FIGURE 5.4. *Trench B: top, F.17 and F.25; below, F.9 and F.42 (photographs: G. Lucas).*

F.42 - Lying furthest south and similar in its fills to F.25, was a stepped deep cut with fairly steeply-sloping sides coming down onto a flat base 0.65 m deep and at least 1.1 m wide. The basal fill was a very mixed mid grey-brown silt and orange sandy silt with gravel (*c.* 0.2 m thick) with occasional charcoal, burnt cornbrash and other burnt stone fragments. Near the top of this deposit was a concentration/dump of large animal bone, including mandibles and long bone shafts. The upper deposit (*c.* 0.3 m thick), was a very mixed orange sandy silt with gravel and patches of pale-mid grey silt, which become darker with depth; pottery, flint and bone occurred in this fill.

Bedding within the top of this was possibly the uppermost fill and/or the base of the lower buried soil (they being identical). Associated with this, perhaps as a separate dump within the same backfilled pit, was F.20 ([047]), a compact, dark grey-brown clay silt with occasional sub-angular pebbles and flecks of charcoal. Along its southern edge there was a heavy concentration/dump of pottery, totalling some 372 sherds, which was spit-excavated for vertical control.

Another, possibly similar, pit occurred in Trench J:

F.50 - A shallow, but fairly steep-sided cut, *c.* 2 m wide, was filled with a mid-pale grey-brown loam with orange sandy mottling and occasional pebbles (*c.* 0.3 m thick).

Sealing the pits was a buried soil which was exceptionally dark in the middle of Trench B ([001]/[027]) and throughout Trench J ([107]; Fig. 5.2), but was much paler at the southern end of Trench B and in Trenches G and H [003]. In the former areas, it also held high quantities of artefacts, especially pottery which typically consisted of large, unabraded sherds. The dark, organic nature of this soil is almost certainly the product of occupation and/or middening. Its spread, which can be estimated to cover a minimum area of *c.* 200 sq.m, probably extends to the north (where it had already been quarried away) and east (under the former Showcase Cinema car park); however, it also seemed to reflect the extent of the underlying pits and rested directly upon both them and a possibly truncated/de-turfed land surface. Between this horizon and the pits was, however, a slightly paler (and 'cleaner') buried soil ([028]; 0.1 m thick), with associated postholes cutting through it in Trench B and a laid gravel surface in Trench J. These postholes, F.9 and F.13, were quite robust (respectively, 0.43 and 0.65–0.7 m in dia; 0.34 and 0.3 m deep) and included frequent charcoal, bone and pottery within their fills.

In Trench H, a further series of postholes were identified (F.51, F.55, F.57 & F.58) which may or may not be contemporary with those in Trench B; they are of a slightly different proportion, being somewhat smaller (0.05–0.2 m deep).

Material culture
Apart from the site's animal bone and later prehistoric pottery assemblages (reported in detail below), the evaluation yielded relatively few finds. The base from an oblique, later Neolithic, arrowhead was amongst the 23 worked flints recovered. Though some evidence of possible metalworking was forthcoming from the Early Iron Age settlement swathe (all from Trench B and consisting of two pieces of slag, together with a crucible fragment from F.13), 12 further pieces of slag were found within its southwestern Roman 'quarter'. Generally, the metalwork itself was undistinguished (three iron objects of post-medieval attribution), with the only noteworthy find being a mid-second-century Sestertius coin, possible of Faustina Senior, from Trench E.

The later prehistoric pottery
(MATT BRUDENELL *with* J.D. HILL)
The evaluation produced a moderate, but well-preserved, assemblage of Early Iron Age pottery, totalling 455 sherds (4500 g) and with a mean sherd weight of 9.9 g. For this analysis, all sherds were examined and recorded in line with the guidelines of the Prehistoric Ceramic Research Group. Sherds weighing less than 1 g (classified as crumbs) were excluded, and are not quantified in this report.

Fabric series

G1: Moderate medium–coarse grog, sparse medium–coarse shell, sparse quartz-sand.

QS1: Moderate fine–medium sub-angular–sub-rounded quartz sand, sparse medium clay pellets (?), and sparse–moderate medium (shell?); very hard.

QS2: Moderate–common fine–medium sub-angular–sub-rounded quartz sand and sparse–moderate medium voids (shell?); medium–very hard.

QS3: Sparse fine–medium sub-angular–sub-rounded quartz sand, sparse fine shell flecking.

Q1: Common fine–medium sub-angular quartz with sparse medium–coarse sub-angular quartz grits; hard–very hard and abrasive to touch.

S1: Common–very common coarse–very coarse plate-like fossil shell. The shell is poorly-sorted, and often protrudes through the surfaces of sherds. From time to time the shell has leached out from the surface, and is only visible when the sherd is broken open; medium hard to very hard.

S2: Moderate medium–coarse sorted shell, sparse sub-angular–sub-rounded quartz sand, very rare medium–coarse partially crushed and partially burnt flint.

S3: Common–abundant fine–medium shell, rare–sparse quartz sand.

S4: Sparse–moderate finely crushed shell with moderate–common very fine shell flecking, sparse–moderate quartz sand.

V: Common medium–very coarse voids left from the complete leaching of shell; very friable and easy to crush between the fingers.

TABLE 5.1. *Early Iron Age Pottery — fabric frequency, and its relationship to burnishing and vessel counts.*

Fabric	No./wt.(g) sherds	% assemblage by wt. (g)	No./wt. (g) burnished	% Fabric burnished	No. vessels	No. vessels burnished
G1	6/35	0.8	-	-	-	-
Q1	15/62	1.4	-	-	-	-
QS1	65/915	20.3	46/744	81.3	2	1
QS2	45/402	8.9	31/286	71.1	3	3
QS3	12/57	1.3	5/16	28.1	2	-
S1	171/2114	47.0	-	-	7	-
S2	23/149	3.3	-	-	1	-
S3	69/489	10.9	7/63	12.9	13	2
S4	43/250	5.6	22/120	48.0	8	3
V	6/27	0.6	-	-	1	-
Total	**455/4500**		**111/1229**		**37**	**9**

Assemblage characteristics

The assemblage comprised a range of fine- and coarse ware angular jars and bowls of tripartite or bipartite form, alongside a series of vessels with more rounded and slack shoulders. Based on the total number of different rims, the assemblage represents a minimum of 37 vessels (31 rims, six bases). Shell tempered fabrics, and fabrics with shell and sand, dominated the assemblage, notably groups S1 and QS1. Sherds with grog (G1) or common sand inclusions (Q1) were extremely rare, with just 21 examples. Evidence for burnishing was absent from the assemblage. Instead, finewares were characterized by careful smoothing, and were restricted to the finer shell and sandier fabrics (S3, S4, QS1, QS2 and QS3). A quarter of sherds (111 sherds, 1229 g) were smoothed, most displaying well-fired dark grey/black or orangey/buff surfaces. Incised decoration was only present on two small smoothed sherds (total weight of 6 g): one from the lower buried soil [28], the other from posthole F.9. Both had simple incised horizontal lines. More complex geometric patterning, of the kind characterizing the fineware vessels in the Wyman Abbott collection (Hawkes & Fell 1945), and to a more limited extent, the Vicarage Farm pottery (Pryor 1974a), was absent from this assemblage. The extent to which this is chronologically significant is debatable. Vessels of this type are infrequently found in LBA/EIA contexts and their frequency in the Wyman Abbot material may be somewhat unusual/atypical.

Coarseware decoration was prolific, being present on nine per cent of the pottery by sherd count (41 sherds), or 15 per cent by weight (664 g). A range of decorative techniques were employed, including finger-tip/nail decoration to the rim-top, rim-exterior, shoulder, neck, and applied cordons, and diagonal tooling or slashing to the rim-exterior. There was also a single example of a pre-firing perforation, though it was unclear where this occurred on the vessel. In the absence of independent dating evidence or clearly stratified ceramic sequences, the frequency of decoration is often used as a guide to assessing the chronological position of LBA/EIA assemblages, particularly for the distinction between early 'Plainware' and later 'Decorated' Post-Deverel Rimbury pottery (Barrett 1980). Unfortunately, the frequency of decoration cannot be calculated in a straightforward manner, as ornamentation tends to be confined to restricted zones on the vessels (primarily rim, neck and shoulder). Gross counts, such as the proportion of decorated to undecorated sherds/feature sherds tend to either over- or underestimate the incidence of decoration (Needham 1996, 112).

One quantification method which appears more reliable and allows more ready comparison is the frequency of rim decoration. Of the 31 different rims in the assemblage, eight (26 per cent) have some form of rim ornamentation. This figure is slightly greater than that calculated for the highest stratigraphic units (L & M) at Runnymede Bridge Area 16 (Needham & Spence 1996, 12, table 14), dated to the late ninth or early eighth century bc. At a local level, the figure is over double that recorded for the LBA assemblages

from Striplands Farm, Longstanton, and Colne Fen, Earith (dated typologically to the tenth–late ninth century bc), where decoration occurs on just 8–13 per cent of vessel rims (Brudenell 2005b; 2006; forthcoming a). Although comparative figures are currently unavailable for the Wyman Abbott material (Hawkes & Fell 1945) or that from the Vicarage Farm sub-Site (Pryor 1974a), rough estimates of rim decoration can be made using the illustrated ceramics. In total, 14 of the 60 rims published from the Wyman Abbott collection (23 per cent) appear to show rim decoration, whilst eight of the 23 rims from Vicarage Farm are ornamented (35 per cent). The percentage of decoration from Tower Works fits comfortably within this bracket, matching much broader patterns across southern England, where levels of decoration fall around or above the 20 per cent mark during the LBA/EIA transition (whether calculated by the number of decorated sherds, e.g. Potterne (Gingell & Morris 2000, 154), Petter's Sports Field (O'Connell 1986, 63); decorated vessels, e.g. Runnymede Bridge (Longley & Needham 1980, 70–71), Budbury (Wainwright 1970, 138); or decorated rims, e.g. Mucking North Ring (Barrett & Bond 1988, 28).

The assemblage can be considered in more detail by analysing the pottery groups from individual features/layers. Ceramics were recovered from a variety of contexts, most deriving from the pits and the upper buried soil in Trenches B and J (Table 5.2). Around seven per cent of sherds were residual in Roman features and post-medieval gravel extraction quarries. These quarries abutted the group of features in Trench B, and are likely to have disturbed Iron Age pits in the vicinity. Some mixing of Iron Age and Roman material also occurred in the upper buried soil [107], implying that this was a long-lived topsoil. Undisturbed features were stratified below this layer, including the pits, postholes, a gravel surface and the lower buried soil. Although a sense of sequence was evident in the stratification of these buried contexts, there is little difference in the fabrics or forms of the pottery, suggesting that the material is broadly contemporary. The only sherd which could be of later date is the rim of a slack-shouldered vessel from posthole F.51. Whilst the form of this vessel is more emblematic of later Iron Age assemblages (c. 300 bc–ad 50), slack-shouldered vessels are present in LBA/EIA contexts.

One of the most intriguing assemblages was that drawn from the buried land surfaces in Trenches B and J, including pottery deriving from the upper and lower buried-soil horizons ([001], [027], [028] & [107]) and material resting on/in the gravel surface ([122]). Under normal circumstances such deposits are truncated or destroyed by later activity (mainly agricultural), with pottery only surviving in sub-surface features. As such, there are few opportunities to investigate whether pottery groups deposited in features are significantly different to those in other types of 'above-ground' contexts, such as floors, rubbish heaps, or the general ground surfaces surrounding settlements. The recovery of pottery from these surfaces is therefore significant, allowing the characteristics of breakage and discard to be compared with that from the pits and postholes. A comparison

TABLE 5.2. *Context of Early Iron Age pottery groups (MSW: mean sherd weight; MNV: minimum number of vessels).*

Context	Context/Feature no.	No. sherds	Weight (g)	MSW	MNV	No. refits
Pits	F.17, F.18, F.20, F.42	213	2437	11.4	9	99
Postholes	F.9, F.13, F.51, F.55, F.58	32	156	5.0	2	2
Gravel surface	[122]	13	76	5.8	17	2
Lower buried soil	[28]	14	95	6.8	1	2
Upper buried soil	[1], [27], [107]	142	1444	10.2	-	9
Residual (post-medieval quarrying)	[4], [6], [10], [12], [23], [24], [41]	27	188	6.9	5	-
Residual (Roman features)	F.12, F.56	3	15	5	1	-
Bronze Age ditch	F.15, F.34	8	72	9.3	-	2
Other	-	3	15	5.0	2	-
Total		455	4500		37	116

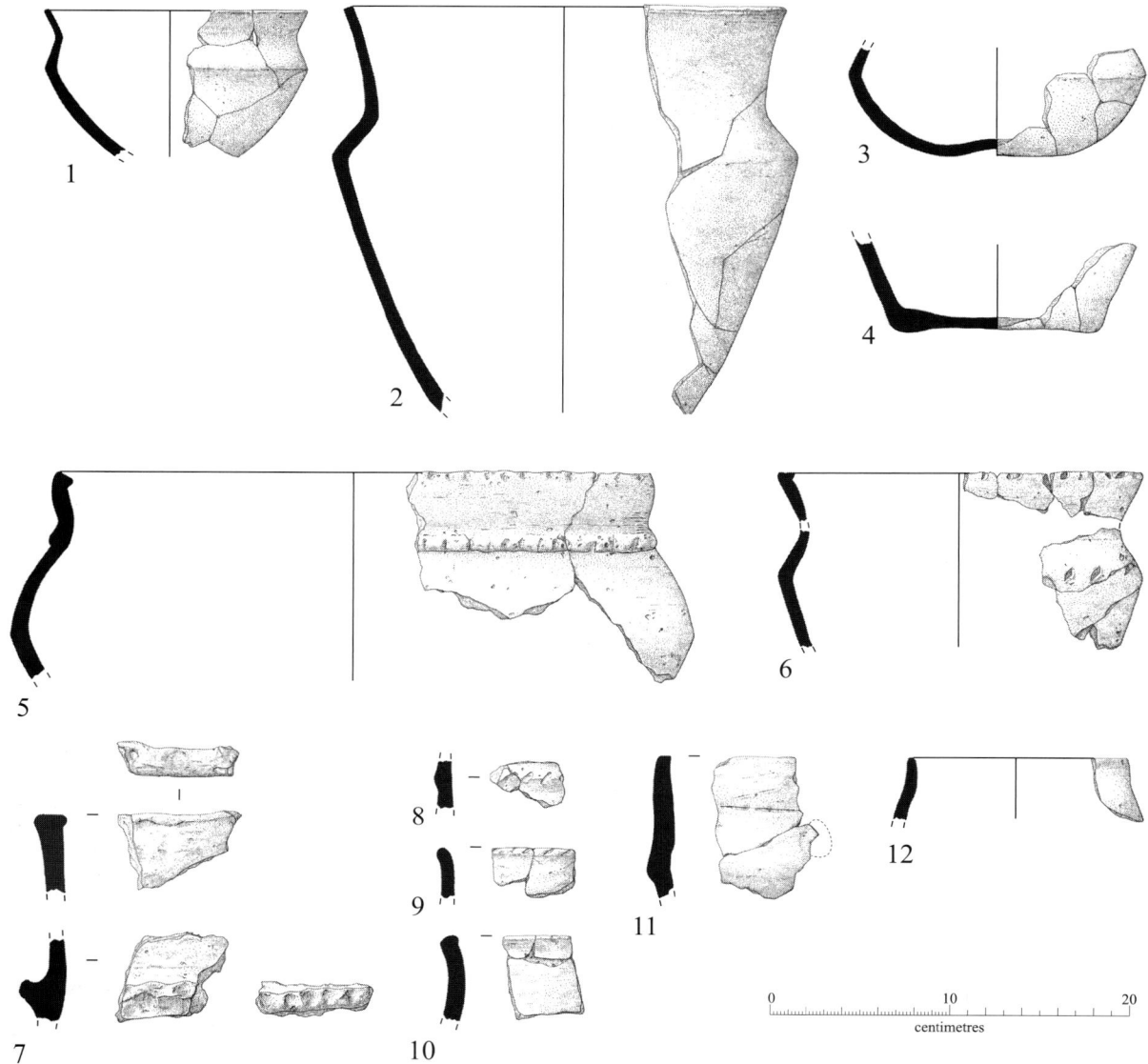

FIGURE 5.5. *Early Iron Age Pottery: 1) Fineware tripartite bowl with smoothed orange/buff exterior surface (rim dia. 13 cm, 11% of rim intact; Fabric QS1, Pit F.20); 2) fineware tripartite jar with smoothed brown to dark grey/back exterior surface, burnt on parts of the rim, shoulder and body (rim dia. 24 cm, 5% of rim intact; Fabric QS1, Pit F.20); 3) lower half of fineware tripartite bowl with omphalos base, with smoothed dark grey exterior surface and burnt along the shoulder and parts of the lower walls (base dia. 5 cm, 90% of base intact; Fabric QS2, Pit F.20); 4) base of fineware jar, with partially burnt, smoothed brown exterior, possibly belongs to the fineware jar (base dia. 12 cm, 40% of base intact; Fabric QS1, Pit F.20); 5) coarseware tripartite jar with finger-tip impressions (showing nail marks) on the exterior rim-edge, and on the applied neck-cordon; has a mid-light grey exterior and shows evidence of burning (rim dia. 33 cm, 37% of rim intact; Fabric S1, Pit F.20); 6) coarseware tripartite jar of 'situlate' form, with diagonally stabbed tooled impression on the shoulder, and vertical tooled impressions on the exterior rim-edge; has a light grey exterior and shows evidence of burning (rim dia. 19 cm, 25% of rim intact; Fabric S1, Pit F.20); 7) rim of coarseware jar with finger-tip impressions along the rim-top, and on applied neck-cordon (mid orangey-brown exterior; Fabric S1, Upper buried soil [01]/[27]); 8) applied cordon with diagonal tooled ornamentation, with dark grey exterior (Fabric QS1, Lower buried soil [28]); 9) rim of coarseware vessel with diagonal-slashed ornamentation along the exterior rim-edge, with dark grey-brown exterior (rim dia. 21 cm, 7% intact; Fabric S3, Pit F.17); 10) rim of coarseware vessel, with dark grey-brown exterior (Fabric S3, Upper buried soil [01]); 11) coarseware bipartite jar with shallow finger-tip impression on the neck, with dark grey-brown exterior (Fabric S3, Upper buried soil [01]); 12) slack-shouldered coarseware vessel, with dark to pale grey exterior (rim dia. 12 cm, 7% of rim intact; Fabric QS3, Pit F.20).*

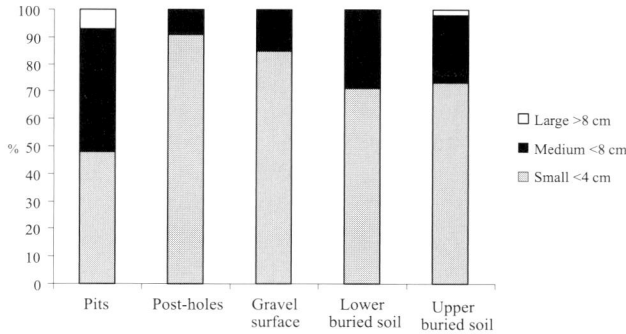

FIGURE 5.6. *Early Iron Age Pottery - Percentage of small, medium and large size sherds from the major contexts/ feature groups in Trenches B, J and H. Weight ranges for small sherds varied from 1–12 g (median 4 g); medium sherds between 6–58 g (median 14 g); and large sherds between 28–148 g (median 44 g).*

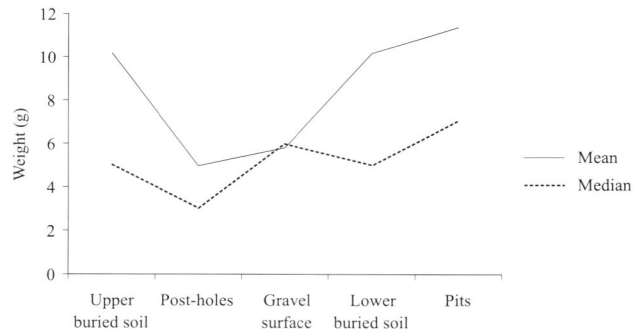

Figure 5.7. Mean and median weight of Early Iron Age sherds recovered from different contexts in Trenches B, J and H. Contexts are arranged in broad stratigraphic order from left (latest) to right (earliest).

of the percentage of different-sized sherds across major context groups has been used to discuss these.

The largest surface assemblage derived from the upper buried soil (142 sherds, 1444 g). A quarter of the sherds in this assemblage were of medium size, with a small fraction falling into the large size range. Other than the pits, this was the only context to contain sherds larger than 8 cm in size, albeit in very small quantities (just two sherds). Perhaps unsurprisingly, the frequency of different sherd sizes most closely resembles that from the lower buried soil, though the MSW was significantly lower. This supports the overall impression that sherds were less fragmented and abraded in the upper horizon. Taken together, the character of the assemblage from the buried soil probably typifies the level and condition of ceramic detritus scattered across the core areas of the settlement. These frequencies are therefore equivalent to the 'background' level of material incorporated into the topsoil or lying strewn across its surface. In totality, such deposits may contain a significant amount of material. For example, the fragments of at least 17 different vessels recovered from this horizon represent 46 per cent of the total recovered from the site. This figure gives some indication of the quantity of pottery concealed in this deposit relative to that in sub-surface features, and allows for some appreciation of how material is lost though truncation.

Sherds from the gravel surface were highly fragmented, with a MSW of just 5.8 g. The vast majority of sherds were of small size, with only a low proportion of medium-sized fragments and an absence of larger sherds. These small sherds probably became incorporated into this horizon through trampling, although it is possible that material was also deliberately added to maintain the surface. The character of the gravel surface assemblage broadly matches that recovered from the five postholes in Trenches B and H (F.9, F.13, F.51, F.55 & F.58). As with the gravel surface, these sherds may have been incidentally included within postholes, perhaps being washed into the hollows left by removed posts, or being accidentally incorporated into the post-packing.

The largest pottery assemblage derived from the pits stratified below the lower buried soil (F.17, F.18, F.20 & F.42). Pit F.20 produced the only significant group of pottery (200 sherds, 2338 g), including fragments from at least seven different vessels. Just under half of the sherds from the pit could be refitted (99 refits), allowing details of several of the vessels to be reconstructed. These included the partial-profiles of two fineware tripartite bowls, one with an omphalos base; a large fineware tripartite jar with tall neck and two decorated tripartite coarseware jars, one with an ornamented

cordon at the base of the neck. With perhaps the exception of the fineware jar, these vessels can be paralleled in the published Wyman Abbott material (Hawkes & Fell 1945). In particular, similarities exist between the form of the fineware bowls and the incised decorated examples from Pits B, L, K and R (Hawkes & Fell 1945, 200, figs. 2:206, 5:209 and 7), omphalos bases being preserved on a number of these vessels. Neck-cordoned coarsewares jars also occurred, with similar vessels from Pit A and G (Hawkes & Fell 1945, 197, figs. 1:204 and 4). This decorative trait was also present on a range of jars at West Harling, Norfolk, dated to the LBA/EIA transition (Clark & Fell 1953).

A variety of decorated tripartite coarseware jars of 'situlate' form are published from the Wyman Abbott collection as well as from West Harling. The rim form of the tripartite decorated jar in F.20 closely resembles that from Pit T (Hawkes & Fell 1945, 211, fig. 8). The closest parallel for the fineware jar from F.20 was found at Loft's Farm, Essex (Brown 1988, 266, fig. 15). The jar from this site displayed an equally tall neck, although it had simple incised lines around the rim, base of the neck and shoulder. A further parallel from Essex was found at Slough House Farm (Brown 1998, 134, fig. 96), though this too was intricately decorated.

In general, the F.20 pit-assemblage was characterized by a range of small and medium-sized sherds, with around ten per cent falling into the large size-range. The high frequency of medium-sized sherds far exceeds those from other contexts, indicating a dump of comparatively 'freshly' broken sherd material. It was clear from the condition of the sherds that a significant number had been re-fired or burnt prior to deposition, including parts of most vessels represented. A shoulder sherd from one of the fineware bowls had become brittle and highly porous through burning, whilst the walls, shoulder and rim of the fineware jar had been discoloured and warped, with evidence of spalling on the body. It is possible that the vessels were wasters, with the broken sherds being gathered up and dumped at the end of an unsuccessful firing; however, refits between burnt and unburnt sherds imply that the re-firing occurred *after* the vessels were broken, perhaps indicating a more complex and protracted sherd history. Whatever the precise details of the post-breakage sequence, it is clear that the dump of pottery in F.20 is both quantatively and qualitatively different to the other pottery groups from the site.

In normal circumstances, a modest-sized assemblage such as this would not require lengthy discussion;

however, the overall importance of this pottery is elevated by its association with the Wyman Abbot material, collected between 1908–23 from gravel pits both within and around the Tower Works site. Despite questions about the dating, contextual reliability and provenance of this material, the Wyman Abbott collection continues to form one of the major type-site assemblages for the Late Bronze Age and Early Iron Age in northern East Anglia, the other being from West Harling, Norfolk (Clark & Fell 1953). Together, these collections have formed the basis for dating ceramics for a 500-year period throughout large parts of northern East Anglia and the East Midlands since the 1940s, mainly because few other sites have been excavated and published in subsequent years; however, neither of these assemblages were recovered in excavations of a modern standard, and in addition, there are no associated radiocarbon or other scientific dates on which to fix the chronological arrangement of the pottery.

As a result there has been considerable debate about the actual date of the Fengate material. The original phasing of ceramics outlined by Hawkes & Fell (1945) has been widely contested; particularly the order of the phase divisions (Champion 1975; Cunliffe 1974; Pryor 1984; Needham 1996). Moreover, the currency of certain decorative schemes remains to be confirmed, namely those found on the fineware bowls. These distinctive ceramics were used by Cunliffe to define his Fengate-Cromer style, which he dated from the fifth to third centuries BC (Cunliffe 1974). Radiocarbon dates from Pryor's excavations have supported a generally late date range; however, a much longer time span for this decorative tradition has been suggested by Champion (1975), and parallels for some of the decorated vessels are found at Loft's Farm, Essex (Phase 2), where a date between the eighth and seventh centuries BC is suggested (Brown 1988, 270).

It is within the context of these debates that the Tower Works assemblage gains importance, providing new evidence from which to address the outstanding problems of the pottery sequence at Fengate. In particular, it is the relative typological relationship between the Tower Works and Vicarage Farm material that is most informative, given the conditions under which the pottery was retrieved and the availability of absolute dates. Even though there are undeniable connections between the Tower Works and Wyman Abbott material, the latter can no longer be seen to offer a reliable guide to the typo-chronological development of Fengate ceramics. We must, therefore, turn to the Tower Works and Vicarage Farm material to address these issues. Fortunately, a useful distinction can be drawn between these two assemblages on

the basis of vessel-base morphology, Vicarage Farm lacking omphalos bases and Tower Works lacking pedestals or foot-rings. The latter base form appears in the ceramic repertoire sometime after 600 BC (Barrett 1980), being more prevalent in assemblages of the fifth–fourth century BC (broadly matching the late radiocarbon determinations for Vicarage Farm). In contrast, omphalos bases have a Late Bronze Age ancestry, and continue to form a component of the earliest Iron Age assemblages. It is therefore likely that the Tower Works assemblage pre-dates that from Vicarage Farm, and probably belongs to the opening centuries of the Early Iron Age, dating from *c.* 800–600 BC. This would make the pottery broadly contemporary with material from West Harling (Clarke & Fell 1953), and the Phase 2 outer enclosure ditch silts at Loft's Farm (Brown 1988), both of which yielded similar vessel forms and decorative schemes.

In summary, the Tower Works assemblage bridges an important gap in the Fengate ceramic sequence from the end of the Late Bronze Age to the later stages of the Early Iron Age. Pottery of this date is often considered to be 'transitional' or of the 'earliest' Iron Age, belonging to Barrett's Post-Deverel Rimbury 'decorated' phase (Barrett 1980). To date, few such assemblages have been identified in northern East Anglia, owing to a general difficulty in distinguishing between Late Bronze Age and Early Iron Age ceramics (Brudenell forthcoming b; Knight 2002; Needham 1996). The combined Tower Works and Vicarage Farm material, therefore, provides a refined local pottery sequence for the Early Iron Age. Moreover, this new material continues to shed light on the Wyman Abbott collections which, by comparison, probably span much of the first half of the first millennium BC. On a more general level, all three pottery groups demonstrate the intensity of activity across a relatively small 'inland' area at Fengate. This can be contrasted with the picture emerging from the 'fen-edge proper', where sites and assemblages of a comparable magnitude are currently lacking.

Given the concentration of fieldwork along the lower fen-edge, it is notable how little Late Bronze Age and Early Iron Age pottery has been recovered from this zone. Only small quantities of EIA pottery were retrieved from Pryor's excavations on Newark Road, Fourth Drove (Pryor 1980a, 106, 156) and Cat's Water sub-Sites (Pryor 1984, 139–53), whilst recent excavations at Edgerley Drain Road and The Elliot Site have yielded a combined total of just 108 LBA/EIA sherds (2064 g). It is against this backdrop that the relatively small assemblages from Tower Works and Vicarage Farm stand out, especially given the limited size of the exposures in this area.

Environmental and economic evidence

Macro-botanical remains (CHRIS STEVENS)

Twelve samples of ten litres were floated for macro-botanical remains, using a 500 mm mesh to catch the flot. The flot was then sorted for identifiable plant remains, using a stereo-binocular microscope. The results are presented in Table 5.3. Relating to this report's immediate focus, the findings from three Roman samples will here be omitted.

Most of the samples produced remains of cereals, with grains of barley, (*Hordeum* sp.) and wheat (*Triticum* sp.) represented within the samples. From the remains of chaff, six-row barley would seem to be present, whilst glume wheats would also seem to be represented.

Several common arable weed species were also present: fat-hen (*Chenopodium album*) and knot-grass (*Polygonum aviculare*) in particular, as well as bindweed

TABLE 5.3. *Charred plant-macros.*

Trench	B	B	B	B	B	J	B	H	H
Feature	7	13	6				9	51	55
Context	27	30	14	95	106	107	20	112	114
Sample	1	2	3	4	5	7	8	9	10
Date	EIA	EIA	EIA ?	EIA	EIA	EIA	EIA	EIA	EIA
Feature type	midden	ph	pit	pit	pit	midden	ph	ph	ph
Chenopodiaceae (undiff.)				2					
Chenopodium urbicum/rubrum					1				
Chenopodium album				10	21				1
Atriplex sp.				1					1
Montia fontana ssp. *chondrosperma*									1
Polygonaceae (undiff.)									
Persicaria maculosa					1				
Polygonum aviculare				8	12				
Fallopia convolvulus					1				
Thlaspi arvense					1				
Vicia cf. *sativa*									
Vicia/Lathyrus spp.									
Medicago/Trifolium sp.									1
Trifolium sp.									
Trifolium cf. *pratense*					1				
cf. *Hyoscyamus niger*					1				
Plantago lanceolata									
Galium sp.							1		
Galium aparine					1				
Festuca sp.									
Poa sp.					1				
Poa cf. *annua*					1				
Lolium sp.					cf. 1				
Bromus secalinus					cf. 1				
buds species indet									
Seed indet small <2.5 mm								1	
Cereals									
Hordeum sp. (grains undiff.)		2							
Hordeum sp. (tail grains undiff.)								1	
Hordeum sp. (rachis fragments)				1	5				
Hordeum sp. (6-row rachis fragments)					1				
Triticum undiff. (grains)						1			
Triticum cf. *dicoccum/spelta* (grains)		4							
Triticum dicoccum/spelta (glume bases)				1				1	
Triticum spelta (glume bases)									
Cereals undiff. (grains)	1	3	3	4		2	1		
Parenchyma	1				4		5	2	
Oak charcoal	1	+++		2	++			5	

(*Fallopia convolvulus*), orache (*Atriplex* sp.), redshank (*Persicaria maculosa*), blinks (*Montia fontanum subsp. Chondrosperma*), field penny-cress (*Thlaspi arvense*), cleavers (*Galium aparine*), perennial rye grass (*Lolium* sp.) and brome grass (*Bromus* sp.).

The samples appear to represent waste from the processing of cereal crops, mainly barley and glume wheats; these may have been grown together as a maslin. The weed species seem to be indicative of lighter sandier soils, especially field penny-cress and blinks (though the latter is more common upon wetter soils). The finding of the spelt glume in the Late Bronze Age sample would seem to confirm the cultivation of this crop at this early date as was also seen at Barleycroft Farm (see Evans & Knight 2000).

The findings of larger numbers of seeds of smaller-seeded species presents an interesting comparison to the samples from Barleycroft Farm, which were dominated to a greater extent by seeds of larger seeded species (see Chapter 2 above). The ratio of large to small seeded species is probably related to the amount of processing carried out prior to storage, with samples high in smaller seeded species possibly attesting to the storing of crops in a more unprocessed state. This, in turn, may be related to the relative size of households, with smaller households unable to process crops to the same stage as those with larger numbers of individuals. The possibility exists, then, that the households at the Tower Works Site may have been slightly smaller in size than those represented at Barleycroft; however, richer and greater numbers of samples from both sites would be needed to confirm this trend. The high numbers of barley rachis fragments at this site would tend to also support the inference that less processing had been carried out prior to storage.

Faunal remains (MARTA MORENO-GARCÍA)

A total of 482 bone fragments (including teeth) were recovered from the Early Iron Age features; in contrast, the Roman contexts were very poor with only 17 bone fragments recovered. This analysis will, therefore, deal only with the former material.

During analysis, re-fitting fragments were unified and counted as one specimen. Of the total 482 specimens, 89 (18 per cent) could be identified to species (Table 5.4). Unfortunately, the bones were highly fragmentary and eroded, limiting the number that could be identified to species. Two general size categories were therefore created: cow-sized (CSZ), which could possibly include the remains of horse, cow and red deer; and sheep-sized (SSZ), which could include the remains of sheep, goat, roe deer and pig. A total of 121 fragments (25 per cent) could be identified

to this level, bringing the total identified portion of the assemblage to 210 fragments (44 per cent).

Identification was aided by the use of material from the CAU and the criteria of Schmid (1972). Bone fragments were recorded individually to give the Number of Identified Specimens (NISP). Minimum Numbers of Elements (MNE) were calculated on the basis of overlapping bone areas, with fusion state taken into account where possible. The highest MNE for each species was used to calculate the Minimum Number of Individuals (MNI). Metric analysis follows von den Driesch (1976). Bones were aged based on epiphyseal fusion dates (Silver 1969) and tooth eruption and wear patterns (Payne 1973).

The highly eroded state of the bone made assessment of butchery marks difficult, but these were recorded where visible. Taphonomic bone changes (such as weathering and carnivore gnawing) were recorded where visible, as were skeletal pathologies.

Species representation

All bones identified were of the domesticates: cow, horse, sheep/goat and pig. The most commonly represented species, both for NISP and MNI is cow, followed by sheep/goat and pig (Tables 5.4–5.5); however, it must be noted that this relationship is dependent upon ignoring the large number of specimens in the sheep-sized category (94), many of which are likely to have belonged to sheep/goat. The overall number of individual animals represented in this assemblage (9) is very low, which means that any conclusions drawn from it must be extremely tentative.

Bos Taurus - Cattle bones made up the largest proportion of both the NISP and MNI, suggesting that they may have been the main providers of meat on the site, especially when the relative size of cow and sheep/goat carcasses are taken into account.

All portions of the carcass are present with the exception of the carpals and phalanges. The lack of these elements may be indicative of the stages of carcass processing, but is much more likely to relate to the hand-retrieval of specimens and the small size of the assemblage. The presence of skull and mandible fragments within the assemblage suggests that these animals would have been butchered on site. Ages could be calculated for four individuals. These indicated the presence of two very old adults, one adult just over two years old and one young adult. Both of the older animals were suffering from malocclusion of the teeth, probably related to their age. The fact that two of four cows identified within the assemblage were in the 'very old' category may indicate that they were being used for traction.

Ovicaprids - Sheep/goat were the second most frequently represented species in the assemblage. Most portions of the carcass were represented, but the numbers of individual elements were not high. Only one individual could be aged (from a right mandible): an adult of 4–6 years. The teeth of this animal had a build-up of calculus on the lingual side and there is evidence of attrition between the fourth premolar and first molar, related to overcrowding within the dentition.

TABLE 5.4. *Animal bone, number of specimens by feature type (the number of loose teeth is indicated in parentheses).*

Species	Pits (F.17 & F.42)	Buried soil [001], [027], [028], [107]	Gravel surface [122]	Postholes (F.13, F.9 & F.55)	Ditch (F.15)	Total EIA
Horse	1	-	5 (1)	6 (1)	-	12 (2)
Cow	7 (1)	9 (1)	10 (6)	3 (1)	1	30 (9)
CSZ	2	9	13	3	-	27
Sheep/Goat	2	6	4 (1)	15 (4)	-	27 (5)
Pig	5	5 (2)	6 (5)	3 (3)	-	19 (10)
SSZ	-	27	-	20	47	94
Human	-	-	1	-	-	1
Unidentified	30	79	145	14 (1)	4	272 (1)
Total NISP	**17** (1)	**56** (3)	**39** (13)	**50** (9)	**48**	**179** (25)
Total	**47** (1)	**135** (3)	**184** (13)	**64** (10)	**52**	**482** (26)

TABLE 5.5. *Animal bone, minimum numbers of individuals (MNI) for the assemblage as a whole.*

Species	MNI	%MNI
Horse	1	11.1
Cow	4	44.4
Sheep/Goat	2	22.2
Pig	2	22.2

TABLE 5.6. *Animal species type by anatomical meat-joint groups.*

	SSZ		Sheep/goat		Pig		Cow		CSZ	
	NISP	%	NISP	%	NISP	%	NISP	%	NISP	%
Best cuts	26	96	5	83	3	60	4	44	9	100
Lesser quality meat bones	1	4	1	17	1	20	3	33	-	-
Waste bones	-	-	-	-	1	20	2	22	-	-
Total	27		6		5		9		9	

Sus scrofa - At least two individuals are represented in the assemblage, one sub-adult and one old adult. Although most portions of the carcass are present, there is an apparent emphasis on the upper limbs, which may indicate a concentration on the main meat-bearing cuts, although the numbers are too small to confirm this.

Equus caballus — A total of twelve fragments of horse were included in the assemblage, all of which may be attributable to a single individual. A single (fused) metacarpal survived intact, allowing measurements to be taken and withers height to be reconstructed according to the conversion factor of Kiesewalter (cited in von den Driesch & Boessneck 1974):

GL: 245 mm
Bp: 48.1 mm
SD: 32.8 mm
BD: 47.2 mm
Reconstructed withers height 1570 mm

The withers height is 12.5 hands, equivalent in size to a modern Dartmoor or Exmoor pony. As the distal metacarpal is fused, this individual must have been at least 15 months old at death (and possibly considerably older)

Homo sapiens - A single human mandible was recovered from the gravel surface.

Pits (F.17 & F.42)

As in the assemblage as a whole, cattle was the most abundant species within the pits. In pit F.17, a left scapula and the diaphysis of a left tibia were recovered. F.42 contains one fragment of right radius, four fragments of mandible (representing at least three individuals) and a lower third molar.

A total of five pig bone fragments were recovered from the pits: a single radius from pit F.17. and a left mandible, two femora and a left scapula from F.42. One femur displayed very fine knife cuts on the anterior and medial sides and was gnawed distally.

The remainder of the assemblage was recovered from pit F.42. A fragment of right mandible and a left tibia are the only ovicaprid remains. In addition, a scapula fragment and a long bone shaft were recorded under the general category of CSZ; a single cervical vertebra constitutes the only horse remains from the pits.

The eroded and very eroded state of all the bones suggests that they were exposed to the elements for some time before they were incorporated into the pits. It is noteworthy that the bones of the three domestic species: cattle, pig and sheep/goat are dominated by mandibles and those bones representing the highest meat content parts of the carcass.

Buried soil

In contrast to the pits, the buried soil is dominated by the smaller species. The identified species were cow (nine fragments), sheep/goat (six fragments) and pig (five fragments). In addition there were 27 fragments from sheep-sized animals and nine from cow-sized animals. Bone preservation in the buried soil is much better than in the pits.

Although the small numbers involved make any conclusions speculative, the NISP for each species were grouped into anatomical meat-joint groups, to investigate whether there was any indication of which activity(ies) produced the assemblage (Table 5.6). Ribs, flanks (thoracic and lumbar vertebrae), hind and fore-quarters are considered as the best cuts of meat. Poorer grade meat comes from the mandibles, neck (cervical vertebrae) and tail (caudal vertebrae). The third group includes those bones identified with butchery waste, bone working and any other 'artisanal' activities: that is horn cores, skulls, metapodials, carpals, tarsals and phalanges.

Table 5.6 shows a prevalence of fragments from the best meat-bearing bones and a paucity of waste debris; however, to draw definitive conclusions from such a small sample would be foolhardy. The differences seen between species may be due to taphonomic factors, rather than variations in the use of different species.

Knife cuts were observed on a cattle calcaneus and metatarsal and on one cow-sized rib; a single fragment of sheep/goat femur was burnt grey/white.

Gravel surface

A scatter of animal bone and a human mandible were found resting on the gravel surface. This material was very eroded, with cracking and often flaking surfaces indicating that it had lain on the surface for a minimum of several years. The poor preservational state of this material hindered its identification: only 21 per cent of fragments could be identified at any level. Larger species apparently dominate the gravel surface sample (Table 5.4) and five of the 12 horse bone fragments in the assemblage were retrieved from it; however, the overall numbers are very low (only 39 identified fragments), and the predominance of larger species may be a statistical artefact of the preservational state of the material.

A horse scapula from the gravel surface was holed at the back and the hole surrounded by a discoloured area of bone. This hole may have been created to hang the joint, or the scapula may have been intentionally burnt or smoked. Other elements of horse are two tibia diaphyses (left and right), a complete metacarpal and a first phalanx.

In addition to the horse remains, at least two cows, two sheep and one pig are represented in the material from the gravel surface. Cow bones incorporated most portions of the carcass and included two mandible fragments (one with an erupting third molar and one with the third molar coming into wear). A left metacarpal showed butchery marks consistent with skinning. Sheep/goat remains were limited to four tibia fragments (two right, two left). Chop marks were visible on one fragment (the bone surface was too badly preserved to allow cut marks to be observed). Two pig humeri and a radius had visible knife cuts. Other pig elements were a loose third molar, a mandible fragment and a third phalanx, possibly suggesting on-site butchery.

The occurrence of a fragment of human mandible is not unusual in British Iron Age sites. As Ellison and Drewett (1971) point out, fragments of human skeletons are often found mixed with settlement debris, scattered across sites or pits (see also Brück 1995).

Postholes

Postholes are associated with small bone fragments, which would have been able to filter down into these small features. This probably explains why the sample was dominated by the bones of small species: 76 per cent of the 38 identified specimens from posthole contexts were sheep/goat, pig or sheep-sized (Table 5.4). Altogether, 15 fragments of sheep/goat, three of pig, six of horse and three of cow were identified. To these can be added 20 sheep-sized and three cow-sized fragments. It is noteworthy that, whilst sheep/goat bones were well-preserved, the bones of cows and cow-sized animals are eroded and have been subject to gnawing. This may indicate that the postholes were the primary deposition place for the sheep/goat bones, but a secondary deposition place for the larger animal bones. Various portions of the carcass are represented in postholes, but not in sufficient numbers to detect any patterning.

Ditch (F.15)

Only five fragments were recovered from this feature. Four were unidentified fragments and the fifth was an extremely eroded cattle left mandible. From its dentition, the latter belongs to an adult individual.

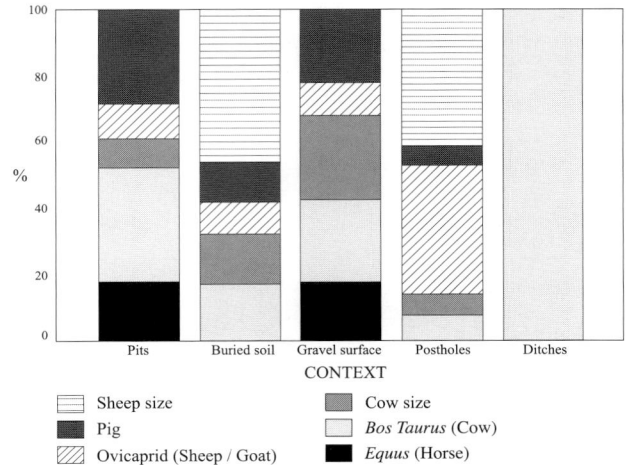

FIGURE 5.8. *Percentage of identified animal species by Early Iron Age feature-type.*

Butchery
A total of eight fragments had indications of butchery. Of these, three were from cow, three from sheep/goat, one from pig and one from a cow-sized animal. All except one butchery mark were produced by a fine-bladed knife. The exception was a sheep tibia with chop marks on its lateral and medial sides. A cow metacarpal from the gravel surface showed evidence of skinning; all other butchery marks were consumption related. It should be noted that the low frequency of butchery marks seen in this assemblage does not necessarily indicate a low intensity of carcass processing: the very poor preservational state of much of the bone has made the identification of butchery marks difficult or impossible in many (if not most) cases.

Discussion
The small size of the faunal assemblage makes it difficult to draw many conclusions; however, it is worth noting those patterns that do appear as they may be of use for later comparison with other sites. The first factor of note is the complete absence of wild species in this assemblage. The lack of fish and bird bones may be related to recovery methods, but the lack of wild mammals is notable. A second absence in the data is that of neonatal and juvenile animals. All of those bones which could be aged indicated the presence of sub-adult and adult individuals. Once again, though, this may be (at least in part) due to the poor preservational conditions and the method of retrieval. A third pattern that emerges is the bias towards the high meat yielding portions of the carcass, together with butchery marks indicating consumption. The presence of older adult cow skeletons, however, sug-

gests that this species may have been used for traction as well as for meat and milk production. Finally, larger species were more abundant in pits and on the gravel surface, whilst sheep-sized species were more abun-

dant in post-holes and in the buried soil (Fig. 5.8). This may indicate some degree of functional diversity, the impact of taphonomic factors, or it may be a statistical artefact of small sample sizes.

Abbott's Iron Age, Vicarage Farm and the 'Diagonal Alignment'

The context and broader affinities of Abbott's Early Iron Age findings will shortly be the subject of a detailed study (by Matt Brudenell) and, therefore, need not overly concern us here. The only point that really warrants emphasis at this time is that, as is evident within his notebooks, Abbott did not actually consider this material to be of 'Early' date, but rather assigned it to 'later Celtic times'. Based on parallels with the Glastonbury assemblage (and presumably also his familiarity with Hunsbury's finds; see Chapter 2 above), this was essentially due to the curvilinear ornamentation on some of his vessels, and it was Leeds who first identified this material as being an earlier, 'Hallstatt-type' (1922; see also Hawkes & Fell 1945).

As discussed above by Brudenell, although there are differences in the pottery recovered from Pryor's 1972 Vicarage Farm excavations, it has the closest recent site-parallels to Abbott's Early Iron Age ceramics; the only other substantive assemblage of that date comes from the subsequent Cat's Water sub-Site. Located some 500 m back/west from Pryor's main Fengate sites, Vicarage Farm is of interest as it lay within the

area's fen-edge hinterland; lying relatively high at 2.5–2.9 m OD, it also straddled the divide between terrace gravels and Cornbrash limestone (Pryor 1974a, 15–22; 1984, 7–10; Fiche Chapter 1). Seemingly comparable to those deep-cut features that were the source of Abbott's finds, essentially the Early Iron Age material derived from a series of large pits scattered across the northwest corner of the site, with later Iron Age and Early Roman pottery coming from its south-centre swathe. Beyond the potential insights the site provides into the settlement context of Abbott's Early Iron Age findings (no structures being recovered in association with the Pryor's pits), what most concerns us from the Vicarage Farm excavations is its double-ditch fieldsystem. Truncated by the Early Iron Age features, despite the intensive, near-total excavation of its boundaries, no dating evidence was retrieved from them. While their arrangement and scale basically matched that of the second-millennium BC fieldsystem, Pryor argued that such an attribution was unlikely based on the difference in their orientation and, instead, remarked that a Neolithic date was possible (1984, 7). ('Off-angle' and not double-ditched, the fieldsystem in Vicarage Farm's Area II was attributed to the later Iron Age [Pryor 1984, 10], and that is also the likely date of the discrete sub-rectangular cropmark enclosures

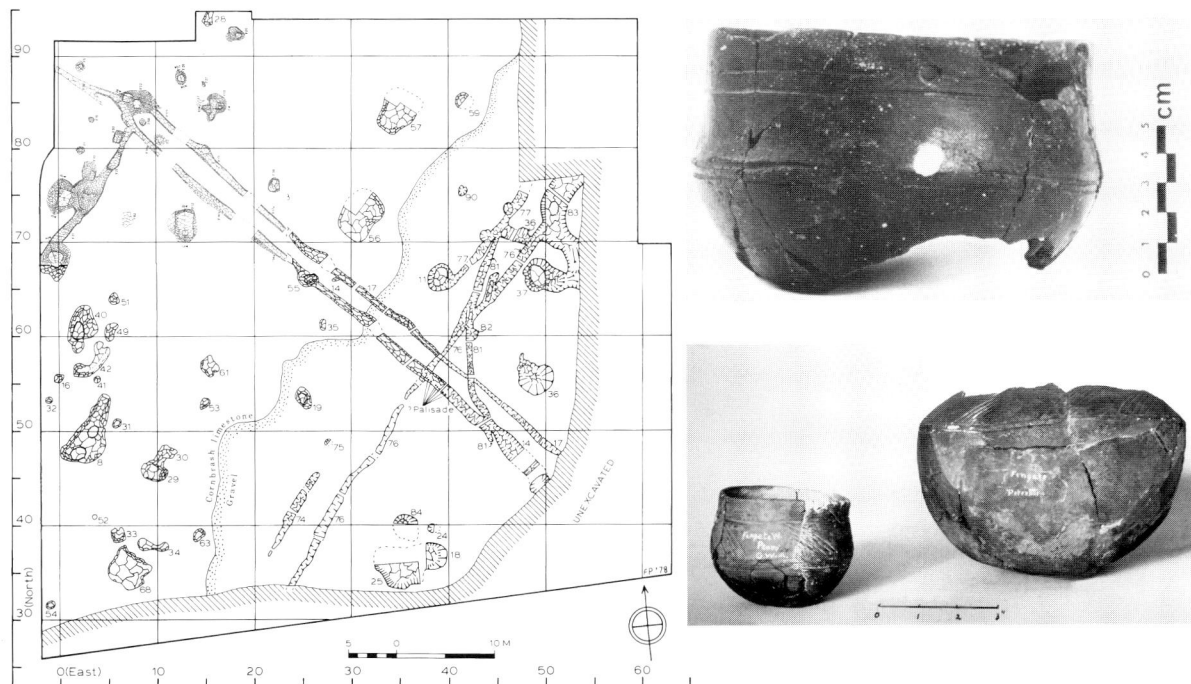

FIGURE 5.9. *Vicarage Farm Ditches and Pottery: Left, Pryor's 1972 site (after Pryor 1974a, fig. 12; 1984, fig. 5); upper right, Early Iron Age bowl from '72 excavations (after Pryor 1984, pl. 1); lower right, selection of Abbott's Early Iron Age pottery from Fengate (photograph from Clare Fell archive and reproduced with permission of Cumberland and Westmorland Antiquarian and Archaeological Society).*

which occur within this hinterland area and are shown on Fig. 6.1:C.) Given a potentially 'early' attribution of the main, Area I Vicarage Farm system, it is surprising that they were not also cited in Pryor's Early Neolithic alignment proposition, as the double-ditches included in his 'axis' northwest of the Site 11 enclosure fell on the same approximate north-northwest/south-southeast orientation (see Inset, Chapter 3). The crucial point here is that, while Site 11 may well have been so early (based on the apparent sealing relationship of its ditches by a Beaker occupation horizon), no positive dating evidence was achieved for the main Vicarage Farm system and 'the alignment's' double-ditch cropmark has never been tested.

Of course, with so little a comparable excavation corpus, an earlier Neolithic assignation of such an extensive (and uninterrupted) boundary system would have seemed much more reasonable in the '70s than it does today (given their layout, the Vicarage Farm ditches are unlikely candidates to relate

to a cursus). Equally, it is only recently that the change in the orientation of *Fengate North's* Bronze Age fieldsystem has been appreciated, and that what appears to be the beginnings of its westward 'fanning' was only recognized with the Broadlands excavations (see Chapter 4 above). From what seems to be the axial 'swing' of the fieldsystem to the northwest across the area, it would now seem much more plausible to assign the Vicarage Farm ditches (together with Pryor's 'alignment pair') to this 'off-angle' portion of the second-millennium BC system. (While Pryor emphasized the extreme compaction of the site's Cornbrash and stressed how difficult it would have been to have cut the Iron Age pits into it (1974, 16–17), the geology was not so 'problematized' in relationship to how the fieldsystem would have been executed, especially if of Neolithic date. As outlined in Chapter 2 above, a Bronze Age fieldsystem has, in fact, now been exposed across higher ground, on the Cornbrash to the west of the City at the Peterborough Prison Site.)

The 2004 investigations

After a delay of some seven years, work on the site only began again in 2004. As the development plans avoided its westernmost quarter (where the Early Iron Age settlement fell) and, otherwise, much of the building work was set to occur within the northern quarried zone, the scale of the archaeological programme was limited and essentially restricted to its southeastern quarter. Nevertheless, given the quality of the site's archaeology and its well-preserved buried soil horizon (which clearly warranted thorough investigation), it was decided to progress the fieldwork in a staged manner.

The first of these stages involved the excavation of three trial trenches: one in the northern half of the development area, and two immediately south of the main area of excavation. Stage 2 comprised a series of buried soil investigations, whilst Stage 3 consisted of open-area excavation (Figs. 5.10 & 5.14). Each phase involved different procedures and slightly different methodologies. Consequently, the various strategies are described individually in the appropriate section below. With the exception of the single trench in Stage 1, all the investigations were conducted in the southeastern quarter of the development area. Therefore, unless otherwise stated, the term 'site' refers to this southern region, where the Stage 2 and 3 investigations took place.

The trial trenching (Stage 1)

In the Stage 1 trenching, nearly 160 m of trenches were excavated (numbered 2–4, following on from the earlier 2004 evaluation; Williams 2004). The first trench (2) was positioned east–west in the northern half of the development area, with the aim of locating further Bronze Age field boundaries and, possibly, settlement

evidence. Due to the presence of trees and major services, this had to be split into two, Trenches 2A (38 m) and 2B (10 m); only a nineteenth-century field boundary was present in these. Two further trenches (3 & 4) were located to the south of the main excavation area, both on a north–south axis. As they are directly connected to the main area of excavation (sub-divided as Areas I and II), their results are discussed along with those from Stage 3 below.

The buried soil (Stage 2)

Across the entire site a buried soil, ranging in thickness between 0.12–0.38 m, was preserved below a layer of partially truncated, dark bluish grey alluvium. Prior to open-area excavation, the buried soil in both Areas I and II was subject to a series of sample-based procedures, involving test pitting, phosphate sampling, metal detecting, and a geophysical survey (Figs. 5.10 & 5.11). Although the sampling methodology remained the same across the two areas, its intensity differed. Consequentially, following French's account of this horizon, the procedures and results for Areas I and II are described separately; this is followed by a more general discussion.

Micromorphological analysis (CHARLES FRENCH)

Across the northern part of the site, the upper palaeosol profile was darker in colour (a 'greenish grey-brown') and contained abundant Romano-British artefacts, whereas away from this 'spread' of archaeological material the soil was a dark orangey-brown colour, more in keeping with the type of soils normally developed on river terrace gravel substrates.

Despite the large areas of the Fengate complex previously investigated in the 1970s using soil and molluscan analyses (French 1980a & b), and more recent micromorphological analyses elsewhere in the Fengate complex (French 1992a & b; 1997; 2001; French & Lewis 2001), there is nonetheless a distinct gap in our knowledge of this northwestern part of Fengate, which is partially addressed by micromorphological analysis at this site.

520702/298744

Area II

Extent of 'artefact enriched'
buried soil [210]

TP 1

TP 8

TP 10

TP 2

Area I

TP 7

TP 9

TP 3

TP 6

TP 4

TP 5

■ Test pit

▲ Metal artefact

0   20
metres

520788/298615

FIGURE 5.10. *The 2004 Investigations, showing Areas I and II, test pit locations and metal-detecting find-spots.*

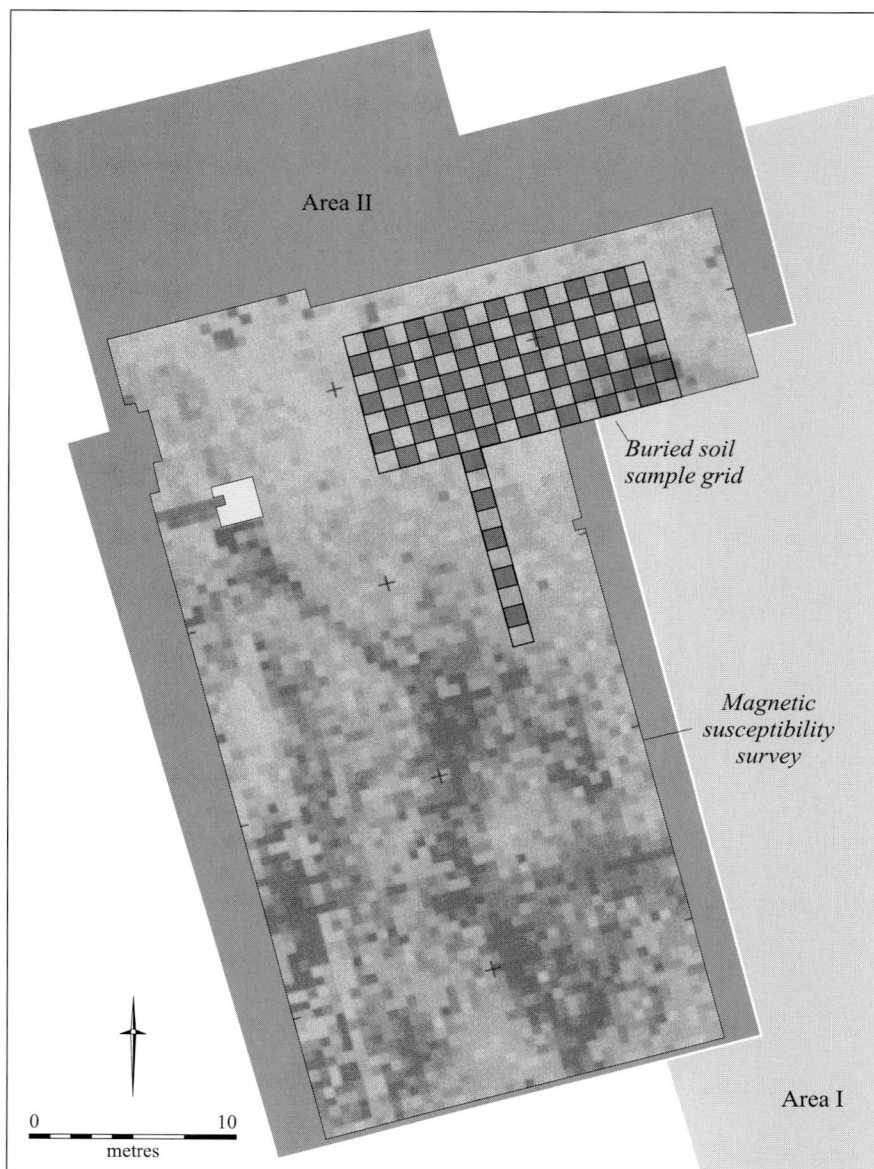

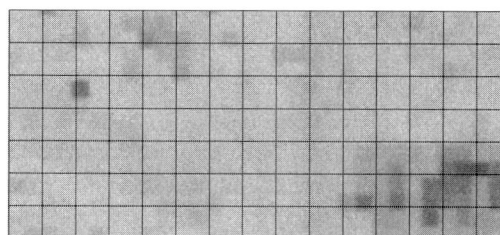

Sample Grid Phosphate   Magnetic Susceptibility

FIGURE 5.11. *Area II showing location of buried soil sample grid and magnetic susceptibility survey (A. Challands; top); below, phosphate and magnetic susceptibility survey.*

Four profiles were sampled (three profiles from the 1997 evaluation and one from the 2004 excavation), but only one monolith (Sample number 217; [268]) was processed for soil micromorphological analysis. This employed the methodology of Murphy (1986), and the descriptive terminology of Bullock *et al.* (1985) and Stoops (2003). The profile chosen for analysis was from the northern part of the site, associated with the Romano-British occupation material, and exhibited a good depth of palaeosol survival (the detailed soil micromorphological descriptions are to be found in the site archive).

The soil profile was cut into three samples to make into thin-section slides; all three exhibit relatively similar characteristics. The soil is a homogeneous, apedal and relatively porous sandy clay loam, with the clay component and porosity decreasing somewhat with depth. It is dominated by very fine, fine and medium quartz sand (*c.* 65–80 per cent), but also contains a strong component of impure or dusty clay (*c.* 10–20 per cent) throughout the groundmass and coating the sand grains. In addition, there are a few discrete zones of illuviated pure (or limpid) clay (*c.* 5 per cent) in the groundmass and void space, sometimes exhibiting micro-laminations. The whole fabric is strongly impregnated with amorphous sesquioxides, and there are occasional vivianite crystal 'flares'. The organic component is very minor, comprising minor amounts of micro-charcoal and some plant tissue replaced by amorphous iron. Notably, one plant stem or root-hole in the uppermost sample is partially infilled with an excremental 'pellety', dark brown sandy loam fabric, with very abundant spherulites (or calcite crystallites produced by digestion in the gut of herbivores such as sheep; Canti 1997; 1999).

This sandy clay loam has a sufficiently well-organized clay fraction to suggest that this is the cambic or lower B (Bw) horizon of a brown earth soil (after Avery 1980). The significant dusty or impure clay component of the fine groundmass probably has several derivations: as a result of a former disturbance possibly associated with tree clearance (Macphail *et al.* 1987) as well as the Romano-British occupation itself, and the down-profile illuviation of fines (silt and clay) associated with post-Roman overbank seasonal flooding and alluviation. The much rarer survival of the micro-laminated pure clay suggests that this soil had supported woodland under stable and well-drained conditions earlier in prehistoric times (Fedoroff 1968; Fisher 1982; Macphail *et al.* 1987). This has been noted and corroborated elsewhere to a limited extent in the Fengate area (French 1997; 2001), especially on First Terrace gravels in the next valley system to the north, in the Maxey and Etton area of the lower Welland valley (French 1990) and the adjacent fen-edge (French & Pryor 1993), and through palynological sequences from the nearby Third Drove (Scaife 1997, in Cutler 1998) and the Flag Fen basin (Scaife 2001).

As is the case on many alluviated sites in this fen-edge area of eastern England (French 2003a), the organic A horizon of this brown earth does not appear to be present. There is every possibility that this became incorporated into and transformed by the subsequent seasonal depositions of alluvial silty clays in the post-Roman period. The only hint of its character comes from the void/root-hole infill of organic sandy loam with spherulites in the upper slide.

The absence of more than a very minor presence of fine anthropogenic inclusions in this soil is surprising given the abundant excavated artefactual evidence that was recovered from this soil. This may partly be due to the subsequent alluvial depositional process, but it would also suggest that a 'dark earth' type of midden deposit containing abundant organic material (after Macphail & Courty 1985) was not deposited on this soil and intermixed through soil faunal mixing processes as one might have expected. Nonetheless, the presence of abundant spherulites in one void created by the oxidation of plant material does suggest the presence of herbivores such as sheep on the surface of this brown earth at some point in the past, and probably prior to the onset of alluviation.

The greenish-grey colouration of this soil noted in the field suggests that this palaeosol has become permanently waterlogged in the past and has subsequently begun to dry out. This is corroborated by the presence of vivianite in this profile. As the palaeosol away from the influence of the modern concrete raft/hardstanding is not so affected, this is most probably a localized feature of this modern construct, involving consequent air-exclusion and a high localized groundwater table.

In conclusion, the pre-alluvial palaeosol is a relatively well-developed brown earth which has hints of once being stable, well-drained and wooded in earlier prehistoric times, but had subsequently become open in later prehistoric times, and gradually seasonally waterlogged and affected by overbank sedimentation in post-Roman times. This alluviation process, as well as the subsequent construction of the overlying concrete raft structure in more recent times, has completely transformed the upper half of the soil profile and rendered it uninformative.

Area I sampling

Covering 0.29 ha, Area I was situated immediately east of the main area of excavation (Fig. 5.10). Although this zone was not scheduled for direct development (i.e. building *per se*), the potential disturbance caused by landscaping warranted a programme of buried soil sampling. Following machine-stripping down to the top of this horizon, a five-metre grid was laid-out and phosphate samples were taken at each point. At 20 m intervals along the same grid, metre-square test pits were then excavated in order to gauge artefact densities and, in addition, the entire surface of the buried soil was metal-detected. Thereafter, Taram webbing was laid across the buried soil to act as a buffer during both the area's immediate backfilling and subsequent construction works.

In total, six test pits were excavated across the area. These yielded a single worked flint, together with 13 fragments of Roman pottery (13 g). The metal-detecting recovered five objects, including a large but heavily corroded first- to second-century AD Roman coin and a biconical steel-yard weight.

In the northern end of Area II three features were visible cutting through the buried soil. These comprised an east–west linear ditch with a dark fill, the terminal of a north–south gully, and a circular pit. In order to gauge their date, the pit (F.124) was half-sectioned. A total of 16 tile fragments weighing 4.7 kg were recovered, together with small sherds of second- to fourth-century AD pottery.

Area II sampling

In the first instance, Area II was subjected to the same sampling strategy as that of Area I, along the same 5 m grid (Fig. 5.10). Covering an area of 0.14 ha, phosphate samples were taken (Fig. 5.11) and four test pits were excavated (Test-Pits 7–10; two further test pits intended for the north portion of the site were abandoned as they fell within the large modern quarry pit). No worked flint was recovered and only eight fragments of Roman pottery were found (20 g). Metallic artefacts were more numerous, with 18 objects retrieved (see Appleby & Hall below).

As the buried soil was exposed across the whole area in a single phase of machine-stripping, geophysical survey was possible and A. Challands undertook a magnetic susceptibility survey over 912 sq.m (the northernmost end of Area II was not surveyed, given that this comprised the backfilled trenches of the 1997 evaluation and the edge of a large, modern quarry pit). The results of the survey are shown in Figure 5.11. Although no features registered on the plot, the higher readings to the north highlight an area of artefact-enriched buried soil (discussed below).

In the centre of Area II, immediately south of the backfilled trenches of the 1997 evaluation, a distinct change in the colour and consistency of the buried soil was apparent (Fig. 5.10). Extending across an area of approximately 270 sq.m, this was an amorphous spread of dark greenish-grey brown silty clay loam. This discol-

FIGURE 5.12. *Top, the buried soil sample grid (looking west); below, stone-packed profile of posthole F.6 (photographs: M. Brudenell).*

oured buried soil ([210]) was first observed in the 1997 evaluation, occurring both between and around the group of cornbrash-lined postholes (Trench E). It was identified as an organic and artefact-enriched upper 'A'-horizon, containing abundant fragments of occupation debris (principally Romano-British pottery).

The discoloured buried soil swathe was subjected to intensive test pitting and phosphate sampling to further investigate the content of this horizon and its potential association with surrounding features (Figs. 5.11 & 5.12). A 7 × 15 m grid was laid-out across the area and divided in to 105 metre-squares. A further transect of ten metre-squares was extended to the south of the main grid-block in order to investigate potential artefact 'fall-off' patterning towards the margins of the spread. Phosphate samples were taken from all 115 squares, and 57 metre-squares of the buried soil were hand-excavated in a *'chequer-board'* fashion (i.e. every other square dug; these test pits will hereafter be referred to as the 'chequer-board grid' to distinguish them from the earlier test pits).

Across the grid-area the buried soil varied in depth between 0.16 and 0.38 m. Although it was occasionally possible to define an upper 'A' and lower 'B'-horizon, these were only visible in section and no distinction could be made during excavation. As a result, finds were collected by square alone, with no further attempt made to sub-divide them.

Four postholes were found during this horizon's sample-excavation, one of which was cornbrash-lined (Fig. 5.12: F.154). Three of these did not penetrate the underlying gravels but were visible in section (F.125, F.136 & F.153).

In total, 640 artefacts were recovered from the buried soil squares, with an average of 11 artefacts per square. In both number and weight, bone and pottery constituted the majority of the finds, accounting for 45 per cent and 47 per cent of the assemblage respectively (see Table 5.7).

In order to investigate the distribution and density of artefacts in the buried soil grid, the number of finds per square was plotted for each major artefact category. Given the fragmentary nature of the pottery and bone, weight rather than number is used (Fig. 5.13; see also plots in Brudenell 2005a). The mean weight per square was also plotted for pottery and bone in an attempt to investigate the distribution of artefact sizes.

TABLE 5.7. *Artefact composition of the buried soil squares.*

Artefact category	Total number	Total weight (g)	Mean number per buried soil square	Mean artefact weight (g)
Worked & burnt flint	6	-	0.1	-
Roman pottery	289	2536	5.0	8.8
Tile	22	1305	0.4	59.0
Burnt clay	5	17	-	-
Bone	301	1497	5.3	5.0
Burnt stone	15	558	0.3	37.2
Slag	2	10	-	-

Total Weights

Mean Weights

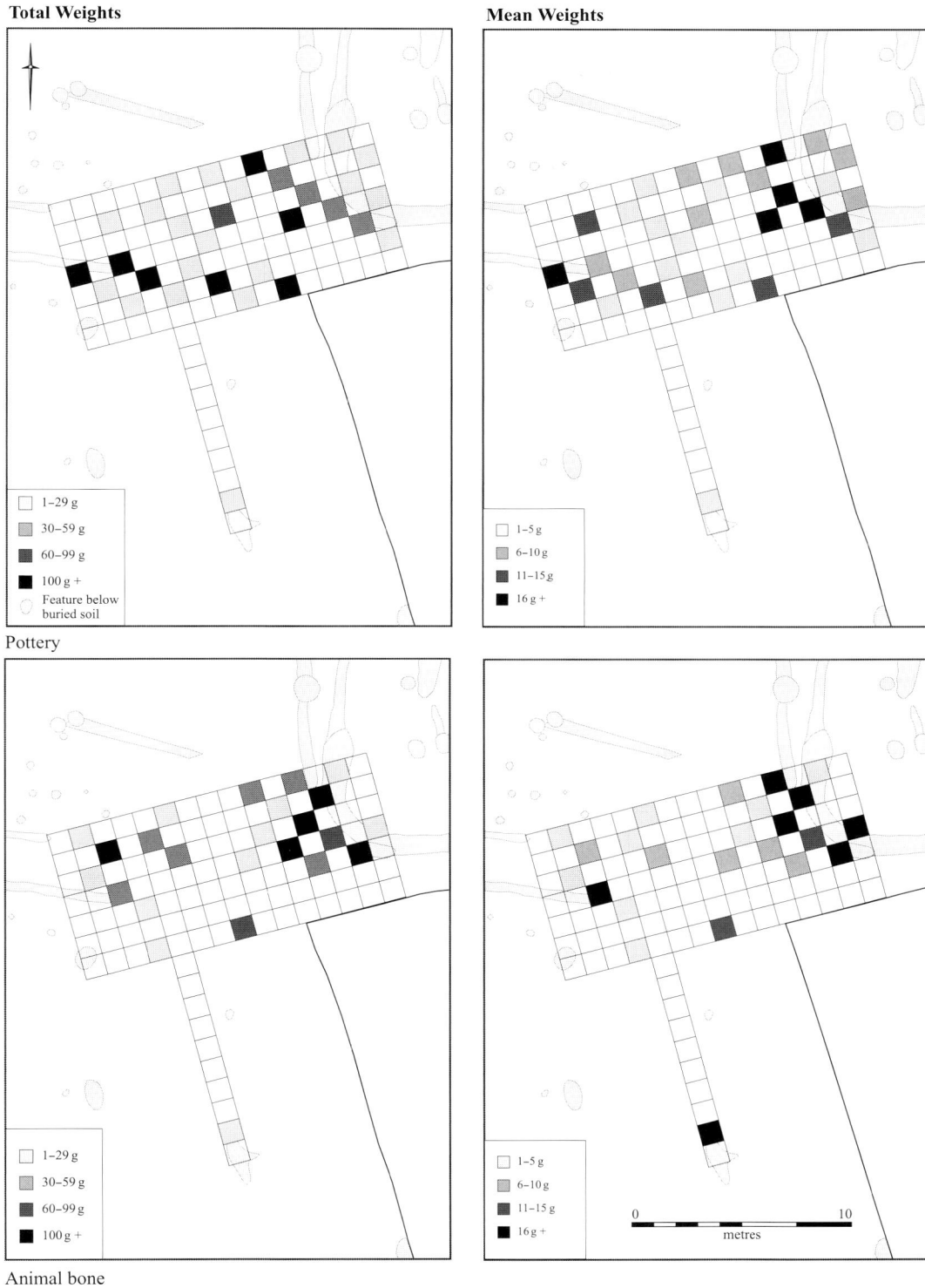

Pottery

Animal bone

FIGURE 5.13. *Buried Soil Grid Densities: Pottery and animal bone.*

The distribution plots for flint, burnt clay and slag show little clustering. Given the relatively low number of finds within these categories, it is no surprise that the distribution appears random; however, the tile plot indicates a slight concentration in the northeast corner of the grid. More informative are the pottery and bone plots (Fig. 5.13). The bone was clearly distributed between two main clusters. The most dense cluster is located in the northeast corner of the grid, where four of the five highest weight categories are situated. A second, lower density cluster is found towards the western side, the two separated by a clear gap where no bone was present. In contrast, pottery appears to be dispersed throughout the grid, with the highest densities towards the southwest.

If the pottery and bone plots are imposed over the excavation plans, the relationship between the artefact densities and the underlying features can be directly assessed. This clearly demonstrates that buried soil artefact weight increases with proximity to features. For bone, this increase correlates with the corner of the ditched enclosure, whereas for pottery, weight increases in relation to the gully. A comparable relationship is evident in the plots for mean pottery and bone weight, demonstrating that artefact-size increases around the features. In effect, artefacts were less fragmented in or around the tops of ditches and gullies (Fig. 5.13). This is hardly surprising, as the more exposed artefacts will break down faster under the effects of weathering and trampling. In particular, bone may be very susceptible to these processes, perhaps accounting for its very low densities beyond feature margins (cf. the more even distribution of the pot).

Together, the plots demonstrate that high artefact densities and large artefact sizes strongly correlate with underlying features. The disposal of domestic rubbish in the ditches, pits and gullies evidently registers in the surrounding buried soil as areas of high artefact density. Presumably resting in the tops of these features, the artefacts were less exposed to the elements and were therefore less fragmented.

Although feature-based refuse disposal accounts for the high artefact densities, it does not explain the lower 'background noise'. In the case of pottery, the lower density spreads were extensive, with ceramics dispersed throughout the grid and not just around features. Likewise, not all the high bone weight categories were on, or immediately adjacent to, ditches and gullies.

The total number of artefacts recovered from the ten main 20 m-interval test pits was remarkably low. Only half yielded finds, and these amounted to just a single worked flint, along with 11 fragments of Roman pottery. Beyond indicating a prehistoric 'presence', little can be discerned. Equally, the minor quantities of Roman pottery recovered attest to only limited activity in the area. With a mean of just 1.1 fragments of pottery per test pit, such densities cannot imply intense occupation *per se*. Rather, the results indicate sporadic use of the southern half of the site, with the finds there most likely entering the buried soil through manuring.

In contrast, artefact densities were much higher from the northern, '*chequer-board*-grid' buried soil squares, with an average of 11 finds per square. A much greater range of artefact types were also present, including tile, bone, slag, burnt stone, and burnt clay, as well as flint and pottery. The lack of bone in the test pits is intriguing, considering its relative abundance in the buried soil grid-squares (present in 42 per cent of the squares). With the exception of Test Pit 8 (which remarkably yielded no finds), none of the 20 m-interval test pits were located on the organically-enriched dark buried soil spread. As the buried soil squares are confined to this spread, the results from the two samples can be compared in an attempt to further understand the nature of the dark deposit (i.e. what sets this horizon apart from the surrounding buried soil). Given the variance in both artefact content and number of test pits excavated, no *direct* comparison is possible; however, as pottery was recovered from both, a comparison between the mean sherd weight per metre-square can be used a rough guide.

The mean sherd weight per square is just 3 g for the test pits, and 9 g for the buried soil squares. Although both weights are relatively small, that from the organically-enriched buried soil ([210]) is three times greater than that from the surrounding buried soil. This indicates that sherd sizes were larger and hence that the pottery was less fragmented. The pottery was also more abundant, occurring in 56 per cent of the buried soil squares, compared to just 40 per cent of the test pits. Given the difference in sample size, the reliability of these results may be questionable, but it is relevant to note that the mean number of worked flints per metre-square is identical across the two sampling grids, demonstrating a degree of consistency.

Overall, there can be little doubt that that the dark, organically-enriched buried soil swathe differed from that surrounding it. The colour and consistency of the deposit, together with the high density of finds, indicates that it was artefact-enriched. The extent of the spread is considerable, registering as a 'high' in the magnetic susceptibility plot (Fig. 5.11). The question is: to what extent was this a deliberate attempt to enrich the soil? Does the high artefact content simply represent the gradual accumulation of detritus across an occupation area, or is this a remnant midden? Certainly, the correlation between features and artefact concentrations indicates that proximity to settlement was a contributing factor in its formation: much of the material derives from the cleaning out of ditches and rubbish disposal within them. Yet this only accounts for the dense concentrations, and does not explain the 'background noise' (which itself is still relatively dense in comparison to the surrounding buried soil). The settlement-edge location (see below) of this horizon makes it unlikely that significant quantities of detritus would randomly accumulate in this area. Therefore it is presumed that the accumulation of debris was a deliberate and purposeful act, suggestive of middening or the creation of a horticultural plot.

The excavation of the buried soil squares also demonstrated that features occurred *within* this hori-

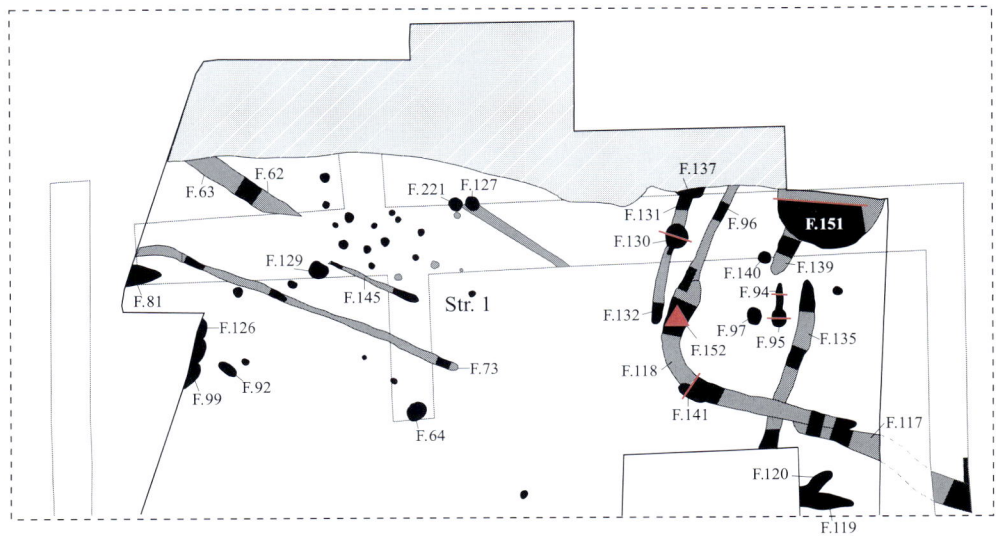

FIGURE 5.14. *2004 area base-plan (with 1997 trenches indicated).*

zon: cutting through it, but not penetrating the natural gravels. Given that a relatively small area was sampled in comparison to that which was finally stripped, the presence of three non-'earth-fast' features (postholes F.125, F.136 & F.153) implies that many more must have existed. Unavoidably, features of slighter construction/scale were lost in machine-stripping, and although F.154 survived this process, its cornbrash lining was removed.

Open-area excavation (Stage 3)

The open-area excavation covered 0.14 ha (Fig. 5.14). Machine-stripping occurred around the buried soil grid, which was then still under excavation. With the squares completed, all features in the southern end of the site were fully excavated. This portion of the site was subsequently relinquished, allowing the machine to track across and remove the remaining unexcavated sections of the buried soil grid. Excavation then focussed on the northern half of the site. Overall, the Stage 3 investigations revealed evidence for Late Roman settlement, with only a limited Bronze Age component. Although a small assemblage of residual Neolithic material was recovered (see below), no features of that date were located. Likewise, Iron Age and Early Roman occupation was absent.

Bronze Age fieldsystem ditches

In total, only four features could be assigned to the Bronze Age: a pit, and three ditches. Although none were directly datable, all were definitely sealed by the buried soil, which contrasts with features of Roman date that cut this horizon.

A re-cut northeast–southwest aligned Bronze Age ditch was located at the extreme southern end of the site. The earlier of the two ditches, F.109, was exposed in both Trenches 3 and 4. The ditch had a steep, but slightly weathered, 'V'-shaped profile with a maximum width of 1.6 m and a maximum depth of 0.73 m (Fig. 5.18). The lower fill of the ditch comprised mid grey silty sands, the upper fill a compact orangey-grey silty sand with frequent weathered gravel inclusions. In Trench 4 these two deposits were separated by a thin lens of dark grey silty sand with charcoal inclusions. In both trenches the ditch was re-cut by F.110, a weathered 'V'-shaped ditch with a narrow concave base. This ditch was 0.78 m wide with a maximum depth of 0.44 m and filled with a mid grey silty sand containing moderately frequent gravel inclusions and charcoal flecks. In total, both ditches ran for over 35 m. It is interesting to note that the northwest–southeast Bronze Age ditch, F.15, discovered in the 1997 evaluation, displays very similar characteristics to F.109. This ditch was 1.25 m wide and 0.87 m deep (Fig. 5.4), and would have run at right angles to F.109, presumably joining this ditch immediately east of Trench 4.

With the exception of a residual Neolithic flint in F.110 (Trench 4) and some fragments of bone, no dating evidence was obtained from the ditches. Their ascription to the Bronze Age is based upon orientation, together with their correspondence to ditches found in the 1997 evaluation. Other features which may be assigned to this period include a ditch terminal, F.99, located on the western edge of

the excavation area, and the abutting pit, F.126. Pit F.126 was 0.48 m wide and 0.52 m deep, filled with gravelly mid grey-brown clayey silt. A similar deposit was found in the adjacent ditch terminal, aligned northeast–southwest. This feature is probably the terminal of ditch F.104, uncovered in Trench 1.

The Roman settlement

The Late Roman settlement consisted of a ditched enclosure containing a series of pits and a well, a possible post-built granary, and a scatter of pits, postholes and gullies. Mainly concentrated in the north of the site, these features represent the margins of a more substantial settlement.

Post-built structure and associated features

In the northwestern corner of the site a cluster of 12 postholes defined Structure 1, the only building discovered during the course of the excavation (Figs. 5.14 & 5.15). This had previously been revealed in Trench E of the 1997 evaluation (see Fig. 5.3). Despite covering this section of the trench with plastic, the backfilled concrete rubble had caused considerable disturbance to the archaeology, with numerous large pieces piercing the sheeting and penetrating the underlying gravels. The rubble made it almost impossible to conduct controlled machining.

After stripping, the former trench was noticeably deeper than the surrounding gravels to the south, being most heavily disturbed towards the west. Two of the postholes recorded in 1997 were completely destroyed and a further four had lost their cornbrash lining. Several other features which were possibly associated with the building had also been severely truncated, including ditches F.63 and F.62, and gullies F.145 and F.73. The degree of damage is best illustrated by ditch F.56, excavated in 1997. No trace of this feature could be found during the current investigations, although it was previously documented as being 0.15–0.2 m deep. Given the truncation, it must be assumed that most, if not all of the postholes, were up to 0.2 m deeper than recorded. Despite the loss and damage, careful cleaning of the area revealed a further four postholes. In order to compensate for the loss of features from the 1997 trial trenching, they have been superimposed on the Structure 1 plan.

Before describing Structure 1, it is worth commenting on the relationship between the building and the buried soil. The 1997 evaluation report states that the cornbrash-postholes cut through a lower buried soil [058], but were themselves sealed by the organically-enriched 'dark earth' buried soil. This implies that any 'enrichment' of the soil or middening post-dated the abandonment/destruction of Structure 1; however, as the formation of a midden would have been a cumulative process, the two may still have been

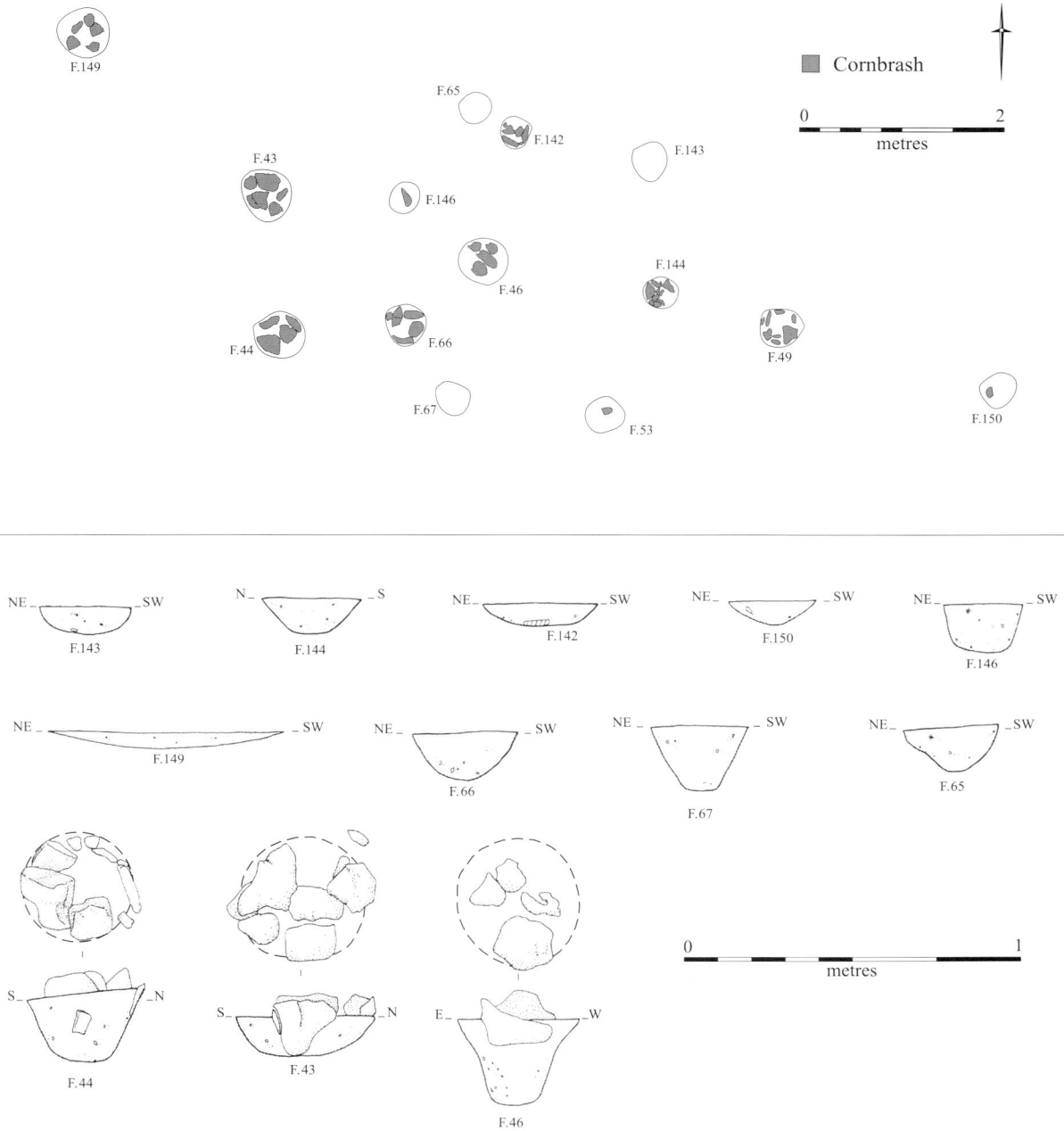

FIGURE 5.15. *Structure 1: top, plan; below, posthole sections.*

contemporary, the adjacent spread of detritus only later encroaching on the structure's footprint.

Although the scatter of postholes clearly relates to a rectangular structure, there is ambiguity concerning its precise size (Figs. 5.15 & 5.16). The best preserved alignment of posts belonged to the central post-row, originally revealed during the 1997 evaluation. Five features constitute this row: F.43, F.46, F.48/F.144, F.49 and F.150. All were previously cornbrash-lined, although only the stone in F.43, and F.46 remained intact. These postholes ranged in diameter from 0.26–0.4 m, and in depth from 0.08–0.26 m; generally they became smaller and shallower toward the southeast. Running parallel to the central post-row, just 1.25 m to the north, was a second post-alignment: F.149, F.65, F.142, and F.143. This row was less complete than the central row, and the depth of features ranged from just 0.05–0.14 m. This indicates severe truncation, presumably with some postholes being completely destroyed. F.149, the most northwesterly posthole in the scatter, appears to represent the northwestern limit of the structure. Likewise, F.150 probably represents the southeastern limit.

Running 1.25 m south of the central post-row were the remains of a third northwest-southeast alignment, comprising F.44, F.67 and F.53. Parallel to this outer post-row, and immediately to the south,

FIGURE 5.16. *Top, Structure 1 with cornbrash-packed postholes (see Fig. 5.2); below, F.151 well (photographs: M. Brudenell).*

shallow circular pits, F.127 and F.128, and ditches F.62/F.63. The pits were almost identical in size, shape and profile, with diameters of 0.65–0.7 m, and depths of 0.04–0.08 m. F.127 was heavily burnt and may have been a hearth. Ditches F.62/F.63 ran broadly parallel to gully F.73, but were heavily truncated. The disturbance to the ditches meant that no relationship with Structure 1 could be established; however, it is likely that the ditches would have stopped short of the building, there being no evidence for their continuation in less truncated areas to the south. To the south of Structure 1 was pit F.129 and two further postholes (F.74 & F.82); no finds were present in these.

Collectively, the surviving postholes of Structure 1 indicate a rectangular building *c.* 10 m long, and 4 m wide (Fig. 5.15). The structure would have originally comprised 18 close-spaced postholes, divided into three northwest–southeast aligned post-rows. Based on the best preserved features, all the postholes would have been cornbrash-lined, and would probably have had an original depth of *c.* 0.4 m (assuming 0.15–0.2 m of truncation in the area). The spacing of the posts, and the presence of a wall trench immediately adjacent, indicates that this was not an aisled barn. Likewise, the paucity of cultural material in the surrounding pits and gullies implies that neither was it a domestic structure in the strictest sense. Rather, this type of architecture is commonly associated with raised granaries, the closely-spaced posts required to hold the considerable weight of grain stored above. A comparable granary structure was uncovered at Orton Hall Farm (Mackreth 1996). As with Structure 1, this granary had stone-lined postholes; however, this was ascribed a Saxon date. Quite why the structure was placed in this phase is unclear. Structurally, the stone-lined postholes were similar to those of the surrounding Roman buildings, and as no finds were recovered, a Roman attribution would seem more logical.

was a remnant narrow gully, F.145, evident for around 5 m, with a maximum depth of just 0.06 m. Given its proximity to the outer post-row, the feature is unlikely to be an eaves-gully; its position was more suggestive of a wall trench.

Several other features in the vicinity demonstrate a relationship to Structure 1. Lying 3.5 m to the south, but on the same alignment, was gully F.73. This, beginning on roughly the same line as the eastern end of Structure 1, ran parallel to the building for 15 m, then turned east–west before exiting the western edge of the excavation area (this feature was not found to continue into Trench 1). Three separate slots were excavated through the gully, which had a maximum width of 0.42 m and depth of 0.09 m. It is interesting to note that ditch F.56 also shared this alignment, but was positioned on the opposite side of Structure 1. Together, these features may have formed a small enclosure around the building, the southeastern side being left open for access.

Other features to the north of Structure 1 included two very

Northeastern compound and associated pits

In the far northeast of the site, the corner of a ditched enclosure was revealed. This was defined by a series of five ditches/gullies, suggesting the compound had several phases of renewal and alteration. None of the relatively shallow features formed a continuous circuit. Instead, the compound was defined by short lengths of ditch and gully, which appear to have been added to, extended or linked, in a fairly piecemeal fashion. Direct re-cutting along the same path was not characteristic of boundary maintenance. The organic development of the enclosure makes separating distinct formal phases problematic. This is compounded by the lack of chronological distinction in the pottery (no feature being more closely datable than late second to fourth century AD); however, stratigraphically two broad phases are evident (Fig. 5.14).

Phase 1

The southern side of the enclosure was defined by the east–west aligned linear ditch, F.117. Only its terminal was exposed in the excavation, although its continuation to the east throughout Area I was noted during the buried soil investigations, and it was also excavated in Trench F as part of the 1997 evaluation. F.117 was 0.73 m wide, and 0.42 m deep, expanding to a deeper 'swollen' terminal, 1.9 m wide and 0.75 m deep. This 'pit-like' butt-end displayed a very different sequence of fills to the adjacent slot, with numerous weathering deposits at its base. The termination of F.117, just 0.5 m to the east of the north–south linear F.135, implies that the two were contemporary

The western side of the enclosure was demarcated by a shallow north–south gully, F.96. Filled with a dark grey sandy silt (not unlike the discoloured buried soil), this was just 0.15 m deep and varied in width from 0.43–0.9 m. Around 6 m of the gully was exposed, being cut by the curvilinear ditch F.118 in the south and the modern quarry pit in the north. Given how shallow this feature was, it is possible that F.118 completely removed any traces of the gully curving east–west. However, the presence of a parallel linear, F.135, just 5.5 m to the west, implies that the ditch never turned, possibly terminating a little further to the south. The shared alignment of F.96 and F.135, together with their stratigraphic relationship to F.118, suggests they formed a compound entrance. How far F.135 continued southward was impossible to gauge. The ditch certainly became shallower as it went north, falling in depth from 0.44 m, to just 0.08 m at its ovoid terminal. On the southern edge of the excavation area, where the ditch was at its deepest point, the feature was 1.11 m deep, containing a lower band of weathered natural capped by clayey silts.

Four features surrounding the perimeter of the compound may be broadly contemporary with this 'first phase' (F.120, F.130, F.137 & F.141; Fig. 5.14). All of these were stratigraphically earlier than ditch F.118 and gullies F.131, F.132 and F.119, the constituent components of the second phase. Two sub-circular pits, F.137 and F.130, were located less than 1 m east of gully F.96. These were the largest and deepest pits on the site, ranging from 1.6–1.2 m in diameter, and 0.6–0.91 m in depth. F.137, the pit with the greatest diameter, had near vertical sides and a flat base, filled with a homogeneous deposit of sand and gravels in a clay matrix. F.130, on the other hand, had a more complex fill sequence, suggestive of it being open for longer (Fig. 5.18). It displayed a deep 'U'-shaped profile, with steep but slightly weathered edges and a rounded base. The lower half of the pits were filled with weathered gravels; the upper deposits included bands of silty sand and a lens of burnt red silt.

Evidence for burning was also recorded in the fills of an elongated pit, F.141. Lying directly in the centre of the putative entrance, this was 1.35 m long, 0.55 m wide and 0.56 m deep, with vertical sides and a slightly concave base. Given the position of this feature, together with its slightly unusual shape, it may well be a small trench dug to hold posts as part of a gate structure; its four fill sequence included a lens of greasy black ash and soot. The only other feature which may be assigned to this phase is a small section of curving gully, F.120, cut by the east–west gully F.119. F.120 was 0.55 m wide, but just 0.1 m deep, filled with mid grey silty sand.

As only 1.75 m of its length was exposed, interpreting its function is problematic.

Phase 2

The second phase in the enclosure sequence is primarily defined by the curvilinear ditch F.118 (Fig. 5.14). Creating a rounded corner to the compound, this would have effectively closed the southwest entrance into the enclosure. The ditch, approximately 14 m in length, appears to have been positioned to link F.96 and F.117, which by this stage would have nearly, if not completely, silted up. The extent to which these earlier features still acted as boundaries is difficult to ascertain. Certainly, the linking of the two together by F.118 (which cut the western terminal of F.117 and presumably the southern end of F.96), implies that they were both at least still visible, possibly as slight earthworks. The ditch itself varied in width between 0.71 and 1.63 m, with a maximum depth of 0.54 m. Of the five slots excavated through the ditch, none contained more than two deposits: the lower contained a relatively thin band of weathered gravels; the upper, dark slightly gleyed silts.

With no evidence to suggest that F.117 was re-cut, it can be assumed that this ditch continued to function as the southern perimeter of the compound, although the former western boundary F.96 was most likely replaced by a new gully, F.131, to the west. Displaying similar characteristics to F.96, this was 0.6 m wide with a maximum depth of 0.43 m. The gully cut through two pits, F.137 and F.130 and terminated on the southern edge of the latter. The gap between F.118 and F.131 was 1.5 m, perhaps implying the existence of a new entrance, possibly leading to Structure 1 in the west. This was subsequently sealed by a second short length of gully, F.132, immediately abutting the southern end of F.131. The gully (just 4.1 m long, 0.48 m wide and with a maximum depth of 0.18 m) had a similar fill sequence to both F.118 and F.131, with a band of weathered gravels capped by dark gleyed silts.

The grave of an adult male, F.152, was found in the upper fill of the F.118 northern terminal (Figs. 5.14 & 5.17). The skeleton was lying in a supine position parallel to the ditch, with the head lying to the north. Although no grave cut was observable, the position of the body suggests that the grave was dug directly into the top of the ditch and backfilled with the same extracted material; its base lay just 0.13 m below the top of the ditch.

The F.152 inhumation (NATASHA DODWELL)

The skeleton is well-preserved, although none of the long bones are complete. The skull and pelvis are fragmentary and there are concretions of iron panning on many of the bones. An estimation of age was based on the degree of epiphyseal union, on dental eruption and attrition (Ubelaker 1989; Brothwell 1981) and on changes to the auricular surface of the ilium (Lovejoy *et al.* 1985). The sex was ascertained from sexually dimorphic traits on the pelvis and the skull and from metrical data.

The body was that of a robust, mature adult male, aged approximately 40–50 years. Cribra orbitalia, indicative of anaemia, was recorded in both orbits. Degenerative changes were recorded in the lower spine, in the shoulder joints and the hips. Osteoarthritis, characterized by marginal osteophytes and Schmorl's nodes, was recorded on the lumbar and thoracic vertebrae. The sternoclavicular joints exhibited an increase in porosity, osteophytes and changes in the joint morphology. Marginal osteophytes were recorded on the right humeral head, both of the glenoid cavities, the left femur head and acetabulum. The right hip joint had undergone severe destructive processes; the acetabulum no longer has the appearance of a socket but is flattened with very ragged margins. There is very little cortical bone on the joint surface (and that which survives has a polished, eburnated appearance) and several sharp-edged erosive lesions were recorded. Only about a third of the right femur head

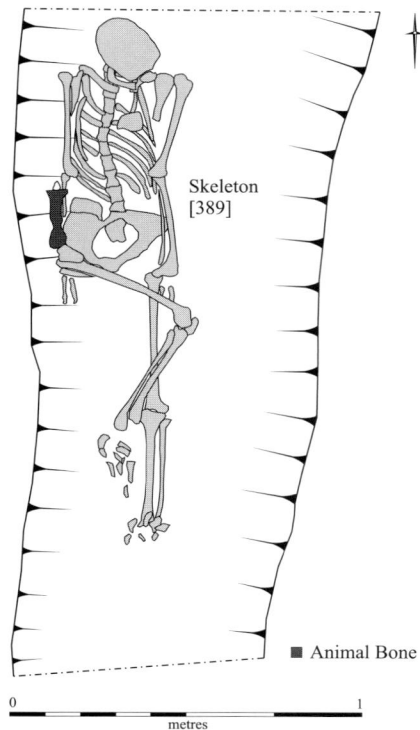

FIGURE 5.17. *The F.152 Inhumation (photograph: M. Brudenell).*

survives; there is both post-mortem damage and destructive, pathological alteration in the form of pitting and smooth edged scalloped lesions. There is also a small area of polishing/eburnation where the bone has rubbed directly on the bone of the acetabulum. These destructive changes in the right hip may be evidence of a septic arthritis or tuberculosis and could explain the awkward position of the right leg. The following dentition was recorded:

8	7	6	5	x	3	\	\		1	2	3	4	5	6	x	x
x	x	x	5	4	\	\	\	\	\	\	3	4	5	x	7	8

Seven teeth had been lost ante-mortem and the left mandibular molar is impacted. Slight to moderate deposits of calculus were recorded on the posterior dentition and the dentine is exposed on the anterior dentition.

A total of seven features were found within the enclosure, including postholes, two pits, two gullies and a well. Well F.151 and gully F.139 are discussed separately below. Without any direct stratigraphic relationship to the compound ditches, no attempt has been made to assign any of these features to a particular enclosure phase.

Lying just 0.5 m apart, F.97 and F.95 were two oval pits with rounded bowl-shaped profiles. Both displayed similar dimensions (max. dia. 0.8 m, max. depth 0.29 m), but different fill sequences. F.97 was 0.9 m long, and had a single fill of dark grey-green clayey silt, reminiscent of the buried soil. F.95 was also capped by a similar deposit, but its edges were scorched and covered with a compact charcoal rich lens of burnt gravel (Fig. 5.14). This burning suggests that the feature acted as a 'fire pit'/hearth. Although the upper fill of pit F.95 appeared to cut F.94, the gully-like feature immediately to the north, the same burnt deposit was evident across its base. F.94 was 1.28 m long, 0.44 m wide and 0.16 m deep, with steep to near vertical sides and a slightly concave base. Running directly into pit F.94, these two features appear to be functionally linked, with F.94 acting as a flue for the fire pit F.95 (Fig. 5.14). Similarly shaped features have been found at Orton Hall Farm (Mackreth 1996), where they were interpreted as furnaces. To the north of the pits, two postholes (F.140 & F.134) were found set 3.5 m apart, there being no indication that they were part of a structure.

Overall, the excavations have clipped the corner of what was probably an extensive enclosure. Judging by the buried soil observations, the enclosure ditch F.117 continued for a least another 50 m to the east. Therefore, the investigations have only provided a small glimpse of the activities which occurred within the settlement. The character of the ditches indicate a 'loosely' bounded space. The ditches were not of heavy construction, and had been 'adjusted' on several occasions. Likewise, the lack of a continuous circuit indicates a fairly permeable boundary, with gaps or 'entrances' occurring around the perimeter. Certainly, without fencing these ditches could easily have been crossed by cattle.

The well

Located in the far northeastern corner of the compound was a large well (F.151), 5.26 m in diameter and

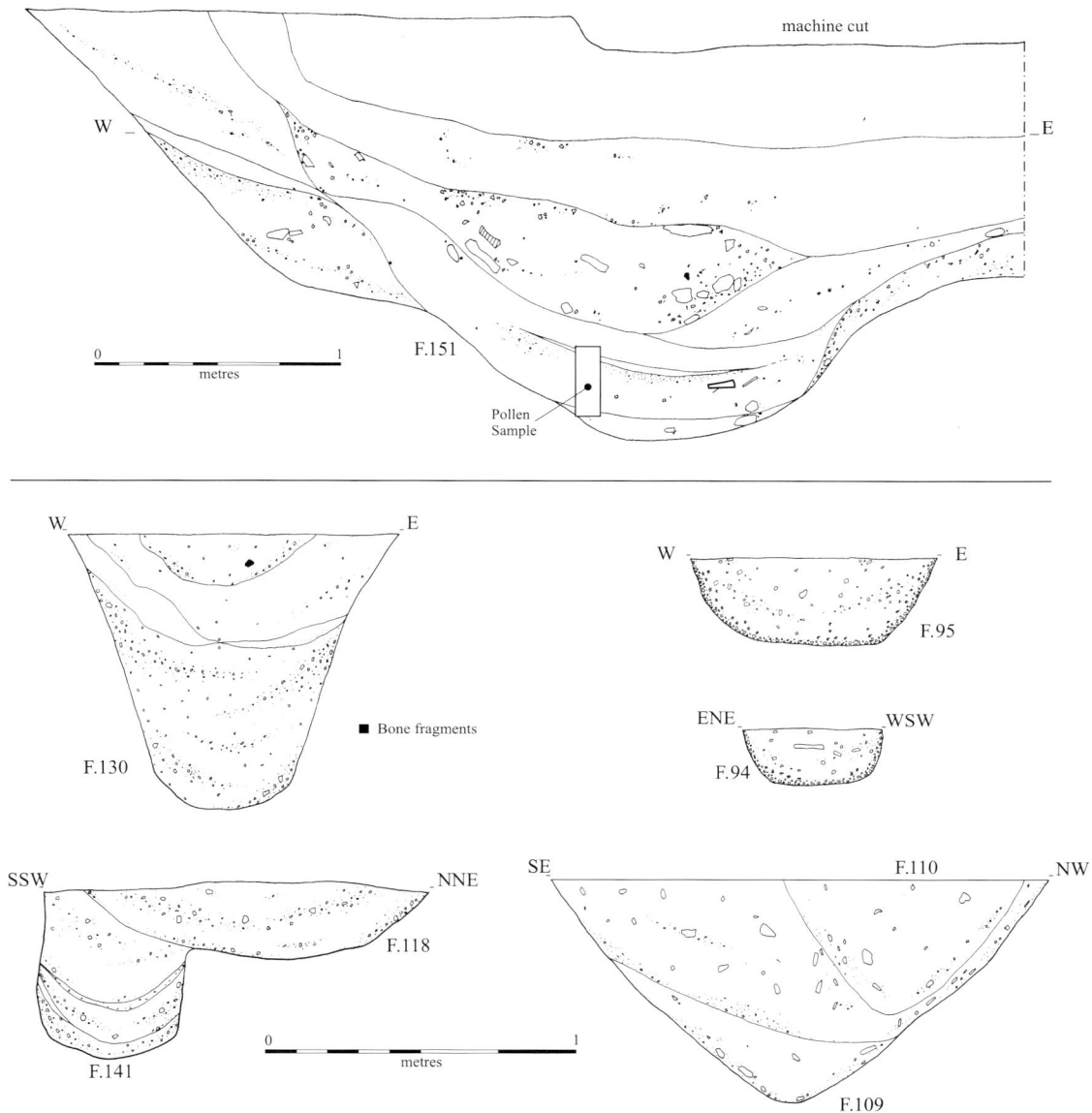

Figure 5.18. *Sections.*

1.88 m deep. Just over half of the feature was exposed, the northern portion being truncated by the modern quarry edge (Fig. 5.14). Initially, a single 2 m slot was excavated through the well, which was subsequently extended to 4.1 m. The far eastern edge of the well was not fully excavated due to the close proximity of a large spoil heap. An informative assemblage of material was recovered from F.151, shedding light on both the status and function of the site. The assemblage included 264 sherds of pottery, representing 57 per cent of the total Roman pottery assemblage; 63 fragments of tile (17.4 kg); two quernstone fragments; 492 fragments of bone (21 kg); four pieces of slag (2 kg) and a near complete hobnailed shoe (Fig. 5.22). During the excavation,

pieces of cornbrash and limestone were separated and counted, the volume of the material being measured. No attempt was made to separate the stone by context, and the material was neither weighed nor retained. In total, 514 fragments of cornbrash were recovered from the well (*c.* 81 litres).

The well displayed a steep-sided profile, dropping sharply to a depth of 1.15 m (Figs. 5.16 & 5.18). At this point, a gently sloping 'ledge', 0.5 m wide, was present. This ledge subsequently fell to a rounded base, 0.97 m across. A total of 16 fills were recorded within this feature. The two basal deposits comprised dark organic-rich silts, containing fragments of brushwood, charcoal, slag, pottery, bone and a near-complete Roman hobnailed shoe. These water-logged deposits were sealed by a lens of fine yellow sand. Further bands of weathering and slumping were also evident on all sides of the well. These consisted of orangey-brown and greyish-brown coarse sandy gravels, occasionally in weathered and banded tips. Although no direct evidence of a wooden lining was found, the occurrence of the distinct ledge-like shelf towards the base of the feature may suggest that a wooden/wattle lining structure had once revetted the well. If this was the case, the 'dirty' gravel slumps could have acted as packing, subsequently slipping when the structure was dismantled.

The central fills of the well ([459] & [458]) were dominated by two thick silty clay deposits. Fill [459] was the most artefact-rich deposit, containing large quantities of pottery, stone, tile, bone and slag within a dark grey silty clay matrix. The assemblage testifies to a range of domestic and industrial activities occurring around the site, as well as indicating the existence of a tiled structure, possibly stone-built. The occurrence of all these artefact groups together, all in relatively large quantities, suggests that the deposits represent dumps of material from the abandonment/destruction/clearance of a substantial building.

The central fills of the well were covered by a lens of greasy black silt, rich in charcoal. Above these, the upper fill comprised a dark grey sandy silt. This was partially truncated by a modern trench, possibly associated with the quarry. On the southwestern side of the well, was a north–south gully/ditch, F.140. On the surface, this feature appeared to be cut by F.151, although, upon excavation, F.140 was found to run into its side. This feature may have functioned as a path to the well's edge.

Pollen analysis (STEVE BOREHAM)

A 30 cm-long monolith from the well was analysed. It comprised a basal dark grey silt unit ([468]; 0–6 cm) containing a little sand and occasional pebbles, from which a pollen sample was taken at 3 cm, and a dark grey sandy silt unit, containing pebbles ([466]; 6–11.5 cm), from which a pollen sample was taken at 9 cm. The upper part of this context appeared to be more oxidized and consisted of three units where grey-buff silty sand graded upwards into sandy silt (11.5–19 cm, 19–24.5 cm and 24.5–30 cm). These upward-fining sequences represent in-wash events, and were not sampled for pollen due to their sandy and relatively oxidized nature. The two samples of sediment were prepared using the standard hydrofluoric acid technique, and counted for pollen using a high-power stereo microscope.

Pollen concentrations were modest at 41,895 and 54,730 grains per ml. Preservation of the palynomorphs was generally good, but pollen grains were rather sparse. The slides contained considerable quantities of algal material and organic debris, which diluted the pollen and hampered counting. Thus, total counts from the slides yielded main sums less than the statistically desirable minimum of 300 pollen grains. The sample from [468] (3 cm) produced a pollen signal dominated by grass (35.3 per cent), with herbs, cereals (7.8 per cent), hazel (9.8 per cent), alder buckthorn (2 per cent), and fern spores (Pteropsida). Pollen of herbs from the goosefoot family (Chenopodiaceae; 11.8 per cent), cabbage family (Brassicaceae; 7.8 per cent) and from mugworts (*Artemisia*; 5.9 per cent) was particularly abundant. The presence of the butterwort (*Pinguicula vulgaris*) in this sample is particularly interesting, since this is a plant associated with acid bogs, rather than alkaline fens. The sample from [466] (9 cm) was also dominated by grass (36.6 per cent) and contained herbs, cereals (7.3 per cent), hazel (9.8 per cent), alder buckthorn (2.4 per cent), and fern spores (Pteropsida). In this sample, pollen of herbs from the goosefoot family (Chenopodiaceae; 12.2 per cent), pink family (Caryophyllaceae; 7.3 per cent) and from strapwort plantain (*Plantago lanceolata*; 7.3 per cent) were more important. Pollen of trees and aquatic plants were apparently absent from both samples.

These samples have broad similarities in their pollen spectra, but differ in the detail of the herbs present. Taken together, they attest to an ostensibly tree-less environment, which comprises grassland, tall-herb communities (meadows), hazel scrub and areas of arable agriculture. The absence of obligate aquatics suggests that there was little or no standing water nearby, although the presence of alder buckthorn, sedges and butterwort hint that damp or boggy ground was not far away. Damp conditions, perhaps in the well itself, are indicated by the presence of ferns, and dock (*Rumex*) is typical of riparian (bank-side) environments. There is certainly evidence for disturbance around the site, with mugworts, goosefoot and strapwort plantain all having associations with trampling, ploughing and other human activity.

It is the absence of trees, aquatic plants and other taxa that hints as strongly as the pollen evidence that this 'well' was within a highly managed environment, showing no signs of abandonment or flooding. This interpretation would fit the Late Roman attribution of the feature.

The presence of a well within the northeast compound is by no means extraordinary. What is significant about this feature is the relatively large assemblage of material recovered from it and the high degree of organic preservation at its base. Once abandoned, the well was rapidly filled by deposits including generally large, unabraded fragments of pottery and quantities of tile, bone and stone. Although this material occurred within nine of this feature's 16 fill-contexts, the vast majority derived from its substantial mid-profile fills, suggesting distinct episodes of dumping. In particular, [459] contained over 50 per cent of the total assemblage, with 465 artefacts. Certainly the quantities of material imply that the well was not simply receiving randomly accumulated rubbish. A comparison between the mean weight of pottery from the well (42 g), and that from the buried soil squares (9 g), demonstrates the difference in weight between that derived from what was presumably the site midden (the discoloured buried soil) and that derived from a single episode of deliberate clearance (the central well deposits). Based on this, it can be assumed that the processes which lead to the formation of these distinct deposits were very different.

The southern pit and posthole scatter

With the exception of those postholes associated with Structure 1, and the two within the northeastern compound, a further 26 postholes were recorded. The majority of these clustered towards the southern end of the site, although no definite structure could be identified. In general, the postholes were small, shallow, and filled with mid grey sandy silts. Other features in the southern half of the site included a series of shallow pits, an unusual gully-like feature, and two tree-throws.

Excluding the large posthole, F.80, which was 0.66 m in diameter and 0.51 m deep, the mean posthole diameter was 0.3 m, with a mean depth of just 0.13 m. Unlike the some of the postholes elsewhere on the site, no cornbrash packing was found in these features and no post-pipes were observed. All the features are tentatively assigned to the Roman period, although no pottery was recovered in association. This is unsurprising given the low number of sherds from the test pits in that area and the location of these postholes away from the settlement 'core' to the north. The only finds recovered from the postholes were two worked flints of Neolithic date. Although there remains the possibility that some of these features are in fact prehistoric, the material is considered residual.

The only indication of patterning in the distribution of postholes is represented by a northwest–southeast line of six (F.68, F.75, F.77, F.80, F.98 & F.133). The interval between these ranged from 2.5 to 4.9 m (centre to centre), with a mean spacing of 3.5 m. It is possible that these features formed a fence line, with wattle panels bridging the gaps; however, this interpretation is highly tentative and, whilst the alignment is similar to that of Structure 1, the dominant Roman axes are north–south/east–west.

Eight pits were excavated in the southern half of the site (F.64, F.84, F.86, F.89, F.90, F.92, F.112 & F.121). These were all characteristically small, shallow and, with the exception of F.84, had only a single fill. The majority were oval and ranged from 0.46 to 1.36 m in length, with none being deeper than 0.34 m. Five of the pits (F.64, F.84, F.89, F.90 & F.92), occupying the central southern region of the site, displayed similar characteristics in both form and fill. These were all oval and filled with grey clayey silt with patches of orange sand.

Other 'miscellaneous' features excavated in the south of the site included an unusual elongated pit/gully (F.85), and two tree-throws (F.138 & F.123). F.85, 4 m long, 0.79 m wide and 0.2 m deep, was filled with a mid orangey-grey silty sand. Its date and function are uncertain, although its fill was similar to that of the surrounding postholes. Tree-throw F.123 in Trench 4 yielded two Neolithic flints and two sherds of Early Neolithic pottery, the only prehistoric ceramics recovered from the site.

The thin scattering of features in the southern half of the site lay beyond the settlement core to the north. The fact that no Roman pottery was recovered from them demonstrates that this was not an area of intensive domestic activity.

Material culture

This section will focus upon the site's Romano-British assemblages. Otherwise, reported upon by Emma Beadsmoore and Mark Knight respectively (in Brudenell 2005a), only 18 flints and two conjoining Neolithic pottery sherds (one a rim) were recovered. Coming from the F.123 tree-throw, the fabric of the rim sherd was soft/medium with frequent small linear voids (dissolved shell) which gave it a 'corky' appearance. The rim is simple but slightly out-turned and, when refitted with its adjoining sherd, suggestive of a neutral or slack form, perhaps from a simple bowl profile characteristic of plain, Early Neolithic vessels (Clark *et al.* 1960); such an attribution would also correspond with the 'corky' fabric (Healy 1988).

Of the worked flints, ten derived from the buried soil sampling, with the remainder recovered from features and as stray finds. The buried soil finds largely comprised flake blanks (chronologically non-diagnostic, although a couple are potentially

Neolithic) and only one tool was present, an earlier Neolithic end-scraper.

Of the material recovered from features or, otherwise, as stray finds, posthole F.78 yielded an earlier Neolithic blade. Two earlier Neolithic flints, a core rejuvenation flake and an edge-used blade, were also recovered from tree-throw F.123. The F.110 Bronze Age ditch yielded a Neolithic edge-used flake, while two Neolithic flakes were recovered as stray finds. The remaining material was chronologically non-diagnostic.

Roman pottery (KATIE ANDERSON)

A total of 758 sherds (16.592 kg) of Roman pottery were recovered, representing 23.41 Estimated Vessel Equivalents (EVEs). Details of their fabrics, forms, EVEs and dates were recorded, along with any other information considered important. For the purposes of this report, the pottery recovered from the test pits will initially be considered separately from the remaining excavation-derived material, although the two groups will later be discussed as a whole.

Buried soil sampling

A total of 300 sherds of Roman pottery, weighing 2557 g, were recovered from 36 of the test pits and buried soil grid squares. The majority of these produced fewer than five sherds, although five yielded much greater quantities.

Grid Square 31 contained 62 sherds (570 g), 49 of which were Nene Valley greywares. This included four sherds from a shallow dish and five rim sherds, representing three different jars. A sherd of Eastern Gaulish samian ware was also recovered from this square. Many of the sherds from this test pit were large and unabraded.

A total of 51 sherds (350 g) were recovered from Grid Square 20. The majority were shell-tempered wares, which appear to be from a single medium-sized jar. This included four rim sherds, three base sherds and 32 body sherds. There were also a single Eastern Gaulish samian sherd and several sandy greyware sherds.

Grid Square 37 contained 31 sherds of Roman pottery (587 g), including 13 Nene Valley greywares, 11 shell-tempered sherds and a Nene Valley colour-coated base sherd. They had a relatively high mean weight of *c.* 19 g.

The pottery from the remaining test pits was comparable to the material discussed above, with relatively large quantities of Nene Valley greywares and shell-tempered wares, and a smaller number of sandy greywares, grog-tempered wares and Nene Valley colour-coated wares. The majority of the sherds were non-diagnostic, although there were a number of rim and base sherds present. Beaded rim jars were the most common vessel types, with at least 16 different vessels represented. There were also two beakers, one mortarium and a dish.

Feature 151 — The well

Feature 151 produced 264 sherds (11,034 g), representing *c.* 57 per cent of the total assemblage. The material came from eight different contexts, although there is no appreciable difference in date between any of these and all contained material dating from the mid-second to fourth centuries AD. This implies that the fills were deposited in relatively quick succession.

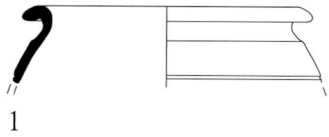
1

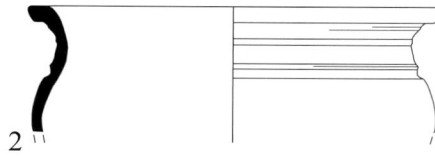
2

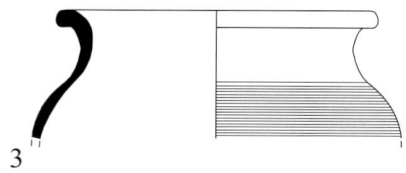
3

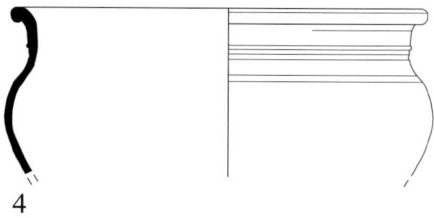
4

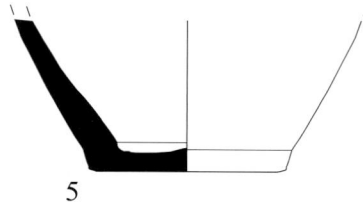
5

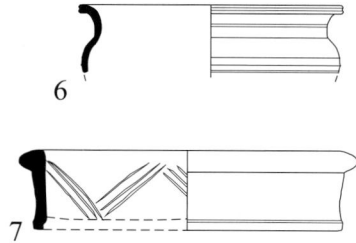
6

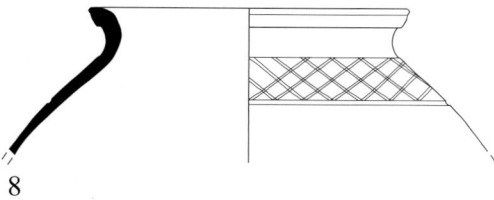
7

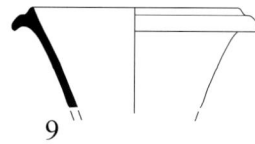
8

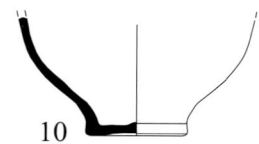
9

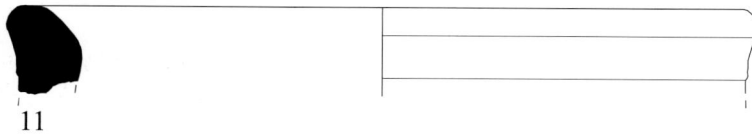
10

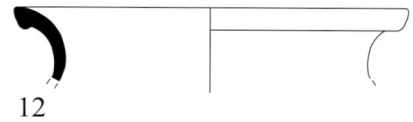
11

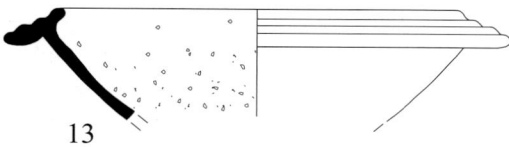
12

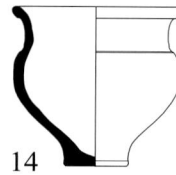
13

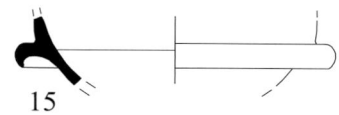
14

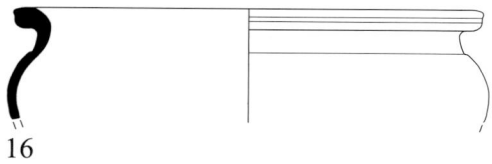
15

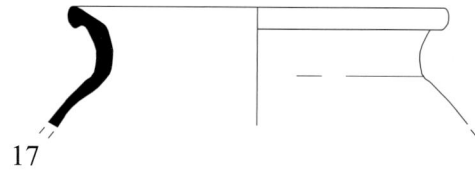
16

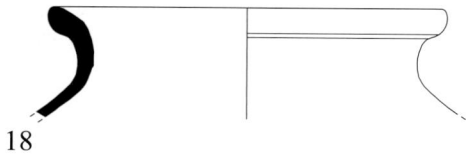
17

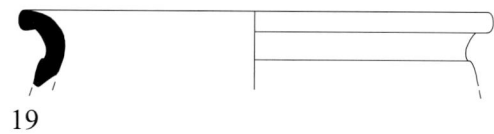
18

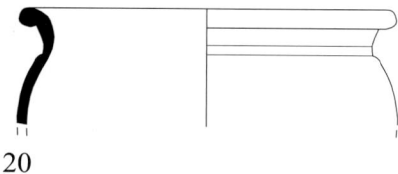
19

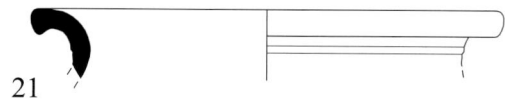
20

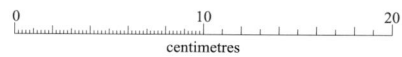
21

0   10   20
centimetres

FIGURE 5.19. *(On left) Romano-British Pottery: 1) Grog-tempered, beaded rim jar with cordon on body (<154> TP.37); 2) shell-tempered jar with angular beaded rim ([468], F.151); 3) shell-tempered rilled jar ([459], F.151); 4) wide-mouth, sandy greyware jar with cordon on neck ([459], F.151); 5) base from a Nene Valley colour-coated jar ([459], F.151); 6) small, wide-mouth Nene Valley colour-coated jar ([459], F.151); 7) a Nene Valley greyware dish, with a beaded rim and incised diagonal lines (<146> TP.31); 8) a sandy greyware jar, with a narrow mouth and incised cross-hatching ([399], F.141); 9) Nene Valley colour-coated, beaded, flanged bowl of third- to fourth-century AD date ([359], F.131); 10) base of a Nene Valley colour-coated beaker ([459], F.151); 11) very large shell-tempered storage jar ([459], F.151); 12) Nene Valley Everted rim jar ([459], F.151); 13) Nene Valley whiteware mortaria ([459], F.151); 14) complete, miniature Nene Valley colour-coated beaker ([459], F.151); 15) Nene Valley colour-coat, imitation Dr38 ([458], F.151); 16) wide-mouth, shell-tempered jar with groove on rim ([459], F.151); 17) sandy greyware jar with constricted neck and everted rim ([459], F.151); 18) shell-tempered everted rim jar ([459], F.151); 19) Nene Valley colour-coated, wide-mouth jar ([459], F.151); 20) shell-tempered jar with beaded rim ([468], F.151); 21) Nene Valley greyware jar with everted, beaded rim with small cordon on neck ([459], F.151).*

The pottery was generally large and unabraded, with a mean sherd weight of approximately 42 g, including one complete vessel, a small Nene Valley colour-coated beaker, dating from the third–fourth century AD. There were, however, a small number of sherds which were heavily abraded.

The most common fabric types from this feature were Nene Valley wares, in particular colour-coated wares (111 sherds). In addition, there were 42 Nene Valley greyware sherds and five whitewares, as well as a significant number of shell-tempered sherds and sandy greywares. Only three samian sherds were present, all of which were from the Eastern Gaulish kilns. These were a Dragendorff 18/31, one Dr33 and a non-diagnostic sherd.

A range of vessel forms were represented. The most common were jars, in particular medium-size necked jars with beaded rims, of which there were at least 27 different vessels present. There were four different Nene Valley whiteware mortaria, as well as three Nene Valley shallow dishes. These range in date from the mid-second century to fourth centuries AD. A number of sherds had evidence of sooting and, on some occasions, there was heavy sooting, of their exterior faces.

Feature 139

A total of 33 sherds were recovered from this feature, including 12 Nene Valley greyware sherds, the majority of which appear to be from a medium-sized, beaded rim jar, dating from the mid-second to fourth centuries AD. Seven grog-tempered sherds were also present, including one which is possibly a lid. There was one non-diagnostic Eastern Gaulish samian sherd, dating from the late second–third century AD. The remaining sherds consisted of eight non-diagnostic shell-tempered sherds, and five sandy greyware sherds, including one necked jar with a small beaded rim, dating from the second–fourth centuries AD.

This feature appears to be cut into by the F.151 well; however, there is no apparent difference in the dates of the pottery from either. This may imply that both were filled within a short period of time. Another explanation is that the pottery from F.139 may have been redeposited from F.151. The latter interpretation could be supported by the mean weight of the pottery from this group, only 7.3 g.

Feature 146

A total of 27 sherds of Roman pottery (99 g) were recovered from this feature. These included only four diagnostic sherds: one Nene Valley colour-coated cornice rim beaker and three sherds from a sandy greyware necked jar. The remaining sherds consisted of ten grog-tempered, eight Nene Valley greyware and five shell-tempered ware sherds. The pottery ranged in date from the second to fourth centuries AD, although some of the sherds could be more specifically dated to the mid-second to mid-third centuries AD.

The mean weight of the pottery sherds from F.146 is only 3.7 g and a number of the sherds were heavily abraded, thus suggesting that they may have been redeposited from elsewhere.

The range of fabric and form types present in this assemblage was relatively limited (see Tables 5.8 & 5.9); it is dominated by Nene Valley products. These are comparable with those recorded by Lucas in the 1997 evaluation (Lucas 1997). He observed that Nene Valley wares were prominent in the small assemblage, with greywares and shell-tempered wares being the only other fabric types of note.

The fabrics and forms are a reflection not only of the nature/function of the site but also the length of occupation. There is no evidence of early Roman occupation in either this assemblage or in the evaluation group examined by Lucas, with the earliest pottery dating (at the earliest) from the mid-second century AD. Even then, there are no definite second-century vessels. Instead, there are vessels with a generic form and/or fabric, which can only be broadly dated to the mid-second to fourth centuries AD. Vessels that could be more closely dated, such as the Eastern Gaulish samian sherds and some of the Nene Valley colour-coated wares, tended to be of third- to fourth-century AD attribution. This suggests that the occupation continued into later Roman times. The later vessels were not present in the 1997 assemblage, with Lucas suggesting a third-century AD date for his material.

Nene Valley wares dominate the assemblage, probably as a result of the site being so close to the production site at Water Newton. Other fabric-types feature much less, which is unsurprising since the Nene Valley repertoire was extensive, with a wide variety of vessel forms for different functions being produced. There would have been little need for wares produced elsewhere. Shell-tempered wares also featured relatively highly in the assemblage. Their exact source is unknown, but similar fabrics and forms are commonly found in later Roman assemblages in Cambridgeshire and beyond.

TABLE 5.8. *Fabrics of all the excavated Roman pottery.*

Fabric	No.	%	Wt (g)	%
Black slipped ware	15	2.6	420	2.5
Buff sandy ware	2	0.3	4	0.02
EG samian	12	1.6	65	0.4
Grog & shell tempered	2	0.3	18	0.1
Grog-tempered ware	31	4.2	341	2
Nene Valley colour-coat	170	22	4829	29.2
Nene Valley greyware	212	28	3770	22.7
Nene Valley whiteware	7	0	419	2.5
Oxidized sandy	13	1.7	13	0.08
Sandy GW	91	12	1497	9
Shell-tempered	201	27	5193	31.4
Unidentified colour-coat	2	0.3	23	0.1
Total	**758**	**100**	**16,592**	**100**

There are many questions surrounding the exact nature of shell-tempered pottery production during the Roman period and, since it is well represented in this assemblage, it provides a useful example for further investigation. Therefore, a series of thin sections were produced (six samples; see Vince below), alongside chemical analysis, in order to assess their fabrics in greater detail and address two specific questions. Firstly, how many fabric types are there and how do they differ from one another? Secondly, are the shell-tempered fabrics local and are any from this site the same as those analysed from other Roman assemblages in the area?

Three different fabric types were identified within the broad 'shell-tempered' category, referred to as Fabrics 1–3, all containing more than one type of shell as well as ironstone and quartz. Fabrics 1 and 2 had a similar range of inclusions, with the main differences being that Fabric 1 contained ostracod shell and microfossils, whilst there was a larger quantity of iron within Fabric 2. Fabric 3 differed from the first two in the smaller range of shell-types present and because the nacreous bivalve shell (a key component in all three fabrics) was larger in size and occurred more frequently within it. Chemical analysis confirmed all three fabrics to be different in composition. Most interesting is the implication that Fabric 1 is similar to a range of fabrics analysed by Vince from the Peterborough area, and in particular, was probably produced to the west, with the Haddon kilns being a likely source (Vince 2003). No previously analysed fabrics matched Fabrics 2 and 3 (including those from Harrold, Beds.). This is not to say that these were not produced locally, but rather that the kilns producing these wares are yet to be found or analysed in sufficient detail.

This study has highlighted the difficulties associated with analysing generic Roman fabrics. Work on similar fabrics recovered from Earith Camp Ground (Evans *et al.* forthcoming) showed further evidence that the shell-tempered industry was diverse in terms of fabrics, ultimately suggesting small, localized industries. Although it is not suggested that pottery production was taking place on a site level, it does imply that there was no single industry supplying the site, or area as a whole, with shell-tempered wares. This undermines the assumption that much of the later Roman shell-tempered wares in and around Cambridgeshire were either produced at the Harrold kilns or in another area of large-scale industry. In reality, it is likely to have been much smaller, perhaps shorter lived industries, which were providing sites in northern Cambridgeshire with shell-tempered wares.

The only imported wares within the assemblage consisted of Eastern Gaulish samian, of which there were only 12 sherds in total. This is probably related to the date of occupation of the site, since the number of wares imported into Britain had significantly decreased by the later Roman period (Tyers 1996); however, the small numbers may also be explained by the fact that the Nene Valley kilns were producing a wide range of both finewares and coarsewares, which may have limited the need and/or desire for imported wares.

The vessel forms present are of a domestic nature, which is supported by the use-wear evidence, including heavy sooting and limescale. The range of vessel-types, though relatively limited, included pots for a variety of functions. The medium-sized jars are likely to have been used for cooking, whilst the fineware beakers and bowls, etc. may have been used as tablewares.

The pottery evidence suggests that the period of occupation at this site was short but relatively intensive. In the cases where Roman pottery was found, there was very little difference in date between that recovered from intercutting features. Features 139 and 151 (see above) yielded pottery of the same date. Features 118 and 135, which also intercut, displayed a slight difference in date. The pottery from the former dated from the mid-second to fourth centuries AD, with a strong likelihood that they are at the latter end of this range. The pottery from F.135, which was cut into by F.118, was of a similar mid-second- to fourth-century AD date; however, this feature included an Eastern Gaulish samian sherd from a Dragendorff 33, which could be more specifically dated to the late second to early third century AD.

The Roman pottery can be compared to the material excavated from the Cat's Water sub-Site at Fengate. Consisting of approximately 60 kg, the majority of this dated from the mid–late second century AD (Hayes 1984). That site, therefore, was not directly contemporary as it was occupied before the Tower Works Site; however, the types of pottery recovered were similar in form, thus suggesting that the two may have had similar functions.

In conclusion, the Roman pottery from the Tower Works Site suggests a late Roman site which peaked in the period between the third and fourth centuries AD. The material recovered implies that the site was of a domestic nature, with a range of vessels related to the preparation and consumption of foodstuffs. The types of pottery found suggest that it was not impoverished, but it was also unlikely to be particularly wealthy. The large number of finewares strongly correlates to the high density of Nene Valley wares. As this is produced locally, to imply that this is evidence of a wealthy site would be misleading. Overall, the assemblage can be considered fairly typical of a rural Roman site. The relatively large quantity of pottery recovered suggests a high level of activity, even if it took place within a short time-span.

Characterization studies of Romano-British shell-gritted pottery (ALAN VINCE)

Samples of Romano-British shell-gritted pottery were submitted for analysis (Table 5.10). Chemical analyses of each sample were made and three of the samples were thin-sectioned. The data were compared with samples of a range of shell-gritted wares from Cambridgeshire and elsewhere. In particular, the possibility of the samples being produced at Earith, Haddon, or Harrold was investigated. Earith is c. 30 miles southeast of Fengate; Haddon is about 10 miles to the southwest and Harrold is about 39 miles to the southwest.

Thin-section analysis

Examination at ×20 magnification using a stereomicroscope indicated that the samples could be grouped into three fabrics (Table 5.10) and a sample of each fabric was thin-sectioned by Steve Caldwell, University of Manchester. These sections were stained

TABLE 5.9. *Vessel forms for all excavated Roman pottery.*

Vessel form	No.	%	Wt (g)	%
Beaker	10	1.3	302	1.8
Beaded, flanged bowl	7	0.9	220	1.4
Body/non-diagnostic	562	74.1	7057	42.5
Bowl	1	0.1	15	0.09
Cornice rim beaker	3	0.4	7	0.04
Shallow dish	8	1	290	1.7
Dragendorff 18/31	1	0.1	19	0.1
Dragendorff 33	2	0.3	17	0.1
Flanged bowl	2	0.3	60	0.4
Flat base	58	7.7	4322	26
Handle	1	0.1	21	0.1
Indented beaker	3	0.4	12	0.07
Lid	1	0.1	22	0.1
Mortarium	5	0.7	232	1.4
Necked jar, beaded rim	55	7.4	2802	17
Necked jar, everted rim	12	1.6	45	0.3
Ring base	7	0.9	346	2.1
Other	20	2.6	803	4.8
Total	**758**	**100**	**16,592**	**100**

using Dickson's method (Dickson 1965). This staining distinguishes ferroan from non-ferroan calcite and dolomite.

Fabric 1 (V4169)

Nacreous bivalve shell; ornamented bivalve shell; echinoid shell; punctate Brachiopod shell; thin-walled shell; ferruginous limestone; ostracods; clay/ironstone; mudstone; angular quartz; voids, moderate euhedral voids were present (up to 1 mm long), however, these are probably either from leached-out sparry calcite or shell fragments rather than selenite crystals, since there are no examples with the distinctive diamond-shape found in a transverse section of selenite crystals.

The groundmass consists of brown, optically anisotropic baked clay minerals, dark brown rounded grains up to 0.2 mm across and sparse microfossils up to 0.1 mm across with ferran calcite filling of the non-ferroan calcite tests.

Fabric 2 (V4170)

A very similar range of inclusions was noted in the thin section of Fabric 2. Only ostracod shell and microfossils were not noted. However, there is a higher incidence of iron, both as rounded grains in the groundmass and coating and staining the shell fragments.

Nacreous bivalve shell; ornamented bivalve shell; echinoid shell; punctate Brachiopod shell; thin-walled shell; ferruginous limestone; ostracods; clay/ironstone; mudstone; angular quartz; voids, as in Fabric 1.

Table 5.10. *Pottery fabric samples submitted for thin-sectioned analysis.*

Action	TSNO	DN NO	Context	Cname	Subfabric	Form	Description
TS; ICPS	V4169	0	330	Shell	FAB 1: Bivalve; Echinoid shell	SJ	Thick-walled
TS; ICPS	V4170	0	408	Shell	FAB 2: Bivalve; Red FE; RQ	SJ	Thick-walled
ICPS	V4171	0	456	Shell	FAB 1	Jar	
TS; ICPS	V4172	0	459	Shell	FAB 3: Bivalve in ironstone groundmass	Jar	
ICPS	V4173	0	459	Shell	FAB 1	Jar	
ICPS	V4174	0	459	Shell	FAB 1	Jar	Rilled ext

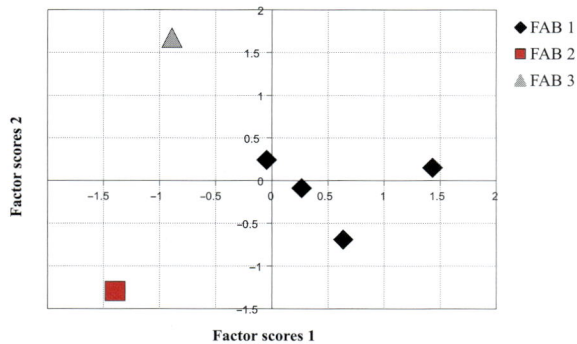

FIGURE 5.20. *Pottery Fabrics: Factor analysis (1).*

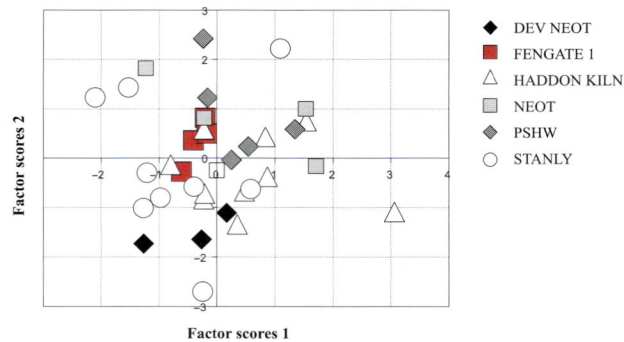

FIGURE 5.21. *Pottery Fabrics: Factor analysis (2).*

The groundmass consists of brown, optically anisotropic baked clay minerals, dark brown rounded grains up to 0.2 mm across.

Fabric 3 (V4172)

There is a lower range of shell types present in Fabric 3 and the nacreous bivalve shell is both larger and more frequent than in the other two fabrics. In addition, rounded quartz, absent from the other two fabrics is present and angular quartz is more frequent.

Nacreous bivalve shell; shelly limestone; ostracods; clay/ironstone; mudstone; angular quartz; rounded quartz; voids, as in Fabric 1.

The groundmass consists of brown, optically anisotropic baked clay minerals, dark brown rounded grains up to 0.2 mm across and sparse microfossils up to 0.1 mm across with ferroan calcite filling of the non-ferroan calcite tests.

Chemical analysis

Samples of each sherd were taken and all surfaces mechanically removed. The remaining block was then crushed to a fine powder and submitted to Royal Holloway College, London, where inductively-coupled plasma spectroscopy was carried out under the supervision of Dr J.N. Walsh. A range of major elements was measured and expressed as percent oxides (Table 5.11) and a range of minor and trace elements was measured and expressed in parts per million (Table 5.12). Silica content was not measured but was estimated by subtraction of the total oxides from 100 per cent. After silica estimation the measured values were normalized to aluminium, to take account of the diluting effect of silica.

Estimated silica content for the four Fabric 1 samples was 59.89 per cent with an SD of 1.60. The Fabric 2 and 3 samples have higher estimated silica: 62.88 per cent and 64.13 per cent respectively. Thus Fabrics 2 and 3 have silica values greater than 1 SD from the mean for Fabric 1; the higher value for Fabric 3 is consistent with the thin section.

The normalized data were examined using Winstat for Excel. All of the measured elements were examined to look for outlying values (greater than 4 SD than the mean) and no such values were noted. In fact, only one value, phosphorus in sample V4169, lay more than 2 SD from the mean, indicating a high degree of similarity in chemical composition.

Factor analysis was undertaken of the least mobile elements (i.e. omitting calcium, phosphorous, strontium and the Rare Earths) and zirconium, which is only partially measured using the RCHL set-up. This analysis found four factors and a plot of the first two factors indicates that the Fabric 2 sample is distinguished by negative F1 and F2 values whilst the Fabric 3 sample is distinguished by high F2 and negative F1 values (Fig. 5.20).

High F2 scores are due mainly to high manganese, lithium and copper values whilst high F1 scores are due to high potassium,

barium and magnesium values and to low lead and titanium values. Examination of the normalized data confirms that Fabric 3 is distinguished by high copper, titanium, lithium and manganese values whilst Fabric 2 is distinguished by high lead and low lithium. Fabric 1 is distinguished by high magnesium and potassium.

The ICPS data were then compared with that from a range of sites in Cambridgeshire and that of a group of waste (of medieval date) from Harrold, Bedfordshire. Factor analysis of this data indicated that the Harrold and Earith samples could be readily distinguished from the Fengate samples and therefore the analysis was repeated omitting these samples.

Factor analysis of this reduced dataset indicates that the Fengate Fabrics 2 and 3 samples do not match any of the *comparanda* whilst the Fabric 1 samples are similar to a range of Peterborough-area shell-gritted wares:

- Ten samples from the Haddon kiln
- Three samples of Developed St Neots-type ware (DEV NEOT)
- Five samples of St Neots-type ware (NEOT)
- Five samples of Peterborough shell-tempered ware (PSHW)
- Nine samples of Lyveden/Stanley-type shell-tempered ware (STANLY)

The Fengate 1 samples and the remaining *comparanda* were then examined again, using both factor analysis and a series of plots of pairs of elements and little patterning was evident (Fig. 5.21). This suggests that that the Fengate 1 samples were probably produced to the west of Peterborough and that the Haddon kiln is indeed a possible source.

The Fengate samples can be divided into three separate fabric groups. Fabrics 1 and 2 contain a similar range of inclusions and might be thought of as variations within a single source. The chemical composition separates the two fabrics quite sharply and instead indicates a similarity between Fabrics 2 and 3; however, these two fabrics have quite different shell inclusions, although in both fabrics there is a high degree of iron both in the body and adhering to the shell fragments.

None of the *comparanda* match either Fabrics 2 or 3 and this is in agreement with their petrology, since none of the comparative fabrics have such high frequency of iron-rich inclusions. Fabric 1 samples, however, match well with a range of shelly wares

TABLE 5.11. *Pottery fabric samples with major elements expressed as percent oxides.*

Fabric	TSNO	Al₂O₃	Fe₂O₃	MgO	CaO	Na₂O	K₂O	TiO₂	P₂O₅	MnO
FAB1	V4169	13.48	6.05	0.92	12.82	0.28	1.99	0.55	2.25	0.09
FAB1	V4171	16.70	6.38	1.15	13.92	0.30	2.43	0.73	0.59	0.08
FAB1	V4173	13.14	5.77	1.01	16.94	0.39	1.77	0.57	0.35	0.11
FAB1	V4174	12.62	5.59	0.80	17.70	0.25	1.62	0.53	0.49	0.07
	Mean	13.99	5.95	0.97	15.35	0.31	1.95	0.60	0.92	0.09
	SD	1.84	0.34	0.15	2.34	0.06	0.35	0.09	0.89	0.02
FAB2	V4170	15.63	6.23	0.57	11.47	0.17	1.36	0.74	0.90	0.05
FAB3	V4172	13.04	5.07	0.56	14.62	0.30	0.88	0.85	0.43	0.12

TABLE 5.12. *Minor and trace elements within pottery fabric samples (expressed as parts per million).*

Fabric	TSNO	Ba	Cr	Cu	Li	Ni	Sc	Sr	V	Y	Zr*	La	Ce	Nd	Sm	Eu	Dy	Yb	Pb	Zn	Co
FAB1	V4169	576	85	21	49	38	13	356	95	22	83	34	61	35	6	1	4	2	10	78	15
FAB1	V4171	514	113	22	62	47	15	404	104	26	60	40	76	41	8	2	4	2	10	101	14
FAB1	V4173	386	88	22	48	49	13	331	84	23	55	31	57	33	6	1	4	2	7	87	15
FAB1	V4174	334	74	22	41	42	11	359	94	23	74	32	59	33	6	1	3	2	8	67	17
	Mean	452.5	90.0	21.8	50.0	44.0	13.0	362.5	94.3	23.5	68.0	34.3	63.3	35.4	6.4	1.3	3.5	2.3	8.7	83.3	15.3
	SD	111.8	16.5	0.5	8.8	5.0	1.6	30.4	8.2	1.7	12.8	4.0	8.7	3.8	0.9	0.2	0.3	0.1	1.1	14.4	1.3
FAB2	V4170	341	76	23	25	47	14	245	111	33	69	39	71	41	9	2	5	3	24	84	18
FAB3	V4172	317	85	30	77	33	12	260	91	21	71	35	67	36	6	1	4	2	14	71	13

found in Peterborough, including material probably produced in the Lyveden/Stanion area and that produced at Haddon. Given the similarity of all of these wares it is impossible to say that Haddon was the source of the Fengate 1 samples, only that there are no petrological or chemical grounds for discounting this source. It may well be that other kilns in the Peterborough area which have yet to be discovered were producing similar wares.

Nevertheless, we can be fairly certain that the Fengate 1 samples have a fairly local source and that neither Earith nor Harrold could have produced this ware.

Roman tile (KATIE ANDERSON)
A total of 120 pieces of Roman tile were recovered (25,941 g). The assemblage had a relatively high mean fragment weight of 216.2 g, with all of the main tile forms represented.

Over half of the tile came from the well, F.151 (63 pieces; 17,361 g). This included some very large and near-complete pieces, with a mean weight of 276 g. The most commonly occurring form was tegula (24 pieces).

A total of 25 pieces of tile were recovered from seven further features, of which 18 pieces came from F.124 (including several very large pieces of tegulae and floor tile). Otherwise, a further 22 pieces were collected from the test pits. These had a mean weight of 59.3 g, which is much less than the material from the excavated features.

TABLE 5.13. *Roman tile by form.*

Form	Number	Wt (g)
Box flue	7	2309
Floor tile	32	11,252
Imbrex	4	499
Non-diagnostic	22	800
Tegula	55	11,081
Total	**120**	**25,941**

The quantity of tile recovered suggests that there was likely to have been at least one substantial building within the immediate area. The size of many of the pieces, particularly those from the well and the other excavated features, indicates the tile had not travelled a great distance and was probably deposited shortly after being removed from the building(s) from which it came.

A leather shoe (QUITA MOULD)
A Roman shoe of nailed construction was found in the basal fill ([468]) of Well F.151.

<257> ([468]; F.151) - Leather shoe of nailed construction (Fig. 5.22). The forepart of the left foot from a shoe of nailed construction. The bottom unit and vamp area of the upper are present; the bottom unit is torn away across the waist and the seat area is missing. The upper and bottom unit are joined, obscuring details of the upper attachment and any constructional thonging. The vamp has an oval toe and is worn away at the toe, the inside toe joint and exterior toe area. The high throat is straight and likely to be broken. The remains of a central, decorative, skeuomorphic toe seam of tunnel stitching is present, originally running from close to the throat to

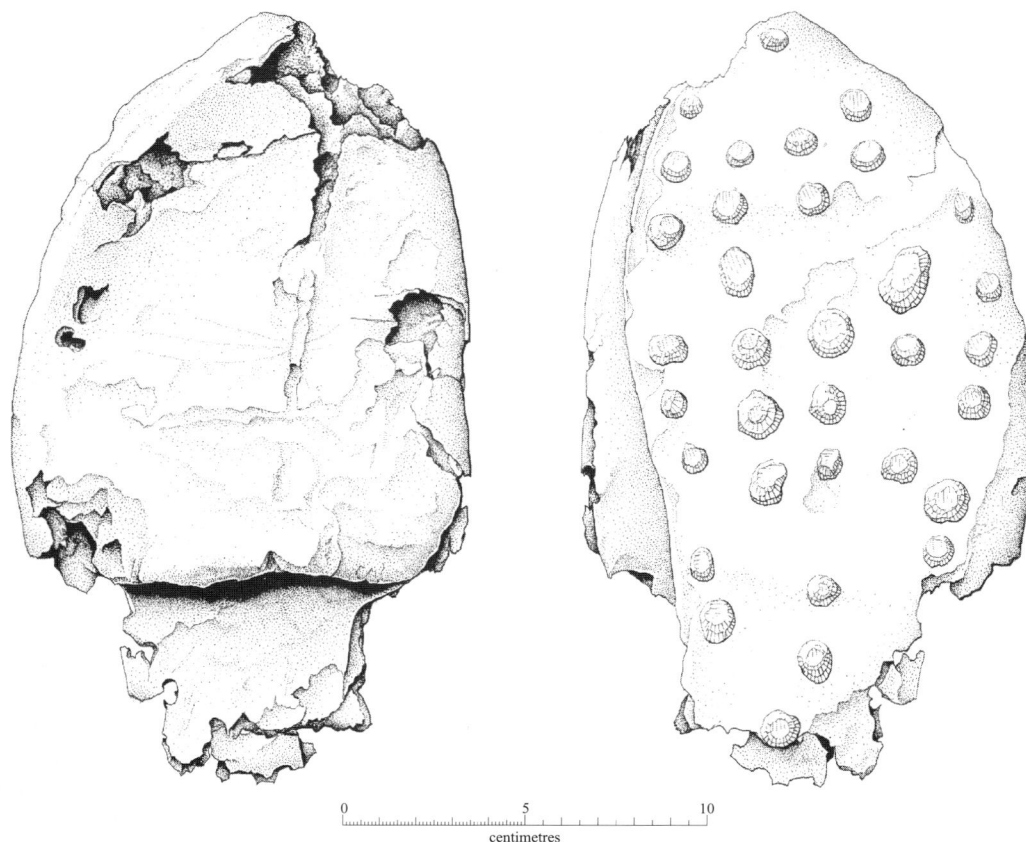

FIGURE 5.22. *Leather shoe from well F.151.*

the toe. A group of three radiating lines on either side of the seam appear to be deliberately impressed to replicate the puckering that would be produced by a real seam. At least two faint lines can also be seen at the toe. It may be that the grain surface of the vamp area of the upper had been decorated with a linear design(s). The bottom unit comprises an insole and nailed sole; a middle or middle laminae cannot be seen at present. No constructional thonging could be observed on the visible insole. The nailing pattern is van Driel-Murray 1A (2001, 351 fig. 21), with a single line along each side and three vertical lines running down the tread. The central line continues down past the waist.

Part of the right side of the lasting margin of the heel stiffener and a small area of upper seat were found separately from the rest of the shoe but are likely to come from it. The total height of the heel stiffener is not preserved. Also present are three small fragments broken from the above.

Bottom unit: surviving length 225 mm, tread width 110 mm: adult size.
Upper: surviving length 150 mm, width 130 mm.
Leather: bovine.

The worn shoe, of adult-size, is for the left foot and, although incomplete, appears to have been whole when deposited. The forepart is well preserved and the surviving vamp area of the upper shows it comes from a closed shoe with a high throat. The remains of a skeuomorphic vamp seam are present, running vertically from the throat to the toe. This feature has been found previously on a small number of shoes of late Roman date in Britain, principally coming from the south of the country.

The skeuomorphic seam on the Tower Works shoe appears to be tunnel-stitched, comparable with stitching down the vamp of a shoe of early/mid fourth-century date from Magor, Gwent (van Driel-Murray pers. comm.) and possibly those from Haynes Park, Beds. and Bancroft, Bucks., both from undated contexts. Decorative stitching running down the vamp was also seen on a shoe from Rectory Farm, Market Deeping, Lincs. This shoe came from the fill of a late Roman well and was associated with pottery dating after AD 250. The stitching on that example appears to be from a decorative stitch of different type, as does that on the Piddington shoe found in a well together with coins and pottery dating to AD 330–360.

The majority of Roman leather comes from military contexts or large urban centres with military associations. Leather from civilian, rural, contexts is relatively rare. The circumstances of the deposition of the shoe are also of interest as a ritual deposition might be implied. The style of this shoe is uncommon and suggests a fourth century date, which is consistent with the attribution of the F.151 well. Finds of footwear from that time are rare, and the shoe may be usefully compared with other examples with skeuomorphic toe seams and the data added to the small amount known about late Roman footwear from civilian contexts.

The author is unaware of the recovery of any leather of Roman date from Peterborough in recent years. Similarly, little Roman leather has been found in the county or those immediate surrounding it. A small amount has been found previously at Rectory Farm, Market Deeping, Lincs (Mould 1996) and at Scole on the Norfolk/Suffolk border (Adams 1973).

Metalwork (GRAHAME APPLEBY & ANDREW HALL)
Metal-detecting was carried out to aid the recovery of metallic finds from the buried soil deposits and the cut features. A total of 23 finds were retrieved from the survey area. Of these, nine were copper alloy, eight were made of lead, two of iron and the remainder consisted of slag/furnace waste fragments (see Timberlake below).

Coins

SmF.1; <231> - Large very corroded bronze Roman coin, recovered from the top of the buried soil. Possible sestertius of the first–second century AD.

SmF.6; <236> - Small copper-alloy coin, mostly illegible, with traces suggesting a late date — Theodosian II, 388–402 AD. Recovered from the quarry.

SmF.7; <237> - Small copper alloy coin, mostly illegible, with traces suggesting a late date — Theodosian II, 388–402 AD. Recovered from the quarry.

Copper alloy

SmF.5; <235> - High lead-content, copper-alloy single-feeder casting jet consisting of a roughly conical reservoir. The feeder has a roughly oval cross-section with a longitudinal ridge and remnant side feeder jet. Casting jets are found on sites where metalworking/casting has taken place, or following middening or manuring activity. The lack of secure dating of this object (recovered from the buried soil) is unfortunate as high lead content bronze is a feature of Late Bronze Age metalworking, several examples of which have been found nearby at Flag Fen (Pryor 2001a). Dimensions: length 23 mm, weight 3 g. Unphased.

SmF.8; <238> - Small irregular fragment of 'dished' shaped copper-alloy sheet; from a crotal bell or similar, or casting waste? Dimensions: 18 mm × 13 mm, weight <1 g. Unphased.

SmF.15; <244> - Irregular five-sided fragment of copper-alloy sheet or plate, slightly dished. The inner surface is smooth (polished?) with a slight bluish/grey patina, possibly indicating that it was tinned. The outer surface has roughly parallel striations that appear to 'radiate' from a point now missing. Probable tinned cooking vessel fragment. Dimensions: 30.5 mm × 31.5 mm, thickness 2 mm, weight 8 g. Dated to the sixteenth–seventeenth centuries AD.

SmF.16; <245> - Small fragment of copper-alloy casting spill. Dimensions: length 22 mm, weight 2 g. Attributed to the sixteenth–seventeenth centuries AD.

Lead

SmF.2; <232> - Very degraded basal fragment of a conical line or net weight. Dimensions: height 15 mm, diameter 22 mm, weight 20 g. A large number of this form (34) of weight, in varying degrees of preservation, were recovered from the Camp Ground, Earith (Appleby forthcoming). Excavations at Stonea produced only two examples (Jackson & Potter 1996, 378, fig. 122). A single example was found at Bancroft (Williams & Zeepvat 1994, 347), three from Camerton (Jackson 1990, 53, pl. 17) and two examples during excavation of the North Somerset Levels (Rippon 2000, 184, fig. 23). Roman.

SmF.4; <234> - Bi-conical steelyard weight with an iron suspension loop at the apex, weighing slightly more than a *Dodrons*, or nine *unciae*. Dimensions: diameter 40 mm, height 49 mm, weight 252 g. This form of steelyard weight is commonly found on Roman and medieval sites, with several Roman examples known from Earith (Appleby forthcoming) and Vicar's Farm, Cambridge (Lucas 2001a). Unphased, though probably Roman.

SmF.11; <240> - Degraded and irregularly shaped flat, roughly rectangular lump of lead (possibly pewter). Dimensions: 22 mm × 17 mm, weight, 12 g. Probable casting waste. Unphased.

SmF.17; <246> - Folded, short rectangular cross-sectioned bar. The bar is folded almost back on itself, as if it has been clamped to another object. Although interpretation is speculative, this artefact may be a line or net weight variant. Dimensions: 16 mm (*c.* 22 m flat) × 11 mm, weight 13 g. Unphased.

SmF.21; <250> - Roughly diamond-shaped fragment with 'sharp' edges indicative of cutting or sheering. Dimensions: 24 mm × 13 mm, weight 5 g. Possible scrap piece. Unphased.

Iron

<167> - Fragment of circular cross-sectioned nail or iron rod. Dimensions: length 33 mm, weight 5 g. Unphased

SmF.3; <233> - Corroded and heavily concreted 'amorphous' unidentifiable iron nodule (plus crumbs); probably iron-pan. Dimensions: length, 69 mm, width 40 mm, weight 108 g. Unphased.

SmF.14 <243> - Irregular rhomboidal flat iron fragment with a surviving rounded corner and edge. There is a distinct burr and distortion of the metal on one edge, suggesting damage caused by another edged object (plough-strike?). Dimensions: 22 mm × 23 mm, weight 5 g. Undiagnostic. Unphased.

<255> F.151 - Small concreted object with everted tip, almost creating a complete loop. The object is flat on one side and there has been considerable mineral loss (there is a bloom of silica salt on one surface). Probable mineral cast of a small bent flat triangular-headed nail (Manning Type 2; Manning 1985) with little remaining iron content. Weight 11 g. Recovered from Well F.151 and dated by associated pottery to the late second to fourth centuries AD.

The date range for the assemblage is broad, with artefacts from the Roman period and others from recent centuries. Several of the retrieved finds are undated due to their undiagnostic nature. The presence of Roman finds, such as the coins, the steelyard and net weights, perhaps implies a commercial or economic aspect to the activities, although both are common finds within Roman settlements. The biconical steelyard weight (<4>) is certainly of a Romano-British type, roughly equivalent to nine Roman ounces (*Dodens*), or ¾ of a *libra*, one Roman pound.

In terms of spatial patterning, the assemblage is too small to allow for any meaningful interpretation. The small group of slag/furnace waste (11, 12, 18 and 22) was recovered from within a zone outside the main area of features (see Timberlake below). This could well reflect an area of small-scale industrial/metallurgical activity situated outside the domestic core of any adjacent settlement.

The presence of still other, more recently dated finds (not listed above), such as a key, tobacco box lid and buckle fragment from within the buried soil, suggest a degree of disturbance to the deposits and the resulting incorporation of this later material. This may have taken place through recent horticultural or agricultural activity, or during the construction/demolishing of the former Tower Works Engineering Plant.

Slag and ironworking debris (SIMON TIMBERLAKE)
Thirteen pieces of slag and other ironworking debris were recovered. These were examined with the aid of a hand-lens, magnet and a steel point for hardness testing.

<241> (M-D Find No. 12; 54 g) - A piece of ferruginous metallurgical waste, found during metal-detecting in Area II. Consists of a cindery surface largely made up of weakly magnetic or non-magnetic iron oxides and hydroxides which on the irregular underside enclose some highly calcined fragments of flint and baked clay, the latter part of the hearth lining. Possibly re-melted iron waste, impurities and hammer-scale from the base of a blacksmith's hearth.

<242> (M-D Find No. 13; 34 g) - A single piece of ferruginous metallurgical waste similar to <247>, found during metal-detecting in Area II. Probably part-melted iron, perhaps hammer-scale or other waste accumulated within the base of a hearth, perhaps associated with blacksmithing. Vesicular top and base, the latter with inclusions of baked clay. Very weakly magnetic, mostly oxidized to iron hydroxides. This may be part of the same hearth fragment as Metal-detector Find No.18. If so, this suggests that these iron slags, and possibly also other items of metallurgical waste and pieces of metalwork found within the same dark soil spread, are mostly re-deposited objects spread out thinly and strewn across the site.

<247> (M-D Find No. 18; 158 g) - Includes six pieces of ferruginous metallurgical waste plus an iron concretion in sand. The broken mass is now highly oxidized, mostly iron oxides/hydroxide, the formation of which has served to cement the underlying sand, clay and fragments of calcined flint, the latter presumably part of the base of an iron-working hearth. The ferruginous mass may

represent the accumulation and accretion of hammer-scale within a blacksmith's workshop, perhaps partly re-melted in a hearth; however, the presence of small slag runnels on the underside at points where these have sunk into the clay/sand and flint base also suggests molten iron-rich slag droplets, perhaps associated with the working of a bloom. The slag was metal-detected within the southeastern part of Area II and, loosely speaking, was associated with a zone of metalwork finds, although not necessarily in numbers which suggest *in situ* workshop activities.

<251> (M-D Find No. 22; 62 g) - A small mass of ferrous metallurgical waste almost wholly oxidized to iron oxides/hydroxide, partly vesicular, and veined with ash and clay. A metal-detector find, apparently found within the 'artefact-enriched' buried soil [210] in Area II. Although it is possible this could be intrusive and therefore post-Roman, the similarity of this to other samples of iron-working slag, plus its association with metalworking in this area, suggests that it is contemporary. The ferrous material is highly oxidized, and thus only very weakly magnetic. Whilst it seems likely that it was never very dense, the sample might be quite oxidized, the iron having been leached out into the soil. The presence of primary gas bubbles suggests metallurgical waste, as does a small area of 'slag skin' runnel on the underside where this had become frozen onto a clay/sand/grit mix lining, possibly the base of a hearth. The remains of this accreted hearth lining includes a small fragment of calcined stone. What is visible of the slag suggests iron-working rather than primary smelting slag, with slag associated with the working of a bloom in a blacksmith's workshop the most likely. Given that this was picked up as a single and isolated find, it is unlikely that it represents the presence of a workshop in the immediate area.

<130> (Test Pit 15; 4 g) - A small fragment of ferruginous waste recovered from Area II and one of the buried soil squares excavated into the 'dark' soil layer ([210]). Little can be discerned of this, aside from the fact that it is probably a fragment of iron-working slag.

<160> (Test Pit 39; 11 g) - A small fragment of black metallurgical waste recovered from Area II and one of the buried soil squares excavated into the 'dark' soil layer ([210]). This appears to be a piece of fairly dense, metallic 'slag' which is moderately magnetic, yet which includes little or no iron hydroxides. This is partly vesicular (contains gas cavities) and the metallic structure of the slag in places is also sub-crystalline. A small particle of charcoal is entrapped within the surface. The structure of this suggests it may be a fragment of tap slag, possibly from the smelting of iron; however, the lack of iron hydroxides is unusual, suggesting that much of the iron is bound up within the silicate fraction. A small fragment like this could have arrived on site attached to an iron bloom brought by iron-working smiths. As an impurity this would have been knocked off during hammering of the bloom in preparation for re-melting and smithing. Certainly, there is no evidence to suggest that the source of this slag lay anywhere close-by; thus it seems quite unlikely that smelting was an *in situ* activity undertaken on site.

<260> ([268], F.151; 14 g) - A pale grey-white coloured lightweight vesicular 'slag' with a chalky to glazed surface and patches of iron-staining. Identical to sample <266> found within basal silt of the well F.151, thus possibly non-ferrous metallurgical waste.

<081> ([450], F.151; 143 g) — A pale grey-white coloured lightweight vesicular 'slag' with a chalky surface and patches of iron-staining. Similar to sample <266> recovered from the base of the F.151 well, this came from one of the upper fills. The metallurgical composition of this material is difficult. This seems to have dripped onto the clay and sandy bottom of a pit or hearth, and is much admixed with charcoal; however, the sand inclusions show little signs of burning. The sample is redeposited, found within one of the silt layers infill-

ing the well. The similarity of this to sample <266> suggests that material from the same area had been used to backfill the well. This may imply that the remains of an 'industrial' workshop hearth(s) existed somewhere close by.

<266> ([468], F.151; 57 g) - A pale grey-white coloured lightweight vesicular 'slag' with a chalky to glazed surface and patches of iron-staining. Found within a black humic silty basal deposit ([468]) removed from the base of well, associated with pottery and bone, but no iron working slag. Probably metallurgical waste, perhaps associated with the melting and refining of a non-ferrous alloy. Small fragments of charcoal have been trapped within the underside of this. An initial visual inspection of a freshly broken surface suggests that the white to blue-white crust might be of tin or lead oxides, most probably the former. This appears to be associated with silicates. A very thin crust of iron oxide (orange) was also noted coating the inside of some of the gas bubbles. This is slightly magnetic, suggesting high enough temperatures for the reduction of iron. This is common within tin smelting or refining.

<114> ([468], F.151; 867 g) - An intact plano-convex slag cake, probably the sub-circular bottom of a metalworking hearth with a very slight conical base (14 × 12 × 8 cm). The weight of this, the slight but variable magnetic content and the presence of iron oxides at the surface suggest a high iron content. The surface of the cake has a bubbly texture indicating the gradual accretion of molten and some solid material. This includes a light to dark grey clay silt plus small fragments of gravel which appear to have fallen in or melted off the hearth sides. Some of this ferrous slag also appears to include lenses of an unidentified metallurgical waste, in some respects similar to the non-ferrous 'slag' sample (<266>) recovered from this same context. This *in situ*-formed slag may be the accreted product of re-using the hearth. Therefore it might represent the re-melting or smithing of several different metals, although most likely iron.

The form of this slag cake reflects the shape and size of the furnace base, perhaps a small shaft furnace no more than 15–20 cm wide and perhaps 20–30 cm high. The raised rim and central depression on the surface of the slag cake appears to reflect the position of the tuyere blast directly above it, whilst the angle of this is from one side of the hearth, as indicated by the flattened concave edge of the rim. The accreting sand and gravel on the underside of the cake suggests that the furnace may not have been floored with clay.

This collection of redeposited slag within the well backfill supports the interpretation, suggested for <081> above, of inadvertent inclusion from the surrounding ground surface. The quite unabraded nature of this slag suggests that the source for this lay close by.

<096> ([459], F.151: <096>a, 516 g; <096b>b, 371 g) - A plano-convex hearth bottom (<096>a). This has been formed by the accretion of layers of charcoal and ferrous waste, possibly some non-ferrous slag, plus some fired and 'frothy', though now largely devitrified chalk and/or silt, clay and gravel lining welded to the underside of the slag cake. Despite its incompleteness, the presence of charcoal inclusions within the ferrous waste, plus the much clearer evidence for a lining, helps with its recognition as a hearth base; however, the upper surface of this slag cake (which might have shown the same sort of molten tuyere blast features witnessed in <114>) appears to be missing. It also seems that this base could have undergone considerable post-depositional leaching whilst buried within the sub-soil.

Sample <096>b is layered and consists of two horizons of whitish bubbly slag (perhaps a non-ferrous type) welded onto an originally vitrified furnace lining. The latter sandwiches a ferruginous layer mixed with sand and gravel and charcoal in between. This suggests re-lining of a hearth and is good evidence for multiple use.

Both pieces could have been part of the same re-lined and

re-used hearth, the upper part of which (<096>a) has since become detached and is missing. Although this could have been for ironworking, it is also conceivable that the iron-working was carried out within a re-used hearth, perhaps one previously associated with non-ferrous metalworking, possibly for lead or for tin (or both). Needless to say, this hearth(s) could have been used for melting down scrap consisting of a mixture of different metals.

Based on the form and the type of technology, and supported in part by good contextual information where this was present, the different types of slag encountered, including iron-smithing waste, nonedescript bloomery waste, slag-accreted furnace lining, non-ferrous metal slag(s), plano-convex hearth bases (slag cakes) and a small fragment of a possible tap slag, are all credible products of small-scale local Romano-British metalworking. Although the total weight of slag and furnace products recovered from this site (2291 g) seems large when compared with that from other Roman rural settlements in Cambridgeshire, such as Vicar's Farm (approx 2000 g, but from an area twice the size of the Tower Works Site; see Cowgill 2001a), this still only represents a small number of pieces with a fairly confined distribution. Moreover, none of these fragments were found associated with any *in situ* evidence for metalworking, although the finds of plano-convex hearth bases and slag from the well probably does indicate redeposition from a metalworking site close by. Roman or Late Iron Age iron-working sites typically produce slags in the order of tens if not hundreds of kilograms; this is certainly the case where there has been smelting from ores (Tylecote 1986; Jackson & Tylecote 1988; Crew 1998; 2002). In this respect, the recovery of just a few hearth bottoms plus fragments of scattered smithing slag suggests non-permanent, perhaps even very occasional metalworking, such as might have been carried out by itinerant smiths or metalworkers passing through the settlement. There is no direct evidence to suggest that any sort of smelting was actually taking place on site.

The somewhat ambiguous evidence for non-ferrous metalworking presented by most of the slag pieces recovered from the F.151 well is worthy of a mention. The two slagged hearth bottoms both have a high iron content, suggesting that they either represent the slag from ironworking, which just happens to be mixed up with a lot of other impurities, or else they represent two different processes (or more likely a re-use of the small metalworking hearth) carried out on different occasions. This sort of ferrous slag could have resulted from the melting and smithing of a rather small raw iron bloom. Alternatively this represents a metalworker's hearth for the re-melting and working of metal scrap. Conceivably, both iron

TABLE 5.14. *Roman charred plant remains (Key: '-' 1 or 2 items, '+' < 10 items, '++' 10–50 items, '+++' >50 items).*

		<204>	<205>	<207>	<209>	<210>	<211>	<212>	<213>	<214>	<215>	<218>	<219>	<220>	<221>	<222>
	Context	[208]	[210]	[210]	[226]	[253]	[250/1]	[266]	[268]	[312]	[333]	[388]	[359]	[353]	[459]	[468]
	Feature	F.104			F.109	F.118	F.117	F.124		F.086	F.095	F.152	F.131	F.130	F.151	F.151
	Feature type	ditch	b. soil	b. soil	ditch	ditch	ditch	pit	b. soil	pit	pit	grave	gully	pit	well	well
	Sample volume – litres	10	15	14	7	14	7	13	16	15	19	8	11	6	14	11
	Flot fraction examined	1/1	1/1	1/1	1/1	1/1	1/1	1/1	1/1	1/1	1/1	1/1	1/1	1/1	1/2	1/2
Silene cf. *vulgaris*	Bladder campion		1													
Rumex sanguineus	Wood dock										1					
Rumex obtusifolius	Broad-leaved dock					3		1			3					
Rumex sp. kernal											1					
Malva neglecta/ sylvestris	Dwarf/common mallow					1		1			2					
Large Leguminoseae indet.	Large legume										0.5					
Galium aparine	Cleavers										2					
Claudium mariscus	Great fen sedge										2			1		
Lolium sp.	Rye grass													1	1	
Bromus sp.	Brome							1								
Small Poaceae indet.	Small grass family					1					1			2		
Medium Poaceae indet.	Medium grass family															2
Large Poaceae indet.	Large grass family							1			2					
Charcoal fragments																
>4 mm		-	-	-		+	-	+		-	+		+		+	-
2–4 mm		+	+	+	-	++	+	++	-	++	++	++	++	+	++	+
<2 mm		+++	+++	++	++	+++	++	+++	++	++	+++	++	+++	++	+++	++
Vitrified		-	+	++		+	+	+	+	+	-	+				
Rootlets				+					+				-	-	-	+

and iron mixed with non-ferrous metal alloy artefacts could be recycled. Temperatures sufficient to fully melt iron, however, could not be achieved within such (small) furnaces, thus metal objects would have to be smithed hot to purify and form a billet after first melting and recovering any other metals. The non-ferrous slag component is most likely to be associated with tin and lead.

Other finds

A total of 12 pieces of burnt clay were found (198 g). Five were found in the buried soil squares, the remaining fragments deriving from well F.151 and pit F.97. Seven of the pieces from these were vitrified, probably as a result of industrial processes. Two fragments of quernstone were retrieved from F.151 ([459] (2050 g)), the smaller of the two showing signs of burning.

A worked bone point was recovered from F.151. This was 65.4 mm in length, oval, pointed at one end and broken off at the other. The diameter of the pointed end was 5.9–6.3 mm, tapering off to 4.2–5 mm diameter at the broken end. This could have been a hair-pin, a stylus or for fixing clothes (Crummy 1983).

Environmental and economic evidence

Macro-botanical remains (ELLEN SIMMONS)

Sixteen bulk environmental samples were processed for charred plant remains using an Ankara-type flotation machine. The flots were collected in a 300 μm mesh, and the remaining heavy residue washed over a 1mm mesh. Flots were dried indoors and sorted for charred plant remains and molluscs. Heavy residue was dried and the greater than 4 mm fraction sorted by eye. Two of the bulk samples, <221> and <222>, appeared to contain material preserved by waterlogging. Sub-samples were therefore taken and processed by soaking and then sieving over a stack of sieves containing 4 mm, 2 mm, 1 mm, 500 μm and 300 μm meshes.

Sorting and identification of plant remains was carried out under a low power microscope. Identifications were made using the reference collection of the George Pitt-Rivers Laboratory, McDonald Institute, University of Cambridge. Nomenclature follows Stace (1997). All environmental remains identified from the bulk samples and the waterlogged sub-samples are listed in full in Tables 5.14 and 5.15.

Preservation of plant remains in these samples was both by charring and by waterlogging. The wa-

TABLE 5.15. *Waterlogged plant remains.*

			<221>	<222>
		Sample number	<221>	<222>
		Context	[459]	[468]
		Feature	F.151	F.151
		Feature type	well	well
		Description	upper	basal
		Phase/date	L Rom	L Rom
		Sample volume – litres	400 ml	400 ml
		Flot fraction examined	1/2	1/2
Culm node	Straw chaff		-	
Nut-shell fragments			4	
Ranunculus acris	Meadow buttercup	Grassland especially damp		-
Ranunculus repens	Creeping buttercup	Wet grassland, stream side, woods marshes		-
Urtica dioica	Common nettle	Many habitats esp woodland, fens, cultivated ground and nitrogen enriched soils		+++
Cheneopodium polyspermum	Allseed	Waste places and cultivated ground		++
Chenopodium album	Fat hen	Waste places and cultivated ground		++
Montia fontana ssp. minor	Blinks	Many kinds of damp places		+
Stellaria media	Common chickweed	Cultivated and open ground		+++
Polygonum aviculare	Knotgrass	Open ground		++
Rumex acetosella ssp. *acetosella*	Sheep's sorrel	Heathy open ground, short grassland and cultivated land		+
Rumex obtusifolius	Broad-leaved dock	Grassland, by rivers, waste and cultivated ground		+
Rumex sp. fruiting tepals			+	+
Malva sylvestris	Common mallow	Waste and rough ground		+
Rorippa cf. *microphylla*	Narrow fruited water cress	In and by streams ditches and marshes		+
Thlaspi arvense	Field pennycress	Weed of arable land and waste places		+
Brassica cf. *nigra*	Black mustard	River banks, rough ground and waste places		+
Rubus fruiticosus	Bramble	Scrub		++
Linum usitatissimum	Cultivated flax	Grown for linen and linseed oil		+
Conium maculatum	Hemlock	Damp ground, ditches, roadside banks and waste ground		+++
Hyoscyamus niger	Henbane	Rough and waste ground especially where manured by cattle		++
Lamium pupurum	Red dead nettle	Cultivated and waste ground		+
Sambucus niger	Elder	Woods, scrub, rough and waste ground		+
Cardus/Cirsium	Thistle			+++
Sonchus asper	Sow thistle	Cultivated soil and waste places		++
Eleocharis sp.	Spike rush	Damp ground, marshes, ditches, pond margins		-
Carex sp. small trilete				+
Fish bone				+
Fish scale				-

terlogged material was very well preserved, enabling identification to species in many cases. The majority of charred cereal grains were relatively poorly preserved, with only fragments of epidermis remaining in many cases, and exhibited some distortion (cf. Hubbard & al Azm 1990). Charred remains of cereal chaff and wild plant seeds were, however, also present, indicating good preservational conditions during charring as chaff and small wild plant seeds are more easily destroyed by fire than grain (Boardman & Jones 1990).

Charred plant remains

The major crop type represented as charred remains in these samples is emmer wheat (*Triticum dicoccum*). Some barley (*Hordeum* sp.) was present and bread wheat (*Triticum aestivum*) may have been present, as indicated by chaff found in Sample <219> taken from gully F.131. This is unusual as spelt wheat almost always predomi-

nates in charred assemblages from the Roman period in England, with only a minor presence of emmer wheat (Greig 1991).

The majority of charred plant remains were found in ditch F.118, the F.131 gully, and the fills of pits F.95, F.124 and F.130. Sporadic finds of charred plant material were also present in the fill of the F.152 grave and the F.117 ditch. The majority of these contexts were located in the northeastern quarter of the site. This suggests that the disposal of waste from crop processing and activities involving the preparation of crops for storage and consumption were carried out in the immediate vicinity.

Processing of glume wheat crops in cooler climates is often carried out piecemeal according to requirements, as the glumes protect the grain from disease and pests while in storage (Hillman 1981). The charred assemblage, including tail grains, glume bases and some small weed seeds, therefore most likely represents waste from the later stages of crop processing such as fine sieving, pounding and hand sorting. Grains, the product of crop processing, are most likely to have been charred during drying or cooking.

The wild plant species represented by charred seeds found alongside the cereal remains were most probably harvested along with the crop and later removed and discarded onto the fire. The presence of great fen sedge (*Claudium mariscus*) and wood dock (*Rumex sanguineus*), therefore indicates that crops were grown in quite damp soil conditions. The other wild plant species represented by charred seeds are all characteristic of open, waste or cultivated ground.

Waterlogged plant remains

Waterlogged plant material was present in the basal fill of the F.151 well (Sample <222>). The seeds of a wide range of plant species were present and represent either plants growing in the near vicinity when the fill was accumulating or material dumped into the well from the surrounding environment.

The majority of the plant species identified were ruderals, characteristic of open, waste and cultivated ground and disturbance. These included annuals which are commonly found where repeated clearance or disturbance has taken place, such as goosefoots (*Chenopodium* spp.), common chickweed (*Stellaria media*) and knotgrass (*Polygonum aviculare*). Perennial plants indicating ground colonization lasting more than a single season were also present, such as docks (*Rumex* spp.), common mallow (*Malva sylvestris*), and the biennial hemlock (*Conium maculatum*), which is associated with established perennial open ground colonizers. Some scrub species were also present such as elder (*Sambucus nigra*) and bramble (*Rubus fruiticosus*), as well as a number of seeds from common nettle (*Urtica dioica*) and henbane (*Hyoscyamus niger*), which both thrive where the soil has been enriched by animal manure. Also present in the well were seeds of cultivated flax (*Linum usitatissimum*) which is commonly found waterlogged on Roman sites (Greig 1991). Flax would have been grown for making linen cloth from fibres, for linseed oil or for food (fish bone and fish scale were also present in the sample from this feature.)

The charred plant remains indicate that the main cereal crop utilized was emmer wheat. Barley and bread wheat were also present, with the charred wild plant seeds suggesting that crops were grown on damp soil. The emmer wheat would have most likely been stored with its protective glumes attached as semi-clean spikelets and processed when needed. The waste chaff, tail grains and small weed seeds then became charred, as did some grains, probably during cooking or drying, and distributed throughout the vicinity where such activities were taking place.

Waterlogged plant remains found in the basal fill of the F.151 well indicate that cultivation of flax, for cloth, oil or food, was being carried out at the site. The environment local to that feature was found to have been largely open, with clearance or disturbance taking place; however, this ceased for long enough for perennial disturbed ground colonizers to be present. Soil enrichment, such as that caused by animal manure, was also indicated.

Faunal remains (CHRIS SWAYSLAND)

A total of 1115 fragments of animal bone (26,530 g) were recovered. The material was identified using the CAU reference collection. The assemblage was quantified using a modified version of the methodology of Serjeantson (1991; 1996), a 'zonal' approach. Bones of

sheep and goats were recorded as sheep/goat. Tooth eruption and wear stages were recorded following Payne (1973) for sheep/goat, Grant (1982) and Legge (1992) for cattle and Hambleton (1999) for pigs. Information on gnawing, butchery and pathology was recorded where present. Butchery was recorded by type (i.e. chop, knife cut, sawn) and location. Pathological conditions were categorized where possible and descriptions made as to form and location.

All the material is of Romano-British attribution, dating between the second and fourth centuries AD. The assemblage is considered for the site as a whole, with the exception of F.151. Yielding the majority of the bones recovered, this is separately considered below.

The identified assemblage is dominated by cattle (23 specimens). Some were of a large size, indicating either the introduction of new species or local improvements in husbandry techniques (Dobney 2001). One metatarsal shows pronounced widening of the distal epiphysis, possibly attesting to the use of cows for traction (Bartosiewicz *et al.* 1997).

Sheep/goat are represented by seven fragments and horse by three. Seven dog bone fragments were recovered from F.108. Representing the articulated back legs of one individual, these were fully fused indicating that the animal was adult. The bones were very fragmentary and no measurements could be taken.

Two fragments of animal bone were discovered in the human grave, F.152 (cut into an earlier ditch, F.118). One was a scapula, a prime meat-bearing bone; the other was a mandible, which holds very little meat. It is uncertain whether these bones represent grave goods or an accidental inclusion of domestic refuse.

Well F.151

The remains from this feature were in good condition, with surface detail preserved on many specimens.

The well's assemblage is overwhelmingly dominated by cattle (80.4 per cent). A range of meat- and non-meat-bearing bones are present in the assemblage although there is an emphasis on the meat-bearing bones. The representation of skeletal elements in the assemblage is interesting: although 19 metapodials were

TABLE 5.16. *Number of identified bone specimens (NISP) for each species identified, excluding well F.151 (* from one articulated dog).*

Species	NISP	%NISP	MNI	%MNI
Cattle	23	57.5	1	25.0
Sheep/goat	7	17.5	1	25.0
Horse	3	7.5	1	25.0
Dog	7*	17.5	1	25.0

TABLE 5.17. *Relative animal species proportions from well F.151.*

Species	NISP	%NISP	MNI	%MNI
Cattle (*Bos taurus*)	127	80.4	9	50.0
Sheep/goat (*Ovis/ Capra*)	21	13.3	5	27.7
Horse (*Equus* sp.)	7	4.4	1	5.56
Cat (*Felis* sp.)	1	<1	1	5.56
Pike (*Esox lucius*)	1	<1	1	5.56
Goose(*Anser* sp.)	1	<1	1	5.56

represented, there was only one first phalange and no second or third phalanges. This may be indicative of a 'consumer' site where carcasses were transported to the site without the lower legs; however, it should be noted that a lack of lower limb bones (carpals, tarsals and phalanges) can be an artefact of hand-retrieval. In addition, the presence of large numbers of mandibles suggests that cows may have reached the site as live animals.

Butchery marks were observed on several cow scapulae, bones which are over-represented in the assemblage as a whole. Four specimens show cut-and-nick damage on the blade and 'shaving' marks on the flat-section of the bone. This is consistent with removal of the last stubbornly attached bits of meat after smoking, or brining of the meat for long-term preservation and storage (Dobney 2001, 41).

An estimation of the age at death can be made by analysis of the state of eruption and wear of the mandibular teeth. Nine cow mandibles could be aged. Although the sample size is small, the data suggests a bimodal pattern with peaks of sub-adult animals at stage 4 (6–15 months) and adult animals at stages 6, 7 and 8 (3–8 years). One cattle mandible showed a congenital deformity of the lower third molar. This tooth was missing the hypoconulid (posterior cusp). This trait has been noted on other Roman cattle material (Maltby 1979; Dobney *et al.* 1996) and may be related to breeding within restricted gene pools (O'Connor 1988).

Sheep/goat are the second most frequently represented species (13.3 per cent). A range of meat- and non-meat-bearing bones are represented in the assemblage. Five mandibles allowed an estimation of age at death from the state of tooth eruption and wear. One mandible was from an animal aged 1–2 years, two were aged 2–3 years and two 3–4 years.

No pig bones were recovered. Otherwise, of the minor species, seven horse elements were recovered: six were teeth and the seventh was a distal tibia. One cat scapula was recovered from [466]. The domestic cat is believed to have been a Roman introduction to Britain; however, this bone is of a large size and may be from a wild cat. One goose bone, a tibio-tarsus, was recovered (from [459]). The large size of this bone indicates it was probably domestic. The bone was complete and had several small cut-marks on the posterior of the distal articulation. Such marks are consistent with dismemberment. A mandible from a pike was also recovered from [466] (see Simmons above concerning the recovery of both fish bone and fish scales from the F.151 well).

The assemblages from the F.151 well and the rest of the site both show a high dependency on cattle. King (1978; 1991) has described a 'gradient' of highly Romanized sites having high percentages of cattle (and pig) through to non-Romanized rural settlements continuing the Iron Age tradition of high sheep percentages. Within this framework, this is clearly a highly Romanized site. In addition, the large size of some of the cattle bones indicates either the introduction of new stock or improvement in husbandry, both being considered aspects of Romanization. Wild species are represented in only very small numbers, the only definite example being the pike jaw; other possible examples are the goose and cat bones.

The adjacent edge: the Sewage Treatment Works

In conjunction with desktop researches (Lucas 1997), in 1997 French and Heathcote undertook coring across this site which straddles the fen-edge some 400m south of the Tower Works (Fig. 5.23). After an interval of six years, further coring again occurred there (Knight & Swaysland 2003). With its ground surface presently lying at *c.* 3.2–3.5 m OD, in general this showed that area's buried topography comprised a basal gravel terrace (see Fig. 5.23) rising from *c.* −1 m OD to 1.5–2 m OD. It forms a 'bluff' to the north of the site, that is overlain by peat and silty peat, and capped by stiff alluvial silty clay. The Sewage Treatment Works (STW) site is bounded to the west by a former area of gravel terrace, once quarried for aggregates and now a landfill site. Now occupied by industrial units, to the east the terrace has also been quarried. The Sewage Treatment Works proper compound lies to the north, and the site is bounded to the south by the canalized course of the River Nene. The site itself is a marshy inlet between gravel terraces that has remained un-drained despite the surrounding development, and provides excellent conditions for sedimentary preservation. It is likely that the inlet marks the confluence of the original course of Cat's Water where the River Nene drains into the Flag Fen basin (French 2003b).

Due to its depth of cover and the shallow nature of the area's intended development, further investigation was considered unwarranted and no trenching was conducted on this site. However, as part of this programme, Boreham also undertook coring and, with Peachey, full pollen/stratigraphic analyses (for the latter's University dissertation project). From this it would appear that, from the Late Bronze Age, the STW inlet began to silt up, with water rising against the gravel 'bluff'. The publication of their study is warranted on the grounds that most of Fengate's fen-edge palaeo-environmental researches have been dominated by the local register of Flag Fen and, thus, potentially somewhat limited when considering anthropogenic activity on drier ground. This study investigated the pollen signal from a somewhat 'removed' locale to determine whether its sequence revealed a more regional, or at least locally broader, record of vegetation and human presence.

Stratigraphy, pollen analysis and palaeoenvironmental reconstructions
(STEVE BOREHAM & MARK PEACHEY)
Based on the results of previous auger surveys, two borehole transects (A & B) were investigated to verify the stratigraphy previously described from the site (see Fig. 5.23). Transect A ran northwest–southeast down the edge of the gravel 'bluff' (Fig. 5.24), whose apex (A2–3) is indicated by sandy silt overlying gravel at *c.* 2 m OD. This was overlain by *c.* 0.5 m of silty peat

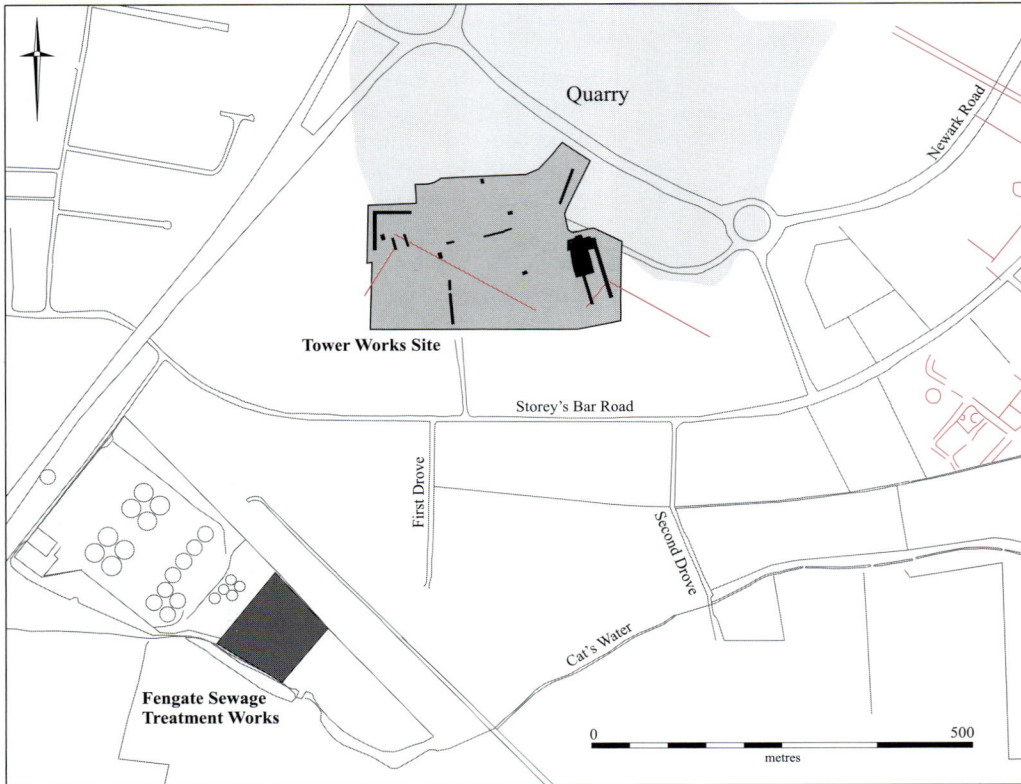

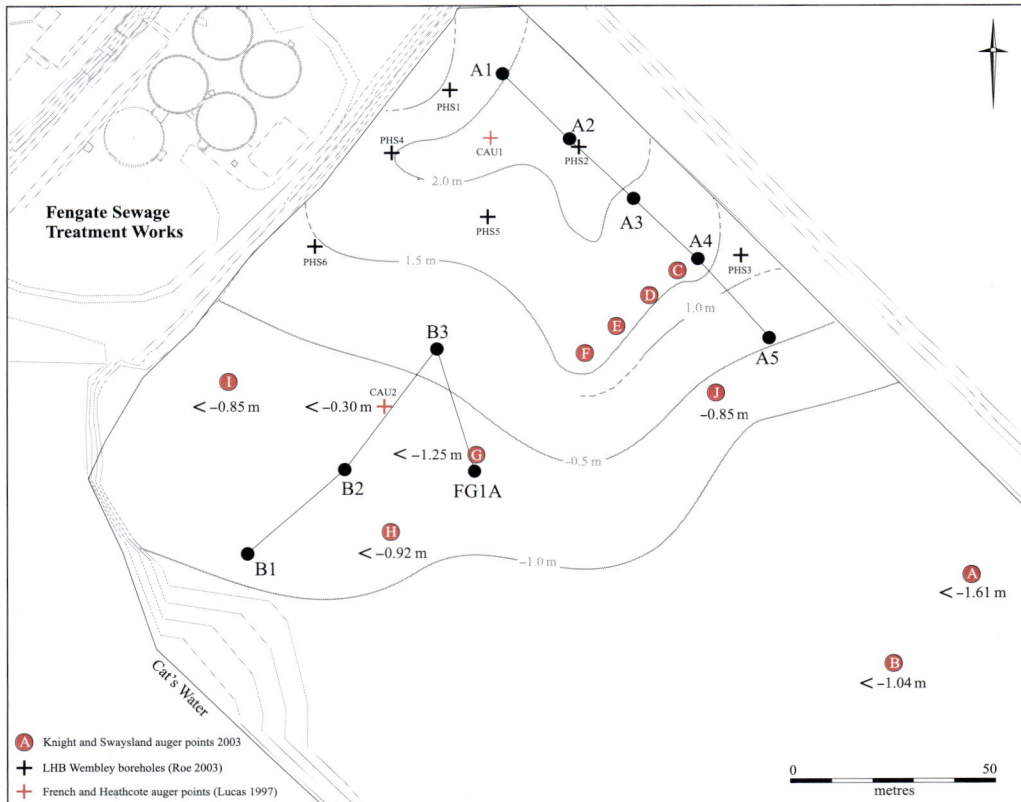

FIGURE 5.23.
*Fengate STW Site,
map showing the
location of boreholes
mentioned and
contours (m OD)
on the surface of
the terrace gravels
(after Knight &
Swaysland 2003).
Reproduced by
permission of
Ordnance Survey
on behalf of
HMSO. © Crown
copyright 2009.
All rights reserved.
Ordnance Survey
Licence number
100048686.*

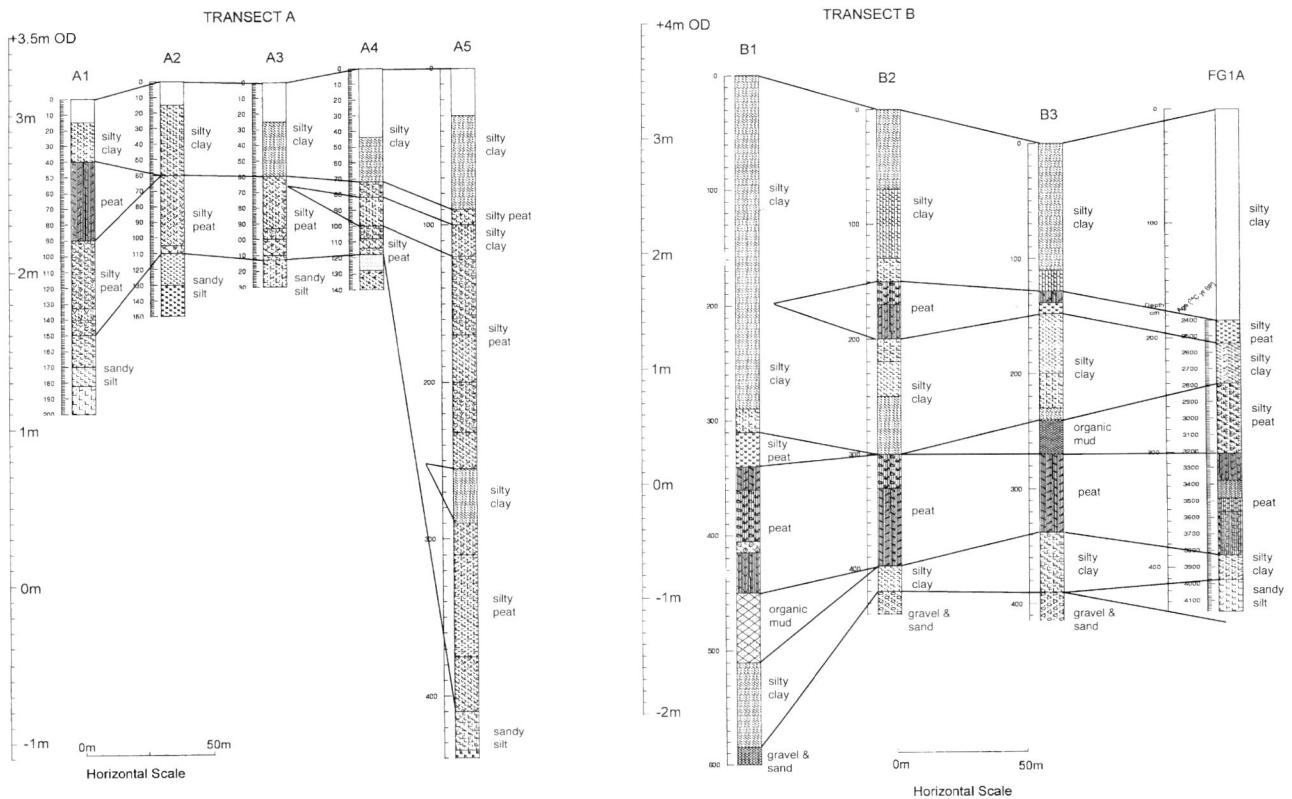

FIGURE 5.24. *Geological cross-section along Transects A and B reconstructed from boreholes.*

and capped by *c.* 0.6 m of silty clay. To the northwest, Borehole A1 showed a deeper sequence, including 0.5 m of peat between the silty peat and silty clay units. However, the sequence at A5 was 4.4 m long, and based on sandy silt over gravel at *c.* –1 m OD. This was overlain by *c.* 3 m of organic silt and peaty deposits, and capped by *c.* 0.9 m of silty clay. The relative steepness of the drop-off adjacent to the gravel 'bluff' suggests that water depths of several metres could have existed quite close to this topographic high.

Transect B ran southwest–northeast along the northwest corner of the site across the modern course of Cat's Water (Fig. 5.24). Borehole B1 provided a 6 m-long sequence based on gravel at *c.* –2.4 m OD. This comprised a basal silty clay unit overlain by organic mud, *Phragmites* peat, silty wood peat and capped by *c.* 3 m of silty clay. Somewhat shorter sequences, with similar stratigraphy, were recorded from Boreholes B2–3, and from the main sequence investigated in this study at Borehole FG1A (Borehole Bii of Boreham 2003). The sequence at FG1A comprised a basal sandy silt unit based on gravel at *c.* –1.2 m OD, overlain by a thin silty clay, *c.* 0.9 m of peat, *c.* 0.6 m of silty clay, a thin silty peat unit and capped by *c.* 1.8 m of silty

clay. It is the lower part of this sequence (below 1.8 m depth) that has been investigated in detail.

A sample of sediment and a sample of wood from FG1A were submitted to the University of Waikato for radiocarbon dating:

Sample	Sample no.	$\delta^{13}C$	% Modern	Result
180–200 cm (organic silt)	Wk-13862	–30.3±0.2	73.8±0.5	2442±54 BP
380–385 cm (alder wood)	Wk-13863	–27.5±0.2	62.5±0.3	3778±42 BP

The calibration of these dates (Stuiver *et al.* 1998, Bronk Ramsey 2001) gives the upper sample of organic silt (Wk-13862) an age range of 400–770 cal. BC (95.4 per cent), on the Late Bronze Age/Early Iron Age boundary, and the lower sample of alder wood an age range of 2340–2110 cal. BC (84.6 per cent), on the Late Neolithic/Early Bronze Age boundary. The implication of these dates is that the *c.* 2 m of sediment between *c.* 1.8 m and 3.8 m depth represents the entire Bronze Age interval. This would agree well with the Bronze Age fen-edge projected by French (2003b).

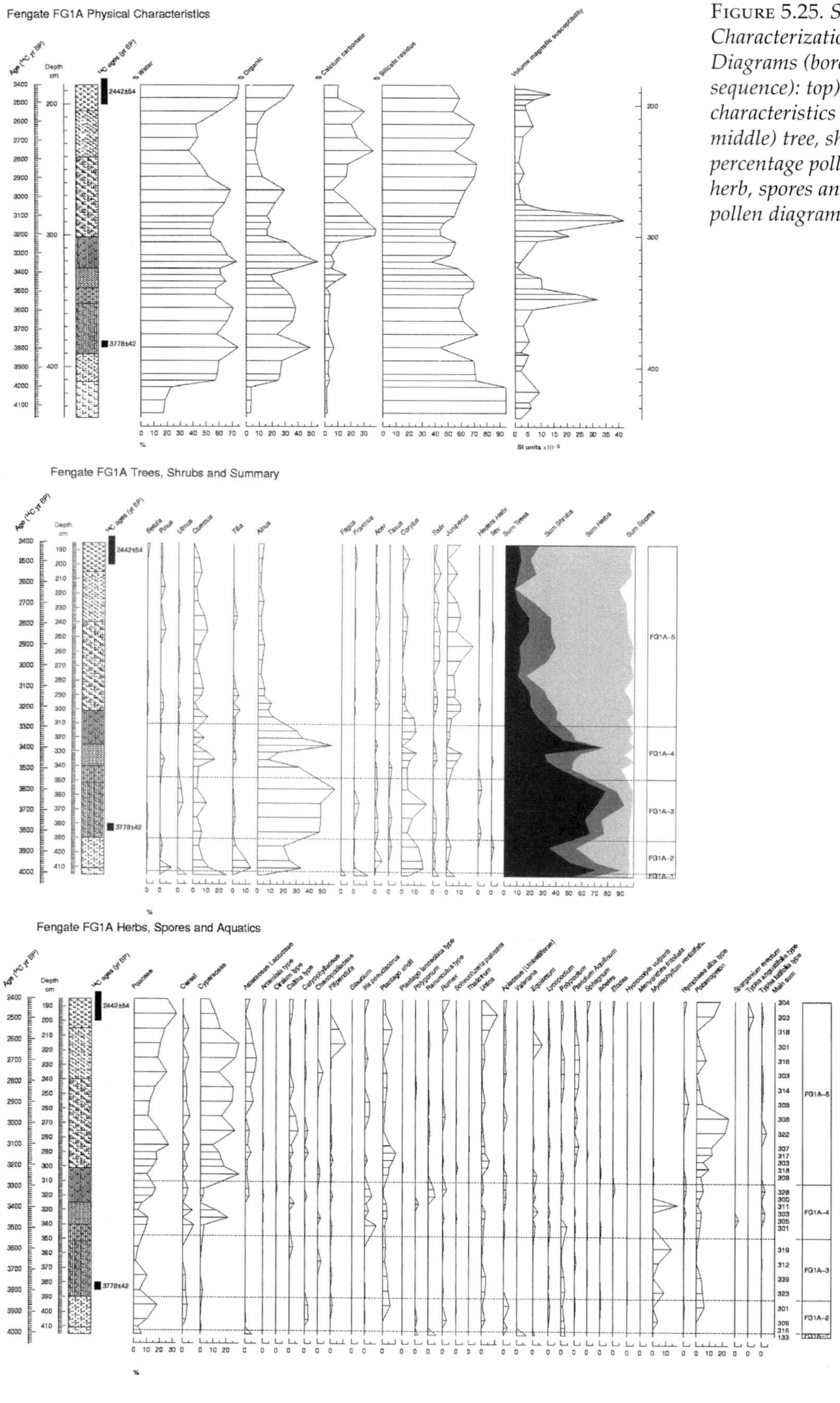

Fengate FG1A Physical Characteristics

FIGURE 5.25. *Sediment Characterization and Pollen Diagrams (borehole FG1A sequence): top) physical characteristics of sediments; middle) tree, shrub and summary percentage pollen diagram; bottom) herb, spores and aquatic percentage pollen diagram.*

Fengate FG1A Trees, Shrubs and Summary

Fengate FG1A Herbs, Spores and Aquatics

Physical characteristics of the deposits

A summary diagram of physical characteristics of the FG1A deposits is shown in Figure 5.25 (top). Note that next to the depth-scale is a time-scale based on a linear interpolation between the two radio-carbon results for the sequence. The water content of the sediment (at 105°C) varied between 18 per cent and 76 per cent, and showed a clear pattern with reduced water content in clastic sediments (silty clays) and increased water content in organic dominated material. Similarly, the percentage organic content (loss on ignition at 550°C) varied between 4 per cent and 56 per cent, with a clear relationship between the data and observed sediment type. However, it is interesting to note that only the sediment above 3 m contained significant amounts (>20 per cent) of calcium carbonate (derived from loss on ignition at 950°C), suggesting deposition in an alkaline fen, whilst the lower silts and peat were generally carbonate-poor. The percentage silicate residue varied between 44 per cent and 94 per cent showing the general dominance of fine-grade clastic (silt) deposition in this fluvially influenced environment. The volume magnetic susceptibility shows generally low values (<10 SI units ×10^{-8}) punctuated by two large peaks (>30 SI units ×10^{-8}) at 2.88 m and 3.48 m. These appear to represent major in-wash (flooding) events which brought magnetic minerals not normally present in the river bed-load to the site from distant parts of the catchment. This release of ferro-magnetic minerals may also relate to the destruction of soils through the progressive clearance of woodland in the catchment.

The changing palaeoenviroments of the sequence could be interpreted as Late Neolithic water-lain sandy silts giving way to quieter organic silty clay deposition. In the Early Bronze Age the area appears to have become a (*Phragmites*) reed swamp with alder carr (wet woodland) affected by at least one major flood episode. A further flood event seems to have marked a change to alkaline fen conditions in the Middle Bronze Age, followed by increasing over-bank alluviation in the Late Bronze Age and Early Iron Age.

Pollen analyses

Pollen diagrams for the FG1A sequence are shown in Figure 5.25. The pollen sequence has been divided into biozones (Bennett 1983). The Late Neolithic sandy silts (zone FG1A-1) have a pollen assemblage dominated by oak (*Quercus*) (*c.* 25 per cent), with elm (*Ulmus*), alder (*Alnus*), hazel (*Corylus*), willow (*Salix*) and juniper (*Juniperus*). This appears to represent a landscape with mixed-oak woodland (post-dating the lime (*Tilia*) and elm decline) just as major woodland clearances began to change the landscape. Above this, the organic silty clay (zone FG1A-2) has a pollen assemblage dominated by alder (*c.* 20 per cent) and hazel (*c.* 15 per cent), with oak, lime and maple (*Acer*). Grass pollen (Poaceae) becomes important, and cereal pollen is present at low levels, together with herbs such as the disturbance indicator *Plantago* (plantain), indicating the establishment of arable activities in the landscape. The presence of aquatic plants of deep slow-flowing open water such as milfoil (*Myriophyllum*), white water-lily (*Nymphaea*) and broad-leaved pondweed (*Potamogeton*) hint at the fluvial environment close to the site.

The Early Bronze Age peats (zone FG1A-3) are dominated by the pollen of alder (>40 per cent), with oak and hazel indicating the spread of local carr vegetation, presumably in response to rising water levels. Grass, cereal and herb pollen are present, but appear to be scarce compared to the wet woodland indicators. The overlying peats (zone FG1A-4) record a major fluctuation in the alder pollen signal, which appears to broadly coincide with the major flood event identified from the magnetic susceptibility signal (Fig. 5.25). The slight lag exhibited by the pollen record tends to suggest that the wet woodland was severely damaged by the flood event, and

that fen vegetation with sedges (Cyperaceae) briefly colonized the area before the alder woodland became re-established. The Late Bronze Age silty peats and silty clays (zone FG1A-5) are dominated by pollen of fen-living sedges and grass (both 10–30 per cent), with the constant presence of cereals, arable weeds and disturbance indicators. Oak, alder, hazel and willow are present at low levels throughout, together with the shade-intolerant shrub juniper. Deeper pools of water are indicated by white water-lily (*Nymphaea*) and broad-leaved pondweed (*Potamogeton*), together with the emergent marginal reedmace (*Typha*), and marsh plants such as marsh marigold (*Caltha*), bogbean (*Menyanthes*) and yellow flag (*Iris*). Towards the top of the sequence (Early Iron Age) there is evidence of riparian (bankside) vegetation with meadowsweet (*Filipendula*) and dock (*Rumex*), with eutrophication and disturbance indicated by nettle (*Urtica*) and plantain.

It is worth noting that, although the interpretations of vegetation change based on the pollen record seem quite clear, there is a lack of modern analogue situations where woodland clearance and arable activity occur at the edge of fenland. Waller (1994) observed that 'sites from within fen communities derived much (almost certainly most) of their pollen from the local environment'. In sites with an element of seasonal or other flooding, however, a certain amount of pollen will be derived from the whole catchment and will represent the regional environment in addition to the local and extra-local environments.

Pollen analysis of the Fengate STW sequence has revealed a story of Late Neolithic woodland decline, Bronze Age arable activity, changes in the aquatic environment at the fen-edge with reedswamp and alder carr giving way to eutrophic alkaline fen, and Early Iron Age inundation of previously dry land. A similar pattern of change was observed at Flag Fen where woodland of lime, oak and hazel was replaced by alder carr, which itself was replaced by fen-living sedge and reedswamp communities, with pools of deeper water (Scaife 1992). The sequence represents the interface between river, fen and dry ground resources, and has an almost continuous presence of cereal pollen, soil disturbance indicators and weeds of cultivated ground. The flooding at the site may have been caused by a combination of rising water levels due to marine incursions backing up water in the River Nene system, and an increase in peak discharge due to woodland clearance in the catchment. The site is of crucial importance since it is one of the few Fenland sites that has remained naturally wet, and hence provides good preservation potential for archaeological remains. In addition, it is possible that the deeper sequence from Borehole B1, apparently occupying a palaeochannel (see also Chapter 3 above), may also represent Neolithic and Mesolithic sediments.

Modes of recording (GAVIN LUCAS)

The context sheet is the lynch pin of recording systems in the UK; it emerged in the 1970s in the midst of the revolution of developer-led excavation and was adopted on most if not all excavations by the 1990s. The idea was to standardize recording methods, providing comparability of deposits and features within and even between sites, and had clear resonance with the wider theoretical developments in archaeology at the time with its concern to make archaeology more scientific (Lucas 2001b). Despite the variability in the precise layout and content of such sheets — indeed debating such matters can become a hobby if not obsession among some excavators — they remain a recognizably uniform phenomenon (Fig. 5.26). During my time at the Cambridge Archaeological Unit, I must have filled out hundreds of such sheets and although it differed somewhat from other units I had worked for, no one needed to explain to me how to fill one out when I first came. However, this very uniformity of the context sheet has often been criticized for imposing an homogeneity on the archaeology, making it all look the same. Take any two context sheets from two projects, miles or years apart, and they will often have an eerie repetition; mix them up, conceal the site code, and you might be hard put to say which came from which site. What began as a positive attempt to control data recovery through standardized descriptions has ended in the creation of an archaeological record, which all too often looks identical – a series of simulacra.

In contrast to this is the more traditional diary form of recording which goes back to the nineteenth century — free style notes and sketches — which outline the important interpretations of a site. The context sheet of course also allows for such open recording (usually on the back of the sheet) in contrast to its more systematic lists and check boxes, but the problem is that most of the more important interpretations transgress context boundaries. A common solution is to create a hierarchy of recording forms, with higher-level/multi-context or group sheets; this is a system I now use in Iceland – but it still does not completely annul the use of a diary. At the Cambridge Archaeological Unit, I used notebooks, a practice encouraged by Chris Evans and indeed most site supervisors practised this kind of recording in some form or another – whether in a notebook or on the back of a beer mat or newspaper. In fact in many ways, it is these *ad hoc* scribblings which bring out what is, perhaps, the underlying point: context sheet and notebook are not just two forms of recording but also two modes of thinking.

It is possible to perceive a certain contrast between two positions on the record of an excavation: an analytical approach which breaks a site down into its smallest components (the context sheet) and requires a degree of standardization and therefore repetition; and a synthetic approach which focuses on connections and usually adopts a narrative and graphic form (the site diary; Fig. 5.26). This distinction is not about description vs. interpretation, or objective *vs* subjective, but rather two very different discursive formations of the archaeological record. These two poles also engender quite different attitudes to the post-excavation process and constructing site reports; for the first, it is a question of building from the bottom up, constructing a matrix, phasing, grouping, and so on (cf. MAP 2). The context sheet becomes the basic building block. Computerization has lent itself well to this, indeed in many ways the development of computer technology is probably closely entwined with this mode of recording and thinking. For the second pole, however, context sheets are almost redundant or only used as a reference in an emergency; it is the diary or more general notes that prefigure the structure of a report. Context sheets are just details and often, useless details at that. This second mode is more akin to an art, characterized by a literary and visual imagination.

These two positions need not be exclusive or antagonistic, though they often are; for the 'analytical archaeologist', the diary might be seen as a throwback to a less scientific and more woolly type of recording. For the 'synthetic archaeologist' however, the context form homogenizes the archaeological record and does not lead to a proper narrative account of a site but merely a dry chronology of cuts and deposits. Indeed, one of the problems with the analytical method is the way it fragments the archaeological process and thinking (Jones 2002); one only has to examine a typical archaeological grey report to see this. It also leads to potentially serious publication problems where literary merit counts for more than the ability to construct an integrated database. On the other hand, the synthetic approach tends precisely to look towards publication, towards narrative and towards the wider academic questions, which help one to make sense of a particular site. However, I would also argue that the interpretation of a site works through the data produced in the analytical mode; it is not the pits or potsherds which we work with at the higher synthetic levels, but our representations of them. The very abstraction and detail of these records, which makes them appear almost valueless to a synthetic account, is precisely what preserves a degree of distantiation and therefore the *possibility of re-interpretation*. The danger of relying solely on one's field notes and sketches when writing up is that it will only reinforce prior interpretations.

Both modes are important, but greater emphasis needs to be put on the synthetic mode, precisely because guidelines, textbooks and manuals tend to focus solely on the analytical mode. The reasons for this would now seem somewhat anachronistic. While the analytical mode clearly fits into the theoretical re-orientations of the 1950s to 1970s, shifts in the perception of fieldwork since the 1980s and especially 1990s, have challenged this focus (Tilley 1989; Hodder 1989; 1997; 1999; Richards 1995; Andrews *et al.* 2000; Lucas 2001b). If this were to occur, it is possible that some of the problems in publishing sites may be overcome. The dilemma between publishing a dry site monograph which differs little from a 'grey report' or a stripped down, coffee-table style narrative with almost no detail to allow a critical reading is partly a product of the over-emphasis on the analytical mode. A publication should ideally be a dialogue between the two modes and for this to happen, the synthetic mode needs to be made a much more central part of the archive production.

FIGURE 5.26. *(On right) Context and Notebook Recording: top, combined single context plan and sheet developed by the author and used in Iceland (pre-printed on A3 permatrace); below, context sheet (right) and, left, notebook page from the author's Tower Works, Fengate excavations.*

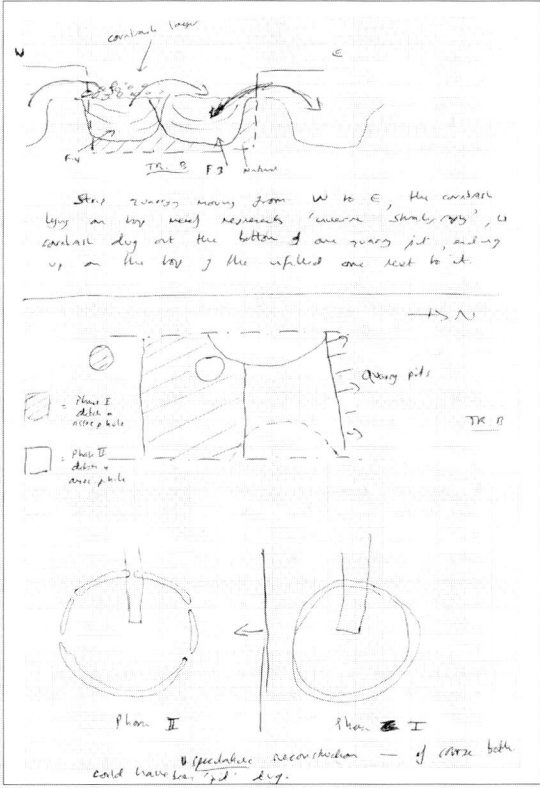

Final discussion

In 1997, sherds from the Tower Works Site's Early Iron Age assemblage were submitted for thermoluminescence dating to the Durham University Laboratory. These, however, failed to yield a determination. A decade later, two radiocarbon assays were achieved (from charred material) and date the site's occupation; these are fully compatible with the assignation of its pottery (calibration to two sigma):

1) F.13 (Beta-229355) — 2410±40 BP/750–690 and 660–640 and 590–400 cal. BC

2) F 42 [095] (Beta-229356) — 2420±40 BP/750–680 and 670–610 and 600–400 cal. BC.

Later prehistoric usage

The importance of the Tower Works Site is defined not only by its position within the Flag Fen Basin, but also by its location on the *periphery* of the fen-edge, the environment most intensively studied. Almost all previous archaeological excavations in the area have been conducted along the fen-edge proper, the 'low-lying' land below the 5 m contour. Beyond this somewhat arbitrary landscape division there have been few opportunities for research, given that much of the land lies in an area of pre-war gravel pits. As such, this 'fen-hinterland' remains chiefly characterized by the artefacts salvaged from the quarries and the limited exposures at Vicarage Farm (Pryor 1974a). The current phase of investigations has provided further context to Abbott's loosely provenanced finds and sketchy field notes, as well as providing the opportunity to discuss (although tentatively) the relationship between the 'lower' fen-edge and its 'higher' hinterland.

Aside from the environs-wide Fengate fieldsystem ditches within the 2004 area (F.15 *et al*; see below), it was only in the western quarter (1997 Trenches B, J, G & H) that later prehistoric evidence was forthcoming to any substantial degree. This is particularly true of the Early Iron Age settlement evidence. There, the earliest features consisted of a group of tightly clustered intercutting pits, F.17, F.18, F.25, F.33, F.42 and F.50. Their near-vertical sides and sharp edges in many instances suggested that they were not open for long but rapidly backfilled, invariably, it seems, with the redeposited natural. A probable purpose behind the digging of these pits was for quarrying-out of the natural sand/gravel; in one instance (F.42) the underlying cornbrash was reached but does not seem to have been penetrated.

Broadly comparable to the later Bronze Age metalled spread at the Edgerley Site, the use to which such gravel was put might be indicated by the laid gravel

TABLE 5.18. *Average sherd quantity by volume of buried soil across the site.*

Trench/Context	Sherd density per 100 litres of soil
B/[027] (upper)	16
B/[028] (lower)	3.4
D/[067]	1.5
E/[025]	2.5
F/[026]	0

layer in Trench J. It was almost certainly an 'original' ground surface and, as indicated by the spread of animal bone and pottery upon it, was later used for dumping refuse. Indeed, the presence of occupation and/or a midden is well attested by the spread of the 'dark earth' in Trenches B and J, which is probably an organically-enriched buried soil that developed after the abandonment of occupation. Of note is a fragment of a human mandible found among the animal bones on the gravel surface (probably from an male adult with periodontal disease; N. Dodwell pers. comm.).

For the buried soil, given the approximate volume known to have been excavated of this layer, we can contrast the artefact densities of its upper and lower horizons: the upper surface produced on average 16 sherds per 100 litres of soil, whereas the lower layer only yielded 3.4. This is an important difference which can be compared to similar values for the buried soil on other parts of the site associated with Roman pottery (see below, and Table 5.18).

Other direct evidence of settlement activity is meagre and based solely on the postholes in Trench B (F.9 & F.13) and H (F.51, F.55, F.57 & F.58). No structural pattern could be discerned within the limited excavation area, but these could easily be part of post-circles or other buildings. Burnt fragments of cornbrash occurred in some quantity in and over the pits in Trench B, and burnt clay (possibly daub) was recovered from posthole F.9. The sheer quantity of artefacts, especially the pottery, would in itself also point to the presence of a settlement which, from all indications, once extended to the west and/or north. The faunal and macro-botanical remains recovered equally attest to occupation, with cereal crop processing (barley and wheat; see Stevens above) and meat *consumption* rather than butchery/processing (cattle, sheep/goat, pig and horse; see Moreno-Garcia above). Some indication of possible metalworking is also given from the fragments of a crucible found in posthole F.13, although no metalwork was recovered.

The final component of the western area is the ditch system (F.34 & F.35). This lay within an area of much 'cleaner', paler buried soil and therefore outside the core/on the margins of any settlement (as, however, did the postholes in Trench H, one of which was apparently cut by ditch F.34). Further discussed below, the alignment of these ditches corresponds with F.15 in the eastern area (Trench F). Both it and ditch F.34 are almost certainly part of a larger fieldsystem and, indeed, align with the Bronze Age droveways and fieldsystem.

Given the density and preservation of the prehistoric remains encountered in the 1997 investigations, the scarcity of comparable finds and features within the 2004 area was somewhat surprising. The test pitting and buried soil squares revealed a very low density of worked flint, testifying to little more than a background Neolithic 'presence'. Only a single flake was found in the test pits, whilst just six pieces of worked and burnt flint were recovered from the buried soil squares. Of the six flints found in features, four were residual; the remaining two were recovered from tree-throw F.123, which also yielded the only two fragments of prehistoric pottery. With no further evidence for early prehistoric activity, the quantity of finds implies nothing more than limited or sporadic use of the area during this period, and this was also true of the 1997 western trenches (the oblique arrowhead being their one diagnostically 'early' finding).

Otherwise, in the eastern area, evidence for later prehistoric activity was confined to the re-cut northeast–southwest ditch F.109/F.110, seemingly sealed by the buried soil. The character and orientation of the ditch indicates a prehistoric date: it ran at right-angles to the Bronze Age linear F.15, found in Trench F. In total, the ditch was traced for 35 m across Trenches 3 and 4. The presence of F.15, just metres to the east, suggests that the ditch either turned abruptly or terminated. Either way, the ditches clearly form the corner of a Bronze Age field block/paddock. The relationship between the ditches is supported by the similarity in fill and profile between F.109 and F.15. The only other candidate for a Bronze Age ditch is F.99, which may be the terminal of the northeast–southwest 'palisade' ditch, F.104, encountered in Trench 1.

The discovery of F.109/F.110 represents the fifth fieldsystem-ditch to be found on the Tower Works Site (Fig. 5.14). F.109/F.110 runs broadly parallel to F.104 (Trench 1) and F.35 (Trench H), but perpendicular to F.15 and F.35 (Trenches H & G). Together, these formed part of an extensive fieldsystem, aligning with the Bronze Age droves and field plots along the fen-edge. The co-axial alignment of ditches at Tower Works appears to *ignore* the curving topography of the area, cutting across the direction of slope. Rather than continuing to run at right-angles to the lower fen-edge, which at first glance appears to be the conditioning factor in the layout of the system to the southeast, the

almost rigid adherence to a northwest–southeast axis *beyond* the curvature of the fen-edge is intriguing.

The reasons for the continuation of the adherence of ditches F.109/F.110 to a northwest–southeast axis remain elusive, although two scenarios can be suggested. Firstly, the field ditches evident around Tower Works may have been laid out later than those towards the southeast (Evans & Pryor 2001, 36). The southeastern droves and field plots appeared to be aligned perpendicularly to the fen-edge, and if constructed first, may have 'set' the orientation for any extension to the fieldsystem. Alternatively, the relationship with the topography may have been over-emphasized, perhaps being more apparent than real. Other recent investigations within the region have demonstrated a lack of correlation between the 'natural' topography and the axis of Bronze Age fieldsystems. As discussed in Chapter 2 above, Bradley Fen's field boundaries were orientated not in relation to the fen-edge, but in respect to pre-existing 'cultural' landscape features. These 'reference points' included a series of round barrows and henges at King's Dyke West, and an extensive ditch and bank traced across both Bradley Fen and Must Farm.

Although the general paucity of prehistoric remains found within the 2004 excavation-area was disappointing, this 'negative' evidence is nevertheless informative, providing limits to both the occupation spreads encountered in the 1997 investigations and those from the pre-war quarry pits. The paucity of later prehistoric material indicates that the settlement spreads are more localized than anticipated. The substantial Early Iron Age occupation remains found in Trenches B and J of the 1997 evaluation clearly do not extend into either Trench 2 or the main area of excavation. Given Abbott's finds to the north of Trenches B and J, any prehistoric settlement swathe must be centred around the western half of the Tower Works Site.

While the Early Iron Age settlement remains at this site clearly resonate with Abbott's findings, it is not a matter of direct equivalence. The 0.2–0.65 m-deep pits here were substantially shallower than the *c.* 1.2–1.8 m-deep features from which he seems to have retrieved the bulk of his material (see Chapters 2 & 4 above). Probably in Abbott's case the material derived from watering-holes/wells. Comparable deep pit-features of the period have been found on Pryor's sub-sites (e.g. Cat's Water and Vicarage Farm). Equally, when one considers that at least 31 individual vessels were evinced from the Tower Works Site's brief evaluation fieldwork, it sets in context the mere 81 vessels of the period listed as being recovered from all the years of Abbott's investigations (see Table 2.1) and certainly indicates his large sherd/near-complete vessel bias.

The larger issue surrounding the later prehistoric features at Tower Works is that of the extent to which they *differ* from the fen-edge sites excavated by Pryor. At least two scenarios might be proposed. In one, the droveways, fieldsystems and minor settlement activity found on the fen-edge would be complemented by a major, probably enclosed, settlement which would lie on the high ground, such as the present site occupies. The alternative is that there is *no* centralized place within the Middle–Late Bronze Age/Early Iron Age landscape of Fengate and that settlement was dispersed and set within the fieldsystems. Certainly fairly substantial occupation remains have been recovered from Tower Works and, in terms of the pottery assemblage, this may well exceed anything found on the lower ground; however, none of the other features displayed anything especially extraordinary and indeed it seems that fieldsystems run across the site in the same manner as those on the fen-edge. As it stands, the evidence from the field evaluation is too slight to favour one scenario over the other, and it is possible that both may be polarising the issue too much (i.e. centralized *vs* dispersed settlement).

Finally, although lacking direct connection with Tower Works, the results of the Sewage Treatment Site palaeo-environmental researches are important on two accounts. Firstly, and further resonating with the Elliott and Materials Recycling Sites' findings, is another probable identification of a palaeochannel of the Cat's Water. Secondly, is the consistent occurrence of cereals throughout the pollen core's sequence, spanning the later Neolithic to the end of the Bronze Age; the implications of this will be further discussed in Chapter Six below.

Romano-British usage

The vast majority of features encountered in the 2004 excavation probably related to a Late Roman farmstead dating from the second to fourth centuries AD. Further chronological refinement was not possible, although the more closely dated ceramics fall between the *later* second and fourth centuries. In essence, the excavations only clipped the edge of this settlement which, judging by observations on the buried soil surface, still survives further to the east. Roman features were primarily concentrated in the north of the site, in particular to the northeast around the area of the compound. A noticeable fall-off in feature density was evident to the south, where only dispersed shallow pits and postholes were located. This fall-off undoubtedly indicates the periphery of the settlement, as shown by the absence of Roman ceramics in features south of gully F.119. The fact that any major settlement features were available for investigation is

itself fortunate, given that their main concentration lay within a narrow (14 m-wide) corridor immediately to the south of the main quarry-zone edge.

The surviving elements of the settlement comprised the enclosure and its associated pits and well, the granary structure partially surrounded by gullies and the scatter of dispersed pits and postholes. By far the most important assemblage of Roman material was recovered from the well. The large quantity of material in its mid-profile fills derives from an episode of dumping, probably from the clearance of a tiled structure. Pottery from these deposits consisted of large unabraded fragments, including a complete Nene Valley colour-coated beaker. That 17.4 kg of tile was recovered is also noteworthy. Despite the fact that just half of this feature was excavated, the quantity of tile nevertheless nearly matches the total of 20 kg recovered from the entire Cat's Water's Roman settlement (Hayes 1984, 179; Pryor 1984, 124–5, fig. 18).

Clearly, the well's deposits were different to those characterising the surrounding ditches, pits and gullies. In order to investigate this further, the mean weight of pottery, tile and bone can be compared across three of the major settlement components: the well, the surrounding enclosure features, and the artefact-enriched buried soil (Table 5.19). It must be noted that sample sizes will obviously vary, which may have some impact upon these calculations; however, these basic calculations are a useful index for comparing gross differences in artefact size, which in turn help elucidate the processes behind their deposition and subsequent transformation.

Table 5.19 demonstrates that mean artefact weights were two to three times higher in the well than in the surrounding enclosure components. The greater weight indicates larger and less fragmented artefacts, expected in an episode of rapid clearance and dumping. Following Schiffer (1976; see Chapter 1 above concerning the context of this citation), the well deposit represents *de facto* refuse, consisting of material still potentially useful that was discarded when a particular phase of activity or occupation was completed or abandoned. The dump is, therefore, considered a 'closure deposit', comparable in its nature, but not in its size, to that found at Orton Longville (Mackreth 2001, 57).

Comparatively, the mean artefact weights from the buried soil are minuscule. The pottery weight was just two-thirds that from the enclosure, whilst that of the bone is four times less. This is probably due to exposure. Whereas those artefacts incorporated into features were afforded a degree of protection by being buried, material left exposed on the surface would have been subject to a series of natural and

TABLE 5.19. *Mean artefact weights (2004 contexts).*

Settlement component	Feature/Context number	Mean pottery weight (g)	Mean tile weight (g)	Mean bone weight (g)
Artefact-enriched buried soil	[210]	8.8	59.0	5.0
Enclosure and associated pits and postholes	F.94–97, F.117–119, F.130–132, F.134, F.139–141	13.9	-	21.0
Well	F.151	41.8	275.6	42.8

cultural processes that continued to break it down. The comparatively low weights from the buried soil indicate considerable artefact fragmentation, perhaps *not* expected in a midden deposit; however, if this spread was an enriched horticultural plot, something akin to a kitchen garden, the low mean weight would be less surprising. Within such a scenario, cultivation would break up and abrade the artefacts, periodically exposing them to the elements. Under these conditions artefact sizes would decrease, accounting for the low values.

As the excavations have dealt with a settlement's fringe, the nature of the features and their associated finds bear witness to types of 'peripheral' activities. The presence of the granary structure suggests that grain storage may have been confined to the limits of the settlement, together with small horticultural plots and/or middens. Other hints of 'functional zoning' are implied by the quantities of slag found (2.3 kg), and the presence of the 'furnace pit' F.94/F.95. Together, this suggests that industrial activities were located in or around the area. Any discussion of zoning is clearly tentative, given that no comparison with the settlement interior is possible. It is, however, worth mentioning that no domestic structures *per se* were found in the excavations, and domestic refuse was relatively rare, occurring in just 22 of the 88 features excavated (25 per cent).

Any estimation of the settlement's original size is obviously near impossible. Clearly extending to the east, its northern extent was presumably destroyed by quarrying. Its western limits are also unknown, although as no Roman features were recovered in Trench 2A, it is unlikely to extend much further in this direction. In 1997, two Romano-British ditches were found to the west in Trench D. No pottery was forthcoming from their fills, their peripheral position suggesting these were field boundaries beyond the settlement limits. The closest known Roman settlement lies *c.* 150–200 m to the northeast, where the remains of buildings, ditches and pits were found by Abbott, dating *c.* AD 200–400 (Fig. 5.27). Falling within broadly the same date range, the Tower Works Site probably represents the southwestern edge of this settlement. If this is the case, then it must have been a considerable

size as, given the proximity of the two 'sites', they are unlikely to have been separate farmsteads and could, together, represent a substantial settlement. Indeed, a functional connection between the Cat's Water sub-Site and that at Tower Works has been suggested by Pryor, who noted that the great 'road-like' drove leading from the fen-edge (and partially excavated at the Storey's Bar Road sub-Site) heads in the direction of the Tower Works/Abbott's settlement (Pryor 1984, 229). Running directly south of the latter, as shown in Figure 5.26, on aerial photographs its cropmark ditches continue to within *c.* 80 m of the Tower Works Site.

To the south, an Early Roman-period fieldsystem was exposed across the Depot Site, which ran parallel with this Cat's Water/Tower Works 'way' (and locally the route of the Fen Causeway) and, also, the immediate length of the fen-edge (Fig. 5.27; Pryor 2001a, fig. 2.6). Evidence of Roman settlement activity, predominately of third-century AD date, was also found across the western side of the Depot field and extended into the area of Pryor's adjacent 1997 trenches (Evans & Pryor 2001, 27, 29–30).

In order to more fully appreciate the situation of Fengate's Roman settlement it is crucial to note that extensive settlement remains of the period have been found at Fletton and Stanground, just southwest of the present, canalized course of the River Nene. A number of kilns of the period have been found, and an 'ancient wharf' reported beside the old, King's Dyke length of the Nene which borders the northern side of the Stanground peninsula, and which has contributed to its identification as the south-eastward Cnut's Dyke route of the Car Dyke canal system (Phillips 1970, 186–7). Therefore, Abbott's settlement lay at a hub within the Roman landscape: at a junction of the cross-fen Fen Causeway road and the confluence of the Car Dyke and River Nene waterways.

Otherwise, relatively little Roman archaeology has been recovered from the immediate 'Fengate North' environs (see though the Parnwell Road Site, Chapter 2 above and Webley 2007). The most likely candidate for any kind of significant settlement presence has been the surface scatter of that period recorded in the Royal Commission volume (1969, fig. 1), that was apparently associated with the

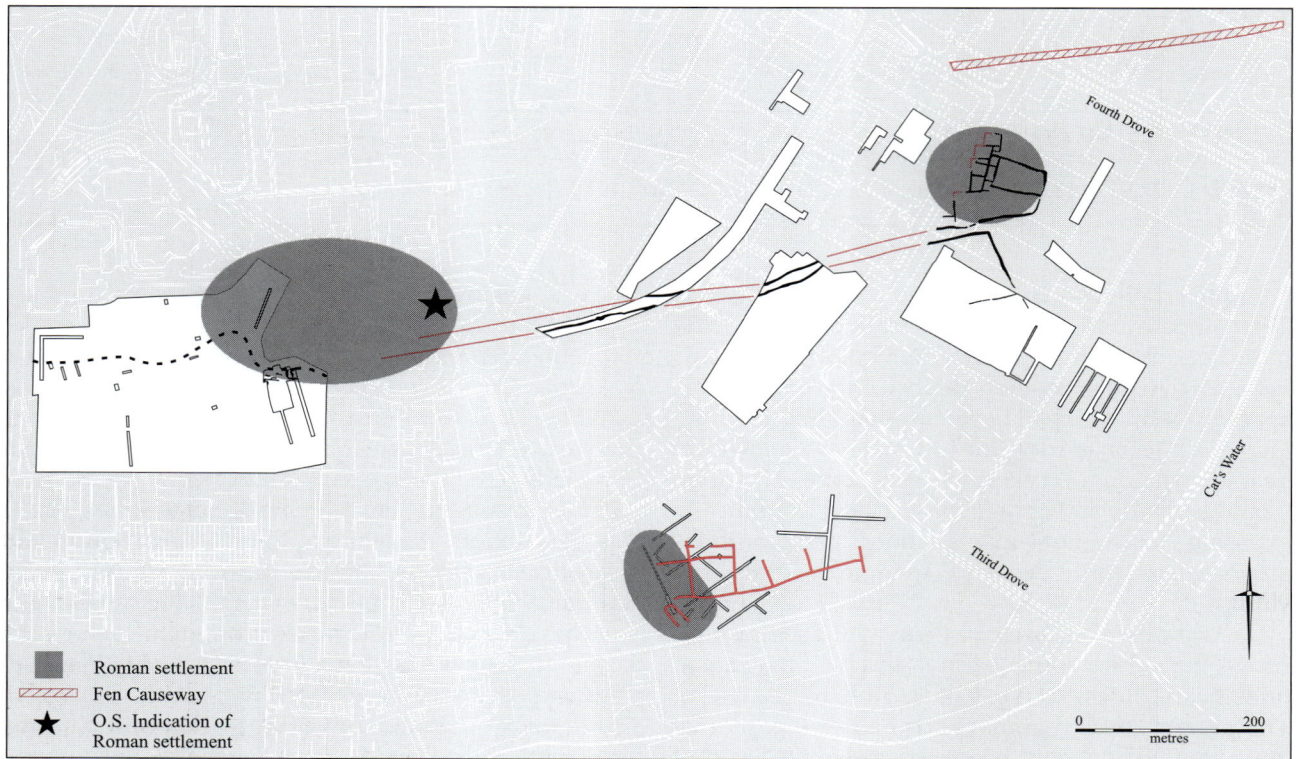

FIGURE 5.27. *Roman Fengate (west-central). Reproduced by permission of Ordnance Survey on behalf of HMSO.*
© Crown copyright 2009. All rights reserved. Ordnance Survey Licence number 100048686.

Flagfen Cottage cropmark enclosure just north and west of the Newark Road Site (Pryor's Ditch 12/13 enclosure; see Figs. 1.1 & 6.1). Otherwise, aside from exposing the Fen Causeway at Fourth Drove (Pryor 1980a, 151–5), some Early Roman features at Vicarage Farm (Pryor 1984, 7) and a few post-Bronze Age ditch lengths and pit features of vaguely first-millennium BC/Romano-British attribution at Newark Road (*ie.* largely undated; Pryor 1984, 66–9, fig. 44), the only substantive occupation evidence has been from the Broadlands Site (Nicholson *et al.* forthcoming); one pit of that date also being found at Edgerley Road (see Chapter 4 above).

Finally, at least for the southwest-central Fengate area, it should be stressed just what a major reorganization of the landscape was represented by the Roman layout: predominantly east–westward as opposed to the northwest–southeast axes of the Bronze Age.

While this might only reflect what portion of the local fen-edge their systems were oriented in relationship to — respectively, the southwest *vs* 'central' — in the case of the Roman, it might show the dominance of the Nene River/Cat's Water 'corridor'; certainly, the route of the north-westward Car Dyke canal seems to have had little immediate influence. Given the scale of this change, what seems extraordinary is the degree to which these Roman landscape components apparently had their roots in the later Iron Age. Not only is this evinced in the continuity of ditch alignment/layout between these periods at both the Cat's Water/Elliott Sites (Pryor 1984, fig. 17 and Chapter 3 above) and, also, the Depot Site's fieldsystem, but also in the apparent Late Iron Age rectangular enclosures arranged sympathetically along the north side of the great droveway at Storey's Bar Road (Pryor 1984, 15, figs. 8–12).

CHAPTER 6

Overviewing Fengate — Matters of Scale, Authority and Community

Christopher Evans

> Time means succession, and succession, change:
> Hence timelessness is bound to disarrange *Schedules of sentiment*.
>
> V. Nabokov *Pale Fire* (1962; emphasis added; see Fig. 6.8)

Under its series' rubric of 'Historiography and Fieldwork', this volume has, in effect, spanned a century of excavation at Fengate: from Abbott's first notebook entries in 1906 to the 2007 investigations at Vicarage Farm Road. This historiographic directive is more than just a matter of vague 'legacy', but involves an *active framing context*. Close scrutiny of the Abbott sources is not just a matter of by rote 'general background'; they have implications that lie at the heart of the interpretation of Fengate's landscape and reflect upon such broad issues as the 'typing' of people and things. Accordingly, to understand today the area's sequence is as much a matter of fully engaging with the context of what has been done before, as what now confronts us in the ground (and also more general/conceptual site genealogies; e.g. Evans 1998). To borrow Foucault's phrase, we now 'dig beyond origins'— always after the fact and the efforts of others — and invariably *re*-read landscape (and the past).

Comparing Abbott's early sketch-map efforts with Pryor's hand-drawn plans of the '70s (which I, myself, rendered a number of) and to today's computer-based mapping, charts an enormous increase in the ability to handle complex data and map land/sites. Yet, by no means is this statement intended to just celebrate archaeology's technological achievement; rather it highlights how vast are the archaeological landscapes we are currently dealing with and that this has implications concerning our knowledge claims and their production. Primarily, that *interpretation is a matter of scale*, and this requires us to acknowledge a greater modesty if we strive towards a validity beyond 'convenient stories' (i.e. Nabokov's 'schedules of sentiment' or the various 'wildwood-to-monuments' landscape narratives now so in vogue; see Evans 2007b). This, in part, is the outcome of having to face up to the sheer density of sites known across the landscape: the number of Bronze Age settlement clusters and fieldsystems which lie distributed across these tracts. Recognizing their numbers/densities — and the population levels that they must have collectively entailed — suddenly makes much more sense of the many thousands of bronzes recovered throughout the region. Certainly, the current picture provides a more realistic basis of their context than could be envisaged, for example, in Fox's day (1923) when only three or four settlements of the period were known within the region, or when Crawford could only document three Beaker settlements nationwide (1912). Put simply, our grasp of later prehistoric settlement densities must affect the nature of interpretation. Through the impact of post-processualism (as opposed to the widespread 'interconnected-ness' of earlier, more systems-based approaches), there has been a tendency to consider the 'site-as-universe', as if all the issues/inventions of any one period were resolved within the confines of its face-to-face community alone. Yet, unless one is extraordinarily lucky, it is unlikely that you are actually going to dig the site where, for instance, bronze technology or agriculture first arose, or gender differentiation emerged. The recognition of settlement numbers/densities means that the interpretation of individual sites (as opposed to broader 'networks', etc.), and the goal of fieldwork generally, should be less a matter of the oft-cited 'explanation of cultural change' than its *transmission*.

A related issue is the size of excavations. Archaeologists now expose landscapes on a scale previously undreamt of. Stripping upwards of 10–50 ha (and often including multiple settlement 'nuclei'), compared, nevertheless, to the hundreds, if not thousands, of hectare-size fieldsystems our sites fall amidst, must challenge the nature of what is considered immediate *causation*. In other words, just what can be realistically interpreted at face value. A droveway or a cursus might pass through these vast site-exposures for many hundreds of metres, but it is improbable that you will dig/'get' the actual determinant of its alignment — the ever-distant barrow or 'ancestral settlement'. Ironically enough, digging 'at scale' forces us to appreciate all the more questions of scope and 'outward-ness', and acknowledge that *something will always lie beyond the edges of our excavations*, no matter how vast.

This is not entirely unlike the writing of books itself, which are invariably acts of investigation in their own right. While theoretically, in systemized modes of chronicling fieldwork, a project's analytical and writing stages should be separate, as soon as sites engage with their landscapes such cut-and-dry approaches quickly dissipate. At the outset you might think the task at hand simple. Yet, akin to walking, one path soon leads to another, where you stumble upon unexpected things, possibilities and avenues of thought/association. This is obviously the case here.

Fixing landscape

In Chapter 1 the argument was made that Pryor's post-1980s linkage of Flag Fen and its Fengate hinterland has been to the detriment of the latter. Certainly, his more recent interpretations have very much focused on the main Newark fieldsystem drove and the Power Station Site timber alignment, seeing its axis as defining the core of Fengate's Bronze Age landscape. In this respect, the recent CAU excavations have expanded the scope/scale of the fieldsystem, especially the archaeology of its southwestern and northern swathes. In fact, the swing of the fieldsystem's axes at the Edgerley Road Site raises the question of whether it actually belongs to the same system as Fengate's Newark Road 'core'. Now, informed by the knowledge of how extensive the period's fieldsystems generally were across the region's low-lying terraces, how are we to know where one fieldsystem ended and another began? This is an issue of 'transformation' and relates to questions of cognitive distinction and where boundaries are drawn amid spectra. It equally resonates with the theme of artefact types: how do we account for variability and then know when one thing becomes another, be it a pottery style or fieldsystem block?

Paying so much heed to the Flag Fen/Fengate linkage, Pryor has equally been concerned with tracing the long-term antecedents of this 'specialness' within its immediate landscape. He has argued for its early expression in the Vicarage Farm/Cat's Water Neolithic alignment and also stressed the range of 'type-representative' Neolithic/earlier Bronze Age pits and settlement longevity at the Birmingham Unit's Site O (2001a, 30–32, 50, 406–7). Yet neither seem

Table 6.1. *Average worked flint densities per metre from buried soil sampling. The 'Fengate Sites' density shows the average of the Table 1.3 figures. For the purposes of appropriate comparison, the Haddenham and Barleycroft Farm densities are only those from their initial 50 and 100 m landscape-wide sample grids and does not include any high value site-'targeting' (Evans & Hodder 2006a, 212–13; Evans & Knight 2000). In the case of the latter, the density-figures are derived from 90 litre buried soil sample-units and should, in theory, be factored upwards by c. 10–20 per cent to equate with a standard metre-square sample of the same. Accordingly, it is better compared to the 'test point' sampling densities from Edgerley Drain Road — 0.27 flints. The Isleham figure is also not directly comparable as it largely reflects flint scatter/site-directed sampling (Gdaniec et al. 2008).*

	CAU Fengate sites	Barleycroft Farm	Upper Delphs, Haddenham	Isleham survey
Worked flint				
Range	0–6	0–6	0–8	0–32
Mean density	0.8	1.6	1.8	3.6

terribly convincing. Of the former, certainly the occurrence of Neolithic houses is rare, but one suspects that, this building form now having been recognized as being of the period, their recovery will soon become more commonplace (see Chapter 3, Inset). As to the latter proposition — the sense of the landscape's pre-fieldsystem 'use-diversity' — recent fieldwork elsewhere shows this not to be so and, if anything, Fengate itself sees a rather low background density of such archaeology. As indicated in Table 6.1, its 'landscape-scale' flint densities are not particularly impressive and, if anything, are rather low (although this may be somewhat biased by the 'targeted' area-specific sampling undertaken to date; i.e. non-grid or site-wide testing).

As outlined in Chapter 3 (Inset), difficulties have also been encountered when trying to distinguish the Cat's Water's pre-Bronze Age fieldsystem usage, and the same is true of the Newark Road sub-Site. This simply reflects the fact that during the 1970s, and really prior to the mid-1990s, the kind of multi-period landscape sequence/palimpsest model we are now familiar with through vast-scale archaeological exposures — wherein all 'type-phases'/'cultures' are to expected if investigation is of a sufficient size (with *density*, rather than 'presence/absence', being the key factor) — was then simply not developed. Rather, a 'predominant-phase' site-based model was still adhered to and, in consequence, concepts of artefact-residuality were often little explored.

As is apparent in Table 6.2 (which also includes Spong Hill's results by way of ready comparison; Healy 1988), and having now repeatedly sifted through the Fengate reports, we can be confident that the marked frequency of 'type' pit clusters found at Edgerley Road did not occur in Pryor's earlier

TABLE 6.2. *Frequency of (pottery-) 'typed' pits (* included 24 pits from Storey's Bar Road; ** excludes the ten Beaker pits from the 1989 Power Station excavations). Obviously, if wishing to directly compare these figures the differences in the areas excavated should, in theory, be factored for; in this case, to establish such equivalence, Edgerley's numbers would have to be multiplied by 6.5.*

	Pryor's '70s Fengate sites (c. 11 ha)	Edgerley Drain Road (1.7 ha)	Spong Hill (1.4 ha)
Early Neolithic	2	1	56
Peterborough	3	3	-
Grooved Ware	28*	27	2
Beaker	5**	11	1
Collared Urn	4	18	1

excavations (the Power Station's Beaker pit cluster being the only exception; Pryor 2001a, 70–72). Indeed, whilst clearly seeing considerable later Mesolithic to earlier Bronze Age activity, the Elliott Site also lacked 'ware-distinct' pit groups (and pre-Middle Bronze Age pottery generally). Rather, it has only been from the fields located down towards the fen-edge east of Cat's Water (i.e. the Co-op Site area) that any kind of range of Neolithic/earlier Bronze Age wares has been forthcoming, but even here only very low numbers are involved. Lying that slight degree higher in the land, only Edgerley's sequence would seem in any way comparable with Abbott's earlier, and more 'inland' findings.

The distribution of Fengate's pre-earlier/Middle Bronze Age sites is indicated on Figure 6.1. Essentially showing swathes of Grooved Ware and Beaker settlement, the area of Abbott's main quarry findings has been assigned to the latter; this attests only to its dominant attribution and, in addition to Beaker features, more minor Neolithic (and also Bronze Age) features/pit groups also obviously occurred there. Equally, Edgerley's Grooved Ware and Beaker occupation are shown as being discrete and not extending either northeast to the zone of Abbott's findings in that area (see Chapters 2 and 4, Inset above), or southwest to connect with the swathe of his main quarry-zone recording (and nor did it apparently run west into the Broadlands investigations; see Chapter 4 above). As will become apparent, the distinction of another major 'early'/Beaker settlement within the larger Fengate environs has potential implications for the (multiple) origins of its fieldsystem(s). Yet, with Bronze Age fieldsystems now known to have been so widespread within the region and across much of Southern England as a whole (Yates 2007; Bradley & Yates 2007), it is rash to only seek strictly locally specific explanations for their advent. In other words, they are unlikely to have been immediately 'invented' and arise as a direct result of local environmental conditions and/or

economic needs. Clearly a mass phenomenon, their explanation must indeed relate to broader socio-cultural factors and *changes in the interrelationship between communities and land*. Nevertheless, they need not have all been a single 'mass event' and, in a Fenland context (if dating to the earlier Bronze Age; see below), land pressure through the region's marine inundation (Waller 1994) could have contributed, as — displaced from the region's low terraces — people bunched-up on its central island and 'edge-lands'.

At this juncture look again at Figure 6.1, for it differs in a number of crucial facets from the Fengate 'master-plan' that introduced this volume (Fig. 1.1) and it is, in effect, the map we've built throughout this book. As outlined in Chapter 1, it was long unease with the interrelationship of Pryor's Ditches 12/13 and 14/15 cropmark compounds north of his Newark Road Site that kindled doubts concerning the accuracy of the cropmark plot in that area. This was furthered when trying to draw together this volume's Roman landscape map. While the position of the Flagfen Cottage's enclosure of that date shown in the 1969 RCHM volume (see Fig. 2.4 above) matches Pryor's Third Report plotting (1980a, fig. 4), both it and the Ditch 16–18 enclosure (and Site 11) had obviously somehow shifted northward in the course of their later large-scale mapping (e.g. Pryor 1992, fig. 3; 2001a, fig. 1.4). As a result, we contacted Rog Palmer who provided us with a master cropmark plot he had earlier prepared of the Fengate and Northey area (Pryor 2003, fig. 60); through comparison (Fig. 6.2) it is clear that, for whatever reason, these cropmarks had migrated northwards by approximately 75 m.

Having identified this error it becomes incumbent to attempt to 'fix' Fengate's plan. (By no means is this a case of any smug 'stone throwing' in proverbial 'glasshouses'; we all make mistakes and invariably have to manipulate plans to a degree, even with much more exact computer- and laser-plotting.) Indeed, combining Palmer's cropmark plot with Pryor's Flag Fen volume 'master' and the results of the recent excavations, allows us to reconstruct quite a different layout and adds new dimensions to Fengate's Bronze Age landscape. Not unsurprisingly, it is the arrangement of the unexcavated cropmark enclosures just northwest of Pryor's Newark Road Site that Palmer's plot has the most significant impact upon. While possibly reflecting a degree of alternation/reuse in Roman times, the southward shifting of the Ditch 12/13 enclosure means that its relationship with the excavated Ditch 14/15 compound, far from being 'uncomfortable', becomes directly complementary. The southern side of the latter now corresponds with the northern corner of the Ditch 12/13 setting. Taken

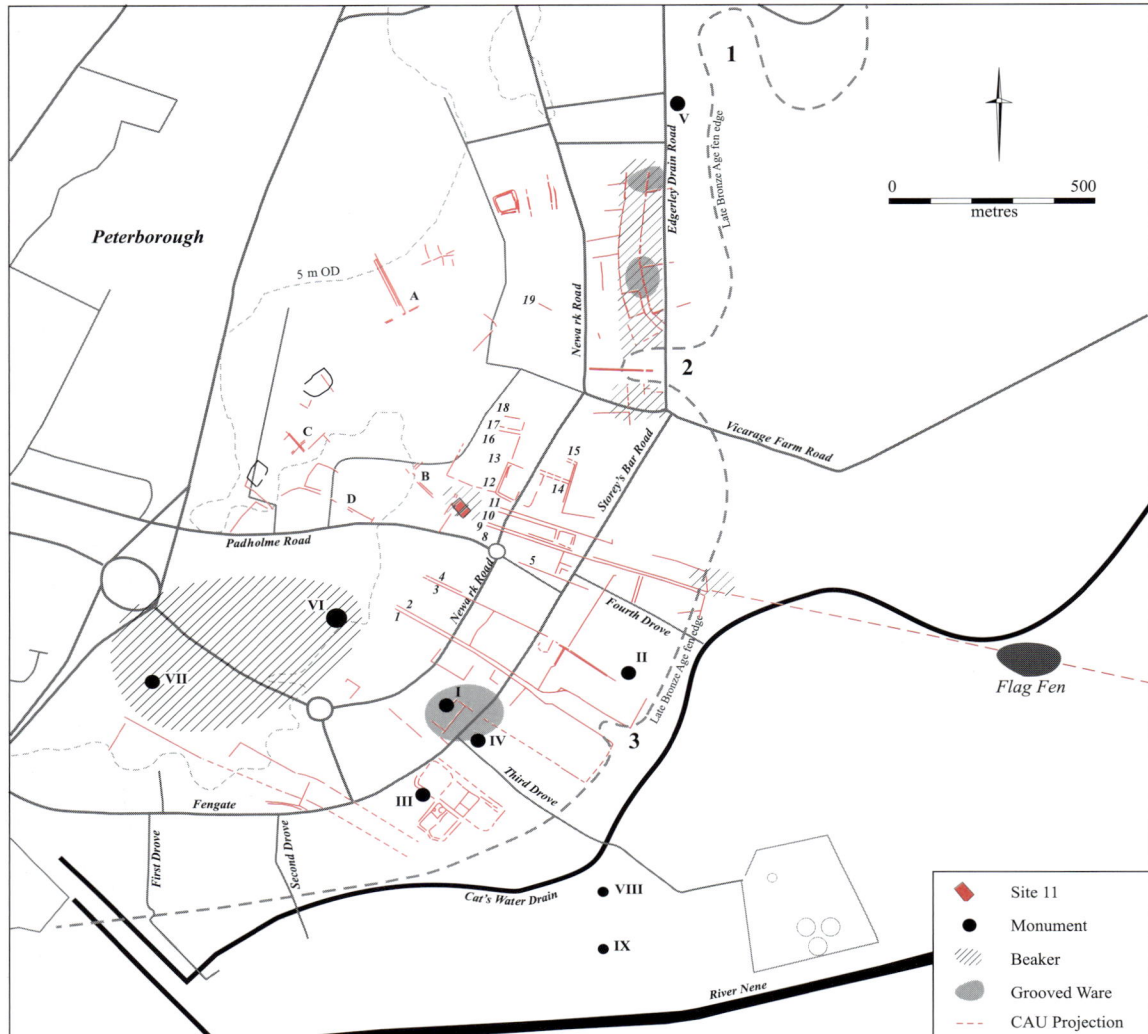

FIGURE 6.1. *Neolithic and Bronze Age Fengate - Amalgamating the evidence of all investigations to date (including Abbott's findings, see Fig. 2.4; 1–3 indicates embayments), this shows the reconstructed fieldsystem and indicates the main areas of Grooved Ware and Beaker occupation/usage. Reproduced by permission of Ordnance Survey on behalf of HMSO. © Crown copyright 2009. All rights reserved. Ordnance Survey Licence number 100048686.*

together, this group now represents a coherent four-/five-compound arrangement; one whose multiple-side double-ditch boundaries and size makes its reminiscent of the Depot Site's 'block' system.

Now being able to appreciate a much greater 'whole' of the lie of Fengate's landscape, the degree to which topography influenced the layout of its fieldsystem becomes clearer. The northwest–southeast orientation of its south-central 'core' basically lay at right-angles to the fen-edge across that area; just as also its paramount north–south alignment across 'Fengate North' was determined by the swing of the fen-edge to that orientation, with the result being a major twist in the fieldsystem's axes (and with the implication that they there continue eastwards around

the Oxney Road embayment; Fig. 6.1:1). In relationship to this, the narrow isthmus-like spit or ridge of gravel that, as shown on the geological maps (and as demonstrated in the clay natural of the Bronze Age 'fieldsystem-less' Parnwell Site to the north (Fig. 2.15; Webley 2007), runs northeast to connect Eye/Thorney to the 'mainland' of the fen-edge, must be considered a significant landscape corridor (see Chapter 4, Inset for its findings).

Where the Fengate system topography does not seem to have been so influential is in the extreme southwest and, though twisting slightly, the orientation of the Tower Works-area ditches seems essentially the same as within the system's 'core'; this being despite that the landscape there shifts more to a north–south slope (i.e. down to the Cat's Water Drain). As discussed in Chapter 3, what might have been the cause of this is that there, in the west, it was no longer a matter of the fieldsystem responding to the fen-edge, but rather the lie of the river/stream valley of the Cat's Water (palaeo-)course of the Nene. In other words, the system's orientation was laid out in relationship to the fen-edge proper and not the river/stream's topography.

The other fieldsystem 'block' or alignment that must be accounted for is what seems to be its radial arrangement throughout the northwest (Fig. 6.1:A & C). In relationship to Edgerley's north–south axis, in the northeast this shift begins at the Broadlands Site, and can be seen progressing in the layout of the cropmarks across this swathe south to the area of the Vicarage Farm ditches (see Inset, Chapter 5). Yes, admittedly, some of the cropmarks within this sector undoubtedly denote discrete Iron Age compounds and the more open, 'organic' layout of others probably suggest accompanying ditch/paddock systems of that period. Nevertheless, a radial pattern of straight ditches can be seen to run throughout this area (including Pyror's putative Neolithic 'pair'; Fig. 6.1:B) and which seem to represent the extension of the Bronze Age system. If so, a certain ambiguity results concerning its determination. Its radial arrangement might simply reflect compensation of its axes as they arced between the northwest–southeast orientation of Fengate's 'core' and the north–south arrangement of its northern sector. In which case, this radial layout could, essentially, have been a secondary phenomenon in relationship to the more fenward portions of the fieldsystem (i.e. laid out after the 'edge-fields' were). Alternatively, as is apparent in Figure 6.1, topography might again have also played a significant role, as the radial system could have been organized from off of the higher ground to the northwest of this area (i.e. *c.* 5 m OD contour). Whatever the case, the interfacing of both the 'edge' and the in-/hinterland radial systems could well have created a 'pinch-point' just west of the Newark Road compounds: the area in which the Ditch 9/10 droves and the Site 11 enclosure should have, theoretically, overlapped (the drove apparently not being present/ identified in Mahany's '69 excavations).

Of Fengate's immediate fen-edge topography, the other factor that needs to be addressed is the role of its *inlets* (Fig. 6.1:1–3). Here, again, the evidence is not entirely consistent. While the embayment just south of the Edgerley Site appears eventually to have been bounded by the massive F.8 boundary (and a bank system along its north side) and to have resulted in a marked eastward swing of Edgerley's drove, it itself

was not a focus of the fieldsystem. (Based on the evidence of Pyror's Boroughby Garage Site, the fieldsystem had evidently shifted to a more north–south orientation well south of the off-Vicarage Road inlet and that the low ground was not itself the focus/cause of this reorientation; see Chapter 4.) Conversely, in the case of the Elliott Site, the Ditch 1/2 drove was clearly oriented upon the inlet proper. As outlined in Chapter 4 (Inset), that 'way' represents the system's prime axis and to appreciate why topography might there have been so influential (and 'suggestive') requires broader discussion of the area's *cultural landscape*, which will duly occur later in this chapter.

Finally, before progressing to consider specific facets of Fengate's fieldsystem and its landscape, the degree to which contemporary attitudes relate to the prehistoric 'fieldsystem question' should here be acknowledged. Do we want to envisage these systems as attesting to egalitarian 'life-ways' (distancing any authority) and as representing a long-continuum of what is rural/'natural' or, alternatively, as an imposed grid-geometry (i.e. anti-'organic') upon land? These could be (mis-) understood as 'good' and 'bad' pasts; although theoretically archaeology should not involve this degree of personal judgement, such factors invariably influence interpretation, given a desire to deeply embed our 'ancestries' (see Evans 1997b on 'sentimental prehistories'). Here, central to this discussion, is the change in attitudes towards *pastoralism* as a cultural category and appellation generally. Though often previously downplayed in favour of the resultant arts of arable economies — in effect, the ancient equation of culture and cultivation — over the last two decades in archaeology it has taken on quite a different role. Attesting to the equally deeply-engrained romanticism of the 'wild other' (see Biddick 1989 on the 'other economy' and e.g. Kitchen 2001's use of Mongolian ethnography *viz.* the British Bronze Age), it has also held a more deep-seated appeal, as pastoral mobilism/transhumance has provided an obvious dynamic to link the subject's far-flung distribution dots (see Evans 1987 and Chapter 2 above).

Cow on the Drove — The how and why of fieldsystems

I've always appreciated Powell's '*Fengate Three*' cover (Pryor 1980a), as it's like no other archaeological reconstruction I know. Oddly hard-edged and other-worldly — and completely unsentimental — it is much more successful than Casper Johnson's impressionistic rendering of the Storey's Bar Road sheepfold that recently appeared in Yates' fieldsystem book (2007, pl. 2). Beyond matters of style, part of the appeal of Powell's *Cow on the Drove* figure is that, highlighting a cow

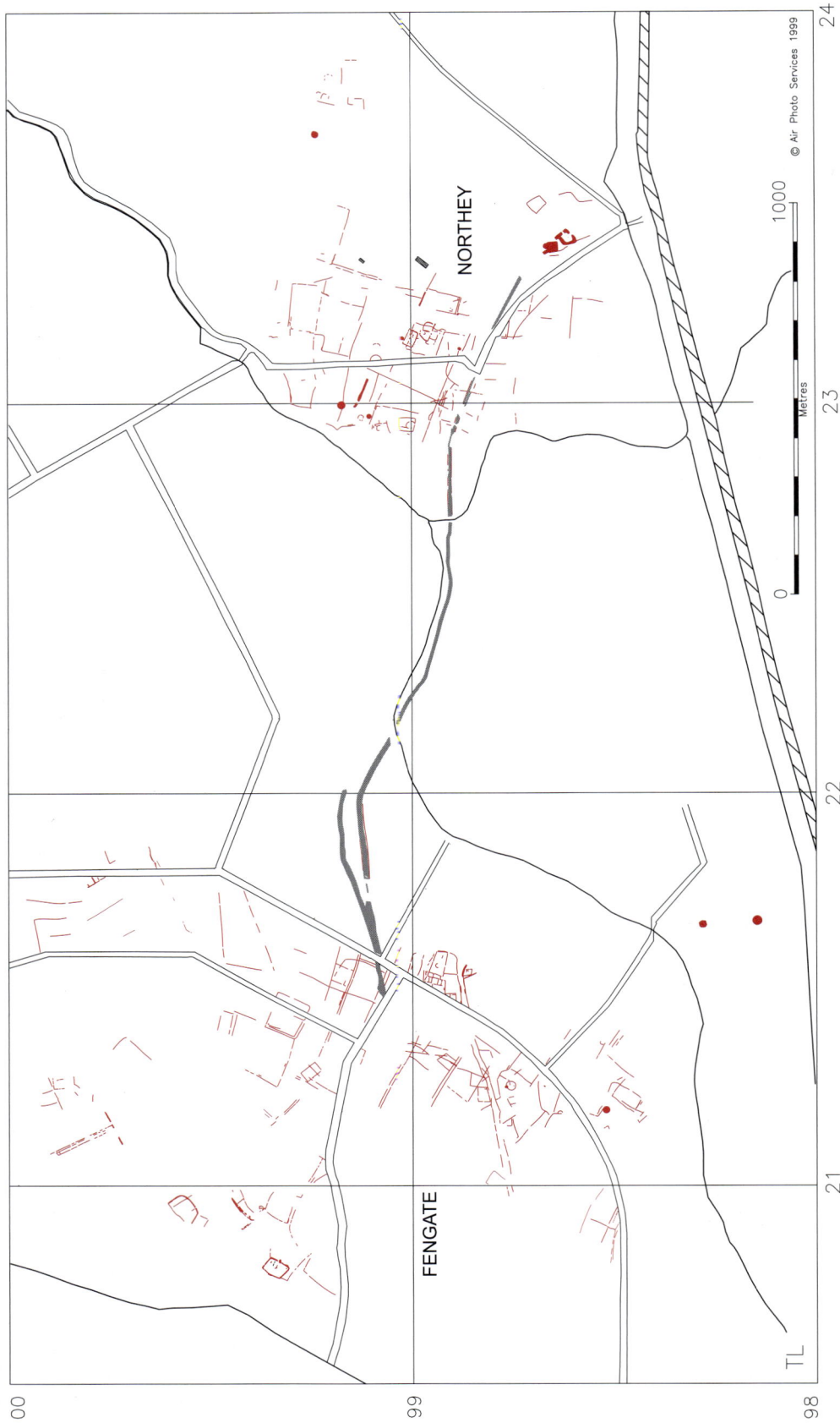

FIGURE 6.2. *Palmer's Fengate/Northey cropmark plot (see Pryor 1999, fig. 60). Reproduced by permission of Ordnance Survey on behalf of HMSO.*
© *Crown copyright 2009. All rights reserved. Ordnance Survey Licence number 100048686.*

and with hedges in the background, it seems much more correct in its essentials (i.e. lone cow *vs* mass sheep). In contrast, the Johnson painting is a product of Pryor's revised sheep-dominated interpretation of the Fengate system (1996), which clearly arose as a result of his experience of becoming a sheep farmer; the root of Pryor's argument being that Fengate and other Bronze Age fieldsystems in the region primarily related to sheep management and that their successful operation required enormous flocks, involving many thousands of animals in a 'climax pastoral farming economy' (Pryor 1996, 317; 2001a, 420).

Pryor's paper appeared (shortly followed by his allied volume of 1998, *Farmers in Prehistoric Britain*) when Mark Knight and I were working on the contemporary Barleycroft Farm fieldsystems. There, we had very similar, 'big-scale' systems of ditched fields, but no droveways whatsoever (Evans & Knight 2000; 2001). Yes, we had narrow double-ditch boundaries, but in some cases these concentrically mirrored three sides of some of its enclosed plots (Fig. 2.20) and there was no conceivable way that these could have been narrow sheep-droves (*cum* 'drafting races'; Pryor 1996). An even greater *apparent* difference lay in Barleycroft's faunal record: only *c.* 3 per cent sheep, as opposed to 58.5 per cent cattle bone (see below). Either our system was very different from Fengate's or something was wrong with the latter's 'new' interpretation. A review of the data was clearly in order.

Questioning the first, would-be 'small droves' issue, is not to imply that the Storey's Bar Road system (whose sheep 'draft race' operation featured in Pryor's 1996 paper; see Fig. 6.3) might not be a specific instance of such. Rather it is to say that, its main droveways aside, Fengate's generally narrow double-ditch systems (having an interval of only *c.* 1.5–2 m between their boundaries) are unlikely candidates for animal 'run ways'. This is especially true when the truncated original upper profile of their ditches is taken into account, narrowing the width of the 'way' to 1–1.5 m. In the Over and Barleycroft Farm systems, not only do such settings 'encircle' the sides of some its rectangular plots (as they do at Fengate's Newark Road and the Depot sub-Sites; see below), but they also, at points, delineate the sides of major field 'blocks'. Based on our work there, we concluded that it was more likely that such narrow ditch pairings related to embanked hedge-lines. In the case of Fengate, the recovery of hedge-wood from the Elliott Site would offer support to such interpretations (despite its being of earlier Bronze Age attribution), and comparable evidence of later prehistoric hedging has recently been forthcoming from other sites in the region (e.g. Pollard 1996).

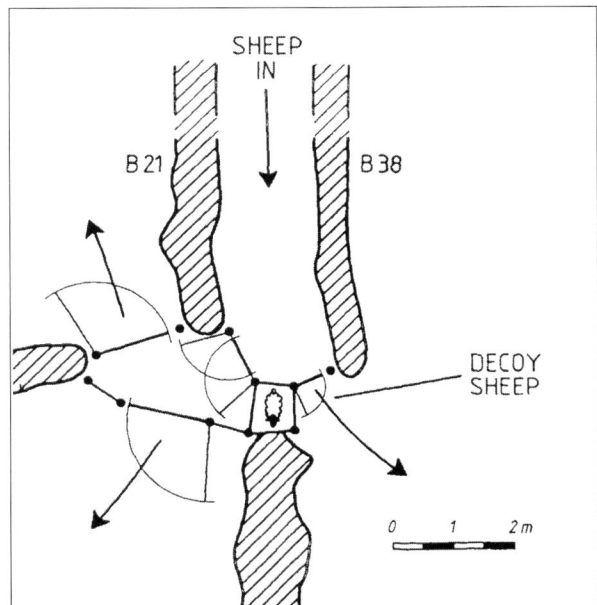

FIGURE 6.3. *Livestock Dynamics - 'The Cow on the Drove' cover of 'Fengate Three' (top; Pryor 1980a); below, Pryor's sheep-run reinterpretation of the Storey's Bar Road system (1996, fig. 3; see Fig. 3.20 for location).*

In much the same way that formally demarcated fieldsystems are not necessary to practise successful agriculture, nor are droves (see Fig. 6.5). This is not just true of Barleycroft but, closer at hand to Fengate, nor does the Bradley Fen system — at least that portion exposed — have any (even the adjacent Northey fieldsystem does not seem droveway-dominated in the manner of Fengate; see Fig. 6.2 and Pryor 2001a, 79–80). At the risk of emphasizing what must seem a truism, the main reason for having such well-defined routes would surely have been to readily take things *through* fieldsystems, essentially related to longer distance transport (the advent and clear frequency of

TABLE 6.3. *Relative species proportions for Bronze Age fieldsystem assemblages from features (including pits) by % NISP (Number of identified specimens; note that the Edgerley Drain Road sample is too small for inclusion). While Pryor's Storey's Bar Road assemblage also saw only low sheep (6.6%, MNI), there pig and cattle occurred in roughly equally percentages (c. 47–49%). Yet, surely reflective of that site's Grooved Ware utilization, of its main 'domesticates' approximately 30% were actually 'wild' (auroch and probably wild pig; see Harman 1978, 177–80 and Chapter 3 above); in other words, it cannot reflect a Bronze Age economy (see Evans & Pollard 2001).*

	Barleycroft Farm	Newark Road	Elliott Site	The Holme, Earith	Bradley Fen
Cattle	58.5	73	78	81.4	86.1
Sheep/goat	2.9	18.8	17	13.2	1.7
Pig	5.9	4.9	1.6	4.2	11.4
Horse	14.9	1.22	0.8	0.8	-
Deer	14.9	-	0.2	-	0.8
Dog	2.9	2.1	1.6	0.3	-

cart transportation could also have been a compelling factor; see e.g. Taylor, in Pryor 2001a, 213–17). Based, for example, on the Barleycroft/Bradley Fen negative evidence, 'user-inhabitants' would not have required droves to take animals around/through their own immediate fields. Instead, the need for droves might have been determined by 'hinterland communities'. In other words, settlements behind or 'inland' from Fengate (or other fen-edge systems) needing to take their animals out onto seasonal marshland pastures. A similar rationale might lie behind the arrangement of *The Holme* fieldsystem excavated at Colne Fen, Earith, which also had a 'great', 13–19 m-wide ditched droveway leading down to the fen (see Figs. 2.21 & 2.24:4).

Another argument relating to the *raison d'etre* of droves might, however, also be applied: the regular, daily-cycle movement of animals between settlements and pasture. This is something that sheep do not generally demand. Driven out to distant pasture and tended by a shepherd, they can potentially be left there for months at a time. Yet, if regular sustenance was provided by cow's milk, then cattle would have been brought into settlements daily for milking and 'herd-routine' would have undoubtedly structured the lives of these communities.

All this returns us squarely to the Bronze Age sheep *versus* cattle economy issue. In the context of our Barleycroft Farm-related review, the most critical problem with Pryor's sheep-arguments was Fengate's own data. As shown in Table 6.3, cattle were the main species within the Newark Road assemblage, as they have been in all of Fengate's subsequent Bronze Age excavations. Indeed, as is also plain in that table, cattle clearly dominate the faunal record of all the main Bronze Age fieldsystems excavated at any scale within the region; in fact, Barleycroft actually had the lowest relative representation of cattle.

This is not to deny the 'participation' of sheep in the Fengate landscape and, indeed, its sites have a higher proportion of sheep than others in the region. Equally, the regular recovery of cylindrical Bronze Age loomwieghts attests to the importance of textile production. We are also fully aware that the smaller bone-size of sheep biases their recovery (*vs* cattle; see Serjeantson 2007). Yet, *contra* Pryor, the Bronze Age pastoral economy *was* primarily cattle-based and it must, therefore, be presumed that milk significantly contributed to the diet (Legge 1981; 1992). Moreover, as Pryor himself explored in his 1976 paper, 'Fen-edge land management in the Bronze Age', given the warrior ethos of the period — with its much evident bronze weaponry — and based on ethnographic parallel (e.g. the renowned African cattle economies of the Nuer, Dinka and Masai), cattle are far more likely to have been the pre-eminent prestige animal and they surely would have been the cause of much raiding/rustling (see e.g. Davis & Payne 1993 concerning the Irthlingborough barrow's mass cattle skull deposit and Bronze Age cattle symbolism). In contrast, the rise of a sheep economy within the region was rather largely a phenomenon of the Iron Age, with the Cat's Water settlement of that period having 42 per cent sheep and 50 per cent cattle (NISP, Biddick 1984; see also e.g. Serjeantson 2006). Returning to the issue of 'bounded-tethering' needs, whilst the landscapes of that period involved a degree of ditch-demarcation, formal gridiron-type fieldsystems as seen in the Bronze Age were not generally used: such systems only re-emerged during the Late Iron Age.

As discussed in Chapter 2 above, there is no necessary reason to presuppose that the prime factor behind Bronze Age fieldsystems actually related to animals, as opposed to crops. The long-term evidence shows that, usually more mobile and 'expansive', pastoral economies could thrive without the need for formal fieldsystems. Rather, fieldsystems would surely have related to *investment within the plot and land*: the long clearance of stones, and manuring to enhance soils (Fowler 1983, 170–71; Johnston 2001). As

Figure 6.4. *Droveway-organized fieldsystem 'spines' (with main droveways indicated in red): Top left, Fengate; top right, Deeping (see Fig. 2.22); below, in contrast, Fleming's apparently 'drove-less' Holne Moor system, Dartmoor (1988b, fig. 34). Reproduced by permission of Ordnance Survey on behalf of HMSO. © Crown copyright 2009. All rights reserved. Ordnance Survey Licence number 100048686.*

such, and given the evidence of the sites' quernstones and pollen record (see Chapter 2 above), Fengate — along with the region's other Bronze Age fieldsystems — would have hosted *mixed farming* regimes and their pastoral component has probably been greatly over-emphasized.

Other factors may well have also contributed to the development of fieldsystems and droveways: one can imagine demarcating coppiced lots to protect young trees from the ravages of animal-browse or closing off systems as a whole from 'the wild', so that wolves did not take stock or aurochs try to breed with domestic cattle. Nevertheless, the evidence of the period's pollen record primarily marks (aside from the rise of open-ground and, thereby, forest clearance) the 'advent' of cereals. Not only is this true of those cores available from the Fengate/Flag Fen environs (see Scaife, in Pryor 2001), but also those from elsewhere. In fact, during the preparation of this volume we received the detailed results of the environmental cores from Colne Fen, Earith (Boreham, in Evans *et al.* forthcoming), which succinctly express the regional second-millennium BC 'trend'. Taken from a deep channel immediately bordering the fen-edge terrace landscape which we had spent years excavating (dotted with earlier Bronze Age ring-ditches and a Middle Bronze Age fieldsystem; see Chapter 2), we first bracketed the column with radiocarbon dates. The initial results clearly showed the onset and then the consistent presence of arable production throughout the second half of the second millennium. Yet, in this case, we wanted greater precision than just a generic sense of pattern and, accordingly, submitted a further sample from the point where arable crops first registered. This produced an assay of 1880–1620 cal. BC (Wk-21083) — some 200–400 years earlier than expected — dating to the time of the area's earlier Bronze Age ring-ditches.

We are not naive in this and fully appreciate that such evidence does not, for example, preclude earlier, Neolithic arable production and that only environmental imprints of a certain intensity are likely to 'show' in such measures. Nevertheless, in this capacity the results of Boreham and Peachy's Sewage Treatment Site palaeo-environmental researches could also be cited (see Chapter 5 above). With cereals essentially occurring throughout its later Neolithic to terminal Bronze Age sequence, its pollen analysis suggested a marked rise of arable activity *estimated* to occur at *c.* 3600 BP (*c.* 2100–1800 cal. BC; Fig. 5.25). Like the surprising results from the Early Bronze Age pit at the Elliott Site (F.302, with its evidence of clearance, hedging and its extraordinary archery-related straps), this highlights the problem of the dating of fieldsystems and the degree to which they may have

formally delineated processes that had already been taking place within their landscapes some centuries before what is currently widely held to be the *c.* 1500 cal. BC fieldsystem 'watershed' (see below).

At *c.* 16 m width, the scale of the droveway at the Edgerley Road Site rivals those at Colne Fen, Earith (see Chapter 2 above), its size explained by the need to convey animals up into that site's 'great' corral-like enclosure (Fig. 4.41). Against this, at only *c.* 5 m width, the core's Ditch 1/2 and 8/9 droves (excavated at Padholme Road and Newark Road) seem considerably more modest. Again, referring back to arguments of 'special-ness', much has been made of the latter drove's unique status, linking as it does Pryor's Newark Road 'communal stockyard compounds' and the Flag Fen post-alignment: the line of the latter and that of the drove are effectively seen as a continuation of each other (despite the fact that their alignment is not exact). Be this as it may, facets of this interpretive connection must now be called into question by the Elliott Site results. With three to four burials known along its drove (including the one excavated at Padholme Road), it rather seems more a focus of burial 'distinction'. Equally, if the massive open-ended compound that funnelled into the fenward-end of its drove was intended for stock management (with animals collected there and driven from hence into the fieldsystem at the end of the summer grazing season), what then of the Ditch 8/9 drove, which at the Power Station Site was without any such broadening/funnel arrangement? If the current interpretation of the Elliott Site's drove-end is correct, then it suggests that the northern, Ditch 8/9, drove had little specific mass stock-handling capacity and this, in turn, could cast further doubt on the communal stockyard interpretation of the Newark Road compounds (see Chapter 4, Inset concerning the respective primary/secondary 'prime-axis' status of these droveways).

Whilst now having an immediate parallel in the Broadlands enclosure (see Chapter 4 above), the arrangement of the two double-circuit compounds on the northern side of that sub-site's Ditch 8/9 drove was really quite extraordinary, and Pryor duly remarked:

> The well ordered rectilinear layout of these enclosures and droves strongly suggests *some form of controlled planning and surveying*. There is very little good evidence for extensive modification or for abandonment of different areas at various times. The whole system seems to have been in use at more or less the same time and there can be little doubt that Structures 1 and 2 were built and used after the main elements of the enclosure system had been laid out, and in use, for some time (1980a, 25; emphasis added).

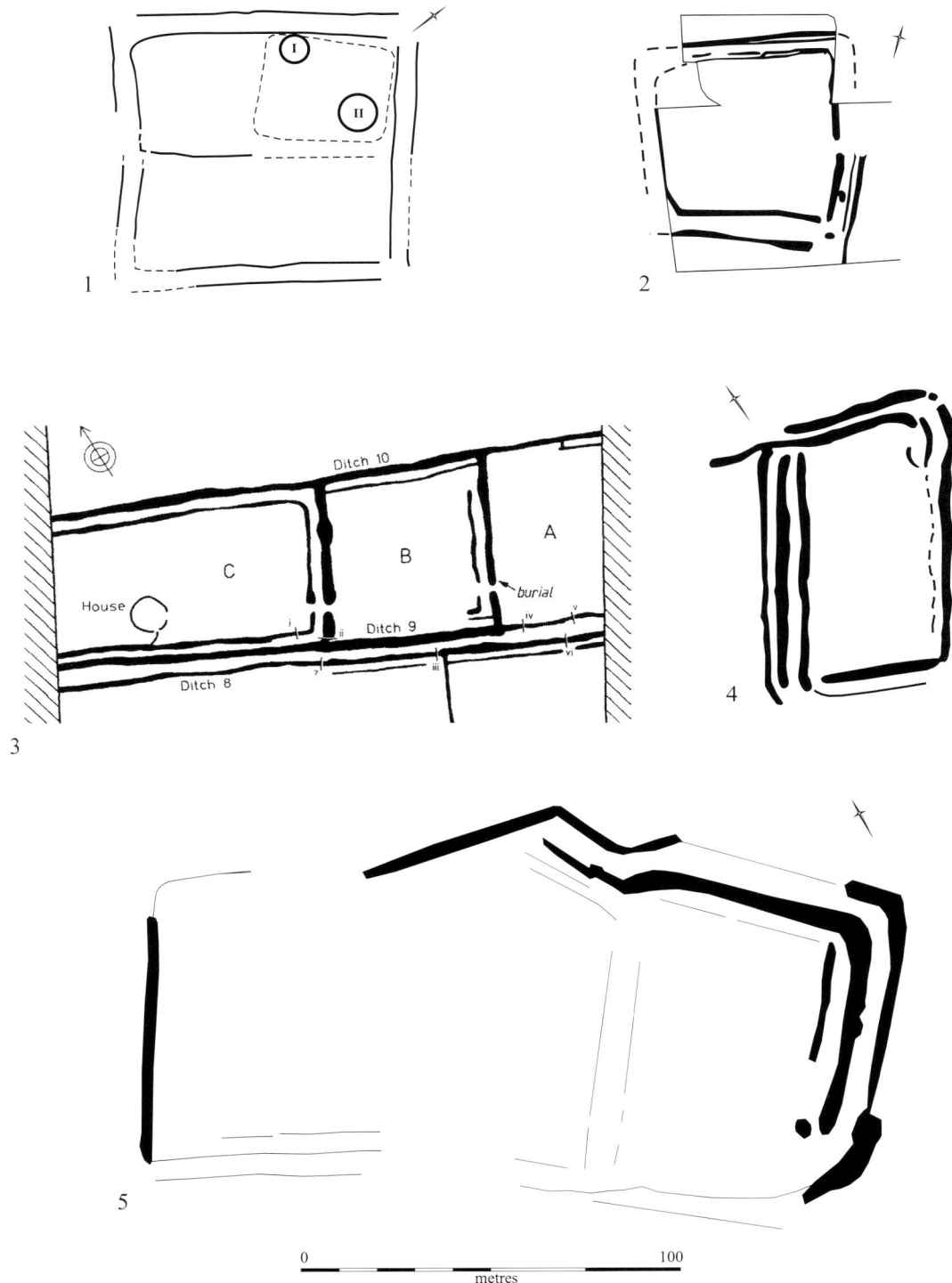

FIGURE 6.5. *Double-ditch Compounds: 1) The Depot Site (after Evans 1992; see also fig. 2.4 in Pryor 2001a); 2) the Broadlands' 'Square' (after Nicholson* et al. *forthcoming); 3) the Newark Road Compounds (after Pryor 1980a, fig. 19; 1996, fig. 1); 4) Welland Bank (after Pryor 2002, fig. 7); 5) the Site I enclosure in the Addenbrooke's environs, Cambridge (Evans* et al. *2008, fig. 4.2).*

As noted above, Pryor originally saw the double-ditch perimeter as reflective of 'internal droves' (Pryor 1980a, 23) but surely, given the logic of their plan-layout, this cannot have been the case and their double-circuit must have flanked upcast banks (Fig. 6.5:3). Probably standing upwards of 1 m high, if hedge- or fence-/palisade-capped, these would have presented a considerable barrier.

Though admitting that the western compounds eventually included settlement, Pryor was not particularly explicit in his original interpretation of their function (Pror 1980a, 171–2). It was only in his 1996 *Antiquity* paper that he interpreted them as a system of 'communal stockyards', and basically as a livestock 'auction ring'. (Further evidence of this stockyard interpretation was thought to be offered by the subsequent excavations at Welland Bank, whose central, partially double-ditched, later Bronze Age rectangular enclosure — with its banks still surviving — provided a parallel as it had little evidence of any interior settlement, its only associated structure being interpreted as a stock-holding pen; Fig. 6.5:4; Pryor 2002, 27.) It is crucial to recognize the linkage that was made to Flag Fen (*via* the drove/post-alignment), as the large, extra-local kin-group social gatherings that would have accompanied these 'markets' also provided a rationale for the platforms' *en masse* ritual activities (Pryor 1996, 317; 2001, 415–16).

Given that Archaeological Solutions have now adopted wholesale the same interpretation for their Broadlands enclosure (Nicholson *et al.* forthcoming), and all that has been made of this 'stockyard-mode' of explanation (*viz.* Flag Fen), some review of the evidence is certainly warranted. For example, it is worth looking again at the phosphate plots of the Newark Road compounds (Pryor 1980a, figs. 111–12), as they certainly do not seem to attest to the occurrence of livestock in the numbers proposed. Considered, moreover, in the light of how poor the evidence of Middle Bronze Age settlement is as a whole (see Chapter 2 above), in having two roundhouses within its interior (Structure 2, though, thought to be a 'barn'; Pryor 1980a, 173–4), the evidence that the Newark Road Compound C

was occupied is actually quite robust and its associated finds seem relatively high (Pryor 1980a, 50–61, figs. 25 & 34). From the array of potential posthole features associated with its Structure 2, there seems no particular reason to consider it a 'D'-shaped barn and it could quite readily have been a 'proper', non-gullied roundhouse. In full fairness, in his '96 paper Pryor did not dismiss the compound's settlement component, but rather implied that it housed the stockyard's 'overseer'. Nor is it here being questioned that stock were not a component of this complex; rather, the key issue is the recognition of just how formal was the layout of these compounds with their concentric circuits and matched/aligned entrances. Indeed, what they are almost reminiscent of is a rectangular form of Essex's Late Bronze Age ringworks, such as have been found at South Hornchurch, Springfield Lyons and Mucking's two 'rings' (Bradley 2007, fig. 4.11). Admittedly, returning us squarely to the issue of the period's weak/non-settlement evidence, the *Late* Bronze Age ringworks clearly saw much higher depositional levels. Nevertheless, given their shared principles/logic of layout (and even associated metalwork; Newark Road's human remains are, however, arguably far earlier; see e.g. Brück 2007 and below), it is reasonable to question whether these Fengate compounds should, in turn, be considered some manner of higher status, defended settlement enclosures.

Recent fieldwork on the south side of Cambridge has yielded a potentially intriguing parallel for this configuration. There, aerial photographs showed two conjoining sub-square compounds, variously with double- and even triple-ditch circuits. Before its evaluation trial trenching we presumed (through analogy with the Orsett Cock complex; Toller 1980) that it probably represented a Romano-British reworking of a Late Iron Age enclosure, and were surprised to find that it was, in fact, of later Bronze Age attribution (its mid second-millennium BC attribution being confirmed by radiocarbon dating). Of course, only its full excavation — which is shortly anticipated — will reveal its detail and full dynamics (Fig. 6.5:5; Evans *et al.* 2008).

'Survey excavation' and redundant information

Undertaken hard on the heels of Fengate, I've always thought that Pryor's Welland Valley fieldwork and Maxey excavations was a great and innovative project (Pryor & French 1985; see also Taylor 1997), being that rare thing, an attempt to do something truly new and different. With its emphasis on sampling techniques, it cannot be said to have been entirely successful, as its artefact numbers were too low to provide much significant patterning. Nevertheless, it was a brave and interesting experiment. Characteristically, Pryor stirred things up when he announced its inception in *Rescue News*: 'I am afraid, however, that enormous set-piece excavations such as Fengate, are a thing of the past; for a start, they cost too much and the post-excavation work … is time-consuming, dull and needlessly repetitive. Vast quantities of data are produced, but there is often precious little information; in short *we are learning more and more about less and less*' (1980b, 6; emphasis added; see also Pryor 1984, 230–31). Considered today, Maxey's excavation-sample seems typical of most rural landscape sites, but in its time (1979–81)

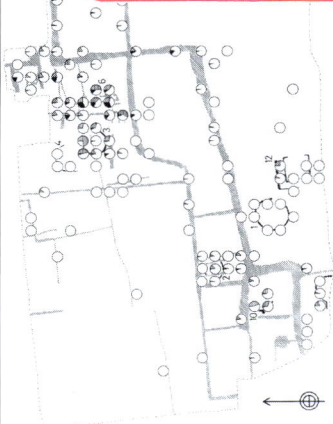

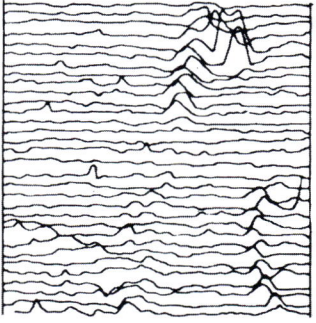

FIGURE 6.6. *A Maxey Miscellanea - The 'Survey Excavation' article that appeared in Rescue News in March 1980, with Ben Booth's piece on 'The Maxey Micro' of later that year ('paper-clipped' upper right along with fig. 31 from Pryor & French's 1985 Maxey report comparing fieldwalking and sub-soil feature Roman pottery densities); inset bottom left, the eastern half of the Maxey base-plan (ibid. fig. 40) showing density of excavation segments (i.e. the 'minimal digging' of the day).*

it was radically 'minimal' and was far less intense than much of Fengate and, most certainly, Mucking. (The forecast of the demise of large-scale excavations was true of those funded from the public purse, but was otherwise premature as it could not anticipate the developer-funding of the next decade.)

In that project, reduced feature-excavation was the compensation for topsoil-surface interrogation (Fig. 6.6). This both involved transect fieldwalking across the broader Welland Valley environs (Taylor in Pryor 1984, 15–23) and the application of a battery of site-topsoil investigation techniques, with the latter inspiring detailed studies of artefact distributional modelling (Crowther 1983; Crowther & Pryor, in Pryor & French 1985, 44–53; see also Lane's artefact-recovery experiments in Pryor & French 1985, 32–3). Although not citing the strict tenets of 'New' or Processualist archaeological practices (post-processualism, effectively, having been born in '82 with the publication of Hodder's 'Brown Book', *Symbolic and Structural Archaeology*), the approach generally, and certainly Maxey's survey procedures, were very formal. This expressed itself in a number of different ways, not least its phasing. Relating to the vexed issue of successive 'typed cultures' raised throughout this volume, in contrast, Maxey's phasing (though having broad period correlates) was strictly numerical: 1–10. Equally, the project embraced computing and the rapid in-field processing of data, so that digging, and information redundancy, could be kept to a minimum, the need

for such 'feedback' being, after all, among the prime planks of systems-based practices (see Evans *et al.* 2006 concerning Great Wilbraham and Haddenham's attempts at the same). (Demonstrating that there is not necessarily a one-to-one relationship between methodology and theory, feedback is of course also a mainstay of Hodder's Çatalhöyük excavations.) It was the related notion of *data-redundancy* — something totally alien to the day's 'rescue' ethos — that, as outlined in Chapter One, Margaret Jones took umbrage with.

What of Maxey's legacy? On the one hand, with the discovery of the splendidly preserved (and deeply buried) Flag Fen platform, Pryor and his teams continued with in-depth dyke survey within its environs (French & Pryor 1993). On the other hand, it and Etton's excavations demanded sustained, painstaking digging which, in many respects, was the antithesis of Maxey's ethos (although the latter site, like Haddenham at the same time, saw the application of innovative sampling of its buried soil horizons). Attempts were made during the Fenland Management Project of the early '90s to investigate the relationship between surface distributions and subsoil features (see Evans 2000). With few exceptions, however, these approaches have not carried much weight in subsequent development-led landscape excavations in the region. Yes, the minimum excavation-sample may have won out, but generally the mass open-stripping used at Fengate (rather than Maxey's staged procedures) has proven the dominant model.

The when (dating) and peoples-as-types

Reviewing the dating evidence for the layout of Fengate's system and that of other such fieldsystems generally within the region, it is crucial to recognize that, whilst today we can essentially recognize them as a second-millennium BC phenomenon, this was not the case during the 1970s. Since then, and especially with the scale of landscape investigation that has taken place post-1990 with developer funding, our familiarity with a range of various settlement and landscape system *types* has become much greater. In the '70s, much of what we now take for granted was unknown, there being then a greater sense of possibility. As outlined above (see Chapter 5, Inset), the Vicarage Farm fieldsystem offers a prime case in point. Excavated in 1973, in contrast to its many pit features which yielded an abundance of Iron Age dating evidence, its ditch system was relatively 'clean' and provided no direct basis for assignation. Because its orientation was not the same as that of the Newark/Padholme Road Bronze Age system (despite the fact that, to all intents and purposes, they looked alike), it was proposed that it might be of Neolithic date. In its time this attribution was a reasonable proposition and it is only over the last decade or so that, through greatly *accrued context/pattern* (see below), we have come to know this to be unlikely.

When first attributing Fengate's Newark Road system to the Bronze Age, Pryor had the incredible

good fortune to be able to draw upon a rare 'type-find' of the period: a Middle Bronze Age spearhead from one of the Newark Road ditches (1976, 41–2, fig. 3.5:11). (The recovery of bronzes in a ditch-context is almost unheard of; while attesting to Pryor's personal 'luck', in hindsight its presence must also be considered an expression of the frequency of metalwork in the wider Fengate/Flag Fen environs and, especially, along the Newark Road drove/Power Station causeway axis.) Based, however, on the results of his Storey's Bar Road excavations (1978), he attributed its origins to the later Neolithic and, since, has consistently advocated the long, millennium-plus usage of the Fengate system. In the radiocarbon dating model offered in *Flag Fen*, he and Alex Bayliss claimed that it was operational for 1340–1890 years, ending in the thirteenth to twelfth centuries BC (2001a, 399). Given a long-maintenance emphasis, he stated that, due to regular mucking-out, the system's prime usage cannot be directly dated as its evidence has been dug away. Instead, in the 2001 model, the origins of the system essentially turn on one date — 4190±90 BC/3030–2500 cal. BC (HAR-780) — from an inhumation within a ditch at Newark Road (see Fig. 6.7). This seems incredibly early and, as explored below, makes little sense in a regional context. Furthermore, having myself been excavating such fieldsystem ditches for more than thirty years now, I can acknowledge that they were clearly recut in their time, but not to the extent that they could have been used for anywhere

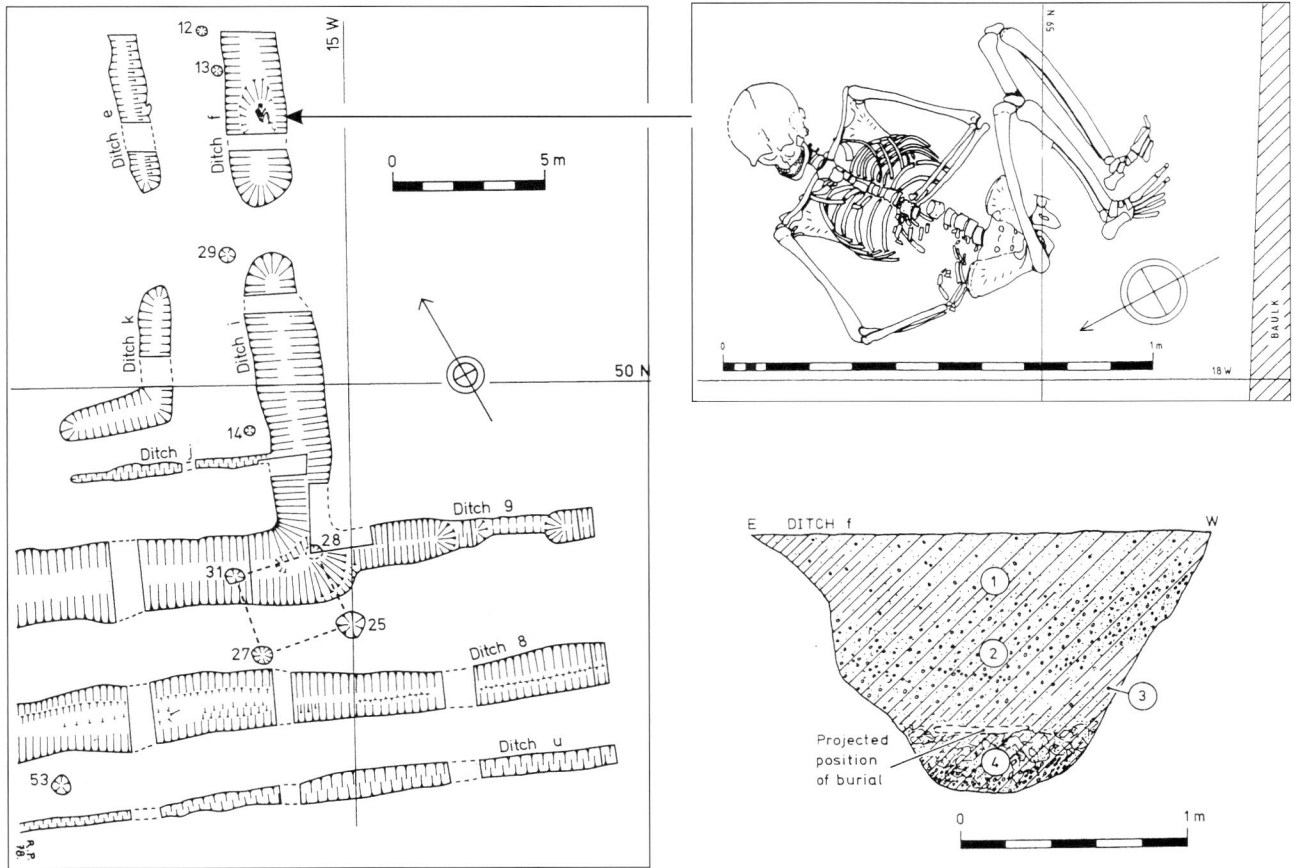

FIGURE 6.7. *Fengate's Dating - The Pivot: The situation of the crouched inhumation near the terminal of Ditch 7 at the Newark Road Compounds (see also Fig. 2.13; after Pryor 1980, figs. 23, 26 & 27); dated 4190±90 BC/3030–2500 cal. BC (HAR-780).*

near a millennium, let alone nearly two. (An additional problem with such explanations is the question of how anyone would know what an actively maintained, millennium-old ditch would actually look like; it seems unlikely to have produced such minor boundaries as those in question here.)

Within the Fenland, and elsewhere in southern Britain, the cumulative weight of evidence associated with 'early' fieldsystems generally points to a mid second-millennium BC date. This would be true of the vast bulk of Fengate's radiocarbon assays and, in other excavated landscapes within the region, complement the association of Deverel-Rimbury cremation cemeteries with the fieldsystems. Yet, as discussed in Chapter 2, the main problem with such an assignation is the distinction of that period's domestic component: in other contexts we have the dead, but the settlements seem to evade us.

This dilemma is well-expressed in Table 6.4, showing the relative frequency of pottery from Fengate's sub-sites, in which there is no obvious 'horizon' to which you would have to attribute its fieldsystem. To be frank, if it was not for the urns accompanying its cremation burials, it would be reasonable to suppose that the Deverel-Rimbury 'era' (*c.* 1500–1200 cal. BC) was essentially aceramic; clearly a substantial portion of the pottery has 'gone' with the dead (and been recycled into the grog-temper of vessels), the representation of later Bronze Age (post-*c.* 1200–1000 cal. BC) ceramics generally being significantly greater. Yet, and as discussed above (see Chapter 2), in the case of Fengate this issue has been further exaggerated by a displacement of settlement evidence in favour of both 'ritual' and 'stock-dominated' interpretation, respectively denying any substantial occupation component for the Flag Fen platform and Newark Road's double-ditch compounds.

Certainly there is something compelling in Pryor's formulation of the Fengate system's *longue durée*, spanning the vagaries of Grooved Ware, Beaker,

Table 6.4. *Comparative Fengate pottery frequencies (sherd number). Note that the figures for Newark and Storey's Bar Road are based on Pryor's attributions (in which complete/semi-complete vessels count as one; 1978, 91–7 and 1980a, 102–6) and only pertain to those sites' illustrated catalogues. Most relevant for Newark Road, this clearly under-represents the assemblage and biases attributions towards decorated vessel-types. For example, whilst 3027 grams of pottery was apparently recovered from Newark Road's ditches (number not provided; Pryor 1980a, table 3), only 45 sherds from these contexts are illustrated. Based on an estimated mean sherd weight of 10–15 grams, this implies that only approximately a quarter to a sixth of the ditch-pottery was attributed (i.e. a further c. 150–250 sherds in addition to the unattributed 42 illustrated sherds from ditch/pit contexts). The 135 generic 'prehistoric' sherds at Edgerley Road are largely grog-tempered and of later Neolithic/Early Bronze Age attribution (M. Knight pers. comm.); given this, and their lack of decoration, they are probably Collared Urn-derived.*

	Tower Works (c. 0.14 ha)	Elliott (1.7 ha)	Edgerley (1.7 ha)	Newark & Storey's Bar Road sub-sites
'Prehistoric' (i.e. pre-Iron Age)				
Sherds (no.)			135	42
Weight (g)			479	
'Neolithic'				
Sherds (no.)	2			
Weight (g)	19			
Earlier Neolithic				
Sherds (no.)			57	5
Weight (g)			119	
Peterborough Ware				
Sherds (no.)			13	
Weight (g)			46	
Grooved Ware				
Sherds (no.)			1066	199
Weight (g)			11,813	
Beaker				
Sherds (no.)			318	8
Weight (g)			1534	
Food vessel (?)				
Sherds (no.)				2
Weight (g)				
Collared Urn				
Sherds (no.)			145	20
Weight (g)			3147	
Middle Bronze Age/Dev-Rim				
Sherds (no.)		165		7
Weight (g)		980		
Late Bronze Age/PDR				
Sherds (no.)		48	59	6
Weight (g)		472	1470	
Early Iron Age				
Sherds (no.)	455	11		
Weight (g)	4500	108		
Middle Iron Age/Late Iron Age				
Sherds (no.)		7		
Weight (g)		196		
Roman				
Sherds (no.)	758			
Weight (g)	16592			

Food Vessel, Collared Urn and Deverel-Rimbury *style* succession, for what is the alternative, but a 'type' attribution? This question highlights the underlying linkages within current British archaeological practices (at least with regard to prehistory) between material culture typologies and *'peoples-as-types'* (Fig. 6.8). When we write of 'Beaker' or 'Grooved Ware pits', is that just a substitute for 'peoples', in effect endorsing a 'Childean' or even 'Kossinnian' perspective of *archaeology as cultural history*? Any one-to-one inter-relationship between material culture types/change and ethnicities (i.e. languages) was first dismissed by Max Muller (see Stocking 1987, 59) and, since, has variously been 'put to bed' by Hodder and Jones (Hodder 1982a; Jones 1997, 15–26), to name but a few. However, in practice British archaeology, albeit inexplicitly, still seems to follow just such a model. In this volume, a certain dichotomy has been established between the Edgerley Road and Elliott sites: the former seeing a classic 'type-logic' succession, the latter a more free-flowing, semi-continuous 'edge-activity' or taskscape expression. Here the crucial point is, what does it mean if we directly associate fieldsystems with mid second-millennium BC Deverel-Rimbury pottery? Are we, actually, saying that only the 'Deverel-Rimbury *people*' were capable of organising fieldsystems (i.e. the 'Collared Urn people' could not), and is this attribution correct?

In the end, in trying to tackle this issue, a balance must be struck between *an archaeology of pattern vs possibility*. Based on the weight of evidence, to ascribe the origins of fieldsystems to the Late Neolithic seems most unlikely. In the case of Fengate, it seems far more reasonable to dismiss its one early 'rogue' burial-associated date than to fly in the face of all established pattern, including what has been understood to be the socio-economic basis of that period. How could a Grooved Ware 'woodland' economy be accommodated to a fieldsystem? (see Table 6.3 and Harman, in Pryor 1978, 177–88). Yates, in his 2007 volume, instead suggests that the origins of the Fengate fieldsystem might lie in the Beaker period (2007, 89). The problem with this 'compromise answer' is that Fengate's Beaker is very localized and it had a very low register in the area of its putative Newark Road-area core. Perhaps even more telling is the broader pattern. As considered in Chapter 4, relatively little Beaker has thus far been found along the wider western fen-edge (where there are extensive fieldsystems), in comparison to the eastern side, where there is little convincing evidence of pre-Iron Age fieldsystems.

Almost by default, we are left with a Collared Urn/Deverel-Rimbury 'overlap' and a dating horizon of c. 1900–1400 cal. BC for the layout of the region's

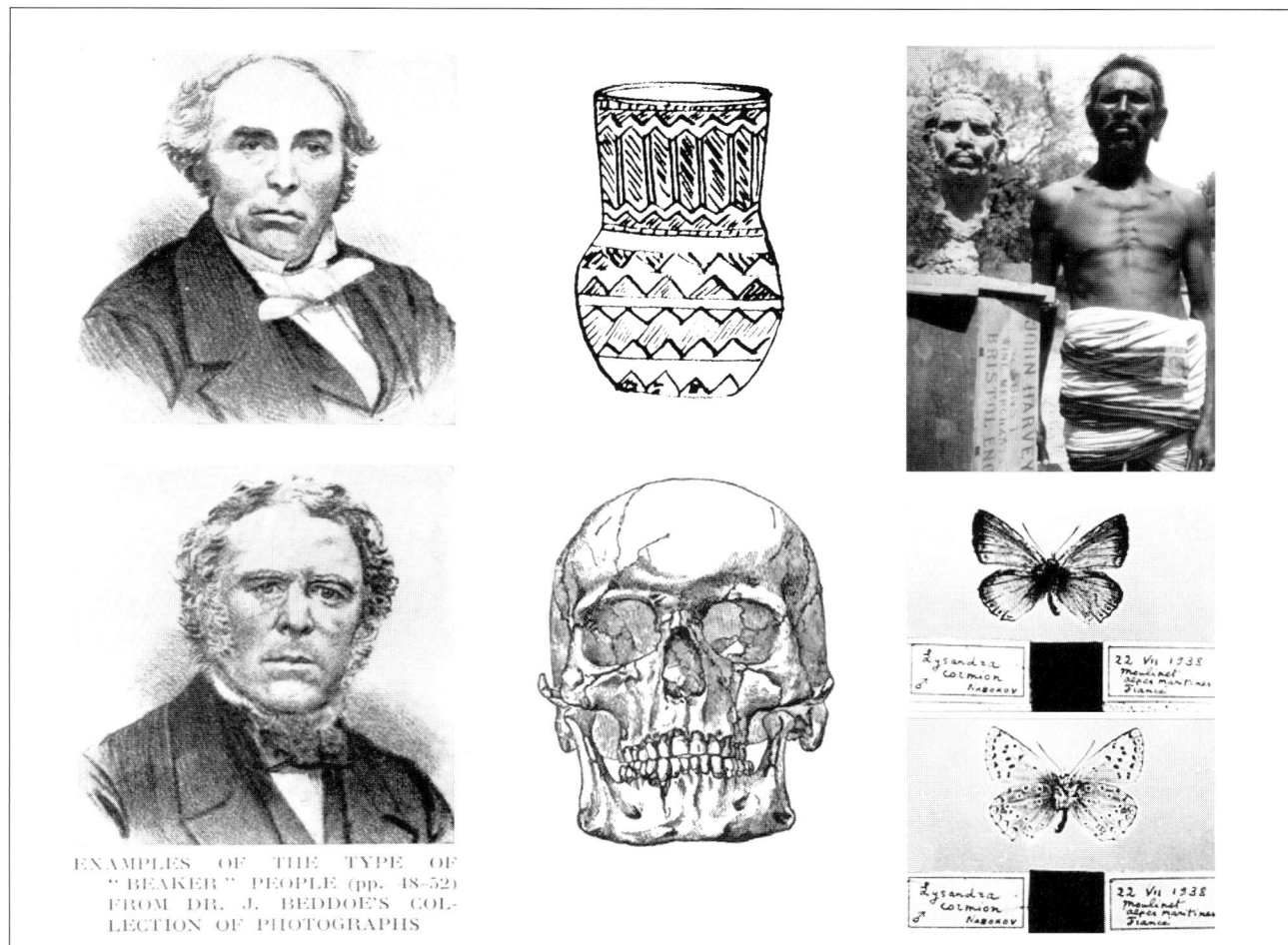

FIGURE 6.8. *Collecting and 'People-as-types' - Beaker Folk: left, Beddoe's portraits from Fleure's* The Races of England and Wales *of 1923; middle, Abbott's Beaker (top; see Fig. 2.5 and Chapter 2) and, below, Brachycephalic skull, from Cowlam, Yorks. in* A Guide to the Bronze Age Antiquities in the Department of British and Medieval Antiquities, British Museum *(1904, fig. 2); upper right, M. Milward's 1936 photograph of 'Jamani, a Pardhi Man' posing beside his portrait bust, the sculpture being one of a series of 100 Indian race, caste/tribal 'heads' done by her in the 1930s (see Elliott, in Herle* et al. *2009, 50–51, reproduced by permission of University of Cambridge Museum of Archaeology & Anthropology; see also Evans* et al. *2009 on 'people-as-types' generally); lower right, a page from one of Nabokov's butterfly albums — the renowned American/Russian-émigré novelist, Vladimir Nabokov (whose work features in this volume), was, aside from being a formidable chess-player, a noted lepidopterist. Working in the Museum of Comparative Zoology at Harvard, he was acknowledged as a butterfly collector and expert, especially for his studies of South American 'Blues' (with a number being named in reference to his literary creations; Johnson & Coates 1999; Boyd & Pyle 2000; see also Gould 2002).*

Bronze Age fieldsystem. Yes, there is an intentional ambiguity here, but that seems only appropriate given the open-ended nature of the evidence. The processes anticipating fieldsystems — clearance, cereal production and landscape-/hedge-division — were clearly under way in the earlier Bronze Age (if not before) and it seems intrinsically wrong to see an absolute distinction or cut-off with the Deverel-Rimbury 'phenomenon', as if there is a necessary linkage between that pottery style and fieldsystems.

(With regard to their 'world-views', both Collared Urn and Deverel-Rimbury were, after all, associated with cremation burial.)

Of course, the problem here may still be an underlying desire to envisage Bronze Age fieldsystems as *a* horizon. As discussed in Chapter 2, across the region their layout sees considerable variability and this might well have related to the local conditions of their immediate origins or, otherwise, to the reception of fieldsystems as an idea. Given this, it would be far more coherent to try, rather, to account for the possible South Lincolnshire/Peterborough grouping of long co-axial, regular drove-interval systems, of which Fengate seems a part (along with Newborough, Market Deeping and Langtoft; Fig. 6.4). Yet, with the others either still unpublished or unexcavated, we will restrict ourselves to Fengate alone (and even then only parts thereof) and admit that, in this specific instance, an alternative, earlier 'reading' of its origins is possible and that certain components of its system could well even date back to the first centuries of the second millennium BC. This would turn on three strands of evidence. First is the frequency of inhumation burials along (at least) the Padholme Road/Elliott Site drove (Ditches 1/2), this being a burial rite that would not easily accord with subsequent cremation practices. Second is the 2300/2200–1960/1880 cal. BC date of the 'hedgewood pit' at the Elliott Site (Beta-230848 & -230849; F.302). Combining these factors, it would not be inconceivable to then see parts of Fengate's landscape as having hedge-divided plots coming off of some of its 'core' droveways. This, in fact, would even raise the possibility that, rather than a later elaboration, some of the system's narrow double-ditch boundaries, such as at Storey's Bar Road or Cat's Water (Figs. 3.20 & 3.22), might actually have fossilized its original embanked-hedge layout.

The third, and final point are the *c.* 1600–1400 cal. BC dates achieved from pits cutting the fieldsystem at both the Elliott and Edgerley Sites, and if the assay from pit F.235 at the latter actually derived from the F.173 boundary and dates the early use of the fieldsystem itself. Not only would this further confirm the Early Bronze Age attribution of the fieldsystem, but could indicate that portions of it had stopped being maintained by the mid second millennium BC. Yet, set against this would be the fact that where system-related boundaries run parallel with the fen-edge, such as at the Elliott and Power Station Sites (and also Bradley Fen), they lie at *c.* 1 m OD. In other words, they delineate the level of 'the wet' during the Middle/later Bronze Age and this could, instead, suggest that other portions of the fieldsystem had been laid out in the second half of that millennium. There need not, however, be anything contradictory in this; it simply indicates a degree of *dynamic* and attests to no more than differential maintenance and system-expansion. As already noted, that ditches may have no longer been recut and/or mucked-out by the mid-millennium need not imply the actual disuse/abandonment of those portions of the system; throughout its overall span, hedge-lines may have been the main basis of boundary continuity (see below).

Obviously, there are still ambiguities concerning the dating of fieldsystems. Yet, in comparison to attributing their origins back to the first half of the third millennium BC, two to five centuries' variation one way or another is not a matter of major consequence (our current excavation and dating techniques may simply be insufficiently subtle to further resolve this question at this time). The crux here is that, compared to a later/Middle Neolithic origin, this resolution recasts the 'project' of fieldsystems. Instead of relating to a millennial-long, generic, farming continuum (as if somehow anticipating 'traditional' practices in the historical British countryside), this would rather frame them as a five to ten century-long *experiment in (hu)man/land relations*, and as something relatively short-term. Although we might want to see farming as almost a long-term constant — evoking all that is nostalgically compelling in rural 'lifeways' — its practice demands that certain socio-cultural infrastructures sustain themselves in terms of relations to *management* (i.e. organizational authority) and *land* (i.e. property/holding). To have people live/farm closely (cheek-by-jowl) requires a certain balance and the presence of regulatory structures and, in this regard, the evidence suggests that the 'world' of Bronze Age Fengate was not the same as our historical present: perhaps they were simply not ready/willing to be our farming ancestors.

Tenure, territory and political geography

Much attention has recently been paid to the social context and potential 'fluidity' of prehistoric land-tenure relations (e.g. Johnston 2001; Kitchen 2001). At Fengate such inferences could be drawn from the frequency of ditch recutting both along the Elliott Site's droveway and the main Newark Road compound (e.g. Pryor 1980a, fig. 32). While theoretically this could be seen as a redefinition or 'enactment' of the compound/plot bounds, essentially it just tells of accruing ditch maintenance (i.e. mucking out); instead, the key point at these sites, and in other fieldsystems of the period, is *the apparent stability of holdings*. True, these systems were obviously not laid out as a whole from the outset, and saw subsequent 'cantilever-'expansion of their axes, but, once established, little significant shift in their boundaries is apparent. Their underlying framework did not break down into some kind of 'organic mess' as might be expected if the plots/compounds were subject to long-term renegotiation and, generally, their structure appears fairly rigid. Equally, whilst inhumation burials occurred alongside Fengate's droves and, at a pinch, Newark Road's bent spearhead could be considered a placed offering (Pryor 1996, 317;

see also Johnston 1998, 319) — and in common with many fieldsystems, its Storey's Bar Road plots seemed laid out to establish an ancestral linkage with that site's ring-ditch/barrow — on the whole, the system's boundaries saw little ritual deposition. Indeed, from this it could be understood that the fieldsystems were not, in fact, a 'problematized arena of social action', but provided a framework that, once in place, could be taken for granted. Whether this is held to directly mirror the period's social structure and to be reflective of its group-cohesion/-conformity, it essentially relates to one's present-day political leanings.

This picture of stability may not have been true of the area's beyond-fieldsystem low ground. With the Fengate, Stanground and Northey/Whittlesey's 'fieldsystem communities' all probably accessing the common resources of Flag Fen's embayment, it could easily have been a more dynamic 'social arena', especially as water levels rose during the later part of the second millennium BC and resource-competition may have become a greater factor (see e.g. Ostrom 1990 and Fleming 1998a concerning 'common dynamics'). The deposition of metalwork along the embayment's boundaries — such as the Power Station post-alignment and Bradley Fen's 'edge'-ditch — would certainly have been votive, perhaps to appease watery deities and/or keep the waters at bay. Yet, equally, they may have pronounced one group's claim to a suite of resources as opposed to another's. In short, it was probably in the intervening low ground, with its variety of common resources — variously seasonal pasture, woodlot and wetland produce — where broader inter-communal group-rights were exercised/negotiated and roles 'performed' (the location of the Must Farm barrow cemetery upon a low-lying terrace within this embayment proper could also be considered as an earlier expression of 'low-ground centrality/collectivity'; see below).

There can be no denying the extraordinary character of the Flag Fen platform, and this is only enhanced by the recent discovery of the timber structure at Must Farm. Along with the ritual deposition of metalwork, all this can only be considered 'special'. Admittedly, there are facets of Barleycroft/Over's Bronze Age that come close to rivalling it; this is not surprising as their landscape situations are broadly comparable: places where the waters of great rivers 'divided' as they entered the Fenland (cf. Figs. 2.12, 2.18 & 6.9). Nevertheless, the Flag Fen basin seems to have been markedly different, to the point that it could, in fact, even be thought of as some manner of place-specific, *later prehistoric polity*. Like the Isle of Ely's northern wetland 'Cove' (i.e. *Cove*-ney) or its land-locked Grunty Fen (Evans 2002; 2003), in the case

of the Flag Fen basin this may well ultimately relate to the intensively utilized Bronze Age landscapes that surrounded it and its central focus as a 'pocketed' marshland — *a singular place*, and one that might also have defined a political geography.

For our purposes here, a pressing issue is whether there is anything in Fengate's archaeology that 'announces' this, and if Flag Fen (*et al.*) was actually a direct expression of the cultural landscape of its immediate fen-edge hinterland. Yes, there are facets of its fieldsystem that seem distinct; specifically, the scale/regularity of its droves and its double-circuit compounds (see below). Yet no great density of contemporary settlement has been found within Fengate's fieldsystem-axes and furthermore, it is now known that comparable fieldsystems of the period extend across much of the region's low gravel terraces, at least within the area of the western Fens. The scale of Fengate's main droves and the settlement evidence from its western, Tower Works area (and north into Abbott's western quarry zone) could be read as indicating that there was a substantial fen-edge hinterland population. If so, it could have been their amassed stock that was seasonally taken down Fengate's droves and out onto its marsh-flanking watermeadow pastures. Though an attractive story, such a scenario seems, if not too fanciful, then perhaps too immediately convenient to convincingly explain the Flag Fen 'phenomenon'.

Quite unexpectedly, some answers might lie in negative evidence; that being the almost complete absence of formal cremation cemeteries (none were encountered during the course of Pryor's Fengate campaigns, or in any fieldwork there since). This is in direct contrast, for example, to the results from both Tanholt Farm, Eye and Barleycroft where, respectively, 12- and 14-interment, 'flat' cremation cemeteries have been excavated. At Barleycroft/Over and Colne Fen, Earith three such cemeteries have been dug associated with ring-ditches (Evans & Knight 2000; Evans *et al.* forthcoming). With their sequences initiated by an inhumation burial, the latter have between 22–35 secondary cremation burials. Whilst their 'small monument' form/elaboration displays considerable variation, there is certainly a general 'type' consistency to these monuments and their accompanying cemeteries (though not all the Lower Ouse environs ring-ditches were mortuary-related). Crucial here is the fact that neither of Fengate's two definite ring-ditches, nor its putative Cat's Water henge, attracted such cemeteries, the Storey's Bar Road monument only having one Collared Urn cremation (see Chapter 4, Inset). All this begs the question of just where Fengate's Middle/later Bronze Age dead were

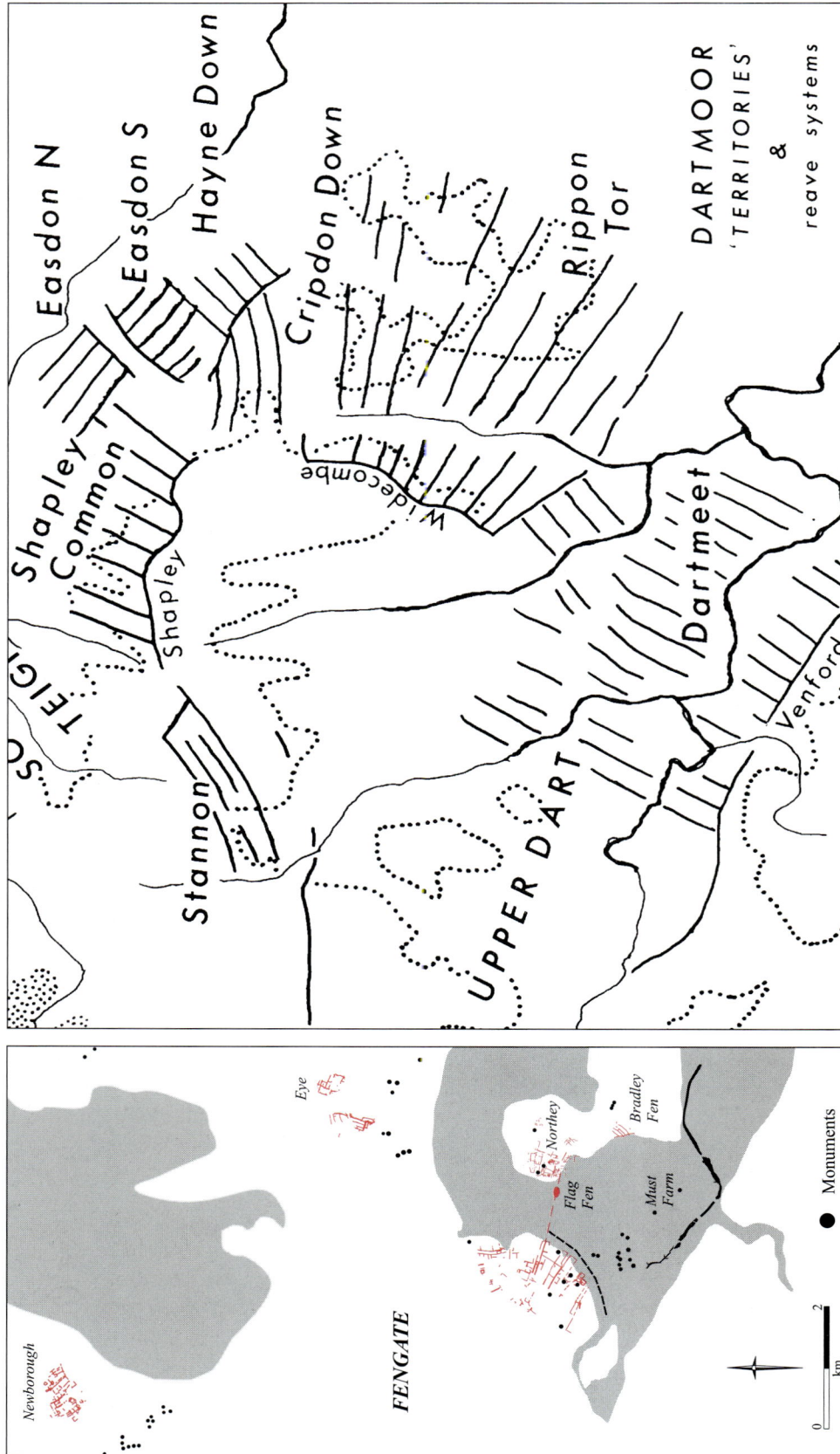

FIGURE 6.9. *The Greater Fengate/Flag Fen Basin environs (left), and extending north to include and the Tanholt Farm (Eye) Peterborough Prison and Newborough fieldsystems and barrow cemeteries (regional base-map after Hall & Coles 1994, fig. 48; Healy & Harding 2007 on wider Nene Valley barrow distributions); right, by way of same-scale areal/'territory' comparison, the core-zone of Fleming's Dartmoor Reaves systems (after 1988b, fig. 30). Note that the full plotting of the latter (extending over c. 700 sq.km), if overlain onto the fen-edge fieldsystem distribution map (Fig. 2.12), would easily encompass both the area of Fengate/Flag Fen (et al.) and the South Lincolnshire systems. Reproduced by permission of Ordnance Survey on behalf of HMSO. © Crown copyright 2009. All rights reserved. Ordnance Survey Licence number 100048686.*

interred. Though it is conceivable that, similar to what has elsewhere been postulated for Iron Age practices, they were deposited in the fen marshes from the Flag Fen platform, currently this argument really cannot be evaluated.

The evidence of Abbott's extraordinary ring-ditch complex, apparently located along the eastern side of his Fengate quarries (near the later Padholme Road Site), is surely relevant in this context. Fully considered in a separate paper (Evans & Appleby 2008) and outlined in Chapter 2 above, whether it is the 80 or 130 cremation figure that is accepted, the scale of this monument's cemetery was clearly remarkable and it could suggest a degree of centralized interment practice. If so, this may well reflect on the character of the Flag Fen platform and the obvious 'authority' that must have co-ordinated its construction and use, and as such, be directly pertinent to the 'polity model'. If, as has been suggested, the Lower Ouse's ring-ditch cemeteries were lineage-based (Evans & Knight 2000), then the much greater scale of Abbott's monument could conceivably attest to multiple-lineage burial rites and, arguably, by the maths, reflects the interaction/amalgamation of two to four lineages. What, after all, lies at the heart of polity formation, if not the breaking (or at least subverting) of the authority of kinship-lineage rights for larger group ends?

The issue of the degree and character of 'social authority' within these Bronze Age landscapes is by no means straightforward, and is much debated. For example, there is the character of the fieldsystems, which effectively seem to 'knit' together their households. Further, there are the houses themselves which generally suggest little differentiation; based on the excavated evidence alone, it would usually be well-nigh impossible to discern the status of one over another. The same would also be true of the period's cremation-burial rite. Though only approximately a third were accorded urn-interment (without accompanying grave goods), the very nature of cremation denies or masks social distinction. It would not, therefore, be unreasonable to see these as relatively egalitarian communities and, after Fleming (e.g. 1985), as exercising co-operative modes of labour organization and decision-making.

In contrast, there is the evidence of the formal planning, and presumably co-ordinated execution, of the fieldsystems themselves. Equally, there are some indications of potentially distinguished households. As outlined above, Newark Road's Compound C could mark such an instance, as might also the longhouse compound at Barleycroft Farm, close to which metalworking moulds were recovered (Evans & Knight 2000); the recently excavated longhouse as-sociated with the Tanholt Farm fieldsystem might also prove comparable. Yet, in a Fengate/Flag Fen context, what most seriously challenges socio-egalitarianism — aside from the co-ordinating authority that seems evident in the very construction of the latter's platform and its enormous draw of timber — is the quality of the metalwork associated with the Power Station alignment (Coombs 2001). With a number of pieces imported and, thereby, raising questions of a prestige goods economy and access to long-distance trade networks promoting local elites (a model much in favour during the 1970s; e.g. Friedmand & Rowlands 1977; Yates 2007, 122–8), this metalwork — and particularly the frequency of weaponry — does not rest easily with the idea of co-operative/egalitarian 'fieldsystem communities'.

The problem of distinguishing the beginning and ends of separate fieldsystems along the region's fen-edges obviously has implications for the definition of any prehistoric 'territory'. Unlike more upland locales, the fen-edge lacks sufficient geographic relief to suggest 'natural' units (e.g. valley systems; see Fleming 1998b and Kitchen 2001 for further discussion). Pryor himself speculated that Newark Road's Ditch 8/9 drove might divide territories on either side (1980a, 23). While certainly marking a major 'seam', this seems to have little justification (though this depends on what is implied by 'territory'; Pryor probably meant no more than the 'fieldsystem-blocks' used here). Although in Fengate's original '70s plan, double-ditch compounds only really occurred north of that drove (and another is now known even further north at the Broadlands Site), the recognition of the square, double-ditched 'block' of compounds at the Depot Site now undermines this pattern. In addition, whilst a further 'landscape-/fieldsystem-seam' may have occurred between that sub-site and Storey's Bar Road (which could relate to the frequency of monuments at their divide; see Chapter 4, Inset), it is actually the occurrence of these square double-ditch compounds across the larger Fengate system that seems to be the unifying trait. A sounder basis of 'blocking' is the north–south orientation of the main droves in the Edgerley/Broadlands sector to the north and this, in fact, might be sufficient to distinguish this as a separate fieldsystem. (The slight northwestward skewing of the Broadlands 'square' could even suggest a quasi-radial arrangement which, westward, might turn further on this axis to match that of the Vicarage Farm ditches.)

Central to any such arguments is the level at which community is thought to 'sit' or be resolved (see e.g. Fleming 1985; Evans & Hodder 2006b). Surely it would have entailed something more than just the daily face-to-face kin-group of immediately adjacent settlement clusters, such as Newark Road's Compound A or the Cat's Water/Elliott Sites' roundhouse pairing? Alternatively, perhaps involving upwards of 20–50 individuals (such as can be estimated for Fengate's 'core'), were 'fieldsystem-blocks' communities, and, if so, were they lineage-based? By any measure, these could not have amounted to a (closed) 'successful' breeding population, but nor would they have constituted any kind of daily 'world', as the entire Depot Site-to-Edgerley length of the Fengate system only extended over *c.* 1.75 km, a distance that could have been traversed in less than thirty minutes. All this indicates that, whilst they represented a distinct sphere of social interaction (no doubt cross-cut by ties of kinship), there must have been a level of community — and even regular gatherings — beyond immediate fieldsystem bounds (see Pryor 1996; Evans & Knight 2001 and Evans & Hodder 2006b for further discussion). If postulating a larger social framework, the known 'fieldsystem communities' of Fengate west to Whittlesey (Bradley Fen, King's Dyke and Northey) and south to Stanground, would have extended over an area of some 25 sq.km and involved, perhaps, as many as 500–1000 people. While this seems a reasonable figure, and is one that could readily supply the labour/surplus necessary to 'generate' Flag Fen, both the area and population of this 'inter-fieldsystem territory' might, of course, have been still greater (by as much as a factor of two to four).

Issues of community 'scaling' are well-expressed in this volume's penultimate figure (6.9). There, the distribution of known fieldsystems and main barrow cemeteries are shown, from the Flag Fen basin north to Borough Fen, and in direct comparison of Fleming's 'core' Dartmoor reave-systems and 'territories' (1988b, fig. 30). This, perhaps more than anything else, underlines that no matter how seemingly vast our open-area excavations may seem, they do not in themselves encompass landscapes; just as the archaeology of Fengate can no longer be approached in any kind of isolation, sites will always have outward connections and we must be wary of over-localizing study. This mapping, furthermore, offers quite a new perspective on the archaeology of the Flag Fen basin itself. Including both our 'restoration' of Abbott's monuments to Fengate proper and the greater Must Farm barrow cemetery recently discovered by Mark Knight and his team, it tells of just what a concentration of monuments occurred within its environs. Indeed, on seeing the broader Bronze Age landscape of the mid-western fen-edge in this manner, what strikes one is the correspondence of major barrow cemeteries and fieldsystems, and this would equally be true, for

example, of Barleycroft/Over. Reflecting, again, on the vexed issue of whether fieldsystems amount to *a* Middle Bronze Age/Deverel-Rimbury 'horizon', this leaves little room for doubt of their *deeper*, early Bronze Age 'interrelations' and, arguably, origins.

The fieldsystem triumvirate — a dialogue
(*with* FRANCIS PRYOR, ANDREW FLEMING & RICHARD BRADLEY)

The following records a series of conversations, held in the autumn of 2007, with 'leading players' concerning their take on the great fieldsystem projects of the 1970s and relevant developments since. It had been hoped that this could have been more a group-conversation and less one-on-one interviews, but, in the end, it proved impossible to get them all in the same room for long enough. Despite this, we still managed to get the voice of, to paraphrase Fleming (see below), the 'Bronze Age fieldsystem triumvirate'.

It was only when transcribing the tapes that the extent to which Mucking featured became apparent. A logical outcome of the CAU commencing its post-excavation work on this site at this time, nevertheless, it has a bit of a feeling that its Director, Margaret Jones (who died in 2001), was an unspoken participant. Others also loom large in these discussions (particularly Christopher Taylor), and various books/texts also lurk in the background: aside from Evans' *Borderlands* volume (with its Fox 1923 agenda; 2008), Bradley had recently published his *The Prehistory of Britain and Ireland* (2007); Pryor was then in the final throes of his 'Hoskins Revisited' Landscape volume for Penguin (Pryor forthcoming b) and Fleming had completed his revised edition of *The Dartmoor Reaves* (2007), having published his review article, 'Post-processual landscape archaeology: a critique' in *Cambridge Archaeological Journal* the year before (2006).

Chris Evans (CE): Francis, in terms of background, when you look back on that time, what of the great scale of Fengate and its earth-moving operations? Where did the immediate inspiration for that come from? Was it Mucking? Of course, Mucking didn't actually do its own machine-stripping.

Francis Pryor (FP): It was partly Mucking, but it was also Peter Grimes who was the chairman of the Nene Valley Research Committee when I started at Fengate. I had read his Defence Ministry excavations before I did the first season of work at Fengate, and his work on the bomber airfields at Heathrow [Grimes 1961], which inspired me. Also, some of the Medievalists' work, because the previous summer (the first Fengate season was 1971) I'd been a supervisor at Peter Wade-Martin's North Elmham, and in order to get a little background reading on that — because I couldn't go into it completely ignorant! — I read some of the work that the Medievalists were doing on open-area excavation at Wharram Percy, which is always said to be an open-area dig, but by the standards of Fengate, was a series of trial trenches. But the Medievalists were doing quite a lot of open-area work, so, actually, it was as much them as Mucking that inspired me.

CE: Based on the '69 *New Town* volume, when you began Fengate what did you think you would get? Were you actually after a prehistoric landscape or, based on that volume's gazetteer, did you think it would largely be Roman? Also, how much did the Wyman Abbott background feature in any of this?

FP: I have to admit that the RCHM volume was something of an add-on for me. I was originally motivated to work at Fengate by the Abbott finds in Peterborough Museum and the Institute of Archaeology. I also talked at some length to Chris Taylor (who wrote the archaeological portions of the RCHM report). I wanted the dig somehow to tie the finds into a coherent story, but to be quite honest I wasn't too certain how I'd achieve it. The Canadians had talked about a two- to three-year project, but I soon realised we'd need longer than that. Like everyone else I thought the RCHM droveways were Romano-British, but in fairness to myself I dropped that idea a few weeks into the first season.

Did I think in terms of landscapes? I'd read Hoskins at least twice by then, but wasn't at all clear how I'd do what he had done simply with an excavation. That came later after talking in '74 with David Clarke, who was the first leading academic (apart from Dave Coombs) to take an active interest in our work. He pointed me in the direction of the Medievalists, such as Father Raftis (of *The Estates of Ramsey Abbey* fame). Conveniently, Raftis was working in the Pontifical Institute for Medieval Studies, in Toronto, where I had many long discussions, along with our bones specialist Kathy Biddick. It was only then that I realised I had the data to be able to think in such broad terms.

It wasn't really until '74 when we did the first really big open-areas that the potential of what we were doing began to hit home. The trouble is it's hard not to see things with the vantage of hindsight — which always makes one seem brighter and more intelligent than was actually the case! Like so much else in life, I suspect that make-do-and-mend, combined with 'muddle through' was actually what motivated much of what we did. That, and a first-rate team, which argued incessantly and constructively.

CE: I always liked the idea that the Royal Ontario Museum's involvement seemed to be a kind of reverse colonialism — how Canada could possibly be coerced into paying for Fengate? How in the world did that come about?

FP: Well, the answer to that is quite simple. I didn't have to persuade them. The Chief Archaeologist there, Doug Tushingham, who was a wonderful man, always wanted to have a Museum dig in England. They had tried to persuade their Roman pot person, Alison Harle-Easton, to do a dig there, but she wasn't a digger at all — she was very much a pot person. Doug was rather disappointed that Alison hadn't come up with a project, so he said to me, 'Go over there, I'll give you $1500' — or was it pounds? — 'and go to this dig and you can bribe them with this money to make you a supervisor.' So I went. I arranged to go to North Elmham. Peter was initially a little dubious, but when I crossed his palm with silver, he welcomed me with open arms. Of course, North Elmham was an extremely well-organised, open-area excavation and I learnt a lot.

CE: And then, thereafter, given its Canadian funding, the pound collapsed didn't it?

FP: Yes, all of that helped. After the Yom Kippur War, when the price of petrol suddenly sky-rocketed, I had managed to keep my money in dollars, rather than pounds. It increased hugely in a few weeks, and I eventually ended up buying, at the end of 1974, a month's worth of plant hire-time from the profit I'd made, and that's why

we stripped the Cat's Water ahead of time. So, if you look at the air photos taken early on, you'll see that some of the areas had gone down to the correct level, but the upper areas of the alluvium had been taken off with a box-scraper.

CE: Changing tack a bit, thinking about the formal Processualist/New Archaeological approach that underpins the second report, where did that come from? Was that your Cambridge background or was that from your time in Canada and exposure to American colleagues?

FP: Exposure to American colleagues, very much so. I'd got very little New Archaeology when I was an undergraduate — I never turned up at lectures!

CE: Can I ask the same thing about your recording techniques, because in '*Fengate Four*' you mention that you changed the recording technique after Storey's Bar Road. In the one you used there the feature numbers changed by area-squares, and I remember using something very similar to it with Keele in West Asia — was that also a New World import?

FP: No, that was partly my own invention. I'd got very interested in computers which, in those days, were entirely main-frame, and had gone on a course in London. I'd learnt Fortran and punch-carding, because I realised that if we were to have many postholes, pits and flints, we would have to computerise it. The first cards which I had printed — and which are published in an appendix in that report — was done with a view to computerizing things.

CE: In terms of the Mucking archive and its correspondence archive, I was wondering if you could talk a little about that. Margaret Jones took quite a lot of umbrage with you and your 'redundant excavation' announcements. That's the line in your *Rescue News* pronouncement about over-digging: 'thinking more, digging less' [1980b]. Of course, that would have been an antithesis to the Mucking approach — how much was Maxey dug as a reaction to Fengate? Did you think that you had over-dug Fengate?

FP: In retrospect, no. I think I did at the time. Maxey rather disappointed me. I was hoping to find more by way of prehistoric archaeology, and the fact that the henge-ditch held nothing, and the henge itself was an odd-looking thing — it was, frankly, a disappointment, which is why I was so very keen to get into Etton.

CE: I've always liked Maxey; it seems like an odd experiment in a formal methodology. It's also interesting for the time it happened, as it coincided with the rise of post-processualism and its apparent lack of methodology. It also has parallels with Haddenham, and, on the whole, during the 1980s there was quite a lot of interest in formal sampling procedures, but the approach taken to the sites wasn't very standardised. There suddenly seemed to be a bit more freedom for how sites were dug — what's your take on it?

FP: Yes, I think that's true. To their credit, English Heritage encouraged me and, thank heavens, in those days you could experiment. You couldn't do that now. Yes, ploughing-over the site before we dug it. I'll never forget bringing the tractor to plough it, because the hydraulics packed-up halfway down the Whittlesey Road, and I was following behind and one of our supervisors was driving the thing, when suddenly there were sparks coming out as the plough hit the road. The old boy driving the thing was half-deaf, so it was quite exciting.

CE: The thing about recent excavations is that they're a lot more professional, but a lot more standardised. Now, something that interests me, with so many Bronze Age fieldsystem reports appearing, is the

WILL IT ALL COME OUT IN THE WASH?
REFLECTIONS AT THE END OF EIGHT YEARS' DIGGING

FIGURE 6.10. *Scrapbook Sources (III) - There is a certain irony that in writing a book where matters of dating loom so large, it is only when reviewing the project's photos that the passage of time really strikes you and conveys a suitable sense of event (and 'humanity') to the entire thing: top, Flag Fen, 2004, with Francis (left, then-CBA president), William 'Bill' Moss (Chief Archaeologist, City of Québec and then-president of the Society for Historical Archaeology) and Charly French (right, Lecturer, Dept. of Archaeology, Cambridge); middle, the 'disreputable' Fengate '75 photo (cf. Fig. 1.5) with a formidable cast: a youthful Francis (1), Charly (2), Dave Cranstone (3; now-Honorary Research Fellow, University of Exeter), Samuel Sidibé (4; now-Director of the National Museum of Mali), Kathy Biddick (5; now-Professor, Dept. of History, Temple University, Philadelphia, USA), Bill Moss (6) and Tony Wilkinson (7; now-Professor of Archaeology, Durham) and, and among the other legendary characters are Boyd Dixon (8) and the late Dermot Bond (9; Fengate, Site Supervisor and Director, North Ring, Mucking excavations); bottom, Fengate 'late phase' - left, Maisie Taylor & Francis, Bob Bourne & Dave Crowther, with a youthful Evans (right) astride the Fourth Drove bank, 1978 (photographs: C. French, F. Pryor, M. Taylor and A. Nother).*

degree to which your livestock-related interpretations are accepted at face-value. What concerns me, in the light of the Mucking, is how on recent sites the excavation-samples are just too low (as opposed to the intense Fengate- or the Mucking-sample) to actually achieve enough data that you can develop a new interpretation for a fieldsystem or challenge an existing one — the numbers are just ridiculously low: 2000 or 3000 animal bones is a big assemblage nowadays, but it's a very small assemblage-size.

FP: What worries me about this, is that it is going to be very difficult for people to challenge some of my assertions, and I want them to. I didn't put forward those ideas to be cast in tablets of stone. I'd love it if somebody turned them upside down and said that I'd got it wrong. But at least I took it a stage further on and there is a tendency to look at something and say that morphologically, on the surface, this looks like it's a drafting-race and, therefore, it's a drafting race. But you've got to prove it. A drafting-race can look very much like a hedge, but if you don't do the phosphates down the middle, you won't know.

Thereafter, having Andrew Fleming (AF) in town for a lecture, the opportunity was taken to specifically talk about his Dartmoor reaves fieldwork, which, of course, was the other great fieldsystem project of the day.

CE: Andrew, when you were first doing the work on Dartmoor, how allied did you feel to the big Bronze Age excavations like Mucking or Fengate, or did you see what you were doing as something really quite different?

AF: I think I probably saw it as fairly different. It depends, really, I was always following Francis' work. We were at the same conferences, along with Richard Bradley, and there was this kind of triumvirate, where I talked about Dartmoor, Francis talked about what was happening at Fengate and Richard would give the overview, and a lot of my thinking was triangulated around those two. Plus the fact that people started getting interested in so-called organized landscapes and it was crystallized at a conference: the quite famous one at Bristol in 1976 [Bowen & Fowler 1978]; an awful lot of things came together briefly at that point and in the BAR volume that came out of it. I wasn't that conscious of Mucking really.

CE: In terms of looking back and the sense of pattern that hindsight can give, what you were doing then, undertaking a sort of earthwork survey research? Did you have any conscious link to someone like Hoskins or, perhaps more appropriately, Chris Taylor, and that it was working in a different manner from the big excavation projects of the day? Was it that you were doing something quite consciously different in terms of landscapes or did that earthwork-survey emphasis come later?

AF: I think I felt I was in the tradition of O.G.S. Crawford and Colin Bowen, really, and in that sense what I was doing didn't feel particularly original. In fact, it definitely wasn't. One of the most important things that happened to me — well, two important things that happened to me, really, in my youth — one was going on an undergraduate field-course to Cranborne Chase and we had a couple of hours with Chris Taylor, who was then, I think, just working on the Dorset Royal Commission volumes. Chris took us out and he talked to us a bit about his recent idea that strip-lynchets were not Saxon, but, in fact, late medieval, and then he talked us through various things. I was absolutely fascinated by it. I sensed that most of my undergraduate contemporaries were not in the least taken by it; on the contrary, he seemed to be boring them. So that was a big influence on me; the whole idea of landscape archaeology was

crystallized for me with Chris Taylor's explanation that you could use your eyes on the surface of the land and make discoveries. Then I think the second big thing was Colin Bowen, who invited me over for a weekend (I was working on Dartmoor at the time). He took me out for, I think, a day and a half on Cranborne Chase, showing me the type of things he was publishing at that period. I was amazed, really; I spent the entire first morning pretending I could see what he was showing me, and it was only later on during the first day, or on the second, that I began to realise that these were not just ordinary humps and bumps. They were very faint, but they were there. So, in a way, I learnt my craft from those two — well, I certainly got my inspiration from them — and I've always felt that I was firmly in the tradition of O.G.S. Crawford, so I didn't feel I was doing anything new in that sense.

CE: On that note, of the question that there now seems to be a Bronze Age coaxial 'horizon' (they seem to be everywhere in southern England) and on the occasion of the Yates' book [2007], how do you see this and to what degree do you consider it as a mass horizon? Do you think there are underlying structural principles shared between somewhere like Fengate and Dartmoor, or do you see the reaves as being removed from that lowland context?

AF: I think that there are two parts to my answer to this question. When I first started talking about Dartmoor, people would say to me, 'Well, this is all on marginal land, isn't it?' with the implication that 'this is some interesting thing you're doing on Dartmoor, but it's not relevant to the Thames Valley or Wessex, so please don't ask me to think too much about its implications'. I went away from that, and started looking for coaxial fieldsystems wherever I could, and insisted that Francis' Fengate stuff was relevant and, also, Tom Williamson's, and Seamas Caulfield's. And I can't help thinking that at the time people must have thought, 'He's doing the usual thing that archaeologists do: extrapolating his own discoveries, exaggerating their importance', and so on and so forth. They could well be excused for thinking that in those days, but now we've got coaxial fieldsystems all over southern and eastern England, not to mention other places. So in a way I was curiously prescient.

The second part of the question, of course, is what coaxiality means, now it's no longer a question of Andrew Fleming appealing to people to put it on the agenda. It is on the agenda now, in various ways. Obviously one of the things that impacted on me was a kind of collective disapproval, really, among post-processualists, because I think they quite approved of the Dartmoor Reaves to start off with, because they said, 'You know, this man is telling it with the authorial voice; he's not hiding from us the agency of the archaeologist'. So they quite approved of it in that sense. But what they didn't like was what they saw as my functionalist/materialist interpretations. They immediately wanted meaning. I remember Ian Hodder was in one of my earlier audiences, and he was quite impatient with my rather functionalist-managerial interpretation; he immediately wanted to know about the meaning of them.

CE: It's quite an interesting idea, isn't it; the notion that fieldsystems have *a* meaning, it almost seems to disavow the idea of landscape fabric.

AF: Yes, perhaps, but I think the rather pointed silence of the post-processualists about Dartmoor does relate to that perception that I've failed to tackle questions of meaning. And so I've come back to it in recent times, partly because I agree with them that we do need to think about meaning, and I've tried to do that in the re-issuing of the Dartmoor Reaves book [2007]. I'm not sure whether I've been very successful, but I have addressed the issue. I draw quite a lot of my inspiration, in a way, partly from Francis Pryor and his notion of a kind of directionality in the landscape, with his Fengate ideas, if you like, and I'm also trying to react to John Barrett's ideas in his book *Fragments from Antiquity* [1994].

You know, the way he talks about fieldsystems as representing a different mind-set, the move from very mobile perceptions of the landscape to people living in fixed domains. Barrett just proposes this change of mind-set and he doesn't explain how it came about. So I've been trying to think about whether you can have transitional phases between a totally fluid, mobile, open landscape and the idea of a very boxed-in landscape.

CE: We're finding much the same, in that the data seems to suggest that.

AF: I think there must be an intermediate phase, where there is directionality in the landscape, and in Dartmoor I can use the stone rows to address that, which, of course, is lucky.

CE: The evidence, though, seems to be that the droves are, perhaps, earlier and hedging also. On that score, it seems to me that there's an interesting kind of dichotomy now. On the one hand, there's a renewed interest in upland earthwork research, of the kind done by Johnston [e.g. 2001] and Kitchen [e.g. 2001]. Of course, it has the advantage that you get to the three-dimensional element in the archaeology. But, on the other hand, there also seem to be the kind of issues we face in the fens and lowlands — primarily questions of territory — and that you can never know their totality because there's no geographic determinants suggesting it, whereas with upland work you have a more dominant geography. But then there also now seems to be problems relating to definition, at least for the post-processualism school, because as soon as you start talking of a stronger sense of system or of territory — in terms of an 'archaeology of paths and clearances' and various Ingold-inspired approaches — they're not themes that are in the greatest favour at the moment.

AF: Absolutely. I don't see that you have to choose, actually. I think those alternatives are too stark. As often with post-processualism, they're promoting half-truths to total truths in my opinion.

CE: But do you think that now, we're seeing a new generation of people interested in upland earthworks survey; but, of course, the one thing about it is that because of the nature of the work and the environment (and also resourcing), it always seems to have very little excavation involved with it — keyhole excavation — whereas now we're seeing vast-scale excavations in the lowlands. How do you see the inter-relationship between the two? Do you think it's one of dovetailing and knitting together, or are they very much split in their fields?

AF: I think there's a complementarity about it, in a way. When I was thinking about David Yates's work on the grey literature, on one level it's very interesting, because suddenly you have all these bits of fieldsystems all over the place on another level, you're very excited because you think, 'there's all this wonderful developer-funding and these people can really open up big areas and do things I couldn't do on Dartmoor'. But there is a problem of scale, because even if you take these big areas that have been opened up in, say, Hampshire or Devon, in terms of one of my big Dartmoor systems, we're still dealing with little windows. In my terms, it's a big excavation, but in terms of the scale of the fieldsystem it's still a keyhole. And in a sense, the advantage of Dartmoor, of course — or the good bits of Dartmoor — is that you can look at a large area and say, 'I will put my excavation there because I do have some advance information about the fieldsystem'.

CE: That's right. A lot of times we're spending enormous amounts of money just chasing ditches, while you get that off the surface

AF: Down here, you're often not sure where you are in the fieldsys-

tem, I imagine, whereas on Dartmoor you've got quite a lot of guidance. Although I wouldn't like to exaggerate, because I think the one lesson of my work is that it's lovely to have the three-dimensional picture, but there's an awful lot under the surface; a huge open area of excavation on Dartmoor would, I think, change perceptions quite a lot, because of all the stakehole features or the wooden buildings and all the things that my excavations have hinted at.

CE: So you would like to do that, if you could?

AF: Not necessarily, no. I'm not a good enough excavator anyway, but I'd like to see it happen.

CE: Finally, it seems to me that in your work there's always been a strong interest in how local past communities operated and their structures of decision-making. It's always underpinned your work from Dartmoor's community working-groups to the St Kilda's parliament, and it's as if your work has an almost ethnographic quality and that there's a sense of desire to write the ethnography of the site. Where does that come from: is it an interest in social anthropology or does it come out of an historic awareness of Medieval working patterns?

AF: I'm not altogether sure, to be honest. I have been interested in it for a long time. I read Tom Steel's book on St Kilda and was interested in it from the point of view of the small rural community long before I got to go to St Kilda; and I've been reading Irish ethnography, things on the Aran Islands and the Blasket Islands, and so on. So I've had the interest for a very long time — I guess, probably since the early 70s. I'm not quite sure where it comes from. I suspect that for me it's probably a convergence. I was brought up in the country and I feel instinctively that I'm a countryman; I'm interested in rural things. I'm also a socialist in a sense, and I like the idea of the rural community: the ideal of the rural community as a kind of organic thing. I know that in many ways this is politically naïve, even sentimental, but at the same time I'm interested in it and I also feel that we need to talk about it because the dominant paradigm in rural studies now is that of private enterprise, the idea of the farmer as the rugged individualist and all of that, which I think fails to recognize past realities. I don't want to sentimentalise past communities, but I do think that we should recognise their strengths and interests, and also probably their dynamic in every epoch until quite recently. So it's partly, you could say, a romantic interest in the rural community; I think it goes back to that emotionally, but I'm intellectually very interested as well.

Finally, with Richard Bradley (RB); starting with a few set questions, the themes quickly became more wide-ranging.

CE: Richard, having done the new book [2007], what would your take now be given the frequency of Bronze Age fieldsystems and what we now know of their metalwork — any new insights on that?

RB: Well, I think the best idea is probably David Yates's [2007]. The major concentrations of fieldsystems correlate, to some extent, with ringworks — he's got a greatly expanded body of them — and also with concentrations of metalwork. The weakness of this is that coaxial fields as a whole have such a finite distribution within the Island of Britain, but the distribution of metalwork extends further. So it's only a partial overlap, really, within the south and eastern part of England.

CE: When I now look at the distributions, not just of fieldsystems, but also the frequency of settlements, it suddenly seems to make sense of the Bronze Age metalwork distributions. I find it quite interesting that if you think back and read Fox [… *Cambridge Region*, 1923], for example, they knew of a couple of Bronze Age settlements, and you have a feeling that they certainly knew there were more, but you don't have a sense that they were expecting that many more — perhaps four or five — in the region. How do they explain that kind of incredible frequency of wealth of metalwork against so few sites?

RB: I think for a long time there were two things. There was a bit of an argument — not very strongly put — for votive deposition and votive deposition in faraway places. But there was also the whole functional approach to hoards — dryland hoards primarily — as meaning that smiths worked out in the wilderness, using locally available fuels. And, of course, we are now finding hoards right next to settlements. So there were two arguments, if you like, which would both favour the metalwork being displaced from the domestic landscape. Of course, there was also the practical point: when we had the settlements, as we did in some cases, quite early on, we didn't know we had them because of chronological problems.

CE: I also find it interesting when one thinks about the pre-War era, but basically the pre-1970s, that with so few sites known no reference was ever made to ethnography as to what should be the expected number of settlements. If you think of the *Cambridge Region* of 1923, no ethnography would ever support such a low density of settlement, whereas it now seems that we're getting realistic numbers, and analogous to what we know and would expect of the fabric of a landscape.

RB: Again, there were two things: one was the dominance of research excavation on standing monuments, which meant that very often you were working on what was a historical margin, investigating sites like hill-forts and standing barrows (as opposed to ring-ditches). So that was one bias. Then, I think, there was a sort of corporate depression caused, particularly, by Chris Taylor saying 'Well, of course you're dealing with a biased sample, but the part you've lost is irrecoverable and there's no point in thinking about it'. I remember hearing that paper and it was totally depressing, completely negative, because he was obviously right in his overall assessment that people weren't living on the margins, they were living where they'd nearly always lived. But he was wrong, as it turns out, in the complete lack of any survival. I think that had a very serious effect at the point when we were looking at ethnography; we just felt the whole game was impossible within an English landscape. A specific case is Fengate: hailed by the Royal Commission as a Roman landscape, because interpreting it as a prehistoric landscape was literally unthinkable.

CE: It's clear, reading their material, there's a kind of incredible urgency around the idea of Rescue. It's interesting that Margaret Jones doesn't talk about 'excavating' Mucking in her letters to Francis, it's 'rescuing' Mucking. Their urgency and the sense that such sites, and such landscapes, are incredibly rare, and really since then there has, I think, been a massive change in expectations.

RB: And we still don't know the full extent of the prehistoric landscape. The National Mapping Programme continues to suggest that there is an extremely high density of archaeology more or less anywhere that's looked at hard enough …. I think that's right and I can see it in my own case. John Barrett and I went digging in Cranborne Chase [Barrett *et al.* 1991], not from any reverence for General Pitt Rivers – because neither of us knew very much about him – but because South Lodge Camp gave us the last chance to look at a Middle Bronze Age enclosure with a fieldsystem and, as it turned out, a cemetery. Of course, the idea is ludicrous. By the time we'd finished digging, so many people had the same thing in

circumstances where we believed there would be nothing remaining, that, in a way, our project was completely unnecessary.

CE: Yes, it's incredible how the whole thing has snowballed. In terms of infilling our landscapes, and the whole idea of pastoral transhumance, re-reading the original Fengate reports (and with Francis very much citing your work on it), do you think the kind of mechanism of pastoralism — life on the hoof, as it were — was that a necessity of the time given how little archaeology was known?

RB: I think it was partly that and it was partly, of course, the influence of Eric Higgs and the notion of mobile animal economies. But a lot of it was trying to find a rational explanation for not discovering what we expected to, and in many cases that was just a false assumption. I remember writing on very, very slender evidence about why hill-fort interiors were empty. Well, most of the hill-fort interiors that have since been excavated weren't empty; they simply had posthole structures rather than pits, so we couldn't pick them up.

CE: I've wondered about the sense of, if you're digging Fengate early in your career and your only analogous site is Mucking, and you have these many metalwork distribution dots and need to make a story; in effect, the only way to link these very disparate and far-flung things is by having people move to tie them together.

RB: People moving, yes; but also remember that it's during this period that Colin Burgess is arguing to international audiences (rather than British) that there was little Middle or Late Bronze Age settlement in England because of climatic factors. We're talking about displacement, but on a massive scale. He had the whole of upland Britain depopulated and a massive population crisis in lowland Britain, for which there was no evidence whatsoever. The idea doesn't even work in the area he originally postulated it for, as we know now. So we also have people on the move in a quite different sense, because of this very doctrinaire climatic determinism, which, curiously enough, gained a lot of adherents.

CE: I can very much remember the impact of it. When we now see such vast tracts covered by various fieldsystem blocks, this certainly seems to have been a very settled landscape. As regards our 'pastoral-phase stories' — with their tales of cattle rustling, *etc.* – today the Bronze Age almost looks more domesticated than it was anticipated at the time.

RB: I think one reason was that, apart from Fengate, Dartmoor and Mucking eventually, we had the chronology of the fieldsystems wrong: they were called 'Celtic fields'. In the 1920s Herbert Toms argued that some Celtic fields were Bronze Age and people wrote to him, saying 'that's impossible because we know the Celts were Iron Age, and these earthworks are called Celtic fields'. Now, I think, we've got to the point where most coaxial fieldsystems are either later Bronze Age or later Iron Age and Roman, and we have a gap in between with something rather different going on. This also applies to the surviving earthworks. Remember that Fowler and Bowen went to Fyfield and Overton Downs to dig the archetypal Iron Age landscape. They had a hill-fort, they had settlements, they had linear ditches, they had Celtic fields – very well-preserved Celtic fields – and when, forty years later, it was published, it turned out that the fields had gone out of use at the beginning of the Iron Age [Fowler 2000]. The settlements weren't firmly attached to the fields, and the hill-fort had nothing to do with them; in a sense, we had been brought up on an image of an Iron Age in which everything was driven by population. An awful lot of that population pressure was created by wrongly dated sites, as we now know; or, not perhaps individual sites, but wrongly dated landscapes, because we didn't know any better. And if we saw 'Celtic fields' and they weren't patently Roman, then they had to be Iron Age. That implied intensification from something simpler and maybe something more mobile. Of course, what's actually happened is that the whole chronology has shifted.

CE: Going back to this issue of intensification, as we were talking earlier about to what degree we're dealing with mixed Bronze Age economies *versus* a more pastoral lifestyle-based system, and the arguments relating to the idea that we're seeing a rise in population by the Late Bronze Age, I certainly think there's a sense that we're seeing a rise in population across the second millennium. That also seems to me a potential factor in all this, as it seems difficult to imagine such a rise in population coming from a pastoral-based system. We just don't have historic analogy for that, whereas we do have greater intensification deriving from mixed production through the fieldsystems. It's not surprising to see, at the end of the millennium, what appears to be, through the record, a suggestion of higher population levels.

RB: I think that's fair enough. The sheer amount of labour that goes into the creation and maintenance of fields is probably equivalent to the amount that was invested in apparently non-practical monuments in earlier periods. But I think there's a missing term in the equation, and we still haven't really picked it up nationally: that's what happens in the Early Bronze Age and Late Neolithic. I think what's hinted at is that much larger areas of the landscape were used. If you can have intensification, then why not talk about 'extensification' — the use of a larger area of land without much input of labour? A lot of the regions first used at that time simply can't have sustained a long period of use. The Early Bronze Age is when you get barrows on heathlands and when you get lithic scatters extending far further than they do subsequently. Quite often the areas that seem to have been cleared in the Early Bronze Age, have very little going on in the Late Bronze Age. So there you've got the displacement Burgess wanted, but it may be over a few kilometres and it's not particularly driven by climate; it's caused by the extension of settlement into areas that simply can't take the pressure. The New Forest is a perfect example. It's hardly got anything, except a Mesolithic and an Early Bronze Age, because, in between, it's just not sustainable.

CE: Yes, I think it's interesting how much, if you look at the pollen data, particularly at around the 1800 BC horizon, there was much more working of the landscape earlier than has been acknowledged.

RB: Yes, I think the fieldsystems, in a sense, are what happens when the extension of settlement really fails to work and people, to some extent, are retreating to the more resilient environments and allocating them in a much more rigid way. Very large parts of the English landscape become unsustainable somewhere between 2500 and 1500 BC. It's a pity we don't know more about the Breckland, as I suspect that, within eastern England, it's probably a good example; whereas in upland Britain, I think that this process is what Burgess mistook for climatic pressure.

CE: Over the last few years, the Unit's been working quite a lot on clays, where the Iron Age seems to have sought out and colonised the heavy soil-lands as quickly as possible. Equally, quite a lot of the summers we've been working at Fengate have been quite dry, and you wonder the degree of risk that farming ran on those light soils and how many years they potentially would have seen drought. It's almost like, once they could cope with it, that the desire was to positively farm and settle on the clays with their perched watertables. You almost feel that in the kind of animal-dominated mixed farming practiced on the gravel terraces during the Bronze

Age, they may have actually kept animals as, in effect, a safety margin against drought.

RB: Yes, I think that's perfectly fair. I think there's another thing that comes in as well, which is probably insoluble with current dating methods. We talk about long continuities of settlement, but lots of people have pointed out that there aren't enough houses and house-replacements for that to have happened. We can have very many sites, but you've probably got long periods in which any particular part of a settlement is deserted. Much of Iron Age studies – certainly the Wessex-centred population-driven models – consists of counting settlements. If you think of the likely lifespan of a house, the question is how many settlements were contemporaneous with each other, given the longevity of one style of pottery.

CE: It's one of the things that I find exciting. I think that, for the first time, we're getting a realistic sense of just how close your neighbours were in prehistory and the fabric of the landscape. There are still problems in terms of the chronology, but just how dense the past was, has been quite severely under-appreciated.

RB: But, again, it's regional. There are perfectly good areas where we just don't have anything and, try as one might to blame it on the local contractors, there are organisations that do not find Iron Age settlements, because they are not there. That happens not just because some regions are aceramic; there are probably very busy areas of the landscape and largely empty ones.

Text after land

Reviewing Fengate's results this book has, through necessity, had to trade in a fair amount of critique; inevitably, working with time, in time we all set ourselves up for reappraisal and each can only await our turn. Yet, behind all this, rests Pryor's unassailable achievement, and it was no banal platitude in Chapter 1 to compare what he did there with Bersu at Woodbury. He did, indeed, invent a new type of grand-scale, open-area landscape archaeology, and that kind of fostering falls to very few. He is, moreover, a 'model' archaeologist: inspiringly larger-than-life and unstintingly enthusiastic, he's embraced the day's key interpretative trends and openly announced his influences (and has not been afraid to revisit his own work), the result being a body of archaeological scholarship closely embedded both in its time and personal experience.

Finally, what then of Fengate itself thirty years on? There can only be something inherently sad about the passing of a celebrated archaeological landscape to industrial-suburban sprawl. While not indulging in nostalgia, its piecemeal-loss since the '80s lacks the compelling drama of either Pryor's grand-scale excavations or even, as elsewhere, the 'total destruction environment' of modern quarries. Having a Auto Body Centre finally sited on the Cat's Water or a Walters Office World on Third Drive gives little sense of any 'majesty' of time/sequence played-out in landscape, and certainly they're no fitting testimonial to great excavations. Now, for the most part, all we have left of its (pre-) history are finds crammed into museum boxes and the accumulated texts. This, if nothing else, hammers home the need for fieldwork historiography — an active awareness of what's been done before to situate present efforts. It is a matter of *site genealogies* and the recognition, in this case, that we're digging after Pryor who dug after Abbott. While certainly no substitution or some kind of 'ennobling' past/present reclamation, today it's not just a matter of *texts on*, but also, *after land*.

Yet, this should not just be a matter of backward gaze, but also future direction. With Peterborough's incessant eastward creep, through projects like Bradley Fen and Must Farm the low 'bottomlands' of the Flag Fen basin are, for the first time, being investigated at a scale which is throwing up completely new dimensions in the area's archaeology. While there is still scope for further discoveries within Fengate proper, the focus of research is shifting: eastward and 'down'. What we've done here is to try to integrate and articulate Fengate's 'upland' or, perhaps better, 'up-edge' archaeology; in effect, a final scene-setting anticipating the future publication of its more deeply buried lowlands. Almost akin to this volume's Herodotus-inspired introductory passage concerning how we grasp the world through cumulative knowledge of neighbours, while maintaining an acute eye on previous efforts/context, it is nevertheless appropriate that the archaeological focus (and 'baton') similarly keeps passing on … .

REFERENCES

Abbott, G.W. & R.A. Smith, 1910. The discovery of prehistoric pits at Peterborough and the development of Neolithic pottery. *Archaeologia* 62, 332–52.

Abercromby, J., 1902. The oldest Bronze-Age ceramic type in Britain; its close analogies on the Rhine; its probable origin in central Europe. *The Journal of the Anthropological Institute of Great Britain and Ireland* 32, 373–97.

Adams, N., 1977. Leather shoes, in *Excavations at Scole, 1973, (Roman Small Town on the Norfolk-Suffolk Border)*, by A. Rogerson. (East Anglian Archaeology 5.) Gressenhall: Norfolk Archaeological Unit, Norfolk Museums Service.

Akerman, J.Y. & S. Stone, 1857. An account of the investigation of some remarkable circular trenches, and the discovery of an ancient British Cemetery, at Stanlake, Oxon. *Archaeologia* 37, 363–70.

Albarella, U., 2004. Mammal and bird bones, in *Excavations at Mill Lane, Thetford, 1995*, by J. Wallis. (East Anglian Archaeology Report 108.) Dereham: Archaeology and Environment Division, Norfolk Museums and Archaeology Service.

Ambrose, T., 1975. The leather, in *Excavations at Portchester Castle (I): Roman*, by B. Cunliffe. (Society of Antiquaries Research Report 32.) London: Society of Antiquaries, 241–62.

Andrews, G., J.C. Barrett & J.S.C. Lewis, 2000. Interpretation not record: the practice of archaeology. *Antiquity* 74, 525-30.

Appleby, G.A. forthcoming. The lead and white metal, in *Process and History: Prehistoric and Roman Fen-edge Communities at Colne Fen, Earith*, by C. Evans with S. Lucy, G. Appleby and R. Regan.

Armour-Chelu, M., 1998. The human bone, in *Etton: Excavations at a Neolithic Causewayed Enclosure near Maxey Cambridgeshire, 1982–87*, by F. Pryor, (Archaeological Report 18.) London: English Heritage, 271–2.

Arnolduseen, S. & H. Fokkens (eds.), 2008. Bronze Age settlements in the Low Countries: an overview, in *Bronze Age Settlements in the Low Countries*, eds. S. Arnoldussen & H. Fokkens. Oxford: Oxbow Books, 17–40.

Ashwin, T., 1998 Excavations at Salter's Lane, Longham 1990 — Neolithic and Bronze Age features and artefacts. *Norfolk Archaeology* 43(1), 1–30.

Ashwin, T., 2001. Exploring Bronze Age Norfolk: Longham and Bittering, in *Bronze Age Landscapes: Tradition and Transformation*, ed. J. Brück. Oxford: Oxbow Books, 23–32.

Avery, B.W., 1980. *Soil Classification for England and Wales*. (Soil Survey Technical Monograph 14.) Harpenden: Rothamsted Experimental Station.

Bamford, H.M., 1982. *Beaker Domestic Sites in the Fen Edge and East Anglia*. (East Anglian Archaeology 16.) Gressenhall: Archaeology and Environment Division, Norfolk Museums and Archaeology Service.

Barclay, A., 2002. Ceramic lives, in *Prehistoric Britain: the Ceramic Basis*, eds. A. Woodward & J.D. Hill. (Prehistoric Ceramics Research Group – Occasional Publication 3.) Oxford: Oxbow Books.

Barrett, J.C., 1976. Deverel-Rimbury: problems of chronology and interpretation, in *Settlement and Economy in the Third and Second Millennia BC*, eds. C.B. Burgess & R. Miket. (British Archaeological Reports British Series 33.) Oxford: BAR, 289–307.

Barrett, J.C., 1980. The pottery of the later Bronze Age in lowland England. *Proceedings of the Prehistoric Society* 46, 297–319.

Barrett, J.C., 1987. The Glastonbury lake village: models and source criticism. *Archaeological Journal* 144, 409–23.

Barrett, J.C., 1994. *Fragments From Antiquity*. Oxford: Blackwell.

Barrett, J.C. & D. Bond, 1988. The pottery, in *Excavations at the North Ring, Mucking, Essex: a Late Bronze Age Enclosure*, by D. Bond. (East Anglian Archaeology 43.) Chelmsford: Archaeology Section, Essex County Council, 25–37.

Barrett, J.C. & R. Bradley (eds.), 1980. *Settlement and Society in the British Later Bronze Age*. (British Archaeological Reports British Series 83.) Oxford: BAR.

Barrett, J.C., R. Bradley, R. Cleal & H. Pike, 1978. Characterisation of Deverel-Rimbury pottery from Cranborne Chase. *Proceedings of the Prehistoric Society* 44, 135–42.

Barrett, J., R. Bradley & M. Green, 1991. *Landscape, Monuments and Society*. Cambridge: Cambridge University Press.

Bartosiewicz, L., W. Van Neer & A. Lentacker, 1997. *Draught Cattle: their Osteological Identification and History*. (Koninklijk Museum voor Midden-Afrika, Annalen, Zoologische Wetenschappen 281.) Tervuren: Koninklijk Museum voor Midden-Afrika.

Beadsmoore, E.L., 2005a. *Edgerley Drain Road, Fengate, Peterborough; Archaeological Excavations*. (CAU Report 686.) Cambridge: Cambridge Archaeological Unit.

Beadsmoore, E.L., 2005b *Fairstead, Kings Lynn, Norfolk: an Archaeological Excavation.* (CAU Report 687.) Cambridge: Cambridge Archaeological Unit.

Beadsmoore, E.L., 2006a. Flint report, in *Excavations at Kilverstone, Norfolk: an Episodic Landscape History. Neolithic Pits, Later Prehistoric, Romano-British and Anglo-Saxon Occupation and Later Activity,* by D. Garrow, S. Lucy & D. Gibson. (East Anglian Archaeology 113.) Cambridge: Cambridge Archaeological Unit, 91.

Beadsmoore, E.L., 2006b. *Elliott Site, Fengate, Peterborough. Archaeological Excavations.* (CAU Report 734.) Cambridge: Cambridge Archaeological Unit.

Beadsmoore, E.L., 2007a. *Feltwell Quarry, Feltwell, Norfolk — A Strip, Map and Record Excavation.* (CAU Report 797.) Cambridge: Cambridge Archaeological Unit.

Beadsmoore, E., 2007b. *Land off Vicarage Farm Road, Fengate: a Watching Brief.* (CAU Report 766.) Cambridge: Cambridge Archaeological Unit.

Beadsmoore, E., forthcoming. Flint, in *Excavations at Linton Village College, Cambridge,* by R. Clarke, *et al.* East Anglian Archaeology.

Bennett, K.D., 1983. Devensian Late-glacial and Flandrian vegetational history at Hockham Mere, Norfolk, England, part I: Pollen percentages and concentrations. *New Phytologist* 95, 457–87.

Bersu, G., 1940. Excavations at Little Woodbury, Wiltshire, part I: The settlement as revealed by excavation. *Proceedings of the Prehistoric Society* 6, 30–111.

Biddick, K., 1980. Animal bones from the second millennium ditches, Newark Road Subsite, Fengate, in *Excavations at Fengate, Peterborough, England: the Third Report,* by F. Pryor. (Northamptonshire Archaeological Society Monograph 1, Royal Ontario Archaeology Monograph 6.) Toronto & Northampton: Northampton Archaeological Society & Royal Ontario Museum, 217–32.

Biddick, K., 1984. Animal bones from Cat's Water Subsite, Fengate, in *Excavations at Fengate, Peterborough, England: the Fourth Report,* by F. Pryor. (Northamptonshire Archaeological Society Monograph 2, Royal Ontario Archaeology Monograph 7.) Toronto & Northampton: Northampton Archaeological Society and Royal Ontario Museum, 245–75.

Biddick, K., 1989. *The Other Economy: Pastoral Husbandry on a Medieval Estate.* London: University of California Press.

Boardman, S. & G. Jones, 1990. Experiments on the effects of charring on cereal plant components. *Journal of Archaeological Science* 17, 1–11.

Boast, R., 2000. 'Pottery', in Excavation of a burnt mound at Feltwell Anchor, Norfolk, 1992, by S.J. Bates & P.E.J. Wiltshire. *Norfolk Archaeology* 43, 408.

Boersma, J., 2005. Dwelling mounds on the salt marshes: the *terpen* of Friesland and Groningen, in *The Prehistory of the Netherlands,* vol. 2, eds. L.P. Louwe Kooijmans, P.W. van den Broeke, H. Fokkens & A.L. van Gijn. Amsterdam: Amsterdam University Press, 557–60.

Boessneck, J., 1969. Osteological differences between sheep (*Ovis aries*) and goat (*Capra hircus*), in *Science in Archaeology,* eds. D. Brothwell & E.S. Higgs. 2nd edition. London: Thames & Hudson, 331–58.

Bond, D., 1988. *Excavation at the North Ring, Mucking, Essex.* (East Anglian Archaeology 43.) Chelmsford: Essex County Council.

Boreham, S., 2003. *Investigation of Ground Conditions and Radiocarbon Dating of Deposits at Fengate Sewage Treatment Works, Peterborough.* Unpublished report. Geography Department, University of Cambridge.

Bowen, H.C. & P.J. Fowler (eds.), 1978. *Early Land Allotment.* (British Archaeological Reports British Series 48.) Oxford: BAR.

Boyd, B & R.M. Pyle (eds.), 2000. *Nabokov's Butterflies.* Uckfield: Beacon Press.

Boyd, W.E., 1984. Prehistoric hedges: Roman Iron Age hedges from Bar Hill. *Scottish Archaeological Review* 3, 32–4.

Bradford, J.S.P., 1942. An Early Iron Age settlement at Standlake, Oxon. *The Antiquaries Journal* 22, 202–14.

Bradley, R., 1978. Prehistoric field systems in Britain and north-west Europe. A review of some recent work. *World Archaeology* 9, 265–80.

Bradley, R., 1984. *The Social Foundations of Prehistoric Britain: Themes and Variations in the Archaeology of Power.* London: Routledge.

Bradley, R., 1998. *The Passage of Arms.* Oxford: Oxbow Books.

Bradley, R., 2007. *The Prehistory of Britain and Ireland.* Cambridge: Cambridge University Press.

Bradley, R. & D. Yates, 2007. After 'Celtic' fields: the social organisation of Iron Age agriculture, in *The Earlier Iron Age in Britain and the near Continent,* eds. C. Haselgrove & R. Pope. Oxford: Oxbow Books, 94–102.

Brandt, R.W., W. Groenman-van Waateringe & S.E van der Leeuw, 1987. *Assendelver Polder Papers (Cingula* 10). Amsterdam: Universiteit van Amsterdam.

Brandt, R.W. & S.E. van der Leeuw, 1987. Conclusions, in *Assendelver Polder Papers (Cingula* 10), eds. R.W. Brandt, W. Groenman-van Waateringe & S.E van der Leeuw. Amsterdam: Universiteit van Amsterdam, 330–52.

Brennand, M. & M. Taylor, 2003. The survey and excavation of a Bronze Age timber circle at Holme-next-the-Sea, Norfolk, 1998–9. *Proceedings of the Prehistoric Society* 69, 1–84.

Britchfield, D., 2001. *Final Report for an Archaeological Watching Brief at Flag Fen Sewage Treatment Works, Fengate, Peterborough.* Soke (Archaeological Services Report No. SAS00/DB/15.) Peterborough: Soke Archaeological Services Ltd.

Britchfield, D., 2002. *A Report on Archaeological Excavations at Oxney Road, Fengate, Peterborough.* Peterborough: Soke Archaeological Services Ltd.

British Museum, 1904. *A Guide to the Bronze Age Antiquities in the Department of British and Medieval Antiquities, British Museum.* London: The British Museum.

Bronk Ramsey, C., 2001. Development of the radiocarbon program OxCal. *Radiocarbon* 43, 355–63.

Brooks, H., 1993. Fieldwalking and excavation at Stansted Airport, in *Flatlands and Wetlands: Current themes in East Anglian Archaeology,* ed. J. Gardiner. (East Anglian Archaeology 50.) Norwich: Scole Archaeological Committee, 40–57.

Brothwell, D., 1981. *Digging Up Bones*. London: British Museum.

Brown, N.R., 1988. A Late Bronze Age enclosure at Lofts Farm, Essex. *Proceedings of the Prehistoric Society* 54, 249–302.

Brown, N.R., 1998. Prehistoric pottery, in *Archaeology and Landscape in the Lower Blackwater Valley*, by S. Wallis & M. Waughman. (East Anglian Archaeology 82.) Chelmsford: Archaeology Section, Essex County Council, 132–41.

Brown, N.R., 1999. *The Archaeology of Ardleigh, Essex: Excavations 1955–1980*. (East Anglian Archaeology 90.) Chelmsford: Archaeology Section, Essex County Council.

Brück, J., 1995. A place for the dead: the role of human remains in the late Bronze Age. *Proceedings of the Prehistoric Society* 61, 245–77.

Brück, J. (ed.), 2001. *Bronze Age Landscapes: Tradition and Transformation*. Oxford: Oxbow Books.

Brück, J., 2006. Fragmentation, personhood and the social construction of technology in Middle and Bronze Age Britain. *Cambridge Archaeological Journal* 16(3), 297–315.

Brück, J., 2007. The character of Late Bronze Age settlement in southern Britain, in *The Earlier Iron Age in Britain and the near Continent*, eds. C. Haselgrove & R. Pope. Oxford: Oxbow Books, 24–38.

Brudenell, M., 2005a. *Archaeological Investigations at the Former Tower Works Site, Mallory Road, Fengate, Peterborough*. (CAU Report 675.) Cambridge: Cambridge Archaeological Unit.

Brudenell, M., 2005b. The later prehistoric pottery, in *Striplands Farm West, Longstanton, Cambridgeshire. An Archaeological Excavation*, by R. Patten & C. Evans. (CAU Report 703.) Cambridge: Cambridge Archaeological Unit.

Brudenell, M., 2006. The later prehistoric pottery, in *Further Excavations at Striplands Farm, West Longstanton Cambridgeshire*, by D. Mackay & C. Evans. (CAU Report 764.) Cambridge: Cambridge Archaeological Unit.

Brudenell, M., 2007. The later prehistoric pottery, in *Past and Present: Landscape and Time on the Bedfordshire Gravels*, by A. Cooper, M. Edmonds & D. Gibson. Cambridge: Cambridge Archaeological Unit, 241–64.

Brudenell, M., forthcoming a. The later prehistoric pottery, in *Process and History: Prehistoric Communities at Colne Fen, Earith*, by C. Evans, with S. Lucy, G. Appleby & R. Regan. (The Archaeology of the Lower Ouse Valley, vol. I).

Brudenell, M., forthcoming b. Reclaiming the Early Iron Age in eastern England, in *Proceedings of the Iron Age Research Seminar, Cardiff 2006*, ed. K. Waddington.

Bullock, P., N. Fedoroff, A. Jongerius, G. Stoops & T. Tursina, 1985. *Handbook for Soil Thin Section Description*. Wolverhampton: Waine Research.

Burgess, C.B., 1974. The Bronze Age, in *British Prehistory: a New Outline*, ed. C. Renfrew. London: Duckworth, 166–232.

Burgess, C., 1980. *The Age of Stonehenge*. London: Dent.

Burgess, C., 1986. Urns of no small variety: Collared urns reviewed. *Proceedings of the Prehistoric Society* 52, 339–51.

Burgess, C. & R. Miket (eds.), 1976. *Settlement and Economy in the Third and Second Millennium BC*. (British Archaeological Reports British Series 33.) Oxford: BAR.

Burkitt, M., C. Fox & G. Wyman Abbott, 1926. The early occupation of Huntingdonshire, in *The Victoria County History of Huntingdonshire*, vol. 1. London: H.M.S.O., 193–215.

Butzer, K.W., 2002. French wetland agriculture in Atlantic Canada and its European roots: different avenues to historical diffusion. *Annals of the Association of American Geographers* 92, 451–70.

Canti, M.G., 1997. An investigation of microscopic calcareous spherulites from herbivore dungs. *Journal of Archaeological Science* 24, 219–31.

Canti, M.G., 1999. The production and preservation of faecal spherulites: animals, environment and taphonomy. *Journal of Archaeological Science* 26(1), 253–8.

Carver, M., 2005. *A Seventh-century Princely Burial Ground and its Context*. (British Museum Press/Society of Antiquaries of London Research Committee Report 69.) London: British Museum Press.

Casa Hatton, R., 1999. *Site 'T', Newark Road, Peterborough: an Archaeological Evaluation*. (Cambridgeshire County Council Archaeological Field Unit Report B62.) Cambridge: Cambridgeshire County Council Archaeological Field Unit.

Casa Hatton, R. & S. Macaulay, 2001. *Prehistoric Field Systems at the Northern Office, March: an Archaeological Evaluation*. (Cambridgeshire County Council Archaeological Field Unit Report A179.) Cambridge: Cambridgeshire County Council Archaeological Field Unit.

Catling, H.W., 1982. Six ring-ditches at Standlake, in *Settlement Patterns in the Oxford Region: Excavations of the Abingdon Causewayed Enclosure and Other Sites*, eds. H.J. Case & A.W.R. Whittle. (CBA Research Report 44.) Oxford/London: Council for British Archaeology, 89–102.

Champion, T., 1975. Britain in the European Iron Age. *Archaeologia Atlantic* 1, 127–45.

Clark, A., 1993. *Excavations at Mucking*, vol. 1: *The Site Atlas*. (English Heritage Archaeological Report 20.) London: English Heritage.

Clark, J.G.D. & C.I. Fell, 1953. The Early Iron Age site at Micklemoor Hill, West Harling, Norfolk and its pottery. *Proceedings of the Prehistoric Society* 19, 1–40.

Clark, J.G.D., E. Higgs & I. Longworth, 1960. Excavations at the Neolithic site at Hurst Fen, Mildenhall, Suffolk (1954, 1957 and 1958). *Proceedings of the Prehistoric Society* 26, 202–45.

Clarke, D., 1970. *Beaker Pottery of Great Britain*. Cambridge: Cambridge University Press.

Cleal, R., 1999. Introduction: the what, where, when and why of Grooved Ware, in *Grooved Ware in Britain and Ireland*, eds. R. Cleal & A. MacSween. (Neolithic Studies Group Seminar Papers 3.) Oxford: Oxbow Books, 1–8.

Cohen, A. & D. Serjeantson, 1996. *A Manual for the Identification of Bird Bones from Archaeological Sites.* Revised edition. London: Archetype Publications.

Connor, A. & R. Mortimer, forthcoming. *Prehistoric and Romano-British Occupation along Fordham Bypass, Fordham, Cambridgeshire.* East Anglian Archaeology.

Coombs, D., 2001. Metalwork, in *The Flag Fen Basin. Archaeology and Environment of a Fenland Landscape*, by F. Pryor. Swindon: English Heritage: 278–80.

Cooper, A., 2003. *Storey's Bar Road, Fengate: Archaeological Desk Based Assessment and Test Pit Survey.* (CAU Report 584.) Cambridge: Cambridge Archaeological Unit.

Cooper, A., 2004a. *Mallory Road, Fengate: Archaeological Test Pit Survey.* (CAU Report 590.) Cambridge: Cambridge Archaeological Unit.

Cooper, A., 2004b. *Land at Edgerley Drain Road, Fengate, Peterborough: Archaeological Evaluation.* (CAU Report 635.) Cambridge: Cambridge Archaeological Unit.

Cooper, A. & M. Edmonds, 2007. *Past and Present: Excavations at Broom, Bedfordshire 1996–2005.* Cambridge: Cambridge Archaeological Unit.

Cooper, L., 1994. Kirby Muxloe, A46 Leicester Western by-pass. *Transactions of the Leicestershire Archaeological and Historical Society* 68, 162–5.

Cooper, S., 1998. *A Ring Ditch at Third Drove, Fengate, Peterborough.* (Cambridgeshire County Council Archaeological Field Unit Cambridgeshire County Council Report 153.) Cambridge: Cambridgeshire County Council Archaeological Field Unit.

Cowgill, J., 2001. The industrial waste, in *Vicar's Farm, Cambridge Post Excavation Assessment Report*, vols. 1 & 2, by G. Lucas. (CAU Report 425.) Cambridge: Cambridge Archaeological Unit, 82–4.

Craddock, P.T., 1984a. A report on the scientific examination of the refractory slag fragments from Iron Age contexts at Fengate, in *Excavation at Fengate, Peterborough, England: the Fourth Report*, by F. Pryor. (Royal Ontario Museum Monograph 7/Northants Archaeological Monograph 2.) Northampton & Toronto: Royal Ontario Museum, Northants Archaeological Society, 174.

Craddock, P.T., 1984b. Soil phosphate survey, Cat's Water, 1973–77, in *Excavation at Fengate, Peterborough, England: the Fourth Report*, by F. Pryor. (Royal Ontario Museum Monograph 7/Northants Archaeological Monograph 2.) Northampton & Toronto: Royal Ontario Museum, Northants Archaeological Society, Microfiche Appendix 4.

Crawford, O.G.S., 1912. The distribution of Early Bronze Age settlements in Britain. *The Geographical Journal* 40, 184–97.

Crawford, O.G.S., 1955. *Said and Done.* London: Phoenix House.

Crew, P., 1986. Bryn y Castell Hillfort — a late prehistoric iron working settlement in north-west Wales, in *The Crafts of the Blacksmith: Proceedings of the Symposium of the UISPP Comité pour le la Sidérurgie Ancienne, Belfast, 1984*, eds. B.G. Scott & H. Cleere. Belfast: Ulster Museum, 91–100.

Crew, P., 1989. Excavations at Crawcellt West, Merioneth, 1986–1989. A late prehistoric upland iron-working settlement. *Archaeology in Wales* 29, 11–16.

Crew, P., 1991. The experimental production of prehistoric bar iron. *Historical Metallurgy* 25.1, 21–36.

Crew, P., 1998. Excavations at Crawcellt West, Merioneth, 1990–1998: a late prehistoric upland iron working settlement. *Archaeology in Wales* 38, 22–35.

Crew, P., 2002. Mapping and dating of prehistoric and medieval iron working sites in north-west Wales. *Archaeological Prospection* 9, 163–82.

Crowson, A., 2004. *Hot Rocks in the Norfolk Fens: the Excavation of a Burnt Flint Mound at Northwold, 1994–5.* (East Anglian Archaeology Occasional Paper 16.) Gressenhall: Norfolk Museum Service, Archaeology & Environment Division.

Crowther, D., 1983. Old land surfaces and modern plough-soil: implications of recent work at Maxey, Cambs. *Scottish Archaeological Review* 2, 31–44.

Crummy, N., 1983. *The Roman Finds from Excavations in Colchester 1971–9.* (Colchester Archaeological Report 2.) Colchester: Colchester Archaeological Trust.

Cunliffe, B., 1968. Early Pre-Roman Iron Age communities in eastern England. *Antiquaries Journal* 47, 1–44.

Cunliffe, B., 1974. *Iron Age Communities in Britain.* London: Routledge & Kegan Paul.

Cunliffe, B., 1978. *Iron Age Communities in Britian.* 2nd edition. London: Routledge.

Cutler, R., 1995. *Marshall's Garage, Boongate, Peterborough: an Archaeological Evaluation.* (Birmingham University Field Archaeological Unit Report 341.) Birmingham: Birmingham: Birmingham University Field Archaeological Unit.

Cutler, R., 1998. *Land off Third Drove, Fengate, Peterborough: an Archaeological Evaluation.* (Birmingham University Field Archaeological Unit Report 515.) Birmingham: Birmingham University Field Archaeological Unit.

Cutler, R. & P. Ellis, 2001. A Bronze Age barrow and Romano-British features at Pode Hole Farm, Cambridgeshire, 1996, in *Four Sites in Cambridgeshire: Excavations at Pode Hole Farm, Paston, Longstanton and Bassingbourn, 1996–7*, eds. P. Ellis, G. Coates, R. Cutler & C. Mould. (Birmingham University Field Archaeology Unit Monograph Series 4. British Archaeological Reports British Series 322.) Oxford: Archaeopress, 5–25.

Darby, H.C., 1940. *The Medieval Fenland.* Newton Abbott: David and Charles.

Darwin, F. (ed.), 1887. *The Life and Letters of Charles Darwin, including an Autobiographical Chapter* (III). London: John Murray.

Davis, S., 1992. *A Rapid Method for Recording Information about Mammal Bones from Archaeological Sites.* (Ancient Monuments Laboratory Report 19/92.) Portsmouth: English Heritage.

Davis, S. & S. Payne, 1993. A barrow full of cattle skulls. *Antiquity* 67, 12–22.

Degerbol, M. & J. Fredskild, 1970. The urus (*Bos primigenius* Bojanus) and Neolithic domestic cattle (*Bos taurus domesticus* Linn) in Denmark. *Kongelige Danske Videnskabernes Selskabo Biologica Skirpta* 17, 1–17.

Dick, W.A. & M.A. Tabatabai, 1977. An alkaline oxidation method for the determination of total phosphorus in soils. *Journal of Soil Science of America* 41, 511–14.

Dickson, J.A.D., 1965. A modified staining technique for carbonates in thin section. *Nature* 205, 587.

Dobney, K., 2001. A place at the table: the role of vertebrate zooarchaeology within a Roman research agenda for Britain, in *Britons and Romans: Advancing an Archaeological Agenda*, eds. S. James & M. Millet. (Council for British Archaeology Research Report 125.) York: Council for British Archaeology Research: 36–45.

Dobney, K.M., S.D. Jaques & B.G. Irving, 1996. *Of Butchers and Breeds. Report on Vertebrate Remains from Various Sites in the City of Lincoln*. (Lincoln Archaeological Studies 5.) Lincoln: City of Lincoln Archaeology Unit.

Dobney, K. & K. Reilly, 1988. A method for recording archaeological animal bones: the use of diagnostic zones. *Circaea* 5, 79–96.

Driel-Murray, C. van, 1999. And did those feet in ancient time… Feet and shoes as a material projection of the self, in *Proceedings of the Eighth Annual Theoretical Roman archaeology Conference, Leicester 1998*, eds. P. Baker, C. Forcey, S. Jundi & R. Witcher. (TRAC 98.) Oxford: Oxbow, 131–40.

Driel-Murray, C. van, 2001. Footwear in the northwestern provinces of the Roman Empire, in *Stepping Through Time. Archaeological Footwear from Prehistoric Times until 1800*, by O. Goubitz, C. van Driel-Murray & W. Groenman-van Waateringe. Zwolle: Stichting Promotie Archeologie, 337–76.

Driesch von den, A., 1976. *A Guide to Measurement of Animal Bones from Archaeological Sites*. (Peabody Museum Bulletin 1.) Cambridge (MA): Peabody Museum of Archaeology and Ethnology.

Driesch von den, A. & J. Boessneck, 1974. Kritische Anmerkungen zur Widerristhohen-Berechnung aus langmassen vor- und fruhgeschichtlicher Tierknochen. *Saugetierkundliche Mitteilungen* 22, 325–48.

Duckworth, W.L.H., 1904. Prehistoric archaeology of Cambridgeshire, in *Handbook to the Natural History of Cambridgeshire*, by J.E. Marr & A.E. Shipley. Cambridge: Cambridge University Press, 238–51.

Dymond, M., T. Lane, F. Pryor & D. Timble, nd. *Assessment Report: Welland Bank Quarry, Deeping St James, Lincolnshire*. Sleaford: Archaeological Project Services.

Edmonds, M., 2004. *The Langdales: Landscape and Prehistory in a Lakeland Valley*. Stroud: Tempus.

Ellison, A. & P. Drewett, 1971. Pits and post-holes in the British Early Iron Age: some alternative explanations. *Proceedings of the Prehistoric Society* 37, 183–94.

English Heritage, 1995. *Guidelines for the Care of Waterlogged Archaeological Leather*. (Scientific and Technical Publications Guideline 4.) London: English Heritage.

Evans, C., 1987. Nomads in 'Waterland'?: prehistoric transhumance and Fenland archaeology. *Proceedings of the Cambridge Antiquarian Society* 76, 27–39.

Evans, C., 1988. Monuments and analogy: the interpretation of causewayed enclosures, in *Enclosures and Defences in the Neolithic of Western Europe*, eds. C. Burgess, P. Topping, C. Mordant & M. Maddison. (British Archaeological Reports International Series 403.) Oxford: BAR, 47–73.

Evans, C., 1989. Archaeology and modern times: Bersu's Woodbury 1938 & 1939. *Antiquity* 63, 436–50.

Evans, C., 1992. *Archaeological Investigations at Fengate, Peterborough. The Depot Site*. (CAU Report 72.) Cambridge: Cambridge Archaeological Unit.

Evans, C., 1993. The Fengate Depot Site. *Fenland Research* 8, 2–9.

Evans, C., 1997a. The excavation of a ring-ditch complex at Diddington, near Huntingdon, with a discussion of second millennium BC pyre burial and regional cremation practices. *Proceedings of the Cambridge Antiquarian Society* 85, 11–26.

Evans, C., 1997b. Sentimental prehistories: the construction of the Fenland past. *Journal of European Archaeology* 5, 105–36.

Evans, C., 1998. Constructing houses and building context: Bersu's Manx roundhouse campaign. *Proceedings of the Prehistoric Society* 64, 183–201.

Evans, C., 2000. Testing the ground - sampling strategies, in *Fenland Management Project Excavations 1991–1995*, eds. A. Crowson, T. Lane & J. Reeve. (Lincolnshire Archaeology and Heritage Reports Series 3.) Heckington: Heritage Lincolnshire, 15–21.

Evans, C., 2002. Metalwork and 'cold claylands': pre-Iron Age occupation on the Isle of Ely, in *Through Wet and Dry: Proceedings of a Conference in Honour of David Hall*, eds. T. Lane & J. Coles. (Lincolnshire Archaeology and Heritage Reports Series 5 and WARP Occasional Paper 17.) Sleaford: Heritage Trust of Lincolnshire, 33–53.

Evans, C., 2003. Britons and Romans at Chatteris: investigations at Langwood Farm, Chatteris. *Britannia* 34, 175–264.

Evans, C., 2004. Modelling monuments and excavations, in *Models: the Third Dimension of Science*, eds. S. de Chadarevian & N. Hopwood. (Writing Science Series.) Stanford (CA): Stanford University Press, 109–37.

Evans, C., 2007a. 'Delineating objects': nineteenth century antiquarian culture and the Project of Archaeology, in *Visions of Antiquity: the Society of Antiquaries of London 1707–2007 (Archaeologia 111)*, ed. S. Pearce. London: Society of Antiquaries of London, 266–305.

Evans, C., 2007b. Review: John Lewis et al. *Landscape Evolution in the Middle Thames Valley: Heathrow Terminal 5 Excavations*, vol. 1: *Perry Oak* (Framework Archaeology Monograph 1). *Antiquity* 81, 809–11.

Evans, C., forthcoming. Archaeology and the repeatable experiment: towards a comparative agenda for development-led practice. *Antiquity*.

Evans, C. & G. Appleby, 2008. Historiography and fieldwork: Wyman Abbott's Great Fengate ring-ditch (a lost manuscript found). *Proceedings of the Prehistoric Society* 74, 171–92.

Evans, C. & I. Hodder. 2006a. *A Woodland Archaeology* (The Haddenham Project, vol. I). (McDonald Institute

Monographs.) Cambridge: McDonald Institute for Archaeological Research.

Evans, C. & I. Hodder. 2006b. *Marshland Communities and Cultural Landscape* (The Haddenham Project, vol. II). (McDonald Institute Monographs.) Cambridge: McDonald Institute for Archaeological Research.

Evans, C. & M. Knight, 1997. *The Barleycroft Paddocks.* (CAU Report 218.) Cambridge: Cambridge Archaeological Unit.

Evans, C. & M. Knight. 2000. A fenland delta: later prehistoric land-use in the lower Ouse reaches, in *Prehistoric, Roman and Saxon Landscape Studies in the Great Ouse Valley,* ed. M. Dawson. York: Council for British Archaeology, 89–106.

Evans, C. & M. Knight. 2001. The 'community of builders': the Barleycroft post alignments, in *Bronze Age Landscapes: Tradition and Transformation,* ed. J. Brück. Oxford: Oxbow Books, 83–98.

Evans, C. & M. Knight, 2004. *Excavations at Over: Chain Bridge Terrace Investigations (Site 2).* (CAU Report 650.) Cambridge: Cambridge Archaeological Unit.

Evans, C. & M. Knight, forthcoming *Further Excavations at Barleycroft Farm, Cambridgeshire.* Cambridge Archaeological Unit.

Evans, C. & D. Mackay, 2005. *Addenbrooke's, Cambridge - The 2020 Lands: Archaeological Evaluation Fieldwork.* (CAU Report 671.) Cambridge: Cambridge Archaeological Unit.

Evans, C. & J. Pollard, 1995. *The Excavation of a Ring-ditch and Prehistoric Fieldsystem at Barleycroft Farm, Bluntisham, Cambridgeshire.* (CAU Report 126.) Cambridge: Cambridge Archaeological Unit.

Evans, C. & J. Pollard, 2001. The dating of the Storey's Bar Road fields reconsidered, in *The Flag Fen Basin: Archaeology and Environment of a Fenland Landscape,* ed. F. Pryor. Swindon: English Heritage, 25–7.

Evans, C. & F. Pryor, 2001. Recent research in south Fengate, in *The Flag Fen Basin: Archaeology and Environment of a Fenland Landscape,* ed. F. Pryor. Swindon: English Heritage, 18–36.

Evans, C., J. Pollard & M. Knight, 1999. Life in woods: tree-throws, 'settlement' and forest cognition. *Oxford Journal of Archaeology* 18, 241–54.

Evans, C., M. Brudenell, M. Knight & R. Patten, 2005. *Must Farm: Archaeological and Palaeo-Environmental Investigations.* (Cambridge Archaeological Report 667.)

Evans, C., M. Edmonds & S. Boreham, 2006. 'Total archaeology' and model landscapes: excavation of the Great Wilbraham causewayed enclosure, Cambridgeshire, 1975–76. *Proceeding of the Prehistoric Society* 72, 113–62.

Evans, C., with D. Mackay & L. Webley, 2008. *Borderlands: The Archaeology of the Addenbrooke's Environs, South Cambridge.* (CAU Landscape Archives: New Archaeologies of the Cambridge Region Series.) Oxford: Cambridge Archaeological Unit/Oxbow Books.

Evans, C., with J. Pettigrew, Y. Tamu & M. Turin, 2009. *Grounding Knowledge/Walking Land: Archaeological and Ethno-Historical Researches in Central Nepal.* (McDonald Institute Monographs.) Cambridge: McDonald Institute for Archaeological Research.

Evans, C. with S. Lucy, G. Appleby & R. Regan, forthcoming. *Process and History: Prehistoric Communities at Colne Fen, Earith.* (The Archaeology of the Lower Ouse Valley, vol. I).

Evans, J., 1860. On the occurrence of flint implements in undisturbed beds of gravel, sand and clay. *Archaeologia* 38, 280–307.

Evans, J., 1876. Note on a proposed international code for symbols for the use on archaeological maps. *Journal of the Anthropological Institute of Great Britain and Ireland* 5, 427–36.

Fedoroff, N., 1968. Génèse et morphologie des sols à horizons B textural en France atlantique. *Science du Sols* 1, 29–65.

Field, D., 2001. Place and memory in Bronze Age Wessex, in *Bronze Age Landscapes: Tradition and Transformation,* ed. J. Brück. Oxford: Oxbow Books, 57–64.

Fincham, G., 2002. *Landscapes of Imperialism. Roman and Native Interaction in the East Anglian Fenland.* (British Archaeological Reports British Series 338.) Oxford: Archaeopress.

Fisher, P.F., 1982. A review of lessivage and Neolithic cultivation in southern England. *Journal of Archaeological Science* 9, 299–394.

Fitch, R.K., 2001. *Winstat for Microsoft* (r) Excel. http://www.winstat.com.

Fleming, A., 1985. Land tenure, productivity and field systems, in *Beyond Domestication in Prehistoric Europe,* eds. G. Barker and C. Gamble. London: Academic Press, 129–46.

Fleming, A., 1987. Coaxial field systems: some question of time and space. *Antiquity* 61, 188–202.

Fleming, A., 1988. *The Dartmoor Reaves: Investigating Prehistoric Land Divisions.* London: Batsford.

Fleming, A., 1994. The reaves reviewed, in *The Archaeology of Dartmoor: Perspectives from the 1990s,* ed. F..M. Griffiths. Exeter: Devon Archaeological Society, 63–74.

Fleming, A., 1998a. The changing commons: the case of Swaledale (England), in *Property in Economy in Context,* eds. A. Gilman & R. Hunt. Lanham (MD): University Press of America, 187–214.

Fleming, A., 1998b. Prehistoric landscape and the quest for territorial pattern, in *The Archaeology of Landscape: Studies Presented to Christopher Taylor,* eds. P. Everson & T. Williamson. Manchester: Manchester University Press, 42–66.

Fleming, A., 2006. Post-processual landscape archaeology: a critique. *Cambridge Archaeological Journal* 16(3), 267–80.

Fleming, A., 2007. *The Dartmoor Reaves: Investigating Prehistoric Land Divisions.* 2nd edition. Bollington: Windgather Press.

Fleure, H.J., 1923. *The Races of England and Wales.* London: Benn Brothers.

Fokkens, H., 2005. Longhouses in unsettled settlements: settlements in Beaker period and Bronze Age, in *The Prehistory of the Netherlands,* vol. 1, eds. L.P. Louwe

Kooijmans, P.W. van den Broeke, H. Fokkens & A.L. van Gijn. Amsterdam: Amsterdam University Press, 407–28.

Fowler, P., 1983. *The Farming of Prehistoric Britain*. Cambridge: Cambridge University Press.

Fowler, P., 2000. *Fyfield and Overton Down: Landscape Plotted and Pieced*. (Reports of the Research Committee of the Society of Antiquaries of London 64.) London: Society of Antiquaries.

Fox, C., 1923. *The Archaeology of the Cambridge Region*. Cambridge: Cambridge University Press.

Fox, G. E. & St J. Hope. 1895. Excavations on the site of the Roman city of Silchester, Hants, in 1893. *Archaeologia* 54, 199–228.

French, C.A.I., 1980a. Sediment analysis of second millennium ditches, in *Excavation at Fengate, Peterborough, England: the Third Report*, by F. Pryor. (Northampton/Toronto: Northamptonshire Archaeological Society Monograph 1/Royal Ontario Museum Archaeology Monograph 6.) Toronto & Northampton: Northampton Archaeological Society & Royal Ontario Museum, 190–202.

French, C.A.I., 1980b. Analysis of molluscs from two second millennium ditches, in *Excavation at Fengate, Peterborough, England: the Third Report*, by F. Pryor. (Northampton Archaeological Society Monograph 1/Royal Ontario Museum Archaeology Monograph 6.) Toronto & Northampton: Northampton Archaeological Society & Royal Ontario Museum, 204–12.

French, C.A.I., 1990. Neolithic soils, middens and alluvium in the lower Welland valley. *Oxford Journal of Archaeology* 9, 305–11.

French, C.A.I., 1992a. Alluviated fen-edge prehistoric landscapes in Cambridgeshire, England, in *Archeologia del Paesaggio, Firenze*, ed. M. Bernardi. Florence: All'Insegna di Giglio, 709–31.

French, C.A.I., 1992b. Fengate to Flag Fen: summary of the soil and sediment analyses. *Antiquity* 66, 458–61.

French, C.A.I. ,1997. Fengate, Peterborough, 1997: Soil Assessment. Unpublished report, Cambridge Archaeological Unit.

French, C.A.I., 2001. The development of the prehistoric landscape in the Flag Fen basin, in *The Flag Fen Basin: Archaeology and Environment of a Fenland Landscape*, by F. Pryor. Swindon: English Heritage, 400–404.

French, C.A.I., 2003a. *Geoarchaeology in Action: Studies in Soil Micromorphology and Landscape Evolution*. London: Routledge.

French, C.A.I., 2003b. The Fengate Shore, lower Nene valley and the Flag Fen basin, Cambridgeshire, England, in *Geoarchaeology in Action*, by C.A.I. French. London: Routledge, 97–113.

French, C.A.I. & J. Heathcote, 1997. Auger survey, in *The Sewage Treatment Works, Peterborough: a Desk-top Study*, by G. Lucas. (CAU Report 234.) Cambridge: Cambridge Archaeological Unit.

French, C.A.I. & H.A. Lewis, 1998. The Depot site: soil micromorphological analysis, in *Excavations at Flag Fen, Fengate, Peterborough*, by F. Pryor, London: HBMC Monograph, 20–22.

French, C.A.I. & H. Lewis, 2001. Soil micromorphological analysis, in *Archaeology and Environment of the Flag Fen Basin*, by F. Pryor. London: English Heritage Archaeological Report, 20–22.

French, C.A.I. & F. Pryor, 1993. *The South-West Fen Dyke Survey Project 1982–86*. (East Anglian Archaeology 59.) Peterborough: Fenland Archaeological Trust.

French, C.A.I. & F. Pryor. 2005. *Archaeology and Environment of the Etton Landscape*. (East Anglian Archaeology 109.) Peterborough: Fenland Archaeological Trust.

French, C., M. Macklin & D. Passmore, 1992. Archaeology and palaeochannels in the Lower Welland and Nene valleys: alluvial archaeology at the fen-edge, eastern England, in *Alluvial Archaeology in Britain*, eds. S. Needham & M. Macklin. (Oxbow Monograph 27.) Oxford: Oxbow Books, 169–76.

Ford, S. 1991. An Early Bronze Age pit circle from Charnham Lane, Hungerford, Berkshire. *Proceedings of the Prehistoric Society* 57, 179–81.

Friedmand, J. & M. Rowlands. 1977. Notes towards and epigenetic model of the evolution of 'civilisation', in *The Evolution of Social Systems*, eds. J. Friedmand & M. Rowlands. London: Duckworth, 201–76.

Friendship-Taylor, D., 1997. Roman/Saxon Mongrels, part 2. *Archaeological Leather Group Newsletter* 5: 2.

Gale, R. & D. Cutler, 2000. *Plants in Archaeology*. Westbury & Kew: Royal Botanic Gardens.

Garner, D.J., 2007. *The Neolithic and Bronze Age Settlement at Oversley Farm, Styal, Cheshire: Excavations in Advance of Manchester Airport's Second Runway, 1997–8*. (Gifford Archaeological Monographs 1. British Archaeological Reports British Series 435.) Oxford: Hadrian Books/BAR.

Garrow, D., 2006. *Pits, Settlement and Deposition During the Neolithic and Early Bronze Age in East Anglia*. (British Archaeological Reports British Series 414.) Oxford: Hadrian Books/ BAR.

Garrow, D.,2007. Placing pits: landscape occupation and depositional practice during the Neolithic in East Anglia. *Proceedings of the Prehistoric Society* 73, 1–24.

Garrow, D., S. Lucy & D. Gibson, 2006. *Excavations at Kilverstone, Norfolk: an Episodic Landscape History*. (East Anglian Archaeology 113.) Cambridge: Cambridge Archaeological Unit.

Garwood, P., 1999. Grooved Ware in southern Britain, chronology and interpretation, in *Grooved Ware in Britain and Ireland*, eds. R. Cleal & A. MacSween. (Neolithic Studies Group Seminar Papers 3.) Oxford: Oxbow Books:

Gdaniec, K., 1996a. A miniature antler bow from a Middle Bronze Age site at Isleham, (Cambridgeshire), England. *Antiquity* 70, 652–7.

Gdaniec, K., 1996b. *Archaeological Investigations at Third Drove, Fengate, Peterborough, Cambridgeshire*. (CAU Report 169.) Cambridge: Cambridge Archaeological Unit.

Gdaniec, K., M. Edmonds & P. Wiltshire, 2008. *A Line across Land: Survey and Excavation on the Isleham-Ely Pipeline*. (East Anglia Archaeology 121.) Cambridge: Cambridge Archaeological Unit.

Geikie, J., 1877. *The Great Ice Age and its Relation to the Antiquity of Man.* London: Edward Stanford.

George, T.J., 1904. *An Archaeological Survey of Northants.* London: J.B. Nichols and Sons.

George, T.J., 1917. Early man in Northamptonshire, with particular reference to the Late Celtic Period as illustrated by Hunsbury Camp. *Northampton History Society and Field Club* 19, 18–19, 29–38.

Gibson, A.M., 1980. A re-interpretation of Chippenham Barrow 5, with a discussion of the Beaker Associated Pottery. *Proceedings of the Cambridge Antiquarian Society* 70, 47–60.

Gibson, A.M., 1982. *Beaker Domestic Sites: a Study of the Domestic Pottery of the Late Third and Early Second Millennia BC in the British Isles.* (British Archaeological Reports British Series 107.) Oxford: BAR.

Gibson, A.M. & I. Kinnes, 1997. On the urns of a dilemma: radiocarbon and the Peterborough problem. *Oxford Journal of Archaeology* 16, 65–72.

Gibson, A.M. & A. Woods, 1997. *Prehistoric Pottery for the Archaeologist.* 2nd edition. Leicester: University of Leicester.

Gibson, C. with J. Last, T. McDonald & J. Murray, 2004. *Lines in the Sand: Middle to Late Bronze Age Settlement at Game Farm, Downham Way, Brandon.* (East Anglian Archaeology Occasional Paper 19.) Hertford: Archaeological Solutions.

Gibson, D., 1998. *Archaeological Excavations at the Co-op Site Fengate.* (CAU Report 264.) Cambridge: Cambridge Archaeological Unit.

Gibson, D. & M. Knight, 2002. *Prehistoric and Roman Archaeology at Stonald Field, King's Dyke West, Whittlesey: Monuments and Settlement.* (CAU Report 498.) Cambridge: Cambridge Archaeological Unit.

Gibson, D. & M. Knight, 2006. *Bradley Fen Excavations 2001–2004, Whittlesey, Cambridgeshire.* (CAU Report 733.) Cambridge: Cambridge Archaeological Unit.

Gould, S.J., 2002. No science without fancy, no art without facts: the lepidoptery of Vladimir Nabokov, in *I Have Landed: the End of a Beginning in Natural History,* ed. S.J. Gould. New York (NY): Harmony Books, 29–53.

Grant, A., 1982. The use of tooth wear as a guide to the age of domestic animals, in *Ageing and Sexing Animal Bones from Archaeological Sites,* eds. B. Wilson, C. Grigson & S. Payne. (British Archaeological Reports, British Series 109.) Oxford: BAR, 91–108.

Greenfield, H.J., 1985. Bone consumption by pigs in a contemporary Serbian village: implications for the interpretation of prehistoric faunal assemblages. *Journal of Field Archaeology* 15, 473–9.

Greig, J.R.A., 1991. The British Isles, in *Progress in Old World Palaeoethnobiology,* eds. W. Van Zeist, K. Wasylikowa & K. Behre. Rotterdam: A.A. Balkema, 299–334.

Grimes, W.F., 1961. Settlements at Draughton, Colsterworth and Heathrow, in *Problems of the Iron Age in Southern Britain,* ed. S.S. Frere. London: Institute of Archaeology, 21–8.

Grove, R., 1981. Cressey Dymock and the draining of the fens: an early agricultural model. *Geographical Journal* 1473, 27–37.

Gurney, D.A., 1980. Evidence of Bronze Age salt-production at Northey, Peterborough. *Northamptonshire Archaeology* 15, 1–11.

Guttmann, E. & J. Last, 2000. A Late Bronze Age landscape at South Hornchurch, Essex. *Proceedings of the Prehistoric Society* 66, 319–59.

Hall, D., 1987. *The Fenland Project,* no. 2: *Cambridgeshire Survey, Peterborough to March.* (East Anglian Archaeology 35.) Cambridge: Cambridge Archaeological Committee with the Fenland Project Committee and Scole Archaeological Committee.

Hall, D., 1992. *The Fenland Project,* no. 6: *The South-Western Cambridgeshire Fenlands.* (East Anglian Archaeology 56.) Cambridge: Cambridge Archaeological Committee with the Fenland Project Committee and Scole Archaeological Committee.

Hall, D., 1996. *The Fenland Project,* no. 10: *Cambridgeshire Survey, The Isle of Ely and Wisbech.* (East Anglian Archaeology 79.) Cambridge: Cambridgeshire Archaeological Committee.

Hall, D. & J. Coles, 1994. *Fenland Survey: an Essay in Landscape Persistence.* London: English Heritage.

Hall, M., 1992. The prehistoric pottery, in *Reading Business Park: a Bronze Age Landscape,* by J. Moore & D. Jennings. (Thames Valley Landscapes Monograph 1.) Oxford: Oxford Archaeology.

Halstead, P., 1985. A study of mandibular teeth from Romano-British contexts at Maxey, in *The Fenland Project,* no. 1: *Archaeology and Environment in the Lower Welland Valley,* eds. F. Pryor & C. French. (East Anglia Archaeology 27.) Norwich: East Anglia Archaeology, 219–24.

Halstead, P., E. Cameron & S. Forbes, 2001. Non-human and human mammalian bone remains from the Flag Fen-platform and power station post alignment, in *The Flag Fen Basin: Archaeology and Environment of a Fenland Landscape,* by F. Pryor. Swindon: English Heritage, 330–50.

Halstead, P., P. Collins & V. Isaakido, 2002. Sorting the sheep from the goats: morphological distinctions between the mandibles and mandibular teeth of adult *Ovis* and *Capra. Journal of Archaeological Science* 29, 545–53.

Hambleton, E., 1999. *Animal Husbandry Regimes in Iron Age Britain: a Comparative Study of Faunal Assemblages from British Archaeological Sites.* (British Archaeological Reports British Series 282.) Oxford: BAR.

Harden, D.B., 1956. Edward Thurlow Leeds, 1899–1955, in *Dark-Age Britain: Studies Presented to E.T. Leeds with a Bibliography of his Works,* ed. D.B. Harden. London: Methuen, ix–xiv.

Harman, M., 1978. The animal bones, in *Excavations at Fengate, Peterborough, England: the Second Report,* by F. Pryor. (Royal Ontario Museum Archaeology Monograph 5.) Toronto: The Royal Ontario Museum: 177–80.

Harris, R.C. & J. Warkentin, 1974. *Canada Before Confederation.* Toronto: Oxford University Press.

Harsema, O., 2005. Farms amongst Celtic fields: settlements on the northern sands, in *The Prehistory of the Netherlands,* vol. 2, eds. L.P. Louwe Kooijmans,

P.W. van den Broeke, H. Fokkens & A.L. van Gijn. Amsterdam: Amsterdam University Press, 543–55.

Hawkes, C.F.C. & C.I. Fell, 1945. The Early Iron Age settlement at Fengate, Peterborough. *Antiquaries Journal* 100, 188–223.

Hayes, J.W., 1984. The Roman pottery from the Cat's Water subsite, in *Excavation at Fengate, Peterborough, England: the Fourth Report*, by F. Pryor. (Northamptonshire Archaeological Society Monograph 2/Royal Ontario Museum Archaeology Monograph 7.) Leicester: Northamptonshire Archaeological Society; Toronto: Royal Ontario Museum, 179–90.

Healy, F., 1988. *The Anglo-Saxon Cemetery at Spong Hill, North Elmham*, part VI: *Occupation during the Seventh to Second Millennia BC*. (East Anglian Archaeology 39.) Gressenhall: Norfolk Archaeological Unit, Norfolk Museums Service.

Healy, F., 1995. Lithics report, in *A Late Neolithic, Saxon and Medieval Site at Middle Harling, Norfolk*, by A. Rogerson. (East Anglian Archaeology Report 74.) London/Dereham: British Museum and Norfolk Museum Service, 32–46.

Healy, F., 1996. *The Fenland Project*, no. 11: *Wissey Embayment: Pre-Iron Age*. (East Anglian Archaeology 78.) Gressenhall: Fenland Project Committee and Field Archaeology Division, Norfolk Museums Service.

Healy, F., R.M.J. Cleal & I. Kinnes, 1993. Synthesis and discussion, in *Excavations on Redgate Hill, Hunstanton, Norfolk, and at Tattershall Thorpe, Lincolnshire*, eds. R. Bradley, P. Chowne, R.M.J. Cleal, F. Healy & I. Kinnes. (East Anglian Archaeology 57.) Dereham: Field Archaeology Division, Norfolk Museums Service, 70–77.

Healy, F. & J. Harding, 2007. A thousand and one things to do with a round barrow, in *Beyond the Grave: New Perspectives on Barrows*, ed. J. Last. Oxford: Oxbow Books, 53–71.

Helbaek, H., 1952. Early crops in southern England. *Proceedings of the Prehistoric Society* 18, 194–233.

Herle, A., M. Elliott & R. Empson. 2009. *Assembling Bodies: Art, Science and Imagination*. Cambridge: University of Cambridge, Museum of Archaeology and Anthropology.

Hey, G. & J. Muir, 1997. *Yarnton-Cassington Project: Yarnton Floodplain B 1996 Post-excavation Assessment*. Oxford: Oxford Archaeological Unit.

Hill, J.D. & L. Horne, 2003. Iron Age and Early Roman pottery, in *Power and Island Communities: Excavations at the Wardy Hill Ringwork, Coveney, Ely*, by C. Evans. (East Anglian Archaeology 103.) Cambridge: Cambridge Archaeological Unit, 145–84.

Hill, R., 1983. *The History of Wyman and Abbott*. Privately published pamphlet.

Hillier, R., 1981. *Clay that Burns: a History of the Fletton Brick Industry*. London: London Brick Company Ltd.

Hillman, G., 1981. Reconstructing crop husbandry practices from charred remains of crops, in *Farming Practice in British Prehistory*, ed. R. Mercer. Edinburgh: Edinburgh University Press, 123–61.

Hinman, M., 2001a. *Late Bronze Age and Iron Age Settlement and Earlier Prehistoric Activity at the Plant Breeding Institute, Hauxton Road, Cambridge, an Evaluation*. (Cambridgeshire County Council Archaeological Field Unit Report 190.) Cambridge: Cambridgeshire County Council Archaeological Field Unit.

Hinman, M., 2001b. Ritual activity at the foot of the Gog Magog Hills, Cambridge, in *Bronze Age Landscapes: Tradition and Transformation*, ed. J. Brück. Oxford: Oxbow Books, 33–40.

Hodder, I., 1982a. *Symbols in Action*. Cambridge: Cambridge University Press.

Hodder, I., 1982b. *Wendens Ambo: the Excavation of an Iron Age and Romano-British Settlement. The Archaeology of the M11*. (Passmore Edwards Museum Monograph Series 2.) London: Passmore Edwards Museum.

Hodder, I. (ed.), 1982c. *Symbolic and Structural Archaeology*. Cambridge: Cambridge University Press.

Hodder, I., 1989. Writing archaeology: site reports in context. *Antiquity* 63, 268–74.

Hodder, I., 1997. 'Always momentary, fluid and flexible': towards a reflexive excavation methodology. *Antiquity* 71, 690–700.

Hodder, I., 1999. *The Archaeological Process*. Oxford: Blackwell.

Hounsell, D., 2007. *Papworth Everard Bypass Project: Post-Excavation Assessment and Updated Project Design*. (Report 971.) Cambridge: CCC AFU.

Hudson, K., 1981. *A Social History of Archaeology*. London: Macmillan.

Hubbard, R.N.L.B. & A. al Azm, 1990. Quantifying preservation and distortion in carbonised seeds; and investigating the history of Friké production. *Journal of Archaeological Science* 17, 103–6.

Hummler, M., 2005. Before Sutton Hoo: the prehistoric settlement (*c.* 3000 BC to *c.* AD 550), in *Sutton Hoo: a Seventh-century Princely Burial Ground and its Context*, by M. Carver. London: British Museum, 391–4.

Hunn, J., n.d. Excavations on a Multi-period Landscape at Rectory Farm. West Deeping. Unpublished manuscript text.

Hunn, J. & R. Palmer, 1993. The Block Fen fieldsystem: 1992 investigations. *Fenland Research* 8, 10–13.

Hutton, J., 2008. *Excavations at Langtoft, Lincolnshire: the Glebe Land*. (CAU Report 837.) Cambridge: Cambridge Archaeological Unit.

Ingold, T., 1980. *Hunters, Pastoralists and Ranchers*. Cambridge: Cambridge University Press.

Jackson, D.J. & R.F. Tylecote, 1988. Two new Romano-British iron-working sites in Northamptonshire — a new type of furnace. *Britannia* 19, 275–98.

Jackson, R., 1990. *Camerton: the Late Iron Age and Early Roman Metalwork*. London: British Museum.

Jackson, R.P.J. & T.W. Potter, 1996. *Excavations at Stonea, Cambridgeshire 1980–85*. London: British Museum Press.

Johnson, K & S.L. Coates, 1999. *Nabokov's Blues: the Scientific Odyssey of a Literary Genius*. Cambridge (MA): Zoland Books.

Johnston, R., 1998. The paradox of landscape. *European Journal of Archaeology* 1, 313–25.

Johnston, R., 2001. 'Breaking new ground': land tenure and fieldstone clearance during the Bronze Age, in *Bronze*

Age Landscapes: Tradition and Transformation, ed, J Brück. Oxford: Oxbow Books, 99–109.

Johnston, R., 2005. Pattern without a plan: rethinking the Bronze Age coaxial fieldsystem on Dartmoor, south-west England. *Oxford Journal of Archaeology* 24, 1–21.

Jones, A., 2002. *Archaeological Theory and Scientific Practice* (Topics in Contemporary Archaeology.) Cambridge: Cambridge University Press.

Jones, M. & D. Bond, 1980. Late Bronze Age settlement at Mucking, Essex, in *Settlement and Society in the British Late Bronze Age*, eds. J. Barrett & R. Bradley. (British Archaeological Reports British Series 83.) Oxford: BAR, 471–82.

Jones, S., 1997. *The Archaeology of Ethnicity: Constructing Identities in the Past and Present*. London: Routledge.

Kapuscinski, R., 2007. *Travels with Herodotus*. London: Allen Lane.

Keepax, C. & M. Robson, 1978. Conservation and associated examination of a Roman chest: evidence for woodworking techniques. *Conservator* 2, 35–40.

King, A.C., 1978. A comparative survey of bone assemblages from Roman sites in Britain. *Bulletin of the Institute of Archaeology, London* 15, 207–32.

King, A.C., 1991. Food production and consumption-meat, in *Britain in the Roman Period: Recent Trends*, ed. R.F.J. Jones. Sheffield: University of Sheffield/J.R. Collis Publications, 15–20.

Kinnes, I., 1992. *Non-Megalithic Long Barrows and Allied Structures in the British Neolithic*. (British Museum Occasional Paper 52.) London: British Museum.

Kinnes, I., 1993. 'The role of the Site 11 enclosure', in Excavations at Site 11, Fengate, Peterborough, 1969, by F. Pryor, in *The Fenland Project, no. 7: Excavations in Peterborough and the Lower Welland Valley 1960–1969*, eds. W.G. Simpson, D.A. Gurney, J. Neve & F. Pryor. (East Anglian Archaeology 61.) Peterborough: Fenland Archaeological Trust, 138.

Kirk, T. & G. Williams, 2000. Glany Cross: a later prehistoric monumental complex in Carmarthenshire, Wales. *Proceedings of the Prehistoric Society* 66, 257–95.

Kitchen, W., 2001. Tenure and territoriality in the British Bronze Age: a question of varying social and geographic scale?, in *Bronze Age Landscapes: Tradition and Transformation*, ed. J. Brück. Oxford: Oxbow Books, 110–20.

Knight, D., 2002. A regional ceramic sequence: pottery of the first millennium BC between the Humber and the Nene, in *Prehistoric Britain: the Ceramic Basis*, eds. A. Woodward & J.D. Hill. Oxford: Oxbow Books, 119–42.

Knight, D. & A. Howard, 2004. The later Bronze and Iron Ages: towards an enclosed landscape, in *Trent Valley Landscapes*, eds. D. Knight & A.J. Howard. King's Lynn: Heritage Marketing & Publications Ltd.

Knight, M., 1999. *Prehistoric Excavations at King's Dyke West Whittlesey, Cambridgeshire*. (CAU Report 301.) Cambridge: Cambridge Archaeological Unit.

Knight, M., 2000. Henge to house — Post-circles in a Neolithic and Bronze Age landscape at King's Dyke West, Whittlesey, Cambridgeshire. *Past* 34, 3–4.

Knight, M., 2002. *Excavation at the New Prison Site, the former Rockwell and APV Works, Westfield Road, Peterborough*. (CAU Report 471.) Cambridge: Cambridge Archaeological Unit.

Knight, M. & A. Cooper, 2004. *Land North of Broom Grange, near Biggleswade, Bedfordshire; an Archaeological Evaluation*. (CAU Report 595.) Cambridge: Cambridge Archaeological Unit.

Knight, M. & D. Gibson, 2006. *Excavations at Bradley Fen, Whittlesey*. (CAU Report 733.) Cambridge: Cambridge Archaeological Unit.

Knight, M & D. Gibson, in prep. *Process and Pattern: Excavations at Bradley Fen, Whittlesey*.

Knight, M. & C. Swaysland, 2003. *Fengate Sewage Treatment Works, Peterborough: Auger Survey*. (CAU Report 573.) Cambridge: Cambridge Archaeological Unit.

Law, R., 2008. The Development and Perpetuation of a Ceramic Tradition: the Significance of Collared Urns in Early Bronze Age Social Life. Unpublished PhD dissertation, University of Cambridge.

Leeds, E.T., 1910. Communication on objects from a Bronze Age tumulus at Eyebury, near Peterborough. *Proceedings of the Society Antiquaries of London* 23, 283.

Leeds, E.T., 1912. Excavation of a round barrow at Eyebury, near Peterborough. *Proceedings of the Society of Antiquaries of London* 24, 80–94.

Leeds, E.T., 1913. *Archaeology of the Anglo-Saxon Settlement*. Oxford: Oxford University Press.

Leeds, E.T., 1915. Further excavations in round barrows near Eyebury, Peterborough. *Proceedings of the Society of Antiquaries of London* 27, 116–55.

Leeds, E.T., 1922. Further discoveries of the Neolithic and Bronze Ages at Peterborough. *The Antiquaries Journal* 2, 220–37.

Leeds, E.T., 1923. A Saxon village at Sutton Courtney, Berkshire. *Archaeologia* 73, 47–192.

Leeds, E.T., 1927. A Neolithic site at Abingdon, Berks. *Antiquaries Journal* 7, 438–64.

Leeds, E.T., 1956. *The Leeds Collection of Fossil Reptiles from the Oxford Clay of the Peterborough*. Oxford: Basil Blackwell.

Legge, A.J., 1981. The agricultural economy, in *Grimes Graves, Norfolk: Excavations 1971–72*, ed. R. Mercer. London: HMSO, 79–103.

Legge, A.J., 1992. *Excavations at Grimes Graves, Norfolk, 1972–1976, fasc. 4: Animals, Environment and the Bronze Age Economy*. London: Trustees of the British Museum, British Museum Press.

Levine, P., 1986. *The Amateur and the Professional: Antiquarians, Historians and Archaeologists in Victorian England, 1838–1886*. Cambridge: Cambridge University Press.

Lewis, H.A., 1998. The Characterisation and Interpretation of Ancient Tillage Practices through Soil Micromorphology: a Methodological Study. Unpublished PhD, University of Cambridge.

Liddle, P., 1982. *Leicestershire Archaeology: the Present State of Knowledge*, vol. 1. *To the End of the Roman Period*. (Leicester Museums, Art Galleries and Records Service Report 4.) Leicester: Leicester Museum.

Longley, D. & S. Needham, 1980. *Runnymede Bridge 1976: Excavations on the Site of a Late Bronze Age Settlement.* (Surrey Archaeological Research 6.) Guildford: Surrey Archaeological Society.

Longworth, I.H., 1984. *Collared Urns of the Bronze Age in Great Britain and Ireland.* Cambridge: Cambridge University Press.

Longworth, I.H., A. Ellison & V. Rigby, 1988. *Excavations at Grimes Graves, Norfolk, 1972–76: The Neolithic, Bronze Age and Later Pottery.* London: British Museum.

Longworth, I.H., G.J. Wainwright & K.E. Wilson, 1971. The Grooved Ware site at Lion Point, Clacton. *Prehistoric and Roman Studies* 1971, 93–124.

Lovejoy, C.O., R.S. Meindl, T.R. Pryzbeck & R.P. Mensforth, 1985. Chronological metamorphosis of the auricular surface of the ilium: a new method for the determination of age at death. *American Journal of Physical Anthropology* 68, 15–28.

Lucas, G., 1997. *An Archaeological Evaluation at the Tower Works, Fengate, Peterborough.* (CAU Report 206.) Cambridge: Cambridge Archaeological Unit.

Lucas, G., 2001a. *Vicar's Farm, Cambridge Post Excavation Assessment Report,* vols. 1 & 2. (CAU Report 425.) Cambridge: Cambridge Archaeological Unit.

Lucas, G., 2001b. *Critical Approaches to Fieldwork: Contemporary and Historical Archaeological Practice.* London: Routledge.

Lucy, S., J. Tipper & A. Dickens, 2009. *The Anglo-Saxon Settlement and Cemetery at Bloodmoor Hill, Carlton Coville, Suffolk.* (East Anglian Archaeology 131.) Cambridge: Cambridge Archaeological Unit.

Lynch, A.H., J. Hamilton & R.E.M. Hedges, 2008. Where the wild things are: aurochs and cattle in England. *Antiquity* 82, 1025–39.

Mackay, D., 2006a. *Archaeological Evaluation at the Darlow Depot Site, Fengate, Peterborough.* (CAU Report 723.) Cambridge: Cambridge Archaeological Unit.

Mackay, D., 2006b. *Archaeological Evaluation and Test Pits at the Darlow Depot Site, Fengate, Peterborough.* (CAU Report 751.) Cambridge: Cambridge Archaeological Unit.

Mackay, D. & M. Knight, 2007. *Further Archaeological Excavations at Striplands Farm, West Longstanton, Cambridgeshire.* (CAU Report 764.) Cambridge: Cambridge Archaeological Unit.

Mackreth, D.F., 1996. *Orton Hall Farm: a Roman and Early Anglo-Saxon Farmstead.* (East Anglian Archaeology 76.) Manchester: Nene Valley Archaeological Trust.

Mackreth, D.F., 2001. *Monument 97, Orton Longueville, Cambridgeshire: a Late Pre-Roman Iron Age and Early Roman Farmstead.* (East Anglian Archaeology 97.) Manchester: Nene Valley Archaeological Trust.

Macphail, R.I. & M.A. Courty, 1985. Interpretation and significance of urban deposits. *Proceedings of the Third Nordic Conference on the Application of Scientific Methods,* 71–83.

Macphail, R.I, J.C.C. Romans & L. Robertson, 1987. The application of soil micromorphology to the understanding of Holocene soil development in the British Isles, with special reference to early cultivation, in *Soil Micromorphology,* eds. N. Fedoroff, L.M. Bresson & M.-A. Courty. Plaisir: L'Association Française pour l'Étude du Sol, 647–56.

Mahany, C., 1969. Fengate. *Current Archaeology* 17, 156–7.

Malim, T., 2001. Place and space in the Cambridgeshire Bronze Age, in *Bronze Age Landscapes: Tradition and Transformation,* ed. J. Brück. Oxford: Oxbow Books, 9–22.

Malim, T. & I. Panter, 2008. Protection of waterlogged sites: by whom, for whom? *The Archaeologist* 70, 36–7.

Maltby, M., 1979. *Faunal Studies on Urban Sites: the Animal Bones from Exeter, 1971–5.* (Exeter Archaeology Report 2.) Sheffield: Department of Prehistory and Archaeology, University of Sheffield.

Maltby, M., 1985. Assessing variations in Iron Age and Roman butchery practices: the need for quantification, in *Palaeobiological Investigations: Research Design, Methods and Data Analysis,* eds. N.J.R. Fieller, D.D. Gilbertson & N.G.A. Ralph. (British Archaeological Reports International Series 266.) Oxford: BAR, 19–32.

Manning, W.H., 1985. *Catalogue of the Romano-British Iron Tools, Fittings and Weapons in the British Museum.* London: British Museum.

Martin, E. & P. Murphy, 1988. West Row Fen, Suffolk: a Bronze Age fen-edge settlement site. *Antiquity* 62, 353–8.

Martin, E., 1993. *Settlements on Hill-tops: Seven Prehistoric Sites in Suffolk.* (East Anglian Archaeology 65.) Ipswich: Suffolk County Planning Department.

McFayden, L., 2000. *Excavations at Eye Quarry, Peterborough. Phase II.* (CAU Report 355.) Cambridge: Cambridge Archaeological Unit.

Mettler, J.J., 1985. *Basic Butchering of Livestock and Game.* Vermont: Storey Books.

Middleton, R., 1990. The Walker Collection: a quantitative analysis of lithic material from the March/Manea area of the Cambridgeshire Fens. *Proceedings of the Cambridge Antiquarian Society* 79, 13–38.

Miller, S.H. & S.B.J. Skertchley, 1878. *The Fenland Past and Present.* Wisbech: Leach and Son.

Moore, W.R.G., 1980. Northampton Museum and T.J. George. *Northamptonshire History News* 45, 14–17.

Morris, E., 2004. Later prehistoric pottery, in *Green Park (Reading Business Park): Phase 2 Excavations 1995 — Neolithic and Bronze Age Sites,* by A. Brossler, R. Early & C. Allen. (Thames Valley Landscapes Monograph 19.) Oxford: Oxford Archaeology, 58–91.

Morris, E. & C. Gingell, 2000. Pottery, in *Potterne 1982–5: Animal Husbandry in Later Prehistoric Wiltshire,* ed. A. Lawson. (Report 17.) Salisbury: Wessex Archaeology.

Mortimer, J.R., 1905. *Forty Years' Researches in British and Saxon Burial Mounds of East Yorkshire.* London: A. Brown and Sons.

Moss, W., 1978. Sites, Circuits and Benders: Networks and Networking on British Archaeological Sites. Unpublished BA Course Paper, University of Waterloo, Canada.

Mould, Q., 1996. The Leather from Rectory Farm, West Deeping. Unpublished manuscript.

Mudd, A., 2001. *Archaeological Excavation on Land at Barnack UK Ltd, Newark Road, Peterborough.* Northampton: Northamptonshire Archaeology.

Mudd, A. & T. Upson-Smith, 2006. Middle Iron Age and Late Iron Age/Early Roman enclosures at the former sports ground, Alma Road, Peterborough. *Northants Archaeology* 34, 19–32.

Murphy, C.P., 1986. *Thin Section Preparation of Soils and Sediments.* Berkhamsted: AB Academic.

Murphy, J. & J.P. Riley, 1962. A modified single solution method for the determination of phosphate in natural waters. *Analytica Chimica Acta* 27, 31–6.

Murray, T. & C. Evans, 2008. Introduction: writing histories of archaeology, in *Histories of Archaeology: a Reader in the History of Archaeology*, eds. T. Murray & C. Evans. Oxford: Oxford University Press, 1–12.

Needham, S., 1996. Post Deverel-Rimbury pottery, in *Excavations at Stonea, Cambridgeshire, 1980–85,* by R.P.J. Jackson & T.W. Potter. London: British Museum Press, 245–57.

Needham, S. & T. Spence, 1996. *Refuse and Disposal at Runnymede Bridge Area 16.* (Runnymede Bridge Research Excavations 2.) London: British Museum Press.

Nicholson, K. *et al.*, forthcoming. Above the Fen-edge: Late Bronze Age to Early Iron Age and Early Romano-British Activity on Land off Broadlands, Peterborough. Unpublished paper.

Northants Archaeology, 1999. *Archaeological Excavation on Land off Vicarage Farm Road, Peterborough, Cambridgeshire.* Northamptonshire Archaeology: Northamptonshire County Council.

Northants Archaeology, 2001. *Archaeological Evaluation on Land at Barnack UK Limited, Newark Road, Peterborough.* Northamptonshire Archaeology: Northamptonshire County Council.

O'Connell, M., 1986. *Petters Sports Field Egham. Excavation of a Late Bronze Age/Early Iron Age Site, Guildford.* (Surrey Archaeological Society Research 10.) Guildford: Surrey Archaeological Society.

O'Connor, T.P., 1988. *Bones from the General Accident Site, Tanner Row [York].* (The Archaeology of York 15/2.) York: York Archaeological Trust.

Ostrom, E., 1990. *Governing the Commons: the Evolution of Institutions for Collective Action.* Cambridge: Cambridge University Press.

Parker Pearson, M. & C. Richards, 1994. Architecture and order: spatial representation and archaeology, in *Architecture and Order: Approaches to Social Space*, eds. M. Parker Pearson & C. Richards. London: Routledge, 38–72.

Parker Pearson, M., R. Cleal, P. Marshall, *et al.*, 2007. The age of Stonehenge. *Antiquity* 81, 617–39.

Patten, R., 2002. *An Archaeological Excavation at Tanholt Farm, Eybury Quarry, Eye, Peterborough, Phase 1.* (CAU Report 464.) Cambridge: Cambridge Archaeological Unit.

Patten, R., 2003. *Excavation at Eye Quarry: Prehistoric and Roman Fieldsystems, Tanholt Farm, Peterborough, Phase II.* (CAU Report 545.) Cambridge: Cambridge Archaeological Unit.

Patten, R., 2004. *Bronze Age and Romano-British Activity at Eye Quarry, Peterborough, Phase 3.* (CAU Report 633.) Cambridge: Cambridge Archaeological Unit.

Patten, R., 2009. *Excavations at Eye Quarry: the Southern Extension.* (CAU Report 869.) Cambridge: Cambridge Archaeological Unit.

Patten, R. & C. Evans, 2005. *Striplands Farm, West Longstanton, Cambridgeshire: an Archaeological Excavation.* (CAU Report 703.) Cambridge: Cambridge Archaeological Unit.

Payne, S., 1973. Kill-off patterns in sheep and goats: the mandibles from Asvan Kale. *Anatolian Studies* 23, 281–303.

Payne, S., 1985. Morphological distinction between the mandibular teeth of young sheep *Ovis* and goats *Capra*. *Journal of Archaeological Science* 12, 139–47.

Payne, S. & G. Bull, 1988. Components of variation in measurements of pig bones and teeth, and the use of measurements to distinguish wild from domestic remains. *Archaeozoologica* 2, 27–66.

Pendleton, C. & A. Gibson, forthcoming. *An Excavated Beaker Assemblage, including a Bronze Flat Axe, from Worlingham, Suffolk.*

Phoenix Consulting, 2003. *Report on a Programme of Archaeological Watching Brief and Excavation.* Phoenix Consulting documents for Aggregate Industries (UK) Ltd.

Phillips, C.W., 1970. *The Fenland in Roman Times: Studies of a Major Area of Peasant Colonization, with a Gazetteer Covering All Known Sites and Finds.* (Royal Geographical Society Research Series 5.) London: Royal Geographical Society.

Pitt Rivers, Lt-Gen. A.H.L.F., 1898. *Excavations in Cranborne Chase* (IV). Privately printed.

Pollard, J., 1996. Iron Age riverside pit alignments at St. Ives, Cambridgeshire. *Proceedings of the Prehistoric Society* 62, 93–115.

Pollard, J., 1998a. The prehistoric pottery, in *Archaeological Excavations at the Co-op Site Fengate*, by D. Gibson, (CAU Report 264.) Cambridge: Cambridge Archaeological Unit, 20–22.

Pollard, J., 1998b. *Excavations at Over: Late Neolithic Occupation (Sites 3 & 4).* (CAU Report 281.) Cambridge: Cambridge Archaeological Unit.

Pollard, J., 1999. 'These places have their moments': thoughts on settlement practices in the British Neolithic, in *Making Places in the Prehistoric World: Themes in Settlement Archaeology*, eds. J. Brück & M. Goodman. London: UCL Press, 76–93.

Pollard, J., 2001. Aesthetics of depositional practice in archaeology and aesthetics. *World Archaeology* 33, 315–33.

Pollard, J., 2006. Pottery, in *Marshland Communities and Cultural Landscapes from the Bronze Age to the Present Day* (The Haddenham Project vol, II), by C. Evans & I. Hodder. (McDonald Institute Monographs.) Cambridge: McDonald Institute for Archaeological Research, 35.

Pryor, F., 1974a. *Excavations at Fengate, Peterborough, England: the First Report.* (Royal Ontario Museum Archaeological Monograph 3.) Toronto: Royal Ontario Museum.

Pryor, F., 1974b. *Earthmoving on Open Archaeological Sites.* (Archaeological Handbook 1.) Peterborough: Nene Valley Research Committee.

Pryor, F., 1976. Fen-edge land management in the Bronze Age: an interim report on excavations at Fengate, Peterborough 1971–4, in *Settlement and Economy in the Third and Second Millennia BC*, eds. C.B. Burgess & R. Miket. (British Archaeological Reports 33.) Oxford: BAR, 29–49.

Pryor, F., 1978. *Excavation at Fengate, Peterborough, England: the Second Report.* (Royal Ontario Museum Archaeological Monograph 5.) Toronto: Royal Ontario Museum.

Pryor, F., 1980a. *Excavation at Fengate, Peterborough, England: the Third Report.* (Royal Ontario Museum Monograph 6/Northants Archaeological Monograph 1.) Northampton & Toronto: Royal Ontario Museum, Northants Archaeological Society.

Pryor, F., 1980b. Survey excavation. *Rescue News* 21, 6.

Pryor, F., 1980c. Will it all come out in the wash? Reflections at the end of eight years' digging, in *The British Later Bronze Age*, eds. J. Barrett & R. Bradley. (British Archaeological Reports 83.) Oxford: BAR, 483–500.

Pryor, F., 1984. *Excavation at Fengate, Peterborough, England: the Fourth Report.* (Royal Ontario Museum Monograph 7/Northants Archaeological Monograph 2.) Northampton & Toronto: Royal Ontario Museum, Northants Archaeological Society.

Pryor, F., 1987. Etton 1986: Neolithic metamorphoses. *Antiquity* 61, 78–80.

Pryor, F., 1988. Earlier Neolithic landscapes and ceremonial in lowland Britain, in *The Archaeology of Context in the Neolithic and Bronze Age: Recent Trends*, eds. J. Barrett & I.A. Kinnes. Sheffield: University of Sheffield Department of Archaeology & Prehistory, 63–72.

Pryor, F. 1991. *The English Heritage Book of Flag Fen: Prehistoric Fenland Centre.* London: Batsford.

Pryor, F., 1992. Current research at Flag Fen, Peterborough. *Antiquity* 66, 439–57.

Pryor, F., 1993. Excavations at Site 11, Fengate, Peterborough, 1969, in *The Fenland Project, no. 7: Excavations in Peterborough and the Lower Welland Valley 1960–1969*, eds. W.G. Simpson, D.A. Gurney, J. Neve & F. Pryor. (East Anglian Archaeology 61.) Peterborough: Fenland Archaeological Trust, 127–40.

Pryor, F., 1996. Sheep, stockyards and field systems: Bronze Age livestock populations in the Fenlands of eastern England. *Antiquity* 70, 331–24.

Pryor, F., 1997. *Peterborough East: a Guide to Curation in an Area of Outstanding Archaeological Importance.* Peterborough: Fenland Archaeological Trust for English Heritage.

Pryor, F., 1998a. *Etton: Excavations at a Neolithic Causewayed Enclosure near Maxey Cambridgeshire, 1982–87.* (Archaeological Report 18.) London: English Heritage.

Pryor, F., 1998b. Welland Bank Quarry, South Lincolnshire. *Current Archaeology* 160, 139–45.

Pryor, F., 1998c. *Farmers in Prehistoric Britain.* Stroud: Tempus.

Pryor, F., 2001a. *The Flag Fen Basin: Archaeology and Environment of a Fenland Landscape.* Swindon: English Heritage.

Pryor, F., 2001b. *A Report on Archaeological Excavations at Boroughby Garage Ltd, Storey's Bar Road.* Peterborough: Soke Archaeological Services.

Pryor, F., 2002. The Welland Valley as a cultural boundary zone: an example of long-term history, in *Through Wet and Dry: Proceedings of a Conference in Honour of David Hall*, eds. T. Lane & J. Coles. (Lincolnshire Archaeology and Heritage Reports Series 5; WARP Occasional Paper 17.) Sleaford: Heritage Trust for Lincolnshire, 18–32.

Pryor, F., 2003. *Britain B.C.* London: Harper Collins.

Pryor, F. (ed.), forthcoming a. *Excavations at Flag Fen, Peterborough, 1995–2006.* Oxford: Oxbow Books.

Pryor, F., forthcoming b. *The Making of the British Landscape.* London: Penguin Books.

Pryor, F. with R.M.J. Cleal & I. Kinnes, 1998. Discussion of Neolithic and earlier Bronze Age pottery, in *Etton: Excavations at a Neolithic Causewayed Enclosure near Maxey Cambridgeshire, 1982–87*, by F. Pryor. London: English Heritage, 209–13.

Pryor, F. & C.A.I. French, 1985. *Archaeology and Environment in the Lower Welland Valley* (Fenland Project no. 1; East Anglian Archaeology 27.) Cambridge: Fenland Project Committee and Cambridgeshire Archaeological Committee.

Pryor, F., M. Taylor & D. Britchfield, 2001. *Archaeological Investigations in Advance of Works Associated with the Green Wheel Cycleway at Flag Fen and Northey. Peterborough (1998–2001).* (Soke Archaeological Services Report SAS01/30.) Peterborough: Soke Archaeological Services.

Pryor, F. & D. Trimble, 1999. *An Archaeological Evaluation at the Premises for Designation Ltd, Newark Road, Fengate Peterborough.* (Soke Archaeological Services Report 99/1.) Peterborough: Soke Archaeological Services.

Pryor, F. & D. Trimble, 2000. *Archaeological Evaluation and Excavation at TK Packaging Ltd., Fengate, Peterborough, 1999.* Peterborough: Soke Archaeological Services and Archaeological Project Services.

Rackham, D.J., 1999. Animal bone, in *TK Packaging Plant, Peterborough TPP99 Environmental Archaeology Report*, by D.J. Rackham, R. Gale, J.A. Giorgi & R.G. Scaife. The Environmental Archaeology Consultancy.

Renfrew, C. (ed.), 1974. *British Prehistory: a New Outline.* London: Duckworth.

Richards, C., 1995. Knowing about the past, in *Interpreting Archaeology: Finding Meaning in the Past*, eds. I. Hodder, M. Shanks, A. Alexandri, *et al.* London: Routledge, 216–19.

Richards, C. & J. Thomas, 1984. Ritual activity and structured deposition in Later Neolithic Wessex, in *Neolithic Studies: a Review of Some Current Research*, eds. R. Bradley & J. Gardiner. (British Archaeological Reports British Series 133.) Oxford: BAR, 189–218.

Rippon, S., 2000. The Romano-British exploitation of coastal wetlands: survey and excavation on the North Somerset Levels, 1993–7. *Britannia* 31, 69–200.

Rowley-Conwy, P., 2007. *From Genesis to Prehistory.* Oxford: Oxford University Press.

Royal Commission on Historical Monuments (RCHM), 1969. *Peterborough New Town: a Survey of the Antiquities in the*

Area of Development. London: Royal Commission on Historical Monuments.

Scaife, R.G., 1992. Flag Fen: the vegetation environment. *Antiquity* 66, 462–6.

Scaife, R.G., 1999. Pollen analysis, in *TK Packaging Plant, Peterborough TPP99 Environmental Archaeology Report*, by D.J. Rackham, R. Gale, J.A. Giorgi & R.G. Scaife. The Environmental Archaeology Consultancy.

Scaife, R.G., 2001 Flag Fen: the vegetation and environment in *The Flag Fen Basin: Archaeology and Environment of a Fenland Landscape*, by F. Pryor. Swindon: English Heritage, 351–81.

Schiffer, M.B., 1976. *Behavioural Archaeology*. New York (NY): Academic Press.

Schmid, E., 1972. *Atlas of Animal Bones*. Amsterdam: Elsevier.

Serjeantson, D., 1991. 'Rid Grasse of Bones': a taphonomic study of the bones from midden deposits at the Neolithic and Bronze Age site of Runnymede, Surrey, England. *International Journal of Osteoarchaeology* 1, 73–89.

Serjeantson, D., 1996. The animal bones, in *Refuse and Disposal at Area 16 East Runnymede. Runnymede Bridge Research Excavations*, vol. 2, by S. Needham & T. Spence. London: British Museum.

Serjeantson, D., 2006. Animal remains, in *Marshland Communities and Cultural Landscape* (The Haddenham Project vol. II), by C. Evans & I. Hodder. (McDonald Institute Monographs.) Cambridge: McDonald Institute for Archaeological Research, 213–45.

Serjeantson, D., 2007. Intensification of animal husbandry in the Late Bronze Age? The contribution of sheep and pigs, in *The Earlier Iron Age in Britain and the Near Continent*, eds. C. Haselgrove & R. Pope. Oxford: Oxbow Books, 80–93.

Serneels, V. & P. Crew, 1997. Ore-slag relationships from experimentally smelted bog-iron ore, in *Early Ironworking in Europe: Archaeology and Experiment. Abstracts of International Conference, September 1997*, eds. P. Crew & S. Crew. (Occasional Paper 3.) Plas Tan y Bwlch: Maentwrog, 78–82.

Seymour, W.A. (ed.), 1980. *A History of the Ordnance Survey*. Folkestone: Dawson.

Sharpe, K.E., 2007. The Lady of the Lakes: Clare Isobel Fell and the role of local societies or women in archaeology, in *Studies in Northern Prehistory: Essays in Memory of Clare Fell*, ed. P. Cherry. (Cumberland and Westmorland Antiquarian and Archaeological Society Extra Series 33.) Kendal: Titus Wilson & Son, 1–23.

Silver, I.A., 1969. The ageing of domestic animals, in *Science in Archaeology*, eds. D. Brothwell & E.S. Higgs. 2nd edition. London: Thames and Hudson, 283–301.

Silvester, R.J., 1991. *Fenland Project, no. 4: The Wissey Embayment and the Fen Causeway, Norfolk*. (East Anglian Archaeology 52.) Gressenhall: Norfolk Archaeological Unit.

Simpson, W.G., D.A. Gurney, J. Neve & F. Pryor, 1993. *The Fenland Project, no. 7: Excavations in Peterborough and the Lower Welland Valley 1960–1969*. (East Anglian Archaeology 61.) Peterborough: Fenland Archaeological Trust.

Skertchley, S.B.J., 1877. *The Geology of the Fenlands*. (Memoirs of the Geological Society of the United Kingdom.) London: H.M.S.O.

Smith, I.F., 1956. The Decorative Art of Neolithic Ceramics in South East England and its Relations. Unpublished PhD thesis, Institute of Archaeology, London.

Smith, M.A., 1959. Some Somerset hoards and their place in the Bronze Age of southern Britain. *Proceedings of the Prehistoric Society* 25, 144–87.

Smith, P.J., 1997. Grahame Clark's new archaeology: the Fenland Research Committee and Cambridge prehistory in the 1930s. *Antiquity* 71, 11–30.

Spence, C., 1990. *Archaeological Site Manual*. London: Museum of London.

Stace, C., 1997. *New Flora of the British Isles*. Cambridge: Cambridge University Press.

Stocking, G.W. Jr, 1987. *Victorian Anthropology*. London: Collier Macmillan.

Stone, S., 1857. Account of certain (supposed) British and Saxon remains. *Proceedings of the Society of Antiquaries of London* 1st series, 4 (1856–9), 92–100.

Stoops, G., 2003. *Guidelines for Analysis and Description of Soil and Regolith Thin Sections*. Madison (WI): Soil Science Society of America.

Stuiver M., P.J. Reimer, E. Bard, *et al.* 1998 INTCAL98 radiocarbon age calibration, 24000–0 cal BP. *Radiocarbon* 40, 1041–83.

Taylor, E. & J. Aaronson, 2006. *Archaeological Trial Trench Evaluation at Stanground South, Peterborough, Cambridgeshire, September–December 2005*. (Northamptonshire Archaeology Report No 06/35.) Northampton: Northamptonshire Archaeology.

Taylor, J., 1997. Space and place: some thoughts on Iron Age and Romano-British landscapes, in *Reconstructing Iron Age Societies*, eds. A. Gwilt & C. Haselgrove. (Oxbow Monograph 71.) Oxford: Oxbow Books, 192–204.

Taylor, M., 1996. 'Worked wood', in Iron Age riverside pit alignments at St. Ives, Cambridgeshire, by J. Pollard. *Proceedings of the Prehistoric Society* 62, 93–115.

Taylor, M., 2001. The wood, in *The Flag Fen Basin: Archaeology and Environment of a Fenland Landscape*, by F. Pryor. Swindon: English Heritage, 167–228.

Thomas, J., 1991. *Rethinking the Neolithic*. Cambridge: Cambridge University Press.

Tilley, C., 1989. Excavation as theatre. *Antiquity* 63, 275–80.

Timby, J., R. Brown, E. Biddulph, A. Hardy & A. Powell, 2007. *A Slice of Rural Essex: Archaeological Discoveries from the A120 between Stansted Airport and Braintree*. (Oxford Wessex Archaeology Monograph 1.) Oxford and Salisbury: Oxford Wessex Archaeology.

Toller, H.S., 1980. Orsett Cock. *Britannia* 11, 35–42.

Trotter, M. & G.C. Gleser, 1958. A re-evaluation of estimation of stature based on measurements of stature taken during life and of long bones after death. *American Journal of Physical Anthropology* 10, 463–514.

Tyers, P., 1996. *Roman Pottery in Britain*. London: Batsford.

Tylecote, R.F., 1986. *The Prehistory of Metallurgy in the British Isles*. London: Institute of Metals.

Ubelaker, D.H., 1989. *Human Skeletal Remains: Excavation, Analysis, and Interpretation*. Washington (DC): Taraxacum Press.

Urry, J., 1984. Englishmen, Celts and Iberians: the ethnographic survey of the United Kingdom 1892–1899, in *Functionalism Historicized: Essays on British Social Anthropology,* ed. G.W. Stocking. (History of Anthropology 2.) Madison (WI): University of Wisconsin Press, 83–105.

Van de Noort, R., S. Ellis, M. Taylor & D. Weir, 1995. Preservation of archeological sites, in *Wetland Heritage of Holderness – an Archaeological Survey*, eds. R. Van de Noort & S. Ellis. Hull: University of Hull, 341–56.

Vaughan, T. & J. Last, 1999. *Land off the Broadlands, Peterborough: an Archaeological Excavation*. (Hertfordshire Archaeological Trust Report 334/1.) Hertford: Hertfordshire Archaeological Trust.

Vaughan, T. & M. Trevarthen, 1998. *Land off Vicarage Farm Road, Peterborough, Cambridgeshire: Archaeological Evaluation*. (Hertfordshire Archaeological Trust, Report 322.) Hertford: Hertfordshire Archaeological Trust.

Vince, A., 2003. The Later Iron Age and Roman pottery, in *A Late Iron Age and Romano-British Site at Haddon, Peterborough*, by M. Hinman. (British Archaeological Reports British Series 358.) Oxford: Archaeopress: 73–5.

Wade-Martins, P., 1980. *Excavations in North Elmham Park, 1967–1972. Norfolk*. (East Anglian Archaeology 9.) Gressenhall: Norfolk Archaeological Unit, Norfolk Museums Service.

Wainwright, G.J., 1970. An Iron Age promontory fort at Budbury, Bradford upon Avon, Wiltshire. *Wiltshire Archaeology and Natural History Magazine* 64, 108–66.

Wainwright, G.J., 1979. *Mount Pleasant, Dorset: Excavations 1970–1, Incorporating an Account of Excavations Undertaken at Woodhenge in 1970*. (Reports of the Research Committee of the Society of Antiquaries of London 37.) London: Society of Antiquaries of London.

Wainwright, G.J., 2000. Time please. *Antiquity* 74, 909–43.

Wainwright, G.J. & I.H. Longworth, 1971. *Durrington Walls: Excavations 1966–1968*. (Reports of the Research Committee of the Society of Antiquaries of London 29.) London: Society of Antiquaries of London.

Waller, M., 1994. *The Fenland Project, no. 9: Flandrian Environmental Change in Fenland*. Cambridge: Cambridge Archaeological Committee.

Wallis, S. & M. Waughman, 1998. *Archaeology and Landscape in the Lower Blackwater Valley*. (East Anglian Archaeology 82.) Chelmsford: Archaeology Section, Essex County Council.

Webley, L., 2007. Prehistoric, Roman and Saxon activity on the Fen hinterland at Parnwell, Peterborough. *Proceedings of the Cambridge Antiquarian Society* 96: 79–114.

Whitlock, R., 1983. *The English Farm*. London: J.M. Dent & Sons.

Whittle, A., 1981. Later Neolithic society in Britain: a realignment, in *Astronomy and Society in Britain*, eds. C.L.N. Ruggles & A.W.R. Whittle. (British Archaeological Reports, British Series 88.) Oxford: BAR, 297–342.

Whittle, A., 1997. Moving on and moving around: Neolithic settlement mobility, in *Neolithic Landscapes*, ed. P. Topping. (Oxbow Monograph 86/Neolithic Studies Group Seminar Papers 2.) Oxford: Oxbow Books: 15–22.

Williams, P., 1979. Waterlogged wood remains, in *Fisherwick: the reconstruction of an Iron Age landscape*, ed. C. Smith. (British Archaeological Reports British Series 61.) Oxford: BAR, 71–7 & 173–83.

Williams, S., 2004. *An Archaeological Evaluation at Land Off Mallory Road (Formerly Tower Works), Fengate, Peterborough*. (CAU Report 603.) Cambridge: Cambridge Archaeological Unit.

Williams, S. 2005. *An Archaeological Evaluation at Land East of Tanholt Farm, Eye Quarry, Peterborough*. (CAU Report 674.) Cambridge: Cambridge Archaeological Unit.

Williams, R.J. & R.J. Zeepvat, 1994. *Bancroft: a Late Bronze Age–Iron Age Settlement, Roman Villa & Temple – Mausoleum*. Aylesbury: Buckinghamshire Archaeological Society

Wilson, J.M. (ed.), 1988. *Lawrence, T.E.: Letters to E.T. Leeds, with A Commentary by E.T. Leeds, and with a Memoir of E.T. Leeds by D.B. Harden*. Leominster: The Whittington Press.

Wotherspoon, M., 2003. *Archaeological Investigations, Land off the Broadlands, Peterborough, Cambridgeshire*. (Hertfordshire Archaeological Trust, Report 1272.) Hertford: Hertfordshire Archaeological Trust.

Wright, R.P., 1940. Roman Britain in 1939. *The Journal of Roman Studies* 30, 155–90.

Wymer, J.J. & F. Healy, 1996. Neolithic and Bronze Age activity and settlement at Longham and Beeston with Bittering, in *Barrow Excavations in Norfolk, 1984–88*, by J.J. Wymer. (East Anglian Archaeology 77.) Gressenhall: Field Archaeology Division, Norfolk Museums Service, 28–53.

Yates, D.T., 2007. *Land, Power and Prestige: Bronze Age Field Systems in Southern England*. Oxford: Oxbow Books.

Zohary, D. & M. Hopf, 1994. *Domestication of Plants in the Old World*. Oxford: Clarendon Press.